The
CRASH
and Its Aftermath

The
CRASH
and Its Aftermath

A History of
Securities Markets
in the United States,
1929–1933

Barrie A. Wigmore

Contributions in Economics and
Economic History, Number 58

Greenwood Press
Westport, Connecticut
London, England

Library of Congress Cataloging in Publication Data

Wigmore, Barrie A.
  The crash and its aftermath.

  (Contributions in economics and economic history,
ISSN 0084-9235 ; no. 58)
  Bibliography: p.
  Includes index.
  1. Stock-exchange—United States—History—20th
century. 2. Depressions—1929—United States. I. Title.
II. Series.
HG4910.W425   1985   332.64′273   84-8961
ISBN 0-313-24574-6 (lib. bdg.)

Copyright © 1985 by Barrie A. Wigmore

Library of Congress Catalog Card Number: 84-8961
ISBN: 0-313-24574-6
ISSN: 0084-9235

First published in 1985

Greenwood Press
A division of Congressional Information Service, Inc.
88 Post Road West
Westport, Connecticut 06881

Printed in the United States of America

10 9 8 7 6 5 4 3 2 1

To my wife, Deedee

Contents

Preface

This book was born out of my own desire for a detailed outline of financial events following the Crash in 1929. For those who anticipate or fear another financial breakdown, there is no other period from which to learn. Most books on the Crash have succumbed to the drama of the event and have concentrated on hyperbole, extreme market changes, and personalities. And there are no comprehensive books on financial markets following the Crash, which is difficult to believe since studying the ruins of a crash is as important as recognizing signs of an impending crash and avoiding it. The available books focus on narrow areas such as bonds, monetary policy, or swindles.

The period covered in detail is from the Crash in 1929 to the end of President Franklin D. Roosevelt's "First Hundred Days" in June 1933, a period of decline and disarray in the financial markets. After the First Hundred Days, the financial markets began a recovery that continued until late 1937.

The data base for much of this book, especially for details of particular industries, consists of 142 leading companies. Financial tables for these companies are in the Statistical Appendix, accompanied by annual tables that apply to each company or its stock the traditional financial measures, such as price-earnings ratios, dividend yields, market price relative to book value, return on equity, and bond ratings. The annual tables also measure each company's stock performance on various bases.

These 142 stocks constituted approximately 77% of the market value of all New York Stock Exchange (NYSE) stocks and include the principal Curb Exchange (now the American Stock Exchange) and Over-the-Counter stocks. (NYSE stocks had a market value of $64.7 billion on January 2, 1930, compared with $49.8 billion for these 142 stocks.) They were chosen on the basis of their volume of trading and market value, and whether they were representative of industries that deserve mention and illustrated general investment principles. The result is a group that illustrates the general stock market. Concentration on this group results in a clear picture of market swings in this period and of valuations of various companies. The data on all the companies come from Moody's manuals for railroads, public utilities, industrials, and banks and financial companies. These manuals were available to investors at the time.

I have presented the entire picture of the credit markets by focussing on bonds of all ratings and types and on short-term investments of all types. Here again I focussed on major bond issues or industry groupings as illustrative of a broader population.

Statistics never tell the whole story of financial markets, so I have woven into the story the personalities riding on events and the structural changes taking place in the financial industry itself. For example, the momentum of the stock market after the Crash had as much to do with the large number of brokers recently employed to sell stocks as it did with human nature in search of a bargain. People made a difference too, for it is clear that during this period companies in comparable industries fared quite differently depending on the skill of their managers.

This book could have been shorter were it not for the summary of events taking place in the broader economy provided for each year, but these events were too epochal to ignore. For example, how can one understand the securities markets apart from monetary policy, the collapse of sterling, the Smoot-Hawley Tariff, and the banking crises of 1932 and 1933?

Perspective has been my goal at all points. I have concentrated on the securities markets in their broad forms and assumed that if the major events as they affected leading companies are clear, the facts are well served. Some securities markets are hardly touched on, such as small companies traded on the Curb Exchange or Over-the-Counter, real estate bonds, convertible securities, puts and calls, and "junk bonds," because I consider them of minor importance. I have indulged in a considerable degree of highlighting in order to cover the whole horizon of financial events.

Herbert Hoover would have liked this book. He believed that the Depression was the result of a series of shocks—collapse of speculation in the stock market, collapse of international trade and finance, collapse of the banking system. I agree, except that the shocks were even more multifarious. Simplistic explanations of the causes of the Depression pale when the many problems of the period are looked at in perspective. Hoover would also have appreciated the constraints on macro-fiscal and monetary policies that become evident when one probes the details of industry losses, bond rating reductions, securities price declines, and public policy constraints. One gets the uncomfortable feeling that macro-fiscal and monetary policies had slight opportunity to affect the course of events in this chain of disasters.

On a personal note, I owe a great debt to David Darst, a colleague at Goldman, Sachs & Co. and author of *The Complete Bond Book*, whose early enthusiasm for and attention to this book meant a great deal to me. Professor Tom Ferguson of the University of Texas has shown similar attention and enthusiasm in the later stages and has saved me from numerous errors. My thanks to Peter Temin of M.I.T. for introducing me to Tom. Vince Rossiter, a learned country banker in Hartington, Nebraska, was also an enthusiastic early supporter who helped to spur me on. Sidney Homer provided a helpful interview and guidance in the beginning. He was also kind enough to review my conclusions. Above all I must thank my wife, Deedee, who was supportive of this time-consuming effort over 12 years, despite the burden it imposed on our free time.

Abbreviations

Banking & Monetary Statistics	The Board of Governors of the Federal Reserve System, Banking and Monetary Statistics, Washington, D.C.: The National Capital Press, 1943.
Historical Statistics	Historical Statistics of the USA, Colonial Times to 1970, 2 parts, Washington, D.C.: U.S. Department of Commerce, U.S. Bureau of the Census, 1975.
Monetary Statistics	Milton Friedman and Anna Jacobson Schwartz, Monetary Statistics of the United States Estimates, Sources, Methods, New York: National Bureau of Economic Research, 1970.
Moody's Railroad Manual	John Sherman Porter, editor in chief, Moody's Manual of Investments American and Foreign Railroad Securities, New York: Moody's Investors Service, annual publications.
Moody's Utility Manual	John Sherman Porter, editor in chief, Moody's Manual of Investments American and Foreign Public Utility Securities, New York: Moody's Investors Service, annual publications.
Moody's Industrial Manual	John Sherman Porter, editor in chief, Moody's Manual of Investments American and Foreign Industrial Securities, New York: Moody's Investors Service, annual publications.
Moody's Financial Manual	John Sherman Porter, editor in chief, Moody's Manual of Investments American and Foreign Banks-Insurance Companies-Investment Trusts-Real Estate-Finance and Credit Companies, New York: Moody's Investors Service, annual publications.

National Income Accounts	National Income & Product Accounts of the United States 1929–65 Statistical Tables a Supplement to the Survey of Current Business, Washington, D.C.: U.S. Department of Commerce, 1966.
NYSE Year Book	New York Stock Exchange Year Book, New York: New York Stock Exchange, Inc., annual publication.
Statistical Abstract 1939	Statistical Abstract of the United States 1939, Sixty-First Number, Washington, D.C.: U.S. Government Printing Office, 1940.
Stock Exchange Practices	Stock Exchange Practices, Hearings before the Committee on Banking and Currency, 73rd Congress, 1st Session, 1933.

The
CRASH
and Its Aftermath

The Crash

INTRODUCTION

The year 1929 was an epic year in financial markets, but its prominence could hardly have been predicted as the year began. When the New York Stock Exchange (the Exchange or NYSE) opened on January 2nd, the Dow Jones Industrial Index was at exactly 300, and it rose 7 points. That was the best gain of the month, although daily trading volume averaged a high 4.6 million shares.[1] The Dow Jones Industrial Index (DJII) closed January at 317, its high for the month. In the following five months there was little change from these January levels. The daily close on the DJII hovered between 300 and 320 with few exceptions until the last week in June. Trading volume and prices soared through the summer, however, until the DJII hit 381 on September 3rd. The Crash began approximately six weeks later and within a month battered the Dow Jones Industrial Index down almost one-third from its 1929 high, to 257. The Dow Jones Railroad Index dropped much further—down 55%. The sample group of stocks which is the data base for much of this study averaged a decline from 1929 high to low prices of 52%, but this was calculated as if all the stocks hit their lowest price on the same day. (Henceforth our sample group will be referred to simply as ''stocks'' or ''all stocks.'' If some larger group is meant, the text will make this clear.)

The market had been very high at its peak. Stock prices averaged 30 times 1929 earnings per share and 425% of 1929 book value per share. At their highest prices, stocks yielded a bare 2 1/2% on average. A few stocks had reached unbelievable heights. Columbia Graphophone Co.'s stock price had reached 165 times 1929 earnings per share and over 50 times book value per share. The National City Bank of New York's stock reached a price 120 times 1929 earnings per share and 13 times book value per share. Other stocks, such as Burroughs Adding Machine Co., Commercial Solvents Corp., International Nickel Co. of

Canada, Ltd., Standard Brands, Transamerica Corp., and United Aircraft and Transport Corp., reached prices over 10 times book value per share.

In 1929 new issues of securities set a record that lasted until the 1960s. Total issues were $11.6 billion, up from an average of $5.8 billion between 1924 and 1928. Common stock issues of $5.1 billion, dominated by investment trust issues, were 10 times the $0.5 billion annual average of common stock issues between 1924 and 1928. This huge volume pushed aside traditional bond issues.

THE COURSE OF EVENTS IN THE STOCK MARKET LEADING UP TO THE CRASH

Stock market prices in the first six months of 1929 were at levels so high that many observers thought them overinflated. Felix M. Warburg and Roger Babson were already publicly predicting a destructive decline in stock prices. Observant market speculators such as Bernard Baruch and Eugene Meyer, who soon became Governor of the Federal Reserve Board in Washington, D.C., were getting out of the market. Percy Rockefeller, a nephew of John D. Rockefeller, and a leading stock market speculator, had begun to sell out his stock positions in 1928, as had John J. Raskob, National Chairman of the Democratic Party and the financial authority on the boards of both E. I. Du Pont de Nemours & Co. and General Motors Corp. (GM). Raskob sold 150,000 of the 153,000 GM shares he owned in 1928. But other professionals believed the price levels were justified by the nation's prosperity and progress. Charles E. Mitchell, Chairman of the National City Bank, said stocks were cheap. Irving Fisher, a reputable Yale economist, backed him up.

There was some room for debate over whether stock prices were too high in the first half of 1929. The Dow Jones Industrial Index was between 300 and 320 throughout the period, which was about 24 times 1929 earnings per share. Twenty-four times earnings was a high average, but at least it was not rising. It appeared that prosperity might catch up with stock prices, since the latter barely rose during the six months. The volume of trading also suggested that investors were marking time. It had averaged 4.6 million shares per day in January, 3.9 million shares in February, and 4.8 million shares in March, but it had trailed off to 3.4 million shares in April, 3.8 million shares in May, and 3.1 million shares in June.

This atmosphere changed decisively in the last week of June. The Dow Jones Industrial Index rose to 333 by the end of the month. The same index closed July at 347, its high for the month, and closed August at 380, again the high for the month. Average daily volume in July was 3.9 million shares and in August was 4 million shares. These should have been "dog days," when both brokers and their customers took vacations, but the former could not afford to leave and the latter did not want to. Making money in the market was more fun than the beach.

The peak in the market occurred on the first trading day in September at 381 on the Dow Jones Industrial Index. Thereafter the market closed steadily lower each week, down to 343 at the end of the month. Trading volume increased, however. It averaged 4 1/2 million shares daily for the month.

September witnessed a record volume of new issues—$1.6 billion, of which $1 billion was common stocks. Common stock issues in this one month were almost double the total for any previous complete year except 1928. This comparison even understates the volume of common stock financing, because debt and preferred stock financing at the time had an unusual emphasis on equity features, such as warrants or conversion rights, which appealed to common stock investors. Virtually every significant common stock offering that month was for an investment company.

Doubt was widespread that the September level of stock market prices could be maintained. Roger Babson had become shrill in predicting the coming collapse of prices. His United Business Service recommended selling stocks in September and again in October because of ''tight money.'' Alexander Dana Noyes, the wise and experienced financial editor of the *New York Times*, was equally pessimistic. Brokers' monthly letters predicted a setback for stocks, and brokers found their inventories of unsold new issues rising as the buying public hesitated.

In the first week of October there was a sickening drop in stock prices. The Dow Jones Industrial Index declined in two days from 344 to 325. Volume reached 5.6 million shares on the second day, and there were touches of panic in the trading as bids for some stocks momentarily disappeared.

Margin calls were numerous. Some brokers were rumored to be in trouble because of the heavy slate of initial public offerings which continued unabated, particularly a $50 million common stock offering which created the Marine Midland bank system. Speculators were active on both sides of the market, so that the Exchange tape was often late. Jesse Livermore, Wall Street's most prominent bear, was rumored to be heavily short.

In the second week of October, however, prices bounced back to 352 on the Dow Jones Industrial Index, and this helped to restore confidence. In the third week of the month stock prices again dropped sharply, so that the DJII was again back to the 320 level. The market was behaving in an erratic manner. The professionals in the market became very uneasy and tried to reduce their commitments. On October 23rd, stock prices suddenly dropped 20 points on the DJII to 305. The volume was 6.4 million shares. At that point, stock prices equalled their level at the first of the year, and a number of investors were in trouble at this level. Investment trusts which had been floated in the summer and had immediately bought common stocks suddenly found they had bought at the highest prices of the year. Instead of making trading profits to pay interest and preferred stock dividends, they would incur trading losses if they dared to sell. Individuals who had pyramided their summer profits by buying on margin were suddenly being asked for more margin by their brokers. Stupendous portfolio profits were turning into losses. This is where our story begins.

THE CRASH

On Thursday, October 24, 1929, which ever since has been known as "Black Thursday," 1,100 members of the New York Stock Exchange were on the floor for the 10:00 a.m. opening bell. Usually, 750–800 members started the day, but the Exchange had directed that all employees were to be in their places at the opening because of heavy margin calls and sell orders placed overnight. Extra telephone staffs had been assembled at the members' boxes around the floor. Opening trades were at prices not far from Wednesday's closing prices. On the Curb Exchange, now the American Stock Exchange, Cities Service Co. stock opened at $55 3/4 on a block of 150,000 shares worth $8.4 million, the largest block in the history of any exchange. Cities Service stock traded over 1 million shares by the end of the day. Price levels wilted quickly after the opening trades, when the volume of stock for sale became apparent. There was a tidal wave of panic, not a gradual loss of confidence. By 10:30 the New York Stock Exchange was in pandemonium and the ticker tape was 16 minutes late. Prices dropped $5 and $10 per trade. Bids disappeared completely for less-active stocks. United States Steel Corp. plunged through its expected support level of $200 down to $194 1/2.

The members of the Federal Reserve Board assembled in Washington, D.C., for the first of two meetings that day in an effort to keep pace with events. This first meeting lasted from 10:45 a.m. to 1:00 p.m. The second lasted from 3:30 to 5:00 p.m., with Treasury Secretary Andrew Mellon presiding. The first meeting received reports from the New York Federal Reserve Bank and Thomas W. Lamont of J. P. Morgan & Co. on the course of stock prices.

The streets of the financial district were in an uproar from shortly after the opening of the Exchange as investors heard of the disaster and, unable to gain information through normal channels, went to the Exchange to seek information firsthand. Thousands of people milled about at the intersection of Wall and Broad streets. Winston Churchill made his way through the crowd to observe the collapse on the NYSE trading floor from the Visitors Gallery.

The Federal Reserve Board, brokers, and bewildered customers had to rely on flash reports from the Exchange floor to keep track of prices during the day. The ticker tape was useless; it was 16 minutes late at 10:30 a.m., 47 minutes late at 11:30, and 92 minutes late at 1:00 p.m. The 3:30 p.m. closing prices were not available until 7:35 p.m. There were 12,894,650 shares traded in 974 issues during the day—both records.

At about 12:00 noon the first organized effort to restore the market began at J. P. Morgan & Co. on the corner of Wall and Broad streets, across from the New York Stock Exchange. Several leading bankers assembled for the meeting. Thomas W. Lamont, the operating head of J. P. Morgan & Co., attended with his partner, George Whitney, the heir apparent. Albert Wiggin, Chairman of The Chase National Bank (not yet a Rockefeller bank), William Potter, Chairman of the Guaranty Trust Co. of New York, and Seward Prosser, President of

Bankers Trust Co. of New York, were there, along with Charles E. Mitchell, President of National City Bank. George F. Baker, Jr., Vice Chairman of The First National Bank of New York, joined the group later in the day when it met again after the close. Many prominent Wall Streeters were not part of the group. The four Guggenheim brothers, Daniel, Murray, S.R., and Simon, were the only people formally acknowledged as being added to the group later, but they never participated in the daily discussions. The group was the WASP blue blood of Wall Street and was made up of bankers, not brokers, except for the Guggenheims.

This small group, from then on known as "the Bankers' Pool," was the first to attempt to restore order on the New York Stock Exchange. The group committed $125 million to buy stocks initially, split 4/25ths from each participant, except 1/25th from the Guggenheim brothers. Everyone named the stocks he wanted to support, and the orders to buy them were prepared and given to Richard Whitney and Warren B. Nash, Treasurer of the New York Stock Exchange, to execute with full discretion. At midday Richard Whitney strode to the Exchange post for U.S. Steel and bid $205 for 25,000 shares (over $5 million) when it was trading at $195. The Morgan broker was supporting the queen of the Morgan stocks. Whitney moved to place bids at the top of his voice in other stocks, and support bids appeared throughout the list.

The effect was electrifying. The leading stocks had been down 15%–20%, but they now bounced back in leaps of $2 and $5 at a time, just as they had gone down. Professionals, speculators, and coolheaded investors swooped in to capitalize on the return to order. The Dow Jones Industrial Index bounced back 26 points from a low for the day of 272 (down 33) to close at 299 (down 6). Some stocks such as American Can Co., Bethlehem Steel Co., and Kennecott Copper Corp., even gained. Table 1.1 shows the changes that took place in stocks with the largest volumes on the New York Stock Exchange and the Curb Exchange.

There is a sense of order to Black Thursday when the events are put on paper, especially because the support of the Bankers' Pool was a focal point in the day's activities, but the day was in fact totally disorganized. There was mayhem in every market, as brokers and dealers struggled to cope with the volume and investors were frantic to find out what was going on. Volume was 12,894,650 shares on the NYSE and 6,337,415 shares on the Curb Exchange. Each was triple normal volume, and there was a large bond volume on the NYSE as well— $23 million.

Attention focused on the NYSE during Black Thursday, but activity was violent on numerous other exchanges. Volume on the Chicago Stock Exchange exceeded 1 million shares for the first time. The Toronto Stock Exchange and the Montreal Stock Exchange also had record volumes and price declines, the 382,521 share volume on the latter including 153,652 shares of International Nickel and 114,414 shares of Brazilian Traction Light & Power Co., both of which were also listed in New York. Taking advantage of their closer access to

Table 1.1
Prices of Stocks with the Highest Volumes on Thursday, October 24, 1929 (Black Thursday)

NYSE:	Close Wed.	Low Thurs.	Change	Close Thurs.	Change	Volume (shares)
General Motors	$ 57⅜	$ 49	$− 8⅜	$ 53½	$− 3⅞	543,900
Radio Corp.	68½	44½	−24	58¼	−10¼	443,700
U.S. Steel	204	193½	−10½	206	+ 2	358,400
Montgomery Ward	83¼	50	−33¼	74	− 9¼	338,700
Anaconda Copper	102	92	−10	102	no change	307,900
Packard Motor Car	20⅞	13½	− 7⅜	18⅝	− 2¼	252,800
Standard Oil (N.J.)	73½	61⅝	−11⅞	68½	− 5	252,300
Commonwealth & Southern	18⅜	13	− 5⅜	16¾	− 1⅝	247,900
International Nickel	47	41	− 6	44½	− 2½	220,200
United Corp.	47	31½	−15½	41⅞	− 5⅛	209,800
Consolidated Gas Co. of N.Y.	121½	108½	−13	118½	− 3	206,300
Bethlehem Steel	101¼	92½	− 8¾	101½	+ ¼	190,800
Sinclair Consolidated Oil	30¼	26½	− 3¾	28⅛	− 1⅛	178,200
Columbia Graphophone	39½	27⅛	−12⅜	35	− 4½	170,500
United Gas Improvement	38¾	30	− 8¾	35½	− 3¼	169,000
Columbia Gas & Electric	97¾	80	−17¾	91½	− 6¼	168,000
IT&T	110¾	79	−31¾	106	− 4¾	160,200
Alleghany Corp.	38	33	− 5	36	− 2	152,800
American Can	154½	137	−17½	157½	+ 3	145,900
Kennecott Copper	67	69	+ 2	75	+ 8	132,600

CURB:						
Cities Service	59	45	−14	51½	− 7½	1,151,900
American Superpower	36⅞	25	−11⅞	32¾	− 4⅛	315,600
Electric Bond and Share	112½	93	−19½	107½	− 5	296,000
Goldman Sachs Trading Corp.	84½	65	−19½	80	− 4½	170,100
Transamerica	63	62	− 1	62	− 1	142,300
Pennroad Corp.	20	18⅛	− 1⅞	18½	− 1½	139,000
Niagara Hudson Power	18¼	15	− 3¼	17⅛	− 1⅛	112,500

events, New York brokers rushed to buy in both Toronto and Montreal when the turn in prices came in New York. The other exchanges in Boston, Philadelphia, Washington, Baltimore, San Francisco, Los Angeles, and Spokane also set trading records. In London, pandemonium dominated a rain-soaked Shorters Court, where Anglo-American securities dealers met after the close of the London Stock Exchange at 4:00 p.m. to follow and trade their stocks based on New York prices. There was an uproar until well after dark.

Chaos reigned in the commodities exchanges as prices broke there, partly in sympathy with stock prices and partly because stock speculators sold out commodity positions to protect their capital for stocks. In Winnipeg, December wheat dropped to a low of $1.25 per bushel, down 12 1/2¢. In Chicago, corn dropped to a low of 88¢ per bushel, down 2 3/8¢. There were wild scenes in the commodities pits as traders struggled to cope with the record volume. Orders to sell 500,000 bushels of wheat were frequent during the morning. Rumors distorted everyone's perspective. Arthur W. Cutten, the leading bull in the press lexicon of speculators, was reported to have sold 10 million bushels of wheat in Winnipeg from a long position. As in stocks, money was to be made in the upturn after the Bankers' Pool came into the stock market, and the scramble to buy, or to cover short sales, continued just as in the early scramble to sell. Wheat closed the day down 4 1/2¢ for December deliveries; corn closed up 1 1/4¢ at 91 5/8¢ per bushel.

The Federal Reserve Board searched for some wise and statesmanlike act it could undertake to preserve orderly markets, which was one of its responsibilities, but it was as disorganized as Wall Street, for it relied on secondary sources, such as bankers and the New York Federal Reserve Bank, for information about the markets at a time when these sources had troubles and responsibilities of their own to attend to. At one point in the day the Federal Reserve apparently told Thomas Lamont of J. P. Morgan & Co. that it would cut the discount rate. Lamont passed this news on to reporters, but it was rescinded, if it was ever intended, and Lamont denied mentioning it. The most the Federal Reserve could do was blame the break on "speculation" and welcome its demise.

The Bankers' Pool was no better organized than other people. At the first meeting no organized support was decided on. Each person selected stocks, and orders were placed for them across the board. The amount of money to be spent was not clarified, nor was the sharing of liabilities. No one in the group knew what prices were as they met.

Some of the participants must have been as worried about their personal affairs as they were about the general market. Richard Whitney, almost bankrupt from injudicious stock investments and high living, had previously prevailed on his brother George, and others outside the meeting, for loans exceeding $1.25 million.[2] Charles E. Mitchell was worried about his merger with the Corn Exchange Bank because the market price of National City Bank of New York stock fell below $400 during the break. Below $400, Corn Exchange Bank stockholders could demand $360 per share, cash, rather than 9/10ths of a share of National

City Bank, and National City Bank would be faced with paying substantially more than the market value of Corn Exchange Bank stock or calling off the deal. On Monday, October 28th, Mitchell obtained from J. P. Morgan & Co. a personal loan of $12 million to support National City Bank stock in the Over-the-Counter market.

The Bankers' Pool met again in the afternoon, following the 3:30 close of the NYSE, and formalized the support effort with each bank participant committing $20 million. The members agreed to meet daily. J. P. Morgan & Co. was appointed to manage the pool, setting the prices to be bid and the amounts. Prices were stepped down in stages in order to fill what Thomas W. Lamont first described to the press as "air holes" in the market, a euphemism for no bids. Morgan narrowed the stocks for which they would bid to the stocks listed in Table 1.2. The next day, the Guggenheims offered to join the Pool, and shortly thereafter commitments were increased to $40 million from each member, except for $10 million from the Guggenheims.

In addition to the stocks in Table 1.2, Black Thursday buying by the Pool included Alleghany Corp., Allied Chemical & Dye Corp., the Chesapeake Corp., Columbia Graphophone Co., International Nickel Co. of Canada, Du Pont, Johns-Manville Corp., The Pennsylvania Railroad Co., Public Service Corp. of New Jersey, Southern Pacific Co., Southern Railway Co., The Texas Corp. (later Texaco), Union Pacific Railroad Co., United Aircraft, The United Gas Improvement Co., and Western Union Telegraph Co., but these companies were dropped from the list in buying on subsequent days.

At the end of Black Thursday, a second organized effort to help the market was begun. Some 35 leading brokers accounting for 70% of NYSE business assembled at the offices of Hornblower & Weeks and agreed that the worst was over and that they should act to reassure their customers. In the *New York Times* the next day, they sponsored a full-page recommendation that the public buy stocks—the largest of many such brokerage recommendations that traced a baneful history until the mid-1930s, when pessimism took full root and recommendations ceased to be published where they were easily recorded.

On Friday, October 25th, the stock market was steady. President Hoover told the nation: "The fundamental business of the country, that is production and distribution of commodities, is on a sound and prosperous basis." He recognized that the stock market drop was critical enough that the nation needed presidential reassurance. Early Friday, stock prices were strong, and the Bankers' Pool was able to sell some of its Thursday purchases. Prices were weaker later in the day, and the Pool had to support some stocks again. Some odd-lot buying began— anxious, but late, to take advantage of yesterday's bargains. The Dow Jones Industrial Index closed at 301, up almost 2 points from its recovery level on Black Thursday. Volume was 5.9 million shares, and the tape was late 1 hour and 34 minutes at the close.

Saturday's volume of 2 million shares was normal for the half day of trading. Prices had an even tone. The Dow Jones Industrial Index was down 2, but there

Table 1.2
Stocks Bought by the Bankers' Pool, October 24–November 11, 1929

	Shares	Average Price	Cost
American Can	106,200	$122.854	$ 13,047,100
American Smelting & Refining	17,100	76.957	1,315,970
AT&T	71,400	232.313	16,586,805
Anaconda Copper	76,200	85.488	6,514,215
Atchison, Topeka & Santa Fe Ry.	15,000	239.316	3,589,750
Baltimore and Ohio R.R.	10,000	118.540	1,185,400
Bethlehem Steel	12,700	101.852	1,293,525
Columbia Gas and Electric	60,000	66.940	4,016,425
Consolidated Gas Co. of N.Y.	88,700	104.407	9,260,940
General Electric	66,600	238.769	15,902,050
General Motors	54,000	43.940	2,372,788
Great Northern Ry. (pfd.)	13,400	100.973	1,353,050
IT&T	92,400	78.423	7,246,290
Kennecott Copper	32,300	60.720	1,961,278
Montgomery Ward	47,100	60.487	2,848,943
N.Y. Central R.R.	25,900	182.698	4,731,900
Radio Corp.	27,000	48.123	1,299,325
Sears Roebuck	28,269	105.705	2,988,200
Standard Oil (N.J.)	27,000	59.471	1,605,725
U.S. Steel	148,400	182.450	27,075,700
Westinghouse	18,400	155.828	2,867,250
Total	1,038,069		$129,062,629

Source: Stock Exchange Practices, part 1, p. 283.

were no dramatic gains or losses. There was a general view that the speculators had received their just due and that the Crash would not hurt business, except for a few luxuries and the Christmas trade. The brokers' weekend letters were mostly optimistic, except for a few small, cautious firms such as Chisolm & Chapman, Morrison & Townsend, and Wade Bros. & Co., names now unknown. Presidents James A. Farrell and Charles Schwab of U.S. Steel and Bethlehem Steel Co. deplored the pessimism they found in so many circles and told the assembled general meeting of the American Iron & Steel Institute at New York's Commodore Hotel that the steel industry was operating at 110% of capacity, that prices were stable, and that inventories were reasonable.

Brokers worked Saturday afternoon and Sunday to clear trades for the week, to balance accounts, and to send out margin calls on accounts which had been weakened. The financial district was active long into the night. Many workers rented rooms in town, and there were high spirits at the overtime pay and the excitement of seeing high stakes played.

A dark note in the two days of calm was the sudden activity in the credit markets. Bankers acceptance rates were cut by 1/8% for the third time in three days, to 4 3/4%, and foreign banks were reported switching out of brokers call loans and buying bankers acceptances. Prices were bid up for U.S. government and high grade railroad bonds. Suddenly there was wide agreement among brokers that the boom conditions of 1928–29 were over. London dealers were very pessimistic, as was Alexander Dana Noyes of the *New York Times*, who had been predicting a bust for months. Bond men suddenly looked forward to the first good bond market in over a year and predicted that call loan money would start to come into the bond market. Those knowledgeable about the heavy out-of-town lending to the $8 billion call loan market to carry stocks were concerned that an abrupt shift might indeed be made to other lending instruments.

Stocks opened weak on Monday morning. U.S. Steel opened off $1 1/4, International Telephone & Telegraph Corp. (IT&T) off $3, General Electric Co. off $7 1/2. Within minutes, U.S. Steel broke through $200, and during the day it touched $185; it closed at $186, off $17 1/2, and was the second most active stock. The volume leaders sank 10%–25%, dropping $1 and $2 in a single trade. Stocks closed near their lows for the day. The Dow Jones Industrial Index dropped 38 to 260, the largest drop on record. Volume was 9.2 million shares, and the NYSE tape was almost three hours late at the close. The *New York Times* described the day with full capital letters in its front page headline:

STOCK PRICES SLUMP $14,000,000,000 IN NATIONWIDE STAMPEDE TO
UNLOAD.

The day's trading in the most active stocks on the NYSE is shown in Table 1.3.

The decline on the Curb Exchange was led by utilities. One, Middle West Utilities Co., closed with no bid or ask quotes. Table 1.4 shows Curb trading of the most active stocks on October 28th. Bank stocks dropped 10%–15% in the Over-the-Counter market.

Margin calls over the weekend were a substantial factor in the decline. Foreigners were also heavy sellers, partly because the London bankruptcy of Clarence Hatry's miscellany of financial enterprises was freezing funds there, but also because the end of the U.S. boom was clearer to foreign investors. Foreign exchange markets were active all day as foreigners repatriated funds.

Much of the selling came from brokers who suddenly had their loans called by corporate lenders who panicked when the Exchange announced that call loans for the prior week were up $15 million. Wall Street had expected a decline in call loans because of the heavy liquidation of stocks during the week. Brokers appealed to the New York banks to replace the called loans. The Bankers' Pool met and resolved to replace part of the called loans. The Federal Reserve Bank of New York bought $25 million in U.S. securities to inject funds into the

Table 1.3
Most Active Stocks on the NYSE, October 28, 1929

	High	Low	Last	Change	Volume (shares)
Radio Corp.	$ 58	$ 39¾	$ 40¼	$ − 18⅜	342,500
U.S. Steel	202½	185	186	− 17½	285,800
Montgomery Ward	72¼	58½	59½	− 15⅜	197,100
Commonwealth & Southern	18¼	15	15	− 3⅛	180,400
Anaconda Copper	102½	92	93½	− 9	162,300
Packard Motor Car	21¾	18	18	− 18½	157,900
Consolidated Gas Co. of N.Y.	116	97	97¼	− 20	157,900
United Corp.	48	46	46	− 1¾	150,800
International Nickel	45⅛	37⅝	38	− 7⅞	144,900
Columbia Gas & Electric	91½	70	70¾	− 22	140,500
Transcontinental Oil	9½	7	8	− 1½	121,700
American Radiator	38	28	28	− 10⅜	116,600
IT&T	100	85	88	− 15	110,700
Alleghany Corp.	36	29	29⅛	− 7½	100,600
Bethlehem Steel	102⅝	94	94⅛	− 9⅜	93,900
Chrysler Corp.	44½	38⅛	40	− 5	93,900

Table 1.4
Most Active Stocks on the Curb Exchange, October 28, 1929

	High	Low	Last	Change	Volume (shares)
Cities Service	$ 46⅛	$27	$27⅛	$ − 18¾	976,800
Electric Bond and Share	105⅞	85	85	− 22⅛	189,300
American Superpower	35¼	25⅛	25⅛	− 10½	101,000
Transamerica (new)	62⅞	62¾	62⅛	− ⅞	84,300
Arkansas Natural Gas A	15	7	8⅞	− 6⅜	77,400
Middle West Utilities (new)	33¼	25⅜	27	− 7½	66,400
Niagara Hudson Power	18⅞	16¼	16¼	− 2½	60,100

banking system so the banks could increase their call loans. The Bankers' Pool did not put in significant bids for stocks in this decline, because the group did not consider its purpose to be to prop up prices, as Lamont and Whitney told the press. There were bids available throughout the day.

On Monday night, margin calls were enormous, and heavy Dutch and German selling came in overnight for the Tuesday morning opening. On Tuesday morning, out-of-town banks and corporations called $150 million of call loans, and Wall Street was in a panic before the Exchange opened. The Federal Reserve Board was in session at 10:00 a.m. when the Exchange opened, and stayed in session until 4:00 p.m. Andrew Mellon, Secretary of the Treasury, chaired the meeting from the start. At the Exchange opening 630,000 shares traded in 26 blocks. In the first 30 minutes, a normal day's trading of 3 million shares was completed. The *New York Times* described the day as the "most demoralized conditions of trading in the history of the Stock Exchange and the Curb." The Federal Farm Board offered loans of $100 million on wheat stocks to try to stem the spread of panic to the commodities pits. A record volume of 16.4 million shares traded during the day. At one time, the Dow Jones Industrial Index was down 48 points and it closed down 30 points at 230.

The *New York Times* attributed the sudden decline in values to several immediate causes: the Massachusetts Public Utility Commission had refused permission to Boston Edison to split its stock because it was too high, the Hatry bankruptcy in London was causing foreign liquidation, and a pool had been caught seriously long in Combustion Engineering stock when it skipped its dividend. These causes pale in comparison with the decline in values, however.

The combined decline in the Dow Jones Industrial Index for Monday and Tuesday was 60 points, or 20%. Leading stocks were down 20%–30%. Numerous stocks were down 40%–50%. Tuesday's results were worse on the Curb Exchange. Utility and investment trust stocks were decimated. Cities Service again traded over 1 million shares and dropped as low as $20, having traded at $46 only two days before. A. P. Giannini removed the support bid for Transamerica Corp. at $62, and the stock dropped to $20 1/4 before it recovered to close at $38 7/8. Transamerica traded over 600,000 shares in the two days, and Giannini bought so much of it in sister corporations to support the stock that he was later ousted as Chairman.

The Curb volume leaders were off 30%–40% at their lows from Monday's close. After a slight recovery before the market closed, Curb stocks were down one-third for the two days. Table 1.5 outlines the staggering losses incurred over the two days for the most active stocks on both exchanges.

The leading bank and trust company stocks dropped so fast in the Over-the-Counter market that all other Over-the-Counter stocks were ignored. National City Bank of New York dropped $155 to $300, despite Charles E. Mitchell's buying support with his Morgan loan. First National Bank of New York dropped $1,600 to $5,200, Chase National Bank dropped $53 to $135, Bankers Trust Co. dropped $40 to $130, Equitable Trust Co. dropped $135 to $425, and

Table 1.5
Trading in Most Active Stocks, October 28 and 29, 1929

NYSE	10/28/29 close	10/28/29 decline	10/29/29 close	2-day decline	2-day volume (shares)
General Motors	$ 47½	$ 6¾	$ 40	$14½	1,355,600
International Nickel	38	7⅞	31	14⅞	814,517[a]
Radio Corp.	40¼	18⅜	38½	20⅛	694,700
U.S. Steel	186	17½	174	29½	593,100
Anaconda Copper	93½	9	85	17½	548,700
Commonwealth & Southern	15	2¼	12¼	5	504,600
Standard Oil (N.J.)	64¾	8	51¾	15	450,200
Packard Motor Car	18	3⅝	16¼	5⅜	448,200
United Corp.	33½	8¾	25¾	16½	427,100
Alleghany Corp.	29⅛	7½	20⅝	16	324,700
IT&T	88	15	71	32	302,000
Consolidated Gas Co. of N.Y.	97¾	20	91½	25¾	287,500
Union Carbide	84	20	73	31	276,800
General Electric	250	47½	222	75½	230,400
AT&T	232	34	204	62	218,600
E. I. Du Pont	150⅛	16⅜	116	50½	135,900
N.Y. Central R.R.	186	22⅝	189½	19⅛	123,300
Pennsylvania R.R.	90	6½	82	14½	103,100

CURB

Cities Service	27½	18¾	22½	23¾	2,082,700
Transamerica	62⅛	⅞	38⅞	24½	653,000
Electric Bond and Share	85	22⅛	59½	47⅜	638,800
American Superpower	25⅛	10½	19	17	482,300
Middle West Utilities	27	7½	18½	16	471,050[b]
Niagara Hudson Power	16¼	2½	13	5¾	243,900
Adams Express	30	7¾	25	12¾	214,600
Goldman Sachs Trading Corp.	60	16	35⅛	40⅞	205,900
Standard Oil (Ind.)	51½	4	47¾	8⅛	198,800
United Light & Power A	28	8	24⅞	11⅛	176,800

[a] Includes volume on Toronto and Montreal stock exchanges.
[b] Includes volume on Chicago Stock Exchange.

Guaranty Trust Co. of New York dropped $120 to $580. The bankers in the Pool witnessed both the shredding of the financial structure they led and the rapid decline of their own fortunes, for they all held substantial interests in their own banks.

The Bankers' Pool met at 12:00 noon on Tuesday, October 29th. Owen D. Young, Chairman of General Electric Co. and a director of the New York Federal Reserve Bank, joined the group, as did Chellis Austin, President of the Equitable Trust Co. (the Rockefeller bank). Shortly thereafter the leading banks announced that margin requirements for their loans were reduced to 25%. Many brokers also dropped their requirements to 25%, some even to 10%. However, it was the banks whose action was most important in this respect because the liquidation of call loans was forcing borrowers to the banks for loans.

Opportunistic buying came into the market on this second day of liquidation and restored some order to the decline. Stocks ticked up at various points during the day before they resumed their decline. Other forces of order began to marshal spontaneously. John J. Raskob announced that he was buying stocks again after staying out of the market for several months. U.S. Steel and American Can declared extra dividends of $1.00 on their stocks, to pay $8.00 and $5.00 respectively. U.S. Steel also announced September nine-month earnings of $15.82 per share compared to $8.17 for the same period in 1928. Julius Rosenwald, Chairman of Sears, Roebuck & Co., guaranteed the stock accounts of his 40,000 employees, irrespective of the stocks they held, to save many from forced liquidation. Samuel Insull, the Chicago utility baron, guaranteed his employees' stock loans the next day. Albert Conway, New York State Superintendent of Insurance, exhorted the casualty insurance companies to buy common stocks and met with the presidents of Prudential Life, Mutual Life, New York Life, and Equitable Insurance to discuss what support they could give the stock market. He undertook to request a change in the New York State law which forbade life insurance companies to buy common stocks.

Some members of the Bankers' Pool strongly favored closing the NYSE but could not carry the group. As it was, the market rallied in the last 15 minutes, buoyed by the converging forces mentioned above, support bids from the Bankers' Pool, and the attraction of many stock yields which had previously been 1% or 2% and now exceeded bond yields. American Can rallied $10 in the last 15 minutes. U.S. Steel rallied $7 1/2, General Electric $12, New York Central Railroad $14 1/2, Anaconda Copper $9 1/8, Chrysler Corp. $5 1/4, Montgomery Ward $4 1/4, and Johns Manville Corp. $8. The NYSE ticker tape finished at 5:32 p.m., the Curb tape at 6:17. As the brokerage clerks worked on, orders began to come in.

On Wednesday morning, October 30th, the stock market opened strong. U.S. Steel was up $3, AT&T up $6 1/8, The North American Co. up $10, Westinghouse Electric & Manufacturing Co. up $4, Cities Service up $1 7/8, and Electric Bond & Share up $10 5/8. American Tobacco Co., Bon Ami, Dictaphone, and National Supply Co. declared extra dividends during the day. At John D. Rockefeller's announcement that he and his sons were acquiring selective common stocks, a surge of public buying came into the market. Investment trusts were heavy buyers. Odd-lot buyers outnumbered odd-lot sellers two to one. Odd-lot volume was 6 million shares over and above the NYSE volume of 10.7 million shares. The tape was over one hour late all day. The Dow Jones Industrial Index was up 28 points to 258. Cotton closed up $1, wheat up 3 1/2–4 1/8¢, and rubber up 10¢–20¢ in sympathy with stocks. Leading stocks closed the day with gains of 15%–20%. (See Table 1.6.)

The NYSE announced after the close that trading on Thursday, October 31st, would begin at noon and that the Exchange would close on Friday and Saturday to catch up on paperwork. There had been opposition to closing the NYSE in the midst of the liquidation because it would have been an admission that its leaders could not cope with the panic. Everyone welcomed the closing now that the market had moved up.

Several bullish events occurred on Thursday morning before the noon opening. The Federal Reserve Bank of New York cut its discount rate from 6% to 5% in coordination with the Bank of England, which cut its bank rate from 6 1/2% to 6%. The *New York Times* called the latter a "gesture of reassurance to America." It was the first positive reaction of public authorities to the crisis of confidence created by the Crash. The Federal Reserve also announced that call loans were down $1.1 billion for the week that ended Wednesday.

The announcements stimulated strong buying when the Exchange opened. Some 2 1/2 million shares traded in the first half hour. Volume for the abbreviated 3 1/2-hour day was 7 million shares. The Dow Jones Industrial Index was up 15 points for the day to 273. Odd-lot purchases were estimated at 4 to 5 million shares. There was generally broad public buying, supported by investment trusts and brokers trying to share in the bargains. There was a rash of dividend declarations during the day. Extras were declared by Consolidated Gas Co. of New York, Standard Oil Co. of New Jersey, New Jersey Zinc Co., Yale & Towne Mfg. Co., U.S. Dairy Products Corp., Warner Bros. Pictures, Inc., and Claude Neon Co. Initial dividends were declared by Bulova Watch Co., United Carbon Co., F&W Grant 5–10–25 Cent Stores, Inc., and National Public Service Corp. Marmon Motors Corp. declared its dividend ahead of time, and Best Products Co. promised an increase when it took dividend action the next month. Corporations fought the confidence crisis in stocks the best way they knew.

The Bankers' Pool did not intervene in the market during the day, nor did it even meet. Prices were up 10% for many of the most active stocks, such as Anaconda Copper Mining Co., Commercial Solvents, Commonwealth & Southern Corp., Consolidated Gas Co. of New York, Montgomery Ward Co., United Corp., and United Gas Improvement Co. Only General Motors was down, among the ten most active, and on the NYSE, in general, only the thinly traded stocks were down. The market closed for the next three days with confidence. Much was made of the fact that no NYSE member firm had been suspended in the crisis. The brokerage community worked from Friday to Sunday to clear orders

Table 1.6
Most Active Stocks, Wednesday, October 30, 1929

NYSE	High	Low	Last	Change	Volume (shares)
General Motors	$ 49⅞	$40	$ 49¾	$+ 9¾	414,700
International Nickel	38	32	38	+ 7	237,100
Commonwealth & Southern	16⅞	11¾	15	+ 2¾	221,200
Standard Oil (N.J.)	65⅝	57	65⅜	+ 7⅞	201,300
Anaconda Copper	95	85	95	+ 10	186,700
United Corp.	34	26	33	+ 7¼	184,400
Packard Motor Car	19½	16	19½	+ 3¼	182,900
Radio Corp.	46	38½	45⅞	+ 7⅜	180,700
United Gas Improvement	33¾	27	33⅛	+ 6⅛	163,600
Montgomery Ward	67	55	66	+ 12¼	146,100
Standard Brands	29	24⅞	29	+ 5	132,600
Commercial Solvents	32½	25⅛	31⅞	+ 7⅞	131,700
Consolidated Gas Co. of N.Y.	100¾	92¾	100	+ 8½	130,900
IT&T	84⅝	72	84	+ 13	125,000
Sinclair Consolidated Oil	28	23½	28	+ 4	124,000
Alleghany Corp.	29	22½	28	+ 7⅜	122,200
Warner Bros.	39	32	38¾	− 5¼	117,800
P. Lorillard	17	14⅞	17	+ 2	113,900
Kennecott Copper	74⅞	76	74⅝	+ 8⅞	110,400
Bethlehem Steel	96¼	86⅛	94¾	+ 10¾	109,300

CURB

Electric Bond and Share	80	67	79⅞	+ 20⅜	202,000
Cities Service	32	23⅝	32	+ 9½	193,700
American Superpower	26	20	26	+ 7	142,955
Niagara Hudson Power	16½	12⅛	15⅝	+ 2⅝	110,120
Commonwealth & Southern					
Wts.	5	4⅛	5	+ 1⅛	108,400
Transamerica	49¼	37⅛	47	+ 8⅛	106,900

and paperwork, despite that the exchanges were closed. Brokers reported during the three days that "buy" orders were voluminous, and there was talk of a reviving bull market.

The desire to talk the market up was intense, but the three days with the NYSE closed gave investors considerable time to think. The very nature of the rally on Wednesday and Thursday threw doubt on whether it could be sustained. Volume was too high, and the pace was too hectic. An odd-lot volume of 3 to 4 million shares was unsustainable, and stories of brokers opening thousands of new accounts suggested that this odd-lot volume was unsophisticated and speculative. The investment trusts bought heavily in the week and were rumored to have exhausted their cash reserves. This industry had been expected to provide a base for the stock market, employing its $3.25 billion[3] in assets to buy stocks whenever they dropped unreasonably low. The market insinuated that the trusts had troubles of their own, however, for most of their stocks sold at a discount from the per share "break-up" value of their portfolios. Other industries were also in trouble. The Foshay Companies, an amalgam of utilities headquartered in Minneapolis and selling securities directly to the public, were ordered into bankruptcy. The brokerage industry too had its first failures during the week. Two members of the Curb failed, one in Boston and one in Wisconsin.

If stocks were going to be strong on Monday, it looked like a good market into which to sell, which is what happened. There was a stampede to unload when the NYSE opened on Monday, November 4th. The decline continued all day. U.S. Steel was off $9 3/4 to $183 1/2 on 108,700 shares. The Dow Jones Industrial Index was down 15 points to 257. Volume was over 6 million shares in the three hours on Monday, and a record 976 issues were traded. Trading was orderly, however, with reasonably close bids available all day. The NYSE announced that sessions would be cut to three hours a day for the week, with closings at 1:00 p.m.

On Tuesday the exchanges were closed for Armistice Day, but on Wednesday, November 6th, the stock markets opened with heavy selling. U.S. Steel was off $2 1/4 to $181 1/4 on the opening. During the day, it plunged to $165, as sellers desperately looked for the Bankers' Pool to support the stock. U.S. Steel closed at $169, off $14 1/2. The Dow Jones Industrial Index for Wednesday closed down 25 points at 231. NYSE volume was 5.9 million shares. The Bankers' Pool did not meet and was not in the market. Stocks were generally off 10%–15%.

Utility stocks on the Curb Exchange were off 15%–20%. Some of the less active stocks were off 30%. Bank stocks dropped 10%–20% in the Over-the-Counter market, and the National City Bank and Corn Exchange Bank called off their merger. Wheat trading in the Chicago grain pits verged on panic.

The sale at public auction of 189,760 shares of Webster-Eisenlohr & Co., one of the largest U.S. cigar companies, illustrated the disarray in the stock market. The stock was auctioned at $2 1/8, when the last NYSE sale had been $7 1/8. The $2 1/8 price represented a paper loss in excess of $21 million for the block from the stock's high price in 1929. Rumors said the block was from the estate of Anthony Schneider, President, who died on October 30th in a fall from his apartment window. The block represented 41% of the outstanding shares.

The next day, Thursday, November 7th, the stock market opened demoralized. Volume in the first half hour was 2.4 million shares, and the NYSE tape was late from the opening. The Dow Jones Industrial Index was down 14 points at the low before noon. Trading ceased to be orderly. J. P. Morgan & Co. thereupon placed bids in a number of stocks, acting on its own discretion, for no meeting of Bankers' Pool members was held Thursday. At that point the market rallied. Volume for the day was 7.2 million shares, and the NYSE tape finished two hours late. Stocks ended the day with small gains. The Dow Jones Industrial Index was up 6 points from Wednesday.

On Friday, November 8th, the stock market was quiet. Close bids were available all day. Volume on the NYSE was only 3.2 million shares; on the Curb Exchange it was 1.3 million shares. The Dow Jones Industrial Index was down 1 point, but the Dow Jones Rail Index was up 0.47. Even though the *New York Times* announced on Saturday, November 9th, in its headline that trading was back to normal, three-hour trading sessions were ordered for the next week. The exchanges were closed on Saturday.

This third week of liquidation again took a heavy toll of stock values. The leading stocks on the NYSE that traded over 100,000 shares during the week were mostly off 10%–15%. A few were off 20%. Utilities led the declines. Despite the decline, brokers and bankers also felt that trading had returned to normal. New York bank and industrial leaders took Friday afternoon off to play golf. The Federal Reserve Board announced that Federal Reserve district surveys of member banks indicated bright business prospects for the holiday season. Only a slight recession, concentrated in the luxury markets, was expected.

The weekend papers also carried the news that James J. Riordan, President of the County Trust Co. and an intimate of Al Smith, had committed suicide because of stock losses. Riordan had died on Friday, but John J. Raskob, one of the leading political and business powers of the period and a member of the board, prevailed on the media to keep the suicide quiet while he strove to prevent a run on the bank Saturday morning. Over the weekend outside auditors were called in to make an immediate audit of County Trust's assets, which were found to be sound. Riordan's stock losses had been personal. Raskob assumed temporary chairmanship of the bank, rallied a group of directors, including Al Smith, to buy 3,800 shares to support County Trust's stock in the market on Monday, and arranged a loan for the group at Bankers Trust Co., where he was a director. They subsequently bought 2,564 shares. Four years later, when Raskob explained his actions to the Senate Committee on Banking and Currency, the group still owned all its shares with a book loss of over $300,000 on an investment of $649,000.[4]

Salvaging the reputation of County Trust was particularly important at this time. Fear was pervasive that a run on the banks might follow the stock panic. There had already been two small bank failures in Germany. Bankers and brokers in Brussels were in serious trouble because European stocks had followed Wall Street down. The principal source of optimism that the economy might not follow the stock market into a depression rested on the absence of a credit panic and the strong loan and capital positions of the commercial banks. A trade depression had never occurred in the United States without being preceded by a banking crisis.

The market opened on Monday, November 11th, in a state of apprehension. The expected sharp sell-off did not materialize, however, as the market was orderly with only slight selling on balance. The Bankers' Pool saw no need to intervene. Volume was light up to the last hour, when heavy selling suddenly materialized. U.S. Steel dropped to a new low of $159 1/2, down $11. General Electric and New York Central Railroad hit lows for the year. Still, the volume was not large—3.4 million shares for the session. The selling was a mystery to brokers, since the decline appeared to be the result of prices fading away as bids were hit rather than to heavy selling pressures. The Dow Jones Industrial Index closed off 16 points at 220.

The cumulative impact of the decline in stock prices began to awaken concern in the Hoover Administration and at the New York Federal Reserve. Initially, both had blamed the decline on excessive speculation and had said that the economy would be better off if speculation was squeezed out. Treasury officials now leaked word that a tax cut was being studied to restore confidence.

On Tuesday, November 12th, Governor George L. Harrison from the New York Federal Reserve Bank met with Treasury Secretary Mellon to discuss the stock market. Liquidation began again as they met. U.S. Steel hit a low of $152 1/4, off $7. Other high-quality stocks joined the decline. Volume exceeded 6.4 million shares in the three hours. When the NYSE closed at 1:00 p.m. the Dow Jones Industrial Index was down 10 points. The commodities markets raged out of control. Wheat futures were off 6 3/8¢ to 6 5/8¢, depending on the delivery month. A number of bankers in the Bankers' Pool wanted to close the NYSE. Lamont was expected to make a public statement in that respect on behalf of the Bankers' Pool but then cancelled the press conference. Nobody seemed to be in control of events. New York City banks admitted that they were selling out weak accounts.

On Wednesday, November 13th, stocks opened down again. Trading was orderly, however, as bids were close, and there were intermittent rallies in prices. Support was organized for individual stocks beyond the Bankers' Pool, but sales broke the bids. A pool supported American Can, one of the leading stocks of the period, but it closed down $10 at $86. Volume for the day was large—7.8 million shares—and the Dow Jones Industrial Index closed down 11 points at 198; but the forces of recovery were marshalled together for the first time this Wednesday, November 13th. John D. Rockefeller placed a bid for 1 million shares of Standard Oil (N.J.) at $50, down $33 from its 1929 high of $83. The New York Stock Exchange called for detailed information from its members on the stock they had borrowed for their own account and those of others. It was widely discussed that the information would be used to discourage short sales. After the close, Treasury Secretary Mellon announced that the United States would reduce corporate and individual income taxes by 1%, equivalent to $160 million, to stimulate confidence and business. He projected that the federal government would still have a budget surplus in fiscal years 1930 and 1931. The proposal received bipartisan support in both houses of Congress.

On Thursday morning, Standard Oil of New Jersey opened at $59 on 40,000 shares, up $8 1/4. U.S. Steel opened at $155, up $3 1/2. Odd-lot business was normal and on the buy side. General Motors announced a dividend extra of 30¢ per share. Standard Oil Co. of Kansas announced that it would resume paying common dividends. During the morning, the New York Federal Reserve Bank announced a second cut in its discount rate from 5% to 4 1/2%. The Federal Reserve said that the readjustment from abnormal credit conditions was completed. Many agreed. The market closed up 18 points. Volume was 5.6 million shares.

This Thursday, November 14, 1929, marked the end of the Crash. Few realized it was over. Those who thought it might be over could place no confidence in their judgment after having been teased and betrayed by one- or two-day recoveries during the Crash. However, it was the end, exactly three weeks after Black Thursday, October 24th.

Within the next five days, the stock market moved up to 248 on the Dow Jones Industrial Index, an improvement of 25% from the closing low in the Crash of 198 on November 13th. In the first week of December, stocks sprinted further to 263 points on the Dow Jones Industrial Index, the high for the month. This December high was still down roughly 100 points from the pre-Crash level, however. Stocks closed the year at 248. Daily volume dropped back to around 3 million shares for the last two weeks of November and averaged 3 1/2 million shares in December. Everyone, including Dana Noyes at the *New York Times*, agreed that the previous selling had been overdone.

Aggressive businessmen resumed their expansion plans. Samuel Insull made several small utility acquisitions in December 1929. Public Utility Holding Corp. of America acquired Portland Gas & Electric Co. U.S. Steel acquired Atlas Portland Cement Co. United Gas Improvement Co. acquired Magnolia Petroleum. The $350 million merger to create Republic Steel was closed on December 18th.

The speculators resumed their past activities, as well. Albert Wiggin, Chairman of the Chase National Bank, reinvested heavily in stocks to his later public regret. William Durant created a new pool in Radio Corp. of America stock. Harley Clarke, Chairman of General Theatres Equipment, Inc., organized a new pool in his own company's 6% convertible debentures with Chase Securities

Co., Pynchon & Co., West & Co., and W. S. Hammons. Pynchon, West, and Hammons were broken by the pool, and Harley Clarke and Chase Securities were ultimately discredited.

TECHNICAL FACTORS BEHIND THE CRASH

How great was speculation in 1929? Many of the best indications of the extremes to which speculation was carried are found in the technical details of the brokerage business. The excesses developing in the stock market were quite clear in this respect in 1929 before the Crash. Daily trading volume on the NYSE in the first 9 1/2 months of 1929 averaged 4.1 million shares, as compared with 3 1/2 million shares in 1928 and 1.7 million shares as recently as 1925. Curb Exchange volume for the year of 476 million shares exceeded 40% of the NYSE's 1.125 billion shares. As recently as 1927, Curb volume was only 125 million shares.

Trading volume relative to outstanding shares assumed unusual proportions. Up to October 15, 1929, over 872 million shares traded—approximately 90% of all shares listed. The trading volume of 1.125 billion shares for the year as a whole exceeded the 1 billion shares listed. This average turnover of more than once per year per share compares with an average of only one-third of all shares per year in 1980. Exchange listings of new issues, reflecting the trading fever, rose almost 100 issues in 1929 to 842 issues.[5]

The brokerage industry had expanded substantially with this volume. NYSE members established 599 new branch offices in 1928 and 1929 combined, for a total of 1,658 offices. In 1925, member firms had only 706 offices, and the trend was for the number to decline slightly.[6] The boom in stock volume sent the price of NYSE seats skyrocketing. A top price of $625,000 was paid for a seat in 1929, up from a range of $290,000 to $595,000 in 1928 and a low of $99,000 in 1925.[7] Curb seats sold at a peak price of $254,000.

Brokers fueled the rapid expansion of their business in a classic fashion—by offering easy credit terms and building large inventories. Margin trading, as the credit was called, expanded to serve both large and small traders. Small investors could borrow up to 75% of the value of stock they bought. Large investors had to put up as little as 10% and in some cases opened trading accounts like charge accounts to be settled periodically with no margin requirement at all. The volume of call loans, which were used to finance brokers' margin loans and their inventories of stocks and bonds, expanded from $4.4 billion on January 1st, 1928, to $8.5 billion on October 1, 1929. These borrowings represented 9.8% of the value of all NYSE stocks on October 1, 1929. This ratio had been relatively constant from 1926 to 1929, despite a 180% expansion in call loans during the period, which for some observers obscured the importance of the growth in call loans.[8] Banks expanded their loans on securities to nonbrokers as well. Securities loans of all member banks to others than brokers were $5.8 billion on October 3, 1928, and $7.2 billion by October 4, 1929.[9]

Brokers loans and bank loans directly to investors peaked at a combined total of $15.7 billion in early October 1929. This total represented 18% of the value of all listed stocks at the time, an enormous proportion to be held on credit.[10]

Small investors and sophisticated financial professionals were both caught up in the speculative mania. Savings bank deposits in the first half of 1929 declined $195 million for the first decline in 20 years as small investors directed savings into the stock market. Normally sober investors, such as J. P. Morgan & Co. partners, were tempted into pools to trade stocks.[11] Walter P. Chrysler even organized a pool with Goldman, Sachs & Co. and Bache & Co. in his own company's stock.[12]

Common stock issues were a record $5 billion, and most corporate debt and preferred stock issues had equity "kickers." Initial public offerings abounded in this atmosphere, and brokers indulged the temptation to scalp an overwilling public. For example, General Theatres Equipment was capitalized at over $40 million in its initial public offering, compared with historic asset costs of less than $4 million.[13] The company's initial 500,000-share public offering piled greed on greed, for the stock price was marked up from $20 per share to $32 per share between the managers and the selling group.[14]

Albert H. Wiggin had a reasonably accurate description of the market's tenor, although it was not appreciated much by the Senate Committee on Banking and Currency investigating stock exchange practices:

MR. WIGGIN: I think the market was a God-given market.

MR. PECORA: What is that?

MR. WIGGIN: I think it was a God-given market.

SENATOR ADAMS: Are you sure as to the source?

MR. WIGGIN: No, sir.

MR. PECORA: God-given market, did you say?

SENATOR COUZENS: That is a new one.

MR. PECORA: Was it "God-given" because the price of the stock [Chase Bank] went up nearly 400 or more points . . . ?

MR. WIGGIN: The market in bank stocks was just like the market in other stocks, as you know, in 1928–29. There developed a great demand for stocks, a great demand for securities. That applied to bank stocks just the same as everything else.[15]

Whoever created the market, it was evident to sober people whose minds had not been formed by the desire for quick profits that stock prices were too high. One could perhaps account for the booming volume, the massive public participation in the stock market, the high NYSE seat prices, the high call loans, and the flood of speculative new issues as adjuncts of a new industrial prosperity which would last indefinitely, but even then stock prices were too high. The average peak stock price was 30 times 1929 earnings per share, while the average

Table 1.7
Stocks with the Highest Price-Earnings Ratios at Their 1929 Peak Prices

	Price-earnings ratio	Market price as % of book value	Return on equity in 1929
Adams Express Co.	153	250%	1.6%
Alleghany Corp.	108	671	2.5
American & Foreign Power	50	390	7.9
Burroughs Adding Machine	42	1,386	33.4
Chase National Bank	62	438	7.4
Cities Service	69	782	11.6
Columbia Graphophone	165	5,086	30.9
Electric Bond and Share	96	233	3.3
Goldman Sachs Trading Corp.	129	295	2.3
International Nickel	50	1,043	21.0
IT&T	51	324	6.4
Middle West Utilities	90	456	5.0
Montgomery Ward	60	476	7.9
National City Bank	120	1,318	11.0
Radio Corp.	73	1,669	22.9
United Corp.	105	255	1.3

Source: Table A.2 and Table A.1 in the Statistical Appendix.

return on equity was 16 1/2%. (See Table A.2 in Statistical Appendix.) This equation is eloquent proof that stock prices were too high. A 16 1/2% return on equity in the business boom of 1928–29, compared to the 5%–6% yields available on corporate bonds, did not justify a multiple 30 times earnings. The same stocks were 420% of book value at their peak prices, (see Table A.1 in Statistical Appendix) which meant that the stockholder's earnings on the underlying equity equalled less than 4%. Such stock prices were clearly dependent on further price rises rather than on the income generated and distributed by the companies.

The incongruity between stock prices and business reality can be seen in Table 1.7, which sets forth the highest-flying stocks. As the low returns on equity of most of the companies show, these high valuations placed little emphasis on earnings.

There is no need to resort to the high-flying stocks to illustrate the specifics of overvalued stock prices. The stocks in Table 1.8 were valued at 30 to 50 times earnings and had equally mundane earnings. This list is more impressive, however, in that it includes numerous stable utilities, banks, and manufacturers that lacked the glamour of the holding companies, investment trusts, and companies with new products; yet these stable companies also received outrageous valuations. Stocks with such prices simply had to come down.

The intense speculation in the stock market created a variety of liquidating

Table 1.8
Other Stocks with Price-Earnings Ratios 30–50 Times Earnings per Share in 1929

	Price-earnings ratio[a]	Return on equity
J. I. Case	34.0	8.1%
Columbia Gas & Electric	44.9	11.1
Commonwealth Edison	35.1	9.4
Commonwealth & Southern	45.7	10.6
Consolidated Gas Co. of N.Y.	38.5	9.0
Continental Illinois Bank & Trust	38.2	13.4
Detroit Edison	34.5	8.9
First National Bank of Chicago	39.1	10.5
General Electric	43.0	16.8
Guaranty Trust	41.4	9.0
Irving Trust	39.1	9.7
National Power & Light	46.5	7.1
North American Co.	37.2	15.7
Public Service Corp. (N.J.)	35.1	8.9
Radio-Keith-Orpheum	32.4	7.6
Union Carbide & Carbon	35.5	13.1
United Gas Improvement	40.0	10.3
Warner Bros.	36.7	8.0

Source: Table A.2 and Table A.1 in the Statistical Appendix.

[a] At 1929 high prices.

pressures that began before the Crash but became pervasive once the Crash occurred. For example, most brokers became concerned about the extent of their margin loans at the high stock prices in midsummer 1929. Brokers began to raise the margin requirements on loans until they were generally up from 10%–25% to 50% by the Crash. In some cases, margin requirements were raised as high as 60%–75%.[16] This dramatic change illustrates brokers' concerns about stock market levels much better than their advertisements or weekly letters. In raising margin requirements, brokers were protecting their own credit exposure and limiting their own business. This was probably a significant factor in creating the market top in late August and early September and in the slow decline in stock prices until the Crash. AT&T also protected its credit exposure at the same time by changing its traditional stock purchase plan of $20 down and $10 per month to $50 down and $10 per month.[17] Once the Crash began, some brokers raised margin requirements further for their customers and refused new margin accounts.

Much of the selling at the worst points of the Crash, when selling appeared senseless, occurred as brokers sold out undermargined accounts. Call loans, which financed margin loans and inventories, dropped from $8.5 billion on

October 1, 1929, to $4 billion on December 1, 1929, where they stayed until the end of the year, at which time they were down to 6.2% of the market value of all listed stocks. As far back as 1925 this ratio had never been below 8%.

The decline of stock prices in the Crash and thereafter created a group of undermargined investors who became a liquidating force whenever stock prices improved. Many banks did not sell out major speculators and brokers that had become undermargined on their loans because the banks considered the decline in securities values unrealistic. Each time during the Crash when stock prices improved, however, the banks sought liquidation of these loans. Individuals or partnerships who saw most of their equity in stocks wiped out needed little encouragement to sell out when prices rose and restored some equity.

A similar liquidating force existed in those who supported the market in the Crash. The Bankers' Pool was the most prominent example, with its accumulation of $129 million in stocks, but others supported stocks on a lesser scale. J. P. Morgan & Co. supported United Corp. independently of the Bankers' Pool because of its role in the creation of the company. A. P. Giannini spent $68 million in four weeks to support Transamerica Corp.; Charles E. Mitchell borrowed $10 million personally to support National City Bank's stock. Many others, alone and in pools, tried to support stocks for long and short periods. None of these were buying stocks as investors; they were buying only to sustain the market and sell when it developed independent strength.

Pools that were caught with long positions in the Crash were sellers in a similar manner. The pools were formed originally to capitalize on the stock market trend with a view to selling higher, not for investment purposes. Pools were organized like syndicates, with up to 20 participants, each taking a small share of the risks.

There were infamous pools in Radio Corp. of America (RCA), Chrysler, Anaconda, Air Reduction Co., Combustion Engineering, and Chase National Bank. Chase itself was a member in 15 pool accounts in 1929. Percy Rockefeller, a reticent nephew of John D. Rockefeller whose voice was so low he could hardly be heard, showed a surprising assertiveness in the stock market, where he was in the Anaconda and Air Reduction pools, even though he was a director of the latter, and in other pools with "Sell 'Em" Ben H. Smith. John Raskob, Bernard Baruch, Eugene Meyer, and Al Smith were also in pools. Nathan Brush, an unknown hotel clerk and machinist in 1921, pyramided a small investment into $15 million by 1929 by speculating in pools. All the brokerage houses participated in pools, including J. P. Morgan, Dillon, Read & Co., Brown Bros., and Kuhn, Loeb & Co. William Durant, founder of General Motors, led repeated pools in RCA. Fellow Detroit auto men, the Fisher brothers, were also leading market speculators.

Usually a prominent market professional managed each pool, such as Arthur W. Cutten or Mike Meehan, the specialist in RCA. The manager used the pool proceeds to support the pool's stocks and to make trading profits. Sometimes the pool was used to "churn" stocks to create an impression of activity that would attract the public as investors. After the Crash, criticism of the markets focussed on the manipulative aspects of these pools, but the pools could manipulate only because the market was moving in their direction; they lost, like others, when the market dropped. In one case, J. S. Bache and W. E. Hutton had to sue W. F. Kenny, a big speculator and intimate of Al Smith, for his share of the $1.6 million loss in a Chrysler Corp. pool.[18] Raskob, Durant, Fred Fisher, Al Smith, Percy Rockefeller, Ben Smith, and Ben Bragg had shocking losses in a $32 million pool in Anaconda stock. The pools were trapped in the Crash and could do nothing about it. They cut their losses when stocks recovered, if they still had the stocks, because they were not permanent investors in the first place.

The speculative spirit did not lapse with the Crash. Speculators sold stocks short to capitalize on the down trend or to hedge long positions which they could not sell for personal or tax reasons. Several Morgan partners and Albert Wiggin of the Chase were included in the latter case. Percy Rockefeller was short Standard Oil Co. (Indiana), Matthew Brush was short up to 130,000 shares at one time. Thomas Bragg anticipated the Crash and built up a large short position. No comprehensive data on short sales is available for this period. The NYSE did not begin to collect steady data on short sales until May 1931.

Some short sales were made by brokers to hedge their trading inventories or put and call operations, but all short sales were publicly condemned because they appeared to capitalize on the nation's problems. The attention to short sales in the press and other commentary verged on sensationalism or a search for a scapegoat. There was little sentiment on the side of short-sellers, whose philosophy Matthew Brush disdainfully outlined before the Pecora Committee:

SENATOR BUCKLEY: You still think you are justified as a patriot in selling short at the present time?

MR. BRUSH: Patriotism has nothing to do with it. But if I sell long, I feel that I also can sell short.

SENATOR GLASS: That's the game.

MR. BRUSH: That's life.[19]

THE BROKERS SURVIVE THE CRASH INTACT

The brokerage community suffered surprisingly light damage in the Crash. The only bankruptcies were small firms in Boston, Providence, Cincinnati, and the state of Wisconsin. The commissions generated by the tremendous volume of stock business were profitable to the brokers even if their customers suffered, but this is an inadequate explanation of the lack of brokerage failures. The brokerage firms held stocks which lost value just as their customers did. They were no less infected by the optimism and prosperity of the period than their customers. There was an active Over-the-Counter market in bank stocks, utilities, investment trusts, insurance stocks, aviation stocks, and many others, in all of which market-makers held inventories. Partners of the brokerage firms also were large stockholders on their own. Often the capital of firms was in the form of securities contributed by the partners. Numerous brokers suffered losses as they tried to support individual stocks in which they were interested during the Crash, operating in a manner smaller than but similar to the Bankers' Pool. Brokers also suffered losses on margin accounts which could not be sold out fast enough to preserve the equity in them.

There were isolated examples of individuals on Wall Street who did not survive the Crash. Richard Whitney, Vice President of the NYSE and popularly recognized as the "Morgan broker," lost heavily in 1929, before and during the Crash. He remained solvent only because his brother, George, a J. P. Morgan partner, lent him over a million dollars. Charles E. Mitchell, President of the National City Bank, was caught with an enormous long position in National City Bank stock. He borrowed $10 million from J. P. Morgan to support National City's stock, as it threatened to decline below the $425 exchange price in a current merger agreement with the Corn Exchange Bank. For his efforts, he ended up overextended and a hapless creditor of J. P. Morgan & Co. for $6 million. He too stayed solvent only because his loan was not called. James Riordan, Chairman of the County Trust Co. and a pal of Al Smith and John Raskob, was destroyed by the Crash and committed suicide. Numerous others who qualified as professionals on Wall Street were broken because they owned stocks on credit.

One might have expected the rights offerings under way during the Crash to have bankrupted some of the investment bankers underwriting them. The North American Co. had a rights offering at $100 per share under way, and the stock dropped as low as $69. Lee, Higginson & Co. underwrote the U.S. portion of a $24 million participating debenture issue sold on a rights offering by Kreuger & Toll. (A participating debenture gets increased interest as earnings increase above a specified level.) The offer was announced October 23rd, to expire December 2nd. It was eventually announced as 97 1/2% subscribed, even though Kreuger & Toll common hit a low of $22 1/8 on November 13th, compared with $33 1/2 when the issue was offered. Middle West Utilities was similarly able to complete a $147 million refinancing which included $92 million of common stock on a 1 for 4 rights offering that expired on November 16th. The underwriters of a rights offering for Grigsby, Grunnow Co., a phonograph manufacturer, were less successful. On November 24th they were forced to pay $40 per share for $9 million of Grigsby, Grunnow common, which had dropped to $17 per share. Their losses must have exceeded $5 million. Dillon, Read & Co. and Ladenburg, Thalman & Co. managed a rights offer by Seaboard Airline Railroad Co. which suffered a similar fate. Some 1,892,630 shares were offered at $12, but the stock dropped to $9 1/8 and closed the year at $11. The underwriters had to take up 1.6 million unsubscribed shares. The Pennroad Corporation, an affiliate of the Pennsylvania Railroad, underwrote 25% of the issue and was forced to take up 400,000 shares.[20] Underwriters also had to take up 40% of a Bethlehem Steel rights offering of 800,000 shares at $110 when the stock had dropped to a low of $78 1/4 on November 13th. It closed the year at $94 3/4. The loss at $94 3/4 was still almost $5 million.

Several factors account for the high survival rate among brokers. Their own stockholdings were light because the speculative froth in the market was recognized. Early in September the brokerage community had become pessimistic and had liquidated many of its holdings. Some of the firms had already gone to extreme lengths, such as Gilbert, Elliott & Co., a small firm which switched its whole business from trading bank stocks to trading bonds—about as ideal a redeployment of capital as could be imagined.[21]

Once the Crash came, brokers sold their own inventories and reduced their exposure to losses on margin accounts drastically, as already discussed in part. Individual margin speculators were squeezed mercilessly by the brokerage scramble to liquidate. There were few opportunities for the victimized investors to respond or to renegotiate their loans. Many employers came to their employees' aid to prevent hardships. Julius Rosenwald, of Sears, Roebuck & Co. and Samuel Insull personally guaranteed their employees' stock loans, even when the stock was in other companies. Standard Oil Co. (New Jersey), U.S. Steel, and Kroger Grocery & Baking took over their employees' stock loans from the brokers. Thus, one way or another, brokers sharply reduced their exposure to stock market losses during the Crash.

The brokers were also saved because the commercial banks showed mercy when their call loans became undermargined, a mercy not extended by the brokers to their own customers. There was widespread recognition in the Crash that banks were ignoring many undermargined loans, and the banks formally reduced margin requirements from 50% to 25% to avoid further liquidation. This banking attitude may have been the principal reason that the brokers remained solvent, because stock prices naturally recovered as the panic subsided, thereby restoring the brokers' equity. In past crises, the problem had been to retain the lenders in anticipation of the recovery. This was the first panic in which brokerage failures were not an important component of the liquidation. The change in circumstances was due to the creation of the Federal Reserve Board. For the first time, the major banks were in a position to extend themselves in a panic, rather than contract in order to save themselves, because they had a lender of last resort. So the presence and the actions of the Federal Reserve acted to save the brokerage industry from collapse in the panic.

Many companies also saved their brokers by cancelling or extending underwritten rights offerings. Cities Service Co. and Sharon Steel Hoop Co. cancelled their offerings, as did Great Lakes Corp., a new investment trust sponsored by Guardian Detroit Union Group. The trust refunded $26 million received out of the $35 million offering, with the wise admonition that "no additional financial burdens should be incurred either by individual or financial institutions at the present time,'' thereby relieving the underwriters, Fisher & Co., of a considerable burden. Pacific Associates, J. I. Case Co., and Allis Chalmers extended their rights offerings so that the market prices of their stocks had time to rise again above the subscription prices and thereby make exercise of the rights profitable again.

SPECIFIC INDUSTRIES AND INDIVIDUAL STOCKS IN 1929

The generalities in which we have been discussing the stock market provide a perspective on events but do little to indicate how particular industries and stocks performed. We now turn to how stock prices changed for various industries and individual companies in 1929, and to how industry and company economic performance fared behind the stock price changes. To keep a balanced perspective, the emphasis will be on the larger industries, with some diversion to less important stocks that were attracting attention.

The data on individual companies can be found in Table A.1 in the Statistical Appendix, which provides per share earnings, dividends, book values, and stock prices as well as returns on equity, capitalization ratios, and cash and equivalents for 1929 to 1933. Table A.2 provides ratios for each company's high and low 1929 stock prices.

The Railroad Industry

Railroads constituted the largest U.S. industry by a considerable margin. The market value of all railroad stocks was $10.1 billion on October 1, 1929, compared with the value of all NYSE stocks of $79.1 billion. The petroleum industry, the next largest, had a value of only $7.2 billion. Several railroads had capitalizations that made them among the largest corporations in the nation, particularly the Pennsylvania Railroad Co., the stock of which had a market value of $1.2 billion on October 1, 1929, and New York Central Railroad, which had a value of $1 billion. (See Table 1.9 for data on specific railroads.)

The railroad industry was in many respects a benchmark of U.S. business conditions. Data on freight-car loadings were published weekly, and data on revenues, revenue-freight miles, and commodities shipped were published monthly. Regulation of the industry by the Interstate Commerce Commission produced steady data on railroad operations.

The railroad industry had done reasonably well in the late 1920s. Industry net income was a record $883 million in 1926, down slightly in 1927 and 1928, and up to another record in 1929 of $977 million.[22] The nine leading railroad companies averaged a 9.7% return on equity in 1929, and their 1929 dividends appeared well protected by earnings per share more than double their dividends.

In this period railroad stocks stood for stability as investments. They offered the highest current income in contrast to a speculative reliance on capital gains. They also fluctuated less in value than other industries. Historically, they rep-

Table 1.9
The Railroad Industry in 1929

	Price-earnings ratio		Market price as a % of book value		Dividend yield (%)		Low price as a % of 1929 high price	Return on equity (%)	Moody's bond ratings	Cash & equivalents ($ millions)
	High price	Low price	High price	Low price	High price	Low price				
Atchison, Topeka & Santa Fe	13	9	130	85	3.34	5.13	65	9.9	Aaa	38
Baltimore and Ohio	14	10	99	72	4.83	6.65	72	7.1	Aaa	(19)[a]
Canadian Pacific	24	16	136	92	3.68	5.40	68	6.6	Aaa	70
Chesapeake and Ohio	13	7	184	106	3.57	6.25	57	14.3	Aaa	7
New York Central	15	10	156	97	3.11	5.00	62	10.1	Aaa	(22)
Norfolk & Western	10	7	144	95	2.76	4.19	66	14.5	Aaa	6
Pennsylvania	13	8	121	80	3.64	5.50	66	9.7	Aaa	34
Southern Pacific	12	8	71	47	3.80	5.70	67	5.7	Aaa	28
Union Pacific	15	10	136	91	3.36	5.00	67	9.3	Aaa	16
Averages	14.3	9.4	131	85	3.57	5.42	66	9.7	—	—

[a] Brackets indicate short-term borrowing.

resented solid value because of the tangible nature of their investments in track, equipment, and station facilities. For this reason the railroads were the first U.S. industry able to do public bond financing. All the leading railroads had Aaa ratings on their mortgage bonds when they were secured by their best track and equipment. (Individual bond issues were secured by specific trackage, property, and equipment.) To many investors, the regulated nature of the business promised stability and security. This general attitude had its roots in the industry's historic importance and perhaps in a perverse twist of logic that argues that what is not exciting must be conservative. The high ratings on the industry's bonds had similar roots.

Rail stocks were widely considered income stocks bought for their dividend yield. The average yield of the nine leading railroad stocks was 3.57% at their 1929 highs, compared with the broad stock average of 3%. Most of the railroads had very stable dividends. Canadian Pacific, Southern Pacific, and Union Pacific paid the same dividend rates throughout the decade, and most of the other railroads had raised their dividends only slightly.

An irony of the railroads' situation was that despite their position as income investments they paid out a low proportion of earnings in dividends. The dividend rates of the leading railroads averaged 51% of net income, compared with the average for all industries of 67%. Only oil, chemical, and heavy manufacturing companies came close to the railroads' low dividend payout ratios. Unlike the railroads, however, which had not expanded their tracks, locomotives, or passenger cars since 1914 and had barely expanded their freight car capacity,[23] these other companies generally needed their income to finance growth. The railroads were forced to retain a high proportion of net income because of their low return on equity, poor cash flow, and difficulty selling common stock. They were already too highly leveraged, with 40% debt, whereas many retail and industrial companies had no debt and utilities kept their debt below 40%. The capital necessary simply to stand still dictated railroad dividend policies rather than opportunities for growth.

The industry was burdened by numerous well-known problems. It ran a large passenger business on which it lost money. Its employee unions were militant and highly paid, and they restricted adaptation of work practices. Automobiles and trucks were beginning to cut into railroad business. Trucks creamed off many of the most desirable, easily managed freight loads. Pipelines were also beginning to attract oil business from the railroads. Changes in competitive practices should have eased the effect of these developments on the railroads, but the Interstate Commerce Commission (ICC) was slow to permit changes. Freight prices were quite rigid and unadaptive to individual situations. For years the ICC had been studying the advisability of creating four or five eastern trunk line systems out of the many competing railroads, but little progress was apparent.

If these problems were exacerbated and the ICC remained unresponsive, the effect on the railroads was bound to be dramatic because they were highly leveraged. The New York Central's capitalization was only 54% common equity, and the Baltimore and Ohio's was 43% common equity. The Pennsylvania's common equity, along with that of the others, was around 60%, which was still low compared to other industries.

These problems of the railroad industry caused the relatively low stock market valuation of railroad earnings and investments. The industry had become the "poor boy" of the stock market by 1929. Rail stock prices had only doubled since 1919, while industrial stock prices had tripled and utility stock prices had quadrupled. Railroad stocks' price-earnings ratio of 14 compared with an average of 30 for all stocks. The railroad stocks' peak price valuation of 131% of book value compared with an average valuation of 420% of book value for all stocks. Railroad stocks were accorded only roughly one-third the value of stocks in general.

In the Crash railroad stocks declined less than others because of the lower level of speculative trading in them. The nine leading railroad stocks dropped to 66% of their 1929 highs, compared with 48% for all stocks. At these low prices, the average railroad dividend yield of 5.42% was below the 6% average for all stocks. However, the railroad industry's relative valuation was still the lowest, at 9 times earnings and 85% of book value, compared with the averages for all stocks of 12 1/2 times earnings and 181% of book value. The industry's lower investor appeal was further reflected in a slower stock price recovery in November and December than other industries experienced. The Dow Jones Railroad Index recovered only 18.6% in November and December, compared with 32.6% for the Dow Jones Industrial Index and 45.2% for the Dow Jones Utility Index. But the railroad recovery was strong enough for the Pennsylvania Railroad to have a $90 million common stock offering in December.

Among the leading railroads, Baltimore and Ohio and Southern Pacific stood out as the most vulnerable. The Baltimore and Ohio (B&O) earned only a 7.1% return on equity, despite its high leverage, because of its heavy dependence on trans-shipments from other lines (37% of its freight), relatively short hauls, and close ties to the coal and steel industries. Its $19 million in short-term debt as it finished 1929 also made it more vulnerable than other railroads.

Southern Pacific had an even worse stock price performance than the B&O; its stock sank to a mere 47% of book value. It deserved such treatment, for Southern Pacific management had fallen asleep at the switch. The line had earned only a 5.7% return on equity and had not increased its dividend since 1907, despite the benefits of a wide diversity of freight and long hauls of freight that the line itself had originated. It had neither the quality of track and equipment nor the midwestern extensions of its chief competitor, the Atchison, Topeka & Santa Fe, and lesser railroads were beginning to encroach on Southern Pacific territory.

The Chesapeake & Ohio and the Norfolk & Western railroads stood out as the two best railroads. Both earned more than a 14% return on equity and still had stock prices close to book value at the lows of the market. Both were built around the bituminous coal freight of Appalachia and carrying it for relatively

long hauls. A financial superstructure had been developed on the strength of the
Chesapeake and Ohio which, if traced upward, led through the Chesapeake Corp.
to the Alleghany Corp., the Van Sweringen Corp., and finally to the Van Sweringen brothers, Cleveland real estate developers. The C&O moved along with
little regard for this weight it carried on its back.

The Operating Public Utility Industry

Electric utilities were still relatively new in 1925. Central city generating units
of 50,000 to 100,000 kilowatts serving a large surrounding area had been developed only within the last 20 years at the behest of Samuel Insull, President
of Commonwealth Edison Co. There were a few large operating utilities with a
capitalization in excess of $250 million, such as Consolidated Gas Co. of New
York, Public Service Corp. of New Jersey, Pacific Gas & Electric Co., Detroit
Edison Co., and Commonwealth Edison, but there was still a separate electric
company in most cities, and sometimes more than one company in a city. Holding
companies often knitted these separate operating utilities together, sometimes
very effectively when the holding companies provided strong management, as
the North American Co. did; but still a great many operating utilities were
independent, only partially owned by a holding company or loosely managed
by one.

Both the technology and the finances of the industry were developing quickly.
Larger generating units and higher voltage transmission lines were reducing the
costs of electric power, and expanding wealth and population provided growing
markets for the new technology. As a result, operating electric utilities had large
capital requirements. They averaged approximately $1.7 billion in public fi-
nancing in 1926–29[24] which accounted for almost one-quarter of all corporate
financing.

By 1929, utilities had become prominent stocks. (See Table 1.10 for data on
specific companies.) According to the New York Stock Exchange, operating
utility stocks were worth $5.1 billion by October 1, 1929, and Consolidated Gas
Co. of New York was the stock most widely held by investment trusts. The
market interest in and valuation of utility stocks were somewhat paradoxical in
that the companies' returns on equity averaged a relatively low 9.7%, compared
with the average of 16 1/2% for all companies, and yet the market valuation of
utility stocks was close to the averages for all companies. Utility stock prices
at their peak were 34 times 1929 earnings per share and 325% of book value,
compared with the averages for all stocks of 30 times earnings and 420% of
book value. The dividend yield on utility stocks at these prices averaged 2.11%,
compared with 3% for all stocks.

In the Crash utility stocks declined in line with the averages. At their lowest
prices, utility stocks were 14.6 times 1929 earnings, slightly above the average
for all stocks of 12 1/2 times earnings, and 137% of book value, compared with
181% for all stocks. The average decline in utility stocks was 42% versus 48%

Table 1.10
The Operating Public Utility Industry in 1929

	Price-earnings ratio		Market price as a % of book value		Dividend yield (%)		Low price as a % of 1929 high price	Return on equity (%)	Moody's bond ratings	Cash & equivalents ($ millions)
	High price	Low price	High price	Low price	High price	Low price				
Commonwealth Edison	35	16	331	149	1.78	3.96	45	9.4	Aaa	20
Consolidated Gas Co. of N.Y.	39	17	345	151	2.19	5.00	44	9.5	Aaa	(9)[a]
Detroit Edison	35	14	306	120	2.08	5.30	39	8.9	Aaa	(8)
Pacific Gas & Electric	28	12	330	140	2.02	4.76	42	11.7	Aa	20
Public Service of N.J.	35	14	314	123	2.46	6.30	39	8.9	Aa	1
Averages	34.4	14.6	325	137	2.11	5.06	42	9.7	—	—

[a] Brackets indicate short-term borrowing.

in all stocks. (The Dow Jones Utility Index is misleading in this respect because it included both operating utilities and holding companies. It declined 55%, compared with 32% for both the Dow Jones industrial and railroad indices. The same distortion occurred in the Utility Index's rise from January to September 1929.) The market's attraction to utilities was still evident at the lows of the Crash in the average dividend yield of 5% on utility stocks versus 6% on all stocks.

Holding and Investment Companies

Holding companies and investment trusts enjoyed unprecedented popularity in 1928 and 1929. Six of the 16 companies in these categories studied here were formed in 1929: Alleghany Corp., Commonwealth & Southern Corp., Lehman Corp., Tri-Continental Corp., United Corp., and United Founders Corp. Goldman Sachs Trading Corp. and Transamerica Corp., were founded in late 1928. Dillon, Read & Co. created the first significant U.S. investment trust, United States & Foreign Securities Corp., in 1924, but there were only $175 million in investment trust issues by 1927. The explosion began in 1928 when investment trust issues totalled $790 million and then grew to almost $2.25 billion in 1929, some 22% of all corporate issues.[25]

Goldman, Sachs & Co. managed initial public offerings in late 1928 and in 1929 for the Goldman Sachs Trading Corp. and its affiliates, Shenandoah Corp. and the Blue Ridge Corp., which became infamous because of their quick demise. Shenandoah skipped its barely established 1 1/2% stock dividend in December 1929, and Blue Ridge was the recipient of a rumored cash infusion during the Crash from Harrison Williams, one of its co-sponsors. But other investment bankers were equally involved in sponsoring such companies. J. P. Morgan & Co. sponsored United Corp. and Alleghany Corp., the former to establish a J. P. Morgan & Co. position in the financing of utilities in the mid-Atlantic states of New York, New Jersey, and Pennsylvania, and the latter on behalf of the Van Sweringen brothers, who controlled the Chesapeake & Ohio and Missouri Pacific railroads. Harris, Forbes & Co., which was the preeminent investment banking firm in the utility industry, underwrote United Founders Corp. and Public Utility Holding Corp. of America, which controlled a maze of domestic and foreign utilities for which Harris, Forbes & Co. managed financing. Kuhn, Loeb & Co. underwrote the Pennroad Corp., an investment and trading affiliate of Kuhn, Loeb's preeminent client, the Pennsylvania Railroad. Lehman Bros. created the Lehman Corp., which turned out to be one of the best-managed investment trusts.

The Public Utility Holding Companies

The various investment trusts and holding companies differed in their operations in some respects. The public utility holding companies controlled operating electric and gas utilities spread out across the nation and typically owned 100% of these subsidiaries' stock. Commonwealth & Southern Corp., whose president,

Wendell Willkie, ran against Franklin Roosevelt in 1940, controlled the subsidiaries of the present-day Southern Co. (Alabama Power, Mississippi Power, Gulf Power, and Georgia Power) as well as Ohio Edison Co., Consumers Power Co., Southern Indiana Gas and Electric Co., and others.

Electric Bond and Share Co. (Ebasco), which had been founded in 1905 by General Electric to take over its utility holdings, controlled five holding companies with subsidiaries in 32 states and 13 foreign countries. Ebasco was the largest electric utility holding company and had the best credit standing. In 1930 its preferred stock was rated Aa, comparable with General Motors, American Can Co., International Harvester Co., and Allied Chemical & Dye Corp. The most prominent operating companies in the Ebasco system were the present-day subsidiaries of Middle South Utilities Co. and Texas Utilities, plus Utah Power & Light, Idaho Power, United Gas Corp., Florida Power & Light, Kansas Gas & Electric, Minnesota Power & Light, Montana Power, Pacific Power & Light, Washington Water Power Co., Carolina Power & Light, Houston Lighting & Power, and many others, the names and corporate structures of which have changed. This was clearly a formidable system.

Cities Service Co. controlled over 90 utility subsidiaries operating in 39 states, Canada, and abroad, as well as 50 oil and gas subsidiaries that produced, transported, refined, and marketed petroleum and by-products. It was run by E. L. Doheny who had been heavily involved in the Teapot Dome Scandal. Cities Service's debt and preferred equity constituted 67% of capitalization, and its bonds were appropriately downgraded to Ba in 1930. It was easily the favorite stock on the Curb Exchange, however, where it often traded in volume surpassing the NYSE volume leader.

Other public utility holding companies were Columbia Gas & Electric Corp., which was built around the industrial area covered by Ohio, western Pennsylvania, and West Virginia; International Telephone & Telegraph, which had a principally foreign telephone network; North American Co., which began in Milwaukee and expanded to include chiefly Cleveland and St. Louis; Standard Gas and Electric Co., which was built around utilities in Pittsburgh, Minneapolis–St. Paul, Louisville, and Oklahoma City; United Gas Improvement, which was based on Philadelphia Electric Co.; and Middle West Utilities, which was spreading rapidly into the small towns of the rural Midwest from North Dakota to Texas.

The distinguishing feature of these holding companies was the role they played in managing their subsidiaries. Many exercised tight operating control over their subsidiaries, such as the North American Co., Columbia Gas & Electric, Commonwealth & Southern, Standard Gas and Electric, and United Gas Improvement. The holding companies played important roles in operations practices, engineering, construction, budgets, financial controls, and financing. Companies such as Commonwealth & Southern had centralized engineering, construction, purchasing, legal, tax, insurance, rate, and finance staffs. The North American Co. included significant coal-mining operations to supply its subsidiaries. Columbia Gas & Electric had six operating divisions, in each of which there was a full organization to cover all operating details. International Telephone & Telegraph managed its telephone and telegraph subsidiaries, constructed facilities and distributed electrical equipment, and carried on research and development work in electronic and cable technology.

Ironically, these companies were held up by Franklin Roosevelt and others as spectacles of financial abuse and confusion, which led to the Public Utility Holding Company Act of 1935 and the subsequent dissolution of the companies in the 1940s. However, in addition to being well founded financially, they were more stable, useful, and operationally oriented than the investment trusts and purely financial holding companies, which were attacked less directly. The public utility holding companies were typically set up before World War I, when the growth of public utilities was helped by central expertise. Most of these holding companies had securities ratings of A or Aa. Most of their securities investments were acquired at costs reasonably close to book value. Prominent men led them. And while the companies did have an interest in buying and selling securities and in financial maneuvers to create gains, they were not narrow financial constructions.

There is no gainsaying the enthusiasm of the financial markets for these public utility holding companies, however. (See Table 1.11 for data on specific companies.) Their trading volume in 1929 exceeded 100% of their outstanding shares. At the high point in the market, their stocks averaged prices 57 times earnings per share, with Electric Bond and Share, which was most prominent because of its size and its relationship with General Electric, selling at 96 times earnings per share. These stocks averaged 444% of their book value at the same high prices, and a dividend yield of merely .87%, with three of the companies paying no dividends at all. Investors may have reasoned that leverage, professional management, and the rise in value of these holding companies' utility investments justified such heady valuations, but their valuations are difficult to understand in the light of these companies' average 1929 return on equity of only 9 1/2%.

The vulnerability of these holding company stock prices became clear in the Crash. They dropped to one-third their highest 1929 prices, which was a negative performance exceeded only by investment trust stocks, and to 148% of book value, compared with 181% of book value for all stocks. The resulting price-earnings ratio of 18 for the group, compared with the average for all stocks of 12 1/2, suggested that the public utility holding company stocks might still be vulnerable to further relative price declines—which indeed they were, but at least there were no rumors that the companies were in financial trouble, as was the case with some investment trusts and other holding companies (see below).

The Investment Trusts

The purpose of investment trusts was purely financial, in contrast to the public utility holding companies. George Howard, President of the United Corp., de-

Table 1.11
The Public Utility Holding Companies in 1929

	Price-earnings ratio		Market price as a % of book value		Dividend yield (%)		Low price as a % of 1929 high price	Return on equity (%)	Moody's bond ratings	Cash & equivalents ($ millions)
	High price	Low price	High price	Low price	High price	Low price				
Cities Service	69	20	782	235	0.44	1.50	29	17.1	Ba	(60)[a]
Columbia Gas & Electric	45	17	500	185	1.43	3.85	37	11.1	A	(8)
Commonwealth & Southern	46	15	485	155	0	0	32	10.6	A pfd.	53
Electric Bond and Share	96	25	233	62	0	0	32	3.3	Aa pfd.	93
IT&T	51	18	324	115	1.34	3.75	36	6.4	A	(23)
Middle West Utilities	91	32	456	160	1.23	3.50	35	5.0	Ba	(1)
North American	37	13	584	210	0	0	36	15.7	A pfd.	4
Standard Gas and Electric	37	11	224	68	1.43	4.73	30	6.0	Baa	23
United Gas Improvement	40	14	413	147	1.94	5.45	35	10.3	Aa pfd.	36
Averages	56.9	18.3	444	148	0.87	2.53	33	9.5	—	—

[a] Brackets indicate short-term borrowing.

scribed the purpose of the corporation to the Senate committee investigating stock exchange practices as follows:

My idea of the United Corporation has been that it is a holding company, with interests in these various other utility operating or holding companies, without management, without supervision, without engineering of any kind, deriving its income wholly either from interest or dividends, whatever they might be, in connection with its investment. It is never building up any organization, leaving complete control in the separate and independent units.[26]

Despite Howard's disclaimer that the United Corp. sought any control over companies in which it invested, the United Corp. was a means for J. P. Morgan & Co. to gain a foothold in the utility business. United Founders served the same purpose for Harris, Forbes & Co. through large indirect holdings in Standard Gas and Electric. Goldman Sachs Trading Corp., Lehman Corp., and Tri-Continental Corp. held influential stock positions in utility, retail, and industrial stocks and exercised control in a few cases, but the portfolios of these investment trusts were more broadly diversified, like a modern mutual fund portfolio.

The underwriters' interest in trusts was in the commissions earned by selling them, and in the fees earned managing their portfolios; but the underwriters also expected these trusts to be successful playing the market and took major shareholdings in the trusts for their own accounts. The underwriters were just as caught up in the optimism of the bull market as their customers were.

The trust stocks traded on asset or portfolio values, rather than on earnings or dividends. Otherwise, they would never have gotten off the ground, for none paid a dividend, and their average return on equity in 1929 was only 4.1%. As stock prices rose, the value of the investment trusts' portfolios rose, which resulted in the trusts' own stocks rising. Some investment trust stock prices got ahead of their asset values in anticipation of the results that professional financial managers could achieve by good management, manipulation, or leverage. (See Table 1.12 for details on specific trusts.) The relationship of market values to book values for these stocks is not a helpful measure, because book values were based on historic costs. These historic costs reflected stock prices whenever the holding company had bought its portfolio, and they were out of line with market values by the end of 1929. The apparent ratio of market to book value at 1929 high prices varied from 356% for Tri-Continental Corp. to 149% for Lehman Corp., yet the latter endured as one of the most successful trusts. None had a bond rating, even though they had debt outstanding.

The investment trust stocks were hit worst by the Crash. They prospered in the market's optimism and suffered in its pessimism. The average stock in this group dropped to 30% of its 1929 high, and, according to market commentators, most investment trust stocks sold at prices below the per-share breakup value of their assets.

Numerous trust stocks were still in underwriters' hands when the Crash hit.

Table 1.12
The Investment Trusts in 1929

	Price-earnings ratio		Market price as a % of book value		Dividend yield (%)		Low price as a % of 1929 high price	Return on equity (%)	Moody's bond ratings	Cash & equivalents ($ millions)
	High price	Low price	High price	Low price	High price	Low price				
Goldman Sachs Trading	129	34	295	78	0	0	26	2.3	NR[b]	(24)[c]
Lehman Corp.	NA	NA	149	69	0	0	46	NA[a]	NR	33
Tri-Continental Corp.	NA	NA	356	63	0	0	18	NA	NR	20
United Corp.	155	39	205	51	0	0	25	1.3	NR	18
United Founders	22	7	245	81	0	0	33	8.6	NR	(10)
Averages	102.0	26.7	250	68	0	0	30	4.1	—	—

[a] NA = Not Available.
[b] NR = No Rating.
[c] Brackets indicate short-term borrowing.

Lehman Corp. was underwritten in September 1929, in a declining market, which may have been the source of its wisdom. Twenty-four investment trusts offerings were made in October. When prices began to drop, many underwriters tried to escape their liabilities by selling their positions in the open market, which drove prices down sharply. Several trusts reacted by buying in their own stocks at the depressed levels. These efforts had little impact on the trend of prices. The stocks of the five trusts followed here sold at 68% of the book value of their investments at their lowest prices in the Crash.

The trust stocks were slow to recover in December, as the market rose again. Observers expected the industry to go through a shakeout in which the strongest trusts absorbed the others. Some trust stocks with prominent sponsors began to rise near the end of the year, but there were rumors that Goldman Sachs Trading Corp. was in serious trouble because of its $24 million in short-term debt and the decline in its portfolio.

The Non-utility Holding Companies

It was to be expected amid the enthusiasm over public utility holding companies and investment trusts that a hybrid between the two types would develop— holding companies designed to control operating companies through passive ownership of a minority or majority stock position without providing managerial or operational leadership. Alleghany Corp. was such a hybrid, sponsored by J. P. Morgan & Co. in 1929 and controlled by the Van Sweringen brothers from Cleveland as the holding company for their railroad stocks, especially the Chesapeake and Ohio and the Missouri-Pacific, from which they hoped to construct a fifth eastern trunk line. Alleghany's principal stock holding was 1.3 million of the 1.8 million outstanding shares of the Chesapeake Corporation, which in turn owned 4.1 million of the 7.1 million outstanding shares of the Chesapeake and Ohio Railway Co. The Van Sweringens, in turn, owned a majority of the Alleghany Corp. common stock. As trouble arose in 1930, they built this pyramid even higher by adding the Van Sweringen Corp., which took over 750,000 of the Van Sweringen brothers' Alleghany Corp. shares and sold bonds and stock warrants to the public.

A. P. Giannini built a large bank holding company system around the Bank of Italy in California and the Bank of America in New York, with the Transamerica Corp. at the apex controlling both these banks and numerous other small banks. (Today's Bank of America was formerly the Bank of Italy mentioned here. The Bank of America name was not transferred to California until after Giannini sold the Bank of America in New York to National City Bank there.) The Bank of Italy was founded by Giannini in San Francisco as a small bank in the Italian produce section, but through aggressive loan policies and high interest rates on deposits, he built it into the largest branch banking system in California. Giannini was thwarted in his efforts to expand into a national branch banking system, partly because banking authorities questioned the soundness of Bank of Italy's lending and capital practices. Giannini's highly personal control over the bank and his secretive habits did not increase the confidence of banking authorities. He came close to his goal, however, by setting up Transamerica Corp. and acquiring the Bank of America. In 1929, he acquired Blair & Co., Inc., a successful investment banking firm, as well.

Other companies formed holding companies along the lines of Alleghany Corp. and Transamerica Corp., often as a preemptive measure to prevent other newly formed holding companies from coming after them. The Pennroad Corp. was formed for this purpose to control the Pennsylvania Railroad, and there was a mass of regional holding companies. None of them achieved the prominence of the two studied here, however.

Stock prices of Alleghany Corp. and Transamerica Corp. soared to heights in 1929 which in some respects even exceeded the stocks of the other holding companies and investment trusts. (See Table 1.13 for details.) Alleghany's stock price reached 108 times earnings per share despite a return on equity of merely 2 1/2% and no dividend. Transamerica stock rose to over 13 times book value despite a return on equity of only 4 1/2% as a result of the enthusiasm of its officers and depositors. Giannini halfheartedly tried to dampen speculation in the stock by proclaiming it overpriced, but he took pride in the avid following of the bank's depositors who were part of the speculation.

When the Crash came, the stocks of Alleghany Corp. and Transamerica Corp. were among the hardest hit. They dropped to 30% of their highest 1929 prices, paralleling the declines of the other holding companies and investment trusts that suffered the worst declines in the market. Alleghany stock dropped to 81% of book value, and its $27 million short-term debt position created some concern about its overall financial position.

The Banks

Bank stocks are of unusual interest in this study because financial causes of the Depression are frequently emphasized rather than causes related to political, industrial, or trade problems. Under the circumstances, banks reflected trends early, and they were directly enmeshed in the most striking events of the period. The leading banks on which we focus are listed in Table 1.14.

There was an air of mystery about the banks' operations, even for the well informed. J. P. Morgan & Co., the leader in prestige both as a bank of deposit and an underwriter of new issues, was a private bank, the financial statements of which had been revealed only once in the century, to the Pujo Committee of the U.S. Senate, which investigated the 1907 market crash. Central Hanover Bank & Trust Co. and the First National Bank of Boston, both among the top ten banks in the nation, consistently did not reveal their earnings, and most of the banks did not reveal the earnings of their securities affiliates. Stocks of all the banks were traded Over-the-Counter rather than on the New York Stock Exchange so that they did not have to offer even the minimal information required by the Exchange. The principal market-makers in the stocks were the banks'

Table 1.13
The Non-utility Holding Companies in 1929

	Price-earnings ratio		Market price as a % of book value		Dividend yield (%)		Low price as a % of 1929 high price	Return on equity (%)	Moody's bond ratings	Cash & equivalents ($ millions)
	High price	*Low price*	*High price*	*Low price*	*High price*	*Low price*				
Alleghany Corp.	108	32	271	81	0	0	30	2.5	Baa	(27)[b]
Transamerica	21	6	1,345	402	2.39	8.00	30	4.5	NR[a]	4
Averages	64.5	19.0	808	242	1.20	4.00	30	3.5	—	—

[a] NR = Not Rated.
[b] Brackets indicate short-term borrowing.

Table 1.14
The Banks in 1929

	Price-earnings ratio		Market price as a % of book value		Dividend yield (%)		Low price as a % of 1929 high price	Return on equity (%)	Moody's bond ratings	Cash & equivalents ($ millions)
	High price	Low price	High price	Low price	High price	Low price				
Bankers Trust	31	21	367	244	1.90	2.86	66	10.9	—	—
Central Hanover	NA	NA	525	265	1.14	2.26	50	NA[a]	—	—
Chase National	62	29	438	208	1.30	2.74	47	7.1	—	—
Continental Illinois	38	23	493	301	1.54	2.52	61	13.4	—	—
First National (Boston)	NA	NA	404	213	1.50	2.83	53	NA	—	—
First National (Chicago)	39	19	412	204	1.55	3.13	50	10.5	—	—
Guaranty Trust	41	17	371	151	1.58	3.88	41	9.0	—	—
Irving Trust	39	17	378	167	1.57	3.56	44	9.7	—	—
National City	120	37	1,318	409	0.69	2.22	31	7.1	—	—
Averages	52.9	23.3	523	240	1.42	2.89	49	9.7	—	—

NA = Not Available.

[a] NA

own investment banking subsidiaries, and because they did not hesitate to trade in the parent's stock to push up its price or to aid officer-stockholders, the outsider never knew what influences might be affecting bank stocks. Banks also lent money broadly to customers who wanted to purchase the bank's stock, and employees were encouraged to become stockholders on margin.

At their peaks the banks were probably the most overvalued stocks in the market. National City Bank stock traded at 120 times 1929 earnings per share and over 1300% of book value. Chase National Bank stock traded at 62 times 1929 earnings per share and 438% of book value. These two were the favorite bank stocks and the most affected by speculation.

The Chase was led by Albert H. Wiggin, its chairman and largest stockholder and the most popular banker on Wall Street. He had joined the bank as a lower-level employee in 1911, when its capital was only $13 million. Once Wiggin became the bank's moving force, he created one of the leading banks in the world through mergers, new branches, offices in Europe and the Caribbean during the 1920s, and the Chase Securities Corp. A solid, bullheaded man with pince-nez glasses, Wiggin radiated an air of confidence and friendliness, which he added to high competence. He was on more than 50 boards of directors by 1929 and an active participant in stock market pools and new-issue syndicates, either personally or through several family trusts established in Canada.

Charles E. Mitchell led National City Bank of New York as its Chairman through the force of his personality rather than large stock holdings. Good-looking, suave, at ease with the press and the radio, Mitchell was a supersalesman of prosperity. His personality seemed more suited to an investment banker than a commercial banker, and he was publicly suspected of excess and vulnerability in his position even before the Crash. None doubted his ability, however. When he became President of the bank in 1921, National City Bank had capital of only $40 million and one office. He made his first acquisition within a year, and during the 1920s he expanded the bank to include 72 branches in New York City and 99 in 24 foreign countries.[27] Its capital in 1929 was $240 million, and its securities affiliate, National City Co., had 60 branches, 11 of them foreign, and was the largest underwriter of new issues and a challenge to J. P. Morgan & Co. Mitchell was even up to challenging the Board of Governors of the Federal Reserve, which he did in May 1929 by publicly making $40 million available to the call loan market when the Board of Governors was trying to reduce stock market credit.

All the bank stocks were overvalued, however, whoever their leaders happened to be. The nine largest at their highest stock prices averaged 53 times 1929 earnings per share, 523% of book value, and a dividend yield of only 1.42%. The banks had no earnings history to justify such valuations. Profits for 1929 for the banking industry were a record $729 million,[28] but for the nine leading companies return on equity averaged only 10.2%, compared with 16 1/2% for all companies, and the banks' history was one of stability rather than rapid growth. Their high stock prices were stimulated entirely by intense merger activity among the banks in 1929 and by the trading of their own securities affiliates.

An extreme version of this merger activity occurred in Detroit, where ultimately two holding companies, the Guardian Detroit Union Group and the Detroit Bankers Co., controlled the city's banking and much of the banking in the rest of Michigan. When the Guardian Detroit Union Group was created in December 1929 by a merger of the Guardian Detroit Group and Union Commerce Corp., the two companies had acquired 27 banks. Eight more were quickly added. Officers later testified that remarkably little heed was paid to the assets of banks acquired in this hectic process. The Guardian Detroit Union Group had two securities affiliates—Keane, Higbie & Co. and the Guardian Detroit Co. Both had heavy inventories of securities at the time of the Crash, and the Guardian Detroit Co. had $3.4 million of the parent company's stock, which it had bought from Goldman Sachs Trading Corp. at the apparent bargain price of $189 per share when the stock was quoted at $230 to $240. The stock was down to $120 by November 29th, when a group of prominent stockholders of the parent took the stock off the Guardian Detroit Co.'s hands at its purchase price in order to protect the company's financial position.[29]

The Guardian Detroit Union Group was poorly managed and showed signs of trouble early. Much of its stock was held by directors, officers, and employees, or on margin loans within the Group's banks. The effect was demoralizing as the stock's price fell. Various directors guaranteed a $1.6 million loan from Bankers Trust Co. to refinance distress loans of officers and employees to counter this effect. The Group and its competitor, Detroit Bankers Co., would make headlines in 1933 when they caused Michigan to be the first major state to declare a bank holiday.

The nine banks' stocks averaged a decline to 49% of their 1929 high prices during the Crash, which was identical to the decline for all leading stocks, despite their high reputation and the support bank affiliates gave to their stocks. National City Co. bought a substantial amount of its affiliated bank's stock as it fell to 31% of its highest 1929 price, but it was able to reduce its holding to normal trading volume before year's end. Chase Bank stock dropped to 47% of its highest 1929 price and traded very heavily. Between September and December, Wiggin sold over 42,500 shares himself through pool agreements managed principally by Dominick & Dominick. (In principle, Wiggin "shorted against the box" by having one trust sell short what another trust owned.)

Price recovery in the bank stocks was limited in December because of the relative overvaluation which still prevailed for these stocks. The nine bank stocks' lowest prices still averaged 23 times 1929 earnings per share, compared with 12 1/2 times for all leading companies, and the banks' dividends provided a yield of 2.89% at their lowest stock prices, versus the average yield for all companies of 5.92%. The banks' reputations were exceedingly high, however.

They had organized the Bankers' Pool to support the market, acted as lenders of last resort when call loans were called, and now appeared as bastions of financial strength which would limit the depths of any trade recession.

The Oil Industry

The oil industry grew dramatically in the 1920s because of the growth of the auto industry. Gasoline production quadrupled between 1919 and 1929 to 18.3 billion gallons, and gasoline determined the oil industry's output and profit performances. The industry's net income of $583 million in 1929 was second only to that of the railroad industry and well ahead of the auto, electric utility, and steel industries, which earned approximately $400 million.

The oil industry was dominated by the Standard Oil companies, principally Standard Oil Co. (New Jersey), Standard Oil Co. of California, Standard Oil Co. (Indiana), and Socony-Vacuum Oil Co. (formerly Standard Oil Co. of New York). Standard Oil of New Jersey already had assets of $1.8 billion. Its bonds were rated Aaa, and its stock was the tenth most active in 1929. The Standard Oil companies were financial powers as well as oil powers because of their large cash positions and strong cash flows. (See Table 1.15 for details on the companies.)

At the other extreme among the oil companies was Sinclair Consolidated Oil Corp., whose Chairman, Harry F. Sinclair, was a principal in the Teapot Dome Scandal and later led manipulations in Sinclair Consolidated stock with Arthur Cutten. The company survived and grew, but much about it was questionable.

Between these two extremes were major companies like Gulf Oil Corp. of Pennsylvania and Texas Corp., which compared in size with Standard Oil of California and Shell Union Oil Corp., controlled by Royal Dutch Shell Co. The Atlantic Refining Co. and Phillips Petroleum Co. were considerably smaller at about one-third the size of Gulf Oil and only one-tenth the size of Standard Oil of New Jersey.

Despite the size and growth of the oil industry, oil company stocks were on a par with railroad and steel company stocks as the lowest-valued stocks in the market. The ten leading oil company stocks at their high prices averaged only 17 1/2 times 1929 earnings per share and 161% of book value, compared with the averages for all companies of 30 times earnings per share and 420% of book value. Oil stocks yielded a relatively high 3.45%, compared with 3% for all stocks. The cause of the poor valuation of oil stocks was the companies' low return on equity, which averaged only 9.7% in 1929. Even the four leading Standard Oil companies averaged only 9 1/4% return on equity.

The pressure on profits came from the dramatic increases in oil reserves, which forced prices down from $2.24 per barrel in 1926 to $1.70 per barrel by October 1929. Prices of gasoline, the oil industry's most important product, dropped from a peak of 15¢ per gallon in 1925 to 7 1/2¢ per gallon in 1929.[30] Seismic

Table 1.15
The Oil Companies in 1929

	Price-earnings ratio		Market price as a % of book value		Dividend yield (%)		Low price as a % of 1929 high price	Return on equity (%)	Moody's bond ratings	Cash & equivalents ($ millions)
	High price	*Low price*	*High price*	*Low price*	*High price*	*Low price*				
Atlantic Refining	13	5	144	56	2.56	6.67	38	11.5	Aaa	13
Gulf Oil of Pa.	21	12	282	155	0.72	1.30	55	13.2	Aaa	27
Phillips Petroleum	9	5	121	62	4.26	8.33	51	13.2	A	6
Shell Union Oil	25	15	145	86	4.38	7.37	59	5.7	A	8
Sinclair Consolidated	16	7	90	42	4.44	9.50	47	5.6	Baa	17
Socony-Vacuum	22	14	155	103	3.33	5.00	67	7.2	Aaa	(3)[b]
Standard Oil (Calif.)	23	14	178	113	3.05	4.81	63	7.9	NR[a]	27
Standard Oil (Ind.)	14	9	166	113	5.16	7.56	68	12.1	NR	123
Standard Oil (N.J.)	17	10	169	98	2.41	4.15	58	9.7	Aaa	242
Texas Corp.	15	10	160	111	4.17	6.00	69	10.9	Aa	78
Averages	17.5	10.1	161	94	3.45	6.07	58	9.7	—	—

[a] NR = Not Rated.
[b] Brackets indicate short-term borrowing.

techniques had revolutionized the industry after their introduction in 1926, increasing oil discoveries so that oil reserves doubled between 1927 and 1939.

In the Crash oil company stocks dropped to only 10 times 1929 earnings per share and 94% of book value, compared to 12 1/2 times earnings per share and 181% of book value for all stocks. The only good point to be made for the oil stocks was that their average decline to 58% of their 1929 peak prices was modest compared with the average of 48% for all stocks. The lack of selling pressure merely reflected that there had been little speculative interest in the industry's stocks during the boom.

The Chemical Industry

Chemicals also went through a major expansion in the 1920s, especially in basic products like soda ash and sulphur. Chemical prices too had declined by almost 45% from their peak in 1920,[31] but financial and profit positions of the chemical companies were excellent. Industry profits were $157 million in 1929 on sales of $4 billion. None of the leading chemical companies had any debt to speak of. Chemical company stocks performed close to the averages for all companies, and at their highest prices they averaged 32 times 1929 earnings per share, 600% of book value, and a dividend yield of 1.88%. (See Table 1.16 for details on the industry.)

E. I. Du Pont de Nemours & Co. was the superior chemical company. It earned 22% on its equity, and its stock accordingly sold at 660% of book value, well above the average of 420% for all stocks. Du Pont was principally in explosives, plastics, paints, rayon, cellophane, dyes, and ethyl alcohol, but it also owned almost 10 million shares (22.9%) of General Motors Corp.—an investment begun in 1917 and completed in 1920 when it had acquired the shares of GM Chairman, William Durant, who found himself overextended in the market decline of that year. The 10 million shares equalled almost one General Motors share per Du Pont share. Du Pont's $43 million income from its General Motors stock exceeded operating income from its regular business by $8.5 million in 1929 and by $15 million in 1928.

Commercial Solvents Corp. was the most highly valued among the chemical stocks because of its 31.9% return on equity, but it was a small company. It had total assets of only $13 million, 2 1/2 million shares outstanding, and two plants in Illinois which produced butyl alcohol and other solvents through the Weizmann Process, on which it held worldwide exclusive license rights. However, Dow Chemical Co. and Monsanto Chemical Co. were also small companies, with total capitalizations of only $19 million and $15 million respectively but with returns on equity roughly half that of Commercial Solvents. Commercial Solvents stock sold at 46 times 1929 earnings per share and almost 1500% of book value at its peak price in 1929.

Chemical stocks in the Crash declined in line with the averages for all leading stocks. At their lowest prices chemical stocks were down 50% to 14 times 1929

Table 1.16
The Chemical Industry in 1929

	Price-earnings ratio		Market price as a % of book value		Dividend yield (%)		Low price as a % of 1929 high price	Return on equity (%)	Moody's bond ratings	Cash & equivalents ($ millions)
	High price	Low price	High price	Low price	High price	Low price				
Allied Chemical	28	16	374	207	1.69	3.05	55	13.3	Aa pfd.	87
Commercial Solvents	46	13	1,477	425	1.43	5.00	32	31.9	NR[a]	6
Dow Chemical	20	15	400	300	2.50	3.33	75	17.5	NR	1
E. I. Du Pont	33	11	660	250	2.25	6.50	35	22.2	Aa	34
Monsanto Chemical	28	16	253	147	1.54	2.66	58	9.0	Baa	2
Union Carbide	36	15	467	197	1.86	4.40	42	13.1	NR	68
Averages	31.8	14.3	605	254	1.88	4.16	50	17.8	—	—

[a] NR = Not Rated.

earnings per share, 254% of book value, and an average yield of 4.16%. Commercial Solvents fell furthest in the Crash to 32% of its highest price, and Du Pont fell to 35% of its highest price, reflecting that the two stocks had the highest valuations before the Crash and so the farthest to fall. Dow Chemical stock proved remarkably resistant to the overall trend, declining only 25%.

The Food Industry

The leading companies in the food industry ranged from the larger fruit and dairy companies, with capitalizations of over $150 million, such as United Fruit Co., National Dairy Products Corp., and the Borden Co., to the milling companies one-third their size, such as General Mills Inc. and Pillsbury Flour Mills, Inc.

Table 1.17 shows that the food companies had average returns on equity of 19.6%, and their stocks at their highest prices averaged 466% of book value, compared with the average for all stocks of 420%. Food industry stocks received an average valuation in other respects, as well, during 1929. The companies' highest stock prices averaged only 22 1/2 times earnings, compared with the average of 30 for all leading stocks, and dividend yields on food stocks at their highest prices averaged 3.16%, versus 3% for all leading stocks. The Crash dropped food stocks to an average of 51% of their highest 1929 prices, versus 48% for all leading stocks. At these low prices, food stocks were only 11 1/2 times earnings and yielded 6.46%, compared with the averages for all stocks of 12 1/2 times earnings and 6.90%. Only the market-to-book relationship of 283% for food stocks at their low prices was better than the average of 181% for all stocks.

Standard Brands stood out in the industry. It earned over 34% return on equity, and its stock at its high was over 1100% of book value. The company was created in June 1929 by the merger of Fleischmann Co., Royal Baking Starch Co., and E. W. Gillett Co., Ltd., and by the subsequent acquisition of Chase & Sanborn, Inc., in August 1929 and Widlar Food Products Co. in December. The merger was managed by J. P. Morgan & Co., as was the initial distribution of 722,600 shares of Standard Brands at $32 per share on June 24, 1929, near the peak of the bull market. The distribution was effected through a private list of individuals, brokers, and investment bankers which became contentious in later years, occupying much of the cross-examination of J. P. Morgan & Co. partners in the 1933 hearings on stock exchange practices before the Senate Committee on Banking and Currency. There is considerable evidence in the correspondence on these placements, tabled with the Senate Banking and Currency Committee hearings on stock exchange practices, that the participants knew a "hot stock" was being created and that they were grateful for the opportunity to buy it at its original price. Standard Brands stock did not disappoint its sponsors. It began trading on September 6th at slightly over $40 per share, compared to its $32 issue price. The prestige of J. P. Morgan & Co. was a

Table 1.17
The Food Industry in 1929

	Price-earnings ratio		Market price as a % of book value		Dividend yield (%)		Low price as a % of 1929 high price	Return on equity (%)	Moody's bond ratings	Cash & equivalents ($ millions)
	High price	Low price	High price	Low price	High price	Low price				
Borden	19	10	291	151	2.95	5.66	52	15.7	NR[a]	11
General Foods	22	10	631	269	3.66	8.57	43	28.7	NR	9
General Mills	18	10	234	132	3.93	7.00	56	12.8	Ba pfd.	(3)[b]
National Biscuit	29	17	594	350	3.95	6.70	59	20.5	Aaa pfd.	23
National Dairy	22	9	458	225	2.30	5.55	42	21.3	A	21
Pillsbury	13	6	188	88	3.13	6.67	47	15.0	Baa	(4)
Standard Brands	33	15	1,125	462	3.33	7.50	45	34.3	Aa pfd.	32
United Fruit	24	15	204	127	2.52	4.04	62	8.7	NR	24
Averages	22.5	11.5	466	226	3.16	6.46	51	19.6	—	—

[a] NR = Not Rated.
[b] Brackets indicate short-term borrowing.

powerful stimulus to attach to a new company that was highly profitable and appeared bent on a course of acquisitions to improve its earnings further. The stock jumped to $45, and in the remaining four months traded almost 6 million shares, which ranked it 36th in volume on the NYSE for all 1929. At $45 it was 33 times 1929 earnings and yielded 3.33% compared with National Biscuit Co., a very strong company, which sold at 29 times 1929 earnings per share and yielded 3.95%.

United Fruit was apart from the other food companies in its low return on equity of only 8.7% in 1929, and its extensive South and Central American landholdings that produced bananas, cocoa, and sugar. However, the company remained surprisingly stable during the Depression for such a heavy dependence on agricultural production.

The Mining Industry

The mining stocks had strong followings on the New York Stock Exchange. In 1929, Anaconda Copper Mining Co., which owned more than one-third of the world's copper reserves and accounted for 20% of world copper production, was fourth in volume of trading on the Exchange. It traded 18 1/2 million shares, double its capitalization. International Nickel Co. of Canada, Ltd., was fifth most active, Kennecott Copper Corp. was 16th, and Nevada Consolidated Copper was 29th.

In 1929, Anaconda Copper was the object of one of the largest pool operations. National City Co. set up an account for 300,000 shares in early August, when the stock was selling between $120 and $135, and initiated a campaign to sell the stock to its customers. In October it bought an additional 50,000 shares to support the market when it weakened before the Crash, and sold this stock as well to customers. Much of the original stock sold to customers was also owned by National City Co. The ethics of the whole affair were made further suspect because Charles E. Mitchell, the head of National City Co., was a director of Anaconda, and was aware that copper prices had peaked earlier in the year and were now artificially pegged at about 17 3/4¢ per pound.[32]

The mining companies were an unusually disparate group. Returns on equity varied from only 4 1/2% at Phelps Dodge Corp. to 58.6% at Texas Gulf Sulphur Co. Anaconda, Phelps Dodge, Homestake Mining Co., and Kennecott Copper Corp. paid out virtually all their earnings in dividends, while National Lead Co. paid out only 20% and Alaska Juneau Gold Mining Co. paid no dividends at all. Except for Texas Gulf Sulphur and International Nickel, earnings were depressingly low for an industry that had such large capital investments and was at the peak of a widely fluctuating cycle in metals prices. (See Table 1.18 for details on the industry.)

In absolute terms the metals mining industry was one of considerable substance in 1929. Its sales of $1.2 billion exceeded all other natural resource extractive industries. Industry profits on these sales were $278 million, which exceeded

Table 1.18
The Mining Industry in 1929

	Price-earnings ratio		Market price as a % of book value		Dividend yield (%)		Low price as a % of 1929 high price	Return on equity (%)	Moody's bond ratings	Cash & equivalents ($ millions)
	High price	Low price	High price	Low price	High price	Low price				
Alaska Juneau Gold	14	6	100	43	0	0	43	7.1	Caa	0
American Smelting	13	6	197	94	3.08	6.45	48	15.2	Aa	23
Anaconda Copper	18	9	230	110	5.00	10.40	48	12.8	NR[a]	(35)[b]
Homestake Mining	22	16	96	67	7.53	10.77	70	4.3	NR	5
International Nickel	50	17	1,043	352	1.23	3.60	35	21.0	A pfd.	17
Kennecott Copper	19	9	318	149	4.76	10.20	47	16.8	NR	47
National Lead	8	5	99	61	2.38	3.88	61	12.0	A pfd.	8
Phelps Dodge	30	12	133	52	3.75	9.68	39	4.5	NR	18
Texas Gulf Sulphur	14	7	773	391	4.71	9.30	51	58.6	NR	5
Averages	20.9	9.7	332	147	3.60	7.14	49	16.9	—	—

[a] NR = Not Rated.
[b] Brackets indicate short-term borrowing.

the telephone and telegraph business and the chemical, tobacco, textile, paper, printing, rubber, timber, electrical machinery, and numerous other industries. Profits of $278 million exceeded half of all electric and gas utilities profits and was one-third of the railways' profits.[33]

Most of the mining stocks were basically copper companies and derived their market attention from the high price of copper. Electrolytic copper sold in New York at over 21¢ per pound in March 1929 and was pegged by the producers, in a collusive effect that should have given the Justice Department apoplexy, at about 17 3/4¢ per pound from May 1929 through the end of the year, compared with 13¢–14¢ per pound in prior years.

The stock market was unwilling to put a large premium on earnings at such prices. If we exclude International Nickel and Texas Gulf Sulphur, mining stocks at their highest prices in 1929 were only 17.7 times earnings per share and 167% of book value, the latter representing a dramatic discount from the average market to book value ratio of 420% for all stocks. However, International Nickel's stock was over 1000% of book value at its highest price. International Nickel had a special market reception because of its position in nickel technology. Its peak price-earnings ratio in 1929 was 50, and its dividend yield was only 1.23%. Texas Gulf Sulphur's 58.6% return on equity gave it a stock price that was 773% of its book value.

In the Crash, mining stocks dropped to an average of 49% of their highest prices, and International Nickel dropped to 35%. The support bid for copper at 17 3/4¢ per pound gave the appearance of a stable industry, but behind this publicly visible price, copper exports dropped sharply in the last quarter of 1929 from close to 40,000 tons per month to 25,000 tons, and domestic copper production dropped from a peak of 190 million pounds in April 1929 to 150 million pounds in December.[34] Investors anticipated that these pressures would reduce copper prices and so gave little credence to the high dividend yields averaging 7.14% on mining stocks at their lowest prices. Anaconda and Kennecott stocks both bore yields over 10% at their Crash lows. Mining stock valuations were well below the averages for all stocks at their lowest prices, with mining stocks averaging only 9.7 times earnings per share, compared with 12.4 times, and excluding International Nickel and Texas Gulf Sulphur, only 83% of book value compared with 181% for all stocks.

Among the poorest stock market valuations in the industry were the stocks of Alaska Juneau Gold Mining Co. and Homestake Mining Co., companies whose recent history could only be described as dull. Neither their stocks nor their earnings had run up in the 1927–29 enthusiasm, and their stable returns on equity of 7.1% and 4.3% respectively inspired no hope for the future. Neither company's stock exceeded book value at the market peak, and at their low points Alaska Juneau's stock was only 43% of book value and Homestake's was 67% of book value. At the moment few saw the opportunities for profit in gold stocks that devaluation of the dollar would produce in 1933.

The Motion Picture Companies

The motion picture companies had prominent speculative stocks because of the new technological developments in movie sound systems and America's general love affair with Hollywood. What is more, they were making money. Motion picture company earnings had risen from $12 1/2 million in 1927, when sound came in, to $35.7 million by 1929. However, the convoluted finances and garish personalities of the leaders of the industry prevented the stocks from having high relative values. Paramount-Publix Co., which had become the largest company in the industry with assets of $215 million under the businesslike leadership of Adolph Zukor, sold at only 13 times earnings and twice book value at its highest price in 1929 because of a modest 12.3% return on equity. Loew's Inc. and Fox Film Corp. stocks sold on approximately the same basis but had 50% better returns on equity. Warner Bros. Pictures, Inc., and Radio-Keith-Orpheum Corp. sold at 37 and 32 times earnings and 295% and 247% of book value, despite returns on equity of only 8% and options or convertible privileges outstanding equal to one-third their common stock, which should have reduced their valuations. RKO paid no dividend and Warner Bros. earnings were only $1.77, versus a $4-per-share dividend. (See Table 1.19 for details on specific companies.)

The low values and difficulty of establishing reasonable comparative values for motion picture stocks reflected the unusual finances of the industry. The companies were highly leveraged with capital structures averaging 43% debt, and large commitments for leases and contingent payouts on acquisitions. Besides, the companies' balance sheets and earnings were questionable indications of their financial positions. Book values of theaters were inflated because of the high prices paid to acquire them when sound movies began. Film inventories were of unknown value since their revenues depended on their popularity. Profits could be arbitrarily set by capitalizing costs as part of film production and by the rate at which film and property costs were amortized. The latter was unusually low for Paramount and RKO, which charged off less than 5% annually of their investments, whereas Warner Bros. charged off 10% and Loew's charged off over 30%.

The personalities of leaders in the industry appeared as unusual as its finances. Moguls like Louis B. Mayer and Sam Goldwyn at Loew's, William Fox at Fox Films, and the Warner brothers had flamboyant reputations unlikely to attract sober-minded investors, and motion picture successes were personalized, artistic achievements that were difficult to institutionalize. Only Adolph Zukor at Paramount had the financial background and personality likely to attract other businessmen. The closest the industry came to institutionalization was in the intermarriage of numerous children of the moguls.

Film stocks were pushed down to unusual depths by the Crash. Their low prices were 35% of their highs and averaged only 7.4 times 1929 earnings per

Table 1.19
The Motion Picture Companies in 1929

	Price-earnings ratio		Market price as a % of book value		Dividend yield (%)		Low price as a % of 1929 high price	Return on equity (%)	Moody's bond ratings	Cash & equivalents ($ millions)
	High price	Low price	High price	Low price	High price	Low price				
Fox Film	10	2	180	32	0.94	5.26	18	17.4	Ba	(41)[b]
Loew's	12	4	224	84	3.82	10.20	38	19.2	Baa	10
Paramount-Publix	13	6	200	75	3.95	8.55	46	12.3	Baa	6
Radio-Keith-Orpheum	32	8	247	63	0	0	26	7.6	NR[a]	3
Warner Bros.	37	17	295	167	6.15	13.35	47	8.0	Baa	5
Averages	20.8	7.4	229	84	2.97	7.47	35	12.9	—	—

[a] NR = Not Rated.
[b] Brackets indicate short-term borrowing.

share. Loew's stock price was only 4 times, and Fox Films only 2 times, earnings per share. Only Warner Bros. stock was above book value (167%). The others averaged 64% of book value.

William Fox, who controlled Fox Film Corp. and Fox Theatres Corp., ran into unusual problems which threatened the whole movie industry in the Crash. Fox had purchased 400,000 shares of Loew's stock early in 1929 for $50 million, plus 260,000 shares in the open market. The two Fox corporations incurred $72 million in short-term debts for these purchases and expanded their debt to over $150 million from under $15 million at the end of 1928. They had both bought the Loew's stock and spent $20 million to buy British Gaumont Co., a chain of 300 U.K. theaters.

These debts began to mature in October, November, and December of 1929 when the Fox companies had no hope of obtaining alternative funds. The Loew's stock, bought at an average cost of $110 per share, was trading below $40 and provided insufficient collateral to justify extension of the loans.

Rumors began to circulate that Fox was going bankrupt. Fox Films Corp. stock dropped from a high of $106 to $19. Fox Theatres Corp. stock dropped from a high of $38 to $5. Before the year ended, both Fox Films and Fox Theatres were in technical default and at the mercy of the bankers, principally Chase National Bank, even though the two corporations earned $12 million combined in 1929. The Fox enterprises were reorganized into General Theatres Equipment, Inc. without William Fox, which is part of the 1930's story.[35]

Motion picture stocks recovered quickly after the Crash. RKO was up over two-thirds from its lowest price, and Paramount, Warner Bros., and Loew's were up about 40%. They were on the verge of becoming the favorite speculative stocks of 1930.

The Steel Industry

In 1929 the iron and steel industry was the second largest manufacturing industry in the United States, second only to the oil industry. Steel industry net income of $409 million compared with $583 million for the oil industry and equalled that of the electric and gas utility industry. Steel sales of $8.3 billion were 6% of all industrial sales and were exceeded only by the food industry.[36] Monthly steel production figures were considered the most important economic data along with freight-car loadings.

United States Steel Corp. and Bethlehem Steel Co. were the two leading steel stocks. U.S. Steel had $2 billion in assets and was rated Aaa. Bethlehem Steel had assets of $735 million and was rated Aa. Their prominence in the financial markets was considerable. U.S. Steel's assets made it the largest unregulated company in the United States and second only to American Telephone & Telegraph Co. It controlled 60% of the country's steel capacity, and its 8 million shares outstanding had a market value of approximately $1.3 billion (the fourth largest). It was in the ten most active stocks every year. Three Morgan partners sat on U.S. Steel's board of directors. It was natural that Richard Whitney made the first bid for the Bankers' Pool in U.S. Steel and that the Pool's position in U.S. Steel of $27.1 million was almost double the next largest—$16.6 million in AT&T.[37]

The quality of U.S. Steel was overrated by the press and later commentators, however. Table 1.20 shows that U.S. Steel earned only a 10.4% return on equity in 1929, when its earnings were 50% above its average for the prior four years. Its stock sold at only 12 times earnings and 128% of book value at the peak of the stock market frenzy and had not sold as high as book value in the previous five years. The company had raised its regular dividend only once since 1916 and did not offer a prospect of better results. All that could be said for the company was that it was large and dominated a fundamental industry. Even its Aaa rating appeared weak, because the company had earned its interest charges only 4 1/2 to 5 1/2 times in 1925–28.[38]

Bethlehem Steel had an even worse financial record and stock market position. Its stock did sell at a peak of 13 times 1929 earnings per share, slightly higher than that of U.S. Steel, but Bethlehem Steel stock was only 98% of book value at this price, and in prior years Bethlehem Steel stock rarely sold at a price above 50% of its book value. Bethlehem Steel earned only a 7.6% return on its equity in 1929 when earnings were nearly double the average of the four previous years. It had one of the worst returns on equity of any leading company. It is a mystery why its long-term debt was rated Aa, for the company earned its interest only 2 1/2 times in 1925–28. Bethlehem Steel's highest dividend rate was established during the high profits of the war years, after which it declined steadily until 1924, when it was eliminated. Dividends were reinstated in 1929, but investors treated them with some skepticism. The stock bore a relatively high yield of 4.26% at its peak price.

Inland Steel Co. and Youngstown Sheet & Tube Co. had better financial performances than either U.S. Steel or Bethlehem Steel. Inland Steel had a 17.8% return on equity in 1929 and increased its per share dividend from $2.50 to $3.50, having paid regular dividends since before World War I. Inland Steel stock sold at only 12 times earnings per share at its highest 1929 price, compared with 30 times earnings per share for all stocks, but at this high price Inland Steel stock was 205% of book value. Youngstown Sheet & Tube earned a 15.9% return on equity in 1929, second only to Inland Steel, and also increased its 1929 dividend rate from $5.00 to $6.00 per share, having paid regular dividends since before the war. At the peak in the market its stock had the highest valuation among the steel stocks at 20 times earnings and 316% of book value. Both these companies were much smaller than U.S. Steel and Bethlehem Steel, however. Inland Steel's capitalization was only 5%, and Youngstown Sheet & Tube's was 10% of the capitalization of U.S. Steel.

In the Crash the major steel stocks declined to 51% of their peak prices, they averaged 85% of book value and only 6 1/2 times 1929 earnings per share. These levels were approximately half the average market-to-book-value ratio of 181%

Table 1.20
The Steel Industry in 1929

	Price-earnings ratio		Market price as a % of book value		Dividend yield (%)		Low price as a % of 1929 high price	Return on equity (%)	Moody's bond ratings	Cash & equivalents ($ millions)
	High price	Low price	High price	Low price	High price	Low price				
Bethlehem Steel	13	7	98	54	4.26	7.70	56	7.6	Aa	118
Inland Steel	12	7	205	129	3.10	4.93	63	17.8	Aa	15
U.S. Steel	12	7	128	74	3.05	5.30	57	10.4	Aaa pfd.	191
Youngstown Sheet & Tube	20	5	316	83	1.45	5.49	26	15.9	Aa	13
Averages	14.3	6.5	187	85	2.97	5.86	51	12.9	—	—

and the average price-earnings ratio of 12 1/2 for all stocks. In the Crash the steel stocks did not decline as much as the averages because the weaknesses of the companies were so clear that they deterred the extreme overvaluation common to other stocks in the first place.

The Automobile Manufacturers

The auto industry sold a record 5.6 million cars and trucks in 1929, compared with 4.6 million in 1928. The still-private Ford Motor Co. sold 2 million Model A cars and earned $82 million, while General Motors Corp. sold virtually the same number of cars domestically and had three times the profits of $247 million. The two companies had over two-thirds of the domestic automobile market. The great difference between them was Ford's reliance on a single, inexpensive model, whereas General Motors had already developed its policy of many models covering the spectrum of buyer tastes. General Motors offered the Buick, Cadillac, Marquette, La Salle, Oakland, Pontiac, Oldsmobile, and Viking, in addition to its mass market car, the Chevrolet, which alone sold 1 million units in 1929. The superiority of the General Motors approach was obvious in its income of three times Ford's on only twice the assets. The lesser automobile companies—Chrysler Corp., Hudson Motor Car Co., and Nash Motors Co.—all earned substantially less in 1929 than in prior years in the face of the competition between General Motors and Ford. Only Packard Motor Car Co. had a record year in 1929. General Motors and Nash Motors stocks hit records in 1929 by a few dollars over 1928, but the stocks of Chrysler, Hudson Motors, and Packard Motors were below their 1928 high prices. The auto industry was one of the few which did not establish significant new stock records in 1929. (See Table 1.21 for details on specific companies.)

The stock market valuation of the major public automobile companies was just average, which was somewhat surprising because it was a burgeoning new industry. Mass middle-class buying of automobiles, the closed body, and major improvements in roads had all occurred in the mid-1920s and might have been expected to produce flights of fancy among investors, especially since the auto companies' average return on equity of 27.6% in 1929 was third highest of any industry. The case was otherwise, however. The auto stocks at their 1929 high prices averaged only 19 times earnings and 518% of book value. The latter was just above the average of 420%, and the former was much below the average price-earnings ratio of 30. The companies' stocks had an average dividend yield of 3.96%, compared with 3.7% for all leading companies.

It is even more surprising that General Motors was not more highly valued. As recently as 1920, the company was a loosely run motley of various subsidiaries, dominated by William Durant and without claim to preeminence in any line of the industry. It controlled a minor share of the automobile market, compared with Ford Motor Co.'s 60% share. Durant lost control of the company in the 1920 slump because of his efforts to support GM stock. Thereafter, General

Table 1.21
The Automobile Manufacturers in 1929

	Price-earnings ratio		Market price as a % of book value		Dividend yield (%)		Low price as a % of 1929 high price	Return on equity (%)	Moody's bond ratings	Cash & equivalents ($ millions)
	High price	Low price	High price	Low price	High price	Low price				
Chrysler Corp.	27	5	519	100	2.22	11.55	19	19.0	NR[a]	39
General Motors	17	6	511	190	3.91	10.75	36	30.5	Aa pfd.	127
Hudson Motor Car	13	5	247	100	5.32	13.16	40	19.4	NR	17
Nash Motors	18	6	595	200	5.04	15.00	34	32.6	NR	42
Packard Motor Car	20	8	716	282	3.33	8.45	40	36.4	NR	18
Averages	19.0	6.0	518	174	3.96	11.78	34	27.6	—	—

[a] NR = Not Rated.

Motors was dominated by the E. I. Du Pont de Nemours Co. and the auto professionals growing up in the company—Alfred P. Sloan, Jr., the Fisher brothers, Charles F. Kettering, W. S. Knudsen, C. S. Mott, Fritz Opel, and Samuel McLaughlin. E. I. Du Pont de Nemours Co. had developed a sophisticated, decentralized and modern management structure as a result of its diversification after World War I which Pierre S. Du Pont now brought to General Motors as its Chairman with the help of John Raskob and several other financial Du Pont men who moved to General Motors. The Du Pont organization introduced strict financial controls, formal planning procedures, and disciplined inventory policies. Management functions were heavily decentralized, along with decision-making authority. The Du Ponts also brought in their policy of creating wealth for key employees by setting up the Management Securities Corporation for 80 executives who each owned an average of $50,000 of General Motors stock through it. This $50,000 was worth over $3 million by 1930.

The new management team was able to capitalize on changes in the automobile industry to catch up with Ford, particularly at the advent of a mass market for its product. General Motors concentrated on closed cars, which were only 17% of the U.S. market in 1920 but were 89% by 1929, and on annual model changes, while Ford persisted with open cars and the static Model T, which adapted poorly to a closed body. General Motors developed lines of cars for all incomes and fostered installment buying through General Motors Acceptance Corp. General Motors sales grew from 457,000 units in 1922 to 1,899,000 units in 1929, while the total market only grew from 2,646,000 to 5,622,000 units. When Ford shut down in 1927 to engineer the Model A car, Chevrolet sold 792,000 units and regularly held first place in single model sales thereafter.[39]

In 1929 General Motors was an exceedingly large and strong corporation. It was the third largest industrial company in the nation. It had 43 million shares outstanding, no debt, and $127 million in cash, and the 14% of its capitalization represented by preferred stock was rated Aa. The company earned 30% on its equity and had profits of $247 million in 1929, compared with $112 million for the rest of the industry.[40] Alfred P. Sloan, Jr., as chief executive of General Motors, had developed a system of controls and planning that would keep the company strong. Its board of directors included representatives of J. P. Morgan & Co., the First National Bank of New York, and Bankers Trust Co., which provided strong financial backing.

Automobile stocks were hard hit in the Crash, even though their prices had not been inflated during the boom. The first effect of the Crash was expected to be on sales of luxuries, such as automobiles. Auto stocks fell to an average of 34% of their 1929 high prices, compared with 48% for all stocks, and to only 6 times earnings—half the average. Only the auto companies' market-to-book-value ratio was an average at 18%. Auto stocks had an average yield of over 11 3/4% at their lowest prices, which clearly illustrates the stock market's estimation of the industry's earnings vulnerability.

The high level of speculative activity in Detroit may also have had an impact on auto stocks as many of the fortunes created by the auto business found their way into high-powered stock market activities. The Fisher brothers created their own brokerage firm and were participants in numerous large pools. William Durant was one of the great plungers of stock market history. The Detroit banks were heavily involved in the stock market. The activities of these Detroiters may have been disproportionately focussed on auto stocks.

Automobile and truck production declined rapidly following the Crash, bearing out investors' expectations. Passenger car production in December 1929 was 96,920 units, down from 211,087 in December 1928 and the first month below 100,000 units since at least 1923. Truck production in December was 28,582 units, down from 32,454 units in December 1928.[41]

Auto stocks recovered in late November and December and closed at 135% of their lowest prices, which was better than the average of 129% but little consolation since they had dropped further than others in the Crash.

The Consumer Products Companies

The consumer products companies so prominent today were much less so in 1929. *Moody's Industrial Manual* categorized most of these companies as ''unclassified,'' but they had already developed a defined form by 1929. Most of the companies had grown rapidly following World War I through a combination of acquisitions, aggressive marketing as personal income rose, and dynamic leadership like that of R. W. Woodruff at Coca-Cola Co. or William Wrigley, Jr., at his namesake company. All these companies had become national in scope, with plants and sales offices from coast to coast, and most of them had become international, with subsidiaries in Canada, England, Europe, Australia, and South America.

The economic advantages of the consumer products companies vis-à-vis basic industry had already become apparent, although economic and financial emphasis was still on basic industries. For one thing, the consumer products companies were still surprisingly small in capital terms because of their low capital intensity. Coca-Cola had a total capitalization of only $58 million, William Wrigley of $57 million, Colgate-Palmolive-Peet Co. of $56 million, Gillette Safety Razor Co. of $54 million, and Lambert Co. of $8 million. The mighty Procter & Gamble Co.'s capitalization was only $119 million. This low capital requirement was translated into excellent profits. The group averaged a 35% return on equity in 1929, with Lambert Co. earning an astounding 133% return on equity. (See Table 1.22 for details.)

Most of the consumer products company stocks were outside the limelight in 1929, partly because of their small capitalizations and partly because their economic performance had peaked prior to 1929. Coca-Cola reduced its dividend in 1929; Kodak had relatively stable earnings from 1926 through 1929, as did Gillette, International Shoe Co., and Colgate-Palmolive-Peet. Colgate, International Shoe, and Wrigley hit a higher stock price in 1928 than in 1929, and

Table 1.22
The Consumer Products Companies in 1929

	Price-earnings ratio		Market price as a % of book value		Dividend yield (%)		Low price as a % of 1929 high price	Return on equity (%)	Moody's bond ratings	Cash & equivalents ($ millions)
	High price	Low price	High price	Low price	High price	Low price				
Coca-Cola	17	10	778	439	2.23	3.96	56	25.2	Baa pfd.	7
Colgate-Palmolive-Peet	22	10	450	200	2.22	5.00	44	19.8	A pfd.	7
Eastman-Kodak	28	16	421	238	3.02	5.33	57	15.2	Aaa pfd.	50
Gillette	28	15	596	350	3.50	6.25	56	18.4	NR[a]	11
International Shoe	18	12	312	216	3.85	5.56	69	17.2	Aaa pfd.	27
Lambert Co.	16	8	1,963	1,000	5.10	10.00	51	132.6	NR	4
Procter & Gamble	33	14	891	391	2.04	4.65	44	26.0	Aaa	9
Wm. Wrigley Jr.	14	11	386	310	4.94	6.15	80	27.7	NR	22
Averages	22.0	12.0	725	393	3.36	5.86	57	35.3	—	—

[a] NR = Not Rated.

1929 high stock prices for the other companies were only modestly above 1928's highest price.

The high returns on equity of the consumer products companies nonetheless resulted in superior stock market valuations in 1929. Their stocks averaged 725% of book value at their highest prices, compared with 420% for all stocks, and in the Crash consumer products stocks fell to only 57% of their high prices, versus 46% for all stocks. In other respects, consumer products stocks ranked close to the averages for all stocks.

The Retailers

The retailers, like the consumer products companies, experienced their peaks in 1928, when profits for 56 public department or variety stores were $186 million. Profits were down $2 million in a light sales decline in 1929.[42] Most retail stocks hit their highest prices in 1928. Only J. C. Penney Co. had an unblemished record of higher sales, profits, and stock price in 1929 (See Table 1.23.) Valuations for the retail stocks were very close to the averages for all stocks, but there were wide variations within the retail industry.

Sears, Roebuck and Co. was already the biggest, with a capitalization of $224 million, 29% larger than Montgomery Ward & Co., its closest competitor, and double most of the other retailers, except F. W. Woolworth Co. Sears and Montgomery Ward had both begun in the 1860–1880s by capitalizing on free mail delivery to farms, but by 1900 Sears had passed Montgomery Ward and built a reputation for guaranteed satisfaction based on quality controls over manufacturers and well-trained, motivated personnel. Eugene Talmadge, Governor of Georgia, campaigned credibly with farmers on the slogan "Your only friends are Jesus Christ, Sears Roebuck, and Gene Talmadge." Robert E. Wood had carried Sears beyond the mail order business into retail store merchandising in 1925, and under his stimulus Sears sales were 50% higher than Montgomery Ward's by 1929; its operating profits were 2 1/2 times higher.

While Sears was the biggest, Montgomery Ward was the speculative favorite. Its peak stock price was 60 times earnings and 476% of book value, both higher than Sears, and its stock trading volume in 1929 was 3 times its total shares outstanding. This volume ranked Montgomery Ward as the most active stock on the New York Stock Exchange. Such attention was unusual, especially since the company's return on equity was only one-half that of Sears Roebuck and earnings per share had declined from $8.49 in 1925 to $2.60 in 1929 because of rights offerings in 1928 and 1929. This speculative interest in Montgomery Ward may have been engendered by the company's rights offerings at a small fraction of market value (one-tenth in 1928 and one-third in 1929) and its high dividend payout relative to earnings; Montgomery Ward paid out 80% of its earnings in 1929, versus 36% paid out by Sears. The differences between the two companies began to appear in the Crash. Montgomery Ward stock dropped to 27% of its high, while Sears stock dropped only to 44%. Montgomery Ward

Table 1.23
The Retailers in 1929

	Price-earnings ratio		Market price as a % of book value		Dividend yield (%)		Low price as a % of 1929 high price	Return on equity (%)	Moody's bond ratings	Cash & equivalents ($ millions)
	High price	Low price	High price	Low price	High price	Low price				
Associated Dry Goods	21	7	237	83	3.52	10.00	35	11.2	Baa pfd.	9
Gimbel Brothers	def.[a]	def.	126	29	0	0	23	def.	B pfd.	4
S. S. Kresge	22	10	387	187	2.76	5.71	48	18.1	Aaa pfd.	4
R. H. Macy	38	16	522	224	1.17	2.73	43	13.8	NR[c]	4
Marshall Field	NA[b]	NA	NA	NA	NA	NA	NA	12.8	A	(5)[d]
Montgomery Ward	60	16	476	129	1.91	7.05	27	7.9	NR	38
J. C. Penney	23	14	583	367	6.67	10.61	63	25.5	A pfd.	7
Sears Roebuck	27	12	453	200	1.38	3.15	44	16.6	NR	(31)
F. W. Woolworth	28	14	650	325	2.31	4.60	50	22.9	NR	6
Averages	31.3	12.7	429	193	2.47	5.48	42	16.1	—	—

[a] def. = Deficit.
[b] NA = Not Available.
[c] NR = Not Rated.
[d] Brackets indicate short-term borrowing.

stock at its low was 129% of book value and carried a dividend yield of 7.05%, while Sears stock was 200% of book value and bore a yield of only 3.15%.

The best financial records among the retailers were established by a quieter couple, F. W. Woolworth and J. C. Penney. They were alone in having returns on equity over 20%, stock prices which at their highest were approximately 6 times book value and at their lowest still 3 times book value, and in experiencing the smallest declines in their stock prices in the Crash. Neither was a speculative favorite, and trading volume in their stocks was far below average.

F. W. Woolworth was more than twice the size of J. C. Penney and was a particularly sound company. In 1929 it had only its second president, Herbert T. Parsons, who had succeeded F. W. Woolworth in 1919. The company had built a reputation by purchasing and selling goods for cash, dealing directly with the manufacturers, and operating with low selling costs, including low wages, low prices, and open displays. Strong management had been built up through an internal training program which provided the executives to run its more than 2,300 stores in the United States, Canada, Cuba, Great Britain, France, and Germany. The company had paid dividends every year since it was incorporated in 1879. F. W. Woolworth stock was to be one of the star performers during the Depression.

J. C. Penney had none of Woolworth's international scope, having been founded in Utah and remaining focussed in the Midwest, but it had established an enviable record of a 131% increase in sales between 1925 and 1929 and a 62% increase in net income. Penney's had made a half-dozen acquisitions of small midwestern and western chains between 1927 and 1929 so that there were 1,453 Penney's stores in 48 states by 1929. Morale was high among employees, who had come to identify closely with the corporation because of its paternalistic policies and wide employee stock ownership.

Penney's strength was evident in its stock, which in the Crash declined only 37%, to 367% of book value, the smallest decline and highest price relative to book value of any of the retail stocks.

The company that clearly qualified as the worst among the retailers was Gimbel Brothers Inc., which had the nerve to pretend to be closely competing with its better-run neighbor, R. H. Macy & Co. Gimbel's had evolved from a Philadelphia department store into a chain based in New York City with stores in Pittsburgh and Milwaukee and control of Saks Fifth Avenue. While it was once dynamic, it had no sales growth from 1926 to 1929, its stock had not hit a new high price since as far back as 1925, and eight Gimbels sat in sinecure seats on its board. The company was alone among retailers in losing money in 1929 and paying no dividends; its highest stock price barely rose above book value, and in the Crash its stock sunk 72% to only 29% of book value.

Gimbel's was the extreme version of a malaise that affected the whole department store industry. As the suburbs began to develop, thanks to the rise of the ubiquitous automobile, downtown stores across the nation had little growth in the last half of the decade. The mail order and other chains had begun to put up stores in the suburbs, quadrupling their market share from 4% to 16% between 1922 and 1929, and the most progressive of the department stores moved to the suburbs too. But stores that had stayed downtown, like Gimbel's, were suffering, and merger talk abounded as failing stores sought strength in size. Lehman Brothers, in particular, among investment bankers was active in mergers, of which Federated Department Stores was the largest.

The Tire Industry

The tire companies had surprisingly poor stock and economic performances for an industry that had grown rapidly under the stimulus of automobile expansion. Unit sales had gone up every year since 1921 except 1929,[43] but the peak in industry earnings had been in 1925. Since then, rubber prices had been cut by one-third and tire prices by one-half, which in 1928 and 1929 created the two worst years for profits for the tire companies since 1921, and very modest returns on equity. As a result, tire stocks at their highest prices had price-earnings ratios and market-to-book-value ratios approximately one-third lower than stocks in general. In the Crash the stocks fared even worse, dropping 62% from their highest prices to an average of only 7.7 times earnings per share and 102% of book value.

The three leading companies were similar. (See Table 1.24 for details.) They were all of similar size, had their headquarters on huge sites in Akron, Ohio, were diversified into footwear as well as tires, were integrated backward into rubber plantations and cotton (for tire fabric), and were spread across North America, Europe, Australia, and South America. The Goodyear Tire & Rubber Co. had a return on equity that was superior to that of the others at 24% in 1929, and therefore a superior stock performance, but as the Depression progressed this margin of superiority became meaningless.

The Farm Equipment Industry

Despite flat farm incomes, farm equipment sales enjoyed dramatic growth in the period from 1926 to 1929 as motorized tractors and harvesters came to the farm just as automobiles came to the city. Farm equipment sales grew from $461 million in 1926 to $607 million in 1929, during which time tractor sales grew 56% to $278 million and harvester sales grew 91% to $88 million. The eight public farm equipment companies reported net income of $76 million in 1929, compared with $43 million in 1926.[44]

International Harvester Co. dominated the farm equipment business with a capitalization of over $300 million. It was four or five times the size of its competitors, its manufacturing plants were stretched across the Midwest and into Canada, France, Germany, and Sweden, and it was integrated back into steel mills, coal mines, and iron ore mines to supply its raw materials. International Harvester also had financial strength, with a 13.2% return on equity, a 72%

Table 1.24
The Tire Industry in 1929

	Price-earnings ratio		Market price as a % of book value		Dividend yield (%)		Low price as a % of 1929 high price	Return on equity (%)	Moody's bond ratings	Cash & equivalents ($ millions)
	High price	Low price	High price	Low price	High price	Low price				
Firestone	23	9	200	81	2.50	6.40	40	8.9	Ba pfd.	30
B. F. Goodrich	22	8	186	67	3.77	10.53	36	8.5	A	(24)[a]
Goodyear	17	6	408	158	3.23	8.33	39	24.6	A	42
Averages	20.7	7.7	265	102	3.17	8.42	38	14.0	—	—

[a] Brackets indicate short-term borrowing.

growth in net income between 1926 and 1929, no debt, $26 million in cash and securities, an Aa-rated preferred stock, and Thomas Lamont of J. P. Morgan & Co. on its board to raise money. (See Table 1.25.)

Deere & Co. had a 29.6% return on equity and had doubled its net income between 1926 and 1929, but the company was a very distant second to International Harvester. Deere & Co. was still heavily committed to the slower-growing plow business and did all its manufacturing in the Moline, Illinois, area. In some respects it was still a local business, with no Chicago or New York directors and an inconsequential dividend.

J. I. Case Co. was also a one-town company, based in Racine, Wisconsin, but its stock gained speculative appeal even though the company's net income did not grow between 1926 and 1929. In the same period, its stock price tripled, rising to a 1929 high price that was 34 times earnings per share, compared with 9 to 20 times for Deere and International Harvester. In 1929 trading volume in J. I. Case stock equalled 164% of all outstanding Case stock, beside which Deere and International Harvester stocks were moribund. But there was nothing to justify such a valuation for Case stock, and it dropped 72% in the Crash as speculators were wrung out, compared with 52% and 54% declines for Deere and International Harvester stocks.

For companies that had virtually no debt and modest valuations to begin with, the farm equipment stocks fared surprisingly poorly in the Crash. The three stocks followed here dropped to 111% of book value, which was only 7.7 times earnings per share—about 60% of the average values for all stocks. Low dividends may have been a factor in these valuations, for the yields on these stocks at their lowest points were also about half the 6% average for all stocks. Or there may have been a realization among investors how much the coming tough times would hurt the commodities businesses and the industries which served them.

The Tobacco Companies

The tobacco companies had unusual financial strength among U.S. industries in 1929, largely as a result of the popularization of mild cigarettes in World War I and their subsequent rapid growth. Cigarette sales doubled between 1923 and 1929, and the industry profited and paid dividends in a fine way because the business was not capital intensive.

American Tobacco Co. was the leading company, with a capitalization almost twice that of any competitor. At one time, American Tobacco was a trust controlling the whole industry, with Liggett & Myers Tobacco Co., R. J. Reynolds Tobacco Co., P. Lorillard Co., and British American Tobacco as subsidiaries, but the trust was broken up between 1912 and 1915. American Tobacco soon bounced back under the tough marketing management of its president, G. W. Hill. Hill increased cigarette production 126% betweeen 1926 and 1929, increasing American Tobacco's market share from 20% to 34%, largely by intro-

Table 1.25
The Farm Equipment Industry in 1929

	Price-earnings ratio		Market price as a % of book value		Dividend yield (%)		Low price as a % of 1929 high price	Return on equity (%)	Moody's bond ratings	Cash & equivalents ($ millions)
	High price	Low price	High price	Low price	High price	Low price				
J. I. Case	34	9	275	77	1.28	4.60	28	8.1	Baa pfd.	(1)[a]
Deere & Co.	9	5	278	135	0.94	1.61	48	29.6	Baa pfd.	(2)
International Harvester	20	9	263	120	1.76	3.85	46	13.2	Aa pfd.	26
Averages	21.0	7.7	272	111	1.33	3.35	41	17.0	—	—

[a] Brackets indicate short-term borrowing.

ducing three heavily advertised brands—Sweet Caporals, Pall Malls, and Lucky Strikes—which were further promoted by price discounts and coupons. Net income increased only 42% under this strategy, but American Tobacco's stock almost doubled between 1926 and 1929.

Liggett & Myers was based on the famous Chesterfield cigarettes and enjoyed a modest 27% growth in net income between 1926 and 1929, but there was none of the savage marketing virtuosity seen at American Tobacco, and Liggett's stock was no higher in 1929 than it had been in 1926. Its highest price was in 1927.

Reynolds Tobacco, insularly based in Winston-Salem, North Carolina, with no outside directors, had started the modern cigarette movement by giving free packs of Camel cigarettes to American soldiers, but it did not expand successfully beyond that one brand. Its 3-year income growth of 23% matched that of Liggett & Myers, although Reynolds stock hit an historic high price in 1929 after being split 2 1/2 for 1.

The three big tobacco company stocks were remarkably similar (See Table 1.26). They were not speculative favorites before the Crash, trading on average only 27% of their outstanding stock during the year and reaching an average price-earnings-ratio peak of 18.3, compared with 30 for all stocks. Their average market-to-book-value ratio of 378% at their highest prices was also below the average for all stocks of 420%, and their dividend yield of 4.53% was unusually high for stocks of such financial stability. In the Crash, the three tobacco stocks ended up uniformly at yields and market-to-book-value ratios much above the averages and with the smallest price declines of any industry (32%). This change in perspective was rooted in the sound fundamentals of the industry. It averaged a 21.4% return on equity, carried no debt, was able to pay out 80%–90% of earnings in dividends, and carried large cash balances. Besides, this was a growth industry with a product that had become a necessity among rich and poor and in which an oligopoly purchased its basic tobacco product from a multitude of unorganized farmers. Tobacco manufacturing was to be one of the most stable industries during the Depression.

The Pulp and Paper Industry

The pulp and paper industry was small, weak, and uninteresting in 1929. Some 35 public companies earned only $26 million, or an average of less than $750,000 each.[45] International Paper & Power Co. was the only large company, with a total capitalization of $640 million, but two-thirds of that was invested in the utility industry. Crown Zellerbach Corp. had capital of $110 million, St. Regis Paper had capital of $80 million, Kimberly-Clark Corp. had capital of $44 million, Mead Corp. had capital of $33 million, and Scott Paper had capital of only $7 million. The industry had been overwhelmed by pulp and newsprint imports from Canada, which had the advantages of extensive virgin timber and cheap hydroelectric power. Newsprint imports had grown from 40% of U.S.

Table 1.26
The Tobacco Companies in 1929

	Price-earnings ratio		Market price as a % of book value		Dividend yield (%)		Low price as a % of 1929 high price	Return on equity (%)	Moody's bond ratings	Cash & equivalents ($ millions)
	High price	Low price	High price	Low price	High price	Low price				
American Tobacco	20	14	374	258	4.31	6.25	69	18.8	Aaa	35
Liggett & Myers	14	10	321	242	4.72	6.25	75	23.8	Aaa	(7)[b]
Reynolds Tobacco	21	12	440	260	4.55	7.70	59	21.5	NR[a]	18
Averages	18.3	12.0	378	253	4.53	6.73	68	21.4	—	—

[a] NR = Not Rated.
[b] Brackets indicate short-term borrowing.

consumption in 1921 to 64% in 1929, while newsprint prices dropped 40%. There was consistently 15%–20% surplus capacity in the United States, with the result that all paper products prices trended down during the decade, with a sharp 10% drop in 1928. International Paper was unable to earn a profit in 1929, and most of the other companies had returns on equity of only 6%–10%, except Kimberly-Clark, which profited from its production of Kleenex and Kotex.

Most of the companies were highly leveraged and carried bond ratings of Baa or lower because of their heavy capital commitments to hydroelectric power. International Paper had only 13% of its capitalization in common equity.

Paper company stocks had some of the worst valuations of any industry—on a par with steel stocks and below oil stocks—with a market-to-book-value ratio of only 85% at the lows of the Crash (See Table 1.27.) The paper stocks only declined 37% in the Crash, as opposed to 52% for all stocks, but this reflected their original low stock prices and the lack of market interest in paper stocks. Trading volume in paper stocks was only a small fraction of their outstanding shares. In many respects, all the companies except International Paper & Power were still regionalized, closely controlled companies tied to the large newspapers and magazine publishers who needed the paper output.

The Office Equipment Companies

The office equipment business was also small in 1929, with the five largest companies—Addressograph-Multigraph, Burroughs Adding Machine Co., International Business Machines Corp. (IBM), National Cash Register, and Remington Rand Inc.—having capitalizations of only $9 to $65 million. But all the companies had already gone international. Nine public companies earned an impressive $44 million, and their stocks had relatively high valuations. Remington Rand, which made typewriters and adding machines, was by far the largest company and the speculative favorite of the group, with a 53% return on equity in 1929. Its NYSE trading volume in 1929 was over 3 times its outstanding shares. The company's profits were also the most variable.

While IBM was much smaller, it was already a growth stock. In the 1920s Thomas J. Watson had led the company into a series of mergers to create a product line of scales, tabulating machines, and timing devices which resulted in 136% earnings growth between 1925 and 1929. IBM stock in the same period moved from a high of $59 to $255, up 332%. Burroughs had an even better earnings record, with net income rising 185% between 1925 and 1929 and its stock rising from the equivalent of $13 to $97, up 646%! The Burroughs performance left National Cash Register, which was somewhat larger, standing still. Its sales and profits had been almost static since 1925. (See Table 1.28 for the details on specific companies.)

Office equipment stocks averaged high prices in 1929 which were 27 1/2 times earnings per share, a remarkable 814% of book value, and a dividend yield of only 2.17%. It is not surprising with these valuations, and the considerable

Table 1.27
The Pulp and Paper Industry in 1929

	Price-earnings ratio		Market price as a % of book value		Dividend yield (%)		Low price as a % of 1929 high price	Return on equity (%)	Moody's bond ratings	Cash & equivalents ($ millions)
	High price	Low price	High price	Low price	High price	Low price				
Crown Zellerbach	17	11	179	114	4.00	6.25	64	10.4	Baa	(1)[d]
International Paper	NA[a]	NA	133	61	5.45	12.00	45	def.[b]	Baa	14
Kimberly-Clark	9	7	102	80	5.26	6.67	79	16.8	NR[c]	3
Averages	13.0	9.0	138	85	4.90	8.31	63	13.6	—	—

[a] NA = Not Available.
[b] def. = Deficit.
[c] NR = Not Rated.
[d] Brackets indicate short-term borrowing.

Table 1.28
The Office Equipment Companies in 1929

	Price-earnings ratio		Market price as a % of book value		Dividend yield (%)		Low price as a % of 1929 high price	Return on equity (%)	Moody's bond ratings	Cash & equivalents ($ millions)
	High price	Low price	High price	Low price	High price	Low price				
Burroughs Adding Machine	42	12	1,386	414	1.86	6.21	30	22.0	NRª	17
IBM	23	10	464	198	1.96	4.59	43	19.6	Aa	4
National Cash Register A	28	11	514	203	2.68	6.78	40	18.4	NR	1
Remington Rand	17	6	892	308	0	0	34	53.3	Baa	8
Averages	27.3	9.8	814	307	1.27	3.60	36	31.6	—	—

ª NR = Not Rated.

activity in their stocks, that they dropped 63% in the Crash; but they still averaged 281% of book value at the lowest prices of the Crash, a reflection of the high returns on equity the companies earned.

Other Stocks

Various other stocks and industries deserve mention because of their importance in the stock market, size, high quality, or prominence later in this period.

General Electric Co. (GE) and Westinghouse Electric and Manufacturing Co. competed with each other with marked differences in their success. Both companies' bonds were rated Aaa, and both had 98%–99% of their capitalization in common equity, but thereafter similarities ceased (See Table 1.29). GE's assets were two-thirds larger than Westinghouse's, and GE had double the sales. General Electric earned 16.8% on its equity in 1929, compared with 11.9% for Westinghouse. General Electric stock sold at a high price, 43 times 1929 earnings per share and 718% of book value, compared with 28 times earnings and 337% of book value for Westinghouse. GE had cash and government securities of $124 million, as well, which made the company a significant factor in the money markets. Westinghouse was inconsequential in this respect.

General Electric's management was considerably more prominent than that of Westinghouse. Owen D. Young, GE's Chairman, was one of the leading financiers and industrialists of his day. He was Chairman of the committee that worked out the Young Plan for dealing with German reparations, Chairman of the New York Federal Reserve Board, and a director of numerous prominent corporations, including General Motors. Ida Tarbell, who tarnished most characters, found him a knight in shining armor in a 1931 biography in which she recommended him for President of the United States. Many took her seriously. GE's President, Gerard Swope, was only slightly less prominent. During the Depression he became known for his support of unemployment insurance, public works, a 30-hour work week, and government loans to industry.

In the Crash, General Electric and Westinghouse stocks dropped to 42% and 34%, respectively, of their highest 1929 prices. Westinghouse dropped to 10 times 1929 earnings per share and only 115% of book value, which indicated a critical market attitude toward the company since both measures were much below the broad averages of 12 1/2 times earnings and 181 1/2% of book value.

General Electric maintained a valuation above the broad averages. At its low price it was still 18 times 1929 earnings per share, 300% of book value, and carried a dividend yield of only 2.85%, as opposed to Westinghouse's 4.0%.

American Telephone & Telegraph Co. (AT&T) was the largest company in the United States, with a total capitalization of $3.2 billion, and its stock was the most widely held. It was not a heavily traded stock, which reflected the conservative nature of its investors. AT&T traded only 5.1 million shares in 1929, some 39% of its outstanding shares, 34th in volume of NYSE trading. The stock's highest price was only 20 times 1929 earnings and 207% of book

Table 1.29
Other Stocks in 1929

	Price-earnings ratio		Market price as a % of book value		Dividend yield (%)		Low price as a % of 1929 high price	Return on equity (%)	Moody's bond ratings	Cash & equivalents ($ millions)
	High price	Low price	High price	Low price	High price	Low price				
American Can	23	11	370	156	2.70	5.80	47	16.0	Aa pfd.	22
AT&T	20	13	207	129	2.90	4.65	62	10.1	Aaa	71
General Electric	43	18	718	300	1.19	2.85	42	16.8	Aaa	124
RCA	73	17	1,669	377	0	0	23	22.9	A pfd.	32
Westinghouse	28	10	337	115	1.71	4.00	34	11.9	Aaa pfd.	29

value, which reflected the company's modest 10.1% return on equity and flat earnings (See Table 1.29). The company had increased its dividend only once since 1907, from $8.00 to $9.00, at which rate it was paying out approximately 75% of its earnings in the period 1925–29.

In the Crash, AT&T stock had one of the smaller declines, to 62% of its 1929 high, at which level it was 129% of book value and carried a yield of 4.65%. This modest yield, when coupled with the company's meager 10.1% return on equity and static dividend history, illustrates how far removed the company was from normal stock market pressures because of the loyalty of its stockholders.

American Can Co. was a highly popular stock that traded in the twelfth largest volume on the NYSE in 1929 (See Table 1.29). It traded 13 1/2 million shares, 5 1/2 times its outstanding stock. At its peak price it was 23 times 1929 earnings per share and 370% of book value. Its dividend yield was 2.70%. In 1929 the company had a 16% return on equity and a good prior income record, in light of which the stock was undervalued, if anything, since the average stock earned a 16 1/2% return on equity, had a 30 price-earnings ratio, and sold at 420% of book value. American Can was a strong company with no debt and 25% of its capitalization in preferred stock rated Aa.

In the Crash, American Can common stock came closer to the averages. It dropped to 47% of its high, versus an average of 49% for all stocks, and its price-earnings ratio of 11 and market price relative to book value of 156% compared with the averages of 12 1/2 and 181% respectively. American Can was one of the first major companies to react to the Crash by raising its dividend from $4.00 to $5.00 to express management's confidence. In subsequent years, American Can's mettle would be recognized.

Radio Corp. of America (RCA) has a special place as a symbol of the stock market of the 1920s and 1930s. It embodied most of the hopes, dynamism, animated leadership, financial excesses, and Depression despair of the period. Founded in 1919 by General Electric to buy out foreign control of the Marconi Wireless Telegraph Co. of America, it became the leading force in U.S. radio research, distribution, and broadcasting in the following decade under the strong leadership of David Sarnoff. In 1928, RCA acquired 64% of Radio-Keith-Or-pheum Corp., which made RCA a force in the development of sound movies, and in 1929 it acquired Victor Talking Machine for $49 million, which broadened RCA's positions in radios and phonographs.

The financial results of RCA's success were explosive. Sales grew from $65 million in 1927 to $100 million in 1928, and earnings went from $2.9 million in 1925 to $19.8 million in 1928. The average price of its stock went from $11 3/4 in 1925 to $50 1/2 in 1928. But financial moderation was not a strong trait. RCA paid no common stock dividends, it was highly leveraged with less than 40% of its capital structure in the form of common equity, it was expanding rapidly through acquisitions, and it had pronounced promotional tendencies.

RCA was the darling of the 1929 stock market with the biggest trading volume on the NYSE. There were many stimuli for such activity. It split its stock 5 for stock 5 for 1 early in the year and acquired Victor Talking Machine; sales vaulted from $100 million in 1928 to $177 million in 1929; and it was heavily involved in negotiations with GE and Westinghouse to take over all of their radio manufacturing rights and facilities. The stock hit a new high of $115, where it was 73 times earnings per share and 1669% of book value (See Table 1.29). It was helped to this peak by its specialist on the New York Stock Exchange, Mike Meehan, who operated large-scale pools in the stock, the most notorious of which was between March 12 and 20, 1929, with such prominent figures as John Raskob, Nicholas Brady, W. F. Kenny, Walter Chrysler, the Fisher brothers, Charles Schwab (Bethlehem Steel), Percy Rockefeller, and J. A. Stillman. Meehan traded 1 1/2 million shares in nine days and was variously reported to have made $1.9 million and $5 million.

Such inflated activity was vulnerable to bad news, however, and in the Crash RCA suffered drastically as its valuation was brought into line and it became more evident that RCA's net income for stockholders was going to be only $10.4 million, as opposed to $18.5 million in 1928, because of the heavy preferred dividend and interest charges for the Victor Talking Machine acquisition. The stock broke to only 23% of its highest 1929 price, compared with the average of 48%, and to more reasonable valuations of a 17 price-earnings ratio and 377% of book value. Its recovery was anemic as well.

Summary

There were wide differences in the valuations and economic performances of various industries in 1929. During the boom, when the average stock price was 30 times earnings and 420% of book value, there was an emphasis on financial stocks, such as the holding companies, trusts, and banks, which had returns on equity below 10% yet price-earnings ratios anywhere from 50 to 100. The other highly exaggerated valuations, for example where market-to-book-value ratios exceeded 700%, were for individual companies rather than whole industries. The stocks of Alleghany, Burroughs, Cities Service, Coca-Cola, Commercial Solvents, Du Pont, General Electric, General Foods, International Nickel, Lambert, National City Bank, Packard, Procter & Gamble, RCA, Remington Rand, Standard Brands, Texas Gulf Sulphur, Transamerica, and Woolworth all sold above 7 times book value at the peak of the boom. Some industries had superior earnings performances, such as the chemical, food, auto, consumer products, tobacco, and office equipment industries, which had returns on equity well above the average of 16 1/2% for all companies, although this seldom led to stock valuations much above the averages for all companies. By contrast, several industries had returns on equity much below the 16 1/2% average, and stock valuations that were well below the averages for all stocks in the boom, such as the railroad, oil, mining, motion picture, steel, pulp and paper, tire, and farm equipment industries. Some of the stocks in these industries were quite prominent and traded in high volume, but they still did not share in the high valuations produced by the boom.

However, the differences in stock valuations and economic performance did not create any sense that companies or industries were in financial trouble. Gimbel Brothers was the only prominent company reporting a loss in 1929. The weaker industries were earning 9%–10% returns on equity, which were certainly satisfactory in absolute terms when bond rates were 4% to 6%. Very few companies had bond or preferred stock ratings below Baa, the bottom of the investment grade rankings, and even the lower-rated securities tended to sell close to par as we shall see in Chapter 3. Companies paid no visible penalty for high leverage other than higher rates on their fixed-income securities.

The Crash eliminated the high valuations for financial stocks, as the holding company and investment trust stocks declined approximately 70%, compared with the average decline of 52%. Most relative valuations tended to fall into line with relative economic performance after the Crash. In the industries with high returns on equity, such as chemicals, food, consumer products, tobacco, and office equipment, stocks declined less than the average of 52%, and the market-to-book-value ratios for their stocks at their lowest prices were well above the average of 181%. By contrast, stock prices dropped well below book value for the railroad, oil, mining, motion picture, steel, tire, farm equipment, and pulp and paper industries, which had below-average returns on equity. The valuations of the weaker industries and the financial companies indicated what would become the critical problem industries of the Depression—except for the banks, whose problems no one yet foresaw.

NOTES

1. All averages of daily trading volumes in this study treat Saturday volume as a half day.

2. John Brooks, *Once in Golconda*, N.Y.: Harper & Row, 1969, p. 135.

3. Sales of investment trust, trading, and holding company securities were $3.285 billion in 1924–29.

4. *Stock Exchange Practices*, part 6, pp. 3043–55.

5. *NYSE Year Book, 1928–29*, p. 132; *1937*, p. 154; *1938*, p. 71.

6. Ibid., *1930–31*, p. 28.

7. Ibid., *1938*, p. 25.

8. Ibid., pp. 61–62.

9. *Banking & Monetary Statistics*, p. 76.

10. *NYSE Year Book, 1938*, p. 62; *Banking & Monetary Statistics*, p. 76.

11. E.g., Thomas Cochran in a General Asphalt pool for 35,000 shares; *New York Times*, 5/20/31.

12. Ibid., 5/20/31.

13. *Stock Exchange Practices*, part 5, p. 3412.

14. Ibid., pp. 3510–12.

15. Ibid., p. 2432.

16. *New York Times*, 10/24/29.
17. Ibid., 11/4/32.
18. Ibid., 5/20/32.
19. Ibid., 4/23/32.
20. *Stock Exchange Practices*, part 3, p. 1341.
21. Sidney Homer interview.
22. *Moody's Railroad Manual, 1931*, p. xxxv. Net income figures throughout this book are from Moody's manuals whenever possible because they are based on reported earnings for public companies and provide the best indication of investors' knowledge. Profit figures differ materially from those in *National Income Accounts*, which are based on tax returns and include many more public and private companies.
23. Ibid., p. xxxi.
24. *Moody's Utility Manual, 1931*, p. xxix.
25. See Table A.26 in the Statistical Appendix.
26. *Stock Exchange Practices*, part 2, p. 318.
27. *New York Times*, 6/15/32.
28. *National Income Accounts*, p. 126.
29. *Stock Exchange Practices*, part 9, pp. 4217–18; part 10, pp. 4947–48.
30. *Moody's Industrial Manual, 1932*, pp. xxxii–vi.
31. Ibid., *1931*, p. xxiii.
32. Ibid., *1931*, p. xxiv.
33. Ibid., *1935*, p. a45.
34. Ibid., *1931*, p. xxv.
35. All sides of the Fox Story are covered in detail in *Stock Exchange Practices*, parts 7 and 8, in the testimony of Murray W. Dodge and William Fox.
36. *Moody's Industrial Manual, 1935*, p. a45; *National Income Accounts*, p. 142.
37. *Stock Exchange Practices*, part 1, p. 282.
38. *Moody's Industrial Manual, 1931*, pp. 717–23.
39. Ibid., *1931*, pp. 2311, xviii.
40. Ibid., *1935*, p. a45.
41. Ibid., *1931*, p. xix.
42. Ibid., *1935*, p. a45.
43. *Statistical Abstract, 1939*, p. 774.
44. *Moody's Industrial Manual, 1931*, p. xvii; *1935*, p. a45.
45. Ibid., p. a45.

2

Political and Economic Influences on Securities Markets in 1929

THE U.S. GOVERNMENT—HERBERT HOOVER TRIES TO RALLY THE NATION

Herbert Hoover had been President only seven months when the Crash occurred. His policies were designed to continue "Coolidge prosperity"—Andrew Mellon continued as Secretary of the Treasury, the decade-long practice of budget surplus continued, and Hoover himself had been Secretary of Commerce before becoming President. He did not hesitate to enter the financial fray after the Crash to preserve prosperity. The day after the Crash he issued his famous statement: "The fundamental business of the country, that is production and distribution of commodities, is on a sound and prosperous basis." This effort to reassure the market had no impact, except to illustrate the seriousness that the country's leaders attached to the decline in stock prices.

The Hoover Administration looked for the bright side in the early days of the Crash and found it in a widely accepted hope that the Crash would destroy the speculators but not the economy. This optimism waned as the Crash progressed, and the Administration resolved to take direct steps to sustain the economy. On November 13th Treasury Secretary Mellon announced an Administration proposal to reduce income taxes by 1%, equivalent to $160 million, as a gesture of confidence in American business. The government was still expected to have a surplus. Congress promised bipartisan support for the measure, and stocks moved up strongly the following day.

In the remaining 1 1/2 months of the year, Hoover orchestrated a variety of efforts designed to restore confidence and mobilize business. On November 15th he outlined the reasons for confidence and called his first meetings of national leaders in Washington. Five conferences were organized for business, organized labor, construction organizations, farm organizations, and public utilities to advise the President. The conferences made public the leaders' sense of responsibility and produced commitments to expand to offset the effects of the Crash. Electric and gas utilities announced record construction budgets of $1.4 billion for 1930, and $0.4 billion for maintenance. The railroads made a commitment to spend $1 billion in 1930, up from $0.8 billion in 1929. The *New York Times* called the railroads "a bulwark of support in a time of need." U.S. Steel announced a three-year mill expansion plan of $250 million, and other steel mills planned expansion. Republic Steel, created in December in a $350 million merger, was a new midwestern giant and a likely focus for expansion.

The resounding success of the first round of conferences confirmed Hoover's reputation for direct action. However, this initial success led him to continue them in the later, more desperate years when their effectiveness was gone and they appeared to be a pallid substitute for fundamental policy changes.

Hoover continued his momentum as the conferences assembled. On November 21st he created a Business Council of Employers and Labor, which was committed to neither increase nor decrease wages, so that purchasing power remained stable. All major businesses were solicited by the council to abide by this wage plan. On November 22nd Hoover sent flash telegrams to all 48 state governors asking them to speed up state construction programs and to ask the same of their cities. Mellon had earlier proposed a federal public works program of $423 million over ten years, up $175 million from previous plans, and Mayor Jimmy Walker of New York had speeded up the city's construction program to $1 billion over four years. Favorable mail poured in to Hoover.

On December 3rd Hoover commenced the tradition of an annual presidential message with a program to abet recovery. He reaffirmed his request for a 1% reduction in income taxes, promised an expeditious push for a new tariff law, which had been held up in Congress, and intensified enforcement of Prohibition, which would raise health and working standards and eliminate waste. The railroad industry was assured prompt development of a new plan for rationalizing competing systems through mergers after years of unproductive debate. The plan was expected to liberate business energies and make transportation cheaper. A committee of 400 businessmen was set up to advise the President on business conditions. It was led by a "Committee of 72," on which sat men who seemed like titans in the business and social atmosphere of the 1920s. Washington supported the President's program in a bipartisan spirit. The tax cut was passed in both houses by December 15th. The Interstate Commerce Commission resolved years of indecision and published a Rail Plan on December 21st, calling for 21 railroad systems in the nation with five trunklines in the East.

The Hoover Administration was remarkably prompt and positive in its reaction to the Crash. As financiers, businessmen, and economists projected economic recovery in 1930, one of their common reasons for doing so was the leadership in Washington. Hoover provided a boost to public and business morale. He coordinated and prompted the efforts of business, local government, and labor to counteract the depressing effects of the Crash. In cases where the federal government was directly involved, he was prepared to expedite resolution of long-standing issues, such as railroad reorganization and tariffs. He was also willing to use the federal budget surplus by reducing taxes and increasing public works. There was none of the hesitation later attributed to him.

MONETARY POLICY, MONEY MARKETS, AND THE BANKING SYSTEM—THE FEDERAL RESERVE AND SPECULATIVE DEMAND CREATE TIGHT MONEY PRIOR TO THE CRASH, BUT CONFIDENCE IS MAINTAINED FOLLOWING THE CRASH BY EASY MONEY AND THE STRENGTH OF THE BANKING SYSTEM

During the Depression the Federal Reserve was frequently accused of having created the "inflation" (by which was meant easy credit conditions) that promoted unwise business expansion and stock market speculation, when in fact the Federal Reserve had done much in 1928 and 1929 to create tight money in an effort to cut off the boom, only to be frustrated by the channels of disintermediation created in the call loan market. Monetary policy appeared to be incapable of having much impact on the stock market boom, as we shall see. The principal role of monetary policy and the commercial banking system with respect to the stock market was to sustain it against panic and complete collapse during the Crash, and to then provide a credit atmosphere afterward which created confidence in the opportunity for recovery.

Money supply data alone provides no insight into the stock market boom, the Crash, the recovery in the succeeding months, or the sudden drop in wholesale, farm, and commodity prices following the Crash. Friedman and Schwartz provide three monthly money supply series in their *Monetary Statistics of the United States* which were substantially constant from early 1928 to April 1930.[1] Money supply, defined as currency held by the public plus demand deposits at commercial banks (MI), was steadily around $26.5 billion for 57 months and only once varied by as much as $1 billion which was in October 1929 in the midst of the Crash. Money supply, defined as currency held by the public plus demand and time deposits at commercial banks (M2), was steadily around $46 billion for 28 months and only varied once by as much as $1 billion which was in October 1929. Money supply, defined as currency in the hands of the public plus demand and time deposits at commercial banks plus deposits at savings banks and with the Postal Savings System (M3), was steadily around $55 billion for 31 months and only varied once by as much as $1 billion which was again in October 1929. All the $1 billion money supply variations from trend were *increases* rather than decreases, which should have raised prices rather than lowering them if any effect at all can be ascribed to 1- to 2-month variations. Since no insight is provided by money supply data, we must turn to other measures of credit conditions.

The Federal Reserve System began tightening credit when the New York Federal Reserve Bank raised its discount rate to 4 1/2% in May 1928. It was raised again to 5% in July 1928, and to 6% in August 1929.[2] The New York bank's buying rates for bankers acceptances show a more even pattern of tightening credit. This was an administered rate at which the New York Federal Reserve Bank undertook to buy bankers acceptances from the dealer market. The practice had been established earlier in the decade when the New York Federal Reserve encouraged the development of acceptance business to create a stronger money market. Earlier in the 1920s, the New York Federal Reserve acted as an acceptance buyer to stabilize the dealer market and limit losses in it, but by 1929 the New York Federal Reserve's buying rate for acceptances had become an instrument of monetary policy. The rate was 3 5/8% on March 30, 1928, and moved up to 5 1/2% by March 25, 1929, in nine separate steps. Five of the rate increases were in the first quarter of 1929. The buying rate had come down slightly to 5 1/8% when the Crash occurred, but it was still higher than any pre-1929 rates since the credit squeeze of 1920–21.[3]

The Federal Reserve System also allowed its portfolio of bills and U.S. Government securities to run down almost completely in this period of credit-tightening. "Bills bought" dropped from $473 million in January 1929 to only $75 million in July. "Bills bought" had normally been $250–$350 million from 1924 to 1928. U.S. securities owned by the Federal Reserve began to decline much earlier. They were as high as $606 million in December 1927, but only $415 million by March 1928 and $147 million by July 1929. A more typical level of Federal Reserve System U.S. holdings was $300–$400 million, which had prevailed from 1924 to 1928. The decline in Federal Reserve System securities holdings between March 1928 and July 1929 was $536 million, and member bank discounts with the System were forced up by an almost equal amount. At these high borrowing levels, bankers and financial observers naturally felt apprehensive.[4]

The expanding economy also created tighter credit conditions. There was a strong business demand for credit, which created most of $1.2 billion in new loans for banks in 101 leading cities in 1929 (up 7%). This was the largest loan expansion of the decade and compared with loan growth of $0.8–$0.9 billion in 1927 and 1928 for these banks. The loan growth in 1929 was also dramatically stronger in business loans than in security loans. Over $1 billion of the loan expansion was for loans other than on securities, while in prior years securities loans accounted for 50%–70% of loan growth.[5] The loan expansion of $500 million in New York City banks was exclusively for loans other than on securities,[6] while the loan expansion of $750 million in banks outside New York City included $300 million in additional securities loans.[7] The banks could not easily refuse or divert business loan demand, since it came from long-term customers, who formed the basis of a solid banking business. Therefore the banks liquidated securities to make the loans, raised their rates for securities loans, and tried to restrain them.

All Federal Reserve member banks had borrowings from the Federal Reserve System of $950 million–$1.1 billion throughout 1929, compared to normal bor-

Table 2.1
Short-term Securities Outstanding, Early October 1929 ($ millions)

Call loans	Commercial paper	Bankers acceptances	U.S. bills & certificates
$8,549	$265	$1,272	$1,500 (est.)

Source: *Banking & Monetary Statistics*, pp. 466, 500, 511.

rowings of $400–$600 million in prior years going back to 1924.[8] New York City banks had peak Federal Reserve borrowings of $341 million the first two weeks in July 1929 and were still borrowing $217 million the first week of September. This level compared with normal borrowings of $50–$100 million throughout most of 1926 and 1927 and the first quarter of 1928. "Credit ease" was interpreted by rule of thumb at the New York Federal Reserve Bank as existing when New York City banks were borrowing approximately $50 million. The pressure on New York City bank funds was further evident in the banks' securities portfolios, which declined $200 million to a level of $1.7 billion in the January-to-October period.[9] Weekly reporting banks in 100 cities other than New York City also had unusually heavy Federal Reserve borrowings. Their borrowings averaged $500–$600 million throughout the last half of 1928 and all of 1929, compared with only $150–$200 million in prior years. These banks' investments declined by $400 million to $3.7 billion under the pressure to raise funds.[10] Country banks outside these 101 cities also had peak Federal Reserve borrowings, which rose from $228 million in January 1929 to $302 million in June. These borrowings were still at $296 million in August. In 1927 and 1928, before credit began to tighten, these country bank borrowings had averaged only $125–$165 million.[11]

Interest rate levels in the summer of 1929 invited comparison with the worst collapses and panics of the century. Commercial paper rates of 6 1/4% established in September 1929 had been exceeded only in the drastic credit squeeze of 1920–21, when dire economic and financial results ensued. Brokers call-loan rates averaging 8 5/8% in September were the highest since 1920, apart from the succession of high rates in prior months of 1929.[12]

The efforts of the Federal Reserve to reduce credit to stock market investors were frustrated by the incredible growth of the call loan market in which brokers financed both their inventories and margin loans to customers. The volume of outstanding call loans to brokers was almost 75% of the short-term market and had risen dramatically in recent years from $4.4 billion in January 1928 to $8.5 billion in October 1929.[13] The relative volume of various short-term instruments can be seen in Table 2.1. A comparison of short-term rates on various instruments in September 1929 (in Table 2.2) shows that call loan rates were 50% higher than competing instruments, which explains how the market expanded.

These high rates had extended the call loan market beyond the New York City

Table 2.2
Short-term Interest Rates

Average week ended	Call loans	Commercial paper	Bankers acceptances	U.S. govt. obligations (3–6 mos.)
Sept. 7	8.65%	6.125%	5.125%	4.58%[a]
Sept. 14	8.09	6.25	5.125	4.58
Sept. 21	8.48	6.25	5.125	4.58
Sept. 28	9.03	6.25	5.125	4.58

Source: Banking & Monetary Statistics, pp. 456, 460.

[a] September average.

and country banks, which were the normal lenders, by attracting funds from new lenders such as corporations, investment trusts, individuals, governments, and foreigners. They accounted for over 60% of the call loan market by October 1929. Corporations provided the largest instance of disintermediation and may have amounted to $5 billion of the $8.5 billion in borrowing reported by NYSE members for September 1929. Corporations had traditionally maintained substantial bank time deposits, which caused this category of deposits in banks in 101 leading cities to grow annually without interruption from $1.6 billion in 1919 to a peak of $6.9 billion in June 1928. However, time deposits began to decline in the second half of 1928, coincident with the rise in call loan rates above 7%.[14] Major corporations in the auto, petroleum, and steel industries, investment trusts, and utilities built up large portfolios of call loans. U.S. Steel, General Motors, AT&T, and Standard Oil Co. of New Jersey had hundreds of millions of dollars in the call loan market, a disproportionate share of their short-term investments, which they normally would never have countenanced.

The diversion of funds into the call loan market by corporations, foreigners, and individuals was prompted by the speculative mania of the period. The banks were unwilling to finance this adventure and maintained their call loans below $2.3 billion throughout 1929.[15] Therefore, the brokerage community had to bid up call loan rates above competing rates and go beyond the banks to their customers to attract the funds the banks would not lend.

There was widespread recognition of the vulnerability of the call loan market to such a large proportion of lending from sources traditionally unfamiliar with the market. The newspapers commented regularly on the unusual size and structure of the call loan market. On October 3, 1929, the Dow Jones Industrial Index dropped 14 points in the worst decline of the year to date in response to an increase in brokers call loans through New York City banks to $6.8 billion. (This is less than call loans as reported by brokers, since the banks reported only loans placed through them or for their own account. The banks' figures were available weekly, however, and show the trend of events best. Call loans reported by brokers were only available monthly.) Again, on October 18th and 19th, the stock market declined sharply after brokers call loans were reported up a further $88 million. Brokers, bankers, journalists, and investors recognized that stock speculation had distorted the credit markets by prompting high call loan rates to attract the funds to finance that speculation. In early October the American Bankers Association passed a resolution supporting brokers call loans as an indirect way of financing industry, since a significant portion of loans to brokers was to finance underwriting positions, but few professionals could have been fooled into believing that day-to-day loans were a wise basis for holding permanent securities issues. The resolution had earmarks of an effort to sustain confidence in an overextended market under public attack.

The Federal Reserve began to ease credit in August 1929, one month before the market hit its peak and two months before the Crash. On August 9th the Federal Reserve Bank of New York raised its discount rate to 6%, but at the same time it reduced its buying rate for bankers acceptances by 1/8%. Since the latter rate was the operative one of the two, it signalled the trend, and the discount rate rise was symbolic. Thereafter the Federal Reserve System's bill portfolio expanded steadily from $66 million on July 10, 1929, to $379 million on October 23rd. Reserves of weekly reporting New York City commercial banks expanded from $703 million on August 7th to $764 million by the end of September, and their Federal Reserve borrowings dropped from over $300 million in July to only $41 million by October 23rd. Levels below $50 million were traditionally held to be a measure of easy credit. Borrowing by Chicago banks also dropped sharply, from a $119 million peak in March 1929 to only $20 million in October.[16] Banks outside these two centers, however, showed no decline in their Federal Reserve borrowings.

Interest rates began to come down under the easier credit conditions. Call loan rates were erratically 6%–9% during September and steadily 5%–6% in the first two weeks of October, compared with an average of over 8% in August. The cooling in the stock market and the economy which began in September 1929 after months of fervid growth had a simultaneous easing impact on credit conditions just as the Federal Reserve was acting to ease credit.

This credit-easing trend was not far advanced by the time of the Crash, however. Banks outside New York City and Chicago still had record borrowings from the Federal Reserve System. Interest rates were still higher than almost any year back to 1920–21. Funds from corporations, foreigners, and individuals traditionally invested in the banking system were still in the stock market directly or indirectly. In any case, the seeds soon to be reaped had been sown over many months prior to this late change in credit conditions.

The Federal Reserve was in a good position to gather information on and evaluate the immediate effects of the Crash. The flow of information to the Federal Reserve from Wall Street was facilitated by the dominant influence then exercised by the New York Federal Reserve, rather than the Board of Governors in Washington. The relationship was informal and close between the New York bank and Wall Street. Benjamin Strong had been prompted to become the first President of the New York bank by leading New York City bankers, particularly J. P. Morgan, and J. P. Morgan's position with the bank was such that he called on officers without appointment. Professionals from Wall Street were also prominent on the bank's board of directors. Owen D. Young, Chairman of General Electric, and Charles E. Mitchell, Chairman of National City Bank, were both directors at this time. These and other financiers recognized quickly that the collapse in stock prices portended a severe financial and economic reaction unless it could be countered promptly, which they successfully communicated to the New York Federal Reserve.

In the Crash the immediate problem to be dealt with by the Federal Reserve and the New York City banks was the collapse of the call loan market. Out-of-town banks and other nonbank lenders to the call loan market panicked as stock prices fell, fearing that the collateral for their loans was lost. They took at least $2.1 billion out of the call loan market in the week ending October 30th, which was 25% of the $8.5 billion previously outstanding. As a result, New York City banks expanded their call loans to the brokerage community as lenders of last resort. In the first week of the Crash, call loans by New York City banks to brokers went up almost 100% from $1.1 billion to $2.1 billion. Loans on securities to other customers went up $0.2 billion as well, as the banks advanced loans to brokers' margin customers forced to look elsewhere. The major banks outside New York City maintained their securities loans at $5 billion.

The New York Federal Reserve acted to accommodate this call loan expansion by purchasing bankers acceptances and U.S. bonds, which enabled New York City banks' reserves to expand from $739 million to $982 million in the week ending October 30th. The Federal Reserve also discounted freely for member banks whose borrowings jumped in the first week of the Crash from $796 million to $991 million, most of the increase coming from borrowing by New York City banks. Once it was clear that the New York Federal Reserve and the New York City banks would act in concert to supply funds to the market, the shortage of funds in the call loan market ceased to be a problem.

The natural question in light of the repetitious decline in stock prices throughout most of November is whether monetary policy played a role in that decline, and if it did not, whether the contraction of the call loan market from $8.5 billion in September to only $4 billion by November 30th represented the breakdown of the financial structure which financed the bull market, and who was to blame.

The answer with respect to the role of monetary policy in fueling the continuing decline in securities prices is conclusive—it did not. The Federal Reserve followed a policy of aggressive credit easing throughout the Crash. The day before Black Thursday the New York Federal Reserve reduced its buying rate for bankers acceptances from 5 1/8% to 5%. Then, during the Crash, the New York Federal Reserve reduced its discount rate from 6% to 5% on November 1st and to 4 1/2% on November 15th. On the same dates, it reduced its buying rate for bankers acceptances to 4 3/4% and 4 1/4%. Another reduction to 4% on November 21st prevailed until January 31, 1930.

The activism of the Federal Reserve in easing credit is also evident in its open market policy of buying U.S. government securities and bankers acceptances to expand commercial bank reserves. The Federal Reserve's holdings of U.S. government securities expanded from $136 million on October 23rd to $511 million at the end of the year, and its bankers acceptance holdings expanded from $379 million to $392 million.[17] Under the impetus of this program, Federal Reserve borrowings of the New York City banks declined to $40 million or less from November 13th through December 4th, a traditional sign of very easy credit, and the New York City banks were even able to increase their short-term investments from $1.7 billion when the Crash began in October to $2 billion by the end of November.

Money market rates reflected these easier credit conditions. The rates on 3- to 6-month Treasury notes and certificates fell from an average of 4.58% in September to 3.03% in December and bankers acceptance rates dropped from 5 1/8% the week of October 19th to 3 7/8% in December. Call loan rates dropped to 4 1/2% in December, which finally restored money market rates to their normal relationships. There was even a significant expansion of short-term instruments, as bankers acceptances outstanding grew from $1.3 billion in September to a record $1.7 billion in December, and commercial paper outstanding grew from $265 million to $334 million. The Treasury felt sufficiently confident about credit conditions to initiate the issuance of Treasury bills in December 1929.

The question remains whether the contraction of the call loan market played a major role in the prolonged decline in stock prices in the Crash. Inexperienced lenders to the market have received the most attention in this respect. Russell Leffingwell, a J. P. Morgan partner, testified in front of the Senate Committee on Banking and Currency in 1933 (the Pecora Committee) that these lenders called loans so heavily that they provided the momentum for the repeated securities liquidations in the Crash. The effect of these lenders' calls is easily seen in the first week of the Crash in the shift of $1 billion of brokers loans to the major New York City banks. The newspapers at the time carried accounts suggesting that $150 million or more of loans were called day after day in that first week. Call loan rates jumped from 4 1/2% to 6% as the brokers bid for funds. This part of the crisis passed smoothly, however, as the New York City banks became lenders of last resort to the brokerage community. More problematic developments in the call loan market occurred after the first week, when the volume of call loans continued to decline. This could have been for any or all of the following reasons:

1. The New York City banks ceased to be lenders of last resort and forced liquidation of their loans.

2. Brokerage firms forced liquidation of their margin loans by selling out weakened accounts, raising margin requirements, or refusing new margin accounts.
3. Brokerage firms sold their own securities inventories and correspondingly reduced their own loans.
4. Customers voluntarily or involuntarily reduced their margin accounts.

There is strong evidence that the banks did not force any liquidation beyond what the decline in collateral values required. They did not panic and try to reduce their exposure to the stock market. Most convincing in this respect is the pattern of their loans on securities to others than brokers. These loans to others than brokers rose during the Crash by $319 million at New York City banks and by $240 million at out-of-town banks. The New York City banks even increased their exposure by reducing their margin requirements to 25% on Tuesday, October 29th, following Monday's decline of 38 points on the Dow Jones Industrial Index. There were some reports that the banks "took over" accounts which became undermargined and subsequently liquidated them when any improvement in the market occurred. This could help account for the prolonged period of liquidation in the Crash. But there were also reports of banks ignoring under-margined accounts, because the decline in stock prices seemed so unrealistic. On balance, the banks appear to have played a responsible role in not forcing stock liquidation.

Whether the brokers were as calm as the banks is a more difficult question. Prior to the Crash, brokers tried to reduce their call loan exposure on margin accounts. Margin practices were unregulated and varied. Many brokerage firms customarily required 25% equity, but sometimes as little as 10%, in a margin account; big trading customers were given open lines of credit equivalent to charge accounts. During the six months preceding the Crash, however, brokers raised these terms, usually to 50% equity, in recognition of the high level of speculation in the market. The newspapers reported a concerted effort by brokers in September and October 1929 to reduce their call loans.

The rates on call loans in the Crash suggest that the liquidating pressure on call loans was from the brokers rather than the banks. On Black Thursday call loan rates jumped from 3% to 6% and stayed there for official purposes until November 18th. However, this rate was pegged by the NYSE in concert with the New York City banks and did not reflect market forces in its normal fashion until November 18th. Call loans were also arranged in the Over-the-Counter market at free market rates which dropped below 6% to 5 1/2% as early as November 4th. Thereafter, through November, call loan rates were often as low as 5 1/2% in the Over-the-Counter market, and there were regular daily reports of $40–$70 million of call money not lent. For at least three weeks of the Crash during November, there was a surplus of call loan funds available, which drove rates down, rather than a scramble for loans.

The brokers' principal methods of reducing their call loans were margin calls and sale of their own securities. Margin calls were frequently mentioned in the newspapers of the period as the dynamic force in many of the sharp declines during the Crash. There appears to have been little sympathy or hesitation in selling out undermargined accounts. Friends and old customers suffered along with new customers. The determination of margin requirements for a given account appears to have been only approximate as well. Customers complained of being unfairly treated, sold out when their accounts were adequate, never contacted, or subjected to valuations below current market prices. Each day through the Crash back offices of the brokerage firms worked into the night evaluating accounts and sending out telegrams for more margin. The deadline for a customer to advance additional equity or give other instructions was 11:00 a.m. the next day, which was an almost impossibly short period, but accounts were sold out on time if no satisfactory response was received. Representatives of the Bankers' Pool later testified that they came to dread this hour of the day.

We have no data to indicate what part of the reduction in call loans may have been due to brokers selling securities they owned. Brokers had substantial inventories of unsold, underwritten securities offerings at the time of the Crash. September 1929 set a record of $1.5 billion for new issues in one month, and new issues in the nine months exceeded $8.5 billion. This was more than brokers could immediately sell, so the unsold balance was in their inventories. It was also a vulnerable balance, heavily distributed among the stocks of investment trusts, public utility holding companies, and initial public offerings of small companies. It would not be surprising if brokers decided to liquidate their inventories of this type. Utility holding companies and investment trust stocks fared among the worst in the Crash.

The brokers were dramatically successful in reducing their call loan exposure. New York Stock Exchange member borrowings had risen to a peak of 9.82% of the value of all stocks on October 1, 1929, and by the end of the year they were down to only 6.17% of the value of all stocks.[18]

There is no doubt that customers also acted to reduce call loans by liquidating their own margin accounts. Demand deposits at New York City banks jumped over $1.5 billion to $6.9 billion in the week ending October 30th as investors left the stock market, but this bulge almost disappeared by year end. The inescapable conclusion appears to be that the brokers were the motivating force behind the reduction in call loans as they sold out both their customers' holdings and their own.

The Federal Reserve's easy money policy helped stem the Crash and created optimism that the nation would recover without undue hardship. The strength of the banking industry was the other pillar of support for this optimism. As 1929 ended, the big banks were in a position of prestige and power. It was a big bank era, just as it was a big band era, and like the bands the banks wrote the music to which others danced. At the end of 1929 the major New York City banks had 16% of all commercial bank loans and investments and over 35% of all loans and investments reported by weekly reporting banks in 101 cities.[19]

Many of the banks had built dominant positions throughout the financial system, which were strengthened in 1929 by numerous mergers. In New York alone, seven mergers took place among major banks:

Guaranty Trust Co. — National Bank of Commerce

Chase National Bank — National Park Bank

Equitable Trust Co. — Seaboard National Bank

National City Bank — Farmers' Loan & Trust Co.

Central Union Trust Co. — Hanover National Bank

Chemical Bank & Trust Co. — U.S. Mortgage & Trust Co.

Bank of America — Blair & Co., Inc.[20]

The leading banks had great strength because they had deposits not more than seven times their capital and surplus. This was a conservative ratio, especially when only 60% of bank assets were typically in loans and advances and up to one-third of those were call loans. The banks also had considerable intangible strength and influence, for their chief executives were leading social, political, and economic figures. Charles E. Mitchell of the National City Bank of New York, Albert Wiggin of the Chase National Bank, J. P. Morgan of J. P. Morgan & Co., and George Baker of the First National Bank of New York were followed in the newspapers like movie stars or politicians. New York bank executives sat on most corporate boards of directors and on the boards of the investment trusts. The bankers influenced investment decisions by life and casualty insurance companies, by other banks, by their own trust departments, and by investment clients. Commercial bankers were prominent directors of their regional Federal Reserve banks, often chose the Federal Reserve banks' officers, and instructed their Reserve Bank governors on attitudes to be taken into Washington Federal Reserve Board meetings.

The banks also began to create investment banking affiliates in the early years of the decade, and these affiliates were among the leading houses handling new securities issues by 1929. These bank affiliates managed 50% of all the new securities issues in 1930, whereas in 1927 they had managed only 12 1/2%.

The leading banks weathered the Crash well. They acted as lenders of last resort to the call loan market during the Crash in a most responsible fashion in concert with the Federal Reserve System. They were also bidders of last resort for common stocks through the Bankers' Pool. Besides these shows of strength, bank finances appeared to be unaffected by the Crash, as net profits of all Federal Reserve member banks were a record $556 million in 1929 and their dividends were $387 million. Most of the major banks posted record 1929 earnings per share.

The broad-based strength of the major banks was a source of confidence that the nation would recover from the Crash, but there was concern about the solidity of very small banks, for 659 commercial banks across the United States suspended deposits totalling $240 million in 1929. Some 604 of the suspended banks had total loans and investments of less than $1 million, and 547 of them were not members of the Federal Reserve System.[21] Over 60% of them were concentrated in the 12 midwestern states north of and including Ohio, Indiana, Illinois, Missouri, and Kansas. But these suspensions were not due to the Crash. This level of suspensions had prevailed throughout the decade and was due to the nation's archaic banking laws. Branch banking was favored by the American Bankers Association to remedy this high incidence of failure, and there was strong support in Congress for a federal branch banking law. Big banks were strong, protective, and public-spirited. Public opinion favored making them bigger.

There were some weak spots in this entrenched image of big bank solidity, however. National City Bank revealed to its stockholders meeting in January 1930 that the bank's investment affiliate, National City Co., had bought and lost heavily in the parent stock in the Crash. There were even rumors that Charles Mitchell might resign because his publicity-prone marketing emphasis on stocks seemed inappropriate. Conservative Detroit financiers questioned the expansionist policies of that city's leading banks and their heavy involvement in stocks. However, these were exceptions in a strong banking picture. Historically minded observers pointed out that the United States had never had a severe depression that was not accompanied by a crisis in the banking system, and the stability of the banking system in 1929 augured a mild recession.

THE U.S. ECONOMY FALTERS BEFORE THE CRASH AND THEN DROPS SHARPLY

The economy rose to record heights in 1929 as industrial output and the Gross National Product reached peaks substantially above 1928 figures. Some 90 billion kilowatt hours of electricity were generated, versus 80 billion in 1928.[22] Auto and truck production was 5.6 million units, versus 4.6 million in 1928. New orders for electric machinery were worth $1.3 billion, up 30% from 1928, and machine tool orders, based on an index of 100 in 1923–24, were at 281, versus 237 in 1928. Crude oil production reached 1 billion barrels for the first time. Railroad locomotive and freight-car orders were double the number of 1928 orders. Steel ingot output was 54.9 million tons, versus 50.3 million in 1928. Production in most other industries was up 4%–5%, except building contracts, which were flat.

With the benefit of hindsight we know that despite the records established in 1929 the trend of the economy had reversed before the Crash. Production peaked in most industries in the first half of the year. Automobile and copper production peaked in April; machine tool orders peaked even earlier; steel ingot production peaked in May; coal and crude oil production did not peak until the summer; freight-car loadings peaked in September. Only electrical equipment orders and retail sales were still better than 1928 in December. Nonetheless, the decline which had begun in some industries in early 1929 became gradually apparent in other industries only as the year progressed. As late as September, Bradstreet's trade review still provided a mixed picture. It reported that steel was strong, that auto production and building construction were down, that shoe production was down slightly, and that there had been the first year-to-year decline in railroad freight car loadings for several years. However, it reported that consumer buying power was high, as were exports and clothing sales.

The changing economic climate was more evident in commodities prices, almost all of which peaked in early 1929. Prices peaked in the first quarter for copper, chemicals, lead, and tin. International ship charter rates also began to decline then. In the second quarter, prices peaked for crude oil, steel, lumber, and cotton. Zinc and fertilizer prices were the only prominent commodities which had price peaks after the first half of 1929, and their peaks occurred in the third quarter.

The Crash immediately produced a sharp change in business conditions, although business pessimism had been building in September and early October, when stocks came under selling pressure. On October 25th, the day after Black Thursday, Presidents Farrell of U.S. Steel and Schwab of Bethlehem Steel deplored the widespread pessimism at the New York general meeting of the American Iron & Steel Institute. They claimed that the steel industry was operating at 110% of capacity, that prices were stable, and that inventories were reasonable (by December, the steel industry produced only three-quarters of the output produced in December 1928). In October, the *Annalist* index of business activity (a weekly magazine published by the *New York Times* and eventually merged with *Business Week*) registered its sharpest drop in 46 years, from 103.5 to 95.4. Auto and truck production in November and December dropped to only half the industry's April peak. Coal production in December was the lowest since 1925. Machine tool orders in December were only half those of December 1928. Employment suddenly shifted from growth to a decline of 1/2% in November and 4% in December.[23]

Despite these sharp shifts in activity, confusion about the course of business persisted. The record construction programs for 1930 announced by the railroads, utilities, local governments, and industry appeared to promise a prompt recovery in the economy. The Federal Reserve banks unanimously predicted a short-lived economic decline in 1930 followed by recovery. The economic decline was expected to be concentrated in the sales of luxury goods and in discretionary consumer items, yet the Federal Reserve reported to President Hoover that Christmas sales were ahead of 1928, although they were erratic. The stock market still expected companies to report record earnings per share for 1929, and this, combined with easy credit and Hoover's pressure on business and local government to expand, made the prospects for 1930 look good.

PRICES ARE STABLE UNTIL THE CRASH, WHEN THEY BEGIN TO DECLINE

Prices were relatively stable from 1927 to the Crash, having come down relatively sharply in the first half of the decade. Several key costs were partic-

Table 2.3
Price Indices, 1925–1929

	1929	1928	1927	1926	1925
Wholesale prices[a]	1.38	1.40	1.37	1.43	1.48
Rail revenues per ton-mile[b]	1.08	1.08	1.08	NA[d]	NA
Building costs[c]	207	207	206	208	207
Farm receipts[c]	138	139	131	136	147

[a]*Source:* U.S. Department of Labor.
[b]*Source:* Moody's *Railroad Manual, 1931*, p. xxxvii.
[c]*Source:* Moody's *Industrial Manual, 1931*, pp. xvi, xxix.
[d]NA = Not Available.

ularly stable, such as wholesale prices, railroad freight rates, building costs, and farm prices. Readers can compare indices of these key costs in Table 2.3.

Other key prices such as those for chemicals, steel, manufactured gas, and cotton goods had been relatively stable. Only street railway fares, among a wide range of general products and services, had gone up in price. Copper, lead, zinc, oil, and scrap steel all rose in price in 1929 as a result of the boom conditions, but in general the prices of these commodities fluctuated during the last half of the 1920s with no clear trend. Coal, cement, tin, imported rubber, and woolen goods showed clear declining price trends during the 1920s.

The overall impact of price trends in the boom years was neutral. There were few rising prices, and a slight trend to declining prices, but this trend was not significant enough to affect business and financial decisions. Increased productivity and expanded output and capacity overcame the slight deleterious effects of a declining price level.

Prices began to decline in the last quarter of 1929 in many industries where prices had been stable or up because of the boom. Prices of sensitive commodities, such as cotton, lead, zinc, wool, oil, and lumber, declined 5%–8% immediately as the active financial markets in most of these commodities were immediately affected by the Crash. Price declines in steel scrap and rubber of over 15% during the fourth quarter were more disconcerting and closely related to the rapid decline in automobile production. The Wholesale Price Index dropped from over 96 before the Crash to 93.3 in December. This was the lowest wholesale price level since World War I, and it clearly put business on notice that a more serious than usual business decline was in prospect.[24]

NOTES

1. *Monetary Statistics*, pp. 24–27. See also Table A.41.
2. *Banking & Monetary Statistics*, p. 441.
3. Ibid., pp. 443–45.
4. Ibid., p. 370.

5. Ibid., pp. 140–42.

6. Ibid., p. 174.

7. Ibid., p. 206.

8. Ibid., p. 400.

9. Ibid., pp. 171–74.

10. Ibid., p. 206.

11. Ibid., p. 400.

12. Ibid., pp. 449–50.

13. Ibid., p. 384.

14. Ibid., p. 450.

15. Ibid., p. 142.

16. Ibid., p. 398.

17. Ibid., p. 384.

18. *NYSE Year Book, 1938*, p. 62.

19. *Banking & Monetary Statistics*, pp. 19, 142, 174.

20. *New York Times*, 12/31/29.

21. *Federal Reserve Bulletin*, September 1937, pp. 871–910.

22. Data on industries reviewed is derived principally from industry reviews in the 1930 editions of *Moody's Industrial Manual*, *Moody's Railroad Manual*, and *Moody's Public Utility Manual*.

23. *New York Times*, 8/9/30.

24. *Statistical Abstract, 1939*, p. 321.

3

Bond Markets in 1929

THE BOND MARKET BEFORE THE CRASH

Before the Crash, credit markets were dominated by events in the stock market. The call loan market which was used to finance stock purchases was the center of money market activity because it offered rates 4%–5% above competing short-term securities. Bond prices declined throughout the year until October. Average yields on long-term government and Aa utility bonds rose 25–30 basis points during the year to 3.70% and 5.05% respectively. Since short-term rates varied from 1%–5% above long term corporate bond rates and the U.S. Treasury bond yield curve was flat, the market was poor for new straight debt issues. Corporate bond issues in 1929 were only $2.1 billion, of which over $1.1 billion were issues with convertible privileges or warrants attached.[1] In prior years, the volume of new annual corporate bond issues reached $4.5 billion, with a much lower proportion of equity-related issues. New issues of bonds in 1929 by foreign governments were reduced to $130 million, compared with $700 million in 1928 and $900 million in 1927. Real estate bond issues were only $527 million in 1929, versus $813 million in 1928. New bond issues of all types in 1929 were the lowest since 1924.[2]

The deflated glamour of the stock market after the Crash was expected to result in renewed interest in the bond market. Following the Crash, long-term interest rates came down 35 basic points from their peaks, but new-issue volume remained small in the closing months of the year.

The new-issue business in normal times was dominated by railroad and public utility bond issues, municipal bond issues, and foreign bond issues. Public utility new issues varied between $1.3 billion and $1.9 billion from 1924 to 1929. Municipal new issues showed little variation between $1.3 and $1.5 billion each year from 1924 to 1929. Foreign new issues varied between $1 billion and $1.6 billion from 1924 to 1928 but dropped to $0.8 billion in 1929. Railroads varied most in their financing, from $0.3 billion to $0.8 billion between 1924 and 1929, but they were considered the premier corporate security. Their bonds sold at yields anywhere from 1/8% to 1/2% below comparably rated utility and industrial bonds. Industrial corporations were not big issuers of debt at this time. In many cases, their plant and equipment or other assets were not considered suitable collateral for bonds, in contrast to the assets of railroads and utilities. Industrials seeking leverage issued preferred stock which often reached 15%–25% of companies' capital structures.

U.S. government bonds were an important sector of the bond market because of the $15.4 billion of public issues outstanding at the end of 1929, but U.S. issues were not important to the new-issue business because the federal government ran a budget surplus from 1920 to 1930. Throughout the 1920s it retired $400–$500 million of debt annually. The attention attracted by the drama of the 1929 stock market distorts the popular image of financial markets at that time, for the bond market was much more important to the capital-raising process than the stock market. In the mid-1920s, new funds raised through common stock offerings were less than 10% of new issues. Common stock was considered highly speculative financing. The amounts of preferred stock sold were as large as common stock, and municipal bond issues were approximately 2 1/2 times common stock offerings. Debt issues of all kinds accounted for over 80% of all new issues. Table 3.1 shows the distribution of new issues of bonds and stocks by the principal sources during the mid-1920s. Figure 3.1 illustrates the novelty of stocks on the New York Stock Exchange in 1930. The prominent position that common stocks occupied on the New York Stock Exchange began to develop only in the 1920s. Prior to that, bond issues listed outnumbered stock issues 2 to 1. Most corporate and many foreign bond issues were listed on the New York Stock Exchange. The U.S. Liberty Bond issues were listed, and so were $12 billion equivalent in Sterling War Loans by Great Britain. Only municipal issues were not listed regularly. This is not to say that all trading took place on the NYSE. Contemporary estimates were that 90% of trading in U.S. securities took place in the Over-the-Counter market between dealers and institutions dealing directly with each other as principals.

The leading underwriting house of this period was J. P. Morgan & Co., but its preeminence is difficult to document. It rested on the quality of the firm's work and personnel and on its selective approach to business. J. P. Morgan & Co. did not do more business than others; it sought only a limited business from the highest quality issuers and still did one of the largest businesses. J. P. Morgan & Co. also appeared to have greater influence over its clients than did other bankers.

There was no lack of competition, however. Harris, Forbes & Co. usually contested J. P. Morgan & Co. for the largest volume of financing and had prestigious clientele. Kuhn, Loeb & Co. was Morgan's equal in snob appeal and nearly its equal in number of clients. The securities affiliates of the commercial banks, such as the Guaranty Co., the National City Co., and the Chase

Table 3.1
New Issues of Bonds and Stocks, 1924–1930 ($ millions)

	1924	1925	1926	1927	1928	1929	1930
Total new issues	$5,593	$6,220	$6,344	$7,791	$8,114	$10,183	$7,023
Corporate debt	2,199	2,451	2,666	3,182	2,385	2,078	2,980
Corporate pfd. stock	318	594	509	874	1,149	1,517	412
Corporate common stock	511	558	578	600	1,812	4,407	1,091
% Total	9%	9%	9%	8%	22%	43%	15%
Municipal bonds	$1,380	$1,352	$1,344	$1,475	$1,379	$ 1,418	$1,434
Foreign issues	1,005	1,095	1,156	1,573	1,325	763	1,020
Other issues	179	169	91	87	64	0	87
Total debt	4,764	5,088	5,257	6,317	5,153	4,259	5,520
% Total	85%	81%	83%	81%	64%	42%	79%

Source: Survey of Current Business (U.S. Dept. of Commerce), February 1938, pp. 16–19.

Figure 3.1
Changes in Issues Listed (as of January 1, 1900–1930)

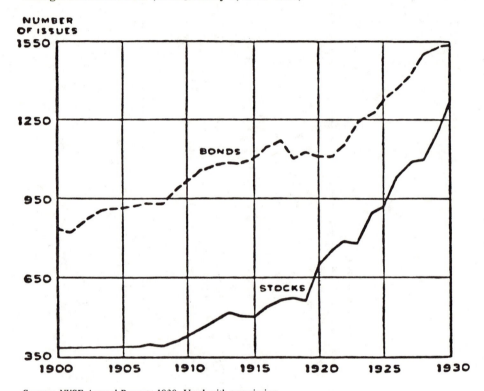

Source: NYSE Annual Report, 1930. Used with permission.

Securities Corp., were not the equal of J. P. Morgan & Co., but neither did they have the history. Most of them became prominent in the 1920s, and by 1929 they were formidable competitors of the traditional investment banking houses. The bank affiliates' market share of new issues rose from 12 1/2% in 1927 to 50% in 1930.

THE BOND MARKET IN THE CRASH

The Crash changed the tone of the bond market immediately. New-issue business of all types came to a stop for three weeks. Total new issues in November and December, excluding municipal issues, dropped to $214 million and $360 million respectively, compared with an average of over $1 billion monthly in the first nine months of 1929. Bond issues were postponed, however, because the brokerage community was preoccupied with common stock trading in the Crash, rather than because of a falling bond market, for, on the contrary, prices of high grade bonds began to rise early in the Crash. On October 22, 1929, before the Crash was in full course, the *New York Times* commented that the "period during which all bond issues had to be 'sweetened' by a convertible feature is drawing to a close." Bond volume on the NYSE in October was the highest in five years. The U.S. Treasury bonds followed in Table A.40 of the Statistical Appendix rose to higher prices each month from October through December until they were $2 1/2 to $6 above their lowest September prices, depending upon the issue selected. High grade utility and railroad bond yields and U.S. bond yields were cut 1/8%–1/4% by the end of the year from the peak yields in August and September. As call loan and commercial paper rates dropped to 5% and bankers acceptance rates dropped to 4%, investors turned to long-term bonds for higher yields. Other investors switched funds from the stock market to high grade bonds, which offered greater security.

Moody's Investors Service, Halsey, Stuart & Co., and other bond dealers predicted a resurgence in bond business after the low 1929 volume. Utilities particularly lined up a large volume of new issues. They issued $228 million in one week of December alone, the largest volume in any week of 1929.

The Crash had a contrary impact on Baa and other lower quality bonds. The yields on Baa industrial and utility bonds dropped little, in contrast to high grade bonds, so that the yield spread between Baa and Aa bonds became the widest in 1929. Baa industrial bond yields were 138 basis points higher than Aa utility bond yields in December, and Baa utility bond yields were 109 basis points higher. Some investors were forced to liquidate bond holdings to cover their losses in the stock market, and their net selling impact was on low grade bonds, which new buyers shunned in a search for security of capital. During the Crash the *New York Times* index of 40 domestic corporate bonds hit its lowest point since 1925, reflecting this impact on lower grade bonds.

The first case of a railroad unable to issue bonds at all occurred in early December, when the bellwether of trouble, the Erie Railroad, applied to the

Interstate Commerce Commission for permission to borrow $12 million short term because of the unreceptive market for its long-term bonds.

The bond market closed 1929 with optimism in the investment banking community that improving prices and a heavy new-issuer calendar were at hand. Bonds were at last reasserting their dominance over the stock market. However, investors who had lost money in the stock market were not prepared to take renewed risks in the bond market by buying low grade bonds. High grade bonds and liquid money market instruments were the desirable investments.

THE MUNICIPAL BOND MARKET DECLINES ALL YEAR UNTIL THE CRASH, AFTER WHICH IT RISES STRONGLY

The municipal bond market often appears dull, and it was no different in 1929. No dramatic sums of money are made or lost in the municipal market. Defaults are rare, and defaults that are not ultimately made good are even rarer. In 1929 only two states were not rated Aaa by *Moody's* (North and South Dakota), and they were rated Aa. All the major cities were rated Aaa. Investors seeking the tax-exempt income offered in the municipal market are presumably quiet, conservative types.

The municipal market is ignored by all but those who participate in it. Scholars ignore it; there are virtually no studies on its history or mechanics. Popular writers ignore it; read contemporary books on the Crash and you would think the municipal market did not exist. Even the newspapers barely touch it, usually mentioning no more than what new issues took place.

We too could ignore it for the moment, but at some point in this period we must confront the municipal market, for the problems of the cities became a central theme in the Depression. The great cities like New York, Chicago, Philadelphia, Boston, and Detroit teetered on the edge of bankruptcy, as did smaller cities and most of the agrarian states. In that condition they were unable to perform the social roles that were massed at the local level, and the long evolution of assigning those responsibilities to the federal government began.

Municipal bonds constituted one of the larger securities markets in 1929. Municipal new issues totalled $1.4 billion, which was 12% of the new issue market. Issues by investment trusts, by public utilities, and by industrial corporations were larger by almost 50%, but that was a reflection of the speculative mania that year. In prior years, only public utilities issued more securities than municipalities.

Moody's estimated that $15.7 billion in municipal bonds were outstanding in 1929, second only to the U.S. government, which had $16 billion outstanding. Utilities, railroads, and industrials each had $10–$12 billion outstanding.[3]

The high ratings of municipal bonds found great favor with conservative investors, especially with corporations and savings banks. Although virtually all the major municipal issuers were rated Aaa, market yields indicated a clear investor preference for the mid-Atlantic industrialized states, whose bonds sold at rates 1/4%–1/2% below those of the less populated, agrarian states.

In 1929 the municipal bond market behaved much like the corporate bond market. Bond prices declined enough to raise yields by 1/4%–1/2% in a steady progression throughout the year in response to the investor surge into the stock market and tightening short-term credit conditions. The yield curve was sharply inverse by November, when short-term municipal notes yielded 5% and comparable quality bonds yielded only 4 1/4%.

This trend was reversed during the Crash as investors departing the stock market created a strong demand for high quality municipals, especially short-term issues. Rates declined by as much as 1/4%, which was $5 in the price of a $100 bond and a large move for one month. At first, new issues were suspended during the Crash while brokers focussed on their stock market problems and issuers awaited more stable conditions, but as municipal bond prices moved up throughout the turmoil of October and November, issuers and underwriters were emboldened to bring new issues, and December witnessed the largest volume of municipal new issues in history—$290 million.

Municipal governments were expected to be an active countervailing force in the anticipated business downturn after the Crash. They were to care for the unemployed who became destitute, and Hoover appealed to all governors and mayors to accelerate their public works construction plans for 1930. Local government construction, which was mostly municipal, was expected to be $3 billion in 1930, equal to that of all private industry and over ten times the U.S. government's plans.[4]

However, many municipalities were not in a position financially to bear the twin burdens of unemployment relief and capital construction if the pressure carried on too long. New York City already had over $2 billion in outstanding debt—almost as much as all states combined. Chicago had $426 million in debts and had to pay the unusual rate of 6% for 1-year notes sold late in the year to cover expenses. The city was turned down by its bankers when it appealed for a second loan in December to cover its $20 million budget deficit. Philadelphia and Detroit also had debts of $400 million, Los Angeles owed over $200 million, and Baltimore over $175 million.

The financial burden of government was disproportionately heavy at the municipal level. The nation's major cities were its major debtors, and they had become increasingly so in the last decade. Municipal debt outstanding had more than doubled in ten years, while federal government debt had decreased by 30% and corporate and individual debts had grown by an estimated 50%.[5] These municipal pressures were quite clear in Florida, where ten municipalities were already in default on debt issued to cope with the state's first massive population influx. More Florida defaults were anticipated, including a default by Miami, whose bonds yielded 5.75%—1% above any other major city's bonds. The financial pressures were also clear in Arkansas, Louisiana, Mississippi, Tennessee, and North Carolina, which had incurred relatively large per capita state debts trying to bring a modern public capital infrastructure to their states. Arkansas had the highest per capita state debt in the nation, mostly because of its road-building programs. From time to time the market for these states' bonds disappeared altogether, despite their Aaa ratings.

These municipal problems were not prominent in 1929 or in 1930, but eventually they were to loom as a major obstacle in dealing with the effects of the Depression.

NOTES

1. Compiled from Otto P. Schwarzschild (ed.), *American Underwriting Houses and Their Issues*, vol. 2, N.Y.: National Statistical Service, no date.
2. *Survey of Current Business*, February 1938, pp. 16–21; and May 1938, pp. 18–20.
3. *Moody's Railroad Manual, 1934*, p. a8.
4. *New York Times*, 1/18/30.
5. *Historical Statistics*, p. 989.

4

Political and Economic Influences on Securities Markets in 1930

The collapse of stock prices in October and November 1929 and the behavior of other securities markets at that time reflected mostly the working of forces and institutions internal to those markets, such as speculative excesses, panic, banking reactions, and monetary policy. In 1930, developments outside the securities markets exerted such profound influences on securities activities that these developments must be reviewed.

The Hoover Administration's efforts to counter the Depression became a principal influence on securities markets, as did the business decline. Other influences, such as the decline in commodities prices, international trade and credit problems, increased failures in the domestic banking system, and local government financial problems also affected securities markets significantly. These influences are interrelated, but they had their own independent momentum as well. We will review each of these areas of politics and the economy before dealing with the securities markets specifically in 1930.

The reader must keep in mind that 1930 was an ambiguous year. It began with a burst of optimism, prompted by the consensus for quick action in business and government to offset the effects of the Crash on the economy. By mid-1930, however, there was increased awareness of the depth of the developing Depression and widespread uncertainty. The Smoot-Hawley Tariff, enacted in June, capped the despair of many businessmen at home and abroad. But even by the end of 1930, opinion was still divided on the strength of the economy and how strongly forces already in motion were acting to restore prosperity, even though the stock market was down over 50% from its high in 1929 and the long-term bond market was disorganized.

HOOVER'S ACTIONS PRODUCE INITIAL OPTIMISM, BUT THE SMOOT-HAWLEY TARIFF MARKS A TURNING POINT FOR THE WORSE

Government, business, and the media recognized promptly that the Crash threatened to bring about an economic decline, and they acted quickly to minimize it. On November 13, 1929, President Hoover proposed a $160 million (1%) cut in personal income taxes, and Congress passed this tax cut before the end of the year. At the same time, he organized the Business Council of Employees and Labor, which agreed not to change wages up or down. The following week, in meetings with national leaders of the utility, railroad, and construction industries, he elicited promises of increased construction programs for 1930. Hoover also exhorted state and local governments to step up their construction programs to offset the effects of the Crash. The federal government expanded its own public works plans to $250 million for 1930. Secretary of Commerce Lamont estimated in January 1930 that public and private construction in that year would be a record $7 billion.

The Hoover policy was to exhort people to think positively, to work harder, and to accept personal and local responsibility to expand in order to offset the effects of the Crash. He tried to carry the message to the nation that business was sound and that he intended to provide a framework in which the nation could continue to prosper. Besides the 1% tax cut, Hoover's annual message to Congress in early December promised a new tariff law to clarify the opportunities open for domestic business, promised intensified enforcement of prohibition to upgrade the health and productivity of workers, and promised new railroad mergers to provide a basis for further expansion in that industry.

These hardly appear as radical gestures to readers today, but they constituted the most active and direct role in the economy taken by the federal government in generations. What is more, the policy appeared to work. Utilities, railroads, the steel industry, and major cities, especially New York, made large public commitments for 1930 investment spending in response to Hoover's requests. The Interstate Commerce Commission reacted to Hoover's prodding and in late December published a plan for reorganization of the railroad industry into 21 systems with five Eastern trunk lines.

The other side of Hoover's policy was to support the Federal Reserve in its policy of credit ease. We shall deal with this policy in detail shortly, but for the moment, it is sufficient to note that Federal Reserve credit policy in the first half of 1930 led to dramatic declines in interest rates and in bank borrowing from the Federal Reserve.

President Hoover's leadership in a combined business and government attack on the impending Depression, and the effects of easy money, were generally expected to produce an economic upswing by mid-1930. Politicians, businessmen, financiers, and independent economists were close to unanimity in this respect. In January 1930 the Department of Commerce told Hoover that there had already been an employment upturn. Slightly later, the New York Board of Trade told Franklin Roosevelt, then Governor of New York, that the spring uplift in economic activity would wipe out any unusual unemployment. These predictions bore little fruit, however.

Doubts about the economy, and suggestions that what we would now call a recession might be ahead, began to develop in May and June. The concern was sufficient to prompt Hoover to try further measures to aid the economy, and he pushed for a conclusion on the tariff considerations which had been before Congress for over a year and were inhibiting business expansion plans. The Senate and the House passed the Smoot-Hawley Tariff bill in mid-June, raising U.S. tariffs by 20% on average, to 44% of the dutiable value of imports, thereby making U.S. tariffs the highest in the world. Hoover immediately announced that he would sign the bill out of fear that there would be a stock market reaction if he prolonged the uncertainty.

The tariff bill did not have the unanimous endorsement accorded Hoover's earlier policies. There was little open discussion of the implications of higher tariffs. On November 12, 1929, Fred Kent, a director of Bankers Trust Co., told a congressional committee that the tariff debate had caused the Crash. This was the first such mention, and it produced a furor in Congress. The auto companies and the Chamber of Commerce opposed higher tariffs,[1] but there was no organized resistance to the high tariff lobby.

The Senate passed the Smoot-Hawley Tariff bill by the slim margin of 44–42, despite the lack of organized opposition. Senator Furnifold M. Simmons (Dem-N.C.) predicted the results accurately: "The most disastrous times this country has ever seen will befall this country as the result of this law." Newton D. Baker later said that in passing the Smoot-Hawley Tariff "war was declared by the Republican Party against the rest of mankind."[2] Thirty nations had protested the new law, and Holland, Belgium, France, Canada, Spain, and England reacted immediately by imposing countervailing tariffs. The delay was barely a week. Hindsight tells us that the Smoot-Hawley Tariff made a significant and perverse contribution to the decline in international trade which characterized the Depression.

The spirit of optimism following Hoover's initial positive actions began to fade rapidly in the summer of 1930 when the tariff bill was passed, and especially as the off-year elections approached, the Administration began to display a more acute awareness of the economic crisis at hand. Richard Whitney, President of the New York Stock Exchange, and white knight of the Wall Street crowd in the Crash, met secretly with Hoover on October 15th to counsel him on financial policy. On October 20th, Hoover set up the Emergency Committee for Employment under Colonel Arthur Woods, who had directed previous relief efforts.

The Democrats swept Congress in the November elections, reflecting the public discontent with economic conditions. The Republicans lost a 17-seat majority in the Senate, which returned with 48 Republicans, 47 Democrats, and 1 Independent. The Democrats gained over 50 seats in the House, erasing a previous Republican majority of 100. Immediately after the election, Hoover and Joe Robinson, the conservative Democratic Senate leader from Arkansas and Al Smith's running mate in 1928, agreed to work together on a nonpartisan program of relief for business and farmers. At the same time, Governor George Harrison of the New York Federal Reserve Bank left for Europe to discuss the problems of the Depression and to seek a basis for mutual attack on its problems.

As the realization developed that Hoover's policy of exhortation and easy money had not produced recovery, rigid principles began to dominate the Administration's reactions and policies. Richard Whitney's reception at the White House betokened a mutual sympathy for his philosophy that the economy should be left alone and the marketplace be allowed to determine the course of events. Colonel Woods was told that unemployment relief was a local responsibility and that the role of his Emergency Employment Committee was to exhort and advise. The Farm Board did intervene directly in the economy to support wheat prices at various levels down to 73¢ a bushel in mid-November, but it was only able to do so over Hoover's objections, and in mid-1931 it had to cease because its resources were exhausted. Eugene Meyer, Chairman of the Federal Reserve Board, privately advised Hoover to cut war debts by 70% and reparations by 40% to improve international trade and financial conditions, but Meyer was rebuffed.[3] The President's policies remained essentially exhortation and setting an environment conducive to local initiative, even though these policies were failing to produce results. He no longer had the initiative in economic policies. Direct intervention in the economy or for relief was taken grudgingly, usually to forestall proponents of more radical measures.

The principle binding Hoover from acting was a balanced budget, and it is easy to see how it limited his action in the second half of 1930. Every fiscal year in the 1920s there was a budget surplus of ordinary revenues over ordinary expenditures averaging $763 million.[4] The surplus was $738 million for the fiscal year ending June 30, 1930, during which Hoover cut taxes, increased public works spending, and expanded the government's apparatus in order to deal with the Depression. Hoover planned a fiscal 1931 budget surplus, but the likelihood of a surplus diminished as 1930 progressed. In the fiscal year ending June 1931 there was a budget deficit of $463 million because of a $1 billion decline in federal receipts. The Federal Gross Debt rose by $616 million during the year for the first time since 1919.[5]

Hoover's budget attitude was reinforced by Treasury Secretary Mellon, whose perception of the tragedies of the Depression rarely rose above abstraction. At this stage Mellon advocated a liquidation of labor, stocks, farmers, and real estate to end the Depression and to form a foundation for renewed expansion.

The Administration's budget focus was not irrational, for as we shall see, welfare expenses were capable of bankrupting local and national governments at the depths of the Depression. However, the budget focus was extreme and debilitating. It prevented effective action which, although it would have required deficit financing, would have caused deficits far short of problematical levels.

MONETARY POLICY, MONEY MARKETS, AND THE BANKING SYSTEM—CREDIT CONDITIONS ARE THE EASIEST IN A DECADE, BUT SMALL BANKS CLOSE IN RECORD NUMBERS AND BIGGER PROBLEMS INCUBATE IN THE LARGER BANKS

The Federal Reserve Bank of New York worked actively to bring down short-term interest rates in the first half of 1930. George L. Harrison, the New York bank's Governor, met with the Bank of England and its Governor, Montagu Norman, in November 1929 and again in February 1930 to coordinate a mutual easing in credit conditions in the two countries. The Federal Reserve banks had eased credit conditions in the Crash in order to position the major commercial banks to act as lenders of last resort to borrowers in the call loan market when lenders outside the banking system withdrew their funds, but the subsequent credit easing in 1930 was more a matter of policy. The New York Federal Reserve Bank reduced its buying rate for bankers acceptances 21 times in 1930 from 4% in January to 1 7/8% by June 30th and to 1 3/4% by year end, and its discount rate was cut five times during the year, from 4 1/2% in January to a record low of 2 1/2% on June 20th, and subsequently to 2%.[6] The decline in short-term rates occurred between January and August, after which rates fell minimally. For example, bankers acceptance rates were unchanged at 1 7/8% from July through December.

The Federal Reserve's policy of steadily reducing rates was paired with an open market policy which maintained total Federal Reserve credit (bills discounted, plus bills bought, plus U.S. government securities bought, plus small other holdings) at a stable level of approximately $1 billion from March through November 1930.[7] Federal Reserve holdings of U.S. governments expanded rapidly following the Crash until March 1930; but as call loan requirements declined and the stock market became more orderly, the Federal Reserve allowed its bill holdings to run down, offsetting its prior U.S. government purchases. The directors of the New York bank and its professional staff wanted to buy up to $200 million long U.S. government bonds to prevent the decline in Federal Reserve credit resulting from the decline in the Federal Reserve's bill holdings and to stimulate the bond market. The New York bank felt, as did the Hoover Administration, that a strong bond market was a precondition for economic recovery. However, the Federal Reserve Board in Washington adamantly opposed the New York bank's requests for permission to buy long-term bonds, out of fear that bond purchases were difficult to reverse and therefore might bring about overly stimulative monetary conditions re-creating the "inflationary" credit conditions of 1929, which meant unsound bank loans, stock market speculation, and overexpansion of business. The New York bank no longer sought to buy long-term bonds after July, when the major banks in New York and Chicago had eliminated their borrowings from the Federal Reserve System.[8]

Whether 1930 should be considered a period of "monetary ease" is a matter of debate. Interest rates declined, but since wholesale prices declined 14.7% and farm prices 29.3% the real burden of interest rates greatly increased for both existing and prospective debtors. Money supply also declined 3.8% to 9.9%, under its various definitions, which seems in contrast to monetary ease. Throughout this book, however, the term "monetary ease" is used with narrow reference to the conditions in the money markets, such as declining interest rates, declining borrowings at the Federal Reserve, rising bank investments, and available load funds. That is not to say that the real cost of funds was affordable to borrowers. In fact, quite the contrary. Two of the conclusions of this book are that interest costs were not responsive to the real cost of borrowing and that the trend of business was such that borrowers could not justify borrowing on any terms.

It is unarguable, despite this debate over easy money, that throughout the year there were few constraints on the Federal Reserve System had it wished to pursue a more vigorous open market policy. The federal budget was still in surplus through most of calendar 1930, which relieved the Federal Reserve System of responsibility for a major financing program, and U.S. gold reserves of $4 billion were rising rapidly, even in November and December of 1930, when banking problems increased.

Money Markets

The call loan market, which had been a source of instability in the 1929 money market, returned to normalcy during the course of 1930 as interest rates on call loans came back into line with those in the acceptance market, after having veered wildly away from them in 1929 because of the massive speculative demand for funds in the stock market. Call loan borrowings declined every month after April 1930 to $1.9 billion in December 1930, compared with $8.5 billion in September 1929.[9] Call loan rates dropped to 2% by June 30th as demand declined, and they stayed at that level until year end. The spread between call loan and bankers acceptance rates in the last half of 1930 averaged only 1/4%, compared with up to 5% before the Crash.

Rates on commercial paper, which along with acceptances and call loans was one of the principal short-term investments, declined to 3 3/8% in June, paralleling the rapid decline in other short-term rates, and dropped a further 1/2% in the second half of 1930. The spread between commercial paper and bankers acceptance rates was stable around 1 1/8% throughout 1930, which meant that commercial paper provided the highest short-term rates. Commercial paper outstanding doubled to $553 million between September 1929 and April 1930, which was a much greater expansion than that of bankers acceptances, then declined steadily as business activity declined until commercial paper outstanding in December 1930 was only $358 million.[10] We will come back to this trend in commercial paper outstanding when we discuss developments in the banking system.

The Banking System

The banking system was broadly considered one of the bulwarks against a depression because the banks appeared to be in sound financial condition following the Crash. Federal Reserve member banks had increased their equity capital from $5.9 billion in 1928 to $6.8 billion in 1929 in their fifth successive year of record net profits. Deposits were 5 to 7 times capital for most banks, which seemed conservative. The banks also had liquid holdings of call loans, bankers acceptances, and government securities equal to 41% of total assets for

New York banks, 48% for Chicago banks, and 35% for other Reserve city banks, which appeared adequate to cushion the banks against most contingencies. The reader might expect that the banks would have suffered losses on call loans during the Crash, but John W. Pole, Controller of the Currency, claimed that he knew of "no instances where bankers have lost anything through loans to brokers."[11] As we have already seen, the New York City Clearing House banks were strong enough to act as lenders of last resort to the call loan markets during the Crash, and it was they who stabilized the stock market through the operations of the Bankers' Pool. There were no runs on the banks in the Crash. Quite the contrary—demand deposits increased as investors sought liquidity.

The banks appeared to be a sound base for the economic system. There had never been a serious economic crisis in the nation unless there had been a banking crisis, so it was assumed that the strength of the banking system would prevent the recent stock market crisis from developing into a deep depression. Now that the Federal Reserve System was in place, it appeared that it would act as a lender of last resort and prevent the credit crises which had hurt the economy in the past.

Confidence in the banking system was further justified because credit conditions were easy throughout 1930. In fact, it was because of easy credit conditions that Federal Reserve monetary policy was not more aggressive. Investments of all member banks expanded steadily through 1930, from $9.8 billion in December 1929, to $11 billion in December 1930. Their investments in U.S. government securities, municipals, railroad bonds, utility bonds, and foreign bonds all expanded throughout the year.[12] The funds for increased investments were created by declining loans of member banks, which dropped from $26.2 billion in December 1929 to $23.9 billion in December 1930.

The extent of credit ease in 1930 is evident in the Federal Reserve borrowings of the banking system. Federal Reserve borrowings in 1930 by New York City banks and banks in 100 other leading cities were the lowest since 1918 and continued this low for 18 months, a record period for such ease. The New York City banks averaged Federal Reserve borrowings of $10 million or less for 16 of the 20 months from February 1930 through August 1931. It was more typical for New York City bank borrowings to be $100–$150 million and in periods of tight money to exceed $200 million. Borrowings had exceeded $600 million for 18 successive months in 1919–21.[13]

Banks in "100 other leading cities" (a series followed weekly by the Federal Reserve) portrayed the same credit ease as banks in New York City. These banks had borrowed a monthly average of over $500 million from the Federal Reserve throughout the last half of 1928 and most of 1929, but dropped to an average of $35–$65 million by April 1930, where they remained for 16 months through July 1931. These low borrowing levels contrasted with peak borrowings of $1.4 billion in most of 1920, and typical borrowing levels of $150–$250 million in periods of easy credit in the 1920s. There were only nine months in the 1920s when Federal Reserve borrowing by banks in these 100 cities averaged less than

$100 million, as they did now. These same banks' investments reached a monthly average of $4.5 billion in December 1930—their highest on record and $868 million above December 1929. These investments had grown every month in 1930 and compared with $4.3 billion in early 1928, before the stock market craze erupted, and $3.6 billion in the mid-1920s.[14]

These credit conditions in 1930 appeared highly conducive to a revival of business and new financing. The only problem with this widely articulated view was that it ignored many uncomfortable facts about conditions in the banking system. Individual important banks had engaged in unsound speculation and had made unsound loans. Other banks were affected by the impact of declining commodities prices on their customers' credit and by the worsening economic conditions, particularly if the banks had large real estate loans. Runs eventually occurred in numerous cities during 1930.

Individual circumstances, such as existed at National City Bank, caused undercurrents of concern among professionals at an early stage, before the problems reached public view. National City Co., the bank's security affiliate, traded heavily in the bank's stock and lost a good deal of money trying to sustain it in the Crash. National City Co. was also a leading competitor in the solicitation of bond issues for South American and Middle European nations, to whom much of National City's appeal was the parent bank's ability to make short-term loans on its own account. This it did in 1930, when foreign issues were difficult to market. Like the bonds, many of these loans defaulted.

An extreme situation existed at the Guardian Detroit Union Group, where the leading stockholders formed an agreement in October 1930 to buy up to $4 million of the company's stock to reduce the selling pressure on it. It had dropped to $60 from $350 in 1929. A smaller group of people bought $400,000 of the security affiliate's inventory to reduce its loans.[15] An Examining Committee of the main bank in the Guardian Detroit Union Group outlined its problems in a report of May 1931, the principal points of which are offered below to provide the reader with an idea of the problems:

The Committee, however, feels called upon to make the following suggestions and recommendations as to future policies . . . .

1. Not sufficient attention has been paid in the past to the character of the respective borrowers and their income capacity . . . .

2. The Committee finds in the list of bad loans many loans that obviously have no other purpose than speculation in the stock market. . . .

3. The Committee finds also in the list of bad loans, loans to officers of this bank and officers in other banks which were clearly made to assist or further stock market operations . . . .

4. One of the major causes of loss has been loans to real estate operators and companies engaged in real estate operations and stock equities in real estate. In almost every instance, the real estate has been subject to prior indebtedness, and the loan, therefore, no matter what form it takes, is certainly no better than a second mortgage.

5. We found on the list of loans a substantial number of individuals who have been recommended by directors of the bank for such loans, loans to friends of directors . . . loans to associates of directors . . . and loans to concerns in which the directors are interested . . . .

6. The Committee finds in the list of bad loans a great many so-called "policy" loans. Judges of courts, referees in bankruptcy, and other political officers have been extended substantial credit. Many of these loans are doubtful.

7. . . . Makers of some slow and doubtful loans have complained that they made the loan in order to buy certain securities recommended by an officer of the bank, or securities in which the bank or some affiliated institution was directly or indirectly interested. . . .

11. The credit files do not contain all the information that the officers desire. . . . [16]

The banking system began to look weaker after mid-1930, when the nation's economic problems became clearer. Runs on banks in Toledo and Omaha in mid-August closed most of their banks. During the same month, U.S. National Bank in Los Angeles closed, tying up $13 million in deposits. Manufacturers Trust Co. cut its dividend from $1.50 to $1.00 in September, which raised concern about its credit. Its business was concentrated in the New York garment trade, which was hard hit by the decline following the Crash, and it was closely tied to the Goldman Sachs Trading Corp., which was visibly in trouble because of the pyramid of investment trusts it had built up in 1929.

The decline in the stock market in the second half of 1930 made some banks especially vulnerable. All Federal Reserve member banks held over $500 million in stocks at the time of the Crash and almost $600 million at the end of 1930. They also held approximately $1.5 billion in long-term debt convertible into stocks.[17] These values were historic book costs that were substantially more than market values at the end of 1930. Chase National Bank set aside reserves of $20 million in 1930 for securities losses, compared with $8 million in 1929.[18] Detroit banks too had to write off substantial investments in stocks. J. P. Morgan & Co., then a private bank, had a decline in its net worth in 1930 from $118 million to $92 million, $21 million of which decline was due to loan and securities losses in the second half of 1930.[19] National City Bank of New York set up a reserve for losses of $20 million in October 1930. Dillon, Read & Co.'s 1930 capital dropped $2.8 million to $12.1 million. There was no panic, but there was no picnic either.

There was also a continuing weakness in the banking system due to unsound country banks. This was a problem greater than the problems incubating in the larger banks which we have just outlined. Both country member banks and nonmember banks lost deposits heavily in 1930 because of the risks depositors perceived in these institutions. A comparison of deposit trends in the various banking sectors is outlined in Table 4.1. The relatively large deposit losses of the country member and nonmember banks stand out clearly as a trend dating

Table 4.1
Total Deposits in Major Banking Sectors, Year End, 1927–1930 ($ billions)

	1927	1928	1929	1930
N.Y.C	$ 8.5	$10.4	$10.2	$ 9.6
Chicago	2.0	2.1	1.9	2.0
Reserve city banks	12.9	13.0	12.9	13.0
Member country banks	13.2	13.6	13.0	12.4
Nonmember banks	12.7	13.6	13.0	11.6
Postal Savings System deposits	0.15	0.15	0.16	0.24
Mutual savings banks	8.3	8.8	8.8	9.4

Source: Banking & Monetary Statistics, pp. 22, 23, 34, 81, 87, 93, 99.

from 1928. New York City bank deposits also declined in 1929 and 1930, but this was a reaction to the large deposit growth in 1928 and not a flight of deposits.

The trend of deposits was away from the small banks to the large ones rather than a flight from deposits to currency. Currency in circulation was relatively stable from 1923 to 1929 at $4.4–$4.6 billion. In 1930, when it dipped to $4.2 billion for many months,[20] currency in circulation was actually at its lowest since 1922.

In 1930 some 1,350 banks suspended operations with deposits of $827 million, compared with 659 banks in 1929 with deposits of only $321 million. Some 1,104 of the 1,350 suspensions were by banks that were not members of the Federal Reserve System, and only 10 of the banks that closed had more than $10 million in combined loans and investments. Suspensions were heaviest in Arkansas (134), Illinois (125), North Carolina (93), Indiana (87), and Mississippi (59).[21] Bank closings reached 256 in November and 352 in December, each of which was a record by over 100.

The problems of the country bank members of the Federal Reserve System were visible in borrowings of close to $250 million from the Federal Reserve by member country banks on four quarterly call dates in 1930. This compared with peak borrowings in 1929 of $438 million and was a typical level throughout much of the 1920s, when money was not tight, but it contrasted with record low borrowings from the Federal Reserve by all other sectors of the system. The contrast with city banks extended to country member banks' investments which remained steady in 1930 at $4.5 billion. Their investments had been $4.7 billion throughout 1928 and part of 1929,[22] whereas city bank investments had grown significantly since 1928.

The problems of the country banks were rooted in their investments and loans, which made them vulnerable to unfolding problems in the economy to a greater degree than the large city banks. Country member banks had absolutely more invested in foreign and railroad bonds than all the larger city banks combined,

Table 4.2
Foreign and Railroad Bond Investments by Federal Reserve Member Banks on December 31, 1930 ($ millions)

	Central Reserve, N.Y.C.	Central Reserve, Chicago	Reserve city	Country
Foreign investments	$148	$23	$162	$382
% of equity capital	7%	7%	7%	17%
Railroad bond investments	$210	$14	$241	$518
% of equity capital	10%	4%	12%	23%

Source: Banking & Monetary Statistics, pp. 81–96.

and double the proportion of equity capital (see Table 4.2). Both these investment areas were deteriorating rapidly.

In rural areas, even the most prudent bankers found it difficult to survive since state banking laws frequently prevented branch banking, which could have provided some diversity in both deposits and loans. As it was, many rural banks found their agricultural base slipping out from under them. Farm prices dropped 29.3% in 1930 eroding both current cash flow and the value of land. Both farming and rural banking had over-expanded between 1900 and 1930. Farm land had grown from 839 million acres to 987 million acres, and perhaps more importantly from a value of $20 billion to $57 billion. At the same time the number of banks had grown from 10 thousand to 24 thousand—the bulk of them rural.[23] The over-expansion in both respects was bound to result in distress and contraction in a difficult economy.

The country banks also had 68% of their equity capital tied up in real estate loans which were particularly illiquid, compared with 5% for New York City banks and 7% for Chicago banks. The only area in which city banks shared credit exposure equal to the country member banks was in the real estate loans of reserve city banks outside New York City and Chicago. These loans equalled 80% of the banks' equity capital and were a fundamental cause of the runs that began on some city banks in the last half of 1930. The relative loan positions of the various categories of banks can be seen in Table 4.3.

We cannot illustrate the decline in the liquidity of nonmember commercial banks with the same detail we can for member country banks, but we do have data which shows that investments of nonmember commercial banks were $3.7 billion on December 31, 1930, a decline from $3.9 billion on June 30, 1930, and no growth from levels back to June 30, 1928.[24]

The biggest blow to the banking system in 1930 was the collapse of the Bank of United States in December. Situated in New York City, it was the biggest bankruptcy to date and a focus of publicity for the next year.

Table 4.3
Loans by Federal Reserve Member Banks on December 31, 1930 ($ billions)

	Central Reserve, N.Y.C.	Central Reserve, Chicago	Reserve city	Country
Open market securities classified as loans & securities loans	$3.7	$0.8	$3.4	$2.3
% of equity capital	185%	267%	170%	105%
Real estate loans	$0.1	$0.2	$1.6	$1.5
% of equity capital	5%	7%	80%	68%
Other loans	$2.1	$0.5	$3.1	$4.2
% of equity capital	105%	167%	155%	191%

Source: *Banking & Monetary* Statistics, pp. 81–96.

The Bank of United States was rumored to be weak in 1929. New York State Bank Superintendent Joseph A. Broderick had ordered the bank to reduce its loans to affiliates from $6 million in August 1929, but the bank actually raised these loans to $13 million within a few months. Bank officers went ahead on an $8 million loan even after the state Banking Department had refused approval.[25] J. & W. Seligman & Co. might have saved the bank at this point. They had planned to buy the bank and install Sloan Colt (later President of Bankers Trust Co.) as President, but the Crash ended this plan. Later, in the spring of 1930, Irving Trust Co. almost acquired the bank, but the price of Bank of United States stock rose and made the acquisition unattractive to Irving Trust.[26]

The optimism that prevailed in the first half of 1930 made depositors in the Bank of United States feel secure despite its problems, but the bank's heavy involvement in garment trade and real estate lending, two weak areas, made the bank highly suspect as the economic decline persisted. The suspicion was justified, for the New York State examiner's report for September 18, 1930, indicated that the bank's surplus had been wiped out. At this point, Broderick sought the assistance of Wall Street leaders to save the bank's depositors. Negotiations for a merger with Manhattan Trust on the basis of 1 share for 3 proceeded through October, but they failed because Bank of United States top executives wanted a 1-for-2 share exchange. A deal was finally worked out when Albert Wiggin pressed the bank's executives to accept. By this point, however, the bank was rapidly losing deposits, and Manhattan Trust insisted on a right to void the merger if deposits of the Bank of United States dropped by more than $50 million before the merger was consummated, even though the Clearing House Association banks were prepared to lend $30 to $40 million to the bank, and a smaller group of banks were prepared to subscribe a guarantee fund of $5–$10 million to cover ultimate loan losses by Manhattan Trust. Failure to agree on the deposit situation led the negotiators to Manufacturers Trust as an alternative, along with two lesser banks. This merger fell through when two Clearing House member banks declined to participate in the $30 million loan fund. A run began on Bank of United States deposits when failure to reach agreement on the merger was announced. Its deposits had declined from $212 million on October 12, 1930, to $182 million on December 5, 1930. They dropped further to $160 million by the time the bank closed on Thursday, December 11th.

Wall Street's leaders were involved down to the wire in seeking a solution to the bank's problem. The leading executives of J. P. Morgan & Co., Chase, National City, Central Hanover, Bankers Trust, Manufacturers Trust, Manhattan Trust, Guaranty Trust, and the New York Federal Reserve Bank each played a role. Ultimately, the unsavory reputations of the bank's management and its heavy involvement in real estate which the Clearing House Association banks did not understand thwarted efforts to save the bank.

The Bank of United States was taken over by the New York State Superintendent of Banks, Joseph A. Broderick. Its stock closed at $3 bid, $7 offered—down from $11 1/2 bid, $13 1/2 offered the day before, and down from a 1929 high of $243. Thus began a tale which was to occupy the front pages of the *New York Times* for over a year. Runs started on the Chelsea Bank because it had a deposit relationship with the Bank of United States, and the Chelsea Bank was forced to close. Manufacturers Trust Company, too, experienced runs at some branches and needed help from the Clearing House Association. Bank stocks plunged. The reputations of U.S. banks suffered abroad, where the Bank of United States was thought to be more important than it actually was because of its name.

Bank Superintendent Broderick, a serious, professional state civil servant with some taste for political attention, suggested that there was a "red" plot in conjunction with brokers selling bank stocks short. Eventually, it was revealed that the Bank of United States had made dubious loans to officers and directors and to their affiliates. A securities affiliate of the bank owned by the officers appeared to have been used to siphon off funds from the bank. Stockholders were assessed the par value of $25 per share to pay depositors, and while few paid, depositors who were stockholders had the assessment deducted from their deposits. It was over a year before the Superintendent of Banks began to pay out deposits, and only after a prolonged court fight in which a committee of depositors fought Broderick's desire to reopen the bank. The principal officers went to jail.

Criticism of the Federal Reserve Role in 1930

Friedman and Schwartz have accused the Federal Reserve System of not acting to counter the rash of bank failures in November and December 1930 and to

Table 4.4
Declines in the Money Supply in 1930 ($ billions)

	M1	M2	M3
Average, first 9 months 1929	$26.54	$46.52	$55.16
Average, first 4 months 1930	26.24	46.04	54.73
Low, December 1930	25.25	44.61	53.71
Decline from first 4 months 1930 to December 1930	3.8%	3.1%	1.9%

Source: *Monetary Statistics*, pp. 24–26.

save the Bank of United States, but the evidence of the System's failure is much less clear-cut than their condemnation.[27]

The Federal Reserve did take the steps which appeared appropriate to the role it had been allocated when bank suspensions accelerated in November and December 1930. It increased its open market purchases aggressively, so that its holdings of bills bought rose to $364 million and its holdings of U.S. government securities rose to $729 million by December 31st. While $364 million in bills bought was not unusual, it was still high. Bills bought only reached $400 million for one period in the prior decade—between October 1928 and February 1929. Federal Reserve holdings of $729 million in U.S. securities was a record by a full $100 million over the highest holdings in prior years. These open market purchases kept bills discounted with the Federal Reserve at $200–$250 million throughout November and December, a low level. Between 1922 and 1930 only four months were as low.[28] If small banks could not survive with credit as easy as this, most observers thought it was the banks' fault and not the Federal Reserve's. The Federal Reserve was doing its job.

Friedman and Schwartz emphasize that the Federal Reserve should have prevented the decline in the money supply in 1930, which in turn would have prevented the country banks from failing and stimulated the economy, but consideration of all the economic trends that were acting parallel to one another at this time discredits this argument. The actual money supply decline in 1930 was modest, despite the deposit decline at the country banks. All the measures of money supply (M1, M2, M3) stabilized in the first four months of 1930 at their pre-Crash levels and in the ensuing eight months declined only 1.9% to 3.8%, depending on which measure of money supply is selected. This data is summarized in Table 4.4. Despite this modest decline in money supply, there was a precipitous decline in prices of 29% for farm products and 35% for industrial commodities, which set in well before money supply even began to decline, and as we have already seen, it was this trend which was destroying the loan and bond asset values of the country banks as well as the incomes of their communities. International trade was also in a sharp decline, with trade and tariff barriers rising rapidly following adoption of the Smoot-Hawley Tariff. These barriers were not amenable to money supply influences either.

Part of the Friedman and Schwartz accusation is justified. The Federal Reserve displayed no leadership effort beyond open market purchases of securities to reduce bank closings. The New York Federal Reserve Bank was the leader of the Federal Reserve System, and its attention was focussed principally on the international currency markets and interest rates. George Harrison took part in deliberations such as those convened to try to save the Bank of United States, but he did little more. There was no active lender-of-last-resort role at the Federal Reserve to smaller regional banks, and the Bank of United States got no lender-of-last-resort loans, even though it might have been saved by them. It ultimately paid depositors 80¢ on the dollar after going through liquidation. Had it not been forced to liquidate at the depths of the Depression, it might have survived. There were also no cases of the Federal Reserve taking over local banks to liquidate them or to recapitalize them. Nor was there any significant behind-the-scenes activity by the Federal Reserve to save banks. The Federal Reserve never suggested that it had any responsibility to preserve the credit of the banking system, and there was no indication that the commercial bankers expected it to exercise such responsibility. Its lender-of-last-resort role appeared to have been reserved for the call money market and the U.S. government market, which is to say that this responsibility was interpreted by all in its narrowest sense.

Several factors account for the Federal Reserve's inactivity as a lender of last resort. For one, the Federal Reserve Board in Washington was inert. Hoover had forced Governor Young to move to the Boston Federal Reserve Bank, and Vice Governor Platt, a New Yorker, to retire, in order to make way for Eugene Meyer as the new Governor. But having forced the resignations in August, Hoover took until November to announce the replacements, which left the organization of the Board in limbo during a crucial period. Meyer was not confirmed in the job until February 25, 1931.

A second factor accounting for Federal Reserve inactivity was that banks in major cities across the nation did not appear to be in trouble. Banks in New York City and 100 other leading cities had relatively small Federal Reserve borrowings through 1930. Investments of these banks were up over 20% from early 1930 to record levels. New York City banks' loans were up for the year, and the decline in loans of other city banks was heavily concentrated in securities loans which no authority felt any commitment to expand.

The banks in trouble were the small, country banks which seemed to merit their demise because of their lack of capital and poor investments in real estate, agriculture, foreign bonds, and railroad bonds. Some 502 of the 608 banks which failed in November and December 1930, were nonmember banks, and deposits in the 608 banks averaged less than $1 million per bank. There was no sense of responsibility for these banks at any level of the financial community. There were a few cases where runs closed all banks in a city, such as Louisville, without discrimination in quality, but in such cases outside banks, such as the

Chemical Bank of New York in this case, made loans to open the best banks. In Detroit, where the Guardian Detroit Union Group was in trouble, Edsel Ford lent the Group $1 million in cash and $5 million in City of Detroit bonds to secure additional borrowings from Bankers Trust Co. in New York City. The Federal Reserve did not need to act as lender of last resort in such cases.

It is not clear whether the failure of the Bank of United States should have led the Federal Reserve into a position of leadership in bolstering the banking system. Events turned out differently. The government spearhead in that crisis was Broderick, the New York Superintendent of Banks, rather than the Federal Reserve. The other banks threatened by the collapse, particularly the Manufacturers Trust Co., were saved by the New York Clearing House banks without the assistance of the Federal Reserve. Leading bankers thought the impact of the default had been localized, and as we shall see, banking conditions in the first half of 1931 following the Bank of United States collapse were much improved over November and December 1930.

Even if we believe, in retrospect, that Federal Reserve lending as a last resort to the Bank of United States would have enabled the bank to pay its depositors in full and that confidence in the banking system would have been sustained, we can hardly blame the Federal Reserve for not doing so. The leadership of the Bank of United States appeared untrustworthy. They had siphoned funds into their own activities and broken banking regulations in making loans to affiliates for which both the Chairman and President subsequently went to jail. The bank's loans were concentrated in the New York garment trade and in real estate, which were both weak areas. The bank was also rapidly losing deposits. In any case, the Federal Reserve could lend only on a restricted list of assets, mostly U.S. government and money market securities which the Bank of United States did not have in adequate amounts to forestall its demise.

In subsequent years, laws and regulations have been developed that permit the Federal Reserve to take over banks and make loans at its discretion, but only recently have we discovered from cases such as those of the U.S. National Bank of San Diego and the Franklin National Bank in New York, where the leading officers were convicted and sent to jail, that even criminal principals can rarely do so much harm to a bank that it cannot pay off its deposits when kept in business.

THE GROUNDS FOR OPTIMISM IN EARLY 1930

Old hands in the securities business remember vividly the optimism that prevailed in the early months of 1930, because many investors were enticed back into the stock market only to be wiped out in the drawn-out market decline which followed. The smart money was lost in this aftermath. At the time, the optimism appeared justified. A business recession similar to those following stock market panics in 1907, 1914, and 1920 was expected, but it was expected to be limited to trade in luxury items. All the Federal Reserve districts predicted an upturn in the economy in the second half of 1930. The commercial banks also forecast an upturn. The Guaranty Trust Co., a perennial optimist, predicted a quick recovery in building construction because of easy money. The Hoover Administration vociferously expressed its confidence in a business recovery, and industry supported the projections. Sophisticated journalists questioned whether there was any connection between securities prices and the business of the United States, and they persuaded themselves that if some vague connection existed Hoover's quick action had been sufficient to restrain it.

There was good cause for optimism at the beginning of the year. In Washington a businesslike administration ran a balanced budget and had acted quickly and decisively to shore up confidence and promote expansion. The United States was the business leader of the world; its business leaders were grasping their responsibility and expanding to offset any momentary decline in business. Business itself was conservatively financed and had not overexpanded, as had the stock market. The commercial banks were sound. The dollar was strong and the nation's gold supply was large. The price level was declining slightly, as it had through most of the 1920s, but only enough to raise real wages without creating a problem of inventories bought at earlier, higher prices. Even the international scene appeared peaceful. The Young Plan promised to restore Germany's credit, and the leading nations had united in goodwill several years earlier to sign the Kellogg-Briand Pact, which forswore the use of arms.

Stock prices boomed in the first quarter of 1930 amid the confidence, many stocks doubling and tripling from their 1929 lows. Trading volume on the New York Stock Exchange recovered to the level of 5–6 million shares a day. Banks and brokers scrambled to rehire the experienced staffs laid off in December 1929. Albert Wiggin, and other speculators like him, got back into the stock market.

The new-issue market for common stocks recovered, too. The first common stock offering after the Crash was an initial public offering of $10 million to create a new company, Federal Neon System, Inc., managed by Charles V. Bob, who was later indicted for securities fraud. Seaboard Airline Railroad Co., which was in bankruptcy, went ahead with a $23 million rights offering of common stock as part of its reorganization plan. The Pennsylvania Railroad Co. had a $90 million common stock offering. Large and small companies had stock offerings with little evidence that the Crash had changed market conditions. Several new investment trusts were even formed, and West & Co. and Thomas F. Lee & Co., two minor brokers, placed privately $80 million of North American Trust shares. Insull Utility Investments, Inc., a trust, used the positive atmosphere to sell $60 million 6% ten-year debentures through Halsey, Stuart & Co.

Wall Street continued to expand as if nothing had happened. There was an office-building boom in the first half of 1930. Stone & Webster Engineering Co. announced a 73-story headquarters at Broad and Beaver streets. Louis B. Adler and Henry L. Doherty each announced they were building a new skyscraper. There were rumors that several others would be announced soon. The Curb Exchange went ahead with plans for a new building. As late as July 31, 1930,

Chase National Bank felt sure enough of the investment banking business that it bought the large and prestigious Harris, Forbes & Co. investment banking organization. The Guardian Detroit Union Group and the Detroit Bankers Co., which together dominated Michigan banking, were both formed in this recovery period.

Outside Wall Street, industry looked strong. Most companies reported record 1929 earnings during the first quarter of 1930, and February dividend payments were $436 million versus $387 million in February 1929. After a two-month hiatus, acquisitions and mergers carried on at a high rate, reflecting business optimism. Republic Steel was created after the Crash. Bethlehem Steel and Youngstown Sheet & Tube would have merged if Cyrus Eaton had not held up the merger in the courts. Chase National Bank merged with the Rockefeller-controlled Equitable Trust Co. to become the largest bank in the nation and create the Rockefeller interest in Chase. National Dairy Products Corp. acquired Kraft-Phenix Cheese Corp. Bigelow Hartford Carpet Co. acquired Sanford & Sons, Inc. Pullman Inc. acquired Standard Steel Car and Osgood Bradley Car Co. Sears, Roebuck & Co. and J. C. Penney announced they were studying a merger, as did the Great Northern and Northern Pacific Railroads. The utility holding companies also carried on their acquisition programs. United Gas Improvement Co. bought Magnolia Petroleum for $50 million; the Public Utility Holding Corp. of America bought Portland Electric Power Co. for $85 million; and the Insull utility system added small companies everywhere. Rumors of major utility mergers abounded. The rate of completed and proposed mergers in the first months of 1930 showed little reduction from 1929.

Optimism was also fostered by the way labor and management worked together to bar a depression. Strikes in 1930 dropped to 637 in number, compared with 921 in 1929, and the number of workers on strike dropped to 182,975, from 288,572 in 1929. Workdays lost because of strikes were 3,317,000 man-days, compared to 5,353,000 man-days in 1929.[29] There was, in fact, a high degree of social unanimity in the early months of 1930.

THE ECONOMY'S DECLINE BECOMES CLEAR BY MID-1930

Hoover's efforts and the widespread optimism might have sustained a business recovery if the decline had been milder. It became clear by mid-year, however, allowing for the time lag in substantiating economic conditions, that the economy was in trouble and its problems were deepening.

Increasing unemployment was the most visible sign of the trend of economic conditions. By mid-March, Senator Robert F. Wagner of New York, who led many of the efforts for social reforms in the Depression, claimed that unemployment had never been worse in the United States. The Director of the Illinois State Employment Agency confirmed in a congressional hearing that Chicago's unemployment was the worst in ten years. The Federal Reserve index of employment dropped to 93.9 in June from a peak of 108.4 in August 1929 and fell further to 83.8 in December 1930.[30]

Employment declines were worst in the durable goods, lumber, rubber products, and transportation equipment industries, in all of which employment declined over 20% during 1930. The most visible declines, however, were in larger industries, such as iron and steel, in which employment dropped by 125,000 jobs; or automobiles, in which employment dropped by 130,000 jobs from less than half the base employment of the iron and steel industry. Railroad employment dropped by almost 200,000 jobs.

There were also job losses in widely diffused small enterprises beyond the more prominent industries. Farms dropped 135,000 workers, textile mills dropped 165,000 workers, and private households dropped 150,000 servants. Almost every industry showed some reduction in employment. The only increased payrolls were in federal, state, and local governments of 130,000 people, and in the gas and electric utility industries of 8,000 people. In aggregate there was the equivalent of over 2,250,000 fewer employees at work in the United States at the end of 1930 than at the end of 1929.[31] The total number of unemployed was greater than this, of course, for to those thrown out of work we must add those previously out of work and new or would-be entrants into the labor force who could not find jobs. The unemployed became painfully visible in 1930, particularly in the large cities.

The most visible indication to businessmen of the trend of economic conditions was the railroad industry, which declined sharply during 1930. Railroad freight revenues were $483.3 million in October 1929, which was close to their peak for that month in October 1928, but in November and December 1929 freight revenues were $60–$70 million below the comparable months in 1928. As 1930 progressed, the comparison with prior year's freight revenues grew progressively worse. By October 1930 freight revenues were down 20% from October 1929, to $385.5 million.

The decline in economic conditions was amply evident in other areas of the economy as well. The index of industrial production dropped almost 20% in 1930, from 119 to 96. The sharpest declines occurred in automobile production, as passenger car sales dropped 39% from 4.8 million cars to 2.9 million, and in steel, plate glass, and rubber production, which were interrelated with automobiles. Copper smelter output dropped 30% from 2 billion pounds in 1929 to 1.4 billion pounds in 1930. In a subsequent analysis of National Income by the U.S. Department of Commerce, every industry, except food, tobacco, and utilities, registered a decline in value added in 1930. Public construction increased from $3.2 billion in 1929 to $3.6 billion in 1930 under Hoover's prodding and local initiatives, but private construction dropped 25% from $7.9 billion to $5.9 billion, despite commitments to expand by the railroads and public utilities, which they did live up to. Gross private investments fell a shocking 36 1/2%, a dismal measure of private expectations for the future.[32]

Incomes fell sharply in 1930 as a result of the economic decline. After-tax net income of corporations dropped 66% to $2.9 billion in 1930, and the deficits of corporations reporting losses widened from $2.9 billion to $4.9 billion. Proprietors incomes dropped 21%. As a result, there was a record 26,355 industrial and commercial bankruptcies during the year, entailing record liabilities of $668 million. Personal bankruptcies were not then in style, although total income of individuals reported on federal income tax returns dropped 25% to $22.4 billion in 1930. Individual income declines were generally a result of layoffs or short work weeks, as wage rates declined only slightly in 1930, perhaps related to the strong efforts made by Hoover to sustain wages.[33]

Prices dropped sharply in 1930 in concert with the decline in economic activity. Those at work enjoyed a continued rise in standard of living, as the cost of living for wage earners and lower-salaried workers declined 1.8% in the first half of 1930 and a further 4% in the last half. Food costs in particular dropped sharply. The benefits were short-lived, however. Businessmen reduced production as they got less for their output and built unsold inventories. The estimated physical volumes of corporate inventories increased slightly, but the value of inventories declined over $3.25 billion, much of which corporations had to absorb as a loss. The declining price level ceased to benefit workers as corporations reduced production and workers lost their jobs and incomes.

Natural forces compounded the nation's economic problems in mid-year as drought swept the Great Plains states from North Dakota to Texas. Farm cash receipts dropped 19 1/2%, beginning a process that wiped out much of rural America. Farmers unsuccessfully sought federal aid, and their plight affected other industries, particularly the railroads which did a significant business carrying farm commodities.

Contemporaries did not have the detailed sector statistics now available on the period, which helps account for why business conditions were as bad as they were amid the optimism which prevailed in the early months of 1930. But the inconsistency is not surprising because the expectation was that the nation would quickly recover from the effects of the Crash. Eventually, the facts eroded that confidence, as data on the economy became available during the course of the year. At first, there was also a willingness to emphasize the optimistic side of divergent indicators or small improvements, but as the Depression forced itself on people's daily lives, there was no need for sophisticated data to interpret its increasing impact. There were still many who expected a recovery imminently, but by the end of 1930 the balance had swung to the more pessimistic souls.

COMMODITIES PRICES DROP PRECIPITOUSLY

Declining commodities prices were a backdrop to the declines in securities prices and economic conditions in 1930. Commodities prices fell so far, and their course was changed so little by disasters which restricted supplies, such as drought, that the decline in commodities prices appeared to have the inexorability of a secular trend. The decline set in motion other economic events, such as bank closings in rural America and bankruptcies in producing nations, which had their own serious contributions to the financial collapse of the 1930s.

Commodities price declines during 1930 from the 1929 highs were 45% for wheat, which was the most prominent commodity, 30% for corn, 50% for cotton, 67% for rubber, 44% for raw sugar, 55% for silk, 50% for copper, and 35% for scrap steel (See Figure 4.1). The decline first attracted nonprofessional attention in February, when wheat dropped from $1.20 per bushel to 99¢ in 11 days. In early February, speculators became concerned that the drop in commodity prices presaged a worse economic decline than was generally expected. On February 21, 1930, the *New York Times* carried stock news on the front page for the first time since December 1929 under a headline which linked the weakness in securities prices to the decline in commodities prices. On February 25th the Farm Board supported wheat in the market at 93 3/4¢ per bushel, which again produced front page news in the *New York Times*. Wheat trading had become hysterical by mid-March because of the unabated decline in prices which was that market's own version of the Crash. The decline in prices continued throughout 1930 with only partial relent in the third quarter for corn, raw sugar, and copper prices. At the end of the year the index of prices for 47 farm products was down 29.3% from pre-Crash prices, and publicly traded industrial commodities averaged a price decline of approximately 35%.[34]

The federal government made no effort to intervene in the commodities markets, except in wheat, which the Farm Board did with uncertain success. It disrupted trading by its interventions because it could deal in such size, and it often trapped professionals "short" wheat or confused them by its arbitrary intervention points. Since the Farm Board had little sympathy from Hoover for its intervention, it was forced to sell abroad the wheat it bought domestically, and it appears to have cut prices in this effort, undoing any sustaining effect it had on domestic prices. The Farm Board tried to restrict crop production by cutting back acreage planted, but it received little cooperation. The most common political reaction to the collapse of commodities markets was hostility toward commodities market professionals. Bills were introduced in Congress to make short selling illegal and to ban futures trading. Hoover declared that speculators who sold commodities short were conspiring against the public welfare. Nonetheless, commodities prices continued to decline without interference in the market.

The decline in farm and industrial commodities prices naturally carried over into other products. The Labor Department's Wholesale Price Index declined steadily all year from 93.3 at the end of 1929 to 79.6 in December 1930, a decline of 14.7% mirrored by a 12.9% decline in retail food prices from December to December. Finished product prices, which naturally adjusted more slowly, declined 9.3%. All these price declines are in sharp contrast to the 2.6% decline in the implicit price deflator for Gross National Product in 1930, which

33. *National Income Accounts*, p. 14; *Statistical Abstract, 1939*, pp. 191, 307, 181 (Table 184).

34. *Statistical Abstract, 1939*, p. 315; *Moody's Industrial Manual, 1935*, blue insert pages on ''The Nation's Basic Industries.''

35. *Statistical Abstract, 1939*, pp. 315, 321; *National Income Accounts*, p. 158.

5

The Stock Market in 1930

The year 1930 was schizophrenic in that the optimistic side prevailed for most of the first half, while the pessimistic side, always looking on and growing in prominence as the months passed, slowly came to the fore. In December 1929, when the stock market first showed strong recovery signs, investors' attitudes were shaded by the memories of what prices and earnings had been. Stocks looked cheap. Many had been sold under duress as investors became overextended, and the extent of the liquidation had been unreasonable. For those who still had money, 1930 held the opportunity for a killing. The rebounds in stock prices after panics had always been profitable, and this one was no exception. There had also been a series of sell-offs in the last several years from which recoveries had been rapid and from which stocks had risen to new high prices. Investors talked themselves into a similar prospect for 1930, especially the new coterie of brokers and portfolio managers at the investment trusts, casualty insurance companies, and brokerage houses.

The stock market fulfilled these expectations by rising strongly in the first four months of 1930. The Dow Jones indices rose steadily until April (see Table A.19 in the Statistical Appendix). The Dow Jones Industrial Index was up 48% from its low in the Crash by April 17, 1930, when it hit a high for the year of 294, although it was still down 22.8% from its September 1929 high of 381. The market declined for the rest of the year until all the Dow Jones indices hit their lowest levels for 1930 on December 15th. The DJII then was 157, down 46.4% from the April high and 58.7% from the 1929 high. The same index was below the low in the Crash by 10.7%. It had made little difference whether an investor had bought his stock in the speculative exuberance of 1929 or as a cool-headed opportunist following the panic. The result was the same—a shocking loss of value.

Investors seeking dividend income still did not feel the full effects of the market decline, however, because total corporate dividends in 1930 fell only

April 1, 1930. Utility holding companies were up 43% between the same dates, but they moved in such violent swings that the monthly figures hide the extent of their rise. Some utility holding companies, such as United Corp., National Power & Light, Electric Power & Light, Electric Bond and Share, and Cities Service, were up 100%–200% from their 1929 lows. Electrical equipment manufacturers and chemical companies posted large recoveries as groups, rising 39% and 33% respectively between December 1, 1929, and April 1, 1930. The amusement group was not a significant part of the market, despite the attention amusement stocks received, for their total valuation was approximately $0.8 billion on April 1, 1930, but operating utilities stocks were worth $4.6 billion, utility holding companies' stocks were worth $4 billion, electrical equipment manufacturers were worth $3.9 billion, and chemical companies were worth $5.5 billion, which made them leading industries.[4]

The poorest recoveries were in the stocks of retailers, mining companies, and U.S. companies operating abroad, which were all below their December 1, 1929, industry values by small amounts on April 1, 1930.

Amid the excitement of recovery, however, notes of concern became sharper. There were numerous comments that the rise was too fast. Both the trend of commodities prices and the international financial scene were becoming matters of serious concern. Wheat had dropped from above $1.25 per bushel to below $1, and trading in Chicago's wheat pits had become hysterical at times. The markets were frequently on the front page of the *New York Times* in headlines linking the intermittent declines within the general rise in stock prices to falling commodities prices. There was a flight from the pound in mid-April as Chancellor of the Exchequer Philip Snowden imposed new taxes to meet the British budget deficit. Optimism began to vanish. Between April 17th and May 3rd the Dow Jones Industrial Index dropped from 294 to 258—over 12%.

In May the characteristics of the end of a strong market emerged, such as high volume with little change in prices, a peak in new issues, a sharp rise in dealer call loans to finance unsold inventories, and then a sudden drop in trading volume as people realize the game is over. Monday, May 5th, in particular, portended the coming decline when the Dow Jones Industrial Index dropped 8 points during the day from the prior close of 258, even though both the Federal Reserve Bank of New York and the Bank of England had reduced their discount rates at the end of the prior week. The stock market recovered from the drop, and the DJII ended Monday up 1 on an enormous volume of 8.3 million shares, but stock market interest tired out quickly thereafter. Volume dropped to 3 million shares a day by Friday of that week and to 2 million shares a day by the following Friday. New common stock issues boomed to $356 million in May, which approximated the 1929 monthly average of $367 million, and borrowings of NYSE members on collateral rose $400 million to a post-Crash peak of $5.1 billion on May 1st. This was 6.7% of the market value of all listed common and preferred stocks. The buildup in call loans attracted wide attention and was indicative both of dealers' inability to sell new issues and of renewed margin speculation.

May also saw the beginning of real damage to the assets of market professionals. Chase Securities Corp., like a barometer of what not to do, formed a trading account in Chase National Bank stock on May 15th for 90,000 shares (almost $15 million) with J. & W. Seligman & Co. and Dillon, Read & Co. When the account closed in August 1930 long 70,000 shares, the loss was approximately $2 million.[5] At the end of May, Waddill Catchings quit Goldman Sachs & Co. and resigned from the boards of directors of various Goldman Sachs clients. At first the resignation was a riddle to the uniformed, for Catchings was one of the stars of the 1920s. He had come out of nowhere at Goldman, Sachs to create a pyramid of investment trusts built on the Goldman Sachs Trading Corp. and its successive offspring, the Shenandoah Corp. and the Blue Ridge Corp. They had been great successes on the Curb Exchange in 1929. But informed traders knew that this structure was in trouble because of the decline in stock prices and the effect of super-leverage on the trusts' net asset values. The resignation of Catchings was a sign that he had lost control of the trusts in an internal controversy over whether to borrow an additional $30 million for investments in California. Walter Sachs and Sidney Weinberg opposed the borrowing, and Catchings was ousted by the controlling partners at Goldman Sachs so they could personally take over the efforts to save the trusts and the firm's reputation. Catchings' exit was a harbinger of the damage soon to be done again to the leading speculators. A pool in Chrysler Corp. stock, which he managed from October 1929 to July 1930, lost $1.6 million, and others suffered similarly.[6]

June was the worst month for the stock market in 1930. The Dow Jones Industrial Index dropped almost 23% in response to commodities prices smashed to their lowest levels since 1914 and the enactment of the Smoot-Hawley tariff. Only 3 of 240 stocks followed by the *New York Times* rose in the month. A reduction in the Federal Reserve Bank of New York discount rate to 2 1/2%, which was the lowest in history, stimulated the stock market for one day, but the gain was lost in the next two days. Stock market news reappeared on the front page of the *New York Times* after an absence of several months. In London, the decline in Anglo-American stocks was worse than in New York, as international-minded investors expressed their fears of the effects of the tariff wars which sprang up immediately after the Smoot-Hawley bill was passed.

The June decline had none of the drama of the Crash, except for during the three days following Hoover's announcement that he would sign the tariff bill in which the stock market dropped almost 26 points on the DJII to 218, with volume over 5 million shares each day. Otherwise, volume was mixed, with numerous days below 2 1/2 million shares. E. A. Pierce tried to stimulate trading by dropping margin requirements to 25% on stocks over $50, and Richard Whitney made a quixotic gesture by bidding $160 a share for 60,000 shares of U.S. Steel on June 11th. Shortly thereafter it passed through $150 per share.

There was an air of inevitability in the June stock market as it declined. New stock issues dropped to $18 million for the month, $20 million in July, and $27 million in August. New stock issues never recovered again in the 1930s. NYSE member borrowings dropped $1 billion in the month to $3.7 billion, a drop exceeded only in November and December 1929. Speculators quit margin accounts, and some firms stopped making margin loans, such as Harvey Fisk & Sons, one of the larger brokerage houses.

Odd-lot investors outweighed sellers in June 1930, a phenomenon which became pervasive in the 1930s. In the following months, leading corporations experienced 15%–20% increases in the number of their stockholders. U.S. Steel's stockholders increased from 117,956 to 141,907 in 1930 alone.

There was some recovery in the market in July and August, but it appeared to be merely technical. The DJII fluctuated between 240 and 218 in July and between 240 and 217 in August. It closed August at 240. NYSE daily trading volume only reached 3 million shares once in July and August, and averaged 1 3/4 million shares per day. August volume was the lowest for any month since July 1927. New securities issues of all types in August dropped to $291 million, an extremely low level. It was equalled only twice going back to 1924—in August 1928 and November 1929. The Federal Reserve made only minor efforts toward lower interest rates, the available alternatives already having been largely spent, since Treasury bill yields were down to 1 1/2% and call loan rates were down to 2%. The stock market marked time for these two summer months and absorbed a variety of bad news: Miami finally defaulted, Warner Bros. and Shell Union Oil omitted their dividends, and a federal budget deficit became a possibility because of the drop in customs duties and corporate taxes and the rise in farm aid. The drought in the Midwest assumed increasing prominence in the stock market. The farm plight received considerable political attention because of the combined effect of the drought and the low commodities prices received by farmers. Foreign trade was off equally sharply. Wholesale trade was off over 20%, and employment had declined by 13%.

Liquidity fears were beginning to arise because of the market losses in stocks and commodities, and the extent of the decline in economic activity began to raise credit concerns among investors. A good illustration of the mood was the wide differential between short-term rates around 2% and high-grade corporate dividend yields around 4 1/2%–5%. There was pronounced investor demand for quality as funds left the stock market, which drove U.S. long-term bond yields down to the lowest levels of the 1920s, around 3 1/4%.

Stocks renewed their declines in the last four months of 1930 as economic and financial difficulties accelerated. The banks began to squeeze their loan customers for the first time, which forced heavy selling of stocks carried with loans. The Dow Jones Industrial Index dropped from 240 on September 1st to 164 on December 31st, a decline of 31%. Stock price declines created further price drops as brokers sold out accounts which became undermargined. Benjamin Block & Co. sold out William C. Durant for the last time beginning October

10, 1930, after two weeks of efforts to get more margin from him,[7] and this famous plunger, who had founded General Motors, lost it, and regained it only to lose it again, was retired from the market involuntarily.

There was a partial recovery in mid-November, but otherwise stock prices declined without relent for the last four months of 1930. The worst declines matched the Crash. Stocks of U.S. companies operating abroad dropped 45%, electric equipment manufacturers' stocks were down 41%, oil companies' stocks were down 37%, public utility holding companies' stocks were down 35%, and bank stocks were down 35%. Stocks in the two best-performing industries— food and communications—were down 17% and 23% respectively. Volume averaged 2.3 million shares daily. It was rarely up to 3 million shares and was often below 2 million shares.

International problems deepened in September, contributing to the decline in stock prices. Investment bankers in the United States were besieged with requests to manage foreign loans, which they mostly refused (See Table A.27 in the Statistical Appendix for the small volume of foreign new issues.) Countries with maturing issues or foreign exchange deficits had to resort to short-term borrowing in New York. There were rumors of defaults in South American bonds, and Germany was widely expected to formally request a reordering of its reparations debts under the Young Plan. Right-wing political unrest in Germany received considerable attention in the United States, as did Adolf Hitler himself, who was considered a principal factor in forcing the government to seek to renegotiate reparations debts. In December, a prominent French financier in the *Coulisse* (Over-the-Counter market) defaulted despite efforts to save him, and more failures were expected. In the same month the Spanish Civil War began.

During the fall of 1930 there was a rash of difficulties in the brokerage community which also depressed stock prices. Kidder, Peabody & Co. was in difficulties which came to a head when Italy and the Bank for International Settlements withdrew $4 million on deposit. J. P. Morgan, Chase, Bankers Trust, Guaranty Trust, and the major Boston banks joined forces to help the firm with a $10 million loan following an infusion of $5 million in new capital from the firm's partners. Goldman, Sachs & Co. contracted sharply because of terrific stock and underwriting losses. A junior partner, Grant Keehn, quit rather than face the losses, and Sidney Weinberg, who became famous as a corporate director and advisor to Presidents, stayed on only because the Sachs family absorbed his share of the losses. Sisto & Co., a well-known NYSE firm, closed on October 1st. A few days later, Piperno & Co. was suspended on the Curb Exchange. On October 10th, Prince & Whitely was unable to meet its obligations and was suspended by the NYSE. Prince & Whitely was a large and respected house whose closing was particularly discomfiting. The firm had become "frozen" in stocks it handled, such as Arlen Department Stores, Atlas Stores, Broadway Motor Lines, P&W Trading Corp., Kelvinator, National Dairy, and Young Spring & Wire. The firm had tried to support these stocks because of the role it had played in distributing them to its customers, but in the degeneration of the market in 1930, and the emphasis on liquidity, such secondary stocks as these were shunned. Prince & Whitely eventually found that by trying to keep a market in these stocks it became the only market. There was no one else to whom to sell them. Otis & Co., a Cleveland firm controlled by Canadian-born Cyrus Eaton, lost $18 million of its capital and was told by the NYSE on October 13th to close or raise $20 million in new capital to replace part of $125 million in loans that it had. Eaton worked out a deal for the money with Continental Co., an investment trust he controlled, which quickly landed him in court.[8] On October 15th, J. Pitblado failed on the Montreal Stock Exchange, and at the end of October, E. A. Pierce & Co. took over C. D. Robbins & Co., as C. D. Robbins wisely retired from the business. Woody & Co., Clothier Jones & Co., Roberts & Hall, and Bower, Poque, Pond & Vivian also closed during 1930. Behind the scenes an effort was going on to save Pynchon & Co., the largest firm ever to suspend, which it eventually did in April 1931. For the moment it was saved by the Chase National Bank, which led a group in taking over Pynchon's securities against loans for which they were pledged. Some $20 million in new equity was put into the firm to keep it in business.

Investment bankers and securities affiliates of banks were in less public distress than the brokers but were hurt badly by the markets. New issues of $1.5 billion in the last four months were lower than in any four consecutive months since 1924, so income was poor. Naturally, investment bankers' inventories were producing substantial losses. J. P. Morgan & Co. had a $22 million loss in 1930, most of which was incurred in the market break from June to December. Kuhn Loeb's capital was reduced $3.75 million to $21.25 million during the year.[9] Dillon Read's capital was reduced $2.6 million to $12.1 million.[10] These were three of the leading investment banking houses. Chase Securities Corp. set up 1930 reserves of $20 million, and the Guardian Detroit Co. pulled through the year only with the help of $5 million from Edsel Ford.

The banks, too, showed signs of financial trouble in the last four months of 1930, which had an unfavorable impact on stock prices. National City Bank of New York set up a reserve of $20 million on October 1st, and Manufacturers Trust Co. cut its dividend at the same time. Bank failures accelerated dramatically in November as 256 banks closed, and a further 352 closed in December. On December 12th the Bank of United States failed. Observers wondered if the financial structure of the nation was falling apart.

The list of corporations cutting or eliminating dividends grew considerably during the last quarter with an obvious unfavorable impact on stock prices. Kennecott Copper, Anaconda Copper, Manufacturers Trust, and the recently created Republic Steel Co. cut their dividends. Pure Oil Co. and Montgomery Ward eliminated their dividends. American Radiator & Standard Sanitary Corp. cut its dividend from $1.50 to $1.00, Packard Motor Car from 15¢ to 10¢, Chrysler from $3.00 to $1.00. Both General Motors and Bethlehem Steel failed to earn their dividends. U.S. Steel barely earned its dividend.

Speculators sold some stocks heavily because other stock market participants, such as the Van Sweringen brothers, appeared to be in considerable trouble because of the decline in stock prices. The Alleghany Corp., the kingpin of their railroad holding company empire, had to meet the 150% collateral requirement of its debentures, and the brothers had to repeatedly post collateral of their own and sell stocks to raise cash. Short-sellers sold mercilessly Alleghany Corp., Missouri Pacific, Chesapeake and Ohio, and Nickel Plate railroads, which were in the Van Sweringen group, to capitalize on their difficulties.

There was no panic, no rush to sell. The stock market groped downward through the last four months of 1930 with an air of inevitability which suited the circumstances. Opinion was widespread that the nation was entering a period of permanently reduced prosperity. Those who stayed in the stock market stayed because they had lost too much to get out. After such a decline, it seemed that there would be more to be gained from a recovery than to be lost in further declines. But there was nothing to prompt buying on the other side. There were token incentives, such as an NYSE cut in commission rates on inactive stocks, and Shields & Co.'s offer to margin stocks under $10, but there was a countervailing tendency on the part of other brokers to stop giving margin accounts at all.

The Hoover Administration did nothing in those last months of 1930 to influence events, except to admit that the Depression was becoming a problem. Governor Harrison of the New York Federal Reserve was dispatched to Europe in November to discuss coordinating an attack on the Depression, and Hoover named a Committee on Unemployment but insisted that unemployment remained the responsibility of industry and local government.

The economic and financial structures were being debilitated without any countervailing forces. The stock market, the bond market, the banks, the international markets, the economy—all were locked in downward drift. Markets of all types showed signs of drying up. Not that they had dried up. Business of all types—financial, industrial, and trade—continued, but in the decline in the volume of business and the destruction of mutual confidence we can see in this period (with the benefit of hindsight) the development of the trends which within the next 18 months were to bring all economic and financial activity closer to a dead halt than they had ever been before.

SPECIFIC INDUSTRIES AND INDIVIDUAL STOCKS IN 1930

The changes in values of NYSE stocks by major industries from the Crash through December 1930 are listed in Table 5.1 in order of the magnitude of their declines. These are averages, of course. Individual stocks generally had better recoveries from the Crash, and sharper declines by the end of 1930, than the comparisons in Table 5.1 indicate. Data on individual companies can be found in Table A.1 in the Statistical Appendix. Table A.3 provides ratios for each company's high and low 1930 stock prices.

Table 5.1
Values of Common Stocks Listed on the NYSE, by Major Industries,
1929–1930 ($ billions)

	Value (10/1/29)	Value at 1930 recovery peak	Change from 10/1/29	Value 12/31/30	Change from 10/1/29
All common stocks	$ 79.1	$ 67.5	− 15%	$ 41.8	− 47%
U.S. companies operating abroad	2.5	1.6	− 30	0.6	− 74
Electric equipment manufacturers	4.8	3.9	− 19	1.6	− 67
Banks[a]	306.46	224.05	− 27	121.88	− 60
Mining companies	2.7	1.9	− 30	1.2	− 56
Automobile companies	5.5	4.0	− 27	2.4	− 56
Retailers	4.7	3.2	− 32	2.1	− 55
Machinery and metals companies	2.8	2.3	− 18	1.3	− 54
Utility holding companies	4.4	4.0	− 9	2.2	− 50
Petroleum companies	7.2	7.1	− 1	3.8	− 47
Chemical companies	6.3	5.5	− 13	3.4	− 46
Railroads	10.1	9.5	− 6	6.0	− 41
Operating utilities	5.1	4.8	− 6	3.0	− 41
Steel companies	3.1	3.0	− 3	1.9	− 39
Communications companies	4.8	4.8	no change	3.7	− 23
Food companies	3.2	3.3	+ 3	2.5	− 22

Source: NYSE monthly bulletins.

[a] Moody's index of bank stock prices. No industry values are available because most bank stocks were traded over-the-counter.

The Railroad Industry

During 1930 there were striking differences in the stock market valuations of various industries. In many respects, railroad stocks were among the worst in the market, with high dividend yields, low price-earnings ratios, and low prices relative to book values. Yields on railroad stocks were approximately 5% at the start of 1930 and dropped to 4 1/2% at the peak of the recovery in stock prices, but by the end of 1930 their yields had risen to over 7%. The reader can best grasp relative yields by studying Table 5.2, which compares railroad, industrial, utility, and bank stocks. (For data on specific railroad stocks, see Table 5.3).

The stock market valuation of railroads was most evident in the relationship

Table 5.2
Yields on Common Stocks, 1930 (in percentages)

	December 1929	December 1930
New York City banks	2.30	4.00
Industrials	4.90	6.21
Railroads	5.01	7.17
Utilities	2.97	4.91

Sources: Moody's Financial Manual 1974, p. a 45, Moody's Industrial Manual 1974, p. a 60, Moody's Railroad Manual 1972, p. a 55, Moody's Utility Manual 1974, p. a 13.

of railroad stock prices to their book values. Southern Pacific common stock at its 1930 high price was only 57% of book value, and the stock of Pennsylvania Railroad, which was broadly considered one of the best in the industry, was only 96% of book value at its high. The Chesapeake and Ohio had the best market valuation, at only 134% of book value. These poor valuations compared with 302% of book value for all stocks at their highest stock prices in 1930. At their 1930 low prices, the railroad stocks averaged 66% of book value. Southern Pacific was 39%. The average for all stocks at the same low point was 139%.

Railroad stocks declined less than those of many other industries in the Crash, but they also recovered less. The Dow Jones Railroad Index rose only 18.9% from its November low of 128 to a high on March 29, 1930, of 157.

The recovery was slight and short-lived because railroad revenues and earnings began to drop in the fourth quarter of 1929 and continued to drop through 1930. The likely earnings trend was highly visible in the weekly reports on freight car loadings. Railroad revenues in 1930 dropped to $5.4 billion from $6.4 billion in 1929. Net income dropped from $977 million to $578 million, producing a 38 1/2% decline in earnings per share.

It became increasingly difficult for railroads to finance in the last quarter of 1930. Investors feared that the decline in income would cause many roads to fail the New York State earnings test of 1 1/2 times fixed charges to qualify their bonds as legal investment for savings banks. Sellers drove rail bonds to new low prices in anticipation of bank sales of bonds which were no longer legal. Common stock financing was equally difficult. In November the Missouri Pacific withdrew an ICC application to sell $38.7 million in common stock. There was an ominous sign at both the Baltimore and Ohio and New York Central railroads when they ended 1930 with approximately $25 million of short-term debt.

The major railroads adamantly maintained their common dividends in the face of this decline in net income and stock prices, with the exception of one line. There was widespread expectation of dividend reductions as each line's dividend meeting approached, but the dividends were paid even when unearned because

Table 5.3
The Railroad Industry in 1930

	Price-earnings ratio		Market price as a % of book value		Dividend yield (%)		Low price as a % of 1929 high price	Return on equity (%)	Moody's bond ratings	Cash & equivalents ($ millions)
	High price	Low price	High price	Low price	High price	Low price				
Atchison, Topeka & Santa Fe	19	13	104	72	4.12	5.95	56	5.5	Aaa	34
Baltimore and Ohio	16	7	83	38	5.70	12.70	38	5.2	Aaa	(23)[a]
Canadian Pacific	22	14	133	81	4.40	7.15	52	6.2	Aaa	39
Chesapeake and Ohio	11	7	134	84	4.90	7.80	46	9.3	Aaa	10
New York Central	27	15	117	64	4.15	7.60	41	4.5	Aaa	(25)
Norfolk & Western	12	8	125	86	3.77	5.49	63	10.4	Aaa	5
Pennsylvania	16	10	96	58	4.60	7.55	48	6.1	Aaa	53
Southern Pacific	15	11	57	39	4.70	6.80	56	3.7	Aaa	30
Union Pacific	16	11	108	75	4.12	5.99	56	7.0	Aaa	20
Averages	17.1	10.7	106	66	4.50	7.45	51	6.4	—	—

[a] Brackets indicate short-term borrowings.

railroad stocks were bought for income, and the managements greatly feared the impact of a dividend reduction on their stock prices. This rigidity resulted in higher railroad dividends in 1930 than in 1929—$603 million versus $561 million—because of the annualized effect of dividends increased during 1929. The resulting payout ratio for the railroad industry was 86% in 1930, compared with 51% in 1929.

The Operating Public Utility Industry

Utilities came into prominence in 1930 as a premier investment for both stocks and bonds because of the relative stability of the industry's earnings. The year 1930 was one of general improvement for the electric utility industry. Sales grew 4% to $69 billion, and net income hit a record $423 million—up from $414 million in 1929. Dividend rates increased 18.4% in 1930 from an average of $3.04 per share in December 1929 to $3.60 in December 1930, although they began to decline slightly in August 1930.[11] Buoyed by this performance and by faith in the benefits of improving technology for both generation and transmission, utilities spent a record $872 million for construction in 1930, increased the number of their employees by 3%,[12] increased wages slightly, and cut the average price of a kilowatt-hour from 4.3¢ to 4.2¢,[13] continuing a trend that had carried through the 1920s. (See Table 5.4 for data on specific operating public utility stocks).

Operating utility stocks underwent a reappraisal in 1930 which changed their relative investment valuation from average to above average. However, this is only a crude generalization for what took place, since the stocks of most of the companies under consideration here attracted considerable investor interest in 1929. Consolidated Gas Co. of New York was the 7th most active stock on the NYSE in 1929, and Public Service Corp. of New Jersey was 22nd. There were also a large number of Aaa bond ratings in the industry, which indicated its high credit standing. But a reappraisal is evident. During the recovery, when the speculative interests of pre-Crash market forces still predominated, operating utility stocks recovered to only 28 times 1930 earnings and an average 251% of book value, but in the subsequent decline, operating utility stocks dropped to only 44% of their 1929 highs and to 16 times 1930 earnings per share, compared with the averages of 36% and 13 times earnings per share respectively for all stocks. The difference in dividend yields is even more striking. The yield on operating utility stocks at the lowest prices in 1930 was 4.78%, compared with 7.75% for all stocks. At the peak of the recovery, the average operating utility yield of 2.77% was much closer to the average for all leading companies of 3.56%. Operating utility stocks also swung from a market price to book value relationship in the recovery period that was below average—251%, compared with 302%—to one above average at the end of 1930—145% compared with 139%.

The stability and creditworthiness of the utility industry appears to have swung

Table 5.4
The Operating Public Utility Industry in 1930

	Price-earnings ratio		Market price as a % of book value		Dividend yield (%)		Low price as a % of 1929 high price	Return on equity (%)	Moody's bond ratings	Cash & equivalents ($ millions)
	High price	Low price	High price	Low price	High price	Low price				
Commonwealth Edison	27	17	251	162	2.38	3.69	48	9.4	Aa	20
Consolidated Gas Co. of N.Y.	27	15	260	148	2.90	5.15	43	9.5	Aaa	(66)[a]
Detroit Edison	29	18	217	136	3.13	4.97	42	7.4	Aaa	4
Pacific Gas & Electric	24	13	250	137	2.67	4.88	41	10.2	Aa	12
Public Service of N.J.	32	17	276	144	2.75	5.20	47	8.7	Aa	11
Averages	27.8	16.0	251	145	2.77	4.78	44	9.0	—	—

[a] Brackets indicate short-term borrowing.

in its favor in relative terms as the decline in stocks grew worse. Our five leading utility companies before the Crash earned a mundane 9.7% return on equity, compared with the average of 16.5% for all leading companies, and the industry could be made exciting only by leveraging holding companies on the operating companies. But in 1930 these operating utilities still earned 9%, while the other leading companies' return on equity had fallen from 16.5% to 11.6%, and the stability of utilities became an asset (see Table A.1 in the Statistical Appendix).

The developing change in attitude toward utilities is best seen in the corporate bond market in the last quarter of 1930, when Aa utility bonds began to sell at lower rates than comparable railroad bonds. Historically, railroads had sold at the lowest rates in the corporate bond market, a position they permanently relinquished to utilities at this point. The utilities were able to dominate the new-issue corporate market as a result of this change in credit standing. Utilities issued $2.6 billion in securities in 1930 out of a total of $5.5 billion, 47% percent of the total, which was their largest market share of new issues to date.[14]

The utilities were not without problems, however. There was a vocal public element which considered electric utilities to be excessively profitable and abusive of the public interest. Public power became a political issue. Franklin Delano Roosevelt, as Governor of New York, and his counterpart in Pennsylvania, Gifford Pinchot, received national attention for their attacks on private utilities and their espousal of public power. In November 1930, voters in Washington and Oregon passed public referendums favoring public power amendments to their state constitutions. These political problems were not great in 1930, but they were to reach significant proportions in 1933 once President Roosevelt assumed office.

Holding and Investment Companies

Investment company stock recoveries were behind the market in the initial stages of the recovery but were assisted soon by active market efforts of their sponsors and by the companies' own activities, so that these stocks rose more than the average of 67% in early 1930. Sponsors actively pushed their stocks once the general rise in prices had created greater underlying value in the companies' portfolios. In some cases companies aided this process by buying their own stock. Lehman Corp. bought approximately 78,000 of its shares for $5.6 million. Transamerica bought $7.9 million of its own stock through various subsidiaries and an affiliated public investment company created by A. P. Giannini. Numerous lesser trusts bought in their own stock. Several companies assisted recovery in their stocks by initiating dividends. Commonwealth & Southern, United Corp., and Lehman Corp. initiated cash dividends in 1930. Cities Service, IT&T, and Adams Express kept up their cash dividends, but over half the leading holding companies and investment trusts still did not pay cash dividends.

Financial gymnastics did nothing for these stocks in the longer run, however.

The companies were vulnerable because of their leverage, particularly their high levels of short-term debt, so 1930 was a year of reckoning for many of them.

The Public Utility Holding Companies

The operations and profits of the public utility holding companies were little changed in 1930 from 1929. Cities Service and Electric Bond and Share actually had higher earnings in 1930, and most of the companies continued to make small acquisitions. Cities Service even joined in the sponsorship with Standard Oil of New Jersey of the construction of the 900-mile ''Big Inch'' (24-inch) pipeline to bring natural gas into Chicago. There was one dividend reduction among the group and two dividend increases. The group earned a respectable 9% return on equity. (See Table 5.5 for data on specific companies.)

Despite this apparent stability, the securities of this group fared poorly. The stocks averaged a decline to 23% of their highest 1929 prices, compared with 36% for all stocks and 44% for operating utilities, which had an identical return on equity. The group's market-to-book-value ratio was also depressed at only 115%, compared with 139% for all stocks, at their lowest 1930 stock prices.

Investor attitudes toward all financial stocks were changing, and the perceived risk of the high leverage of the public utility holding companies became a negative feature. Standard Gas & Electric had a capital structure with only 19% common stock, Commonwealth & Southern had only 22% common stock, and North American Co. had only 25% common stock. Even a company as solid as United Gas Improvement had only 47% common stock in its capital structure. By contrast, operating utilities tended to have common stock equal to 50%–60% of their capital structures. There was also a worrisome buildup in the short-term debt of the public utility holding companies. Electric Bond and Share's subsidiaries, American & Foreign Power and Electric Power & Light, had almost $200 million in short-term debt, which forced them into the market on poor terms for refinancing in 1930 and 1931. Cities Service had $92 million in short-term debt, Columbia Gas & Electric went from $8 million to $67 million in short-term debt, and North American Co. went from $14 million cash to $24 million in short-term debt. IT&T and United Gas Improvement also had high short-term debt. The trend bothered Moody's Investors Services as well, because the rating agency reduced ratings for Cities Service, Electric Bond and Share, and IT&T securities.

Samuel Insull's utility holding company system got into severe problems because it was caught with too much short-term debt. Insull had found himself in a struggle with Cyrus Eaton for control of the Insull utility system. Eaton, a Nova Scotian who ran Otis & Co., investment bankers in Cleveland, had put together Republic Steel by merging a number of midwestern steel producers and had thwarted the merger of Bethlehem Steel and Youngstown Sheet & Tube in the courts. He was a hard, cynical player in the financial game. It appeared that Eaton had taken on Samuel Insull in 1928, when Eaton began to accumulate stock in Commonwealth Edison Co., Northern Illinois Public Service Co., and

Table 5.5
The Public Utility Holding Companies in 1930

	Price-earnings ratio		Market price as a % of book value		Dividend yield (%)		Low price as a % of 1929 high price	Return on equity (%)	Moody's bond ratings	Cash & equivalents ($ millions)
	High price	Low price	High price	Low price	High price	Low price				
Cities Service	30	9	520	152	0.68	2.31	19	17.1	Ba	(92)c
Columbia Gas & Electric	49	18	310	111	2.30	6.45	22	8.8	A	(67)
Commonwealth & Southern	33	13	304	114	3.00	8.00	23	7.6	Baa pfd.	41
Electric Bond and Share	49	15	NAb	NA	0	0	20	4.1	A pfd.	52
IT&T	37	9	167	39	2.60	11.10	12	4.7	Baa	(21)
Middle West Utilities	NMa	NM	302	119	0	0	26	8.6	Ba	(18)
North American	29	13	420	180	0	0	30	13.3	A	(24)
Standard Gas and Electric	21	9	119	49	2.71	6.60	22	5.6	Baa	23
United Gas Improvement	32	16	328	160	2.65	5.40	39	11.0	Aa pfd.	(31)
Averages	35.0	12.8	309	115	1.55	4.43	23	9.0	—	—

a NM = Not Meaningful.
b NA = Not Available.
c Brackets indicate short-term borrowing.

Middle West Utilities—three key companies in Insull's empire. Insull was exposed to such a raid because he had only minority control of his system. He began to create a series of holding companies with the aid of Halsey, Stuart & Co. to counter Eaton's acquisitions. Insull Utility Investments, Inc., was created in December 1928 and financed in 1929 through public offerings of bonds and preferred stock totalling $57 million. The proceeds were invested in stock of Commonwealth Edison, Middle West Utilities, Peoples Gas Light & Coke, and Public Service Co. of Northern Illinois. Corporation Securities Co. of Chicago was incorporated almost a year later with $60 million in common and preferred capital. It bought a $35 million position in Insull Utility Investments, as well as positions in the other Insull companies. According to *Moody's*, "The company was organized for the specific purpose of acquiring and holding securities of the above-named companies in order to insure continuity of policy and management."[15] Insull came closer to control of his operating companies through these holding companies which he and his friends controlled. He also became a truly wealthy man for the first time when these holding company stocks soared, but he never owned close to majority control of the operating companies.

When Eaton tried to sell out to him, Insull was able to turn him down five times until Donald R. McLennen, Eaton's emissary, founder of Marsh & McLennen insurance agents and a director of Commonwealth Edison and Continental Illinois National Bank & Trust, finally persuaded Insull to buy the stock. Complete control was too difficult to resist. Insull bought the stock in June 1930 for $56 million, of which $48 million was borrowed short term by Insull Utilities Investments and Corporation Securities Co. of Chicago. Insull also continued to buy up companies all around the nation, using the same two holding companies. Their short-term debts totalled almost $115 million by the end of 1930, plus $30 million in notes due serially over the next five years. The timing for such debt purchases was not propitious. The holding companies were unable to get permanent financing at the time as the stock market dropped in June more sharply than at any other time in the Depression except the Crash itself, and as the debt markets deteriorated permanently. Insull found his companies holding stocks which dropped steadily in value, while he was trapped with an amount of short-term debt which was gigantic for that period.

Reputations are made in such moments, and this trade between Cyrus Eaton and Samuel Insull was an ironic illustration of life's fortunes. Eaton sold the stock to the only person who would be interested in it at the last possible moment. In May 1930 the market appeared to be on a recovery path from the Crash, and new-issue business had revived substantially to fortify that belief. One month later, after the June collapse in prices, a depression appeared likely, opinion in Wall Street had become pessimistic, and the Insull holding company system was seriously overextended.

The Investment Trusts

The reaction against financial stocks was strongest against investment trust stocks. Investment trust stocks had traded at prices based on asset values in the boom which placed little emphasis on cash flows or dividends, but this theory was suddenly reversed in 1930 and the trusts traded at discounts to asset values because the trusts were squeezed for cash. Trading losses had to be accepted as stocks were sold to generate cash for operations and, in a few cases, new dividends. This kind of cash generation was financial cannibalism, however, and few investors gave much weight to the dividends so paid. (For data on specific investment trust stocks, see Table 5.6.)

The companies paid the price of their typically speculative origins. Their leverage which had pushed their stocks up now pulled them down. The heavy trading volume in the stocks in 1929 now became heavy in the opposite direction. Early in 1930 the *New York Times* suggested that Wall Street observers expected many investment trusts to go bankrupt and the industry to be reorganized and consolidated. This was a harsh judgment for such a new industry and such a recent crisis. Suggestions of bankruptcy did not circulate about any other industry, but the performance of investment trust stocks suggested that such critical attitudes were widespread. For example, stocks of the group recovered in 1930 to only 54% of their highest 1929 prices, compared with 75% for all stocks, and there was wide divergence in the recoveries of trust stocks, with the stock of J. P. Morgan's United Corp. rising 174% and Tri-Continental Corp. stock rising 100%, while Goldman Sachs Trading Corp. stock only rose 47%. Once the market began to decline, the investment trust stocks were pummelled, dropping to 19% of their highest 1929 prices and only 56% of book value. This tied with nonutility holding companies as the worst record for any group of stocks. Goldman Sachs Trading Corp.'s stock dropped to only 4% of its highest 1929 price. Lehman Corp. and United Corp. initiated dividends to help their stocks, but it had little effect.

Suspicions of the investment trusts were well founded. Many of them could not sustain the decline in securities prices that had taken place, even after the recovery, because of the companies' high leverage and the highly speculative securities they held. Goldman Sachs Trading Corp. began liquidating assets during 1930, when it sold control of three small New York fire and casualty insurance companies to the Home Life Assurance Co. Near the end of 1930, Goldman Sachs Trading Corp. negotiated the sale for $7.3 million of 200,000 shares representing control of Manufacturers Trust Co. to a group headed by Harvey D. Gibson, who became President. Goldman Sachs Trading Corp. took a loss of approximately $48 million on the trade.[16] Goldman Sachs Trading had contracted to buy the stock originally at $200 per share and sold it to Gibson's group at approximately $26.35 per share.

During 1930, Goldman Sachs Trading also liquidated C. F. Childs & Co., its government bond trading subsidiary in Chicago which it had purchased earlier, and sold the name back to C. F. Childs. Other assets were sold where markets could be found, such as an interest in Guardian Detroit Union Group in Detroit, which was sold back to the Group. Goldman Sachs Trading wrote down its portfolio value $165 million at the end of 1930 in order to bring it to market

Table 5.6
The Investment Trusts in 1930

	Price-earnings ratio		Market price as a % of book value		Dividend yield (%)		Low price as a % of 1929 high price	Return on equity (%)	Moody's bond ratings	Cash & equivalents ($ millions)
	High price	Low price	High price	Low price	High price	Low price				
Goldman Sachs Trading	NM[a]	NM	379	35	0	0	4	5.1	NR[c]	(10)[d]
Lehman Corp.	NM	NM	131	70	3.09	5.77	38	0.1	NR	17
Tri-Continental Corp.	def.[b]	def.	199	56	0	0	28	def.	NR	8
United Corp.	67	18	185	50	1.00	3.60	18	2.4	NR	(15)
United Founders	NM	NM	489	67	0	0	8	9.9	NR	(12)
Averages	NM	NM	277	56	0.82	1.87	19	4.4	—	—

[a] NM = Not Meaningful.
[b] def. = Deficit.
[c] NR = Not Rated.
[d] Brackets indicate short-term borrowing.

value. Almost half the write-offs were on securities for which no adequate public market existed. The stock of Shenandoah Corp., which Goldman Sachs Trading controlled, had dropped from $39 in 1929 to $3 5/8, and the stock of Blue Ridge Corp., which Goldman Sachs Trading also controlled, had dropped from $29 to $2 5/8. Losses of $165 million on a portfolio with a book value of $237 million placed considerable doubt on the value of "professional management" of a portfolio.

In 1930, Goldman Sachs Trading Corp.'s stock dropped to lower levels than any other leading stock in this group as a result of the company's troubles. Its low price for the year was $4 3/8, only 4% of its 1929 high of $121. At this price, the stock was only 35% of the underlying portfolio value, even though the portfolio had been reduced on the books to market value.

United Founders Corp. also ran into trouble, although the company looked sufficiently attractive that it was able to take over American Founders Corp. in March 1930, thereby doubling in size. United Founders at this point had two relatively well defined areas of activity. American Founders and its subsidiaries managed highly diversified portfolios, while two other companies—United States Electric Power Corp. and Public Utility Holding Corp. of America—controlled and managed various utilities. United Founders investment policies appeared conservative at first glance. The company had only $12 million in debt and positions in a number of prominent operating electric utilities—Duquesne Light Co., Empire Gas Co., Northern States Power Co., Wisconsin Public Service Corp., Louisville Gas & Electric, Oklahoma Gas & Electric, San Diego Consolidated Gas & Electric, and California-Oregon Power Co. Yet United Founders stock dropped to $6 in 1930 from its 1929 high of $76, one of the worst performances of any leading stock. Its portfolio value dropped from $266 million book value in 1929 to a market value of $138 million in 1930,[17] and to a net value per share of $8.96.

The sources of United Founders' problems were in its utility holdings. One—Public Utility Holding Corp. of America—amounted to 15% of its assets and held almost exclusively foreign securities, which rapidly lost value in 1930. Public Utility Holding Corp. of America stock dropped from a 1929 high of $39 to $4 5/8. United Founders' other utility investment, United States Electric Power, controlled solid assets, but through many intermediaries and with extreme leverage. It controlled Standard Power & Light with H. M. Byllesby & Co., which in turn controlled Standard Gas and Electric, which in turn controlled the operating companies mentioned above, sometimes through a further intermediary. Standard Power and Light reported a 1930 consolidated balance sheet in which only $215 million of common equity supported $1.2 billion in total assets. United Founders was simply too high up on the pyramid.

Lehman Corp. was unique among the trusts in that it was formed at the peak of the 1929 bull market but avoided the excesses of many trusts. It had no debt and no subsidiaries. At the end of December 1929 it also had $33 million in cash, call loans, and U.S. government securities—one-third of its portfolio. At the end of 1930 Lehman Corp. still owned $15 million in U.S. government securities. It had also bought back 77,700 of its own shares for $5.6 million and had been listed on the New York Stock Exchange—one of the few investment trusts there. The Lehman Corp. portfolio was widely diversified among industrial, railroad, and utility stocks, so it could not perform much differently from the general market, but it did avoid the most prominent pitfalls in the market. It held virtually no foreign securities and only a few of the best holding companies. The Lehman reputation for shrewd investing was already on its way.

The Non-utility Holding Companies

Non-utility holding companies fared much like other companies in the initial recovery of stock prices in 1930, but they had catastrophic stock price declines later in 1930—to only 16% of their highest 1929 prices and 24% of book value— which placed them on a par with investment trust stocks. (See Table 5.7 for data on specific companies.) Alleghany Corp. is an excellent case history of this transformation. The market attitude during the first half of 1930 was sufficiently positive that Alleghany Corp. was able to sell $25 million in 5% debentures and $12.5 million of 5 1/2% preferred stock in March 1930, and the related Van Sweringen Co. sold $30 million of 6% debentures to buy 500,000 shares of Alleghany Corp. from the Van Sweringens and a further 250,000 shares in the open market.

The Van Sweringen railroad empire had become highly leveraged by this point. The system was based on the Chesapeake and Ohio and Missouri Pacific railroads, which were controlled by Chesapeake Corp., which in turn was controlled by Alleghany Corp., which in turn was controlled by the Van Sweringen Co. These companies had combined debt of $260 million at the end of 1930. Chesapeake Corp. had $83 million of combined long- and short-term debt, versus $85 million of common equity. Alleghany Corp. had $97 million of debt, versus $155 million of equity. The Van Sweringen Corp. and it subsidiary, Cleveland Terminals, had $80 million of debt, versus approximately $32 million of con- solidated equity.[18]

This structure could not stand the decline in security values which occurred after the spring of 1930. The Van Sweringen Corp. was squeezed by the terms of its recent $30 million debt issue, which required 50% in collateral. The company was forced by the decline in the price of its 750,000 shares of Alleghany stock to sell some of the stock in November 1930 and to replace it with U.S. Treasury notes worth $15 million, to which the 50% collateral requirement did not apply. Alleghany Corp. began to be squeezed under covenants on its $85 million long-term debt, which required much higher collateral of 150%. Some 540,000 shares of Chesapeake Corp. worth $49 million had originally provided collateral for much of Alleghany Corp's. bonds, but even though 1,205,000 shares had been put up by the end of 1930, they were worth only $38 million. A further 320,000 shares of Missouri Pacific were added to the collateral, along with various smaller holdings. Chesapeake Corp. did not have the requirement

Table 5.7
The Non-utility Holding Companies in 1930

	Price-earnings ratio		Market price as a % of book value		Dividend yield (%)		Low price as a % of 1929 high price	Return on equity (%)	Moody's bond ratings	Cash & equivalents ($ millions)
	High price	Low price	High price	Low price	High price	Low price				
Alleghany Corp.	NM[a]	NM	167	27	0	0	10	NM	Ba	(17)[b]
Transamerica	60	13	100	21	2.13	10.00	21	1.7	Baa	6
Averages	NM	NM	134	24	NM	NM	16	NM	—	—

[a] NM = Not Meaningful.
[b] Brackets indicate short-term borrowing.

in its long-term debt indenture to maintain collateral at a specific market value, probably because it issued its debt in 1927, when fears of overvaluation of its holdings were less, but Chesapeake Corp. had $36.7 million in short-term debt with commercial banks on which collateral had to be maintained.

The Van Sweringens struggled to cope with the squeeze on them by trying to create new value through reorganizing operations. The Pittston Co. was created to own and operate the Erie Railroad's coal properties and the Pittston stock distributed to Alleghany Corp. and other Erie stockholders. Terminal Shares was created to own the terminal and office properties of the Van Sweringen railroads in Cleveland, and its notes were similarly distributed to Alleghany Corp. and other railroad stockholders. The banks, led by J. P. Morgan & Co., were persuaded to extend their loans despite the poor collateral for them. The ultimate step, however, was to sell off the stocks held by the various companies. The Van Sweringens had simply tried to go too far too fast by expanding their empire on debt.

The market began to anticipate the outcome of the Van Sweringens' problems in 1930, and Alleghany Corp. common was sold heavily. Alleghany common dropped from $35 to $5 3/4 by the end of 1930, at which point it was only 10% of its 1929 high price of $57 and 27% of book value. The stock had one of the poorest performances on the basis of these two parameters of any stock in 1930. Alleghany's bonds also declined to an extent that indicated coming problems. Its three issues dropped from prices over $100 to approximately $60 by the end of the year.

Transamerica Corp. also felt the squeeze during the year, particularly in its Bank of Italy subsidiary, which was overleveraged and had heavy real estate and agriculture loans. Elisha Walker and Jean Monnet, who had taken over as Chairman and Vice Chairman respectively in February 1930 when A.P. Giannini retired, were forced to cut the Transamerica dividend from $1.60 to $1.00 in July after the Bank of Italy reduced its dividend, and they took other measures to improve the liquidity of Transamerica and its subsidiary banks. Fortunately, Transamerica had no leverage itself, but the decline in its stock price to only 21% of book value indicated that the stock market foresaw considerable trouble ahead for the company.

The Banks

Recoveries in bank stock prices in early 1930 were considerably below the average stock recovery of 67% from the 1929 lows, but the industry remained highly overvalued. Trading in bank stocks was still stimulated by prominent bank mergers, such as that between Chase National Bank and the Equitable Trust Co., and by bank securities affiliates trading in the parent company's stock. Chase Securities bought $112 million and sold $114 million in Chase Bank stock in 1930.[19] At their 1930 high prices, many bank stocks were still 275%–400% of book value. The stock of National City Bank, which was the most aggressive bank and attracted the most attention under Charles E. Mitchell, was at 630% of book value and had a peak price-earnings ratio of 67. (See Table 5.8 for data on specific bank stocks.)

During the Crash and in 1930, there was much talk about the strength of the banking system and the distinction between this and other financial crises. The strength of the banks was expected to limit the duration of the trade depression, just as their strength had eased the market decline in the Crash and the flight of lenders from the call loan market. Most of the leading banks bore out this generalization. Their earnings per share generally declined only 25%–30% in 1930, and four of the top ten paid higher dividends in 1930. Only First National Bank of Chicago among the top ten banks lowered its dividend rate. The ratio of these banks' deposits to capital plus surplus was also reassuring. At the end of 1929, First National Bank of Chicago had the highest leverage, with deposits 7.1 times capital plus surplus. The other banks had deposits generally 5 or 6 times capital plus surplus. The Guaranty Trust Co., which was the most conservative, had deposits only 4 1/2 times its capital and surplus.

These leading banks belied the general trend in the industry, however. Net income of all Federal Reserve member banks declined 45% in 1930, from $556.5 million to $306.5 million. A significant factor in this earnings decline was undoubtedly the easy money policy of the New York Federal Reserve Bank. At the resulting short-term interest rates of 2%–4% during 1930, the banks could not even earn above the deposit rates they paid to investors because savings deposit rates stayed up at 4 1/2% until October, when the first reduction to 4% occurred. By that time, market short-term investment rates were 1 7/8%–3%. Bank dividends declined 5.3% from 1929, but *Moody's* monthly statistics on the dividends of a wide group of New York City banks indicate that the banks' dividends began to decline as early as September 1929. There were only 2 months in the subsequent 15 months that these dividends did not decline.[20] Member bank suspensions during 1930 doubled to 1,350, and deposits affected more than tripled to $837 million, culminating in the collapse of the Bank of United States in December 1930.

The decline in bank stock prices to a more normal valuation reflected a realization that the financial excesses of the 1920s were over, despite some last flings in entertainment, holding company, and utility stocks. Bank stocks continued to decline through December 1929, when other stocks were rising, and in early 1930 they were still one-third below their prices before the Crash. National City Bank's stock was less than half its pre-Crash price. Bank stocks began to decline again in March 1930, before most other stocks, and by the year end Moody's index of bank stocks had declined 50% from March 1930.

Bank stocks at the end of 1930 when the Bank of United States crisis had become acute sold at prices 15–20 times earnings and 120%–200% of book value and bore yields of 4%–5%. National City Bank and Chase National Bank stocks fared poorly in the readjustment of values because they had been the focus of the most speculation and manipulation in the boom. National City Bank's stock

Table 5.8
The Banks in 1930

	Price-earnings ratio		Market price as a % of book value		Dividend yield (%)		Low price as a % of 1929 high price	Return on equity (%)	Moody's bond ratings	Cash & equivalents ($ millions)
	High price	Low price	High price	Low price	High price	Low price				
Bankers Trust	38	20	400	210	1.65	3.20	36	10.4	—	—
Central Hanover	NAª	NA	400	186	1.70	3.65	37	NA	—	—
Chase National	NA	NA	285	120	2.22	5.25	27	NA	—	—
Continental Illinois	37	18	345	166	2.08	4.32	36	9.3	—	—
First National (Boston)	NA	NA	310	151	2.40	4.90	30	NA	—	—
First National (Chicago)	34	19	263	146	2.15	3.90	36	10.4	—	—
Guaranty Trust	34	16	260	123	2.33	4.93	34	7.7	—	—
Irving Trust	39	15	279	104	2.15	5.70	27	7.1	—	—
National City	67	21	630	195	1.55	5.00	14	NA	—	—
Averages	41.5	18.2	352	156	2.03	4.54	31	9.0	—	—

ª NA = Not Available.

at the end of 1930 was only 14% of its 1929 high. Chase's stock price was 27% of its 1929 high and only 120% of book value.

The Oil Industry

The oil companies were exposed to a severe decline in oil prices in 1930 as wellhead prices for crude oil dropped to $1.30 per barrel from a peak of $2.24 in 1926 and $1.70 in 1929.[21] In some southwestern states, oil sold for 40¢ per barrel in 1930. There was a tremendous surplus of oil, even though consumption of gasoline, the industry's principal product, continued to rise in 1930 and 1931. In response to the surplus, the oil-producing states attempted to pro-ration production for the first time.

Competition to sell crude oil was so cutthroat that there were fears of widespread defaults among even large companies. Richfield Oil was close to bankruptcy, and Shell Union Oil tried desperately to conserve cash by eliminating its common stock dividend. *Moody's* dropped Shell's bond rating to Ba (speculative quality) during the year. Like other commodities industries, the oil industry needed controls on production and prices to stay profitable, and this began to push oil executives toward favoring pro-rationing schemes.

Industry net income from crude oil and natural gas dropped from $583 million in 1929 to $255 million in 1930, and the companies in this study averaged a return on equity of only 3.8%. No company escaped the impact. (See Table 5.9 for data on specific companies.) Earnings per share of Atlantic Refining, Gulf Oil, Phillips Petroleum, Standard Oil of New Jersey, and Texas Corp. (later Texaco) declined approximately 75%. Shell Union Oil Corp. registered a deficit, which was to be expected since it was more highly leveraged than the others. Richfield Oil Co. of California hovered on bankruptcy all year after earning $8.5 million in 1929. The company was not in deficit, but developed severe working capital problems. After borrowing $10 million on short term, it was put into receivership on January 16, 1931.

There was a considerable range for the stock price performances of the oil companies, with the largest companies' stocks performing the best, but overall the valuations of oil stocks were very low. Despite high oil company bond ratings and strong cash positions, investors fared poorly in the stocks. The recovery in the stocks in early 1930 was below average, with the stocks of Socony-Vacuum and Texas Corp. recovering less than 25%. In the subsequent decline, oil stocks dropped to 36% of their highest 1929 prices and only 57% of book value. Not one oil stock was above book value at its lowest price in 1930, and Atlantic Refining, Phillips Petroleum, Shell Union Oil, and Sinclair Consolidated were below one-third of book value. Most of the companies tried to keep stockholder confidence by maintaining their 1929 dividend rates despite the sharp decline in 1930 earnings, but this had little effect as yields on many of the stocks rose to over 10%.

Table 5.9
The Oil Industry in 1930

	Price-earnings ratio		Market price as a % of book value		Dividend yield (%)		Low price as a % of 1929 high price	Return on equity (%)	Moody's bond ratings	Cash & equivalents ($ millions)
	High price	Low price	High price	Low price	High price	Low price				
Atlantic Refining	50	17	98	33	3.92	11.76	22	2.0	Aaa	11
Gulf Oil of Pa.	71	25	223	79	0.90	2.54	28	3.1	Aaa	28
Phillips Petroleum	63	17	125	33	4.44	16.67	26	2.0	Baa	(12)c
Shell Union Oil	def.a	def.	118	24	0	0	26	def.	Ba	7
Sinclair Consolidated	18	6	64	20	3.10	10.00	22	3.7	Baa	36
Socony-Vacuum	44	22	129	65	4.00	8.00	42	2.9	Aaa	45
Standard Oil (Calif.)	26	15	164	92	3.33	5.95	51	6.5	NRb	16
Standard Oil (Ind.)	22	11	150	75	4.17	8.34	48	6.9	NR	88
Standard Oil (N.J.)	52	27	174	90	2.35	4.55	53	3.5	Aaa	226
Texas Corp.	40	18	135	62	4.92	10.71	39	3.5	Aa	63
Averages	42.9	17.6	136	57	3.10	7.85	36	3.8	—	—

a def. = Deficit.
b NR = Not Rated.
c Brackets indicate short-term borrowing.

The Chemical Industry

Chemical industry net income in 1930 declined from $158 million to $113 million, but the largest companies had only one modest change in dividends. (See Table 5.10 for data on specific companies.) Du Pont cut its dividend 50¢ from $5.20 to $4.70 per share. Price-earnings ratios of the companies' stocks ranged between 29 and 37 at their recovery highs and between 11 and 18 at their year-end lows. All the stocks except Monsanto had prices which were very favorable relative to their book values, averaging 440% of book value at their highest prices and 198% of book value at their lowest prices at year end.

The chemical company stocks had declined at their lowest point in 1930 to 37% of their highest 1929 prices, which was about average for all stocks, but they represented a very high quality segment of the stock market, as was evident from their high market-to-book-value ratios and in other respects. The companies averaged a 13 1/2% return on equity compared with 11.6% for all companies; they had little leverage and strong cash positions, and at their lowest stock prices they carried dividend yields averaging only 5.40%.

The industry showed none of the stress of other commodities-based industries, such as oil or mining, even though most chemical production was of a commodity nature.

The Food Industry

In 1930 the food industry had the third highest return on equity as General Foods and Standard Brands earned better than 30% returns on equity and National Dairy and National Biscuit earned better than 20%. Borden earned almost 15%, which was better than the average for all stocks but looked ''sleepy'' in this industry. (See Table 5.11 for specific data on food industry stocks.)

The food companies made only modest dividend changes in 1930, both up and down, and their stocks accordingly sold at high valuations relative to book value. The stocks of Standard Brands, General Foods, and National Biscuit at their recovery peaks were over 5 times book value, and at their lowest prices in December they were still over 3 1/2 times book value.

Food industry stocks provide a good measure of how earnings were valued in the Depression, because the industry had an 18.2% return on equity, which was relatively stable, and the industry was not part of the speculative mania in 1929 (except for Standard Brands). This combination led to a below average recovery from the Crash by food stocks of only 47%, but once the focus shifted in the last half of 1930 to quality and stability, the industry's stocks did very well. They declined to only 46% of their highest 1929 prices and to 218% of book value, compared with 36% and 139% for all stocks.

Standard Brands stock did less well than the other food company stocks in 1930 because of the speculative attention it received in 1929. Its low stock price for 1930 was only 31% of its 1929 high price, much below the other companies'

Table 5.10
The Chemical Industry in 1930

	Price-earnings ratio		Market price as a % of book value		Dividend yield (%)		Low price as a % of 1929 high price	Return on equity (%)	Moody's bond ratings	Cash & equivalents ($ millions)
	High price	*Low price*	*High price*	*Low price*	*High price*	*Low price*				
Allied Chemical	35	17	370	183	1.75	3.53	48	10.4	Aa pfd.	87
Commercial Solvents	36	13	800	295	2.65	7.15	20	27.6	NR[a]	5
Dow Chemical	29	14	455	223	2.00	4.08	61	15.6	NR	NA[b]
E. I. Du Pont	31	18	454	253	3.25	5.80	35	11.6	Aa	63
Monsanto Chemical	37	11	206	58	1.95	6.94	22	5.6	A	2
Union Carbide	34	17	352	177	2.45	4.90	38	10.4	NR	46
Averages	33.7	15.0	440	198	2.34	5.40	37	13.5	—	—

[a] NR = Not Rated.
[b] NA = Not Available.

Table 5.11
The Food Industry in 1930

	Price-earnings ratio		Market price as a % of book value		Dividend yield (%)		Low price as a % of 1929 high price	Return on equity (%)	Moody's bond ratings	Cash & equivalents ($ millions)
	High price	Low price	High price	Low price	High price	Low price				
Borden	18	12	258	172	3.33	5.00	59	14.6	NR[a]	17
General Foods	17	12	508	367	4.92	6.82	54	30.2	NR	13
General Mills	16	11	155	105	5.08	7.50	45	9.8	Ba pfd.	13
National Biscuit	27	20	580	430	3.55	4.78	73	21.3	Aaa pfd.	25
National Dairy	15	9	326	184	4.20	7.45	40	21.6	A	20
Pillsbury	9	6	106	69	5.26	8.00	39	11.4	Baa	(6)[b]
Standard Brands	24	12	725	350	4.15	8.55	31	30.3	Aa pfd.	25
United Fruit	25	11	150	67	3.81	8.51	30	6.1	NR	23
Averages	18.9	11.6	351	218	4.29	7.08	46	18.2	—	—

[a] NR = Not Rated.
[b] Brackets indicate short-term borrowing.

stocks. At that level its yield was 8.55%, the highest in the group. Its price-earnings ratio of 12 was only average, even though Standard Brands had a return on equity 50% higher than most of the other companies.

The Mining Industry

The mining industry fared poorly in 1930 as metal prices fell. Copper prices fell from 17.78¢ per pound, where they had been stabilized since May 1929, to a low of 9.6¢ in October 1930, a record low price for the century. Lead prices dropped 25% to 5¢ per pound, and zinc prices dropped 33% to just over 4¢ per pound. A dramatic overcapacity was evident in the mining industry, and the United States bore the brunt of the world surplus because of the recent expansion of large, high grade and low cost mining in Canada, South America, and Africa with which the older, lower grade U.S. mines could not compete. Domestic copper production dropped 30%, lead output dropped 14%, and zinc output dropped 20%, while production in the rest of the world barely dropped at all.[22] Net income for the metal mining industry under these adverse conditions dropped from $278 million in 1929 to $97 million in 1930. The major companies, excluding Texas Gulf Sulphur, averaged a return on equity of only 5 3/4%, and Phelps Dodge had a deficit. The industry's dividend payments dropped from $194 million to $92 million[23] as Anaconda, Kennecott, and Phelps Dodge cut their dividends by over 50%. (See Table 5.12 for data on specific mining industry stocks.)

Mining stocks had been among the most actively traded on the New York Stock Exchange in 1929, and they remained active in 1930, except now it was on the down side as the dismal economics of the business prompted investors to rush from the stocks. Only Texas Gulf Sulphur, International Nickel, and Homestake Mining had stocks above book value at the end of the year, when prices were lowest. The rest averaged barely 50% of book value. The copper stocks were down to 25% of their highest 1929 prices or less. Yields on the mining stocks shot up to around 10%, even though dividends had been cut savagely. Since dividends were still above earnings for most of the companies, investors expected further reductions.

The industry looked very sick if nothing could be done to raise prices and to agree on worldwide capacity reductions. Fortunately, the industry had no debt—with the exception of Anaconda, which was about to be squeezed severely.

The Motion Picture Companies

The motion picture stocks had a dramatic recovery from the Crash, and an equally dramatic collapse by the end of 1930. (See Table 5.13 for data on specific stocks.) Radio-Keith-Orpheum, in which Joseph Kennedy made a fortune, rose 317% in the 1930 recovery to a new high of $50 and then dropped to $14. Loew's Inc. also hit a new high in 1930 at $96—up 200% from its 1929 low—

Table 5.12
The Mining Industry in 1930

	Price-earnings ratio		Market price as a % of book value		Dividend yield (%)		Low price as a % of 1929 high price	Return on equity (%)	Moody's bond ratings	Cash & equivalents ($ millions)
	High price	Low price	High price	Low price	High price	Low price				
Alaska Juneau Gold	16	8	91	45	4.40	8.90	45	5.2	NR[b]	0
American Smelting	21	10	140	67	5.00	10.53	29	6.6	Aa	25
Anaconda Copper	40	12	135	41	3.05	10.00	18	3.5	NR	(48)[c]
Homestake Mining	14	12	124	107	8.43	9.72	77	8.9	NR	6
International Nickel	66	19	630	185	2.05	6.95	18	6.9	A pfd.	10
Kennecott Copper	38	12	191	61	3.20	10.00	19	5.5	NR	26
National Lead	25	15	90	54	4.21	7.02	54	3.6	A pfd.	10
Phelps Dodge	def.[a]	def.	90	41	4.55	10.00	25	def.	NR	13
Texas Gulf Sulphur	12	7	558	333	5.97	10.00	47	44.3	NR	6
Averages	29.0	11.9	228	104	4.54	9.24	37	10.6	—	—

[a] def. = Deficit.
[b] NR = Not Rated.
[c] Brackets indicate short-term borrowing.

Table 5.13
The Motion Picture Companies in 1930

	Price-earnings ratio		Market price as a % of book value		Dividend yield (%)		Low price as a % of 1929 high price	Return on equity (%)	Moody's bond ratings	Cash & equivalents ($ millions)
	High price	Low price	High price	Low price	High price	Low price				
Fox Film A	14	4	139	39	1.75	6.25	15	9.9	Ba	(1)[c]
Loew's	11	5	252	110	4.15	9.50	49	20.2	Baa	8
Paramount-Publix	13	6	163	75	5.20	11.40	46	11.8	Baa	7
Radio-Keith-Orpheum	def.[a]	def.	263	74	0	0	30	def.	NR[b]	4
Warner Bros. Pictures	def.	def.	445	57	3.75	30.00	13	def.	B	5
Averages	12.7	5.0	253	71	2.97	11.43	31	14.0	—	—

[a] def. = Deficit.
[b] NR = Not Rated.
[c] Brackets indicate short-term borrowing.

and then dropped to $42 by the end of 1930. Paramount-Publix, Fox Film, and Warner Bros. all recovered over 100% in 1930. The motion picture industry was the only industry in which new highs were broadly established in 1930, and it thereby produced tremendous momentary fortunes. But it fell with almost equal grandeur. Fox Film's stock was worth only 15% of its high by the end of 1930, Warner Bros. was worth only 13%, and Radio-Keith-Orpheum only 30%.

In many respects, the motion picture industry was a speculative vehicle of the brokerage business, based on popular fascination with talking films. Warner Bros. recognized this well enough to sell 231,000 shares in the first six months of 1930 at inflated prices and buy them back later at a $7.4 million profit.[24] The industry never had the earnings quality to justify the interest it received. It earned a 12.9% return on equity in 1929, and two companies were in deficit in 1930. Besides, the industry was highly leveraged as a result of the inflated prices it paid to acquire other companies. Warner Bros. had only 41% common equity in 1929, RKO had only 45%, Loew's had 47%, Fox Film had 51%, and Paramount had 62%. Much of the companies' debt had speculative ratings by the end of 1930. After 1930, the industry was visibly sick and lost importance in the market. There is every sign that investors realized it was sick in the first place from the valuations placed on earnings and the general contempt for book values. The stocks of Fox Film, Paramount, RKO, and Warner Bros. averaged only 61% of book value by year end.

The story of Fox Film's reorganization in 1930 and again in 1933 can be told here, for it illustrates many of the problems and excesses of securities markets in this period. The company was founded in 1915 by William Fox and by 1929 had become one of the largest film companies under his leadership. It produced, distributed, and exhibited films in over 500 theaters. Fox Film had net income of approximately $10 million in 1929, and its affiliated corporation, Fox Theatres, had a net income of $2.7 million. The two companies had little debt and no preferred stock at the beginning of 1929, and an unblemished reputation.

The Fox tragedy began in April 1929, when Fox Theatres purchased 400,000 shares of Loew's Corp. for $50 million from the estate of Marcus Loew. The 400,000 shares gave Fox control of 42% of the outstanding stock of one of his most profitable competitors. An important aspect of this profitability was Loew's motion picture source: Metro-Goldwyn-Mayer (MGM). The purchase also gave Fox Theatres a considerable short-term debt burden, which was increased further when Fox bought 260,900 additional shares on margin in the open market.

At this early stage, the transaction appeared to be a coup for William Fox. He paid $125 per share for the Loew's estate stock, compared with a market price of $50–$60, but the deal had the blessing of prudent financial heads. Halsey, Stuart & Co. was Fox's advisor, and AT&T lent $15 million through its subsidiary, Western Electric, to facilitate the transaction. The Western Electric loan had been obtained in half an hour of discussion with E. S. Bloom, the company's President, partly, Fox later suggested, because the deal thwarted Warner Bros., which was also competing for the stock but was fighting with AT&T. Harold

Stuart of Halsey, Stuart & Co. and John Otterman, Treasurer of AT&T, suggested to Fox that the purchase be supplemented by buying up stock in the open market.

Flushed with the enthusiasm of such effortless expansion, Fox went $20 million further into debt to buy control of Gaumont–British Picture Corp., a chain of 300 theaters in Great Britain, where sound films were only beginning to show. Otterman and Stuart were again voices of encouragement. Stuart arranged United Kingdom bank loans for Fox of approximately $6 million for the purchase. Prudence had fled by this point, however, for the two Fox companies now owed over $150 million, of which at least $90 million was short-term debt.[25]

Misfortune suddenly befell William Fox at this high point in his career. Enroute to a golf game with Adolph Zukor of Paramount, an auto accident disabled Fox from July to October 1929. Since Fox essentially ran a one-man show, no steps were taken to fund the two companies' debt while he was idled. His release from the hospital coincided with the Crash and a sudden decline in the value of Loew's stock and his own Fox holdings. Loew's stock declined from a high of $85 to $32. Fox Film B stock, which controlled Fox Film, dropped from $105 5/8 to $19 1/8. Fox companies' margin loans were severely "under water," and nervous brokers were suddenly after William Fox for more money. But Fox had little leeway, having purchased Loew's stock, in his own words, until he ran out of money. Fox canvassed Halsey, Stuart & Co., AT&T, and New York commercial bankers for further loans on the collateral of Fox companies' real estate to satisfy the brokers but found the climate sharply changed. The banks and AT&T were unwilling to make new loans. Halsey Stuart had its own problems in bailing out a recent Insull Utility underwriting caught by the Crash. The Fox companies' position had also changed with the change in attitudes. What had been coups in buying out a competitor and a major U.K. chain became millstones, as the value of the Loew's investment shrunk to a fraction of its cost and permanent financing became impossible. The Fox companies now appeared overextended, vulnerable to the economic downturn because of their luxury nature, and led by an eccentric rather than a genius.

Fox was saved in the short run by the intermediation of Albert M. Greenfield, a rough Philadelphia banker-millionaire who built City Stores Corp. and who intruded on the Fox story at numerous points, always to Fox's benefit. Greenfield lent Fox $10 million for the original purchase of Loew's stock and led Fox to Louis B. Mayer, head of the California Republican Party and of MGM, when Fox inexplicably developed a problem with the Justice Department over the purchase of Loew's, having earlier received informal approval. Now Greenfield tendered an offer of $10 million from Warner Bros. for various Fox West Coast properties which William Fox had previously considered valueless. Fox used the proceeds to meet the brokers' margin demands and to tie up these loans to year end as long as there was 35% equity in the accounts. Financing for the Fox companies by year end appeared reasonable.

In November and December Fox found to his surprise not only that financing was unavailable but also that his demise was being reported well in advance of its realization. Murray W. Dodge, Executive Vice President of Chase Securities Corp. and a key figure in subsequent Fox financings, later testified before the Pecora Committee:

The figures we looked into at that time of the Fox Film Co. led us to believe that the Company over a period of 10 and 15 years had been a successful and profitable concern, and its troubles at that time were caused only because it had capital obligations coming due which it could not meet.[26]

The first maturity in the Fox companies' bank loans was $1.6 million on December 9, 1929. Harry Stuart of Halsey, Stuart & Co., and John Otterman from AT&T approached Fox even before this date with the proposition that he was in default and that his control of the Fox companies should be turned over to a voting trust of Fox, Stuart, and Otterman. Such concessions were hardly in the Fox character, but when the December 9th due date passed and Fox was too sick and harassed to cope with the situation, the companies suddenly found their bank deposits set off against their loans by the Harriman National Bank and then by all the other bank lenders. On the advice of Charles Evans Hughes, Fox acceded to a trusteeship for the Fox companies.

In early 1930 the Fox companies were taken into court by bank lenders who were unwilling to extend their loans and sought performance on the Fox companies' notes. However, the judge was unwilling to put the companies in receivership because of their strong earnings, and Fox had wisely hired as his counsel Samuel Untermeyer, who brought in Bancamerica-Blair and Lehman Brothers with proposals for permanent financing. This confusing picture at least promised some succor for the Fox companies, so their stocks rose with the general market recovery of early 1930 until Fox Film stock stood at $57 3/8, versus its 1929 high of $105 5/8 and low of $19 1/8. Both William Fox and the market were highly unstable in this period, however, and when both became too much to handle in April 1930, all the investment bankers resigned from the effort. Left without choice, Fox sold out for $15 million to General Theatres Equipment, Inc. (GTE).

This might have been the end of the story, and the moral might have been the evils of excessive confidence, short-term debt, buying on margin, relying on bankers, buying stock at twice its market price, dealing with shadowy intermediaries, and borrowing from AT&T. But the tale has only just begun. The purchaser, GTE, was much more extreme than the Fox companies. It was organized in August 1929 by Harley Clarke to develop and market new projectors for sound films and wide screens. GTE was created by a series of mergers and acquisitions, which resulted in its assets being carried on its books at 10 times their historic costs because of the premium paid over book value in each successive merger.[27]

The Fox companies were refinanced in April 1930, with the help of GTE after it acquired them. Fox Film sold 1,600,000 A shares at $30, of which GTE bought

1,160,000, and Halsey, Stuart & Co. and Pynchon & Co. led a group buying 440,000 shares. The bankers bought Fox Film A stock at $30 when the market for it was at $40, and they immediately began a pool in the stock for 150,000 shares in hopes of creating enough activity and interest to move the 440,000 shares into investors' hands. The deep discount from the market price of $40 later drew critical comment from Senate investigator Ferdinand Pecora, but it appears reasonable in light of the tenuous position of the Fox companies, the uncertain stock market, and the importance of the equity infusion.[28]

The additional $48 million in equity in Fox Film enabled it to sell $55 million in 1-year notes through Halsey Stuart and to pay off its defaulted bank and other short-term debts. A subsidiary, Wesco Theatres, was able to sell a further $10 million note for one year.

The financial burden was passed in this process to GTE, which had to come up with $15 million for the original stock purchase from William Fox and $35 million for the 1,160,000 Fox Film A shares. We have already noted GTE's recent and weak entry on the corporate scene. At this point its 1929 net income was only $2.5 million. Nonetheless, in April 1930 it was able to sell 617,000 shares of common stock at $40, to realize $23 million, and $30 million of 10-year 6% convertible debentures. Chase Securities was able to sell the $30 million convertible debentures by charging an unusually high underwriting fee of 9 1/2%.[29] Halsey, Stuart & Co. and Pynchon & Co. were less fortunate with GTE common stock, which they bought along with the 440,000 shares of Fox Film A Stock. Six months later they still held almost 600,000 shares of GTE and were in desperate straits to meet margin calls on the stock from the bankers lending against it.[30] GTE exchanged the common stock for preferred stock, which would be more marketable, to bail out the bankers in October 1930.

At the time of the Fox Film and GTE financings in April 1930 the stock market was at its recovery peak. However, the market was not strong enough to support this large amount of financing for two weak credits. The market was also more prone than before the Crash to look critically on the flimsy enterprise represented by GTE.

If 1930 was difficult, April 1931 was a disaster when the $65 million in Fox Film and Wesco Theatres 1-year notes matured. GTE had added $44 million to its debts during the intervening year, $6.4 million of which it incurred buying 177,000 Fox Film shares to support the market, and was no longer in a position to help the Fox companies' refinancing. The companies therefore turned to Chase National Bank, which had been an instigator of the GTE takeover and had lent GTE $15 million in 1930. Chase National Bank had added other loans related to the Fox takeover. Pynchon & Co. had come so close to bankruptcy in November 1930 that Chase National Bank had taken over an unknown amount of GTE securities in forgiveness of the loans against them, and Halsey, Stuart & Co. was simply refusing to pay on its Chase loans against GTE stock.

The 1931 Fox refinancing resulted in the financial burden finally being transferred to Chase National Bank, where it came to rest as in a game of poisonous musical chairs. The refinancing of the $65 million of Fox Film and Wesco notes was accomplished by the sale of $30 million Fox Film convertible debentures due in 1936, a subsidiary's sale of $10 million of 7% preferred stock and $20 million of 6% 2-year notes secured by the original 660,900 shares of Loew's which started all this trouble, and $15 million of 2-year Wesco notes. Virtually nothing in this package sold successfully. Underwriters were left holding $28.2 million of the $30 million Fox Film debentures, of which Chase Securities held $23.6 million. The market for the $15 million Wesco notes was so bad that no effort was made to sell them publicly, and Chase National Bank ended up with all $15 million. GTE bought the $10 million 7% preferred stock by borrowing the funds from Chase National Bank. The $20 million of 6% 2-year notes secured by the Loew's stock were never reoffered by the underwriters either. Western Electric took $8.5 million to satisfy its earlier loan to Fox Film. Chase Bank's share of the remaining syndicate liability was $4.4 million.

In the next two years GTE went bankrupt, the Fox companies were reorganized again, Pynchon & Co. went bankrupt along with several other members of the Fox-GTE syndicates, and Halsey, Stuart & Co. refused to pay Chase National Bank on the loans against GTE stock. Chase National Bank ended up with total exposure in loans, stocks, or bonds of GTE, Fox, or syndicate members in their issues of almost $90 million, of which it had written off $70 million by October 1, 1933, when questioned in the Pecora investigation. The losses destroyed the career of Albert Wiggin, Chase's Chairman. Chase National Bank's earnings and reputation were badly hurt. The whole affair was held up to public view as a model of self-dealing, speculative excesses, inadequate disclosure if not deception, influence peddling, bad management, and profiteering. In the evidence presented to the Senate committee investigating stock exchange practices in 1933, Chase National Bank appeared to have been in collusion with Harley Clarke of GTE for the personal profit of Albert Wiggin, and Halsey, Stuart & Co. and Clarke appeared to have conspired against William Fox, and the U.S. Justice Department was subject to outright manipulation.

Few abuses of the securities market were missed in the Fox-GTE drama. Underwriters formed pools to influence stock prices, insiders dealt heavily in their own stock, Chase National Bank underwrote poor securities to pay off its own loans, information was concealed or misrepresented, conspiracies were carried out, enormous fees were charged, assets were overvalued, and influential figures were enriched. Mysteriously, Loew's thrived through it all.

The Steel Industry

The fundamental weakness of the steel industry became clear in 1930 despite all the attention and power credited to such giants as U.S. Steel and Bethlehem Steel. Steel industry sales dropped from $8.7 billion in 1929 to $5.9 billion in 1930, beginning a trend that threatened to bankrupt the industry. By year end, production was down to 2 million tons per month, only 35% of capacity. Profits of the industry dropped from $409 million in 1929 to $189 million in 1930, as the leading companies averaged a return on equity of only 5.7%.[31] (See Table 5.14 for data on specific stock.)

The steel stocks were depressed in the general decline in stocks to only two-thirds of book value, which put them closely in line with other heavy capital goods industries such as the railroads, mining companies, tire manufacturers, oil companies, and farm equipment manufacturers. U.S. Steel cut its dividend modestly from $8.00 to $7.00, but otherwise all the companies kept up their dividends, and Inland Steel even increased its dividend. Nonetheless, the plight of Bethlehem Steel was symptomatic of the industry's future. Bethlehem Steel stock had dropped to 33% of book value and a dividend yield of 12.75% as investors anticipated a rough future. The high securities ratings and strong cash positions of the steel companies were both about to be liquidated.

The Automobile Manufacturers

As the economy declined in 1930, the automobile industry suffered quickly and more severely than other industries, reflecting a cyclicality present from the industry's infancy. Sales of cars and trucks were down almost 40% in 1930. The decline was only down to 1928 levels in the first five months, but after June 1930, production was only half the levels of 1928. The industry adapted quickly to cut costs—137,000 employees, one-quarter of the work force, were laid off, with 60,000 of the layoffs at General Motors, which eliminated its Marquette and Viking auto lines to cut costs. Despite such efforts, industry net income dropped from $359 million to $163 million and to a return on equity of 9.7%. (Table 5.15 gives data on specific auto industry stocks.)

General Motors, Ford, Nash Motors, and Packard coped reasonably well with the decline in business. Their profits remained at approximately half their 1929 levels. General Motors continued its regular $3.00 dividend and even made some small acquisitions. GM was not without pain, however; General Motors Acceptance Corp., its finance subsidiary, had over $200 million in short-term debt outstanding, and Moody's lowered the Aa rating on GM's preferred stock to A. Chrysler and Hudson Motors suffered worst. Their earnings were virtually eliminated, and both cut their dividend by $2.00.

The cyclical nature of the industry was reflected in its stocks, which sold down to prices averaging only 21% of their highest 1929 prices, the worst performance for any heavy industry. Chrysler's stock dropped to only 10% of its highest 1929 price. Dividend yields on the auto stocks were a heady 12.16%. Nonetheless, the stocks did receive some recognition for the dynamic future of the auto industry—at their lowest prices they averaged 111% of book value, which was approximately 65% higher than the other heavy capital goods industries.

Table 5.14
The Steel Industry in 1930

	Price-earnings ratio		Market price as a % of book value		Dividend yield (%)		Low price as a % of 1929 high price	Return on equity (%)	Moody's bond ratings	Cash & equivalents ($ millions)
	High price	Low price	High price	Low price	High price	Low price				
Bethlehem Steel	21	9	76	33	5.45	12.75	33	3.8	Aa	55
Inland Steel	18	11	175	104	4.08	6.90	51	9.6	Aa	11
U.S. Steel	22	15	98	66	3.50	5.20	51	4.7	Aaa pfd.	188
Youngstown Sheet & Tube	29	14	138	64	3.33	7.14	48	4.8	A	5
Averages	22.5	12.3	122	67	4.09	8.00	46	5.7	—	—

Table 5.15
The Automobile Industry in 1930

	Price-earnings ratio		Market price as a % of book value		Dividend yield (%)		Low price as a % of 1929 high price	Return on equity (%)	Moody's bond ratings	Cash & equivalents ($ millions)
	High price	Low price	High price	Low price	High price	Low price				
Chrysler Corp.	NM[a]	NM	165	54	2.30	7.15	10	0.2	NR[b]	42
General Motors	17	10	300	178	5.56	9.38	35	18.1	A pfd.	179
Hudson Motor Car	NM	NM	197	56	4.76	16.67	19	0.6	NR	14
Nash Motors	21	8	328	117	6.78	19.05	18	15.6	NR	38
Packard Motor Car	38	12	500	152	2.60	8.55	21	13.9	NR	19
Averages	25.3	10.0	298	111	4.20	12.16	21	9.7	—	—

[a] NM = Not Meaningful.
[b] NR = Not Rated.

The Consumer Products Companies

The popular wisdom following the Crash was that 1930 would be a year of economic stagnation principally because of consumer retrenchment, but the economic change had little impact on consumer goods companies. (Table 5.16 gives data on specific industry stocks.) Earnings gains among the consumer products companies were registered by Coca-Cola, Procter & Gamble, and Wm. Wrigley Jr. Co., and return on equity for the group as a whole averaged 28 1/2% (19.8% excluding Lambert Co.), which was the best of any industry group. Coca-Cola increased its dividend 50%, Colgate increased its dividend 25%, and Procter & Gamble increased its dividend 10%. Only Gillette Safety Razor Co. was in its own particular form of trouble. Most of the companies carried on business as usual in 1930, continuing their earlier pattern of acquisitions, as Gillette acquired AutoStrop Razor Co. Inc., Lambert acquired Prophy-lac-tic Brush Co., and Procter & Gamble acquired James S. Kirk & Co., a Chicago soap manufacturer, and Thomas Hedley & Co., an English soap manufacturer.

Investors treated the companies' stocks well also. Coca-Cola's stock price exceeded its highest 1929 price in the early 1930 recovery, and Wrigley's stock equalled its highest 1929 price. Then in the decline in stock prices which ensued, only Gillette's stock declined over 10% beyond its lowest 1929 stock price, and the stocks of Coca-Cola, Procter & Gamble, and Wm. Wrigley did not go below their lowest 1929 prices. The consumer products stocks at their lowest 1930 prices still averaged 12 times earnings per share, 319% of book value, a 6.25% dividend yield (excluding Gillette), and 60% of their highest 1929 prices (again excluding Gillette). These valuations provide interesting insight into what investors would pay for the most promising stocks during the lowest point in the market in 1930.

Gillette Safety Razor was an interesting exception to these generalizations. Gillette began production of the first safety razor in 1902, and by 1926 the company had 80% of the safety razor and blade market in the U.S. It was also firmly ensconced internationally, selling over one-third of its production abroad through 44 branch offices and agencies. Although Gillette's earnings had declined from $13.7 million in 1927 to $11.4 million in 1929, it was still realizing over 20% return on equity, and its stock was highly valued in early 1930 when it hit a peak price of $106 which was 460% of book value and over 30 times 1930 earnings per share.[32]

This fine performance had begun to unravel several years previously, however. Gillette's market share had peaked in 1926 and was declining rapidly due to very sharp price cutting by foreign and small domestic blade producers. The company was also threatened technologically by Henry J. Gaisman's AutoStrop Safety Razor Co. which had developed a two-edged razor blade which could be produced in continuous strips rather than individually sharpening each blade as Gillette had been doing for years. Gaisman had tried to sell the patent on his process to Gillette in 1928 for $5 million, but Gillette refused and then turned

Table 5.16
The Consumer Products Companies in 1930

	Price-earnings ratio		Market price as a % of book value		Dividend yield (%)		Low price as a % of 1929 high price	Return on equity (%)	Moody's bond ratings	Cash & equivalents ($ millions)
	High price	Low price	High price	Low price	High price	Low price				
Coca-Cola	17	12	764	532	3.14	4.51	74	25.6	Baa pfd.	10
Colgate-Palmolive-Peet	17	12	295	200	3.85	5.68	49	15.3	A pfd.	7
Eastman-Kodak	29	16	392	218	3.14	5.63	54	13.5	Aaa pfd.	36
Gillette	31	5	663	113	3.80	22.20	13	21.6	Baa	10
International Shoe	19	15	238	185	4.84	6.25	62	12.7	Aaa pfd.	28
Lambert Co.	12	7	1,027	645	7.08	11.27	45	89.4	NR[a]	5
Procter & Gamble	24	16	564	379	2.78	4.15	54	23.6	Aaa	16
Wm. Wrigley Jr.	13	11	352	283	4.94	6.15	80	26.6	NR	25
Averages	20.3	11.8	537	319	4.20	8.23	54	28.5	—	—

[a] NR = Not Rated.

around and copied him. Gaisman brought a patent suit against Gillette in April, 1929, and by July, 1930, Gillette was in such fear of losing the suit that it agreed to buy AutoStrop for 310,000 Gillette shares with a market value at the time of approximately $20 million.

Things rapidly went wrong from this point on. Gillette tried to buy the 310,000 shares of common stock in the open market through a pool organized by its New York investment banker and chairman, John Aldred, which entailed borrowing by selling $20 million of 5% convertible debentures. This tactic was confounded by an auditors' investigation of Gillette's books which revealed that its earning had been overstated by $12 million in the last 5 years by booking the profits on transfers to foreign subsidiaries before final sales occurred. The reversal of this practice was part of substantial write-offs in 1931, but at the moment it led to a renegotiation of the AutoStrop merger in October, 1930, substituting 310,000 5% convertible preferred shares with a market value of approximately $30 million for the 310,000 common shares previously agreed upon. Gillette had nonetheless retired 200,000 of its 2,200,000 common shares and assumed $20 million of convertible debt. The effect of the whole transaction was to reduce earnings per share by almost 15%, aside from the restatement of earnings. Gillette also had incurred a stockholders' suit for $21 million over the terms on which it bought its stock from the Aldred pool and other self-dealings by directors.

Gillette's stock was so severely depressed by its own affairs and the general market decline that it dropped to $18 versus a high price of $143 in 1929. At this price the stock was down 87% and was 113% of book value, compared with a decline of 40% and 349% of book value for the other consumer products companies. The dividend was reduced from $5.00 to $4.00 per share, and the current yield of almost 22% indicated a further reduction was expected.

In this difficult environment Henry Gaisman took over as chief executive of the company which had acquired him and promptly removed John Aldred, the prior chairman, Frank Fahey, the chief financial officer, and Thomas Pelham, the head of sales, from the executive committee. The next spring they were removed from the board of directors as well. Five AutoStrop executives became vice-presidents, and a new president was soon recruited from outside, Gerard B. Lambert, son of the founder of Lambert Co., another consumer products company. The new team took over the management of Gillette. Even the previous advertising agency, Batten, Barton, Durstine & Osborne, was fired as Gaisman brought in his own advertising firm, Detroit-based Maxon, Inc.

Unfortunately, neither the change in management, the change in manufacturing, nor the financial house-cleaning which took place in 1931 was able to turn around Gillette's fortunes. Gillette's share of the blade market had dropped from 80% in 1926 to 55% after the merger with AutoStrop under competition from blades as cheap as 1¢ versus 10¢ for a Gillette blade. By 1938 Gillette had only 20% of the blade market, despite repeated price reductions to as low as 2 1/2¢ for a Gillette blade.

The Retailers

Retail sales declined only 5%–10% in 1930, and accordingly retailers' operations and profits did not change greatly. The nine principal retailers averaged a satisfactory 11 1/2% return on equity, approximately the average for all companies. But this result masked the different trends among mail order stores, department stores, and five-and-tens. (See Table 5.17 for data on the specific companies.)

Mail order stores had a sharp decline in sales which amounted to over 25% for Montgomery Ward's mail order business. The company had a deficit for the year and eliminated its common stock dividend in November 1930, which knocked the stock down to only 10% of its highest 1929 price, one of the worst declines for any stock. Montgomery Ward's stock price was only 45% of its book value at the lowest price for 1930. Sears too was hard hit, as its earnings were cut in half and its stock dropped to 24% of its highest 1929 price, but Sears maintained its dividend and a 7% return on equity, which kept its stock price over book value. There was a wide gap between the results of the two companies.

The department stores had a lesser sales decline of approximately 8% in 1930, but earnings declined by one-third to one-half for most of the department stores, and their stocks were pushed down to approximately 25% of their highest 1929 prices, compared with the average for all stocks of 36%. The stock of Gimbel Brothers, which had a deficit in 1930 as it had in 1929, dropped to only 9% of its highest 1929 price. J. C. Penney cut its dividend, and Associated Dry Goods was expected to do so too, as it was not earning its dividend.

Sales of the five-and-ten stores declined only 3% in 1930, so these stocks did relatively well. Woolworth, which persistently shows up as one of the best companies of any type throughout the Depression, earned almost a 21% return on equity, and its stock at its lowest price was still 50% of its highest 1929 price and 3 1/4 times its book value. S. S. Kresge was less fortunate, earning a 12.6% return on equity, which was only slightly above the average for all companies of 11.6% in 1930, but Kresge's stock in 1930 declined to only 45% of its highest 1929 price, where it was still at 173% of book value. The strength of the five-and-ten stores was foreseen, as Moody's had previously rated Kresge's preferred stock Aaa.

The Tire Industry

The economic decline in 1930 hit especially hard on the tire companies, which had a 15% decline in sales and considerable profit problems as a result. The nine public companies reported a loss of $23 million, compared with profits of $29 million in 1929.[33] Both Firestone Tire & Rubber Co. and B. F. Goodrich Co. reported deficits for 1930 and cut their dividends, Firestone from $1.60 to $1.00 and Goodrich from $4.00 to zero. Goodyear earned $3.16 per share while

Table 5.17
The Retailers in 1930

	Price-earnings ratio		Market price as a % of book value		Dividend yield (%)		Low price as a % of 1929 high price	Return on equity (%)	Moody's bond ratings	Cash & equivalents ($ millions)
	High price	Low price	High price	Low price	High price	Low price				
Associated Dry Goods	25	9	170	63	4.90	13.16	27	6.7	Baa pfd.	8
Gimbel Brothers	def.[a]	def.	57	11	0	0	9	def.	B pfd.	6
S. S. Kresge	19	14	247	173	4.32	6.15	45	12.6	Aaa	11
R. H. Macy	33	17	338	174	1.89	3.66	32	10.2	NR[c]	2
Marshall Field	26	13	123	62	5.21	10.42	NA[b]	4.6	A	17
Montgomery Ward	def.	def.	152	45	0	0	10	def.	NR	28
J. C. Penney	28	10	500	175	6.88	19.64	27	17.9	A pfd.	12
Sears Roebuck	34	14	251	107	2.50	5.80	24	7.3	NR	(17)[d]
F. W. Woolworth	20	15	450	325	3.30	4.60	50	20.9	NR	17
Averages	26.4	13.1	254	126	3.22	7.05	28	11.5	—	—

[a] def. = Deficit.
[b] NA = Not Available.
[c] NR = Not Rated.
[d] Brackets indicate short-term borrowing.

paying a $5.00 dividend which was obviously in jeopardy. (Table 5.18 gives data on specific companies.)

The markets reacted quite violently to this decline in earnings and dividends because all the companies were highly leveraged with an average of less than 50% of their capitalization in common equity. All three stocks sold below book value at their lowest 1929 prices, where they averaged only 26% of their highest 1929 prices, compared with 36% for all stocks. Moody's dropped the ratings on the three companies' securities, rating Firestone's preferred stock a mere B, which represented a "speculative" security.

The Farm Equipment Industry

Farm equipment stocks had dramatic recoveries in early 1930; they all rose by an average of 140% to over double book value and a price-earnings ratio of 30. (See Table 5.19 for data on individual company stock.) Deere's stock, which rose to $163, even exceeded its highest 1929 price of $128. These companies had one of the better recoveries from the Crash for an industry group, but the optimism was dashed during the year as the combined impact of drought in the Midwest and sharply declining farm commodities prices cut into farm income and reduced farm equipment sales by 17%. Near the end of 1930, industry observers got an inkling from the low monthly sales levels of the decline in sales in 1931 to only one-third of 1929 sales. Such a dramatic decline threatened earnings and dividends, but it also affected liquidity, since the companies took back notes from their dealers for a substantial amount of dealer inventories. Notes receivable jumped from $25 million to $38 million at Deere, and all the companies increased their reserves for bad debts. Farm equipment companies' stock prices were pushed down to only 24% of their highest 1929 prices under these circumstances, and each of the stocks followed here sold well below book value. There were no dividend cuts or securities ratings reductions among the companies in 1930, but their stock prices accurately anticipated such events in 1931.

The Tobacco Companies

The year 1930 was an excellent one for the tobacco companies. Cigarette production and sales held up at their record 1929 levels, which was 50% above just five years ago, and other tobacco production declined only slightly. The manufacturers' raw tobacco costs dropped 50% during 1930, even as cigarette export prices rose 20% to a record of $2.43 per thousand. In this favorable environment, two of the three major companies had higher earnings per share and higher stock prices than in 1929, and the group averaged a remarkable 22.8% return on equity. Moody's reported that six cigarette companies had a record net income of $106 million.[34]

Tobacco stocks continued to perform well when the market decline set in

Table 5.18
The Tire Industry in 1930

	Price-earnings ratio		Market price as a % of book value		Dividend yield (%)		Low price as a % of 1929 high price	Return on equity (%)	Moody's bond ratings	Cash & equivalents ($ millions)
	High price	*Low price*	*High price*	*Low price*	*High price*	*Low price*				
Firestone	def.[a]	def.	114	52	3.03	6.67	41	def.	B pfd.	12
B. F. Goodrich	def.	def.	169	46	0	0	15	def.	Baa	10
Goodyear	31	11	269	97	5.15	14.29	23	8.8	Baa	37
Averages	NM[b]	NM	184	65	2.73	6.99	26	NM	—	—

[a] def. = Deficit.
[b] NM = Not Meaningful.

Table 5.19
The Farm Equipment Industry in 1930

	Price-earnings ratio		Market price as a % of book value		Dividend yield (%)		Low price as a % of 1929 high price	Return on equity (%)	Moody's bond ratings	Cash & equivalents ($ millions)
	High price	*Low price*	*High price*	*Low price*	*High price*	*Low price*				
J. I. Case	38	9	225	49	1.65	7.15	18	5.4	Baa pfd.	(4)[a]
Deere & Co.	27	5	326	58	0.74	4.14	23	12.2	Baa pfd.	(5)
International Harvester	25	10	215	83	2.15	5.55	32	8.6	Aa pfd.	30
Averages	30.0	8.0	255	63	1.51	5.61	24	8.7	—	—

[a] Brackets indicate short-term borrowing.

Table 5.20
The Tobacco Companies in 1930

	Price-earnings ratio		Market price as a % of book value		Dividend yield (%)		Low price as a % of 1929 high price	Return on equity (%)	Moody's bond ratings	Cash & equivalents ($ millions)
	High price	Low price	High price	Low price	High price	Low price				
American Tobacco	15	12	400	300	3.79	5.05	85	25.9	Aaa	29
Liggett & Myers	16	11	335	226	4.39	6.49	73	21.1	Aaa	33
Reynolds Tobacco	17	12	390	268	5.10	7.50	61	21.4	NR[a]	33
Averages	16.0	11.7	375	265	4.43	6.35	73	22.8	—	—

[a] NR = Not Rated.

during the second half of 1930. They declined to only 73% of their highest 1929 prices, compared with 36% for all stocks, and to only 265% of book value. There was no threat to the companies' earnings, dividends, or liquidity. Table 5.20 shows that the tobacco companies established themselves at this point as the soundest industry in this study and one of the most uniform.

The Pulp and Paper Industry

The pulp and paper companies established themselves in 1930 as the worst of America's heavy industries, as idle capacity for the year rose to an average of 31% and net income for 35 public companies fell from $26 million in 1929 to $15 million.[35] Most of the larger companies plunged into deficits. Their decline in business was doubly troubling for them because they were unusually highly leveraged. (Table 5.21 gives data on specific companies.)

Crown Zellerbach had only 25% of its capitalization in the form of common equity, and International Paper had only 13%, which was absurd for companies so weak competitively alongside the new Canadian pulp and paper mills. As a result, their stocks were very depressed. Crown Zellerbach's stock dropped to 17% of its highest 1929 price and only 30% of book value, and International Paper's stock dropped to 13% of its highest 1929 price and 17% of book value. The market anticipated that Crown Zellerbach would eliminate its dividend, since the stock yielded 23.53% at its lowest price. International Paper eliminated its dividend in 1930. Only Kimberly-Clark, which manufactured Kleenex tissues and Kotex, and a few of the smaller, more specialized paper manufacturers were able to operate profitably, but most of their stocks still sold below book value.

The Office Equipment Companies

Office equipment companies had a mixed experience in 1930 as reported net income fell from $44 million to $27 million.[36] IBM and Burroughs did well, as they earned approximately 20% returns on equity, and IBM even had improved earnings. But Remington Rand had almost no earnings, and National Cash Register and Underwood Elliott Fisher Co. had approximately 50% declines in earnings. (See Table 5.22 for data on specific companies.)

The office equipment stocks had been popular in 1929 when their highest stock prices had averaged 8 times book value, and they more than doubled in the early 1930 recovery in the stock market. Therefore, as market valuations became more realistic, the stocks with premium valuations were brought more into line. The stocks of Burroughs, National Cash Register, and Remington Rand fell an average of 80%, and their market-to-book-value ratios assumed a more reasonable relationship, as Table 5.22 shows.

IBM's stock performed better, dropping to only 51% of its highest 1929 price. This was partly due to IBM's 4% increase in earnings and the increase in its dividend from $5.00 to $6.00, but it was also a reflection of the lesser speculative

Table 5.21
The Pulp and Paper Industry in 1930

	Price-earnings ratio		Market price as a % of book value		Dividend yield (%)		Low price as a % of 1929 high price	Return on equity (%)	Moody's bond ratings	Cash & equivalents ($ millions)
	High price	Low price	High price	Low price	High price	Low price				
Crown Zellerbach	def.[a]	def.	136	30	5.26	23.53	17	def.	Ba	(6)[d]
International Paper	NA[b]	NA	97	17	0	0	13	def.	Baa	(26)
Kimberly-Clark	12	8	105	68	4.24	6.58	67	8.9	A	1
Averages	NM[c]	NM	113	38	3.17	10.04	32	NM	—	—

[a] def. = Deficit.
[b] NA = Not Available.
[c] NM = Not Meaningful.
[d] Brackets indicate short-term borrowing.

Table 5.22
The Office Equipment Companies in 1930

	Price-earnings ratio		Market price as a % of book value		Dividend yield (%)		Low price as a % of 1929 high price	Return on equity (%)	Moody's bond ratings	Cash & equivalents ($ millions)
	High price	*Low price*	*High price*	*Low price*	*High price*	*Low price*				
Burroughs Adding Machine	35	12	745	257	1.92	5.56	19	22.0	NR[b]	19
IBM	17	11	340	226	3.05	4.58	51	19.7	Aa	4
Remington Rand	NM[a]	NM	940	280	3.40	11.43	24	2.3	Ba	7
National Cash Register A	37	12	300	100	4.76	14.29	19	8.0	NR	—
Averages	26.0	11.5	675	254	2.79	7.19	31	14.7	—	—

[a] NM = Not Meaningful.
[b] NR = Not Rated.

activity in IBM's stock in the first place. While the other stocks had sold as high as 14 times book value in 1929, IBM's stock price was less than 5 times book value. By the end of 1930, the market valuations of IBM and Burroughs were remarkably similar for similar profit results.

Other Stocks

In 1930, General Electric opened a significant performance gap between itself and Westinghouse Electric. General Electric earned over 16% on its equity in 1930, while Westinghouse earned only 5.2%, and GE's stock price ranked as one of the best, at 680% of book value in the recovery and 300% of book value in December 1930; Westinghouse's stock price was below average, at 232% of book value in the 1930 recovery and only 101% of book value in December 1930. Westinghouse sank to 30% to its 1929 high price by December 1930, GE only to 42% of its 1929 high price. (See Table 5.23 for data on GE and Westinghouse.)

American Telephone & Telegraph Co. (AT&T) remained a strong company in 1930 (See Table 5.23.) It still had the largest capitalization and the largest short-term investment portfolio—$419 million on December 31, 1930. AT&T's return on equity of 6.7% was more reasonable than that of U.S. Steel, its competitor for size and public recognition, and the better earnings were reflected in AT&T's stock, which sold as high as 266% of book value and fell only as low as 165% of book value. It had declined to only 55% of its 1929 high by December 1930, compared with 36% for all stocks, and its yield was only 5.3%. Its $9 dividend was obviously expected to continue, even though earnings per share had dropped from $15.22 in 1929 to $10.26 in 1930. The dividend rate of $ 9.00 did continue right through the traumatic events of 1929–33.

American Can Co. was also a high quality stock (see Table 5.23). The company increased its 1930 earnings slightly to $8.08 per share, at which point it was earning a healthy 15.2% return on equity. Its stock was still at 57% of its 1929 high price and 210% of book value at its low price in 1930, and yielded only 4.75%. American Can was among the ten most active stocks from 1930 to 1933.

Radio Corp. of America (RCA) was able to consolidate its position in radios strongly in 1930 by consummating an accord with GE and Westinghouse to take over all their radio manufacturing facilities, licenses, and patents as well as their positions in National Broadcasting Co. and Victor Talking Machine and $32 million of RCA debt they accepted in the latter's acquisition. The price for this gain, however, was 6.6 million RCA shares split 60–40 between GE and Westinghouse and giving them combined control of 51.3% of the stock. This heavy dilution of existing stockholders and a sharp decline in RCA's sales from $177 million to $132 million, which produced a break-even year, put a damper on the stock. It recovered to only 60% of its highest 1929 price in the early part of 1930; then it was sold heavily later in the year down to only 10% of its highest 1929 price, compared with the average for all stocks of 36%. Moody's lowered

Table 5.23
Other Stocks in 1930

	Price-earnings ratio		Market price as a % of book value		Dividend yield (%)		Low price as a % of 1929 high price	Return on equity (%)	Moody's bond ratings	Cash & equivalents ($ millions)
	High price	Low price	High price	Low price	High price	Low price				
American Can	19	13	314	210	3.20	4.75	57	15.2	Aa pfd.	16
AT&T	27	17	266	165	3.30	5.30	55	6.7	Aaa	419
General Electric	48	21	680	300	1.25	2.85	42	15.9	Aaa	142
Radio Corp. of America	NM[a]	NM	1,062	169	0	0	10	0	Baa pfd.	16
Westinghouse	45	20	232	101	2.50	5.70	30	5.2	Aaa pfd.	32

[a] NM = Not Meaningful.

RCA's preferred stock rating from A to Baa as the preferred dividends became less secure. (See Table 5.23 for data on RCA.)

Summary

The themes which would distinguish among various industries during the Depression became clearer in the steep stock decline in the second half of 1930. In particular, the financial companies which had employed high leverage with apparent impunity in 1929 paid a heavy price for it in 1930. The holding company and investment trust stocks, which involved the greatest leverage through both senior securities and their pyramid structures, dropped to approximately 20% of their highest 1929 prices, compared with the average for all stocks of 36%. Goldman Sachs Trading Corp. became the first company to pay the price for its leverage as it was forced into liquidating major investments in Manufacturers Trust and several insurance companies. Troubles within the internal structure of financial markets began to reverberate when the Bank of United States failed and the most aggressive banks of the boom years began to have troubles. Companies with large short-term debts, particularly among the holding companies, but also among railroads and motion picture companies, began to be squeezed by their lenders, just when the public markets would not accept their permanent securities, which carved on the business mind for many decades the evils of short-term debt.

Most of the heavy industries suffered disproportionately in 1930. Auto production dropped to 50% of capacity, and auto stocks dropped to 21% of their highest 1929 prices, compared with the average for all stocks of 36%. Several heavy industries which had satisfactory earnings in 1929 suddenly registered deficits or virtually break-even levels of earnings in 1930 and were revealed to have much greater economic problems than anticipated. Railroad, steel, and tire companies fell into that group, and their stock prices dropped to two-thirds of book value, compared with the average for all stocks of 139%. The heavy, commodities-based industries, such as the oil, mining, farm equipment, and pulp and paper industries, had similar profit and stock price performances, and the companies' problems were exacerbated by sharp commodities prices declines and intense foreign competition with cheaper costs.

The industries which emerged in 1930 with small profit declines, or even profit increases, were less capital intensive and oriented toward consumers rather than business, as in the food, consumer products, and tobacco industries. These industries still had returns on equity of 20% or more, compared with the average of 11.6% and their stocks generally declined 50% or less from their highest 1929 prices. The chemical and operating public utility industries were not as profitable as these consumer-oriented industries, but were clearly stable, profitable industries whose stocks were undergoing a favorable reevaluation.

NOTES

1. *National Income Accounts*, p. 126.
2. *NYSE Year Book, 1938*, p. 71.
3. Ibid., p. 62.
4. New York Stock Exchange *Bulletin*, Volume 1, Number 1, April 1930, New York City: New York Stock Exchange, pp. 2–3; and *New York Times*, 12/21/29, p. 32.
5. *Stock Exchange Practices*, part 6, pp. 2839–42.
6. *New York Times*, 5/20/31.
7. Ibid., 6/5/31.
8. Ibid., 6/17/31.
9. *Stock Exchange Practices*, part 3, p. 1087.
10. Ibid., part 4, pp. 2160–61.
11. *Moody's Utility Manual, 1974*, p. a12.
12. *Statistical Abstract, 1939*, Table 381.
13. For a 250 kilowatt-hour user.
14. *Survey of Current Business*, May 1938, Table 57. (See also Table A.26 in the Statistical Appendix).
15. *Moody's Financial Manual, 1931*, p. 2615.
16. Ibid., p. 2629.
17. Ibid., *1932*, p. 2152. *Moody's* gives two values: $189 million or $12.24 per share if U.S. Electric Power Corp. is valued at book value, and $8.96 per share if U.S. Electric Power Corp. is valued at market value. I have extrapolated $8.96 per share to produce $138 million market value for the portfolio.
18. See *Moody's Railroad Manual, 1931*, and *Moody's Financial Manual, 1932*, under the names of each company.
19. *Stock Exchange Practices*, part 5, p. 2839.
20. *Moody's Financial Manual, 1974*, p. a45.
21. *Moody's Industrial Manual, 1931*, p. xxxvi.
22. Ibid., *1934*, pp. a10, a19.
23. *National Income Accounts*, pp. 142, 130; *Moody's Industrial Manual, 1935*, p. a45.
24. *New York Times*, 5/22/31.
25. *Moody's Industrial Manual, 1931*, pp. 3124, 3129.
26. *Stock Exchange Practices*, part 7, p. 3558.
27. Ibid., p. 3412.
28. Ibid., pp. 3587, 3605–6.
29. Ibid., p. 3442.
30. Ibid, part 8, pp. 3793–3800.
31. *National Income Accounts*, p. 142; *Moody's Industrial Manual, 1934*, p. a30; Ibid., *1935*, p. a45.
32. I am indebted to Russell B. Adams, Jr., *King C. Gillette The Man and His Wonderful Saving Device*, Boston: Little, Brown and Company, 1978 for background information on Gillette Safety Razor Co.
33. *Moody's Industrial Manual, 1935*, p. a45.
34. Ibid., *1933*, pp. a98-a99; Ibid., *1935*, p. a45.
35. Ibid., *1933*, p. a86; Ibid., *1935*, p. a45.
36. Ibid., *1935*, p. a45.

6

Bond Markets in 1930

The fixed income markets revived strongly following the Crash and began again to receive prominent investor attention after languishing in the background of the stock market in 1929. Call loan rates dropped from an average of 8 5/8% in September 1929 to 4 7/8% in December and to 2% by late 1930. The Federal Reserve's monetary policy was principally responsible for this decline. At the same time, however, rates in the long-term bond market changed very little during 1930. Aa utility bonds yielded approximately 5% in September 1929, 4 7/8% in December 1929, and 4 3/4% in December 1930. The volume of new bond issues rose sharply from the depressed levels of 1929, and foreign governments were able to borrow again, after being virtually shut out of the public debt market during 1929. This surge of financing lasted only into the summer, however, for thereafter the seriousness of the economic decline began to affect investors' judgments of creditworthiness. The volume of new issues in the last six months of 1930 shrank to half the level of the first six months, as many issuers, particularly foreigners, were unable to finance publicly. In the last half of 1930 the difference between yields on Baa and Aa utility bonds widened from 100 basis points to 180 basis points, and the difference between short-term and long-term interest rates reached 285 basis points, reflecting investor concern for safety and liquidity.

THE NEW ISSUE BUSINESS IS STRONG UNTIL CREDIT FEARS DEVELOP IN THE LAST QUARTER

The stability in long-term rates of high quality debt issuers during 1930 contrasted with the sharp decline in short-term rates. The slight changes in long-term bond rates during the year are evident in Table 6.1.

The volume of new bond issues for the first five months of 1930 averaged $643 million per month, which exceeded the monthly averages of bond financing

Table 6.1
Yields on High Quality Long-Term Bonds, 1929–1930

	December 1929	December 1930
U.S. governments	3.36%	3.22%
Aa utilities	4.87	4.74
Aa railroads	4.74	4.85
Aa industrials	4.84	4.85
High grade municipals	4.22	4.05

Sources: *Banking & Monetary Statistics*, p. 469–470, Moody's Utility Manual 1974, p. a7, Moody's Railroad Manual 1972, p. a51, Moody's Industrial Manual 1974, p. a51.

in both 1928 and 1929. Corporate and municipal bonds accounted for the bulk of this financing. Corporate bond issues rose to levels of $300–$400 million per month, which compared with the highest levels ever achieved in the past, and municipal issues rose to $100–$150 million per month, typical of the steady volume which had prevailed in the municipal market for years. Within the corporate bond sector, public utilities issued the largest volume, including a record $569 million in May, but railroads and industrials issued almost as much.

Holding and investment companies were able to raise over $230 million publicly in the first 9 months of 1930. Samuel Insull, the Chicago-based head of a sprawling nation-wide utility empire, took advantage of the good market to have his Chicago investment banker, Halsey, Stuart & Co., sell $60 million of 6% 10-year debentures for Insull Utility Investments. Corporation Securities Co. of Chicago, another Samuel Insull company, raised $34.4 million through yet another Insull company, Utility Securities Co., by selling 1 1/4 million common shares. The Van Sweringen brothers also arranged longer term funding for their holding company structure set up to control the Chesapeake and Ohio Railway Co. They had Alleghany Corp. raise $37.5 million in March through issues of 5% 20-year convertible debentures and 5 1/2% preferred stock with warrants. The next month Van Sweringen Corp. sold $30 million of 6% 5-year notes with warrants, and in June a Van Sweringen Corp. subsidiary sold a $10.5 million mortgage on the Cleveland Terminals Building which dominated downtown Cleveland.

The volume of new corporate bond issues declined in June 1930 in conjunction with the decline in stock prices, and thereafter the trend in corporate bond market conditions followed the stock market closely. Corporate long-term debt issues were only $648 million in the last half of 1930, barely one-quarter of the volume in the first half of 1930. The volume of financing was halved for railroads and foreign issuers, and bond issues for holding and investment companies were soon eliminated.

The last quarter of 1930 witnessed the beginnings of changes in the bond markets which were part of the secular trends of the ensuing years. The most marked trend was the spread that developed between yields on high quality Aa bonds and Baa bonds in all industries. Aa bond yields rose approximately 1/4% during the last quarter to between 4 3/4% and 5%, but Baa rates rose approximately 1%, so that the resulting Baa debt rates were approximately 2% above Aa utility rates, compared with an historic difference of approximately 1%.

An emphasis on quality in the last quarter produced this spread between Aa and Baa bonds and resulted in a long list of deferred issues at the end of the year. Halsey, Stuart & Co., one of the largest, most successful bond houses, said in its market letter that bond buyers' temperaments were such that they would buy only gilt-edged bonds with high liquidity; buyers lacked confidence in their own judgment and would not look at issues outside the best class. Because of this attitude, even yields on A-rated issues began to diverge sharply from yields on Aa-rated issues.

A reappraisal of the quality of railroad bonds began at this time, although the impact was slight and focussed on the smaller bond issues. Railroad bonds had been considered the premier investment because of their security (often specific trackage) and economic importance. Railroad bonds traded at yields 5–30 basis points below yields on comparably rated utility bonds, and carried more Aaa and Aa ratings than any other industry. However, the poor profit performance of the railroad industry, and its problems with regulatory restrictions and competition, which bedevilled railroad common stocks, now initiated doubts about the general creditworthiness of the industry. Traffic and earnings declined so sharply in the second half that some railroads were expected no longer to qualify as legal investments for New York savings banks because the railroads could not meet the test of earning their fixed charges 1 1/2 times. Railroad financing in the last quarter of 1930 was only $27 million, the lowest quarterly volume since 1924.

Many railroads wanted to issue bonds. They had extended themselves after the Crash to provide construction work to bolster the economy—"Bulwarks of the Economy" the *New York Times* called them—and now there were many railroads with significant short-term debt, but the market would not absorb their bonds. The Erie, Missouri Pacific, and New York Central were publicized examples of railroads that could not sell securities. Railroads issued only $145 million in securities in the last five months of 1930, compared with $882 million in the prior seven months of the year. Concern over how the railroads would handle their 1931 debt maturities began to grow, and suggestions were made that the federal government should make special loans to the industry to ease its liquidity problems.

The gradualness of investors' reactions to the railroad's problems is surprising, however. Moody's did not reduce the rating of any large railroad bond issues during 1930, and railroad issues traded at lower yields on average than comparably rated utility and industrial bonds. Our knowledge after the event of the decline in railroad credit during the Depression naturally leads us to foresee this trend in the last quarter of 1930, but it was a gradually developing realization that was evident only in the bond issues of the smaller railroads and in the new-issue market at this time.

This gradual development of quality perceptions was also evident in other sectors of the corporate bond market. As in the railroad industry, Moody's did not reduce any large utility or industrial bond ratings during 1930, and the large utility and industrial issues in the appendix generally traded within a compact yield range for each bond rating and within the traditional yield ranking of railroads lowest, utilities second, and industrials third. The bonds of several weaker oil companies, such as Royal Dutch Co., Shell Union Oil Corp., and Pure Oil Co., were alone in diverging to prices sharply below other comparably rated bonds because of the sharp decline in crude oil prices and therefore in income.

The emphasis on quality by bond investors had a favorable impact on U.S. Treasury bond prices. U.S. Treasury bond prices began hitting new highs in June 1930, just as the stock and bond markets turned down, and moved up another dollar by November while prices of Baa issues wilted. (See Table A.40). U.S. issues were aided in their price movement by a federal budget surplus of $225 million for the fiscal year ending June 30, 1930, and budget plans for a surplus for fiscal 1931, including public debt retirements of over $400 million. The Administration was committed politically and emotionally to a strong bond market, which helped the government bond market, if nothing else. Secretary Mellon and his Deputy Secretary of the Treasury, Ogden Mills, repeated frequently that economic recovery was dependent on a strong bond market in which the capital for expansion would have to be raised. They returned repeatedly to this point when demands arose for public works spending, deficit financing of welfare, or immediate cash redemption of the Veterans' Bonus Bonds awarded soldiers at the end of World War I.

THE DEMISE OF THE FOREIGN BOND MARKET

The United States had been a debtor nation throughout its history until World War I turned it into a creditor nation, and the 1920s saw the center of international finance shift from London to New York. Table 6.2 shows that international securities issues in New York became approximately five times those in London. The foreign bond market was divided into issuers from Canada, Western Europe, South America, and Eastern Europe in that rough order of acceptability to U.S. investors and therefore in order of ascending interest rates.

Investors treated Canadian bond issuers as if they were part of the United States, as indeed they were for purposes of raising capital, since the domestic Canadian bond market had not yet developed. The government of Canada, the provinces of Ontario and Quebec, and Canada's principal cities, Montreal and Toronto, were rated Aaa by Moody's, and all the remaining provinces were rated Aa. The yields on Government of Canada bonds were right in line with

Table 6.2
International Securities Issues, 1925–1930 ($ millions)

	New York	London
1925	$1,316	$164
1926	1,361	272
1927	1,738	379
1928	1,583	349
1929	785	168
1930	1,147	334

Sources: New York data is from *Survey of Current Business*, February 1938, pp. 16–17. London data is from Ilse Mintz, *Deterioration in the Quality of Foreign Bonds Issued in the United States, 1920–1930*, National Bureau of Economic Research Publication No. 52, New York: National Bureau of Economic Research, 1951, p. 19.

the lowest corporate yields in the market, and lesser Canadian governments were so well received that they were able to bid their bonds competitively.

All the countries of Western Europe and the United Kingdom had dollar-denominated bond issues after the war. They were rated either Aaa or Aa by Moody's in 1929 and 1930, and their bonds traded at yields 1/2%–1% higher than comparably rated railroad bonds.

Bond issues by South American governments were surprisingly well received in the U.S. market. Argentine bonds were rated Aa by Moody's, which also gave an A bond rating to Buenos Aires, Chile, Cuba, Peru, Rio Grande do Sul, and Uruguay. Bolivia, Brazil, Colombia, and Rio de Janeiro were rated Baa, which still implied investment quality in contrast to speculative securities. Rates on these bonds were only 1%–2% over comparably rated domestic corporate issues when optimism prevailed.

The weakest market reception was for bonds of East European countries. Only Austria and Czechoslovakia were rated A by Moody's. Bulgaria, Hungary, Poland, and Rumania were rated Baa, while Yugoslavia was rated Ba. Their bonds traded at yields slightly higher than similarly rated South American bonds, because these newly created East European countries were considered politically unstable and economically truncated.

South American and East European bond issues made up the outer fringe of the foreign bond market. Many South American issues were based on the pledge of toll road or customs revenues, commodities receipts, or similar revenue flows to service the issues. The East European issues were frequently sponsored by the League of Nations to promote reorganization of Europe's finances, although no guarantee by the League was implied. The speculative nature of these issues was evident in the fees paid to the brokerage houses selling them of 7% to 8 3/4%. These fees compared with 1 1/2%–2% for domestic issues and 2 1/2%–4% for the more creditworthy foreign issues.[1]

The willingness of both brokers and investors to deal in these lesser bonds is understandable, however, for international trade and financial conditions on which these credits depended had improved throughout the decade. There had been an almost uninterrupted increase in U.S. exports and imports of goods and services annually since 1923. Exchange rates for virtually every South American and East European country were either stable or up from 1925 onward, once the major West European countries had stabilized their currency rates. Since 1927, commodities prices had been unusually stable for metals, meats, cotton, wool, lumber, and oil, with only tin and rubber prices dropping sharply (mostly affecting Bolivia and Brazil), and those being offset by a sharp rise in copper prices from 14¢ a pound to 18¢. Gold reserves were stable in most countries, and up dramatically since 1925 in the Argentine (from $450 million to $600 million), Brazil (from $54 million to $150 million), France (from $700 million to $1,600 million), and Germany (from $288 million to $650 million). Only Canada and Australia lost gold between 1925 and 1929, but they backed their currencies with pounds or dollars. It was a remarkable period in which everyone gained and none lost because of a worldwide expansion in gold reserves from $9 billion to $10 billion.[2] The international financial mechanisms worked to redistribute savings, and there was concerted international action through the League of Nations to keep the machinery running smoothly, as in the cases of the League loans for Eastern Europe and the Dawes and Young plans to assist Germany's external finances. U.S. private income on investments abroad rose every year after 1921 from approximately $400 million to almost $1 billion in 1929.[3]

During the Depression, many of these countries defaulted on their U.S. bond issues, and the outcry against the brokers who had handled them was intense, but the brokers were judged under later, changed conditions, much different from the optimism which prevailed when the issues were undertaken. Indeed, there would have been an earlier outcry around the world against these same brokers had they not been willing to handle these foreign bond issues, for U.S. gold reserves had tripled between 1914 and 1922 and accounted for almost half the world's gold reserves; in addition, the United States had a steady $1 billion annual balance of payments surplus during the 1920s which had to be recycled back to the rest of the world so that the system would not break down.

In the 1920s the international financial system was working adequately in that the shift had been smoothly made from London to New York as the center of export capital and that American wealth was being successfully channelled into the debtor countries of Europe and South America. But underneath this satisfaction lurked widespread concern that the system was inherently unstable because of the financial arrangements that came out of the world war. France and Great Britain were heavily in debt to the United States, and they insisted on assessing Germany with reparations payments sufficient to repay the United States and to assist in restoring their own economies. At the same time, France wanted to keep Germany too weak to recover its dominant position on the

Table 6.3
International Gold Reserves at Year End, 1926–1930 ($ millions)

	1926	1927	1928	1929	1930
Argentina	$ 451	$ 529	$ 607	$ 434	$ 412
Belgium	86	100	126	163	191
France	711	954	1,254	1,633	2,100
Germany	436	444	650	544	528
Italy	224	242	266	273	279
Netherlands	167	161	175	181	172
Spain	493	502	494	495	471
Switzerland	91	100	103	115	138
U.K.	729	737	748	710	718
U.S.	4,083	3,977	3,746	3,900	4,225

Source: Banking & Monetary Statistics, pp. 544, 545, 550–51.

Continent. As J. M. Keynes pointed out when he resigned from the team sent by Britain to the Versailles Treaty conferences, the two goals of high reparations and a weak Germany were incompatible, since reparations could be earned only by a strong German export performance.

The three countries followed quite different courses during the 1920s:

— Britain tried to restore the pound sterling to its previous parity of $4.86 (U.S.) in order to regain its old glory and the City of London's position as the world's financial center. This parity relationship was now seriously overvalued, however.

— France manipulated the exchange rate for the franc and then pegged it at an artificially low level of 125 francs to the pound in order to gain a competitive trade advantage.

— Germany tried to rebuild its economy and to pay its reparations debts, borrowing wherever it could (mostly in London and the United States) to permit both to go on together.

England's economy was constrained to slow and sporadic growth in the 1920s by its financial policies. In 1926 the exchange rate was reestablished with the aid of a $200 million loan to the Bank of England led by J. P. Morgan & Co., and thereafter England had a constant problem maintaining adequate reserves. They usually hovered around $700 to $800 million, in contrast to U.S. gold reserves, which were over five times as large, and French gold reserves, which grew to be three times as large starting from the same base in 1926. Table 6.3, showing reserve data for major countries, is helpful at this point because of the importance that international financial problems later assume.

No other country had returned to its prewar exchange rate, but in England even those aware of the handicap this rate would place on British industry favored it. Reginald McKenna, who had once served as Chancellor of the Exchequer and who foresaw the results of returning to the old parity, told Winston Churchill in 1926 that he had no choice but to reestablish the old rate. There was a widespread conviction that London's financial reputation was tied up with restoring the old parity.

Ironically, England's role as a center of world finance was frustrated by the policy statesmen thought necessary to that end, for the overvaluation of sterling prevented the growth of an adequate foreign trade surplus to lend abroad, and the poor economy fostered the success of the Labour Party, which held office twice in the period 1926–1931. Investors doubted the Labour Party's desire and ability to maintain England's financial role. These effects combined to render the English capital markets highly unstable, so that bond issues were often impossible and New York replaced London as the center for raising international capital.

The greatest source of instability in the international financial system was Germany which had built up massive international short-term debts that it could not service. Germany had a reparations burden equivalent to $28.7 billion (59 payments of $487 million each under the Young Plan), it lacked foreign exchange reserves, the savings of individuals had been wiped out by hyperinflation in the early 1920s, and the rest of Europe so feared a rebirth of German militarism that it was unwilling to participate in any plan that restored Germany's productive might. Since hyperinflation and reparations payments eliminated domestic savings, both German industry and government were forced to borrow abroad, which was fostered by the German federal government to raise the foreign currency necessary for reparations. German politics alternated between trying to make the reparations payments and giving in to popular resentment at the limitation which reparations placed on domestic prosperity. The popular sentiment was fanned by Hitler and gained prominence at every election. These problems prevented long-term foreign financing by German issuers on any large scale, as a result of which Germany built up massive floating short-term debts, principally to London and New York banks. The instability of these short-term debts twice threw Germany's financing into disarray, first in 1925, after which Charles Dawes led an effort to restructure the country's finances, and again in 1929, when a committee chaired by Owen D. Young (Chairman of General Electric Company, a director of the Federal Reserve Bank of New York, a Wall Street professional, and a prominent, responsible political leader) worked out a new plan. Germany's economic relations with Austria, Bulgaria, Hungary, Poland, Rumania, and Yugoslavia were so fundamental to their prosperity that Germany's problems carried over into these countries, not to mention the problems they suffered from the fragmentation of the Austro-Hungarian Empire into small nations with disrupted historic economic relations.

Foreign bonds had some noticeable problems in 1929. Yields on Aaa foreign issues ranged between 5% and 5 1/2%, which was only 1/2% above Aaa railroad bonds, but whereas lesser rated domestic bonds right down to Baa rated issues carried yields within 1/2% of Aaa railroad bonds, the lesser-rated Aa and A foreign issues bore yields up to 2% higher than Aaa foreign bonds, and the Baa rated foreign bonds yielded up to 5% more. Foreign securities issues in the United States dropped in half from $1.6 billion in 1928 to $0.8 billion in 1929 because of heavy flow of domestic funds into stocks and call loans. Foreign government issues within these totals, as distinct from foreign corporate issues, were cut even further, from $0.7 billion to $0.1 billion. Charles E. Mitchell, Chairman of National City Bank of New York, described the market for foreign bonds in the months before the Crash as one of outright hostility.

The failure of the U.S. market to accept foreign bond issues provided considerable embarrassment for many countries. Some had debt maturities they had anticipated refunding. Many countries had initiated large capital plans in the expectation that the funds would be available. U.S. investment bankers had solicited foreign business aggressively in 1927 and 1928, encouraging foreign governments to believe that large loans were possible in New York. The stock boom, however, drew from the bond market the speculative funds which would have been invested in foreign bonds (an hypothesis suggested by Ilse Mintz in *Deterioration in the Quality of Foreign Bonds*). The New York banks advanced short-term loans to issuers under these circumstances or took a large share of short-term public debt issues. The U.K. market was too weak to provide an alternative source of funds. During the first half of 1930 the general resurgence of interest in bond investments pushed foreign bond prices up to or higher than their highest prices in 1929. Aaa foreign bond yields were generally under 5%, and A bond yields were under 6 1/2% (see Table A.15 in the Statistical Appendix). This bond market recovery gave foreign issuers access to the U.S. bond market again. The first foreign government long-term debt issue in 1930 was $40 million of 5 1/2% 15-year A rated bonds for Cuba in February through Chase Securities, after which there was a surge of foreign borrowing. The Cuban issue subsequently became infamous when the Pecora investigation into stock exchange practices revealed the circumstances of the issue. The proceeds were used to refund $30 million of Cuban notes and serial bonds held by Chase National Bank and other banking members of the syndicate. The banks appeared to have an unseemly interest in refunding their own loans and earning the underwriting fees of almost $1.75 million, to the point that the offering circular made no mention of Cuba's budget deficit or difficulties in servicing the debt.

Foreign government issues exceeded $100 million per month for April–June 1930, and a number of significant issues were made in that period. Chile sold $25 million of A rated bonds to yield 6.7% through National City Co. in April. The State of São Paulo, Brazil, sold $35 million to yield 7.58% through Speyer & Co. the same month. In May, Japan sold $50 million of Aa rated 35-year bonds to yield 6.20% through J. P. Morgan & Co., and Uruguay sold $17.6 million of A rated 34-year bonds to yield 6.14% through Hallgarten & Co.

Two other major issues were handled by J. P. Morgan & Co. In 1929, Morgan began behind the scenes to raise $200 million or more for Germany as part of the Young Plan reorganization of Germany's finances. This issue hung over the foreign bond market for six months, preventing other German issues for local governments and corporations until, in June 1930, Morgan led a five-nation syndicate offering $98.5 million of the bonds to yield 6.20% (then a high rate). The amount of $98.5 million was the most that could be raised. In the meantime, Germany's most prominent financier, Hjalmar Schacht, resigned in protest from the presidency of the Reichsbank. The attitude toward Germany's bonds under such conditions was, as a Rothschild representative remarked, ''No one wants any.'' Richard Whitney bought $9.2 million of the issue on the NYSE in 20 days' bidding for the syndicate to sustain the issue. Morgan also raised $25 million at 7.43% for Aa rated Austria in July. Austria's issue marked the end of significant foreign financing in the United States for a decade.

The foreign bond market prospered during the first half of 1930 as investors moved out of stocks into bonds and interest rates declined. The visible decline in economic activity was expected, and not yet prolonged enough or severe enough to raise fundamental doubts about the creditworthiness of either domestic or foreign bond issuers. During the course of the year, however, South American countries were particularly affected by a 25% decline in U.S. foreign trade and declines of over 40% in the prices of copper, cotton, tin, and rubber, which cut sharply into the export revenues of South American countries.

Hope for recovery in international trade and commodities prices was doomed in June 1930, when Congress passed the Smoot-Hawley Tariff bill and Hoover made clear that he would sign it. The bill raised tariffs by 20%. Canada and Europe responded immediately with countervailing tariffs, at first in an effort to provide bargaining tools which could force the United States to rescind the increases, but ultimately in the spirit of an eye for an eye and a tooth for a tooth.

This combination of economic decline and the Smoot-Hawley Tariff bill raised such fundamental questions about the creditworthiness of the less-developed nations that their access to the U.S. bond market was virtually shut off. Non-Canadian foreign corporate and government issuers sold only $64 billion in securities in the last five months, compared with over $579 million in the first seven months.[4] The only long-term foreign issue in the last four months of 1930 was $1.9 million for Bergen, Norway, even though New York investment bankers were besieged with demands for loans from foreign governments, particularly from countries dependent on revenues from commodities exports.

The best that foreign issuers, except Canada, could achieve in these circumstances was to sell short-term debt. Argentina sold $50 million of 1-year notes in September at 4 5/8%; the Argentine province of Córdoba sold $4.5 million of 6-month notes in November at 6%; Bremen sold $1 million of 3-month notes privately in September; Hungary sold $5 million of 1-year notes at 5 3/4% in November. Even short-term bank borrowing was difficult. Right at the end of the year the Chatham-Phenix National Bank & Trust refused to extend a $16 million loan to Buenos Aires for six months, although Central Hanover Bank & Trust Co. ultimately led a syndicate which made the loan indirectly through

Banco de la Nación, the Brazilian central bank. Colombia was able to borrow only $20 million from a National City Bank group after it put its house in order by revamping customs, raising railroad rates, and balancing its budget.

Mexico, which was already in default and negotiating with a bondholders' committee headed by Thomas Lamont of J. P. Morgan & Co., was unable to rearrange its finances because of declining commodities prices and so continued to pile up debt service payments in pesos in blocked accounts in anticipation of future availability of foreign exchange.

Economic and financial problems were quickly translated into social problems in South America. In September there was a revolt in Chile and a revolution in Argentina. In October a rebel coup in Brazil succeeded, during which the banks were closed for 15 days. During the fourth quarter of 1930, Moody's lowered Peru's bond rating to Baa and the ratings of Bolivia, Brazil, and Venezuela to Ba, but the market was far ahead of these changes in bond ratings. Peru's bonds had dropped from a high price of $90 in 1929 to $33 in 1930, and the bonds of Bolivia, Brazil, Rio de Janeiro, and Rio Grande do Sul had all dropped well below $50 from high prices between $90 and $100 in 1929 (see Table A.15 in the Statistical Appendix). Such prices represented investors' expectations of extended difficulties for these issuers. This story would be repeated in several major categories of bond issuers during the Depression, as economic events proved to be more overwhelming than the rating agencies were able to anticipate. For many countries and industries the rating agencies were clearly willing during good times to accord them higher ratings than were justified in difficult times.

While South America was actively in the throws of crisis, in Europe the crisis was still brewing. The $98.5 million that J. P. Morgan & Co. had raised for Germany was an insignificant contribution toward eliminating Germany's short-term debt, which exceeded $3 billion at this point. Within three months rumors originated in Germany that it would have to renegotiate its external debts. The Reichsbank raised the Reichsbank rate from 4% to 5% in October to retain short-term funds, and Hitler was again creating a domestic problem for the governing Social Democrats in both the Reichstag and the local elections. German capital fled to Paris and New York, and by the end of the year Germany's gold reserves had dropped from $675 million to $528 million. In November, Dr. Julius Curtius, Reich Foreign Minister, announced that the Reich was considering suspending reparations payments. The price of the recent German bond issue dropped to $68.

A financial crisis simmered in Britain apace with Germany's, albeit on a lesser scale. Britain had a current account deficit in foreign trade, British business was dour, and unemployment was its highest since 1922. When Philip Snowden, Labour Party Chancellor of the Exchequer, raised taxes in April 1930 to meet a budget deficit principally due to the cost of welfare payments, there was a flight from the pound in which Great Britain lost $55 million in gold, mostly to France, within a month. The British securities markets were completely distracted and unable to sustain new issues. The summer brought relief from the massive gold outflow, but the drain continued on a lesser scale. In the fall, Britain echoed Germany's complaints that reparations payments needed to be renegotiated.

Thus, the international scene was unsettling at the close of 1930. Britain and Germany appeared to be encumbered by their historic inheritances. Eastern Europe was weakened by dependence on Germany and artificial boundaries which disrupted historic economic ties. France pursued a lonely, selfish way accumulating gold, and the United States sought to isolate itself from the old world in a self-contained market. The South American countries were impoverished by declining commodities export revenues and doomed to no recovery by the trade policies of the great powers. Revolutions of the right or left were growing out of the resulting social conditions around the world. None of the participants was aware of it, but the foreign bond market in the United States was about to close for a generation.

MUNICIPAL BOND PRICES RISE UNTIL CREDIT FEARS DEVELOP IN THE LAST QUARTER

Municipal bonds and municipal governments appeared to enjoy a hearty revival in 1930. Municipal bond prices rose from January through October by a total of $5–$7 until the best bonds yielded 3 3/4%, compared with a previous high yield of 4% or more. Virtually all municipal bonds participated in the price rise, and yields on the whole range of state and major city credits were within a relatively tight range of 3 3/4% to 4 1/2% all year (see Table A.16 in the Statistical Appendix). New issues during the year were a steady $1.5 billion, closely in line with prior years. Municipal governments in general took a prideful role in accelerating construction budgets to offset any lag in the economy due to the Crash. State and local government employment rose from 2 1/2 million persons to 2.6 million and was backed up by an 8 1/2% increase in revenues. There were exceptions to this pattern, but there appeared to be clear reasons for the exceptions.

Most cities in Florida had defaulted on their bonds because they had overbuilt community services in anticipation of a population surge that did not materialize. The Florida land business had boomed and collapsed in 1925–26, leaving behind it acres of half-developed property which the finances of the communities involved could not support. Miami finally defaulted in May 1930 to complete the Florida denouement.

Chicago and Cook County were also in trouble, mostly because of irresponsible municipal government structures and management. There were eight major governments within Cook County—the county itself, the City of Chicago, the Chicago School Board, the Sanitary District, the County Preserve District, South Park District, Lincoln Park District, and West Park District—as well as 418 small taxing bodies in the county. Political responsibility was diluted in the extreme, administration was unwieldly, and taxing powers had been stymied by a successful taxpayer resistance to taxes in the courts on the basis of faulty assessments. The City of Chicago had floated a high rate 6% 1-year note issue in 1929 to meet current expenses, and when the banks refused to handle further issues, the city borrowed from its building fund to pay teachers in December 1929 and got Commonwealth Edison Co. to advance its tax payments to the city. In January 1930, Silas H. Strawn, the prominent head of the First National Bank of Chicago, declared publicly that "Chicago and Cook County are broke," although this was hyperbole since the city's bonds did not yield over 4.40% during the year and it had not defaulted. It was, however, four to six weeks behind in wages due to civic employees.

There were emerging signs of fiscal problems in local governments beyond Florida and Cook County late in the year as the pressures of a declining economy and rising welfare burdens converged on city governments, and drought and declining commodity prices squeezed rural economies. In Detroit, where unemployment was high and tax arrears mounting, the city lost access to the public market during much of the year. Senator James Couzens and Edsel Ford combined at one point to buy $5 million of the city's bonds to help it carry on. New York City had to raise its tax rate 10% and undertake a private charity drive that raised $5 million for the unemployed. In the South, Mississippi was rumored likely to default, and there was a strong disposition in the Democratic legislature to let it do so. Mississippi, too, was behind in paying public employees' wages. The state banking system was in such disarray that the risk of default was increased. Neighboring states of Arkansas, Louisiana, and Tennessee were also having financial troubles, and the bonds of this group bore the highest yields among the states by the end of the year—4.50% to 4.85%. Such yields reflected anticipations of credit strains rather than serious default situations, but the rapidly declining agricultural situation took much of the control of events out of the hands of these rural states.

In the last two months of the year, municipal bond prices generally declined $2 1/2 to $5 as the economic problems were reflected throughout financial markets.

SUMMARY OF 1930

The year 1930 began with optimistic faith in the nation's power of economic recovery and confidence in the policies of the Hoover Administration and the Federal Reserve System. These policies fueled the rise in the stock and bond markets and led to record-low short-term interest rates of 2%. But 1930 ended in a tone of dismal pessimism with the economy apparently heading into a period of permanently reduced prosperity. England and Germany, two of the world's leading nations, appeared politically and financially unstable. Lesser countries in Eastern Europe and South America appeared to be plunging into chaos. International trade was declining sharply, and commodities prices were at their lowest points in the century. At home, the Dow Jones Industrial average closed December 31st at 164, less than half its 1929 high of 381. Other stock indices were equally depressed. Volume on the New York Stock Exchange had contracted from the regular 3- and 4-million share days of 1929 to an average of barely 2 million shares per day. Everything else financial appeared to have contracted as well. Call loans shrank from $8.5 billion at their peak in 1929 to $1.9 billion in December 1930. New-issue markets contracted, especially for common stocks and the debts of issuers judged to be risky—investment trusts, holding companies, railroads, and most foreign issuers. Bond rates for the best issuers had not changed much, but the definition of the best issuers was changing from the railroads to the utilities. Bond rates for riskier issuers had begun to diverge sharply from the best issuers. Many foreign issues outstanding sold at prices that reflected anticipated default.

The nation's institutions appeared to be at a loss to cope with the impending crisis which the securities markets reflected. The Hoover Administration had exhausted its resources in exhorting business and local initiative to solve the employment problem. The Administration was determined to balance its budget and equally determined not to destroy federal credit by assuming the burden of unemployment relief which was breaking England. Its one strong step was the adoption of an unwise tariff policy. Banks were closing at a record rate, not just in the South and West, where small banks were exposed to the vicissitudes of local economies, but in New York as well, where the Bank of United States had just been declared insolvent. Bankers were suspected of holding many frozen foreign, real estate, railroad, and investment loans and acted as if this were the case in their search for safety and liquidity in the short-term market, even though long-term yields were 3 to 4 times short rates.

It is a testimony to the optimism of Americans that at the end of 1930 probably a majority of those in finance and business were predicting that there would be an economic recovery in 1931 despite this multitude of problems. Economists' predictions at the American Economics Association annual meeting in Chicago over the year end were heavily weighted toward a 1931 economic upturn. Bank chairmen at the banks' January 1931 annual meetings universally predicted a business recovery during 1931, as did politicians, financiers, businessmen, and even Europeans, who had been the most skeptical of similar predictions in early 1930.

NOTES

1. See summary of all J. P. Morgan & Co. issues in *Stock Exchange Practices*, part 1, pp. 228–30, and of all Dillon Read issues in part 4, pp. 2275–76.

2. *Banking & Monetary Statistics*, pp. 544–45.

3. *Historical Statistics*, p. 864.

4. *Survey of Current Business*, May 1938, table 57. (See also Table A.27 in the Statistical Appendix.)

7

Political and Economic Influences on Securities Markets in 1931

Financial trends in 1931 were divided by the international financial crises of midsummer in Austria, Germany, and the United Kingdom. Prior to these crises, both short-term and long-term interest rates were declining. Thereafter, all securities prices declined, so that by the end of the year the markets were dominated by such unmitigated pessimism that they almost ceased to function. By December 1931, the prices of leading stocks averaged only one-third of their 1931 highs and one-sixth of their 1929 highs. New securities issued during the year were only half the volume of 1930, and one-third that of 1929; new issues almost disappeared in the fourth quarter of 1931.

The decline in business conditions accelerated sharply after the international crisis. Bank failures were at record levels in the last quarter of 1931, and many industries, particularly railroads, began to suffer severe losses. American industry as a whole lost $870 million for the year. The Gross National Product dropped 7.7% in constant dollars. Unemployment approached 25% by the end of the year.

The Hoover Administration, which presided over this breakdown of financial markets and decline in the economy, declared a moratorium on war debts in June and created the Reconstruction Finance Corporation in December, but the Administration's efforts were insignificant before the momentum of the financial and economic events which swept the world. The public rightly felt that events were out of control.

HERBERT HOOVER TRIES TO RESPOND TO THE PROBLEMS OF THE ECONOMY, EUROPE, AND THE BANKS BUT IS CONSTRAINED BY THE BUDGET DEFICIT

The U.S. Treasury was committed to the proposition that business recovery could occur only if there was a good bond market in which corporations could raise capital. Ogden Mills, Undersecretary of the Treasury, made the point directly in February: ''It is to the bond market that we look primarily today in laying the foundation for a business recovery. Capital spending must lead recovery and it is strictly dependent on the bond market.''[1] The Administration's concern for the bond market did not lead to a reflex demand for a balanced budget, however. There was a budget deficit for fiscal 1931 of $462 million[2] because of a $900 million decline (20%) in revenues from the prior year, but Hoover did not propose to raise taxes or to cut expenses during fiscal 1931. The deficit could be financed without disrupting the bond market and so created no problem for Administration policy.

The Hoover Administration's emphasis on financial markets did produce a period of political inactivity. Hoover exhorted employers and employees to neither increase nor decrease wages, but otherwise his policy forced him to wait passively for the economic fruits of a good bond market. There was not sufficient sense of crisis in the first half of the year to produce further action by the Administration. Financial markets held up reasonably well, at least through June. Governor Harrison of the Federal Reserve Bank of New York thought that the commercial banking system was stronger than ever because of its increased liquidity. No major industries appeared to be in danger of bankruptcy, and the economy appeared to be moving sideways.

Hoover was reawakened to action as new crises appeared. On June 20th, under prodding principally from J.P. Morgan & Co. and Montagu Norman, the strained and secretive Governor of the Bank of England, Hoover proposed a one-year suspension of all war debts in order to halt the run on German and Austrian gold and foreign exchange reserves. Hoover further suggested that outright reductions in war debts could be considered if they were tied to reductions in European armaments. The stock market rose 13% in three weeks in a ''moratorium rally'' in response to this leadership. Hoover continued to be an active participant in the efforts to resolve this crisis, even though it did not directly involve the United States. Hoover and Mellon later encouraged J. P. Morgan & Co. to lead a syndicated loan of $200 million to the government of England.

In the last months of 1931, as the domestic and international crises became overwhelming, the Hoover Administration was willing to commit its own funds to banks, railroads, or other ailing industries. It was willing to commit additional funds to farmers through the Federal Land Banks and to homeowners through new Federal Home Loan Banks. It was willing to defer war debts and even reduce them. It was willing to use the Federal Reserve banks to extend further credit to the banking system and to free deposits in closed banks.

President Hoover's focus at home was on the banks and the railroads. He proposed a $500 million credit pool in October to aid banks in trouble by lending to them on assets ineligible for discount at the Federal Reserve banks, particularly real estate. Under Hoover's prodding, the major banks accepted responsibility for funding the credit pool themselves. New York City Clearing House banks committed $150 million, and by November 6th the facility was in place with $400 million subscribed. Hoover had made clear in his proposal that the government was willing to set up the pool if the banks did not. At the same time, Hoover proposed that the Federal Reserve banks be given broader authority to discount commercial bank assets, that a mechanism be created to facilitate loans to depositors in closed banks, and that additional funds be authorized for Federal Land Bank loans to farmers.

In Hoover's annual message to Congress on December 9th, he proposed a Reconstruction Finance Corporation to aid creditworthy banks, railroads, and other companies in danger of default. On the same day, bills were introduced in both houses of Congress for a Reconstruction Finance Corporation with $500 million equity and authority to borrow a further $1 1/2 billion. The bills were passed before month's end with bipartisan support. The corporation was to operate for one year and have its authority extended for a second year at the President's discretion. It could make loans for up to three years, extendable for a further two years, on good collateral. Hoover proposed at the same time a system of Federal Home Loan Banks which would channel mortgage funds into the private sector to build 3 million additional houses in five years, and funds for the Federal Land Banks, for which $100 million was appropriated by December 20th.

Railroad earnings and credit were declining precipitously in the fourth quarter of 1931 and appeared to be a major element in the economic decline. Hoover had tried to move toward a solution to railroad problems early in 1931, but now redoubled his efforts. His annual message to Congress called for legislation to forward consolidation of competing rail lines. Shortly thereafter the Interstate Commerce Commission, with Hoover's endorsement, proposed a series of measures to aid the railroads. It asked Congress to repeal a recapture provision in railroad rates which allotted half of any railroad returns on capital over 5 1/2% to the U.S. government and advocated changing rate-making from a fair-value basis to historic cost (which favored the railroads, since prices were declining). The ICC also recommended greater cooperation among railroad lines, despite the anti-trust implications, and regulation of air, water, and highway competitors of the railroads.

In this period of action, President Hoover addressed a special message to Congress, calling for extension of the war debts moratorium and adjustment of war debts to each nation's capacity to pay, which would have corrected the principal destabilizing factor in international currency markets. The proposal was unpopular domestically, opposed by both Republicans and Democrats, and got little support.

President Hoover also proposed to cut expenditures in the 1932 budget $280 million below those in 1931 in order to reduce the impending deficit of $2.1 billion. Treasury Secretary Mellon followed with a proposed list of new income and excise taxes for fiscal 1933, which appeared likely to have a deficit of $1.4

billion. From our perspective, these budget proposals appear wrongheaded, but some empathy must be engendered when one realizes that the projected 1932 deficit of $2.1 billion exceeded total 1932 revenues of only $1.9 billion.

The problem with the Hoover Administration's policy in this period was its exclusive focus on financial measures. The crises loomed as financial problems—such as the stock market crash, the collapse of the Austrian, German, and English currencies, bank suspensions, threatened railroad bankruptcies, and property foreclosures under mortgages—but these reflected fundamental economic problems of declining income and production as much as they reflected failures in the financial fabric. President Hoover was unwilling to take direct aim at income and production by assuming federal responsibility for welfare payments and a massive public works program. England had just been broken by the burden of the dole on the national budget, in the opinion of many observers. Both welfare and public works on a scale sufficient to serve all the United States presented burdens on the financial strength of the federal government which Hoover felt it could not sustain. Franklin Roosevelt assumed these obligations for the federal government, but not on a scale sufficient to affect the economy dramatically. However, President Hoover was unwilling to make the venture at all.

MONETARY POLICY, MONEY MARKETS, AND THE BANKING SYSTEM—LOW INTEREST RATES PREVAIL UNTIL THE STERLING CRISIS, WHICH IS FOLLOWED BY RECORD FAILURES AMONG SMALL BANKS

Federal Reserve policy and credit conditions in 1931 are controversial topics, largely because of the sharp attack on Federal Reserve policy made by Friedman and Schwartz in their *Monetary History of the United States 1867–1960* and the faith they hold in the economic powers of monetary policy. We will therefore take pains here to trace monetary policy and credit conditions within a larger financial perspective.

The most detailed view of bank conditions in 1931 is provided by data on the weekly reporting Federal Reserve System member banks in 101 leading cities which accounted for almost 75% of all Federal Reserve member bank deposits. These banks' total deposits reached a peak in April 1931 of $25.4 billion and declined 19.3% to $20.5 billion in December.[3] Over three-quarters of the decline in demand and time deposits, which were 84% of all deposits, was in the September–December period.

Nonmember commercial banks' deposits declined much faster than did deposits of member banks. Nonmember banks' deposits, on the semiannual basis for which data is available, peaked in December 1928 at $13.6 billion and had already declined to $11.6 billion by December 1930. This contrasts with the deposit experience of weekly reporting member banks, which on a comparable basis rose to an historic high of $26.1 billion in December 1930. Nonmember banks' deposits dropped further, from $11.6 billion to $8.8 billion (24%) between

December 1930, and December 1931. Three-quarters of the decline was in the last half of the year.

Total investments and Federal Reserve borrowing of the weekly reporting banks behaved during the first six to nine months of 1931 as if the decline in deposits in that period put little pressure on the banks' resources. Their total investments rose from $6.7 billion in January to $7.9 billion at the end of September with little interruption. Securities investments of all member banks, which had been approximately $9.8 billion at the time of the Crash, had grown to $12.1 billion by June 30, 1931. Relative to deposits, therefore, the banks had increased their investments in liquid securities by 20%–25% between 1929 and 1931. These increased investments were in both U.S. government and other securities until April 1931, but thereafter the increase was completely in U.S. securities because the volume outstanding of the principal alternatives — bankers acceptances, commercial paper, and call loans — declined due to the decline in the business on which they were based.

Federal Reserve borrowing by the banking system also indicated little pressure on the banks. Federal Reserve borrowings by weekly reporting banks remained in the area of $20–$60 million until mid-August, which qualified as low borrowing in the minds of Federal Reserve officials. During this period, "Central Reserve City Banks" in New York and Chicago had excess reserves and no Federal Reserve borrowings. "Reserve City Banks" in other major cities had excess reserves which almost exactly equalled their Federal Reserve borrowings.[4] Country member banks' borrowings declined to $186 million on June 30, 1931, the lowest level on a call date since World War I. The volume of bills discounted by the Federal Reserve banks (usually at members' request to obtain reserves) dropped to $149 million at the end of June 1931, the lowest level since 1917.[5] The nonmember banks again diverged from the member banks, however. Investments of nonmember banks peaked at $3.9 billion on June 30, 1930, and were down to $3.6 billion by June 30, 1931. No data are available on their borrowings.

The commercial banking system in the first half of 1931 was relatively stable. We have already noted concerns about the stability of the banking system in 1930, which carried over into 1931, and of course the relatively low level of economic activity reduced bank business and undermined the security of bank loans in some instances. Nonetheless, there was no atmosphere of crisis surrounding the banks. Deposits in closed banks were not growing, and runs on banks were few. As early as February 1931 the Federal Reserve Board declared that the banking system was much stronger than 18 months earlier. Loans were of better quality than when speculative pressures were greater and bank liquidity had been rebuilt substantially from 1929 levels.

If the banks had any particular problem at this time, it was the low level of short-term interest rates. Bankers had a difficult time making a profit on the investment of idle funds on short-term deposit. Short-term interest rates declined in mid-1931 to the lowest levels on record as yields on U.S. Treasury 3- to 6-

Table 7.1
Short-Term Interest Rates, December 1930 to December 1931 (month end)

	December 1930	March 1931	June 1931	September 1931	December 1931
U.S. 3–6 months	1.48%	1.38%	0.55%	0.45%	2.41%
Bankers acceptances, 3 months	1.88	1.50	0.88	1.06	3.00
Commercial paper, 4–6 months	2.88	2.50	2.00	2.00	3.88
Call loans (new)	2.04	1.58	1.50	1.50	3.00
Time loans, 3 months	2.38	1.88	1.63	1.75	3.50
N.Y. bank commercial loans (average rate)	3.82	3.67	3.66	3.50	4.48

Source: Banking & Monetary Statistics, pp. 456–57.

month obligations dropped below 1/2%. Short-term rates in 1931 are outlined in Table 7.1.

The Federal Reserve Bank of New York played an active role in the decline in short-term rates. It reduced its discount rate from 2% to 1 1/2% on May 8, 1931, and reduced its buying rates for bankers acceptances ten different times between January 16th and May 19th in an aggressive policy which led dealer rates rather than followed them.[6] The Federal Reserve did not increase its open market activity in this period, however, holding its U.S. government securities portfolio at $700–$750 million.[7]

Thus, the impression created in credit markets prior to September is one of considerable ease. Banks were able to build substantial investments, and interest rates dropped. Even the country member banks appeared highly liquid. Only nonmember banks appeared to be under any stress as they lost deposits, but this was not severe enough to force borrowers out of country banks and create a surge of extra borrowing at member banks.

This is not to say that borrowers could afford the available credit, however, as the real cost of borrowing was rising dramatically. Wholesale prices declined 9% from 79.6 in December 1930 to 72.1 in June 1931 and farm prices declined 17%. Industrial commodity prices were experiencing similar declines in the first half of 1931. (See p. 231.) Credit market conditions changed sharply following the Sterling Crisis. Three different factors converged in the short-term credit market: a six-week run on U.S. gold reserves, acceleration in the decline of the economy, and a run on the banks of the most serious proportions to date.

The U.S. gold stock held by the Federal Reserve Banks at the end of August 1931 was $4.6 billion, which approximated 41% of the world's gold reserves.

Table 7.2
U.S. Gold Reserves Held by Federal Reserve Banks, 1920–1931 ($ millions)

	Owned	Earmarked for foreign banks
1920 December	$2,451	$ 22
1921 December	3,221	—
1922 December	3,506	4
1923 December	3,834	3
1924 December	4,090	45
1925 December	3,985	13
1926 December	4,083	39
1927 December	3,977	199
1928 June	3,732	106
December	3,746	80
1929 June	3,956	80
December	3,900	135
1930 June	4,178	115
December	4,225	138
1931 June	4,593	32
July	4,587	61
August	4,632	77
September	4,364	356
October	3,905	464
November	4,031	436
December	4,052	459

Source: *Banking & Monetary Statistics*, pp. 537, 544.

As Table 7.2 shows, U.S. gold reserves had grown steadily since 1920, when they were $2.5 billion. The reader can also follow monthly changes in the U.S. gold stock shown in Table A.35 in the Statistical Appendix.

U.S. gold reserves increased right up to the week ending Saturday, September 19, 1931—the day before the United Kingdom decided to suspend gold payments. The U.S. gold outflow began on the following Monday, when foreign banks, including the Bank of France, bought almost $100 million in gold from the Federal Reserve to be held under earmark. During the week, U.S. gold losses were $183 million. Thereafter, the Federal Reserve lost gold daily in amounts up to $40 million per day. Within three weeks of the suspension of sterling, the United States lost $423 million, or approximately 10% of its reserves. An end to the losses was not in sight, for foreign bankers were in a panic over Hoover's October 6th proposals to create a $500 million credit pool to aid commercial banks, to give the Federal Reserve banks broader lending powers, to create Federal Home Loan Banks, and to lend to the railroads. His proposals made foreign bankers aware of the growing crisis in U.S. finance and industry.

To counter the gold outflow, the New York Federal Reserve Bank raised its discount rate from 1 1/2% to 2 1/2% on October 8th, but foreign concern had reached a pitch which was not affected by mere changes in interest rates. Safety of capital was at issue, rather than return on it. Rumors abroad that the United States would go off the gold standard prompted a record one-day gold outflow of $49 million on October 14th. The New York Federal Reserve Bank discount rate was raised a further 1% to 3 1/2% the next day. The next week following friendly and well-publicized meetings in the United States, Premier Pierre Laval of France and President Hoover agreed on a program of cooperation in financial matters. France agreed not to withdraw any more gold from the United States, and both countries agreed to consult each other before advancing any new proposals for extending the war debts moratorium or revising reparations obligations. Gold loss in the week of October 26th slowed to $6 million, but the gold loss in the six weeks since September 20th had amounted to $747 million, reducing U.S. gold stocks at the end of October to $3.9 billion.

The Federal Reserve did not go beyond raising interest rates to tighten credit. It could have instead used open market operations in this crisis, but it held its holdings of U.S. securities and bills constant at approximately $1.2 billion from September to December (with a brief increase in October which reflected borrowing by the United Kingdom under its $200 million line of credit). These Federal Reserve holdings of U.S. securities and bills had previously increased from $750 million in July 1931 to $1.2 billion in September because the Federal Reserve had bought U.S. long bonds heavily in the open market as the currency crisis developed (see Table 7.3).

Some aspects of the money market give the appearance that the Federal Reserve conducted a massive credit tightening policy in the fourth quarter—the sharp decline in the volume of outstanding bankers acceptances, commercial paper, and call loans of $2.1 billion—but these money market securities shrank in volume because the underlying business purposes that created them contracted sharply. Some 79% of the $582 million reduction in bankers acceptances outstanding was due to the decline in financing of U.S. exports and goods stored in foreign countries. Commercial paper declined $238 million because of the decline in business inventories, which it usually financed. Call loans contracted over $1.3 billion because of the reduction in stock market speculation. Amounts outstanding of these securities are outlined in Table 7.4.

This relatively mild Federal Reserve impact on the money markets is corroborated by interest rates for various money market securities and by bank loan rates. Bankers acceptance rates rose 200 basis points to 3%, but commercial paper and call loan rates were virtually the same as bankers acceptance rates. There was not the wide spread in yields on various short-term investments which one would have expected in such a crisis. The same is true of the limited reaction that banks made in their commercial loan rates. The New York banks, which were more sensitive to market conditions, raised their loan rates roughly 1% but rates on loans in other regions rose only 40 to 50 basis points.[8] The mild Federal

Table 7.3
Federal Reserve Securities Bought 1931 (month end), ($ millions)

	U.S. bonds	Other U.S. securities	Total U.S. securities	Bills bought	Total
January	$ 84	$526	$610	$125	$ 735
February	76	523	599	109	708
March	67	532	599	124	723
April	61	537	598	163	761
May	69	529	598	125	723
June	192	476	668	106	774
July	211	467	678	73	751
August	292	436	728	215	943
September	309	433	742	469	1,211
October	317	410	727	681[a]	1,408[a]
November	316	401	717	452	1,169
December	360	457	817	339	1,156

Source: Federal Reserve bulletins, February 1931 to January 1932.

[a] Appears to include approximately $200 million lent to the United Kingdom and repaid before the end of the year.

Reserve impact is also visible in other markets. The stock market rose 35% between October 5th and November 9th, and wheat prices doubled within the same period. Tight money should have had the opposite effects.

The Federal Reserve was prevented from following an actively restrictive credit policy to stem the gold loss—other than raising interest rates—because the banking system began to appear too weak to sustain such stress almost

Table 7.4
Open Market Short-Term Securities Outstanding, December 1930 to December 1931 ($ millions)

	December 1930	March 1931	June 1931	September 1931	December 1931
Bankers acceptances	$1,556	$1,467	$1,368	$ 996	$974
% decline	—	6	7	27	2
Commercial paper	358	311	298	251	120
% decline	—	13	4	16	52
Call loans	1,894	1,909	1,391	1,044	587
% decline	—	+1	27	25	44

Source: *Banking & Monetary Statistics*, pp. 466, 500.

simultaneously with the acceleration of the international currency crisis. There were rumblings of concern about the banking system in mid year, when National City Bank set aside reserves of $20 million for the six months and Chase National Bank reserved $35 million, but these two banks stood out as the most aggressive in preceding years, and their stocks, as well as their loan and investment positions, were taking a drubbing. More concern was aroused by events in Chicago, where the First National Bank of Chicago bought the Foreman State National Bank in June after a reorganization effort failed. Central Trust Co. of Illinois and National Bank of the Republic in that city merged as well to fend off runs. There were runs on numerous suburban Chicago banks, and, on June 8th and 9th, 19 banks were forced to close. During August, runs closed most of the banks in Toledo and Omaha and banks in Los Angeles, New York, and Brooklyn. Bank failures accelerated in July and August. By the end of August, 932 banks had failed, which was up to the record annual rate of 1,350 in 1930. Deposits in closed banks reached $699 million at the end of August; on an annual basis, this was 25% above 1930's record level of $837 billion.

Crisis levels were reached in the banking system in the last four months as the international currency system collapsed and the economy nose-dived. In the last four months of the year, 1,361 banks with deposits aggregating $991 million closed, so that by year end 70% more banks (2,293) with over twice the deposits ($1.7 billion) had closed than in 1930. Suspensions by months in 1931 are outlined in Table 7.5, and those over a longer period in Tables A.28 and A.29 in the Statistical Appendix.

In September the Bank of Pittsburgh suspended payments on $47 million in deposits when Treasury Secretary Mellon refused President Hoover $1.5 million to keep it going. The Baltimore Trust Co. would have suspended $83 million in deposits at the same time had it not received loans of $15 million from New York and $7.5 million from local businesses. In October banks in Philadelphia had to support the Integrity Trust Co. (deposits of $43 million) when it threatened to suspend. In December the Federal National Bank of Boston suspended payments on $58 million in deposits. These were large banks in major cities. Clearly the bank crisis had escalated beyond the problems of rural banks based on narrow economies.

There was a sharp contraction in bank deposits generally during the last quarter of 1931. Demand deposits in the major banks in 101 leading cities, from which the Federal Reserve collected weekly data, dropped 10% to $11.9 billion during the last quarter of 1931. Time deposits dropped 13% in the same period to $5.9 billion. Interbank deposits, which had continued to grow to $3.5 billion in June 1931, suddenly dropped $1 billion in the last half to $2.5 billion at year end.[9] Deposits by foreign banks in the United States dropped almost 50% in the last quarter, from $775 million to $424 million.[10] There was a sharp increase in member borrowing from the Federal Reserve banks in the last quarter as bills discounted by the Federal Reserve jumped from a daily average of $223 million in August to $774 million in December. The peak borrowing from the Federal

Table 7.5
Bank Suspensions, 1931

	All Banks	Nonmember banks	All deposits ('000)	Nonmember deposits ('000)
January	198	164	75,712	52,266
February	76	52	34,179	18,024
March	86	63	34,320	22,882
April	64	41	41,683	19,180
May	91	61	43,210	25,455
June	167	126	190,480	118,628
July	93	68	40,745	29,464
August	158	110	180,028	93,894
September	305	231	233,505	121,495
October	522	384	471,380	236,932
November	175	130	67,939	35,466
December	358	267	277,051	162,261
Total	2,293	1,697	$1,690,232	$935,947

Source: *Federal Reserve Bulletin*, September 1937

Reserve at the end of December reached over $1 billion.[11] Particularly significant was Federal Reserve Bank borrowing by banks in Philadelphia, where borrowings jumped from near zero to $65 million; in Cleveland, where borrowings rose from $5–$10 million to $44 million; and in San Francisco, where borrowings rose from $15–$20 million to $70 million. Country banks in the New York and Philadelphia districts also increased their borrowings from levels around $20 million to $100 and $50 million respectively.[12]

Various factors produced the sharp bank contraction in the last quarter of 1931. The international crisis played an important role. We have seen the $350 million reduction in U.S. deposits by foreign banks, following the collapse of sterling, and the outflow of nearly $750 million in U.S. gold between September 20th and November 1st. Both movements drained reserves from the U.S. banking system. The foreign crisis also stimulated fears of domestic depositors. U.S. banks were thought to be heavily exposed to losses on their international loans and investments, although no reliable estimates of the magnitude of these loans and investments were available. Loans of $1 billion to Germany were frozen by the Standstill Agreement announced in August except for limited monthly withdrawals, which it did not appear Germany could sustain. The collapse of the creditworthiness of banks in Austria, Germany, and England, especially the Bank of England, which was refused further foreign loans in September, undoubtedly instilled in observers everywhere an awareness of the weakness of financial institutions which had appeared impregnable. Currency in circulation, including gold and silver, jumped from around $4.5 billion in June 1931, where it had been since World War I, to $5.4 billion in December, as people began to hoard currency rather than accumulate bank deposits.[13] This increase in currency took place completely in Federal Reserve Bank notes and was therefore a direct drain on member bank reserves.

Some depositors shifted their funds from commercial banks to the postal savings system, which almost doubled its deposits in the last half of 1931 from $347 million on June 30th to $606 million on December 31st. This growth in postal savings bank deposits continued until mid-1933, when they reached $1.2 billion—a level at which they remained until World War II.[14]

The combined effect of the gold loss ($750 million), the shift in foreign deposits ($350 million), the currency increase ($900 million), and the shift to postal savings ($259 million) had the potential, if there was no double counting, to reduce bank reserves by over $2.25 billion. This reduction was offset only by the Federal Reserve's purchases of $400 million of government securities and bills between July and December.

The collapse of real estate values also generated uneasiness toward the banks, particularly in the San Francisco and Cleveland Federal Reserve districts, where real estate loans were 33% and 23% respectively of loan portfolios. The banks subject to runs in larger cities tended to be those that had prominent positions in real estate lending and which therefore had illiquid collateral on which neither Federal Reserve nor other banks were willing to lend if a run on deposits developed. Concern that real estate loans were threatening the banking system's liquidity reached a high pitch similar to the fear about illiquid foreign loans. In September 1931 an article in the *New York Times* reported that real estate loans by national banks had burgeoned from 5% of loans in 1928 to 10% in 1930 and equalled 104% of the equity in all national banks.[15] I am unable to verify this data, but it was a good example of the half-true inferences about the condition of the banking system. The member banks of the Federal Reserve System, which constituted over 75% of all commercial bank deposits, held a relatively constant portfolio of approximately $3 billion in real estate loans from 1928 through 1931. The proportion of these loans in total loans and investments of member banks did increase, but only from 8.7% in 1928 to 9.9% in 1931, and all of the increase reflected a reduction in total loans and investments rather than an increase in real estate loans. Nor did real estate loans approximate 100% of the banks' capital. They were 54% of capital in both 1928 and 1931.[16] There was, however, a significant change in real estate lending by commercial banks over the ten-year period 1921–31. Real estate loans in that time had steadily increased from 4.7% of all loans and investments to 9.9%.[17] The soundness of this growth was irrelevant in late 1931. The weakness of real estate loans and the resultant vulnerability of the banking system were hearsay gospel not to be contradicted.

Changes in major banks' securities businesses also highlighted that banks' financial problems were on a scale which merited concern. The most striking case was Chase Securities, the securities affiliate of Chase National Bank, which announced on December 10, 1931, that it planned to reduce its capital of $120 million to take account of losses in securities still carried at pre-Crash values, especially the securities of General Theatres Equipment, Fox Film, and Fox Theatres, which totalled $125 million. These securities had been acquired as part of the reorganization of the bankrupt Fox Film Corp. in 1930 in which Albert Wiggin had been instrumental. General Theatres Equipment common stock closed at 50¢ on December 31, 1931, down from an all-time high of $15 1/2 in February 1931. Fox Film A closed at $2 5/8, down from its all-time high of $105 in September 1929. The reduction in Chase Securities' capital from writing off such declines in values was sure to be significant. Other banks dissolved their securities affiliates because of losses or lack of business. Chatham-Phenix National Bank & Trust dissolved its affiliate first and was followed in October by Bankers Trust Co., which absorbed its securites affiliate after writing down its investments and closing offices in Buffalo, Newark, Minneapolis, Cincinnati, and St. Louis. The Bank of Manhattan Trust Co. dissolved its securites affiliate in December, and Chemical Bank & Trust Co. announced plans to dissolve Chemical Securities Corp. at its January 1932 stockholders meeting.

Banks' problems were also evident in their net profits, which were reduced from over $556 million in 1929 and $306 million in 1930 to virtually zero in 1931. Securities losses were a record $264 million in 1931 (compared with $109 million in 1930, $95 million in 1929). Loan losses were a record $295 million ($195 million in 1930, $140 million in 1929). Interest earned on loans, bills, and commercial paper dropped from $1.6 billion in 1929 to $1.3 billion in 1930 and $1.1 billion in 1931. The banks were squeezed from every direction.[18].

Various efforts were made to relieve the banking distress. Laws were readily changed to preserve the fiction of profits. A moratorium was declared on removing railroad bonds from the legal investment list in New York State, so that banks did not have to realize losses on the sale of bonds taken off the "legal list," and so that such sales did not further depress railroad bond prices. Federal authorities allowed banks to carry at par all U.S. bonds and other bonds within the four highest credit ratings (Baa to Aaa). President Hoover was anxious to change the powers of the Federal Reserve Banks to permit them to lend on a wider range of collateral to relieve banks in distress. Governor Harrison of the New York Federal Reserve met with the New York commercial banks in mid-October to try to induce them to set easier standards for loans to correspondent banks, in effect asking the New York banks to act as lenders of last resort. At the same time, Hoover proposed the creation of the National Credit Corporation, which opened in November 1931 with over $400 million in subscribed capital to aid failing banks. The Reconstruction Finance Corporation, which Hoover proposed in his December annual message to Congress and which within days was embodied in bills before the House and Senate, was also empowered to lend to banks.

But 1931 closed with no cure in sight for the banks' plight. Friedman and Schwartz blame the Federal Reserve in this period for a misguided policy which they believe exacerbated the declines in banking conditions, in low-grade bond prices, and in the economy. In particular, they point to the directors and the professional staff of the New York Federal Reserve Bank, who in mid-1931 favored an open market policy of purchasing up to $300 million long-term U.S. bonds to create large excess reserves which would prompt banks to lend more freely and force down U.S. bond yields so that investors would divert funds to other parts of the bond market, thereby renewing opportunities to finance there and providing a base for economic recovery. New York's position was greeted with hostility by the Federal Reserve Board in Washington and the newly constituted Open Market Committee. The New York bank was unable to obtain approval of its policy until April 1932.[19]

The struggle for bureaucratic power within the Federal Reserve System undoubtedly had much to do with the New York bank's failure to get approval. The New York bank under Governor Benjamin Strong had dominated the Federal Reserve System despite considerable opposition, until his death in 1928. Harrison, however, had neither the personality nor the understanding to dominate the System as Strong had, and the Federal Reserve Board in Washington was both anxious to dominate and felt it was the Board's responsibility. The Open Market Committee was reorganized in 1930, following the dispute over the New York bank's prerogatives to make open market purchases at its own discretion. The decision-making power on open market activities was taken out of the hands of the New York bank, which remained as the executive agency of the committee, and placed in the hands of the new committee, which was composed of the presidents of all the Federal Reserve banks, the Chairman of the Board, and the Secretary of the Treasury. Harrison was anxious to work harmoniously with this committee and therefore did not push the New York bank's beliefs as hard as he was justified in doing, since it was both at the center of the market and had the only professional financial staff.

The attitudes and beliefs of the various members of the Open Market Committee vacillated widely without strong leadership from either New York or Washington. Besides erring in open market policy because of bureaucratic infighting, the Federal Reserve also erred in placing too much emphasis on the major banks in New York City and Chicago as barometers of credit conditions when they were not much affected by conditions in the last quarter. Table 7.6 shows that Central Reserve City Banks in New York and Chicago had limited Federal Reserve borrowings.

Under Governor Strong, "easy money" had been defined as circumstances under which the major New York and Chicago banks were borrowing no more than $50 million in each city. These conditions were met in the last quarter of 1931, but the focus on them ignored the problems of the smaller banks. Table 7.7 shows that borrowings by Reserve City Banks in other cities, and by country banks, climbed seriously high to over $700 million, which was more than 3 times first half borrowings. Bank suspensions at this time were concentrated in these smaller banks.

Only one of the 2,293 bank failures in 1931 involved a bank with total loans

Table 7.6
Borrowings of Central Reserve City Banks, New York and Chicago, 1931 (monthly averages of daily figures, $ millions)

	New York	Chicago
January	$19	—
February	17	—
March	13	—
April	17	—
May	12	—
June	4	2
July	2	1
August	14	1
September	13	1
October	82	4
November	27	2
December	45	9

Source: *Banking & Monetary Statistics*, pp. 397–98.

Table 7.7
Borrowings of Reserve City and Country Banks from the Federal Reserve, 1931 (monthly averages of daily figures, $ millions)

	Reserve City banks	Country banks
January	$ 67	$166
February	46	153
March	27	136
April	18	119
May	24	126
June	42	139
July	38	128
August	59	148
September	99	167
October	274	248
November	343	311
December	355	354

Source: *Banking & Monetary Statistics*, pp. 398–99.

and investments over $50 million. We have already mentioned that 1,697 of the 2,293 suspensions were by nonmember banks. This combination of small and nonmember banks in trouble permitted leaders of the Federal Reserve System to consider the bank crisis due punishment for the excesses of the 1920s. This was in accord with Treasury Secretary Mellon's view that there was a need to liquidate the results of these excesses before economic progress could resume. Many of the Federal Reserve banks had an emotional commitment, which verged on a class attitude, to seeing this punishment and liquidation carried through. Harrison complained frequently that representatives of the district banks on the Open Market Committee were instructed by their boards, composed of the local business hierarchy, to oppose open market purchases with no discretion to listen to argument or reason.

The tendency is to blame the Federal Reserve for ignoring the problems of the smaller banks, but at the time the Federal Reserve System felt slight responsibility to sustain the banking system in general. Even the New York bank's desires for large open market purchases had more to do with stimulating the economy than with directly helping hard-pressed banks. In November, Governor Harrison did meet with the major New York Clearing House banks to try to persuade them to increase their loans to troubled correspondent banks, but otherwise there was no direct sign of a Federal Reserve sense of responsibility for even its member banks. President Hoover wanted the Federal Reserve to take some such responsibility by broadening its legislative powers to lend so that it could accept illiquid collateral, but many within the Federal Reserve, and the influential Carter Glass in the Senate, opposed the change. Nor did the financial press suggest that the Federal Reserve should take responsibility for the failing banks. Instead the National Credit Corporation and the Reconstruction Finance Corporation were set up for that purpose. Many, including Senator Glass, felt that the Federal Reserve was too new and too much in need of public confidence to shoulder a task which was so fraught with the risk of losses. Nonetheless, Friedman and Schwartz place this responsibility on the Federal Reserve, and with stronger leadership the Federal Reserve might have shouldered it.

There were, however, constraints on Federal Reserve open market activities, which opponents of open market purchases on the Board emphasized. Critics have focussed on the "free gold" constraint which was part of the Federal Reserve Act. It required the Federal Reserve banks to maintain gold backing equal to outstanding Federal Reserve credit (Federal Reserve credit equals the loans and investments of the Federal Reserve banks), and it did not treat U.S. securities as equal backing, which therefore limited reserve expansion through open market purchases. This was a fleeting constraint, however, which was effective only during the September 21st–October 30th gold drain and which in any case could have been removed either by a congressional amendment or a declaration of emergency by the Federal Reserve Board.

A more important constraint on open market policy was the outflow of gold which prompted the Federal Reserve to a classic defense of the exchange rate by raising the discount rate, which in turn raised other interest rates. Had the Federal Reserve not done so, or had it countered the effect by large open market purchases, the European, and particularly the French, reaction would have been profound. No doubt there would have been a rapid withdrawal of foreign deposits in anticipation of an exchange rate devaluation. Foreign short-term deposits in New York were approximately $2 billion, equal to half of U.S. gold reserves.[20] So the Federal Reserve had to pay serious attention to them. Americans and foreign businessmen would have been surprised had the Federal Reserve not defended the dollar in this manner, and if in doubt about its determination would have responded by increasing their non-U.S. investments and trade assets, in the pattern of "leads and lags" which has since become prominent as part of a run on a currency.

The Federal Reserve overdid this fear, however. It appears to have kept its portfolio of U.S. government securities and bills stable at around $1.2 billion, excluding estimated U.K. loans held as "bills bought." Such rigor was uncalled for in the light of the currency hoarding and bank suspensions taking place, particularly when the U.S. gold outflow ceased in early November. Observers questioned whether the New York Federal Reserve Bank had more concern for international considerations than domestic considerations, which it probably did.

Federal Reserve governors were also opposed to extensive open market purchases, fearing that they would drive down interest rates. Bankers welcomed the higher rates, contrary to the usual bankers' reaction. At an October 7th meeting Governor Harrison told his New York directors that higher rates would improve bank earnings and improve bankers' psychology. The New York banks literally demanded that higher rates be maintained because lower rates would threaten the solvency of many banks.[21] Short rates had become so low in 1931 that there was no incentive for investors to make deposits in search of interest, and this abetted the strong hoarding tendency which was developing. The banks also lost income at such low rates. The focus on interest rates rather than on reserves failed to recognize the greater importance of reserves both to the banks and to the economy.

Governor R. A. Young, Chairman of the Federal Reserve Board and later Governor of the Federal Reserve Bank of Boston after he was forced by Hoover to resign the chairmanship in favor of Eugene Meyer, opposed a heavy open market purchase policy of U.S. bonds because of the impact on confidence. This is easily dismissed as compulsive restrictiveness, but it had a better basis in a judgment on bond market capabilities. A large Federal Reserve portfolio of long-term bonds created several market problems for the Federal Reserve. A portfolio of $500–$700 million long-term U.S. bonds probably could not be sold promptly. The dealer market was not strong, and dealers had lost considerable capital and nerve in the decline of most medium and low grade (and some high grade) bond prices in the last two years.

This dealer market could handle large volumes of short-term U.S. obligations which sold quickly, had small price movements, and required little capital margin; but it could not handle similar volumes of long-term bonds. Bonds took longer to sell, had much wider price movements, and probably required 10 times the margin capital of short-term debt. The dealer community simply did not have the capital to inventory and market quickly as much as $500 million in bonds under even the most favorable conditions. The U.S. government itself was subject to doubts. It was running a $2 billion deficit and was likely to fall into the hands of an uncertain Democratic Administration. Other countries had turned out to be unreliable credits with no market acceptance. It could happen to the United States. A declining market could have been turned into a rout if, amid a lack of confidence in the United States, the Federal Reserve became a big seller of long bonds. In such a context, the Federal Reserve's long-term bond portfolio would be frozen and its ability to cope with demands on it put in doubt. Bond dealers knew that a large long-term bond portfolio created this vulnerability in the Federal Reserve, and their confidence in it would have been affected accordingly.

A large long-term bond portfolio in the Federal Reserve's hands might also have affected the Federal Reserve's responsibility to manage the financing of the federal government. There was a $2 billion budget deficit to finance, plus $10 billion in U.S. maturities in 1932–33. If the Federal Reserve had to sell its own long-term bonds it would demoralize the market for these new financings. There is a tendency to assume that, because it did not in fact have to sell a large volume of long-term bonds, the Federal Reserve did not have to be concerned about the problem of a large holding of long-term bonds. But the men on the scene at that time had no such benefit of hindsight. The commitment to large-scale long-term bond purchases required a conclusion that there was no natural potential in the economy for an upturn and that the Federal Reserve would not need the flexibility to restrict the sort of "inflation" which in 1929 had led to unwise loans for business overexpansion and stock market speculation. This conclusion seemed evident to many in 1931, but one of the most striking problems in decision-making at that time was the extent of disagreement about the course of, and proper remedies for, the economy. There was a widespread fear that an economic recovery would be accompanied by the overconfidence and speculation of 1929 if bank reserves were excessive, and that a depression would follow which would shake the foundations of society.

The arguments over appropriate monetary policy then and now probably exaggerate the impact it could have had. The bank failures were due to the decline in bond values, real estate values, commodities values, and business generally, which destroyed asset values and income. Friedman and Schwartz argued that banks with large excess reserves could have lent more freely to failing banks, or bought bonds they were selling, and thereby prevented the declines in bond prices which reduced asset values. Both claims beg the question, however. Many of the failures appeared to be justified because they were concentrated in small banks, and large banks had to be doubtful about their ability to save small banks when so many were failing. The magnitude of the number of suspensions created an atmosphere of *sauve-qui-peut* (each for himself) which militated against further lending to small banks.

There is no sign either that banks could have been persuaded to buy long-term corporate bonds. If interest rate differentials could have created an active buyer interest in low-grade bonds, the differentials in 1931 should have achieved it. U.S. bonds yielded 3.93% in December 1931, when Baa rail bonds yielded 11.96% and Baa industrial bonds yielded 10.50%. Even in June there was a wide spread between U.S. bonds at 3.13% and Baa rail bonds at 7.39% and Baa industrial bonds at 8.08%. The problem with the low grade bond market was that these bonds were losing their status as legal investments for savings banks, insurance companies, and trustees, which required these holders to sell the bonds and certainly prevented them from buying additional bonds. This swath cut wider than those bonds actually rendered illegal, of course, because institutions had to anticipate which bonds might become illegal and sell them early or avoid buying them. Dealers marked down many bond prices in anticipation that bonds might lose their legal status, and lowered their bids to avoid buying such bonds.

It certainly cannot be argued that more and cheaper credit availability would have stimulated business. On the one hand, credit was too expensive in real terms since wholesale and commodities prices were declining 10% to 20%, particularly in the industries which were most affected by the economic decline. Even with interest rates of zero, the cost of more borrowing was very high. Perhaps more pertinent, however, the industries which needed credit could not justify it. Farmers, railroads, real estate, steel, mining, pulp and paper, and other basic industries were unjustifiable credit risks and new loans to them would have called into question the judgment of the lending banks. Those industries which were not such bad risks generally had cash on hand and did not need credit to expand.

The rapidly declining economy which lowered the demand for funds and the credit of would-be borrowers was the determinant of credit market conditions more than monetary policy, just as it was the determinant of the decline in bank earnings and of the illiquidity of many bank loans and investments. A much· easier credit policy could have had only a marginal effect on the economy and the markets. There is no factual basis for a chicken-and-egg argument that if credit policy had been easier the economy would have been better and the credit markets less disrupted. The sudden collapse in stock and credit markets, the banking system, and the economy which paralleled the international currency crisis could not have been offset by a concurrent easy credit policy, which would have taken months to affect the economy in whatever indirect manner such effects are achieved. In the meantime, the structure of business and finance was collapsing, and banks and investors would have faced the same fears and judgments in making loans that actually led them to resist.

In late 1931 the best choice available to those investors with funds was to leave them in some safe, even if nonearning, form. This preserved capital at a time when its preservation was in doubt. It also produced real earnings, since the price level was declining in excess of 10% a year.

There was no leadership in monetary policy in this period, but it mattered little. The most important problems were in other areas of the economy, such as industrial production, real estate, international trade, agriculture, unemployment, and declining price levels.

THE ECONOMY DECLINES ON EVERY FRONT, ESPECIALLY AFTER THE STERLING CRISIS

The economy appeared to be recovering in the first quarter of 1931 without further assistance from the federal government. Informed opinion was almost unanimous that the economy would recover during the year. Economists at the American Economic Association meeting on January 1st predicted an upturn in the second half of the year. Bank chairmen at their annual meetings claimed that recovery had already begun. All the Federal Reserve Banks reported an imminent recovery based on surveys of business in their districts. Even Europeans, who had been skeptical of predictions of U.S. economic recovery in 1930, generally expected recovery in 1931. Signs of recovery were reported in February in every European country except England. The stock and bond markets were strong. As late as April, President James A. Farrell of U.S. Steel told the annual meeting of stockholders that he expected a good year (the company subsequently lost $1.39 per share in 1931). President Walter S. Gifford of AT&T said in April that he saw "immediate signs of returning prosperity."[22] New orders for machine tools surged in March from an index level of 84 in February (1922–24 = 100) to 118. Crude oil production almost returned to levels established in early 1930. Electric output was also stable. The consumer appeared to be buying again, as retail sales in April almost matched 1929 and 1930 sales.[23]

The weakness of the economy became conclusively apparent only in the summer months, as real estate foreclosures accelerated, wage and salary cuts were initiated in major industries, and domestic and international trade fell off sharply. Real estate was one of the weakest areas of the economy and loans on real estate were a significant part of the nation's financial structure. Federal Reserve member banks in 1930 had real estate loans outstanding of $3.2 billion— almost 10% of their total loans and investments, up from 4.7% in 1921. Life insurance companies held $7.6 billion in real estate mortgages—40% of their admitted assets, up from 30% in 1920. Public bond issues secured by commercial real estate were commonplace throughout the 1920s—usually in a volume of $500–$700 million each year. Farm mortgage debt was $1.7 billion. Some 30% of the nation's 3.35 million farms carried mortgages averaging $1,715 per farm and 27% of estimated farm value.[24]

Real estate values had collapsed earlier in some regions, particularly in Florida and South Carolina, where property booms has ended in 1926 in a dismal array of municipal and bank failures. Collapse of the real estate market was more widespread and more fundamentally serious in 1931, however. In New York, foreclosures on commercial properties and rental buildings by savings banks and life insurance companies produced a rash of foreclosure auctions beginning in June 1931. Large parcels of 10–20 properties with values reaching up to $30 million went on the block. In Chicago over $400 million in real estate loans was estimated to be in default, compounding the revenue problems of a city financiers already considered bankrupt. Farmers were seriously in arrears on their mortgage payments because their cash income had dropped from $11.2 billion in 1929 to $6.3 billion in 1931.[25] There was great pressure on rural congressmen to seek indefinite deferral of arrears on farm mortgages held by the Federal Land Banks. All real estate property owners servicing mortgages out of business income were hard-pressed to meet mortgages established at earlier dollar values because rents had declined 25%–35% since 1926 and personal income had declined 23% in just two years.[26].

Different regions were variously affected by real estate foreclosures. On the West Coast, real estate loans were 33% of all bank loans; in the Cleveland Federal Reserve District they were 23%. Real estate problems threatened the financial systems of these regions. Elsewhere in the nation, real estate loans were 6%–16% of all bank loans and therefore less significant.

Wage and salary cuts in major industries began in earnest at the end of July when U.S. Steel cut the pay of salaried, nonunion employees. Republic Steel, Western Electric, Westinghouse, and the Pennsylvania Railroad initiated salary cuts immediately following U.S. Steel. In September, immediately following the suspension of sterling, U.S. Steel led again, cutting wages of 200,000 hourly employees by 10%. Bethlehem Steel made similar wage cuts for 50,000 employees. General Motors cut salaries 10%–20% depending on pay levels. U.S. Rubber put workers on a five-day week and reduced wages by one-eleventh. Jones & Laughlin, Colorado Fuel & Iron, Phelps Dodge and all the other copper producers, Pepperell Manufacturing Co., Northern Pacific, and Alcoa cut wages in the same week. President Hoover was dismayed that his wage pact established after the Crash had been broken, but he was powerless to forestall the cuts. During 1931 hourly wages for unskilled workers were cut in almost all areas of business. Wage rates for unskilled male workers in manufacturing dropped 4%, wage rates of laborers in the building trades dropped 9% and wage rates for laborers on road gangs dropped 8%. Wage rates even dropped in some of the skilled unionized trades, such as for bricklayers, lathers, plasterers, and sign painters.[27] Because of shorter working hours, employed workers of all classes had lower earnings. Income from wages and salaries dropped 15% in 1931 to $39.1 billion, which was over 22% below 1929 wages and salaries of $50.4 billion. Disposable personal income after taxes, including incomes of farmers, businessmen, professionals, dividends, and rental income, dropped 14% in 1931 to $64 billion, 23% below the 1929 level of $83.3 billion.[28]

A radical shift in the distribution of National Income had occurred by the end of 1931. While National Income had declined by 31% in current dollars, the income of all businesses fell from $23.7 billion to $8.3 billion, or 65%—over twice as fast as the economy as a whole. Corporate profits had declined from 10% of National Income to a loss equal to a negative 1 1/2% of National Income. Proprietors' and farmers' share of National Income dropped from 17.3% to 15.4%. Thus, the combined share of all businesses in National Income dropped from 27.3% to 13.9%. Bankruptcies soared to a record of 28,285, involving liabilities of $736 million, and gross private investments dropped 65 1/2% from 1929 under these conditions.[29]

While the industrial production index for 1931 was off 32% from 1929, in line with a similar decline in National Income, the decline was greater in a number of industries related to capital investment, beginning in August and September during the international crisis. Auto, steel, copper, and railway equipment, machine tool orders, and residential construction, were all down more than 50% in 1931 from their levels in 1929. Some 2 million passenger cars were produced in 1931, compared with 4.8 million in 1929. Auto production in the last quarter of 1931 was only one-third of the 1929 level in the same quarter, which was itself an unusually low quarter. The steel industry operated at 46% of 1929 output. The copper industry produced 1 billion pounds of copper, compared with 2 billion in 1929. Machine tool orders on an index equal to 100 for 1922–24 dropped from 281 in 1929 to 74 in 1931. Railroad equipment orders for locomotives, freight cars, and passenger cars almost came to a halt. Orders for 265 locomotives in 1931 were 20% of 1929 orders; orders for 14,838 freight cars in 1931 were 12% of 1929 orders; orders for 43 passenger cars (which was a money-losing business) were less than 5% of 1929 orders. Residential and nonresidential building contracts of $1.9 billion in 1931 were only 44% of 1929 contracts totalling $4.3 billion. Most other areas of business were down to 60%–70% of 1929 production levels such as freight car loadings, nonferrous metal production, public works and utilities contracts, coal production, and lumber production. Only food, tobacco, and utility production showed any stability in the private sector. Fortunately, local government economic activity was still up 7% from its 1929 level in response to the general hardship, employment otherwise would have been even lower than the resulting 30.7 million people. This was down 5.2 million from 1929 and led to a rash of strikes which accounted for a record 6.9 million man-days lost.[30]

The currency devaluations around the world left exporting sectors of the U.S. economy particularly poorly positioned because the United States had not devalued. Exports declined 48 1/2% from 1929, from $7 billion to $3.6 billion. Farm receipts dropped 43 1/2%, as farmers found it impossible to compete abroad and at the same time faced sharply declining commodities prices.[31] Businessmen made no pretense of optimism by the fourth quarter of 1931. Downward trends in production, employment, prices, and financial markets had become so pronounced that false optimism was impossible. The international currency crisis in particular strained financial confidence and rendered the trade and business outlook in Europe negative. At this point, serious business leaders, such as

Gerard Swope, President of General Electric, began to call for national industry associations immune from anti-trust laws to regulate trade practices which were becoming mutually destructive. Edward Filene, a Boston merchant noted for his optimism, returned from Europe in October and announced, "We are not at bottom yet." He predicted two further years of depression and a revolution in Germany.[32]

COMMODITIES PRICES DECLINE ALL YEAR, REACHING LOWS IN THE STERLING CRISIS

Prices of leading commodities declined an average of approximately 50% in 1931 from their highest pre-Crash prices. The price declines were most severe in farm commodities, for which prices at the end of the year averaged only 50% of their prices before the Crash. The price of wheat had dropped from a peak of over $1.40 in 1929 to 48 5/8¢ per bushel, wheat's lowest price since 1852. Corn dropped from over $1 per bushel to 37 5/8¢, a new low for the century. Cotton dropped to 6.15¢ from over 20¢ a per pound. New low prices for farm commodities were established in most successive months, with December prices the lowest of the year.[33]

Throughout the first half of the year, the Farm Board tried to support wheat prices about 15% above world prices, but it received limited support from President Hoover and ran out of funds in midyear. On June 3rd, faced with massive sales of early Texas wheat, it removed its support bid, and wheat prices dropped 10¢ to 13¢ to approximately 57¢ per bushel. Thereafter the Farm Board requested that prices be maintained by reducing supplies. In August it recommended plowing under much of the cotton crop, but it could get agreement from only 3 of the 14 governors in the states affected. Farm commodity prices had a brief resurgence in November. Wheat rose from its 48 5/8¢ low in September to a 1931 high of 84¢ per bushel. Professionals predicted that wheat would hit $1 during the year. The ever-present Arthur Cutten was estimated to be long 100 million bushels, but the run-up was purely speculative.

Industrial commodities prices in 1931 also declined to approximately 50% of their highest pre-Crash prices, with copper and crude rubber being extreme examples that declined 63% and 78% respectively. The most striking characteristic of the declines in industrial commodities prices was their concentration in the first half of the year, when the decline was roughly twice the decline in the second half of the year. Copper, lead, zinc, crude oil, and steel scrap prices declined more in the first half than in the second. Tin and rubber declined more in the second half, but they are notable as the only industrial commodities in the list which were basically imports, and so were affected by the devaluations of most foreign currencies in the second half.[34]

This decline in commodities prices before the Sterling Crisis and sharp economic decline helps fortify the point that the decline in prices was so severe, so widespread among all goods, and so international in scope that it assumed the magnitude of an irreversible secular trend. Understanding of its causes was as limited as our understanding of inflation today. Simply because of the proportions of the price decline, it developed an internal momentum which hampered recovery. Businessmen incurred large losses on inventories and therefore naturally tried to defer production to as close to the sale date as possible, which resulted in a $1.6 billion decline in inventories equal to 2.1% of the Gross National Product (GNP). Businesses were also at a disadvantage if they invested in new plant earlier than competitors when the cost of new plant was declining, so they postponed capital expenditures. And business debtors were cruelly squeezed by declining prices, which reduced profits while their debts stayed constant.

The decline in industrial and farm commodity prices was reflected in the Wholesale Price Index and Retail Food Price Index, both of which declined approximately 28 1/2% from their pre-Crash levels by December 1931. In both these cases the decline in the first half of 1931 was approximately twice the decline in the second half of the year. Again in 1931, the decline in prices is not adequately reflected in the GNP deflator, which declined only 11 1/2%. This pales in comparison with the 50% declines in farm and industrial commodities prices and 28 1/2% declines in food and wholesale prices. In addition, because of its modest size, it fails to impart the terrific negative impact of prices which had declined for 28 months without relent.[35]

NOTES

1. *New York Times*, 2/11/31.
2. *Historical Statistics*, p. 1104; reprinted in Table A.38 in the Statistical Appendix. All budget surpluses or deficits are stated net of debt retirements.
3. *Banking & Monetary Statistics*, p. 144.
4. Ibid, pp. 396–98.
5. Ibid, p. 375.
6. Ibid, pp. 441, 445.
7. Federal Reserve monthly bulletins for 1931.
8. *Banking & Monetary Statistics*, p. 464.
9. Ibid., p. 144.
10. Ibid., p. 78.
11. Ibid., pp. 371–385, 386.
12. Ibid., part 2, ''Member Bank Statistics by Federal Reserve Districts,'' various tables.
13. Ibid., p. 412.
14. Ibid., p. 479.
15. *New York Times*, 9/27/31.
16. *Banking & Monetary Statistics*, pp. 74, 75, 76.
17. Ibid., p. 79.
18. Ibid., p. 263.
19. Friedman and Schwartz, *op cit*, pp. 379, 383–386.
20. *Banking & Monetary Statistics*, p. 574.

21. Elmus R. Wicker, *Federal Reserve Monetary Policy 1919–1933*, New York: Random House, 1966, pp. 165–169.

22. *New York Times*, 4/21/31.

23. *Moody's Industrial Manual*, 1933 p.a90.

24. *Statistical Abstract, 1939*, pp. 250, 294, 624.

25. Ibid., p. 639.

26. *National Income Accounts*, p. 32.

27. *Statistical Abstract, 1939*, pp. 332, 342–45.

28. *National Income Accounts*, p. 32.

29. Ibid., pp. 2, 14; *Statistical Abstract, 1939*, p. 307.

30. *Moody's Industrial Manual*, 1933, pp. a71–a77, a83, a84, a89, a94, a95; *Moody's Railroad Manual*, 1933, p. a25; *Moody's Utility Manual*, 1934, pp. a12, a23; *National Income Accounts*, pp. 2, 18, 102; *Statistical Abstract, 1939*, p. 347.

31. *National Income Accounts*, pp. 2, 28.

32. *New York Times*, 10/11/31.

33. NYSE monthly bulletin, September 1938, charts on prices of commodities; *Statistical Abstract, 1939*, p. 315.

34. *Moody's Industrial Manual, 1935*, blue insert pages on "The Nation's Basic Industries."

35. *Statistical Abstract, 1939*, p. 315; *National Income Accounts*, p. 158.

8

The Stock Market in 1931

Attrition of values in the stock market continued in 1931. Common stock prices equalled slightly less than one-fifth of their peak 1929 values and one-third of their peak 1931 values at their lowest prices at the end of 1931. During 1931 the Dow Jones Industrial Index ranged from a high of 194 to a low of 74, a decline of 62%. New issues of common stock in 1931 amounted to only $195 million, compared with over $5 billion in 1929, and trading volume on the New York Stock Exchange shrunk to half the 1.1 billion shares traded in 1929.

Stocks with the best relative price performance in 1931 were concentrated in the tobacco, food, retailing, communications, automobile, and operating utility industries. Those stocks with the poorest price performances were concentrated in the amusement, steel, electric machinery, and railroad industries, or had operations principally in foreign countries. None of the leading stocks was able to escape the general market trend downward, however. Every industry but tobacco reached its highest monthly valuation on March 1, 1931, and every industry without exception was at its lowest monthly valuation on December 1, 1931. The greatest monthly decline in stock prices for every industry was in September, coincident with the Sterling Crisis.

THE COURSE OF EVENTS—OPTIMISM PREVAILS UNTIL SPRING WHEREAFTER EUROPE'S CURRENCY PROBLEMS LEAD TO A SHARP DECLINE IN STOCK PRICES

The stock market was infused with the perennial New Year's optimism in January and February 1931. Improved economic conditions in numerous industries, and general business expectations of an economic recovery fueled a rise in stock prices from between 165 and 170 on the Dow Jones Industrial Index in December 1930 to 194 in late February 1931. This rise in prices was accompanied by relatively heavy NYSE trading volume in February averaging 3.2 million shares per day (excluding Saturdays). Trading volume began to lag in March, but stock prices held up in general. The DJII was still at 185 in the last week of March.

Stock prices declined quite sharply from the last week of March through April and May 1931 as doubts about the economic recovery accumulated. Brokerage failures also began to assume unusual proportions in the spring. In May, the Creditanstalt crisis in Austria began to affect stock prices. The DJII dropped from the 185 level in March to almost 120 at the end of May, down 35%. This index closed successively lower every week but one between March 21st and May 29th. Utility and railroad stocks declined in parallel with industrial stocks.

The market improved significantly in early June through the most publicized period of the German currency crisis, as events accelerated towards President Hoover's declaration of a moratorium on war debts. The "moratorium rally" which followed Hoover's proposal on June 20th carried the DJII up to 157 on June 27th. The DJII was up 36% from June 1st at this point. Daily NYSE volume averaged approximately 1 1/2 million shares in June prior to the moratorium, but volume surged to between 4 and 5 million shares a day in the June 22nd–27th week of the moratorium rally. Volume fell off again in July to 1 1/2 million shares a day or less and averaged barely 1 million shares on full days throughout August. This was the period in which the currency crisis shifted to England and was met by repeated loans to England. During this period the market declined to the 140 level on the DJII from the peak June level of 157.

The stock market at this point, before the Sterling Crisis accelerated into the September 21st suspension of gold payments, was down modestly from levels at the beginning of 1931. The Dow Jones Industrial Index was down 17%, the Dow Jones Utilities Index was down only 7%. The Dow Jones Railroad Index, however, was down 31%. The market was down considerably from its highs in February. Other stock market indicators in May through August showed the weakness of the market in the midst of the currency crisis. New common stock issues were below $5 million each month, which is to say negligible. NYSE trading volume below 2 million shares per day, except in the moratorium rally, indicated that there was little support for stock market price levels.

Some observers, including President Hoover, later suggested that domestic conditions had been improving until the international currency crisis developed. But the stock market did not reflect this in early September, nor could it be said that the stock market was in an uptrend any time in 1931 after late February. Nonetheless, up to September 1931, the stock market was strikingly different from the following period. The consequences of the collapse of sterling were not yet reflected in stock prices, nor was the severe decline in the economy which took place in the last quarter of 1931. The Dow Jones indices were virtually cut in half in the remaining four months.

September was the worst month of the year in the stock market. Values of NYSE stocks by industry groups registered their largest declines of the year in September, generally around 30% and the DJII declined 38% between September

1st and October 5th from 140 to 87. These stock price declines took place on rising volume. In September, 51 million shares were traded compared with 25 million shares in August and 34 million in July. There was no single cause of this decline in stock prices. England went off the gold standard on September 21st, and a sharp outflow of U.S. gold reserves began, but there were equally important adverse domestic events during the month. Large-scale wage cuts began in industry, and banks closed at a record rate. While there was no panic in financial markets, there was a pervasive air of pessimism and resignation.

Stocks rallied from the September disasters. The DJII rose from 86 on October 5th to 116 on November 9th, up 35%. Most of the rebound was concentrated in the week of October 5th–10th, during which President Hoover came forward with his proposals for a National Credit Corporation and various other provisions to ease the banking crisis. Interest rates rose sharply in this same week as the Federal Reserve Bank of New York increased its discount rate from 1 1/2% to 2 1/2% to combat the gold outflow which followed the suspension of sterling. The gold drain continued throughout most of this month of improvement in stock prices. Commodities prices rose strongly as well. Wheat prices doubled within the same period of rising stock prices. Wheat reached a 1931 high of 84¢ per bushel on November 6th. London also repaid most of its emergency borrowings during the month, which may have undercut the sense of international crisis, even though the United States was losing gold.

Stocks declined sharply for the balance of 1931 following this rally, as bank failures increased, municipal issuers began to have increasing problems, and economic activity declined. The DJII dropped to a new low of 74 in late December.

BROKERAGE FIRMS BEGIN TO FAIL, AND OTHER TECHNICAL ASPECTS OF THE MARKET

The brokerage industry was reduced substantially during 1931 by numerous failures and the cutbacks naturally coincident with the reduced volume of trading. Even during the February recovery, floor members on the New York Stock Exchange suggested that some inexpensive coin be substituted for the $20 gold double eagle which members were obliged to carry to flip to resolve simultaneous bids. Showmanship had given way to economy.

Kidder, Peabody & Co. failed in mid-March and was reorganized by Edwin S. Webster, Jr., Chandler Hovey, and Albert Gordon. It was the most significant brokerage failure following the Crash, and only the name was salvaged. Kidder, Peabody & Co. was founded in Boston in 1865 and was the original manager of AT&T's financing. It had declined considerably by the Crash, however, and was no longer a leading investment banker. The firm previously got into severe difficulties in 1930 because of falling prices of securities it held in inventory and deposit withdrawals of $4 million by the Government of Italy and the Bank for International Settlements. J. P. Morgan & Co. and Chase National Bank at that time led a group of nine banks which advanced $10 million to Kidder

Peabody to save it, and old partners put up $5 million. The firm's problems were too great, however, and it required a second effort in 1931 in which the capital for the new firm was provided by Edwin S. Webster, Sr., who had left Kidder Peabody to found Stone & Webster Engineering Co. Al Gordon, who had worked at Goldman, Sachs & Co. following graduation from the Harvard Business School in 1925, became the driving force in rebuilding Kidder Peabody. Over 40 years later he was still leading a large and profitable firm.

Pynchon & Co. suspended on April 25th, quickly succeeding Kidder Peabody as the largest suspension in the history of the NYSE. Its liabilities were estimated at $40 million. Pynchon & Co. was founded in 1895 and had become one of the largest brokerage houses on the Exchange. In earlier years it had been a leading commodities broker. Pynchon had been a frequent member of Chase Securities Corp. banking groups, and much of its trouble was due to the decline in price of General Theatres Equipment and Fox Films securities. General Theatres 6% convertible debentures due in 1940 had been created in the reorganization of Fox Film Corp. and sold by a Chase Securities group in April 1930 at $99 1/2. They were now at $42 7/8. The same securities forced Chase Securities Corp. to make a massive write-off in December. Pynchon & Co. had earlier been saved by Chase and others in the fall of 1930, when it would have failed if they had not taken over the securities Pynchon & Co. had pledged against loans. The banks also put $20 million of new capital into the firm at that time. The effort to save Pynchon this time was unavailing. Its collapse was rumored in Wall Street for several weeks before it was suspended, although customers in its boardroom were caught by surprise when they were dispersed and it was closed. West & Co., a NYSE member firm closely tied to Pynchon & Co. in its business, failed several days later. Its liabilities were estimated at only $5 million. At the same time, Otis & Co. transferred its brokerage business to E. A. Pierce & Co. and reduced its business to investment banking.

Others changed their brokerage business under the pressure of events. The most notable change was the consolidation in June 1931 of Chase Securities Corp. and Harris, Forbes & Co., which Chase National Bank had bought earlier. Eighteen of 70 offices were immediately closed in the consolidation. In November, Fenner & Beane merged with Ungerleider & Co. to create the second largest brokerage house after E. A. Pierce & Co. The new firm had 60 branches. In time the top two would merge to become Merrill, Lynch, Pierce, Fenner & Beane. Mergers were numerous in the last months of 1931.

The most disquieting failure on the NYSE occurred in mid-October 1931, when Kountze Bros. suspended. It was an old, established firm which did a conservative bond business. The failure was due to the general decline in prices of bonds which it held in inventory for trading purposes. The firm had no speculative business and a sound operating history. No firm was immune when such a firm failed. Palmer & Co. also failed during December, but it had been a prominent speculative operator in the market. Its denouement provoked less apprehension.

We have already noted that the New York banks began to eliminate or consolidate their securities affiliates in the last quarter of 1931. Bankers Trust Co., Manhattan Trust Co., and Chemical Bank & Trust Co. announced dissolution of their securities affiliates, as did Phenix National Bank in Providence, R.I. Political pressures tended toward a division of the commercial and investment banking businesses, but the best reason for these closings was that their operations had become uneconomical.

NYSE data shows the deterioration in the strength of the brokerage industry in 1931. Member firms declined from 665 in 1930 to 649 at the end of 1931, and the 1,658 offices run by member firms at the end of 1929 had shrunk to 1,347 by the end of 1931. The number of cities with NYSE member firm offices shrank from 418 in 1929 to 337 in 1931.[1] The price of Exchange seats fell during 1931, but few members were prepared for the extremity of the decline. In 1929, seats traded for between $350,000 and $495,000, but in 1931 they dropped to $125,000, the lowest since 1925.

The net borrowings of NYSE member firms, which were used to finance margin accounts and inventories, grew slightly during the market rise in February and March 1931 but basically continued to decline as they had since the end of the recovery in April 1930. Member borrowings were $8.5 billion in October 1929 but only $0.6 billion by the end of 1931. This decline may be measured in absolute terms as an $8 billion reduction in the capital-chasing securities, or in percentage terms as a reduction in member borrowing from 9.82% of the market value of all listed NYSE stocks on October 1, 1929, to 2.20% on January 1, 1932. The reduction in purchasing power in the stock market was terrific in either case.[2]

The NYSE began in 1931 to collect systematic statistics on short sales of stocks by members (see Table A.23 in the Statistical Appendix). The first report on May 25, 1931, recorded short sales of 5.6 million shares, which declined to 2.8 million shares at the end of the year.[3]

The short position bore little correlation to the broad movement of stock prices. The 30% decline in stock prices in September was accompanied by a reduction in the short position from 4.4 million shares to 3 million shares. The short position was unchanged during the "moratorium rally," and it increased during the October–November market rise when President Hoover presented his banking proposals and leading commodities prices doubled. Within the period of these records, the short position represented 6%–8% of a month's trading volume; this does not appear to be significant, but the day-to-day changes in the short position by 100,000–200,000 shares amounted to 10%–20% of many days' trading volume. When short sales data became available, however, many observers were surprised that short sales were not larger. At 3–4 million shares, short sales were not the pervasive influence that many commentators looked for.

Besides revealing short sales, several other efforts were made during 1931 to reduce selling pressure on stock prices. Banks reduced margin requirements in June from 25% to 20%, and most of the brokerage houses followed suit. In

October the National Convention of Insurance Commissioners voted to allow insurance companies to use June 30, 1931, market values in their financial statements, and at the same time U.S. Senator N. W. Cheney, Chairman of the Joint Legislative Committee on Banking and Investment Trusts, proposed changes in the laws governing fiduciaries to prevent forced sales of portfolio securities which had become ineligible trustee investments. New York State declared a moratorium on striking railroad bonds from its legal list, and Federal Reserve member banks were allowed to carry bonds in the top four rating categories at par rather than adjust them to current market values in their financial statements.

A miscellaneous item among the technical data of the 1931 stock market was the heavy proportion of odd-lot trading. Brokers reported that 30%–60% of their business was odd-lot orders. Six major corporations reported an 18% increase in the number of their stockholders, following a 35% increase in 1930.[4]

SPECIFIC INDUSTRIES AND INDIVIDUAL STOCKS IN 1931

Data on individual companies can be found in Table A.1 in the Statistical Appendix. Table A.4 provides ratios for each company's high and low 1931 stock prices.

The Railroad Industry

In 1931 railroad stocks continued the poor stock market performance which characterized them in 1930 (see Table 8.1). The stock market reflected the economic problems of the railroads, whose earnings dropped from almost $900 million in 1929 to $135 million in 1931. The combination of market and economic problems for the railroad companies created conditions of such severity that many of the companies were threatened with bankruptcy. Some 19 railroads went into receivership in 1931, compared with 4 in 1930 and 3 in 1929. Only 1914 and 1917, when war disrupted the railroad industry, were as bad. But the industry was not at its nadir. Declining freight traffic and refinancing problems promised a greater number of railroad insolvencies in 1932.

The deterioration of railroad securities prices in both the stock market and the bond market was so severe that it threatened the credit of financial intermediaries and direct investors who had placed their confidence in the industry. The impact of the industry's decline was magnified by the industry's size. The $6 billion in railroad common stocks listed on the New York Stock Exchange as of January 1, 1931, was two-thirds again the size of the next largest industries—communications, petroleum, and chemicals—and at least double that of any other industries. Outstanding railroad bonds of $11.8 billion were almost one-third of all corporate bonds outstanding.[5]

The economics of the railroads in 1931 were fairly straightforward. Revenues dropped to $4.7 billion from $5.8 billion in 1930 and $6.9 billion in 1929 as a result of the general decline in business. The railroads tried to overcome reduced

Table 8.1
The Railroad Industry in 1931

	Price-earnings ratio		Market price as a % of book value		Dividend yield (%)		Low price as a % of 1929 high price	Return on equity (%)	Moody's bond ratings	Cash & equivalents ($ millions)
	High price	Low price	High price	Low price	High price	Low price				
Atchison, Topeka & Santa Fe	29	11	88	34	4.93	12.66	26	3.0	Aaa	20
Baltimore and Ohio	NM[a]	NM	61	10	0	0	10	0.4	Aaa	(43)[b]
Canadian Pacific	NM	16	113	27	2.78	11.36	16	1.7	Aa	24
Chesapeake and Ohio	14	7	98	48	5.32	10.87	33	7.1	Aaa	3
New York Central	NM	NM	83	16	0	0	10	0.3	Aa	(59)
Norfolk & Western	15	7	104	51	4.61	9.43	37	6.7	Aaa	4
Pennsylvania	NM	11	74	18	3.13	12.50	15	1.8	Aaa	41
Southern Pacific	NM	14	48	12	3.64	14.81	17	0.8	Aaa	27
Union Pacific	21	7	93	32	4.88	14.24	23	4.5	Aaa	17
Averages	19.8	10.4	85	28	3.25	9.55	21	2.9	—	—

[a] NM = Not Meaningful.
[b] Brackets indicate short-term borrowing.

revenues by cutting back employees from 1.7 million in 1930 to 1.4 million in 1931. The railroads also reduced maintenance, and they curtailed equipment purchases over 75% ($82 million in 1931 versus $374 million in both 1930 and 1929). The railroads joined to seek a 15% increase in rates at midyear, which they first sought as a temporary increase, then permanently. The initial reaction of the Interstate Commerce Commission was negative, since general business conditions were poor and prices were declining rather than rising, but as the railroads ran into greater credit difficulties, the 15% increase found ICC favor as a source of funds for a pool to aid ailing lines. New York Central asked its employees to take voluntary wage cuts in November after they had become general in other industries, but the strong railroad unions and traditional railroad employer-employee hostility prevented cooperation. Employees of several lines did accept voluntary 10% pay reductions in late December, most notably employees of Southern Pacific.

Dividend reductions were made by many railroads in reaction to their financial problems. The Wabash Railroad skipped preferred dividends as early as January 1931, and the St. Louis-San Francisco Railway Co. and the Chicago, Rock Island & Pacific Railway Co. "deferred" common dividends in February. The Lehigh Valley and New York Central railroads both cut their common dividends in March, catching the stock market by surprise and provoking a critical reevaluation of railroad prospects. The Pennsylvania Railroad reduced its dividend twice—in June and October—to its lowest rate since 1891. At year end, the Baltimore and Ohio, the Lehigh Valley, the Central, and the Southern railroads, among the largest roads, had eliminated their common dividends. The industry paid dividends of $401 million in 1931, compared with $603 million in 1930 and $561 million in 1929, but these dividends in 1931 were paid mostly in the first half of the year.

Railroads' ability to finance had been almost completely destroyed by year end. Total railroad public issues in 1931 were $517 million—half of 1930 volume and the lowest volume since 1926. Almost all the $517 million was in the first half of 1931. Railroads were able to sell only $85 million of securities in the last half of 1931. The St. Louis–San Francisco Railway Co. was unable to refund a $9.3 million bond maturity in June until Chase Securities and Dillon, Read & Co. bought $10 million in bonds due in five years for their own account and went on the board of directors. Dillon, Read & Co.'s rescue mission may have been motivated by its control of U.S. & Foreign Securities Corp., the first U.S. investment trust, an affiliate of which had a substantial interest in the St. Louis–San Francisco Railway Co. F. L. Dick, a prominent railroad finance expert of Roosevelt & Co. and Chairman of the Security Holders' Committee on the Railroad Emergency, testified in July before a congressional committee that it was "impossible to raise new money" for railroads and that, without the proposed 15% increase in rates, 75% of the outstanding $7.5 billion in railroad bonds would no longer be legal investments for savings banks at the end of 1931.[6] At the end of the year the New York Central sought approval of up to $50 million in short-term borrowing because it could not sell permanent securities. Almost simultaneously, the Wabash Railroad was placed in receivership. The Baltimore and Ohio was also building up a serious amount of short-term debt.

Railroad common stock prices reflected these dismal industry conditions. The Dow Jones Railroad Index dropped 72% in 1931 from a February high of 112 to a December low of 31. After February the index dropped to a lower level every month, with two minor exceptions. September and November were particularly difficult months in which the index dropped 23% and 30%, respectively. Leading railroad stocks were 21% of their 1929 high prices in December 1931 and 28% of book value, which was only one-third the valuation of stocks in general.

The Chesapeake and Ohio and the Norfolk & Western railroads occupied a special niche in the industry because of their solid base in the long-haul coal business. The two companies still earned approximately a 7% return on equity and maintained their dividends. Their stocks were still one-third of their highest 1929 prices at the low point in December 1931 and one-half of book value. By contrast, the Baltimore and Ohio and the New York Central were in deep trouble. They had started to report losses in the last half of 1931, eliminated their dividends, and built up large short-term debts. Both stocks were down to 10% of their highest 1929 prices and down to 10% and 16% respectively of their book values. They both needed help to avoid default and were watching anxiously as the Reconstruction Finance Corporation came into being.

The Operating Public Utility Industry

The larger electric and gas utilities fared unusually well in 1931 in the face of the declining economy and turbulent securities markets. The five leading companies in Table 8.2 earned a stable 8 1/2% return on equity, compared with 9% in 1930, and none of them changed its dividends. Moody's reported stable electric and gas utility industry profits between $413 million and $423 million each year between 1929 and 1931.[7] This relatively stable performance was grounded in strong economics because utility revenues, electricity generation, and utility employment all declined less than 10% from their prior peaks.[8] The utilities were also protected from having to write down the values of their properties due to declining price levels, as so many other industries were doing because of earlier U.S. Supreme Court cases (the Bluefield and Hope Natural Gas cases) which established that utilities had a right to returns on their investment calculated at historic costs. There were some signs of stress in the utility industry, such as bond rating reductions at Consolidated Gas Co. of New York from Aaa to Aa and at Detroit Edison from Aaa to A, and Commonwealth Edison in Chicago was somewhat disrupted by the obvious financial problems in Samuel Insull's Middle West Utilities Company. On the whole, however, utility bonds actually gained favor vis-à-vis other corporate bonds, and new issues of utility

Table 8.2
The Operating Public Utility Industry In 1931

	Price-earnings ratio		Market price as a % of book value		Dividend yield (%)		Low price as a % of 1929 high price	Return on equity (%)	Moody's bond ratings	Cash & equivalents ($ millions)
	High price	Low price	High price	Low price	High price	Low price				
Commonwealth Edison	25	11	193	82	3.11	7.34	24	7.6	Aa	14
Consolidated Gas Co. of N.Y.	22	12	200	104	3.64	7.02	31	9.0	Aa	(59)[a]
Detroit Edison	22	12	168	95	4.10	7.27	29	7.7	A	5
Pacific Gas & Electric	20	11	183	100	3.64	6.67	30	9.3	Aa	15
Public Service of N.J.	25	13	220	111	3.51	6.94	36	8.7	Aa	13
Averages	22.8	11.8	193	98	3.60	7.05	30	8.5	—	—

[a] Brackets indicate short-term borrowing.

stocks and bonds constituted 60% of the corporate new-issue market, compared with 24% in 1929.[9]

This economic stability made operating utility stocks fare relatively well in the 1931 decline in stock prices, even while public utility holding company stocks were devastated. The leading operating utility stocks declined only 49%, compared with 65% for all stocks, and were still virtually at book value when all other stocks were at 75% of book value. The highly uniform valuation parameters of utility stocks at their lowest 1931 prices of approximately 12 times earnings, 100% of book value, and 7% yield provide insight into the returns investors expected in this environment from stocks which retained traditional investment merits.

Holding and Investment Companies

Holding and investment companies had the broadest financial troubles, and their stocks had the worst declines in 1931. Many of these financial companies suffered income declines, asset write-offs, bond rating reductions, foreign exchange problems, and management conflicts. These problems made it difficult for the companies to refinance existing debts or raise new funds. Many barely survived 1931.

The Public Utility Holding Companies

The public utility holding companies had everything that had worked for them up to 1929 work against them in 1931. Their stocks dropped to 9% of their highest 1929 prices, compared with 19% for all other stocks, and all but United Gas Improvement had their bond ratings reduced. Most of the companies were clearly on the way to paying no common stock dividends, and many had accumulated large short-term debt positions as well. The companies hit worst, such as Electric Bond and Share and IT&T saw their stocks sink to approximately 15% of book value. (See Table 8.3 for data on specific companies)

The paradox of such market distress was that the very stability of the operating utility companies which had justified the holding company superstructures was realized in 1931, yet the holding company stocks were among the most depressed of all stocks. This was partly because of the general reaction against the holding and investment company stocks, many of which were in real financial trouble, including Middle West Utilities among the public utility holding companies.

But the public utility holding companies were also victims of two other influences—their leverage and their foreign investments. The public utility holding companies were leveraged by over 50% of their capitalizations in debt and preferred stocks, but also many companies owned only a portion of the common stock of their subsidiaries and affiliates. Therefore, as economic conditions worsened, declining values for their investments had to be added to the prospect of reduced dividends from the operating companies. Both the asset value underlying

Table 8.3
The Public Utility Holding Companies in 1931

	Price-earnings ratio		Market price as a % of book value		Dividend yield (%)		Low price as a % of 1929 high price	Return on equity (%)	Moody's bond ratings	Cash & equivalents ($ millions)
	High price	Low price	High price	Low price	High price	Low price				
Cities Service	42	10	259	62	1.43	6.00	7	6.2	B	(69)[c]
Columbia Gas & Electric	32	9	242	63	3.26	12.50	9	7.5	Baa	(44)
Commonwealth & Southern	30	8	212	53	2.50	10.00	9	7.6	Ba pfd.	42
Electric Bond and Share	NM[a]	8	103	15	0	0	5	4.3	B pfd.	33
IT&T	33	6	87	16	1.54	8.42	5	2.7	B	(44)
Middle West Utilities	NM	7	154	26	0	0	4	6.5	NR[b]	(29)
North American	26	8	265	76	0	0	14	10.7	Baa	(11)
Standard Gas and Electric	22	6	81	23	3.98	14.00	10	5.6	Ba	18
United Gas Improvement	26	10	271	107	3.16	8.00	24	10.4	Aa pfd.	20
Averages	30.1	8.0	186	49	1.76	6.55	9	6.9	—	—

[a] NM = Not Meaningful.
[b] NR = Not Rated.
[c] Brackets indicate short-term borrowing.

the holding companies' securities, and the cash flow to service those securities were undermined.

In instances where these operating companies were foreign, the negative impact was even greater because foreign exchange restrictions in South America and Eastern Europe prevented companies from paying dividends even when they were profitable, and the market values of their stocks dropped accordingly.

Electric Bond and Share (Ebasco) was hard hit by these trends because it made a point of not owning all of any companies it controlled and had heavy foreign interests. The market value of its net assets dropped from $1.2 billion on December 31, 1929, to only $0.3 billion on December 31, 1931, when it wrote down their value by $441 million. The prices of Ebasco's holdings in Electric Power & Light and National Power & Light common stocks, its two principal domestic holding company affiliates, had dropped from high prices in 1929 of $103 1/2 and $71 3/4 to $9 and $10 1/4 respectively. The stock price of its foreign affiliate, American & Foreign Power, dropped from $199 to $6 1/8. Foreign exchange restrictions prevented American & Foreign Power from paying any of its second preferred dividends, amounting to $19 million, all of which were due to Ebasco, and what is more, Ebasco was forced to lend the company $30 million to overcome its foreign exchange cash flow problems.

Electric Bond and Share's stock sank to 5% of its highest 1929 price and 15% of its reduced book value under such circumstances, and the proud inheritor of the General Electric utility securities assets had its preferred stock rating slashed from a respectable A to a lowly, speculative B.

IT&T fared as poorly as Ebasco, with its stock dropping to 5% of its highest 1929 price and 16% of book value, and its debt downgraded to a B rating, principally because all its assets were in foreign utilities, most of which were in South America. However, the stocks of the domestic holding companies fared almost as badly as those of Ebasco and IT&T because the domestic companies had substantially higher leverage, offsetting the greater security of their domestic investments.

The decline in securities values and market liquidity in the last half of 1931 doomed the efforts of Samuel Insull's Chicago holding company system to reorganize or refinance. The stocks of Insull Utilities Investments and Middle West Utilities, which it controlled, were subject to such heavy selling that any hope of refunding their combined short-term debts of approximately $120 million was destroyed. Insull Utilities stock dropped from a high of $50 to a low of $4, and Middle West's stock dropped from $25 to a low of $4 3/4. Insull Utilities closed 1931 with debts of approximately $115 million, versus securities it held with a market value of only $78 million. It had lost approximately $125 million on its investments in Commonwealth Edison, Middle West Utilities, Peoples Gas, and the other Insull operating utilities. Middle West Utilities ended the year with short-term debts of $70 million and bankers demanding payment.

Only United Gas Improvement stood apart from the other public utility holding companies in having a low common stock price still 24% of its highest 1929 price and about book value. It maintained both its dividend and its Aa preferred rating. The sources of this strength were virtually 100% ownership of its principal operating subsidiary, Philadelphia Electric Co., and no debt.

The Investment Trusts

The investment trust stocks easily qualified as the most hapless group in 1931, as the stocks of Goldman Sachs Trading, Tri-Continental, and United Founders were battered to $2 or less per share. The United Corp. fared only slightly better, even though it increased its dividend during the year. Although some of the trusts reported profits on the basis of interest and dividend income, they all in fact had enormous losses because of declines in the values of their securities portfolios. The impact of the declines in values varied in relation to the leverage of each trust and the pressures on it to realize its losses rather than wait for a recovery. (See Table 8.4 for data on the specific companies.)

Goldman Sachs Trading Corp. was one of the first trusts to be forced into selling assets when it sold its investments in several casualty insurance companies and Manufacturers Trust in 1930. The company's downfall is prominent in financial history as a dramatic example of leverage in the investment trust industry. Goldman, Sachs & Co., which had sponsored Goldman Sachs Trading Corp. in 1928, created an affiliated investment trust, Shenandoah Corp., in July 1929 at the height of the craze for investment trusts, and Shenandoah sold $67 million in convertible preference and common shares. Goldman Sachs Trading Corp., along with Central States Electric Corp., which was co-sponsor, retained 80% of the common stock of Shenandoah. Then in August 1929, having discovered a good thing, Goldman, Sachs & Co. created Blue Ridge Corp., which sold $72 million in convertible preference and common stock. Shenandoah controlled over 80% of the common stock of Blue Ridge by investing $62.5 million. Blue Ridge invested its new capital in Central States Electric Corp. (already mentioned as co-sponsor of Shenandoah Corp.) and North American Co. (about 10% each), various other utilities (about 13% in total), and a miscellany of industrial stocks.

The leverage in this structure was twofold. Shenandoah and Blue Ridge were each highly leveraged by the convertible preference stock they sold. Shenandoah had outstanding $42.5 million in preference stock at the end of 1929 on a total capitalization of $123 million. Blue Ridge had outstanding $58 million of preference stock at the end of 1929 on a total capitalization of $131 million. The 6% dividend on both issues required a cash outlay just short of $6 million per year. The system, from Goldman Sachs Trading Corp. to Blue Ridge, was also highly leveraged by the pyramid of control which left, as net income for Shenandoah, what was left over after Blue Ridge paid preference dividends, and as net income for Goldman Sachs Trading Corp. the even smaller amount remaining after Shenandoah paid its preference dividends. There was no way for Shenandoah to escape the impact of a decline in Blue Ridge's earnings, as Shenandoah had $62.5 million of its $122 million investments at the end of 1929 invested

Table 8.4
The Investment Trusts in 1931

	Price-earnings ratio		Market price as a % of book value		Dividend yield (%)		Low price as a % of 1929 high price	Return on equity (%)	Moody's bond ratings	Cash & equivalents ($ millions)
	High price	Low price	High price	Low price	High price	Low price				
Goldman Sachs Trading	NM[a]	NM	156	25	0	0	1	1.8	NR[c]	(10)[d]
Lehman Corp.	def.[b]	def.	121	61	4.35	8.57	26	def.	NR	21
Tri-Continental Corp.	def.	def.	NM	NM	0	0	4	def.	NR	8
United Corp.	41	10	344	83	2.42	10.00	10	2.5	NR	(13)
United Founders	NM	NM	446	61	0	0	2	5.8	NR	(3)
Averages	NM	NM	266	58	NM	NM	9	3.4	—	—

[a] NM = Not Meaningful.
[b] def. = Deficit.
[c] NR = Not Rated.
[d] Brackets indicate short-term borrowing.

in Blue Ridge Corp. Goldman Sachs Trading Corp. invested approximately $55 million of its $250 million in investments at the end of 1929 in Shenandoah Corp.

The effects of such leverage were exacerbated by problems arising from the principal investments of Goldman Sachs Trading Corp. and its offspring. American Trust Co. of San Francisco, which constituted almost 50% of Goldman Sachs Trading Corp.'s assets, stopped paying dividends in July 1929, and North American Co., which was a high quality public utility holding company controlled through Shenandoah Corp. and Blue Ridge Corp., never did pay dividends. Thus, these two supporting columns of the Goldman Sachs Trading Corp. empire provided no cash flow to service either the $6 million in preference dividends of Shenandoah and Blue Ridge, or the approximately $1 million in interest Goldman Sachs Trading Corp. had to pay on its debts. The pyramid based on Goldman Sachs Trading Corp. could sustain itself only by raising cash from the public, such as by sales of Shenandoah and Blue Ridge Corp. stocks, or by liquidating its investments. The latter course was forced on Goldman Sachs Trading Corp. in 1930 and 1931 because of the general market reluctance to accept investment trust and holding company new issues and by the problems of Manufacturers Trust Co., the third largest Goldman Sachs investment. Manufacturers Trust was caught up in the turmoil surrounding the collapse of the Bank of United States. Manufacturers Trust was similarly controlled by Jews, was a big lender to the Jewish garment industry, and had reduced its dividend rate in October 1930—a public signal of its problems. A run developed on its deposits just as it did on the Bank of United States, and the one solution was for the bank to join the New York Clearing House Association, in which all members guaranteed each other's deposits. The price of the remedy, however, was the end of Goldman Sachs Trading Corp. control and the imposition of new gentile management in the person of Harvey D. Gibson from Bankers Trust. The loss in this sale was over $32 million.

Other trusts were as leveraged as Goldman Sachs Trading Corp. and its affiliates. Harris, Forbes & Co., one of the leading investment banking firms of the period, sponsored a complex empire based on United Founders, a trust which controlled American Founders and Public Utility Holding Corp. of America. This group also controlled U.S. Electric Power. The investments of the Harris, Forbes & Co. group depreciated, as did those of Goldman Sachs Trading Corp., for they were similar. Most of the trusts and holding companies concentrated their investments in the utility industry, which appeared to have a stable growth in earnings and dividends which could support high leverage. The better cash flow in the Harris, Forbes & Co. group enabled it to get by without the same pressure to liquidate investments in a bad market. United Founders ultimately survived.[10]

Tri-Continental Corp., which was controlled by J. & W. Seligman & Co., fared much like United Founders. Its stock dropped to $2 from a high of $57 in 1929, as the market value of its portfolio dropped to $30 million, leaving almost no margin of value for common stockholders over the $29 million in capital attributable to the corporation's preferred stock. But Tri-Continental still had $2 million in dividend and interest income from prudent investment in domestic industries, so it continued to pay preferred dividends and was thereby strong enough to take over two distressed trusts, Selected Industries and Wedgwood Investing, whose stocks were selling below their net asset values.

J. P. Morgan's United Corp. was able to raise its dividend during 1931, and its investments in eastern utilities remained sound, but its stock nonetheless dropped to only 10% of its highest 1929 price and a slight discount from its asset value per share of $9. Its investment portfolio had a year-end market value of only $269 million, compared with a book cost of almost $600 million. It was really indistinguishable from the other trusts, despite its prominent backer.

Lehman Corp. remained the only investment trust which stood out in an industry with disastrous results. Lehman Corp. stock fell to only 26% of its highest 1929 price, compared with an average of 9% for the other leading trusts, and paid a substantial $3.00 per share dividend. Lehman Corp. had one-third of its investments in U.S. Treasuries, the balance in domestic stocks, and no leverage whatsoever to amplify the impact of its losses. It also freely advertised the market value per share of its assets and shrewdly repurchased 218,000 of its 1 million shares outstanding when they sold at substantial discounts to book value. Nonetheless, at the end of 1931 Lehman Corp. stock sold at a 40% discount from the per share market value of its investments. Such was the shift in the market's valuation of professional asset management from the heady premiums it received in 1929.

The Non-utility Holding Companies

The railroad holding company structure created around Alleghany Corp. by the Van Sweringen brothers got in trouble almost as early as Goldman Sachs Trading Corp. (See Table 8.5 for specifics.) In January 1931, Alleghany Corp. was required to pledge an additional $9.6 million in assets to the trustee for its bonds, Guaranty Trust, because of a covenant in Alleghany's convertible debenture issues that required pledged assets with a market value of 150% of the outstanding debentures. Van Sweringen Corp., which controlled Alleghany Corp., had sold 500,000 shares of Alleghany in November 1930 at a loss of $10.5 million, and the Van Sweringen brothers personally pledged $15 million in U.S. Treasury certificates to the trustee for Van Sweringen Corp.'s outstanding debentures to prevent a default.

Van Sweringen Corp. sold all its interest in Alleghany Corp. by October 1931 and pledged cash and U.S. government securities to its trustee to keep from defaulting. At this point the Van Sweringens did their best to eliminate the outstanding debt in Van Sweringen Corp. by offering $500 plus 20 shares of common stock for each $1,000 6% debenture due in 1935, of which there was $30 million outstanding. At the same time, Alleghany Corp. continued the forced sale of some of its assets to stay solvent, selling a 20% interest in Kansas City

Table 8.5
The Non-Utility Holding Companies in 1931

	Price-earnings ratio		Market price as a % of book value		Dividend yield (%)		Low price as a % of 1929 high price	Return on equity (%)	Moody's bond ratings	Cash & equivalents ($ millions)
	High price	Low price	High price	Low price	High price	Low price				
Alleghany Corp.	def.[a]	def.	68	6	0	0	2	def.	Ba	(7)[c]
Transamerica	NM[b]	8	327	36	0	0	3	4.6	B	(21)
Averages	NM	NM	198	21	0	0	3	NM	—	—

[a] def. = Deficit.
[b] NM = Not Meaningful.
[c] Brackets indicate short-term borrowing.

Southern Railroad to Chicago Great Western Railroad for $13 per share, compared with a cost of $95. Alleghany was forced to eliminate its preferred dividend to conserve cash, and its common stock traded down to $1 1/8 in 1931, compared with a high of $57 in 1929.

The irony of the Van Sweringens' plight was that their role in the railroads they controlled was positive. Popular descriptions of their activities, such as that by Ferdinand Pecora in *Wall Street Under Oath*, portray the brothers as grasping Cleveland real estate operators who incidentally got into the railroad business through a highly leveraged opportunity to buy the Nickel Plate Railroad between Buffalo and Cleveland. On the contrary, the Van Sweringens' principal line, the Chesapeake and Ohio, was one of the best railroads in the nation. It had the highest return on equity, maintained its dividend from 1929 to 1933, and was one of the best-performing railroad stocks. The Van Sweringens made a courageous effort to revitalize the moribund Missouri Pacific Railroad by connecting it with the rest of their system to create a trunkline to the West and by upgrading the management and operation of that railroad, but they were frustrated by the Depression, which again forced the Missouri Pacific into bankruptcy. J. P. Morgan & Co.'s relationship with the Van Sweringens and Alleghany Corp. supports the contention that they ran an operation of quality.

Transamerica Corp., which controlled the Bank of America in New York and the Bank of America National Trust & Savings Association (Bank of Italy renamed) in California, was also subject to great stress in 1931. The California bank was having serious problems with loan losses, and its market share of California deposits had declined from 31% in June 1930 to 25 1/2% by the end of 1931. Its absolute deposits had declined from $908 million to $750 million, and it had been forced to borrow $40 million from New York banks. The bank eliminated its dividend to Transamerica in September, thereby eliminating most of Transamerica's income, and to compound this problem the Comptroller of the Currency asked Transamerica to inject $15 million into the bank to take out bad loans, and warned that he might ask for $20 million more since the bank had reached the high deposit-to-capital ratio of 10 to 1. By June 1931, Transamerica had piled up short-term debts of $52 million and a plan of action was urgently needed.

Elisha Walker, Jean Monnet, and their people in Transamerica worked out a plan to sell off Transamerica's assets which was vigorously opposed by A. P. Giannini, the banks' founder, and his friends on the board of directors. The upshot was a board contest which Walker won and a September board meeting which announced the resignation of Giannini and his supporters, the elimination of Transamerica's dividend, the intention to sell Bank of America to the National City Bank of New York (which it did in October), and the reduction of Transamerica's assets from a book value of $1.1 billion to $300 million. Restrictive new management was put into the California bank to tighten up its liberal loan policies and stop real estate lending.

A. P. Giannini promptly launched a proxy fight for control of Transamerica,

Table 8.6
Data for Federal Reserve System Member Banks, 1929–1933 ($ millions)

	1929	1930	1931	1932	1933
Net income	$557	$ 306	$ 12	$ (255)[a]	$ (356)[a]
Loan losses	140	195	295	403	425
Securities losses	95	109	264	305	344
No. of suspended banks	659	1,350	2,293	1,453	4,000
Deposits in suspended banks	231	837	1,690	706	3,597
Dividends	387	367	335	245	150

Source: Banking & Monetary Statistics, pp. 262–63, 284–85.

[a] Numbers in parentheses indicate a loss.

despite the difficult economic environment and his own failing health. His proxy meetings in towns like Stockton and Sacramento drew 3,000 to 4,000 people, and on February 11, 1932, he was swept back into control with 15 million out of 25 million votes. During the proxy fight the Bank of America in California nearly collapsed, however. Corporate deposits were withdrawn, and the bank had to borrow from the Federal Reserve and the National Credit Corporation. John U. Calkins, Chairman of the San Francisco Federal Reserve and a critic of Giannini, thought the bank would fail. Not surprisingly, it became the first bank to borrow from the Reconstruction Finance Corporation in 1932. It was equally unsurprising that Transamerica's stock sank from $18 to $2, only 3% of its highest 1929 price.

The Banks

The banking industry had few problems in the first half of 1931, but its problems in the last half of 1931 when faced with the devaluation of sterling, the collapse of Germany, tight money in the United States, and a sharp decline in the economy were so great that 1931 was the worst year in history, up to that point, for banking operations in the United States. The net income of Federal Reserve System member banks dropped from $557 million in 1929 and $306 million in 1930 to a mere $12 million in 1931. Loan losses and securities losses of the banks exceeded $550 million, more than double those of 1929. There were suspended payments by 2,293 banks on deposits of almost $1.7 billion. Both were records which almost doubled the records set in the prior year. Table 8.6 outlines the unmitigated decline of the banking system in the five years under study here. Table 8.7 gives data on specific banks.

We know with the benefit of hindsight that 1931 was merely an installment

Table 8.7
The Banks in 1931

	Price-earnings ratio		Market price as a % of book value		Dividend yield (%)		Low price as a % of 1929 high price	Return on equity (%)	Moody's bond ratings	Cash & equivalents ($ millions)
	High price	Low price	High price	Low price	High price	Low price				
Bankers Trust	41	16	310	125	2.42	6.00	19	7.6	—	—
Central Hanover	NA^a	NA	269	105	2.53	6.48	21	NA	—	—
Chase National	21	5	175	40	3.64	16.00	9	11.0	—	—
Continental Illinois	22	6	216	60	3.85	13.91	11	8.3	—	—
First National (Boston)	NA	NA	200	72	3.72	10.32	14	NA	—	—
First National (Chicago)	26	12	163	72	3.49	7.93	18	9.2	—	—
Guaranty Trust	NM^b	NM	172	75	3.53	8.06	21	1.9	—	—
Irving Trust	27	9	159	56	3.72	10.67	15	6.5	—	—
National City	33	10	306	94	3.64	11.76	6	11.0	—	—
Averages	28.3	9.7	219	78	3.39	10.13	15	7.9	—	—

^a NA = Not Available.
^b NM = Not Meaningful.

in the "progress" to the Bank Holiday of 1933, but to contemporary observers 1931 was already as bad a year for bankers as a reasonable person could expect. Loan losses were a record because of failures in the real estate industry, the large number of Latin and South American countries which defaulted, and losses on securities loans. Securities losses were incurred in banks' own security portfolios, particularly on railroad or low quality corporate bonds, but they were also high in securities affiliates. We have already noted the trend to dissolve these securities affiliates which developed in the last quarter of 1931.

There were considerable differences in how individual banks reported their earnings, because income or losses in securities affiliates were reported separately, and securities and loan losses were often charged directly against capital rather than against income. The changes in the capital positions of the leading New York and Chicago banks made clear the direction of events, however. New York banks in the Federal Reserve class of Central City Reserve Banks, which were essentially the New York Clearing House Association banks, suffered a decline in capital in 1931 from $2 billion to $1.7 billion. Capital of the comparable banks in Chicago declined from $210 million to $167 million.[11]

The trend to lower short-term interest rates was a further pressure on bank earnings. Bankers acceptances yielded 1% or less for over half the year, and 3- to 6- month Treasury bills yielded around 1/2%. Call loans averaged 1 1/2% and commercial paper averaged 2% for similar periods. (See Tables A.17 and A.18 in the Statistical Appendix.) Banks reduced their deposit rates, but the spread narrowed sharply between deposit and short-term investment rates. The money banks earned on their float, idle deposits and own capital was reduced as well. The pressure on earnings from lower short-term rates was exacerbated by the banks' tendency to reduce long-term investments and loans in favor of short-term investments in order to maintain liquidity. Almost all that the banks got from this action was liquidity, since the income from short-term investments was minimal.

Despite the industry's problems, the leading bank stocks performed close to the averages for all stocks in 1931. Price-earnings ratios for their stocks were 25 to 30 at their highs and averaged 10 at their lows, although disparities were wider at the low prices because the acuteness of the banks' problems varied. The lowest bank stock prices in 1931 were 15% of their highest 1929 prices, which was below the average of 19% for all stocks, but bank stocks at these same low prices averaged 78% of book value, which almost exactly equalled the 75% average for all stocks.

Chase National Bank and National City Bank were singled out from the other banks for tougher treatment by investors. Chase stock dropped to only 9% of its highest 1929 price, and National City stock dropped to only 6% of its highest 1929 price. These relatively large declines reflected suspicions that the two banks' leaders, Albert Wiggin and Charles Mitchell, had led them into excesses during the late 1920s which would surface as losses in the Depression. There was considerable justification for the attitude towards Chase Bank, for at the end of the year the bank wrote down its net worth from the equivalent of $63 per share to $47. National City Bank had only a small write-off.

The reader will observe that the stock market was already treating these two banks as if they were either guilty of transgressions or badly managed, even though the public revelations of their activities would not be made until 1933 in the investigation of the Senate Committee on Banking and Currency into stock exchange practices.

The Oil Industry

The petroleum industry, like other commodity-based industries, lost money in 1931. Industry net income was $583 million in 1929 and $255 million in 1930, but turned into a loss of $45 million in 1931.[12] Domestic crude oil production dropped from 1 billion barrels in 1929 to 850 million barrels in 1931,[13] which does not appear unusually large in the light of the general economic decline, but prices dropped excessively because of the intense competition in the industry and discovery of the immense East Texas oil field. In 1931 the monthly average per barrel price of crude oil at the wellhead ranged nationally from $1.26 to 70¢ compared with $1.82 to $1.68 in 1929, and one sale was publicized in Texas in which 40,000 barrels were sold for 2 1/2¢ per barrel. By the end of the year, pro-rationing was introduced in Texas, Oklahoma, and Kansas as producers and politicians in oil-producing states pushed for pro-rationing of oil production to reduce the erosion of values in the industry from full production.

The low prices and surplus product in the oil industry were reflected sharply in the industry's securities (see Table 8.8). Oil stocks dropped to 16% of their highest prices in 1929, even though they had not participated in the boom in prices in 1929. After such a decline, oil stocks averaged only 29% of book value, which was one of the worst measures of any industry. Most of the companies reduced their dividends, and Phillips, Sinclair Consolidated, and Shell Union Oil eliminated them totally. Bond ratings were reduced for Atlantic Refining, Gulf Oil, Phillips, and Texas Corp. Bond ratings as low as Ba for Phillips and Shell Union Oil suggested that some of the oil companies were in deep financial trouble. Even the Standard Oil companies, which still had positive earnings and reliable dividends and stood out for much better stock performance than the rest of the industry, had financial results and stock prices which were deplorable relative to other strong companies. The oil giants lacked the profits and power which had made them so prominent in the past.

The Chemical Industry

Chemical industry profits dropped to $83 million in 1931 from $158 million in 1929 and $113 million in 1930, on a sales decline from $4 billion in 1929 to $2.8 billion in 1931.[14] The companies were able to reduce their costs in close

Table 8.8
The Oil Industry in 1931

	Price-earnings ratio		Market price as a % of book value		Dividend yield (%)		Low price as a % of 1929 high price	Return on equity (%)	Moody's bond ratings	Cash & equivalents ($ millions)
	High price	Low price	High price	Low price	High price	Low price				
Atlantic Refining	NM[a]	NM	47	17	4.17	11.59	11	2.8	Aa	6
Gulf Oil of Penna.	def.[b]	def.	112	38	1.97	5.77	12	def.	Aa	14
Phillips Petroleum	def.	def.	49	11	0	0	9	def.	Ba	(13)[d]
Shell Union Oil	def.	def.	53	13	0	0	8	def.	Ba	14
Sinclair Consolidated	def.	def.	89	22	0	0	9	def.	Baa	44
Socony-Vacuum	def.	def.	81	26	3.85	11.94	17	def.	NR[c]	64
Standard Oil (Calif.)	47	21	118	52	4.81	10.87	28	2.5	NR	14
Standard Oil (Ind.)	38	13	100	36	2.56	7.14	22	2.6	NR	89
Standard Oil (N.J.)	def.	def.	110	54	3.77	7.69	31	0.7	Aaa	280
Texas Corp.	def.	def.	82	23	5.56	20.00	14	def.	A	44
Averages	NM	NM	84	29	2.67	7.5	16	NM	—	—

[a] NM = Not Meaningful.
[b] def. = Deficit.
[c] NR = Not Rated.
[d] Brackets indicate short-term borrowing.

concert with their reductions in sales, and they remained profitable despite sizable write-offs to reflect lower asset and inventory values. At these lower profit levels, Commercial Solvents still had a return on equity of 22.6%, and the leading companies averaged a return on equity of 12.1%, even though Du Pont wrote off $14 million, Allied Chemical established a $40 million reserve, and Union Carbide had a $55 million write-off. Du Pont was the only chemical company to change its dividend in 1931, and it only dropped from $4.70 per share to $4 per share. (See Table 8.9 for data on specific companies.)

The industry's financial stability was not at all challenged by the Depression. Du Pont, for example, still had cash assets of $69 million after buying back $8 million of its own common stock, and Allied Chemical had $94 million in cash and equivalents.

The chemical industry provides good insight into investors' valuations of stocks in the severe conditions prevailing after the Sterling Crisis. In this respect, chemicals join the food, consumer products, operating utility, and tobacco industries, which also had stable dividends and high returns on equity. At their lowest 1931 prices the chemical stocks carried a dividend yield averaging 9.43% and a price-earnings ratio of 9.8, which were very close to the averages for these other industries but averaged only 21% of their highest 1929 prices and 108% of book value. Both measures exceeded the averages for all companies of 19% and 75% respectively but fell considerably short of the same measures for the industries mentioned above. In part this was because of the chemical companies' return on equity, which although it averaged 12.1% when U.S. industry was posting a loss, was considerably short of the returns over 20% still earned by many of the food, tobacco, and consumer products companies.

The Food Industry

The leading food industry stocks were among the best in the market again in 1931 as their lowest prices were 29% of their highest 1929 prices (19% average for all stocks) and 139% of book value (75% for all stocks). (See Table 8.10 for data on specific companies.) These food companies maintained an unusually high return on equity, which averaged 16.3% in 1931, exceeded only by tobacco and consumer products companies. The food industry as a whole fared less well. Sales declined from $11.3 billion in 1929 to $9.2 billion in 1931, which reduced industry net income from $410 million to $161 million.[15] The high profits and income stability of the big, publicly owned companies resulted from their superior marketing skills and concentration in profitable, growing product lines rather than in staples. The closer food companies were to staples products, the lower their returns on equity were, as in the cases of United Fruit, Pillsbury, General Mills, and Borden.

All the food companies except United Fruit and National Biscuit retained their 1929 dividend rates in 1931. National Biscuit's dividend dropped in two steps from $3.75 in 1929 to $2.80 per share in 1931, but the company kept its earnings

Table 8.9
The Chemical Industry in 1931

	Price-earnings ratio		Market price as a % of book value		Dividend yield (%)		Low price as a % of 1929 high price	Return on equity (%)	Moody's bond ratings	Cash & equivalents ($ millions)
	High price	Low price	High price	Low price	High price	Low price				
Allied Chemical	27	10	195	68	3.28	9.38	18	9.1	Aa pfd.	94
Commercial Solvents	26	8	567	171	4.55	15.09	9	22.6	NR[a]	5
Dow Chemical	17	10	213	125	3.92	6.67	38	12.5	NR	(1)[b]
E. I. Du Pont	25	12	268	125	3.74	8.00	22	11.2	Aa	69
Monsanto Chemical	10	5	88	48	4.31	7.81	20	8.9	A	2
Union Carbide	36	14	300	113	3.61	9.63	19	8.3	NR	22
Averages	23.5	9.8	272	108	3.90	9.43	21	12.1	—	—

[a] NR = Not Rated.
[b] Brackets indicate short-term borrowing.

Table 8.10
The Food Industry in 1931

	Price-earnings ratio		Market price as a % of book value		Dividend yield (%)		Low price as a % of 1929 high price	Return on equity (%)	Moody's bond ratings	Cash & equivalents ($ millions)
	High price	Low price	High price	Low price	High price	Low price				
Borden	20	9	220	100	3.90	8.57	34	11.9	NR[a]	25
General Foods	16	8	467	233	5.36	10.71	34	29.5	NR	12
General Mills	13	7	128	74	6.00	10.34	33	10.1	Ba pfd.	11
National Biscuit	29	13	525	225	3.33	7.78	38	17.9	Aaa pfd.	29
National Dairy	15	6	283	111	5.10	13.00	23	19.3	A	24
Pillsbury	9	5	100	54	5.41	10.00	31	9.7	Baa	2
Standard Brands	19	10	553	289	5.71	10.91	24	28.4	Aa pfd.	20
United Fruit	29	8	97	26	4.41	16.27	11	3.6	NR	26
Averages	18.8	8.3	297	139	4.90	10.95	29	16.3	—	—

[a] NR = Not Rated.

Table 8.16
The Retailers in 1931

	Price-earnings ratio		Market price as a % of book value		Dividend yield (%)		Low price as a % of 1929 high price	Return on equity (%)	Moody's bond ratings	Cash & equivalents ($ millions)
	High price	Low price	High price	Low price	High price	Low price				
Associated Dry Goods	def.[a]	def.	107	21	3.33	17.39	8	def.	Ba	9
Gimbel Brothers	def.	def.	23	5	0	0	4	def.	B pfd.	6
S. S. Kresge	18	9	200	100	5.33	10.67	26	11.2	Aa	2
R. H. Macy	29	14	241	114	2.59	5.50	20	8.2	NR[c]	(4)[d]
Marshall Field	def.	def.	103	30	7.58	26.32	NA[b]	def.	A	16
Montgomery Ward	def.	def.	97	23	0	0	4	def.	NR	34
J. C. Penney	14	9	265	159	5.33	8.89	26	18.2	A pfd.	14
Sears Roebuck	26	12	154	73	3.97	8.33	17	6.2	NR	(12)
F. W. Woolworth	17	8	429	206	6.03	12.57	34	24.9	NR	23
Averages	20.8	10.4	180	81	3.80	9.96	17	13.7	—	—

[a] def. = Deficit.
[b] NA = Not Available.
[c] NR = Not Rated.
[d] Brackets indicate short-term borrowing.

Table 8.17
The Tire Industry in 1931

	Price-earnings ratio		Market price as a % of book value		Dividend yield (%)		Low price as a % of 1929 high price	Return on equity (%)	Moody's bond ratings	Cash & equivalents ($ millions)
	High price	Low price	High price	Low price	High price	Low price				
Firestone	17	10	85	50	4.55	7.69	35	4.8	B pfd.	15
B. F. Goodrich	def.[a]	def.	64	10	0	0	3	0	Baa	21
Goodyear	NM[b]	NM	196	52	5.66	21.43	9	0	Baa	37
Averages	NM	NM	115	37	3.40	9.71	16	NM	—	—

[a] def. = Deficit.
[b] NM = Not Meaningful.

Table 8.19
The Tobacco Companies in 1931

	Price-earnings ratio		Market price as a % of book value		Dividend yield (%)		Low price as a % of 1929 high price	Return on equity (%)	Moody's bond ratings	Cash & equivalents ($ millions)
	High price	Low price	High price	Low price	High price	Low price				
American Tobacco	14	7	358	169	4.65	9.84	53	25.2	Aaa	40
Liggett & Myers	13	6	253	108	5.49	12.82	49	19.2	Aaa	48
Reynolds Tobacco	15	9	344	206	5.45	9.10	50	22.8	NR[a]	44
Averages	14.0	7.3	318	161	5.20	10.59	51	22.4	—	—

[a] NR = Not Rated.

The Pulp and Paper Industry

Although the pulp and paper industry reported a modest loss of only $2 million in 1931, versus profits of $15 million in 1930, and although imports were reduced from 64% to 55% of consumption, the paper stocks still fared among the very worst of any industry.[23] Following the Sterling Crisis, paper stocks dropped to only 11% of their highest 1929 prices and 14% of book value, ratios which are borne out for other paper companies besides the three in Table 8.20. Companies' bond ratings were uniformly reduced, in many cases to highly speculative levels. The industry's very high leverage, its weak economic position vis-à-vis Canadian producers, and its frequent ties to the troubled public utility holding companies led to a mood of complete despair surrounding the companies' securities.

The Office Equipment Companies

The office equipment companies had highly uneven experiences in 1931, but Moody's still reported the overall industry as profitable, earning $11 million in 1931 versus $44 million in 1929.[24] Remington Rand's sales dropped from $36.5 million in 1929 to $16.8 million in 1931, and it swung from profits over $3.00 per share in 1929 to losses of over $3.00 per share in 1931. Burroughs earnings dropped by almost two-thirds from 1929, and IBM's earnings remained at their 1929 level. The two latter companies still averaged a very high 23% return on equity, however. (See Table 8.21 for details on each company.)

The stocks of IBM and Burroughs ended up with relatively similar valuations at their lowest prices in 1931, particularly if Burroughs' higher dividend yield is reduced by one-third to eliminate a special dividend of 50¢ at the beginning of 1931. IBM stock was one of the best-performing stocks on the NYSE at 36% of its highest 1929 price and a yield of 6.50%. By contrast, National Cash Register and Remington Rand stocks were among the worst-performing stocks, at less than 5% of their highest 1929 prices.

Other Stocks

The differences between General Electric and Westinghouse became quite striking in 1931 as their sales declined 37% and 47% respectively from 1929. (For details on GE and Westinghouse, see Table 8.22.) General Electric had a 43% decline in earnings per share compared with 1929 and an 11.1% return on equity, but Westinghouse swung all the way from earnings per share over $10 in 1929 to a loss of $1.52 in 1931. Westinghouse reduced its work force by 38% from 1929 levels, which was 50% greater than GE's reduction. There was also a sharp difference between Westinghouse's cash on hand of $33 million and GE's $122 million. These differences carried through to the two companies' common stocks. General Electric stock dropped to a low price 23% of its highest 1929 price and a robust 187% of book value, versus averages for all stocks of

Table 8.20
The Pulp and Paper Industry in 1931

	Price-earnings ratio		Market price as a % of book value		Dividend yield (%)		Low price as a % of 1929 high price	Return on equity (%)	Moody's bond ratings	Cash & equivalents ($ millions)
	High price	Low price	High price	Low price	High price	Low price				
Crown Zellerbach	def.[a]	def.	17	10	0	0	5	def.	B	(1)[d]
International Paper	NA[b]	NA	32	6	0	0	4	def.	Ba	(36)
Kimberly-Clark	18	6	73	25	6.10	17.86	25	4.1	Baa	2
Averages	NM[c]	NM	41	14	NM	NM	11	NM	—	—

[a] def. = Deficit.
[b] NA = Not Available.
[c] NM = Not Meaningful.
[d] Brackets indicate short-term borrowing.

Table 8.21
The Office Equipment Companies in 1931

	Price-earnings ratio		Market price as a % of book value		Dividend yield (%)		Low price as a % of 1929 high price	Return on equity (%)	Moody's bond ratings	Cash & equivalents ($ millions)
	High price	Low price	High price	Low price	High price	Low price				
Burroughs Adding Machine	18	6	469	146	4.69	15.00	10	27.8	NR[c]	17
IBM	16	8	300	153	3.33	6.52	36	18.2	Aa	5
National Cash Register A	NM[a]	14	148	26	0	0	5	1.9	NR	4
Remington Rand	def.[b]	def.	1,333	125	0	0	3	def.	Ba	7
Averages	17.0	9.3	563	113	4.01	10.76	14	16.0	—	—

[a] NM = Not Meaningful.
[b] def. = Deficit.
[c] NR = Not Rated.

Table 8.22
Other Stocks in 1931

	Price-earnings ratio		Market price as a % of book value		Dividend yield (%)		Low price as a % of 1929 high price	Return on equity (%)	Moody's bond ratings	Cash & equivalents ($ millions)
	High price	Low price	High price	Low price	High price	Low price				
American Can	25	11	245	109	3.85	8.62	31	9.6	A pfd.	6
AT&T	21	12	132	73	4.46	8.04	36	6.3	Aa	289
General Electric	41	18	448	187	2.91	6.96	23	11.1	Aaa	122
Radio Corp. of America	def.[a]	def.	NM[b]	NM	0	0	4	def.	Baa pfd.	25
Westinghouse	def.	def.	133	27	2.31	11.36	8	def.	Aa pfd.	33

[a] def. = Deficit.
[b] NM = Not Meaningful.

!9% and 75%, while Westinghouse stock dropped below average in all respects, ɔ only 8% of its highest 1929 price and 27% of book value.

AT&T remained a preeminent stock, even though its 38% decline in earnings ·r share since 1929 left its $9.00 dividend barely covered and its return on uity was only 6.3%. (See Table 8.22 for details on AT&T.) These parameters ulted in the company's debt rating being reduced from Aaa to Aa, but con- ?nce in the stock, particularly in the stability of the $9.00 dividend, remained h. The stock sold down to only 36% of its highest 1929 price and a yield of 8%.

American Can also remained a highly attractive company in 1931. (See Table 8.22.) Its return on equity was still 9.6%, despite a 36% decline in earnings since 1929. Even though there were no changes in its common stock dividend, American Can's preferred stock rating was reduced from Aa to A, but the stock market retained a high level of relative confidence in the company, as can be seen in its lowest 1931 stock price, which was still 31% of its highest 1929 price and 109% of book value, versus the averages for all stocks of 19% and 75%.

RCA's excessive leverage and overexpansion produced a sad awakening for the company in 1931 as its sales dropped from $132 million in 1930 to $100 million, and it registered a net loss of $4.4 million. In November the company had to participate heavily in refinancing RKO, its motion picture affiliate, lest RKO default. RCA ended up buying $9.8 million of a $11.6 million bond issue by RKO, just when RCA needed the money itself. In December it failed to pay the fourth-quarter dividend on its B preferred stock, and the following month it wrote off $42 1/2 million, mostly in equipment and inventory costs, thereby wiping out the common stockholders' equity.

Amid such distress RCA's stock slumped to $5, only 4% of its highest 1929 price. (See Table 8.22 for details on RCA.) This approximate price was repeated again in 1932 and 1933, so RCA reached a very depressed and persistent low price early in the Depression. Nor did it have any particularly dramatic recoveries during this period. The zip had gone out of the stock.

Summary

In 1931, following the international currency crisis, financial problems appeared on a massive scale requiring remedial action. In the railroad and banking industries, where these problems impinged heavily on the public and the whole financial structure, the problems led to legislation creating the Reconstruction Finance Corporation at the end of the year with authority to assist these two industries. Among the holding companies and investment trusts where the public interest was less directly touched, remedial action was unavailable and the companies suffered acute cash squeezes. Their stocks generally sank to less than 10% of their highest 1929 prices, compared with an average of 19%, and reorganizations or liquidations were in prospect, particularly for the Van Sweringens and Middle West utilities. The highly leveraged industries, such as motion pictures, had similar cash squeezes.

Many heavy industries registered their first losses of the Depression in 1931, particularly the copper, oil, steel, tire, farm equipment, and pulp and paper industries. Industries whose product prices were determined on international commodities markets, such as oil and mining industries, suffered especially as other countries devalued their currencies, lowering their commodities prices. Most of these industries had little debt and so were not threatened with reorganization, but their stock prices generally sank to less than 13% of their highest 1929 prices and below 30% of book value, compared with the averages of 19% and 75%, respectively. The market had reduced the values of these industries almost to insignificance.

The food, consumer products, tobacco, and some of the retail companies achieved extraordinary results in 1931 by comparison with the heavy industries and financial companies. These consumer-oriented companies had returns on equity which were frequently 20% or higher, and their lowest stock prices were 150% or more of book value, which was twice the average valuation. These companies' results had still not been touched significantly by the Depression.

Although the chemical and operating utility industries had been affected by the Depression, they were proving to be relatively stable and profitable, with returns on equity of 8% to 12%. This produced low stock prices still around book value and other elements of stability such as unchanged bond and preferred ratings and dividend yields of 7% to 8%.

The gold mining stocks assumed a unique place in Depression financial markets for the first time in 1931. Gold stocks established earnings, dividend, and stock price records in 1931.

NOTES

1. See *NYSE Year Book*, 1938, pp. 60–61, 71–72; and Table A.25 in the Statistical Appendix.

2. Ibid., pp. 62–63; and Table A.22 in the Statistical Appendix.

3. Ibid., pp. 56–57.

4. NYSE Bulletin, Volume 3, Number 5, May 1932, p. 1.

5. *Moody's Utility Manual, 1934*, p. a8.

6. *New York Times*, 7/14/31.

7. *Moody's Utility Manual 1974*, p. a23. These *Moody's* statistics contrast with National Income Accounts statistics indicating that utilities' net income declined from $415 million in 1929 to $271 million in 1931, but we have used *Moody's* data as a more current reflection of investor knowledge.

8. *National Income Accounts*, pp. 110, 142; *Moody's Utility Manual, 1974*, p. a23; *Statistical Abstract, 1939*, p. 378.

9. *Survey of Current Business*, May 1938, Table 57. (See also Table A.26 in the Statistical Appendix.)

10. Data on Goldman Sachs Trading Corp. and United Founders is principally from *Moody's Financial Manuals, 1931, 1932, 1933*.

11. *Banking & Monetary Statistics*, pp. 81, 87.

12. *Moody's Industrial Manual, 1935*, p. a45.

13. Ibid., *1932*, p. xxxvi.

14. *National Income Accounts*, p. 142; *Moody's Industrial Manual, 1935*, p. a45.

15. *National Income Accounts*, pp. 126, 142.

16. *Moody's Industrial Manual, 1933*, pp. a77–a78, a85; *National Income Accounts*, pp. 102, 142, 126.

17. *Moody's Industrial Manual, 1935*, pp. a28–30, a45.

18. Ibid., *1933*, pp. a71, a72; *1935*, p. a45.

19. Ibid., *1933*, pp. a90, a101; *1935*, p. a45.

20. *National Income Accounts*, pp. 142, 102; *Moody's Industrial Manual, 1933*, p. a91; *1935*, p. a45.

21. *Moody's Industrial Manual, 1933*, pp. a70, a100; *1935*, p. a45.

22. Ibid., *1933*, p. a87; *1935*, p. a45.

23. Ibid., *1933*, p. a87; *1935*, p. a45.

24. Ibid., *1935*, p. a45.

9

Bond Markets in 1931

BOND MARKETS IN GENERAL

Long-term interest rates declined by 1/8% to 1/4% in the first half of 1931, reducing the yields on Aaa railroad and utility bonds to approximately 4%. However, this trend was reversed by the international currency crisis and the coincident economic decline, which raised questions about the ability of many companies, especially railroads, to pay their debts. The yield on the best Aaa railroad and utility bonds rose during the last quarter to approximately 5%, reductions in railroad bond ratings were numerous, and the sector of the bond market made up of weak A and Baa credits became quite disorganized with yields varying from 8% to 12%. Railroad bonds gave up forever their position as the preeminent corporate bond and began to yield more than comparably rated utility and industrial bonds.

U.S. government bond yields declined and rose in conjunction with the best corporate bond rates during the year. There was no significant threat to the federal government credit, but the market disruption of the last four months of the year halted for a year and a half the efforts of the government to extend the maturity of U.S. debts.

The foreign bond market experienced the largest losses in 1931. Virtually every South American country, except the Argentine, defaulted on its foreign debts, and their bond prices dropped to a range between $5 and $25. Eastern Europe did not default during the year, but the prices of East European external debt issues dropped below $40 in anticipation of the difficulties ahead. Even the bonds of such stable countries as Belgium, Canada, Denmark, Norway, and Sweden dropped $30–$40 in the maelstrom surrounding the international currency crisis. Moody's reduced its bond ratings for 23 foreign countries in response to the year's events.

The municipal bond market also shared in the rising interest rates and credit problems characteristic of the other credit markets in the last half of 1931. High grade municipal bond rates rose approximately 1% during the currency crisis, and the low quality sector of the market showed disruption similar to the corporate bond market. Local governments in particular trouble were the states of the Deep South and several large cities, such as Chicago, Detroit, and Philadelphia. But the municipal market was not to see the depths of its problems until 1933.

THE COURSE OF EVENTS—INTEREST RATES DECLINE TO THEIR LOWEST LEVELS SINCE THE CRASH, UNTIL THE CURRENCY CRISIS DRIVES THEM TO NEW HIGH LEVELS

Bond prices rose to their highest levels since the Crash during the first half of 1931 under the impetus of a liquid banking system, an active Federal Reserve policy to lower short-term rates, and early business optimism. Interest rates on A rated, or better, bonds dropped 1/2% - 1% below their highest levels in 1930, and prices of these bonds were actually $1 to $3 above their highest levels in 1929 and 1930. Interest rates on the best corporate bonds at this point were 4%, and even good Baa rated bonds had yields of only 4 1/2%. Interest rates were neatly arrayed in their customary order, rising from the lowest rates on U.S. government debt, with municipal rates next, through railroad, utility, and industrial bonds to foreign bonds, as follows:

Bonds	*Yields*
U.S. government bonds	3 1/8%
Municipal bonds	3 3/4%
Aaa railroad bonds	4 1/8%
Aaa utility bonds	4 1/4%
Aaa industrial bonds	4 1/2%
Aaa foreign bonds	4 3/4%

At this high point in the bond market, corporate bonds showed little indication of the disaster approaching only three months ahead. The spectrum of interest rates was surprisingly compact, with the range between Aaa railroad bond interest rates and Baa industrial interest rates only spanning from 4 1/8% to 5 3/8%, and within a given rating category of an industry, yields were quite close together.

This orderly market disappeared during the international currency crisis. Long-term interest rates rose 1% within two months on Aaa rated bonds and 2% on Aa and A rated bonds. Interest rates rose approximately 4% on Baa and Ba rated bonds in the distinctive pattern of the Depression bond market, which created a large interest premium on low quality credits during crises. At the same time, the orderly structure of interest rates by bond rating and by industry was shattered, as bond ratings were reduced and individual companies suddenly began to look like high risks for paying off their debts. The yields on railroad bonds shifted from being the lowest in any rating category to being the highest, and interest

Table 9.1
New Issues of Long-Term Debt, 1929–1931 ($ millions)

	1929	1930	1931	Last quarter 1931
Domestic corporate issues	$2,370	$2,811	$1,628	$ 74
Municipal issues	1,429	1,487	1,256	116
Foreign government issues	130	620	51	0
All foreign issues[a]	785	1,147	270	51

Source: Survey of Current Business, February 1938, pp. 18, 19. See also Tables A.26 and A.27 in the Statistical Appendix.

[a] Mostly debt.

rates available within a given industry bond rating became widely divergent, depending on the outlook for individual companies.[1]

The new-issue business puts in sharp relief the magnitude of the change in bond markets in the fourth quarter of 1931. New issues in the last quarter of 1931 came to a virtual halt. Table 9.1 outlines public bond financing in 1929–31 and in the fourth quarter of 1931.

Railroad Bonds Collapse

Railroad bonds suffered in the last half of 1931. Moody's reduced the bond ratings on 18 of the railroad bond issues over $40 million, 11 of which had been Aaa rated. (See Table A.7 in the Statistical Appendix.) Suddenly there were groups of large railroad bond issues rated A and Baa, whereas previously only utility and industrial bonds had occupied these rating categories. There were some shocking losses in railroad bonds, with 19 of the 34 railroad issues over $40 million dropping over $30. Seven of the 19 issues dropped over $40. (See Table A.12 in the Statistical Appendix.) These were particularly stiff losses for smaller banks that were forced to sell bonds to maintain liquidity, bonds they had previously bought thinking they were the most conservative bond investments.

Railroad bond yields suddenly became greater than on comparably rated utility and industrial bonds, having been lower historically. Railroad bond yields averaged 1/2% to 1 1/2% greater than comparably rated utility bonds at their lowest prices for 1931, with the highest differential applying to Baa rated bonds. The railroad bond market in fact became quite disorganized with bond ratings losing much of their meaning and investor opinions of individual systems dominating their bond prices. This disorganization can be seen in the wide variations in yields within a given rating category. (See Table A.12). For example, yields on

Aa railroad bonds varied between 5 1/2% and 8 3/4%, and on Baa railroad bonds between 8 1/4% and 12%, compared with differences of 1/2% or less in better markets. Amid this debacle, the only rail bonds which retained real stability were the best issues of the Atchison, Topeka & Santa Fe, the Lake Shore & Michigan Southern, the New York Central, the Norfolk and Western, and the Pennsylvania railroads. This is not to say that these systems' junior bonds fared as well though—the Pennsylvania had four large junior issues which lost between $34 and $44.

Utility Bonds Become the Premier Corporate Bond Investment

During the last quarter of 1931, with yields 1/2% to 1 1/2% below those on railroad bonds, utility bonds assumed the place they were to occupy for the next four decades as the premier industry in the corporate bond market. Moody's did not reduce its bond rating on a single utility bond issue over $40 million (see Table A.8 in the Statistical Appendix), and the market for utility bonds rated between Aaa and A remained orderly and well organized. Only one of these issues declined over $20, compared with over half the railroad issues dropping over $30. The average yields on Aaa to A utility bonds at their lowest prices in the year ranged between only 5% and 6 1/4%, and within a rating category, yields on various issues were quite close together. (See Table A.13 in the Statistical Appendix for price and yield ranges of utility bonds.) Bell Telephone system subsidiaries, Duquesne Light, Duke Power, and Public Service Electric and Gas stood out as the utility bonds with the lowest yields.

Only the Baa sector of the utility bond market showed signs of disorganization characteristic of the aversion to credit risks in this last-quarter atmosphere of crisis. Baa utility bonds averaged yields 1 1/4% higher than A utility bonds, and within the Baa category, yields ranged all the way from 6 1/4% to 8 1/2%. A yield of 8 1/2% pales by comparison with yields over 12% in the railroad and industrial bond areas, however.

Industrial Bonds

While industrial bond issues were generally too small, too few, and too lacking in homogeneity to allow broad conclusions, some observations about this market sector are possible. Eight of the 20 issues over $20 million were downgraded by Moody's, including three of the six Aaa oil companies (see Table A.9 in the Statistical Appendix). Among industrial bonds rated A or better, only one declined over $20, and industrial bond yields averaged in between those on utility and railroad bonds. However, the Baa and Ba sectors of the industrial bond market showed even greater difficulties than the railroad bond market, with seven of the nine issues declining over $30 and yields rising higher and diverging further. Interest rates on Baa and Ba industrial bonds ranged from 8% on National Steel's 5% bonds due in 1956, to 12 3/4% on Pure Oil Co.'s 5 1/2% bonds due as early as 1940 (see Table A.14 in the Statistical Appendix for price and yield ranges on industrial bonds).

U.S. Government Bonds

Yields on long-term U.S. Treasury bonds rose from 3 1/4% to 4% in the fourth quarter of 1931, as the prices of the U.S. Treasury bonds followed in Table A.40 dropped $5–$14, depending on the issue. The selling pressure was created by active selling of long-term U.S. government bonds by the commercial banking system. Federal Reserve member bank holdings of long-term U.S. bonds declined from $4.3 billion on the September 29, 1931, call date to $3.7 billion at the June 30, 1933, call date before these holdings began to rise again.[2] There is a tendency in retrospect to assume that U.S. Treasury financing was no problem in the Depression because of the ultimate security of U.S. bonds and the demand for U.S. bonds to provide liquidity. But this demand was focussed on the short end of the market during the worst stages of the Depression, which made Treasury officials concerned about their ability to manage the government's financial requirements. The principal cause of concern was the $10.8 billion of Treasury debt maturing in the next two years as a result of World War I Liberty Bond financing. Andrew Mellon as Secretary of the Treasury, and Ogden Mills as his Undersecretary and successor, placed high priority on refunding this short-term debt into midterm obligations and made the state of the bond market a principal concern of federal financial and economic policy.

Besides short and intermediate treasury financings, there were three long-term bond issues announced in 1931 as part of the refunding plan: $1.4 billion of 3 3/8% bonds due in 1943 announced on March 2nd; $0.8 billion of 3 1/8% bonds due in 1946/49 announced on June 1st; and $0.8 billion of 3% bonds due in 1955 announced on August 31st. The first two issues were heavily oversubscribed, the second by a record 750%. The third issue was barely subscribed—$940.6 million for an issue of $800 million. This was in large part because of the low 3% coupon in the midst of the international crisis and a decline of $4 in long-term U.S. Treasury prices in September. After the Sterling Crisis there were no further refundings in 1931 because of the weakness of the market. The U.S. Treasury 4 1/4% bonds due in 1952 dropped from over $114 in June to as low as $102 in October, rose back to $108 in November and fell down again to $100 in December—all of which was too much volatility for successful underwriting.

This refunding concern explains much of the Hoover Administration's attitude toward Veterans' Bonus Certificates, welfare programs, and public works. All these programs threatened to exacerbate the government's heavy financial requirements. The federal government was already running a deficit of $462 million in fiscal 1931 (net of debt retirements) and projected in September that the fiscal 1932 deficit would be $1.5 billion. This projection had risen to $2.1 billion by December, and turned out to be $2.7 billion. At the time, there were examples of national governments that were unable to finance their cash requirements in Germany, South America, Sweden, Hungary, Rumania, and the United Kingdom. These were examples of countries unable to finance in foreign markets, which the United States did not need to do with over $5 billion in gold reserves, but we can at least sympathize with the Administration's concern for its credit in such an atmosphere. It was a mistake in judgment about the proportions of the problem, but not a stupid or hide-bound mistake. When the United States lost $750 million of gold in six weeks following the Sterling devaluation, it appeared that the nation indeed had to be concerned about its international credit standing.

MUNICIPAL BONDS

In early 1931 state and local governments were generally considered strong and creditworthy. Municipal revenues nationwide held up throughout 1931, despite the Depression, at $2.3 billion, compared with $2.2 billion in 1930.[3] Municipal bond and note issues were a record $850 million in the first half of 1931. New York State sold $40 million in bonds due 1932–81 on September 16th at a record low net interest cost for the state of 3.23%. But there were isolated municipal credit problems early in the year. Chicago and Cook County continued on the verge of bankruptcy. Municipal workers there were consistently behind in their pay. Chicago schools almost closed in May because teachers were unpaid. Teachers had not been paid for six months by October. In May and June, advance tax payments by Commonwealth Edison, Illinois Bell Telephone, and other local companies were necessary to avoid default on $2.9 million in bonds due July 1st. Cook County actually defaulted on June 1st on $1,450,000 in bonds and $417,000 in interest, but the obligations were paid by Continental Illinois National Bank & Trust, First National Bank of Chicago, Harris Trust Co., Northern Trust Co., and other local banks. Mississippi was also saved from default in April by local bankers, after the state was expected to fail to meet a bond maturity. Neighboring states to Mississippi had similar credit problems.

Municipalities' credit deteriorated abruptly in the fourth quarter, just as the banking crisis developed and the economy dipped further. Big cities and rural areas were both affected. Sharp increases in unemployment and welfare benefits threatened big-city budgets with impossible deficits, while the business tax base withered. The economies of rural areas were decimated by drought and low commodities prices. Municipal securities issues were only $170 million in the fourth quarter, the lowest quarterly rate since at least 1924. The decline in volume was particularly unusual because municipal new-issue volume was the most stable of any type. Detroit, which was allocating one-third of its $76 million tax roll for debt service on $350 million of municipal debt, was unable to sell bonds in October and borrowed $28 million from banks. Later in the year, it sold $5 million in bond anticipation notes by borrowing $4 million from its own sinking funds and getting $1 million from wealthy Michigan Senator James Couzens.

In December, New York City bonds dropped to 5% yield levels for the first time in a decade as suspicions about the city's creditworthiness developed. The city had proposed a $2 billion construction budget for 1931, but Mayor Jimmy Walker ordered budget cuts in August and warned that a tax increase was in prospect because the city's uncollected taxes had grown from 0.96% of the tax rolls in 1927 to 4.88% in 1930. New York City's credit had become greatly weakened by December, when it sold $60 million in 90-day notes at 5 1/2%, an unusually high rate. Atlanta had difficulty selling bonds because of a deficit of $1 million. Tennessee was able to sell only $17.5 million in 6-month notes at 6%. Chicago and South Carolina were unable to sell bonds or notes at any rate. Civic employees in Chicago, Philadelphia, Tennessee, and Alabama were behind in receiving their pay. Municipal bond dealers in December were unwilling to inventory bonds, and as a result small municipal issues were generally unable to attract bids at competitive sales. Municipalities with short-term debts maturing and unable to borrow from their banks faced the prospect of default.

THE FOREIGN BOND MARKET—THE SOUTH AMERICAN COUNTRIES DEFAULT, AND A CURRENCY CRISIS STRIKES EUROPE

Events in South America and Europe in 1931 broke the back of the weak economic and financial structure of international commerce. Most South American countries suffered social distress and defaulted on their external debts because of the poor international economy and low commodities prices. In Europe, Germany's financial problems brought the countries of Eastern Europe close to default on their foreign debts and forced England and its Scandinavian neighbors to devalue. The devaluation of sterling in September 1931 sent shock waves through U.S. securities markets that pushed prices to new lows in the Depression.

South American countries found both the quantity and the unit value of their commodity exports sharply depressed in the first half of 1931. We have already noted that commodities prices declined most sharply in the first half of 1931. The result was an acute shortage of foreign exchange at the same time that high unemployment and social unrest prevented South American governments from making significant efforts to restrain domestic spending, which might have reduced imports. Indeed, almost every country in South America had a problem with revolution, revolt, or war.

In 1931 virtually every South American issuer but the Argentine defaulted on its U.S. debts. In some cases, such as the bonds of Bolivia and Peru, default had been anticipated in 1930 when prices on their issues dropped to approximately $35. Peru defaulted in March 1931, fulfilling a six-month prophecy, and its bonds dropped to a low price of $5 1/4. Bolivia's bonds dropped to $6 1/2. Chile suspended foreign debt service in July, following President Hoover's declaration of a one-year moratorium on war debts. In August 1931, Cuba defaulted on $170 million in U.S. debts, of which $100 million was to banks on a short-term basis. Brazil suspended all foreign debt payments in October after depositing the equivalent amount in local currency for a short period.

The problems in each case differed, depending on the country's exports and domestic political situation, which were in turn reflected in the prices of each country's bonds at the beginning of the year. While bonds of Peru and Bolivia were no higher than $55, Argentine bonds were at $88, Buenos Aires bonds were at $84, Chile bonds were at $86, Cuba bonds were at $81, and Uruguay bonds were at $89. However, none of these bonds escaped the whirlwind which swept over South America. The major bond issues of nine countries declined 75% or more, and the bonds of Rio Grande do Sul, Rio de Janeiro, Peru, Mexico, Chile, and Bolivia sold below $10. Only the bonds of the Argentine (which did not default) and Cuba sold above $25 at their low prices for the year. All but three of the major South American bond issues were rated Ba by year end, having been A or Baa when they were issued. (See Table A.10 in the Statistical Appendix on Moody's ratings for foreign and Canadian government bond issues and Table A.15 for price and yield ranges for representative foreign bond issues.)

Investors found virtually no protection in diversification, such as one might expect in these low quality countries over such a large continent as South America. Nor did the different paths and timetables to default make any difference. Bonds of the Argentine, Chile, Cuba, Uruguay, and Buenos Aires hit high prices for 1931 at which their yields were only between 6% and 8%, and their bonds held at least some meaningful values as the countries struggled to meet debt service, only to end up in the same position as Peru and Bolivia, which defaulted quickly. Nor did investors receive the usual benefit in a government default that its debts are reorganized with new amounts, maturities, and interest rates that permit a resumption of debt service. The situation was hopeless in every country but the Argentine, and almost every other South American country's bonds sank to prices below $25, which reflected the situation.

Chile's plight illustrates the hopeless position of other South American countries. The original 1931 budget of the federal government of Chile was $126.4 million, but it had been reduced during the first half of the year to $117.3 million when declining copper prices and world trade reduced the country's foreign exchange revenues. In August 1931, when the Chilean government ceased appropriations for foreign debt service, the government was trying to reduce its budget further to $104.6 million. It was also trying to plan a 1932 budget of only $85.2 million based on revenues estimated at $73 million. Ordinary expenditures were estimated at $48.7 million of the $85.2 million. The balance of $36.5 million was to pay interest on Chilean debts. Any revenues in excess of the $73 million estimate were to be placed in a sinking fund to pay principal on these debts. It is hardly surprising that Chile had a revolution and suspended its foreign debt service in the face of this budget reduction of almost one-third.

The investments of holders of South American bonds were simply wiped out with a breadth and finality which defied earlier imaginations. Other countries with commodity-based economies also suffered, although not as much as South

America. Australia's bond rating was cut from Aa to Baa, and its 7% bonds due in 1957 dropped from $98 to $35. John T. Lang, the Socialist Premier of the Australian State of New South Wales, defiantly allowed his state to go into default, but the federal government took over New South Wales debts. The other states and the federal government banded together in a cost-cutting program to avoid further defaults. In Western Canada, where drought created a 1,000-mile dust bowl and grain prices were too low to justify planting, the provinces of Manitoba, Saskatchewan, and Alberta had their bond ratings slashed from Aa to Baa. Cities and towns in these provinces were in arrears on their debts. At the opposite end of the continent, Newfoundland was unable to refinance its maturing debt until England arranged a bank loan on its behalf.

The debacle in South American bonds, in particular, provoked outrage among small investors and country banks who had been the largest buyers of these bonds. The collapse of values was so widespread and total that investors wondered if they had been duped or defrauded by U.S. bankers acting for the issuers. A subcommittee of the Senate Finance Committee was empowered to conduct an investigation into the issuance of foreign bonds in the United States. It began to hold hearings in December.

In the first quarter of 1931, as the South American countries rolled toward default, Europe looked toward an economic recovery, and European bond prices reflected this optimism. The bonds of the United Kingdom, Canada, Denmark, Switzerland, Norway, and Sweden all yielded less than 5% at their highest prices. France and Belgium's bonds yielded between 5% and 6%, and the bonds of Germany, Italy, Czechoslovakia, and Finland yielded between 6% and 7%. Only Poland and Yugoslavia, among the major bond issuers, had bonds which yielded over 8% or 9% at this high point in the market. The same optimism was shared in the United States, where other securities prices rose to a spring peak.

This optimism was short-lived, however. In May, Austria's leading bank, the Creditanstalt, had a run on its foreign deposits which threatened to exhaust Austria's meager reserves of gold and foreign exchange. The run quickly spread to Germany. Ultimately, the same wave engulfed England and led to the devaluation of sterling in September 1931. Within the space of a few months thereafter, many nations made competitive currency devaluations, and those which did not began to hoard gold rather than hold foreign exchange. All countries introduced import restrictions to preserve their trade advantages. By the end of 1931, international trade and foreign exchange were in a shambles that took decades to unravel.

The seeds of this breakdown were planted in the structure of European financial relations established after World War I. Germany was burdened with such heavy reparations obligations that it could meet them only by foreign borrowing, which was mostly short-term because the reparations obligations made Germany's credit too weak to attract long-term capital. The heavy short-term foreign debt, estimated at $3 billion, created as severe a potential for financial disequilibrium among Germany's lenders as it did for Germany—a potential ultimately realized.

The other flaw in the postwar financial structure was the United Kingdom's over-valued foreign exchange rate, which hampered its international competitive trade position and prevented England from running the trade surplus critical to England's role as a financial center. The City of London still followed its prewar practice of taking massive foreign deposits and relending them abroad; this created a potential for disequilibrium since the United Kingdom no longer had a substantial margin of foreign exchange reserves if these deposits were withdrawn or the loans went bad. Both occurred when Germany reached the end of its string in 1931.

The collapse began on May 17, 1931, when the Creditanstalt, the Rothschilds' Vienna bank and the leading bank in Austria, published its balance sheet with sharply reduced capital because of operating losses in almost 250 Austrian companies which it controlled. The bank earlier had been pressed into acquiring the Bodenkreditanstalt when it verged on failure for the same reason, and Baron Rothschild, the Creditanstalt President, now insisted on writing off the losses of these companies on the Creditanstalt balance sheet. The new balance sheet caused some sudden withdrawal of deposits, but the Austrian national government immediately offered to contribute up to $10 million to cover losses in return for a 47% share of ownership. Ten days later, however, the Creditanstalt was still in trouble. Many large foreign deposits and business credits had not been renewed in the intervening two weeks, and the bank was particularly concerned that credits for $30–$35 million advanced by U.S. banks would not be renewed. The government and the Government National Bank combined forces to seek foreign loans for the Creditanstalt in Berlin, Paris, Amsterdam, and England. The Bank of England wanted an Austrian government guarantee of any loan. The Bank of France was outrightly political, demanding that the proposed customs union between Germany and Austria (the *Zollverein*) be dropped as a condition to any loan. France was frightened of resurgent German power in a customs union, but conversely the truncated, landlocked Austrian state created by the Treaty of Versailles was in large part responsible for the present crisis in Austrian industry and finance. Germany was unable to offer significant support to counter the French demands, because shortly after the run began on Creditanstalt deposits it began on German banks. Governor Harrison of the New York Federal Reserve Bank wrote to Montagu Norman, Governor of the Bank of England, saying of the Creditanstalt crisis, "This is the beginning of much to come!" He was rapidly proved correct. But financial circles doubted that the European financial powers would dare let the Creditanstalt collapse and expected politics to intervene in the solution.

The positions of Austria and the Creditanstalt deteriorated through early June, as both local and French depositors withdrew funds. Over half the Creditanstalt's $145 million in deposits was foreign. The Austrian cabinet agreed to guarantee all the Creditanstalt's deposits, but France remained intransigent in its demand that the customs union be dropped. The crisis was resolved only when the Bank of England on June 16th suddenly loaned the $21 million under discussion to Austria, and the Bank of England and Chase National Bank representatives negotiated a two-year extension of $71 million in foreign deposits remaining in the Creditanstalt with an Austrian government guarantee.

By this time, however, the crisis had extended beyond Austria to Germany. In June the Reichsbank's reserves of gold and foreign exchange dropped by one-third, from 2,577 million reichsmarks to 1,721 million reichsmarks—the lowest level in five years.[4]

The proportions of the crisis had become clear to Montagu Norman, Governor of the Bank of England, early in June, and he thereafter played a major role in events of the summer. Norman had been a director of the bank since 1907, prior to which he had built his reputation as a partner in Brown, Shipley & Co., in charge of U.S. trade financing. He later became the Bank of England's first full-time Governor. Norman had a difficult time communicating with others, so friendships became one of his principal paths of influence, especially within the City of London and with foreign bankers, such as Hjalmar Schacht, President of the Reichsbank until March 1930, and Benjamin Strong, Governor of the Federal Reserve Bank of New York until 1928, and his successor, George Harrison. Equally, antipathies were one of his greatest barriers to effectiveness. He was personally incompatible with successive Governors of the Bank of France in the 1920s and 1930s—Emile Moreau and Gustave Moret—and never able to cooperate with them. Norman was a neurotic aesthete, prone to repeated nervous breakdowns. His financial principles were derived from instinct, but he was able to run the Bank of England and influence much of Europe and America by a combination of fear and brilliance. His influence had been paramount in persuading Winston Churchill of the wisdom of reestablishing the gold standard with the pound valued at $4.86, its prewar parity.

Norman now led the effort to maintain the gold standard by renegotiating the reparations agreements entangling Europe. Even while the Bank of England was lending $21 million to Austria in mid-June, Norman had been the principal influence behind a request to President Hoover by Ramsay MacDonald, Labour Party Prime Minister, that Hoover propose that German reparations payments be postponed. At the same time, Norman told Andrew Mellon, then in London, that a three-year moratorium was necessary. He also persuaded Mellon that Hoover's public call for a moratorium should precede consultations with the French, who would oppose it. On June 19th President Hoover proposed publicly a one-year moratorium on Germany's war debts, catching most political observers by surprise.

The international reaction to a moratorium was generally favorable. Commentators expected a moratorium to restore international finances, stimulate trade and end the Depression. Stocks and commodities rose for several days in a "moratorium rally." France expressed agreement, provided that a minimum German payment of $100 million to France was maintained. Terms of a one-year moratorium on war debts to July 1932 were agreed on and signed within slightly over two weeks. The French continued to receive $100 million a year, but these funds were to be reinvested in German Reich rail bonds.

Norman's concern over Germany's credit had a sound domestic motive. London banks had been borrowing heavily on short term in French francs at rates approaching 2%, converting the funds into reichsmarks and relending them to German industry and local government at 8%. Norman thought such loans exceeded $1.2 billion, but they actually exceeded $3.6 billion. England's public and private finances were at risk in Germany.

Norman was busy on various fronts. He persuaded London's bankers to leave their short-term funds in Austria and Germany, despite the crisis, since all knew that only a small portion of the investments could be retrieved if all lenders tried to retract their funds at once. He also organized a $100 million short-term loan to Germany by the Bank of England, the Bank of France, the Bank for International Settlements, and the Federal Reserve banks. Unfortunately, the $100 million was exhausted in less than a week to meet foreign exchange demands, as was $50 million from Bank of Manhattan Trust Co.

On July 11th, only five days after the moratorium was announced, the Reich government appealed to the United States to make further loans and to renegotiate reparations, because short-term investments were still being rapidly withdrawn from the nation and runs on banks had begun. The next day, the Darmstaedter und Nationalbank, the third largest bank in Germany, with deposits of $240 million, collapsed. The German stock exchanges were closed for Monday and Tuesday, the next business days, and on Monday, July 13th, a nationwide bank holiday was declared in Germany. The Reich government guaranteed the Darmstaedter's deposits and began to liquidate it. Banks in Austria and Hungary closed.

Germany's request for additional loans was turned down by all the central banks because the problem had become political rather than financial. Germany clearly could not repay further loans in any reasonable period. Germany's reserves of gold and foreign exchange had dropped from a normal level of $582 million in January 1931 to $383 million by the end of July despite foreign loans of $150 million during the period—a decline of $349 million, or 60%. The German banking system was in chaos. Its deposits had shrunk almost 30% in the last year, from the reichsmark equivalent of $2.5 billion on June 30, 1930, to $1.8 billion on June 30, 1931.[5] The Reich government had cut its budget on successive occasions to restore confidence without that result. Unemployment exceeded 4 million persons. The government was threatened from both the Left and the Right as Communist riots broke out in many cities and Hitler railed against German reparations payments.

Bankers expected Germany to help itself henceforth by mobilizing private assets, restricting credit, and balancing national and state budgets, which Germany tried to do. In the last half of July, the Reichsbank discount rate was raised from 7% to 10% and the companion rate for loans on collateral was raised from 8% to 15%. The Reichsbank monopolized all foreign exchange transactions, and all foreign assets over 20,000 reichsmarks (approximately $4,760) were requisitioned by the government. The bank and stock exchange holidays were extended ultimately to August 5th for the banks (three weeks) and September 3rd for the stock exchanges (seven weeks).

No solution to Germany's financial and economic problems was found, but the public attention on Germany and the air of sudden crisis subsided. This was partly because the crisis shifted to England and partly because money flows were controlled by the government restrictions placed on banks, securities markets, and foreign exchange. A series of ad hoc financial measures were advanced thereafter in Germany to remedy its problems, but as each measure was eased no solutions appeared. At the end of July, as the Sterling Crisis accelerated, the Reichsbank raised its discount rate of 15% and its rate on collateralized loans to 20%. The German government took over the Dresdner Bank, the second largest in the nation, and bought $71.4 million in preferential stock to keep it afloat. The German banks reopened on August 5th and operated amid relative calm, but cash and deposit withdrawals were severely limited. On August 12th the Reichsbank discount rate was reduced from 15% to 10% and the collateral rate from 20% to 15%.

In August, a Bank for International Settlements committee, headed by Albert Wiggin, appeared to be close to a "standstill agreement" with Germany on an estimated $1 billion in foreign short-term bank deposits, under which agreement 25% of foreign bank deposits in Germany could be withdrawn immediately, a further 15% each month. On September 1st, the Reichsbank rate was reduced for the second time in three weeks, this time from 10% to 8%, and the collateral rate from 12% to 10%. But on September 3rd, when the Berlin Stock Exchange reopened, there was a rush to sell. Stocks dropped 25%–40% and sellers had to be rationed. On September 13th, the Reichsbank expropriated all citizens' foreign assets over 1,000 reichsmarks (approximately $235) to meet foreign exchange commitments. It had previously expropriated all foreign assets over 20,000 reichsmarks. When the Standstill Agreement was finally signed with foreign banks on September 17th, Germany lost approximately $80 million in gold and foreign exchange within two weeks. Germany's reserves continued to decline throughout 1931. (See Table 9.2.)

In late November 1931, Germany finally took official action under the Young Plan for relief from reparations by asking the Bank for International Settlements for a formal examination of Germany's finances to determine its ability to pay. As late as December 18, 1931, Thomas W. Lamont, operating head of J. P. Morgan & Co., told a Senate Finance Subcommittee investigating foreign debt issues that he did not expect Germany to default on its private debts (as distinct from war debts suspended under the moratorium). But Charles E. Mitchell believed that unless German war debts were renegotiated there would be a revolt, and already President Hoover had asked Congress to extend the moratorium an additional year, to July 1933. The days of crisis in June and July during which the German financial system threatened to collapse had indeed resulted in col-

Table 9.2
Reichsbank Reserves of Gold and Foreign Exchange, 1931 ($ millions)

Jan.	Feb.	Mar.	Apr.	May	Jun.
$583	583	598	601	613	410

Jul.	Aug.	Sep.	Oct.	Nov.	Dec.
$383	410	343	303	280	275

Source: Banking & Monetary Statistics, p. 646; data there has been
    converted into U.S. dollars at 23.8 cents per reichsmark.

lapse. Newspaper attention to Germany's finances faded, as did the highly visible efforts of bankers and politicians to solve the crisis, but in the quieter period which followed, Germany was forced to endure the economic and social distress resulting from the financial collapse.

Public attention moved from Germany to England in mid-July, following the failure of the Darmstaedter und Nationalbank in which London banks had deposits of approximately $40 million. During July the Bank of England lost $150 million in gold from its June reserves of $793 million, despite an increase in the bank rate from 2 1/2% to 3 1/2% on July 23rd. Sterling recovered to $4.85 7/16 from $4.84 on the foreign exchange markets, which should have stopped the gold outflow since the sterling rate was between the "gold points," but the Bank of England continued to lose gold. Commentators blamed the gold outflow on English Foreign Secretary Arthur Henderson, who had ineptly told French Premier Laval and his colleagues, during meetings to resolve Germany's crisis, that England might have to declare a moratorium on private debts if Germany did. Later opinion placed considerable emphasis on the May Report, published July 31st, as a cause of the crisis which persisted until sterling was devalued on September 21st. The May Report was the product of a government committee study of the national finances, chaired by Sir George May, Secretary of the Prudential Assurance Co. The report predicted a national budget deficit of almost $600 million in the next fiscal year, 1932–33, and recommended sharp reductions in welfare and unemployment benefits. The report provoked a sharp loss of foreign confidence in the Labour Party government. Many foreign financial experts, especially in France, had already privately expressed doubts about the Labour government's financial competence.

The more fundamental and immediate cause of the run on England's reserves was the overextended position of the City of London in Germany and Eastern Europe. Short-term loans by English banks of $3.6 billion in Germany alone, without counting loans in Austria, Hungary, Rumania, Bulgaria, and Yugoslavia, which were all in foreign exchange difficulties, were over five times the Bank of England's $679 million in gold reserves at the start of 1931. Foreign depositors in London began to withdraw their funds coincident with the spread of the Creditanstalt crisis to Germany because they feared for the safety of their deposits. Lazard Frères, a leading London merchant banking house, found itself in serious difficulties because of its loans in Germany and was saved only by a large loan from the Bank of England. On July 27th, before the May Report was published, Montagu Norman wrote in his diary that there was danger that the gold standard would have to be suspended. England's reserves were simply too small to withstand a concerted call on its foreign liabilities. Nor was there a possibility of building those reserves through foreign trade, with the prewar exchange rate of 1 pound = $4.86, which substantially overvalued sterling and made English prices uncompetitive.

The Bank of England mounted a strong defense to the run on sterling, even though Norman was bedridden by a characteristic nervous prostration. The Bank Rate was raised from 3 1/2% to 4 1/2% on July 29th. On July 31st a $250 million loan to the Bank of England was announced by the Bank of France and the Federal Reserve Bank of New York. The sterling exchange rate continued to decline in the first week of August, however, and England continued to lose small amounts of gold. The effect of the rise in the Bank Rate and the new lines of credit should have been the opposite. Historically, a rise in the Bank Rate and in corresponding short-term interest rates had always been sufficient to attract funds to London. In the current atmosphere, however, French bankers openly expressed doubts about the financial ability and responsibility of the Labour Party government, and funds stayed away. There was no public air of crisis because of the magnitude of the $250 million credit on which the Bank of England could draw, but privately Sir Ernest Harvey, Norman's Deputy Governor at the Bank of England, informed Chancellor of the Exchequer Philip Snowden of the continued outflow. Harvey expressed a need for government budget cuts to restore confidence and asked for permission to inform the opposition of the seriousness of the run on sterling. Within three weeks the $250 million loan was almost used up supporting sterling.

Exhaustion of the $250 million loan carried the Sterling Crisis from the financial sphere into the political sphere. Further loans were necessary. Sir Robert Kindersley, a Bank of England director and a partner of Lazard Frères, in France now for the second time in a month seeking loans, was told that any further loans to the Bank of England would have to be guaranteed by the government of England (the Bank of England was then a private bank). Lack of confidence in the Labour government had raised such doubts about the ability of the Bank of England to cope with the financial pressures that the credit of the "Old Lady of Threadneedle Street" was exhausted. The projected U.K. budget deficit had risen to $600 million, the government's floating debt had risen $0.5 billion to $3.5 billion in the last five months alone, and British overseas trade in the first six months of the year was down $1 billion. There appeared to be neither the domestic political-financial competence nor the foreign export earnings to bolster the drain on Britain's reserves caused by frozen loans in Germany and the fears of foreign depositors.

The Bank of England was asked by Snowden to determine the steps the government had to take to restore foreign confidence, particularly in the United States and in France. Over the weekend, J. P. Morgan & Co. and the Bank of France were consulted by the Bank of England, and the government was advised that budget reductions, especially in unemployment insurance, were the only alternative. Sir Josiah Stamp, a Director of the Bank of England, met privately with the King to impress on him the necessity of acting to preserve sterling. The Labour Party cabinet was unable to unite on a policy of cutting the dole (unemployment insurance) and was succeeded by a "National Government" on Monday, August 24th, in which Ramsay MacDonald and Snowden were the principal Labour Party leaders, Stanley Baldwin and Neville Chamberlain were the principal Conservatives, and John Simon and Herbert Samuel the principal Liberals. The National Government's purpose was to bring the budget into balance, restore England's credit, and as soon as was suitable, hold a general election.

The National Government immediately sought a new loan and promised massive budget cuts. This time the loan was directly to the government, since U.S. and French bankers were opposed to further loans to the Bank of England. President Hoover, Andrew Mellon, and Eugene Meyer, Chairman of the Federal Reserve Board, met in New York with representatives of J. P. Morgan & Co., Chase National Bank, Guaranty Trust, and Central Hanover Bank & Trust to encourage them to make a loan to England. A $400 million credit for one year was announced on August 28th. U.S. bankers provided $200 million, French bankers provided $100 million, and a public offering of U.K. bills for one year was to be made in France at 4 1/4% for the French franc equivalent of $100 million. The amount of $400 million appeared to be such a large credit that it was thought unassailable by speculators. The commitment to defend sterling was massive.

There was a slight improvement in the spot sterling exchange rate following these events, but no improvement in the forward market for sterling which best reflected expectations. In the first week of September there were rumors that a $5 million increase in U.K reserves had been accompanied by a $20 million drawing under the U.S. line of credit. On September 10th, the National Government announced budget cuts of $300 million, principally in the dole ($129 million cut), government salaries ($24 million cut), defense ($25 million cut), and education ($51.5 million cut). Tax increases were announced equal to $407.5 million in a full year and $202.5 million in the remaining half year by raising the standard income tax to 25% and placing excise taxes on beer, tobacco, gas, and theater tickets. A projected budget deficit of $850 million was thereby converted into a projected surplus of $7 million. The same day, it was announced that the English public offering of $100 million in France was a success. The bonds rose to an immediate premium which reduced their yield from 4 1/4% to 3 3/4%.

Sterling was clearly in trouble these days, but confidence in England's financial strength still held in many places. Even in this period of stress, U.K. 5 1/2% bonds due in 1937 trading on the NYSE were down only to $104, which hardly reflected credit doubts. Two loans within one month totalling $650 million also evinced the ultimate faith of leading foreign bankers in England. The National Government and its quick action on the budget should have buttressed the faith of those who doubted England's stability.

The drain on the sterling reserves continued, however. The Bank of France supported sterling throughout the week of September 7th–12th, even while the U.K. offering in France was achieving success. On Monday and Tuesday, September 14th and 15th, the newspapers carried reports that England was drawing substantially on its $200 million credits in both France and the United States. Rumors of mutinies in the British fleet against the proposed pay reductions in the budget, just when the fleet was supposed to go on maneuvers, and the subsequent Navy decision to bring the ships home to port to try to resolve the pay grievances, accelerated foreign gold withdrawals. At the end of the week (September 14th–19th), Dutch banks began to call funds heavily from London to meet their domestic cash needs, as they were being squeezed also. They drew $20 million in this week and drove the Dutch exchange rate to a new high for the year. English investors were reported to be making large investments in foreign securities, and businesses were drawing their sterling balances down as low as possible. There was heavy selling pressure on the pound, which dropped to $4.85 15/16. On September 19th sterling dropped to $4.84 1/2—an unusually large decline. Banks refused speculative short sales of sterling as the wolves came in for the kill. The London Stock Exchange was in panic. Financiers reported to the National Government that another sterling crisis was on hand. The government knew that the $400 million credit which was supposed to be too big to challenge was almost exhausted.

Over the weekend, the Bank of England wired Montagu Norman, who was recuperating in Quebec, the cryptic message "Old Lady goes off on Monday." Norman thought the message meant his mother was going to the Continent for a vacation. On Sunday, September 20th, the National Government announced it was suspending gold payments. The Stock Exchange was closed Monday to prevent panic. The Bank Rate was raised from 4 1/2% to 6%. The government statement claimed that gold withdrawals since mid-July had been $1 billion. U.K. gold reserves on June 30, 1931, had been just short of $800 million. Netting out new loans to the United Kingdom in this period, the bank had been broken.

Nothing had availed—not a National Government, not a balanced budget, not $650 million in loans, and not all the skills of the City of London. The Navy unrest exacerbated affairs, as did the withdrawals of the Dutch banks, but the basic point remains that, after the nation had done all that could be asked of it, it was forced to suspend gold payments within the space of a few weeks. London banks' large foreign short-term debts and their large suspended loans to Germany and Eastern Europe overcame all the efforts of politicians and financiers. Germany's finances continued to deteriorate throughout the Sterling Crisis, so that knowledgeable investors realized that the liquidity of U.K. banks was threatened. Depositors naturally tried to protect themselves by withdrawing funds, and these withdrawals were more than the reserves England could muster.

The first day of trading after the suspension of gold payments, sterling dropped as low as $3.71 from the previous parity of $4.86 but closed at $4.20. Thereafter, sterling exchange rates fluctuated widely, from as high as $4.20 to as low as $3.50 during September. Sterling averaged $3.89 in October, $3.72 in November, and $3.37 in December. A devaluation of approximately 31% in the sterling-dollar exchange rate had been achieved by the end of the year.

The collapse of sterling set off reactions throughout Europe. Exchanges in Berlin, Copenhagen, and Vienna closed on September 21st, along with the London Stock Exchange. The Amsterdam Exchange opened in the morning but closed promptly. Only the Paris Stock Exchange was open in Europe. In Athens, the stock exchange asked that trades in September be annulled because all the members would otherwise be rendered insolvent.

There were runs on Yugoslav banks, which were forced to restrict withdrawals to the equivalent of $17.50 per day. Denmark, Sweden, and Norway suspended gold payments, after Sweden had sought a $100 million loan in France to maintain gold payments and been refused. Finland suspended gold payments on October 10th. Latvia took over all foreign exchange trading and forbade exports of precious metals and jewels. Canada forbade gold exports except by chartered banks in order to conserve gold for Canadian debt service to the United States.

Countries closely connected with the United Kingdom in foreign trade tended to devalue their currencies as well. The Scandinavian countries devalued by a percentage similar to that of the United Kingdom—31%—as did Portugal, New Zealand, Egypt, and India. Australia devalued by over 40%, Canada by only 17%. Most South American countries devalued their currencies either before or after the sterling devaluation.

There were a surprisingly large number of countries which did not devalue. These countries fell into two groups—those like France, Belgium, the Netherlands, Czechoslovakia, Switzerland, and Italy, which accumulated gold rather than revalue their currencies upward, and those like Germany, Austria, Bulgaria, Hungary, Poland, and Rumania, which chose to ration their weak currencies rather than devalue.

The differing economic strengths of the countries of Europe after September 1931, was abruptly reflected in their bonds. Bonds of Germany, Austria, and the rest of Eastern Europe, with the exception of Czechoslovakia, sold off drastically. Whereas before the currency crisis East European bond yields were only 2%–3% over those of West European bonds, now East European bonds

Table 9.3
Gold Holdings

	12/31/30	12/31/31
France	$2,176	$2,699
Swiss Confederation	138	455
Netherlands	172	358
Belgium	190	354

Source: Banking & Monetary Statistics, pp. 544, 550.

slumped to prices so low that their yields were meaningless. The prices reflected expectations of default. Austria's bonds dropped to $35, Germany's to $22, Poland's to $32, Berlin's to $14, and Yugoslavia's to $29. (See Table A.15 in the Statistical Appendix for price and yield ranges for representative foreign bond issues.)

Bonds of the Scandinavian countries slumped $9–$16 in one day following the suspension of sterling and continued to decline thereafter, but not to default levels. The bonds of Denmark, Norway, and Sweden bore yields of 8 3/4% to 9 3/8% at their low prices. The bonds of Finland, which was the poorest rated of the Scandinavian countries, dropped to a low price of $34.

One would have expected U.K. bonds to drop like a stone because of the publicity focus, but England's credit was not seriously dissipated by the event. United Kingdom 5 1/2% bonds due in 1937 dropped to $92 immediately, having been $104 a week prior, but $90 was the low price for 1931 and the bonds were back over $100 by year end. At their lowest prices, U.K. bonds continued to rank among the lowest yields on foreign bonds. And Moody's did not alter the United Kingdom's coveted Aaa bond rating in this period when for a while it was the only foreign country with this rating.

England had been so hampered by an overvalued currency that the devaluation acted like a tonic. Stocks in the succeeding month were up 30%, and by the end of October the Bank of England repaid $100 million of its foreign debts as money flowed back into London banks. The $250 million borrowed from the New York Federal Reserve Bank and the Bank of France was reduced below $10 million by mid-November. British industry improved visibly, especially in shipping, coal, and textiles, which were dependent on export markets where prices for these products were now cheaper.

The strong West European countries outside of Scandinavia reacted to the currency upheaval by aggressively converting their foreign exchange assets into, and accumulating, gold. In France, this became a well-publicized government policy. The effect on these countries' gold reserves can be seen in Table 9.3. This display of economic and financial strength, by France and Switzerland in particular, made their bonds unusually stable. France's gold 7% bonds due in

1949 did not drop below $109. Moody's reduced the rating on Swiss Confederation bonds to Aa, but these bonds were the strongest in the foreign market. The 5 1/2% issue due in 1946 varied only between $107 and $99. At $99 its yield of 5.55% was the lowest in the foreign market and within 1/2% of the best Aaa railroad and utility bonds in the U.S. market. Belgium's bond rating was also reduced to Aa, and its bonds hit a low price of $72, where they yielded 8.83%. The Netherlands was downgraded to A but had no U.S. bonds we can follow.

Two bond issues, for Czechoslovakia and for Italy, were among the most stable. Bonds of both these countries were rated Baa, yet they each declined only 20%–30% from their 1931 high prices and yielded 9 3/8% to 10 3/8%. Both countries had good economies and strong currencies which made their bonds stable but high yielding investments that persistently traded at better prices than similarly rated issues for other countries. We should also mention at this point that Canada's 4% bonds due in 1960 were reduced in rating to Aa by Moody's and slumped to $64. However, their yield at this low price was still only 6 7/8%, one of the three lowest yields on foreign bonds.

A turning point was marked in the foreign bond market in 1931 as a result of the financial and social turmoil in Europe and South America. The optimism accorded foreign bonds as a group disappeared, as did the foreign new-issue bond market. Foreign issues totalled only $138 million in the 11 months after January 1931, and of this amount only one issue was over $1 million in the last half of 1931—$50 million for Taiwan Electric guaranteed by the government of Japan in July before sterling collapsed. South American bonds became virtually valueless, as we have already noted, in such a debacle that the U.S. bond market remains closed to them to this day. Among foreign bonds which retained some value, credit distinctions became much wider. Moody's made 26 reductions in countries' bond ratings and reduced ratings on issues of seven Canadian provinces. Whereas most prosperous issuers had been rated Aaa or Aa, suddenly only one was Aaa, and some fell all the way to Baa, such as Germany, Australia, and the provinces of Western Canada. A wide range developed between yields on the best foreign bonds at 5 1/2% to 7% and solvent Baa credits, such as Czechoslovakia and Italy, at 9 3/8% to 10 3/8%, with many credits filling the middle ground as perceptions of risk became more widely graduated. Even the best foreign bonds bore higher yields than they had previously, versus the best U.S. corporate bonds as that premium widened to over 1%.

The destruction of values reflected in this change of attitude was enormous. South American bonds became worthless, but significant amounts were lost on the best foreign bonds too. Every foreign bond hit a new low for the period in 1931, and every issue but those for Switzerland and France declined 20% or more from its 1931 high price. The weighted average decline from 1930's lowest price to the lowest price in 1931 for all the foreign issues studied here was 41%. This was a degree of fluctuation in value for which no bondholders were prepared. As a result, all the United States turned its back on foreign bonds for a generation.

SUMMARY OF 1931 FINANCIAL MARKETS

The focal financial event of 1931 was the international currency crisis which culminated in the collapse of sterling in September. The economic and financial deterioration, which had progressed only slowly before September, grew like a rampant cancer in the remaining four months of the year. The sharpest declines occurred thereafter in domestic industry, wages, and international trade. Bank losses and closings suddenly grew to crisis proportions. The stock market registered its largest losses since the Crash, and bond markets diverged sharply into good and bad credits, all of which had to pay higher rates. Railroad bonds were suddenly thrust into the lowest quality sector of the corporate bond market after having been its best. South American bond issuers defaulted almost universally, and East European bonds sold down to prices which suggested the same impending end for them. Unlike the Crash, when high grade bond prices rose because of the transfer of investor interest to bonds, both bonds and stocks suffered after the Sterling Crisis. It was also the pivotal point in monetary policy which had previously been leading to increasingly lower rates. After September the Federal Reserve acted consciously to raise rates because of the outflow of U.S. gold.

The Sterling Crisis also marked a change in the capital-raising function of the securities markets. New issues of bonds and stocks in 1931 had run about two-thirds of 1930 new-issue volume into September but thereafter were only about one-eighth of 1930 volume. The market for investment trust, foreign, and other low grade issues completely dried up, and remained so for several years. Part of the reason for the decline in new securities issues was the lack of expansion by corporations and local governments, but a vicious circle was also at work, for the failure of many corporations to expand was influenced by the knowledge that the money could not be prudently raised.

Prior to the Sterling Crisis, there was a sense that the nation would be able to cope with the problems at hand. It can hardly be claimed, as President Hoover did, that the economy and financial markets were recovering, but they were not in a precipitous decline. Modest initiatives at the federal and local levels of government and by corporations and charities held some hope for coping and recovering. After the Sterling Crisis, a heavy sense of despair invaded affairs, and the ability of governments or businesses to cope seemed lost. Governments and businesses were limited in their reactions to the crisis by accelerating deficits and increased rigidity of opinion. Class divisions widened as the lower classes suffered more and more. A mantle of despair was pulling over the nation as 1931 ended.

NOTES

1. Moody's bond indices exaggerate the rise in interest rates by approximately 1% at this time for A rated railroad and industrial bonds and most Baa rated bonds, due to the

particular bonds used in the indices. The Baa railroad bond index exaggerates the rise in interest rates by approximately 2%.

2. *Banking & Monetary Statistics*, p. 77.
3. *Statistical Abstract, 1939*, p. 216.
4. *Banking & Monetary Statistics*, p. 646.
5. Ibid., pp. 646, 655.

10

Political and Economic Influences on Securities Markets in 1932

Economic problems and individual hardship reached unprecedented proportions in 1932. Arnold Toynbee called 1931 "Annus Terriblus," which it was for Europe, but 1932 was "Annus Terriblus" in the United States, too, and its hardships exceeded anything in Europe.

The Gross National Product at current prices declined to approximately 60% of 1929 levels, and nonfarm unemployment averaged 36% for the year. Factories and towns closed completely. Corporations en masse lost $2.7 billion during the year. Factory workers, farmers, and veterans turned to violence in sheer frustration. The Wholesale Price Index dropped 32% from 1929 levels. Commodities prices established record lows unseen since the 1870s. Major cities, such as New York, Chicago, Philadelphia, and Detroit, developed severe financial problems, as did many southern states, and they carried on only by cutting budgets, not paying employees, and submitting to the direction of bankers' committees. Problems in the banking system spread beyond small, nonmember banks in many leading cities. Chicago, Cleveland, Detroit, and Baltimore were paralyzed by bank problems. International trade and finance lapsed into anarchy as industrialized nations raised new tariffs to maintain commodity production and ward off imports, and major European countries defaulted on their war debts to the United States.

Financial markets were paralyzed during midyear as these external pressures reached their peaks. Stock prices dropped to approximately 12% of their 1929 high prices. Baa railroad bonds rose to yields over 12%, and similarly rated industrial and utility bonds came close to this level, while U.S. bonds hovered between yields of 3 1/2%–4%, along with a few of the strongest corporate and foreign bonds, which were only 1/2%–1% higher. Many municipal bonds could not get bids during the year. Bonds of foreign issuers outside Western Europe dropped to default prices of $25 or less. Major defaults by the Wabash Railroad, Kreuger & Toll, Middle West Utilities, and several German local governments shook markets which were already demoralized. New securities issues by corporations were only 6% of 1929's volume, and New York Stock Exchange trading volume in the worst period was down to a similar level. Liquidity in many securities was non-existent, and artificial attempts to create it were unproductive.

The real estate market was similarly paralyzed. Values underlying real estate mortgages evaporated, as did the income on properties. Foreclosure auctions of 20 to 30 commercial properties at a time were a weekly commonplace in large cities. Everything related to real estate was fighting for its life—banks, savings and loans, life insurance companies, fire and casualty insurance companies, and of course the owners.

The federal government was forced into active efforts to cope with this disaster despite a frightening budget deficit. The Federal Reserve initiated the largest open market purchases of U.S. bonds in its history. In six months the Reconstruction Finance Corporation approved $1.2 billion in loans to banks, railroads, insurance companies, savings institutions, and farmers. Public works were expanded somewhat. But the end product of these efforts was slight, and by the end of the summer it was clear that Franklin Roosevelt would be the next President and that his attitude toward the financial markets he had overseen as Governor of New York was decidedly hostile.

THE HOOVER ADMINISTRATION IS CONSTRAINED IN ITS ATTACK ON THE DEPRESSION BY THE BUDGET DEFICIT

The Hoover Administration faced 1932 in a highly schizophrenic state of mind. On the one hand, Congress in January passed Hoover's request for a Reconstruction Finance Corporation with authority to lend up to $1.5 billion, but on the other hand the fiscal 1932 budget deficit was estimated at $2.5 billion[1] and the pressures to reduce it were enormous. It turned out to be $2.735 billion.

It would be well to outline the budget position and the pressures on President Hoover to balance the budget before considering the positive acts he took to stem the Depression. The perspective may temper criticism of Hoover's policies. In a nutshell, federal budget revenues were cut in half between fiscal 1929 and fiscal 1932, while federal budget expenditures grew by half. The net budget position swung from a 1929 surplus of $734 million to a deficit of $2.7 billion in fiscal 1932. This $2.7 billion deficit was 50% greater than total 1932 budget revenues of $1.9 billion, a staggering deficit to support. (The budget figures for 1929–33 are outlined in Table 10.1 and in Table A.38 in the Statistical Appendix.)

The Hoover Administration estimated that the fiscal 1933 deficit would approximate $1.7 billion if there was an economic recovery of 15% in industrial production. Accordingly, the Administration began to push for tax increases and expenditure reductions during the first quarter of 1932 as the 1933 budget was being prepared. Treasury Secretary Mellon pushed for a $920 million income tax increase plus other new taxes in January,[2] and his successor, Ogden Mills, sought a $1.1 billion tax bill in March.[3] Mills actually wanted a retroactive tax increase, but was turned down quickly. The Administration also wanted ex-

Table 10.1
Summary of Federal Government Finances, Administrative Budget,
   Fiscal Years 1929–1933 ($ millions)

	Budget receipts[a]	Budget expenditures[a]	Surplus or (deficit)	Total public debt
1929	$3,862	$3,127	$ 734	$16,931
1930	4,058	3,320	738	16,185
1931	3,116	3,577	(462)	16,801
1932	1,924	4,659	(2,735)	19,487
1933	1,997	4,598	(2,602)	22,539

Source: Historical Statistics, p. 1104.

[a] Excludes borrowing, debt repayment, and trust accounts.

penditure cuts, which it eventually placed at $250 million, in conjunction with its tax bill. The onus for selecting these cuts was at first placed on Congress.

Business support for a balanced budget was almost universal. The American Bankers Association and the Investment Bankers Association predictably passed resolutions at their conventions early in the year favoring higher taxes and lower expenditures to balance the budget. The National Industrial Conference Board said, "Government taxes are the only way to avoid disaster in the most serious financial emergency outside of wartime."[4] Owen D. Young described efforts to aid the financial markets as futile without a balanced budget. Alfred P. Sloan, Jr., as head of General Motors, broadcast on CBS that "if Congress will cut down unnecessary expenditure, balance the budget—and then adjourn—there is a possibility of sentiment improving and business likewise."[5] Local business associations and fraternal groups everywhere passed resolutions in favor of a balanced budget.

Political support for a balanced budget was broadly bipartisan. Representative Charles Crisp (Dem-Ga.) introduced a tax bill in March 1932 to raise $1.1 billion; the bill included a 2 1/4% manufacturer's excise tax for the first time. Political attitudes coalesced around this bill, which had Administration support, but because the bill did not pass both houses of Congress until June 1932, there were three months of harmful uncertainty, particularly in international markets. There was still considerable unanimity of opinion on the broad principle of balancing the budget, despite what this prolonged debate might suggest to the contrary. Most of the delay had been due to jockeying for political position since this was an election year. The House Speaker, Democrat John Nance Garner, got a commitment from the House at the end of March, when it first rejected the 2 1/4% sales tax, to a balanced 1933 budget which required a net change of $1.25 billion. Franklin Roosevelt was strongly committed to a balanced budget in New York State, where as Governor he signed a bill in February doubling income taxes to raise $76 million.[6] Bernard Baruch, a prominent financier and Roosevelt advisor, wanted a Democratic platform plank calling for $1 billion in budget cuts. Republicans, Democrats, and even radicals broadly favored the principle of balancing the budget.

It took considerable courage to be against a balanced budget, for those in positions of authority spoke in relatively cataclysmic terms of the dangers of an unbalanced budget. Treasury Secretary Mellon, who was respected, independent, and a banker of note, declared in January that the U.S. government's credit was threatened by the deficit and that no market existed for long-term U.S. bonds.[7] His successor, Ogden Mills, described the stake in a balanced budget as follows: "Our currency rests predominantly upon the credit of the United States. Impair that credit and every dollar you handle will be treated with suspicion."[8] Eugene Meyer, Chairman of the Federal Reserve Board, declared that if the veterans' demand for earlier payment of the War Bonus was met, the resulting deficit would destroy the national credit structure. Charles E. Mitchell said that half the banks in the nation would be bankrupted by the reverberations in the credit markets.

There were supporters of increased federal spending, despite the budget consequences, but these positions were clearly radical or individualistic. The "Bonus Army" of unemployed veterans assembled in the Midwest in May to march on Washington, seeking early redemption of the $2.4 billion in adjusted service certificates given to veterans. These certificates matured, like bonds, in 1945, and their early payment would have increased budget expenditures by the face amount of the certificates. The Bonus Army encamped on the outskirts of Washington with very little support from Congress and was finally dispersed on July 28th by U.S. troops.

Senators Robert F. Wagner of New York and Robert M. La Follette, Jr., of Wisconsin led continuous efforts to pass bills providing for public works, unemployment compensation, and direct welfare grants, with little success. La Follette sought a $5.5 billion "prosperity bond" issue at the beginning of 1932 for these purposes, which the Administration opposed, and when La Follette reduced his aim to a mere $375 million relief bill in February, President Hoover still opposed it. When in June the House and Senate passed a Wagner-sponsored relief bill for $2.3 billion financed by a bond issue, Hoover promptly vetoed it.

Various bills to extend financial aid to hard-pressed New York City and Chicago received no significant support.

Some of the individual demands that budget balancing be attributed less importance are interesting, principally because the men were financiers. Otto Kahn, senior partner of Kuhn, Loeb & Co., which was one of the half dozen leading investment banking firms of the period, recommended in February that both unemployment and old-age insurance programs be adopted. In June, Gerard Swope, President of General Electric Co., pressed for a public works program, work sharing through a 30-hour week, unemployment benefits, and government financing of industry. Late in 1932, when an element of exaggeration had crept into financial discussions because of the pending presidential election, Roger Babson, who had gained wide recognition because of his outright prediction of the Crash and Depression, said:

I strongly condemn the constant talk about economy as carried on by the National Economy League and other organizations.... Their general preaching of economy at this time is, however, both wrong and very dangerous.... Today we need to emphasize the importance of judicious spending. Only as more is spent will there be more produced.[9]

These demands for greater spending were not as sharply in conflict with the broad demand for a balanced budget as they appeared, because budget balancing as a principle was applied only to the Administrative budget and "normal" government expenditures. All spectrums of opinion were prepared for major nonbudgetary borrowing and expenditure by the federal government to relieve the extreme distress.

The most prominent nonbudgetary vehicle for relief of distress was the Reconstruction Finance Corporation (RFC), proposed to Congress by President Hoover in December 1931 and signed into law on January 23, 1932, with authority to spend $1.5 billion. The RFC idea was conceived by Eugene Meyer, Chairman of the Federal Reserve Board, on a pattern following the War Finance Corporation. Like the War Finance Corporation, it was originally an agency to assist business. Railroads and banks requested loans immediately to meet bond maturities or deposits which could not be rolled over. The railroads used the RFC facilities prominently and with full publicity, the first instance being a $12.8 million loan to the Missouri Pacific Railroad, which used $5.85 million to repay half its short-term bank loans from J. P. Morgan, Kuhn, Loeb & Co., and the Guaranty Trust Co. This provoked immediate criticism from the Interstate Commerce Commission and Congress, because the loan proceeds were not used for "productive" purposes. Thereafter, RFC loans typically were used as a lever to negotiate partial payment on maturing debt and partial use for expansion or replacement of facilities.

The RFC was an energetic lender, thanks to Jesse H. Jones, who became its chairman. It exhausted its $1.5 billion authorization before year end and had the amount expanded, including $300 million for loans to local governments for relief and public works.

The banks were not eager to borrow from the RFC and feared publicity about their borrowing. The first RFC loan was for $15 million to Bank of America.[10] Union Trust Co. in Detroit (part of the Guardian Detroit Union Group) got an early loan for $5 million. In June, General Charles Dawes resigned as President of the RFC to help his family bank in Chicago, Central Republic Bank & Trust, which promptly applied for, and was granted, $80 million from the RFC. Union Trust of Baltimore, one of Maryland's largest banks, which had earlier been assisted by local industry and New York banks, also obtained an RFC loan in August 1932. But the opprobrium attached to RFC bank loans prevented all banks except those in serious jeopardy from applying for RFC loans. If word got out that a bank was borrowing from the RFC its condition was immediately suspect and runs on its deposits began. In May, President Hoover prompted formation of an advisory group at the New York Federal Reserve Bank to encourage bank use of RFC facilities so that bank loans could be maintained rather than called. "The Twelve Apostles," as the group was called, was made up of leaders such as Owen D. Young, Walter Gifford of AT&T, Floyd Carlisle of Consolidated Gas Co. of N.Y., and numerous bankers. It was to be copied in every Federal Reserve District. However, the prestige of the group was unable to erase the stain of RFC bank borrowing.

The RFC quickly became Hoover's favored vehicle to aid other distressed areas of the economy such as local governments. During May 1932, Hoover requested a doubling in the RFC authorization to $3 billion, of which $300 million was earmarked for aid to local governments. The first such loan was for $3 million to Illinois in July after its unemployment funds ran out.[11] Most states quickly applied for and received loans, although many of them were for less than a million dollars. The more ambitious states, such as New York, sought up to $100 million to fund housing and public transportation developments. The first large RFC loan to local government was in September 1932, when it advanced $40 million to the Metropolitan Water District of Southern California to build an aqueduct.

President Hoover was rigorously opposed to public works loans which were not self-liquidating through tolls or utility fees, and this prevented RFC public works loans from reaching significant proportions. Treasury Secretary Ogden Mills decried public works loans as "handouts" that would destroy the economy, destroy the government's credit, and deter recovery.[12] Indeed, loans to local governments for any purpose must have galled Hoover. He expressed his attitude as follows in an August 11, 1932, campaign speech:

Thus we have held that the Federal Government should in the presence of great national danger use its powers to give leadership to the initiative, the courage, and the fortitude of the people themselves; but it must insist upon individual, community, and state responsibility to supplement and strengthen the initiative and enterprise of the people.[13]

To alleviate the Depression, the Hoover Administration initiated a number of other measures besides the RFC. John W. Polk, Comptroller of the Currency, instructed bank examiners as early as January 1932 to use par value as the "intrinsic value" of bonds rated Baa or better held by national banks. The powers of the Federal Intermediate Credit Banks were widened in May 1932, and their securities were strengthened by being made joint and several obligations by Federal Reserve rediscount eligibility and by direct Federal Reserve and Treasury financial support. A Commodity Credit Corporation was set up by New York City banks in August 1932 at the behest of Eugene Meyer, Federal Reserve Board Chairman, to lend on the collateral of raw materials. The Home Loan Bank Board also swung into action in 1932. In August it created 12 district banks and assigned them working capital to begin making loans by October. The banks opened with $9 million in stock and $125 million from the U.S. government. The first loan was made in Pittsburgh in late November.

The feebleness of these measures was epitomized by the Farm Board in September 1932, when it ceased supporting commodities prices with the plea that the private sector do something. Arthur W. Cutten, one of the leading speculators in the commodities markets, accused the board of handing over a cadaver after losing $500 million trying to revive it.[14] The Administration also continued its exhortations to the public and to the business world to think positively. This ranked with the RFC as President Hoover's favorite remedy. Hoover and Treasury Secretary Mills regularly chastised the banks for restricting loans and condemned both the public and the banks for hoarding. A new U.S. bond issue, called "Baby Bonds," was created to reduce hoarding by offering $100 bonds at 2% for one year, with the right to redeem them on 60 days' notice. Hoover also called another of his interminable conferences of business and industrial leaders to set action programs to improve credit facilities and promote production.

The focus of the Hoover Administration throughout 1932 was uniquely financial as the Administration's remedies all sought to bridge inadequacies in financial markets or to promote extension of credit. The RFC made loans to railroads, banks, and states. Federal Home Loan Banks bought mortgages. The Commodity Credit Corp. financed commodities. The "Twelve Apostles" promoted increased use of RFC credit. The Baby Bonds were to reduce hoarding and expand credit. The powers of the Federal Reserve banks were expanded to make direct loans and increase credit. The Hoover budgets were designed for financial effect—reducing government financing—rather than economic impact. The Administration was never able to surmount its early preoccupation with credit and the bond market, which it saw as the basis for business expansion. There was virtually no effort by the Administration to influence the investment, production, merchandising, or service parts of the economy. President Hoover resolutely opposed the efforts in these directions, such as the Veterans' Bonus, public works, welfare, and unemployment insurance, as destructive of the national credit.

The Administration had a curious blind spot in this respect. On the one hand, it demanded reductions in government expenses and increased taxes to balance the "regular" administrative budget, and opposed all programs which aggravated this deficit. On the other hand, it promoted or acceded to loan programs outside the administrative budget, particularly for the RFC. Hoover rationalized such loans on the grounds that they were adequately secured, but the impact of these loan programs on government financing requirements was no different than the programs entailing direct government spending. The investing public may have viewed the purposes of the borrowings differently, and so have maintained greater faith in the credit of the United States under Hoover's strict policies, but the market reception of government bonds was so favorable that it raised doubt about the need for this excessive genuflection to the conservative investor.

Hoover was willing to have an unsettled bond market when his own political fortune was at stake. Federal political uncertainties assumed major proportions during 1932, and naturally affected securities markets and the economy. The fiscal 1933 budget was debated in Congress from March through June while Hoover gave little guidance on the budget cuts necessary, trying to place the onus for them on Congress in this election year. Foreign reaction to the indecision was negative and clearly expressed in U.S. gold losses throughout the period.

Franklin Roosevelt opened his campaign in August with a nine-point speech focussed solely on securities abuses and demanding federal control of stock and commodities exchanges. He criticized the Hoover Administration for the speculative securities issues of 1929, for the activities of bank investment affiliates, for Federal Reserve policies, for foreign bond issues, and for stock market speculation. Roosevelt's program shortly escalated to federal regulation of public utilities, regulation of public utility holding companies, and federal development of hydroelectric sites. The Smoot-Hawley Tariff also came under attack. The tone of Roosevelt's campaign was almost exclusively critical of finance and business, even though he was supported by prominent New York financiers, such as Bernard Baruch, Owen D. Young, and Newton Baker.

This tone may account for the exaggerated polemics employed by Roosevelt's opponents. Hoover declared in Madison Square Garden that the New Deal wwould "destroy the very foundations of our Government and crack the timbers of the Constitution," and that the results of a lower tariff would be that "grass will grow in the streets of 100 cities [and] weeds will overrun the fields of millions of farms."[15] Ogden Mills repeatedly declared that Roosevelt's election threatened recovery and that the Democrats would restore the inflation of the 1920s. E. F. Hutton & Co. even went on the radio to support Mills' prophecies. Brokers' letters in October suggested that an industrial collapse would follow Roosevelt's election.[16]

Russell Leffingwell, a respected J. P. Morgan & Co. partner, suggested to the Senate subcommittee investigating stock exchange practices that Hoover further exacerbated financial fears during the campaign when he claimed in a speech in Des Moines that the United States had been within two weeks of going off the gold standard in February, before the Glass-Steagall bill was passed, allowing U.S. obligations as collateral for Federal Reserve notes.[17] If the United States had come that close to the brink, the public could justifiably assume that the financial stakes were still enormous.

The uncertainties which naturally surrounded a new President-elect were unfortunately exacerbated by events after the presidential election. Europe's war debts to the United States became a major controversy as England and France requested a continued moratorium immediately following the election. Roosevelt refused to cooperate with Hoover on a resolution of the war-debts question, on the grounds that Hoover was still President, but Roosevelt was visibly at odds with Hoover's policy of continuing to postpone and to study the war debts.

Rumors circulated that Roosevelt proposed to devalue the dollar, which drove both Hoover and the financial community into consternation. Roosevelt discussed such a step with bankers during this period, and it was openly espoused by Henry Wallace, the pending appointee as Secretary of Agriculture, and by a staunch Roosevelt advisor at Cornell, George F. Warren, and his "Committee for the Nation." Nor would Roosevelt calm the rumors by giving assurances to the contrary to Hoover or Senator Carter Glass when they sought them.

Roosevelt also disagreed with Hoover's budget proposals, particularly his support of a 2 1/4% federal excise tax, even though Roosevelt and House Speaker Garner agreed with Hoover on its necessity at one point in the budget's preparation. Roosevelt was willing to propose a short special session of Congress to provide farm relief and repeal the Volstead Act to allow sale of beer, but Hoover threatened to veto such an act.[18] Hoover also tried to get Eugene Meyer and Justice Charles Hughes to resign from the Federal Reserve Board and Supreme Court, respectively, when Roosevelt won. Mutual respect and communication between the two leaders during the "lame duck" period were impossible, and the nation therefore had to drift until the inauguration in March 1933.

THE ECONOMY DECLINES TO LEVELS THREATENING A BREAKDOWN OF THE ECONOMIC SYSTEM

The broad measures of the economy in 1932 dropped to almost 50% of their 1929 levels at current prices. The Gross National Product was $58 billion, compared with $101.3 billion in 1929 (down 43%), industrial production was down 46%, and National Income was down 51% to $42.8 billion, compared with $86.8 billion in 1929. Corporate sales of $69.2 billion were down 50%, compared with $138.6 billion in 1929. Exports were down further to 36% of 1929. These levels of economic activity represented a decline of approximately 25% from the depressed state of the economy already prevailing in 1931. The decline was less if expressed in constant 1958 dollars—approximately 27%–28% from 1929 and 15%–19% from 1931.

In business, as Alexander Dana Noyes said at the beginning of the year, "it was now no longer merely a question of what shocks must be endured before the recovery should come, but a question of universal bankruptcy." Inventory liquidation of $2.6 billion was a massive 4.5% of GNP as business strived to achieve liquidity. There were a record 31,822 bankruptcies, with liabilities of $928 million. The decline in business squeezed profits mercilessly. Industry as a whole had an aftertax loss of $2.7 billion in 1932, compared with its peak profits of $8.6 billion in 1929. The share of all public, private, and farm business in National Income had shrunk from 27.3% in 1929 to 7% in 1932.[19]

These macro-economic indicators provide little feeling for the extremes reached in the economy, however. Gross private investment had declined 94% from $16.2 billion in 1929 to only $1 billion. The auto, steel, metals, and construction industries, most closely related to the investment cycle, were virtually closed down for part of the year. Auto output dropped to only 1.2 million cars, compared with 4.8 million in 1929. Building contracts were $1.4 billion, versus a peak of $6.6 billion in 1928. New orders for electrical equipment also fell to approximately one-quarter of 1929 levels. Machine tool orders, which could be expected to drop further than other business indicators, dropped to one-eighth their 1929 volume. In the steel industry furnaces shut down for months, plant doors were locked, and all employees were sent home except for a few guards patrolling the property. Mining towns became inert as mines closed and literally all business in the towns came to a halt. Family businesses, which had employed hundreds of employees, again shrunk to employing only the family and its relatives. Shipping docks in the coastal cities lay idle for weeks at a time without a single ship arriving. Trains on many spur lines ran virtually empty of both freight and passengers. Cars and trucks were put on blocks to await better times. Factories in small towns stood inert, boarded up, without even the benefit of guards, as only the wind and playing children whistled through them. Half-finished buildings stood everywhere, like useless monuments to dead ambitions. Only the electric utility industry among major businesses kept some modicum of stability. Its kilowatt-hour output of 63 ½ billion kwh was down only 15% from 1929.[20]

Workers suffered severely from the decline in business, and from the first significant decline in local government economic activity during the Depression, as it cut back 14%. Unemployment averaged 36.3% for nonfarm workers during 1932. Hoover estimated that at the low point in July 1932 the unemployed totalled 12.4 million persons and 18 million were on relief. Employment dropped from 35.9 million persons in 1929 to 27.2 million in 1932. Those who were employed saw their wages steadily cut. The average hourly pay in manufacturing dropped to 31.8¢, compared with 38.3¢ in 1931 and 40.7¢ in 1929. U.S. Steel cut wages by 25% in two stages; New York City builders took a 25% wage cut; and even rail unions, which were the most resistant to employer demands, took a 10% wage cut in late January. Local governments cut wages and in many cases deferred paying wages or issued scrip that could be used locally.

Workers became militant. Man-days lost because of strikes surged to a record 10 ½ million from 6.9 million in 1931 and only 3.3 million in 1930, when the first signs of economic hardship produced compliance among workers. In the River Rouge riots at the Ford Motor Co.'s Dearborn plant in March, 3,000 marchers, including Walter Reuther, advanced on the Ford plant demanding jobs, but were turned back by police and guards who killed 4 and wounded 19 marchers. The next day, a Communist protest rally at the Arena Gardens attracted 6,000 people. There was a riot of unemployed at New York's City Hall the next month in which 15 were hurt, and a simultaneous riot at Harvard where students rushed both Radcliffe and the police station. At the latter they were dispersed with tear gas. Later in the year, 10,000 marched quietly through Chicago's Loop on a hunger march. In Iowa, farmers also took to violence by blocking roads and overturning trucks and wagons to prevent crops from reaching market and further depressing prices. The atmosphere of unrest, if not revolution, unsettled investors, businessmen, and politicians.

Real estate problems became particularly acute as the economy declined because of the high leverage and lack of liquidity inherent in real estate investment. In the major cities, real estate sales came to a halt, except for foreclosure sales. In New York City, outstanding realty bond issues of $800 million were estimated to be approximately $100 million in default. Most of the major hotels were in default. The Pierre filed for bankruptcy in March, only two years after it was built; the Waldorf-Astoria's finances were reorganized, as were the finances of the Bowman-Biltmore Hotel; the Hotel Carlyle was sold at foreclosure auction for $2,655,000 in May; and the Plaza Hotel declared bankruptcy in December. Masses of properties were put into default in March, when Henry Mandel, a noted New York City realtor, declared bankruptcy with assets of almost $400 million. Tax arrears in the city reached 26%, compared with 18% in 1931. In Chicago, tax arrears were $690 million, and a local judge ordered sold at auction 600,000 realty parcels in default on taxes to the extent of $141 million, although this was in part related to a court fight over city taxes. In Cleveland and Detroit, the cities' banking systems were threatened because the decline in real estate values had gone so far that many of the banks' loans were worthless. These cities were particularly affected by the downturn in heavy industry. Major new centers, like the Van Sweringens' Terminal Towers in Cleveland, which had appeared so progressive, operated at tremendous losses. Detroit tax arrears were 36% of the assessed tax levy. As Brooks, Harvey & Co., the leading mortgage brokerage firm, noted, real estate business was at a complete standstill. No new funds were available for mortgages or even for refinancing. All funds were going into the U.S. government and high grade municipal markets. Brooks, Harvey & Co. predicted that conditions would get still worse.

Conditions were even worse in the farm areas, where drought and low prices combined to bankrupt farmers. Farmers' cash receipts were down 59% to $4.6 billion from $11.2 billion in 1929 as corn prices averaged 35¢ per bushel versus 83¢ in 1929 and wheat averaged 60¢ versus $1.03. In Mississippi, which was hit particularly hard, an estimated 25% of the land had been foreclosed. In the plains states to the north, farmers took up their guns and manned barricades on the roads to prevent their farms from being taken. The average farm mortage was not that large—about $3,500—but small rural banks were under terrific pressure to liquidate their loans, and farmers found it impossible to come up with even small amounts of cash.

MONETARY POLICY, MONEY MARKETS, AND THE BANKING SYSTEM—A LIQUIDITY CRISIS DEVELOPS OUTSIDE OF NEW YORK CITY BANKS, DESPITE UNPRECEDENTED OPEN MARKET PURCHASES BY THE FEDERAL RESERVE AND LARGE-SCALE LOANS BY THE RECONSTRUCTION FINANCE CORPORATION

Problems in the banking system dominated short-term money markets in 1932. New York City banks shared some of these problems, but they were most acute in the smaller country member and nonmember banks and in several large cities acutely affected by the Depression. In the early months of 1932, the Reconstruction Finance Corporation played a vital role in keeping these bank problems from surfacing as suspensions. Between April and August 1932, the Federal Reserve instituted an unprecedented open-market purchase program in an effort to create bank liquidity for the same purpose. However, neither effort was successful in preventing the acceleration of a massive liquidity crisis by the end of 1932 which stopped banks from lending and drove short-term rates down to uncompensatory levels.

On the surface the banking system appeared to be recovering in 1932 from the high number of suspensions in the last quarter of 1931. In January, bank suspensions were as high as in late 1931, but in February deposits suspended dropped suddenly to 25% of January's level. The 11 months following January had fewer suspensions than either 1930 or 1931. (Bank suspensions are outlined in monthly detail in Tables A.28 and A.29 in the Statistical Appendix.) Federal Reserve borrowing was relatively low for banks in major cities during 1932, and these banks' investments were stable, which also gave the impression that the emergency in banking conditions had passed.

But these broad numbers for 1932 effectively mask the severe situation in the banking system. The Reconstruction Finance Corporation prevented bank closings in 1932 from being more numerous by lending $1.3 billion by the end of August 1932 to 5,520 financial institutions. Leading banks in Baltimore, Chicago, Cleveland, Detroit, and San Francisco were among the early recipients of these RFC loans. The RFC made its first loan to the Bank of America for $15 million, which it ultimately expanded to $64.5 million. Bank of America's credit had been shaken by its large real estate loan portfolio and by a management conflict which erupted publicly into a proxy battle between A. P. Giannini, its founder and former chairman, and Elisha Walker, who had taken over the bank. The Guardian Detroit Union Group borrowed $5 million from the RFC as soon as it began operations and by the end of the year it had borrowed $19 million. The Union Trust and the Guardian Trust in Cleveland borrowed over $50 million between them, and the Union Trust in Baltimore borrowed immediately from the RFC as well.

In the second quarter of 1932 a crisis in confidence developed which provoked much of the RFC's activity. The economy reached its lowest point in the Depression, which naturally had a severe impact on bank credit and financial markets, but there were also other uncertainties that exacerbated the tension at this point. There was a procrastinated, politically inspired, three-month debate in Congress over the budget, which was now in deficit by $2.7 billion and which neither party wanted to take responsibility for cutting in an election year. Gold loss in the quarter exceeded $500 million, as foreigners reacted against the budget indecision and in fear of a U.S. dollar devaluation. Such gold losses were as high as any experienced in the 1931 currency crisis. The RFC and the ICC had also thrown a disconcerting judgment into the maelstrom that railroad bonds (heavily owned by the banking system) maturing in 1932 should not be paid off in cash lent by the RFC, but rather handled by a combination of cash and refunding bonds which lenders had no choice but to accept.

The Federal Reserve System made an historic effort to counter the effects of this crisis on the banking system through open market purchases which provided increased reserves. The Federal Reserve System's holdings of U.S. government securities expanded from $870 million on March 31, 1932, to $1,784 million by June 30. This three-month program of purchases averaging $100–$150 million per week was publicly announced and deliberately pursued. The Federal Reserve purchased bills, certificates, notes, and bonds across the board. This program's details are shown in Table 10.2. Holdings on this scale were more than double any prior level in the Federal Reserve's history, and the speed with which they were acquired was unprecedented.

The effect on money market rates was electric. Three- to 6-month Treasury securities yields dropped 180 basis points from 2.25% to .30% in eight weeks once the Federal Reserve began its purchases. These rate declines restored short-term rates to the levels that had prevailed in the summer of 1931 before the currency crisis. Other short-term rates, except for bank commercial lending rates, came down proportionately.

Over $500 million of the Federal Reserve's $677 million in purchases in April and May was in bills and certificates under one year, which affected rates in this area disproportionately. Thereafter, the Federal Reserve bought more actively beyond one year, expanding its note holdings from $172 million in May to almost $400 million by August, which brought 1-year rates down to 1.25% in September and .75% in December.

The efforts of the Federal Reserve to provide reserves to the banking system were frustrated by the magnitude of the banking crisis which was developing. The approximately $1 billion in reserves provided by the Federal Reserve's open market purchases was partially offset by a $300 million decline in bills discounted by the Federal Reserve and by a $290 million increase in money in circulation. Most of the balance was reflected in a $400 million increase in the reserves of New York City banks and a $100 million increase in the reserves of Chicago banks during 1932.

The New York banks, in particular, contrasted with the rest of the banking system. During 1932 they expanded deposits in every respect. Demand deposits rose from $4.7 billion in March to $5.7 billion in December, and time deposits rose from $750 million to $890 million. Interbank deposits grew proportionately more than any other category, from $0.9 billion in March to $1.5 billion by December, as lesser banks built up their quick reserves with these large banks. The expansion of the New York banks' deposits was completely reflected in a $1 billion increase in their U.S. government holdings from $1.5 billion to $2.5 billion and in a $400 million increase in their reserves from $650 million to $1.05 billion between March and December. These reserves were roughly 25%–30% larger than any prior year.

Table 10.2
Holdings of U.S. Government Securities by Federal Reserve Banks,
1928–1933 (month end, $ millions)

	Total	Bills	Certificates	Notes	Bonds
1928	$ 228	—	$ 68	$ 100	$ 54
1929	511	$ 56	162	216	77
1930	729	24	315	226	164
1931	817	152	271	33	360
1932—January	746	110	258	59	320
February	740	87	261	74	319
March	872	149	311	84	328
April	1,228	328	454	100	346
May	1,549	400	589	172	389
June	1,784	352	725	270	438
July	1,841	369	783	269	421
August	1,852	326	709	396	421
September	1,854	354	680	398	421
October	1,851	424	643	363	421
November	1,851	400	652	378	421
December	1,855	415	719	300	422
1933—January	1,763	296	724	323	421
February	1,866	300	695	450	421
March	1,838	298	660	458	423
April	1,837	265	637	514	422
May	1,890	222	570	657	441
June	1,998	225	622	708	441
July	2,028	234	625	728	441
August	2,129	362	464	861	442
September	2,277	384	514	937	441
October	2,421	467	517	994	443
November	2,432	436	519	1,034	443
December	2,437	425	516	1,053	443

Source: Banking & Monetary Statistics, p. 343.

The great New York City banks had in effect become the liquidity reserve for the rest of the financial system. Corporations and institutions which feared that their deposits would be tied up in closed domestic banks transferred deposits to New York. Regional banks built up their liquid assets by increasing interbank deposits with New York. This trend is by and large explained by the sheer size of the New York banks. Their reserves were equal to 40% of the reserves of all the banks in the Federal Reserve System and roughly 4 times those of the Chicago banks. The reserve role was also a function historically performed by the New

York City banks, to which they had adapted their operations. They were more liquid than other banks, with fewer bond and real estate investments, higher U.S. government securities holdings, and larger reserves, proportionately. Of course, the New York banks shared in the problems of other banks to some degree, as we shall see.

Outside New York City, the banking system was subject to severe stress during 1932. Even Chicago, the nation's second financial center, felt the pressure. Reserves of the Chicago banks rose from $136 million in March 1932 to $286 million at year end, and excess reserves rose from $5 million to $163 million in the same period, giving the impression of a well-fortified city; on the contrary, however, these reserve increases reflected the liquidity pressures in Chicago. By mid-1932 there were only one-third the number of banks in Chicago that there had been in 1929, as suburban banks, set up under the state's archaic laws allowing no branches, collapsed one after the other. Events reached a crisis during the national Democratic convention in Chicago in June. There were 33 bank closings in seven business days ending June 24th, including the Bank of Commerce, which was the first Loop bank to close. Its deposits had dropped from $10 million to $5 million. The Central Republic Bank was under similar pressure, but it was a much larger bank. Its deposits had dropped from $170 million at the end of 1931 to $95 million at the end of June 1932, and the bank was fruitlessly supporting its own stock to prevent further loss of confidence. When this support for the stock was removed, it plunged from $47 to $4 in the over-the-counter market; it traded as low as $1. The bank and its chairman, General Dawes, who until recently had been President of the RFC, were saved only by an $80 million loan from the RFC and $15 million from Chicago and New York banks. The Continental Illinois National Bank & Trust Co. and the First National Bank of Chicago, Chicago's two leading banks, tried to maintain a proud mien despite their troubles, even lending to banks in other cities, but their positions were forlorn. Continental Illinois had a net worth only half that of the large New York banks, and First National had only one-quarter the net worth, while the deposit-to-capital ratios of the two banks were approximately twice that of the New York banks.

Banks in other major cities had even greater difficulties. Leading banks in Baltimore, Cleveland, Detroit, and San Francisco borrowed from the RFC early in the year and repeatedly throughout it. Demand deposits in large banks in 100 cities (including Chicago) outside New York continued a month-to-month decline from $6.5 billion in January 1932 to a low of $5.8 billion in August. Time deposits followed almost exactly the same trend, declining from $5 billion in January 1932 to $4.8 billion throughout the last half of the year. This decline in deposits of approximately $900 million in the first half of 1932 was reflected in a comparable decline in loans, but unlike the loans of the New York banks less than half of these loans were on securities, with the balance representing a reduction in loans with broader economic purposes. This deposit decline also put pressure on the liquidity of these city banks. Their investments declined almost $200 million from January to July, and their balances with other banks remained at less than half the $2.5 billion level they had been at in the first half of 1931, even though they built up somewhat from year end.

As a group, however, these banks managed some improvement by the end of 1932. Their reserves were up from $822 million in January to $947 million in December. Their balances with other banks, while still low, had doubled from $800 million in January to $1.6 billion in December. Their U.S. government investments had risen from $2.3 billion to $2.7 billion, their total investments from $4.7 billion to $4.9 billion.

As much as the banks in large cities felt the liquidity squeeze in declining deposits, the most devastating impact was on the country member banks of the Federal Reserve System and the nonmember banks, which also tended to be small and outside the major cities. Deposits of country member banks declined from $10.4 billion to $9.1 billion during 1932, and nonmember bank deposits declined from $8.8 billion to $7.3 billion. These banks were ill-prepared to cope with the liquidity squeeze. Each category of banks cut loans $1.1 billion. Reserves of country member banks dropped 10% to $440 million during the year, and cash dropped almost 25% to $232 million. In short, the basic measures of bank liquidity were cut, in contrast to the larger city banks, and accordingly suspensions among small banks in the first half of 1932 were a record for that period, exceeded at any time only by the last half of 1931. On the June 30, 1932, call date, country member bank borrowings from the Federal Reserve were at $556 million, which was a peak since 1921 and much above the level in 1929. By the end of 1932, these borrowings were still only down to $218 million, in contrast to the New York and Chicago banks, which were no longer borrowing, and banks in 100 large cities, which had cut their borrowings to only $75 million.

There were numerous weaknesses of long standing in the country banks—both members and nonmembers—which the Federal Reserve was powerless to affect through its open market purchases. Deposits at member and nonmember country banks had been declining since 1928, when they were a combined total of $27.2 billion. By June 30, 1932, these deposits were only $17 billion. The number of these banks had been declining even longer. In 1921 there were 20,041 nonmember banks, but the number declined every subsequent year until there were only 10,986 at the end of 1932. The number of state member banks (a useful proxy for member country banks) declined similarly from a peak of 1,648 in 1922 to 805 at the end of 1932. These banks were frequently under-capitalized and unduly concentrated in their loans to local farm and real estate customers. With no resources beyond their local community, they were poorly equipped to withstand economic hardships in their community.

The country banks were also poorly equipped to withstand deposit withdrawals or a liquidity squeeze because of their investments. *Member* country banks (for which we have much better data than nonmember banks) had only one-third of their December 31, 1931, investments in U.S. government securities, compared with two-thirds for the New York banks. *Nonmember* banks were even worse off, with 80% of their investments outside U.S. government securities. In the words of Ben Anderson, economist for Chase National Bank, country members suffered "fearful losses" on their investments in long-term corporate bonds, which were 41% of their investment portfolios and 90% of their net worth. Many of these bonds became unmarketable in 1932 because of investors' fears of default. The best railroad bonds traded at low prices in a range of $60–$70, and lesser rail bonds traded in a range of $30–$50. All but the best utility bonds traded at low prices below $75, and many utility bonds traded below $50; most industrial bonds dropped to $50 or less.

Country member banks also found the squeeze difficult because of the nature of their loans. Their loans were heavily concentrated in illiquid real estate and farm commodity loans which could not be foreclosed successfully. Real estate loans made up over 20% of their loans, versus only 3% at the New York banks at the end of 1931. The New York banks also had made almost half their loans to carry securities, which were much easier loans to liquidate (however unpleasant), compared with only 27% loaned on securities by the country member banks.

The Federal Reserve understandably felt powerless to affect the difficulties developing in the country banks. The reserves it provided through open market purchases of $1 billion in U.S. securities flowed into the major New York and Chicago banks, which accumulated excess reserves exceeding $200 million. If the reserves were not going to be gained by the banks that needed them, the open market purchases appeared to provide little benefit and threatened the Federal Reserve's ability to control credit conditions in the future. The problems of the banks outside major cities appeared to be rooted in these banks' real estate and agricultural loans and their portfolios of long-term rail, utility, and industrial bonds. The banks' problems were the mirror image of the economy's problems.

There were critics within the Federal Reserve System of the country banking structure who expected, and in a vague sense approved of, the country bank suspensions. This attitude found broad support in many informed circles. Branch banking to eliminate these small units had wide support among bankers and was officially supported by the American Banking Association before the Crash. Senator Carter Glass was a vocal critic of these small banks, which he referred to as "pawnshops set up over the country, miscalled 'banks.'" J. W. Pole, the Comptroller of the Currency, was an ardent advocate of branch banking and frequently made speeches in favor of it.

In effect, the Federal Reserve washed its hands of responsibility for the troubled banks of almost every size once it found that its open market policy could not solve the banking industry's problems. The rescue job was turned over completely to the Reconstruction Finance Corporation, which had been set up with government capital for that purpose and did not have the hampering responsibilities of the Federal Reserve for bank regulation, bond markets, federal financing, foreign exchange, and currency. The banking crisis was defined by Federal Reserve officials as a political problem, rather than a financial market problem, and the political sphere could accordingly deal with the problem. Henceforth the Federal Reserve limited its involvement to trying to persuade money center banks to lend to smaller correspondent banks when they could provide reasonable collateral, and to rediscounting eligible bills for members.

Despite its early success in reducing closings, however, the Reconstruction Finance Corporation was unable to sustain the banking system because of its need for collateral. As Russell Leffingwell, J. P. Morgan & Co. partner, put it, "For a fatal year and a half the RFC continued to lend money to the banks on adequate collateral security and gradually bankrupted them in the effort to save them."[21] The RFC made large loans to banks on the collateral of real estate loans and securities that many considered to be of questionable value, but the RFC still had to make these loans on some estimation of the fair market value of the collateral and with some margin of surplus collateral. These collateral values were well below the banks' book values in the securities. As a result, the borrowing banks found they had pledged all but their worst assets to the Federal Reserve and to the RFC at a discount from the distress market values prevailing, but had been able to borrow only a portion of their deposits. Many banks would have had their net worth effectively wiped out if all their assets, securities, and loans had to be written down to the low values of mid-1932, but this is effectively what happened when the RFC calculated how much it could lend a bank. As a result, if a bank's deposits dropped further than it could borrow from the RFC after it had sold its highly liquid securities, the bank had no more good assets on which to borrow elsewhere. This process was evident in the Detroit and Cleveland banks. The Guardian Trust Co. in Cleveland finally closed in 1933, at which time it had been able to borrow only $17.5 million directly from the RFC against collateral with a book value of $40.9 million. It had been able to borrow $6.2 million more against collateral with a book value of $19.3 million.[22] The Union Trust Co., also of Cleveland, borrowed $17.4 million directly from the RFC against collateral with a book value of $34.8 million, and it borrowed $21.2 million indirectly against collateral of real estate loans with a book value of $46.3 million.[23] In Detroit, the Guardian Detroit Union Group of banks borrowed $59.5 million from the RFC against collateral with a book value of $147.2 million.[24] When the loans available from RFC were so small relative to the book value of the collateral, the problem was more than borrowing money. The root question was "How much?" and the real need was to prevent the value of loan assets from declining (which is a simple statement, but means avoiding the ravages of the Depression) or to lend on book value in confidence that it would be restored.

The Detroit and Cleveland banks just cited were criticized roundly in the Senate Finance Subcommittee hearings on stock exchange practices and by historians for abusive loans, unwise investments, self-dealing by officers, and political favoritism, but the problems of these banks far exceeded their abuses and unwise investments. It was no coincidence that the most acute problems among major banks occurred in large industrial cities, which suffered acutely from the Depression.

There was a vicious circle set in progress for the banks which borrowed from the RFC on its terms. Directors, officers, other banks, and often major customers were aware of a borrowing bank's plight and the assets that had to be pledged. This information circulated in the business community and naturally caused large depositors to be cautious about the size of deposits they left with the bank. After RFC bank loans were published, the general public discovered the same things that insiders knew more specifically, and small depositors shunned the bank. As deposits declined in this environment, the bank invariably came to the point where it could borrow no more and had to suspend payments.

The squeeze on banks became acute in the last half of 1932. National City Bank described the banking system as the victim of fear which it could do nothing about. The Industrial Conference said this was the greatest crisis since wartime. The run on General Dawes' Central Republic Bank in Chicago in June marked a new scale of seriousness, for it was a large even if not leading bank in the financial center of the Midwest. National City Bank and Chase National Bank also made their second dividend reductions for the year at almost the same time. South Trimble, aged clerk of the House of Representatives, decided in August during the congressional recess that the RFC law required him to make public all RFC borrowers, including banks. He did not actually release the names of borrowers until October, over bitter objections, but the anticipated effect on depositors then occurred as borrowing banks lost depositors rapidly. There was also a prior effect in that banks, knowing their RFC loans would be advertised, tried to liquidate their loans and investments to raise cash rather than borrow from the RFC.

In November the first statewide bank closing occurred in Nevada when 12 banks in 9 cities around the state, owned by a prominent cattleman, George Wingfield, suspended deposits, and the Lieutenant Governor closed all the banks. Nevada's banks had generally been weakened by the decline in livestock prices on which many of the banks' loans were based. Banks closed on a large scale in Oklahoma and Pittsburgh during the same month. The Guardian Detroit Union Group was kept afloat in December only by a $3.5 million loan from Ford Motor Co. Bank examiners for the National Bank of Fort Wayne and the Fletcher American Bank in Indianapolis expected these banks' problems to erupt into public view at any moment.[25]

The federal election campaign exacerbated public fears about the financial system. Roosevelt's speeches emphasized the financial abuses in securities markets and banks' involvement in those abuses. Indeed, he blamed financial excesses for causing the Depression. His proposed reforms were directed mostly toward regulating the stock market, bond markets, and bank lending. The financial system was clearly going to be a victim rather than a partner under his Administration. Hoover, in a Des Moines campaign speech, said the United

States had been within two weeks of going off the gold standard early in 1932 before he got the Glass-Steagall Act passed. Such proximity to disaster unsettled the public, despite counterclaims by Senator Glass himself that no such danger had been imminent. Russell Leffingwell blamed this speech for reversing the summer economic recovery. Following Roosevelt's victory, fears were further increased as it became clear that Hoover and Roosevelt could not cooperate on war debts, the budget, the gold standard, farm policy, or Prohibition in the four-month interregnum.

This visible, developing crisis put an emphasis on bank liquidity which virtually halted bank lending in the second half of 1932. By the end of 1932, the New York City banks built up excess reserves of $283 million and added $500 million to their U.S. government securities, which became $2.5 billion by year end. J. P. Morgan & Co. had 50% of its total assets invested in U.S. governments by year end, and there were rumors of a New York bank 80% invested in U.S. governments.[26] The banks were unwilling to lend even to borrowers facing bond maturities, which forced these borrowers into loans from the RFC or the Federal Reserve directly, or into defaults. Banks outside New York themselves needed loans, which they frequently obtained from local businesses, as from the auto companies in Detroit, rather than the RFC or bigger banks. Banks were frequently too busy trying to save themselves to save their customers.

This intense desire for liquidity created such unusual competition for short-term government securities that Treasury bill yields were negative in much of October, November, and December. The average new-issue rate for Treasury bills in the last quarter of 1932 was 0.15%. Ninety-day bankers acceptances dropped from 7/8% in June to 3/4% in July through mid-October, and to 3/8% by December. Only commercial paper rates stayed high—over 2% until October and down only to 1 3/8% at the end of 1932.[27] This dramatic decline in rates occurred despite the usual tendency for an economic crisis to produce higher rates.

Efforts to counter the liquidity crisis were ineffective. President Hoover frequently appealed to the public to have confidence in the banking system and to cease hoarding cash, which was draining bank reserves. The federal government even had a Baby Bond issue of denominations under $100, which was designed to appeal to small investors in the hope that they would pay for the bonds with hoarded cash. Representative Henry B. Steagall (Dem-Ala.) and Senator Arthur Vandenburg (R-Mich.), among others, began a campaign for U.S. guarantees of bank deposits, but proponents of the idea were unable to agree on the proportion or size of deposits to be guaranteed, and many banks not in trouble fought the idea.

Hoover organized committees of prominent citizens in all Federal Reserve districts to try to encourage the larger regional banks to make loans. Similar committees were set up to encourage banks to borrow from the RFC. Many banks formed regional pools of funds for specific loan purposes, but these pools were ineffective and appeared to take the banks out of the business of making those loans individually. A new form of trade acceptance was created which could be rediscounted at the Federal Reserve to provide an alternative form of loan to business which was highly liquid, but it had little effect on loan volume.

It is paradoxical that in the last half of 1932, as the liquidity crisis accelerated, the stock and bond markets recovered significantly from their low points in the second quarter of 1932. The economy too had begun to recover, not merely in the statistical series but also in the opinion of current commentators. This divergence helps place the bank crisis in perspective amid the numerous other crises which confronted the nation during the year. The banks were latecomers to the party, not an early, causative factor in the economy, as the monetarists have claimed.

PRICES DROP TO THEIR LOWEST LEVELS IN THE DEPRESSION

National City Bank observed in its *Monthly Review* during 1932 that deflation, and the resulting burden of previously acquired debt, was the chief cause of the "psychological depression" spread throughout the land. The index of 47 farm products prices dropped in midyear to only 39% of the pre-Crash level, which produced the lowest grain prices on record since the Civil War. International Harvester found farm prices so unrealistic that it offered farmers credit against their crops on machinery purchases at prices up to 50% above prevailing market prices. At its lowest point, in December 1932, wheat traded below 40¢ per bushel in the face of a worldwide wheat surplus of 745 million bushels, compared with shipments of only 261 million bushels in 1932. In 1929, wheat prices had been as high as $1.40 per bushel. Corn prices reached below 25¢ per bushel, compared with $1 in 1929, and cotton was below 6¢ per pound, compared with over 20¢ in 1929.[28]

Prices of publicly traded industrial commodities reached a low point almost identical to farm commodities prices in mid-1932 at 37% of their pre-Crash prices. Zinc prices averaged a mere 2½¢ per pound in 1932, or 37% of their pre-Crash level, and lead prices were similar. Copper's lowest price was 4.8¢ per pound, which was only 27% of its pre-Crash price, even though copper producers worldwide operated at only 26% of capacity. Rubber prices had the worst decline of all, dropping to only 13% of their pre-Crash price. Only oil and tin prices failed to decline further in 1932.[29]

The lowest point for commodities prices was during the liquidity crisis in May and June, which was also the low point for stock and bond prices and for the economy. In the summer commodities prices rose with stocks and bonds, but the composite index of commodities prices rose only 10% between June and September, while stocks doubled and bond prices were up one-third. Essentially there was no relief for farmers or businesses from the price decline which had now spanned 40 months.

Prices in their own right became a focus of public attention in 1932. Farmers barricaded highways and dumped farm products into roadside ditches rather than sell at market prices. Congress reacted to price level problems by imposing tariffs on imported copper, oil, sugar, and other commodities to protect home producers from foreign price cutting. In May 1932, the House of Representatives passed the Goldsborough Bill, directing the Federal Reserve to act to maintain commodities prices at 1926 levels, but the bill could not get through the Senate, where it was opposed by Carter Glass. The Federal Intermediate Credit Banks were empowered to lend on commodities, the Federal Farm Board tried to support farm prices but exhausted its resources early in the second half of the year, and Eugene Meyer, Governor of the Federal Reserve Board, went so far as to support a $30 million wheat pool led by Arthur W. Cutten, a prominent 1920s speculator, and along more decorous lines pushed New York banks into capitalizing a $100 million Commodity Credit Corp. to help stabilize prices.

Compared with the 63% decline in farm and business commodities prices, at the end of 1932 the Wholesale Price Index for 784 goods was down 35% from its pre-Crash level and the Retail Food Price Index was down 40%. Both indices were at their lowest level at the end of the year and experienced almost no upward change in midyear, when securities prices rose sharply. In 1932 the GNP deflator was down only 21.6% from 1929, compared with the price declines which were generating such political heat and economic hardship.[30]

NOTES

1. *New York Times*, 3/13/32.
2. Ibid., 1/13/32.
3. Ibid., 3/13/32.
4. Ibid., 3/8/32.
5. Ibid., 6/2/32.
6. Ibid., 2/27/32.
7. Ibid., 1/14/32.
8. Ibid., 3/13/32.
9. Ibid., 12/14/32.
10. Susan Estabrook Kennedy, *The Banking Crisis of 1933*, Lexington, Kentucky: The University Press of Kentucky, 1973.
11. *New York Times*, 7/27/32.
12. Ibid., 6/3/32.
13. Herbert Hoover, *Memoirs of H. Hoover: The Great Depression 1929–1941*, New York: Macmillan Co., 1952, p. 37.
14. *New York Times*, 9/10/32.
15. Ibid., 11/1/32.
16. Ibid., 11/11/32.
17. *Stock Exchange Practices*, part 2, p. 951.
18. *New York Times*, 11/29/32.
19. Ibid., 12/31/31; *National Income Accounts*, p. 14.
20. *Moody's Industrial Manual, 1933*, pp. a71–86; *National Income Accounts*, pp. 4, 126, 142.

21. Quoted in Arthur Schlesinger, Jr., *The Age of Roosevelt*, Volume 1, *The Crisis of the Old Order*, 1919-1933, Boston: Houghton Miflin Company, 1957, p. 237.

22. *Stock Exchange Practices*, part 18, p. 8026.

23. Ibid., p. 8253.

24. Ibid., part 10, p. 4756.

25. Ibid., pp. 4653–54.

26. Ibid., part 1, p. 22.

27. *Banking & Monetary Statistics*, pp. 457, 460.

28. *Statistical Abstract, 1939*, p. 315; NYSE monthly bulletin, September 1938, graphs on prices of commodities.

29. *Moody's Industrial Manual, 1935*, blue insert pages on "The Nation's Basic Industries."

30. *Statistical Abstract, 1939*, p. 315; *National Income Accounts*, p. 158.

11

The Stock Market in 1932

Stock prices reached their lowest point in the depression during 1932. In July the Dow Jones Industrial Index dropped to a low of 41, which was only 11% of its high in September 1929 of 381. The Dow Jones Railroad Index dropped to 7% of its 1929 high as the beleaguered railroads fought to stay solvent. Even with some recovery by year end, the three Dow Jones indices were still between 14% and 19% of their 1929 high points. (Table A.19 in the Statistical Appendix outlines the Dow Jones indices monthly for 1919 to 1933.)

The decline in values corresponded to lethargic trading activity. NYSE trading volume for 1932 was only 425 million shares, which averaged approximately 1 1/2 million shares per day, and volume dropped as low as 750,000 shares per day in midyear. Common stock new issues were only $13 million for the whole year. The low level of activity is understandable in the light of corporate financial conditions. Industry as a whole reported a net loss of $2.7 billion in 1932 and cut dividends from $4.1 billion to $2.5 billion.

THE COURSE OF EVENTS—STOCKS REACH THE LOWEST POINT IN THE DEPRESSION IN JUNE AND JULY

The year 1932 began in unrelieved gloom. The effects of the international currency collapse in September 1931 and the domestic banking crisis of the last quarter of that year carried over into 1932 as the United States continued to lose gold reserves and bank suspensions continued above 300 in January. President Hoover's annual message stressed the need for courage rather than hope. Economic forecasts were uniformly negative, stressing the poor business atmosphere, bank defaults, municipal and real estate problems, wage cuts, and the federal budget deficit.

This gloomy outlook was ameliorated momentarily in mid-February when the

Reconstruction Finance Corporation began to make loans to banks and railroads and when Congress passed an amendment to the Federal Reserve statute permitting the Federal Reserve banks to hold U.S. government bonds, as well as gold, as cover for Federal Reserve obligations. The Federal Reserve System was thereby freed to pursue an aggressive open market policy of purchasing government securities without being constrained by the loss of gold to foreigners expected to follow such an "inflationary" policy. The Dow Jones Industrial Index jumped from 71 to 85 in two days—a whopping 19 1/2%.

In March, however, the market sold off again as individual negative events kept affecting it. General Theatres Equipment declared bankruptcy on March 1st. Ivar Kreuger committed suicide on March 12th. Middle West Utilities went into receivership in April. There was a steady stream of bad dividend news as dividends were eliminated by Anaconda Copper, Kennecott, IT&T, Middle West Utilities, and Southern Pacific Company. Other market leaders such as General Motors, General Electric, and U.S. Steel cut their dividends. Fears of social unrest also began to loom, as workers rioted at Henry Ford's River Rouge plant and plant guards attacked and killed several rioters. Young Walter Reuther was injured in the rioting.

The market decline which began in March extended for 11 weeks until the DJII had dropped from 88 on March 8th to 44 on May 31st, a decline of 50%. At the same time, the DJRI dropped 63% from 38 to 14. The record low for the Depression was established on July 8th when the DJII closed at 41. Trading volume that day was 720,000 shares, which was typical in May, June, and July of that year. Every industry category on the NYSE recorded its lowest value for the year in either June or July.

This stock market decline occurred while the Federal Reserve was following an unprecedented open market policy of expanding its holdings of U.S. government securities from $740 million at the end of February 1932 to $1.8 billion at the end of July.[1] As a result of this operation, Federal Reserve Bank credit outstanding expanded from a daily average of $1.8 billion in February to $2.4 billion in July.[2] However, other matters clearly overshadowed this favorable credit policy. Financial commentators focussed on the federal budget deficit as the overriding influence on stock and bond markets. The federal deficit had reached $2.7 billion at fiscal year end on June 30th. There was no period in history to compare with such a deficit, except the wartime deficits of 1918 and 1919, which were $9 billion and $13.4 billion, respectively.[3] Hoover had sought increased taxes, particularly a federal excise tax on manufacturers, and reduced expenditures since March, but the bills required were stalled in the Senate until June, when taxes were finally increased $1.1 billion. In its June review, National City Bank of New York said, "It is safe to say that no single influence has done more to unsettle confidence, check business revival, and offset the good effects of the Federal Reserve credit expansion program than the delay on the part of Congress in dealing effectively with this issue."[4] Since individuals and businesses had to pay the $1.1 billion increase in taxes, however, we may be justifiably skeptical about whether it was the budget deficit or the new taxes which upset confidence and recovery.

In any case, there were other elements in the news that surely upset markets as much as or more than the federal budget deficit. The plight of borrowers was clear to all as the RFC was besieged for loans by railroads and by banks outside New York. By June 30th it had authorized loans of $214 million to railroads and $640 million to banks.[5] Major banks in Detroit, Baltimore, Cleveland, San Francisco, and Chicago were borrowing from the RFC, the most celebrated being the Bank of America and the Central Republic Bank in Chicago.

During the summer, social conditions had reached explosive levels and affected the financial markets. Earlier violence at the Ford Motor Co.'s River Rouge plant was now followed by the Bonus Army's march to Washington, where it encamped through the early summer until it was disbanded forcefully in July by 52-year-old General Douglas MacArthur. Farmers in the Midwest, particularly in Iowa, turned to violence to protest low commodities prices. Milk was dumped into ditches, calves were slaughtered on highways, and roads were blocked to prevent produce from entering market centers. Wage reductions were made for the third or fourth time in many manufacturing industries, and unemployment exceeded 30%. Investors justifiably feared that the social and financial structures were coming apart.

The Dow Jones Industrial Index recovered in August and September to a peak of 79.93 (which was almost double the low hit in July) on hopes of a business recovery. Volume soared to an average of 3.1 million shares per day in August and 2.7 million per day in September, in comparison with volume below 1 million shares per day in each of May, June, and July. Brokers began to rehire laid-off staff. Businessmen sensed an expansion in their activity in July. U.S. Steel reported an increase in its July backlog of orders for the first time in 17 months. Rail car loadings improved beginning in September. Alexander Dana Noyes, business and finance editor of the *New York Times*, predicted, "1932 will be described as the first year of recovery from the great depression." Roger Babson, who had been so prescient in predicting the progress of the Depression, told a Halifax audience that business activity would be back to normal levels by 1934. The Federal Reserve Bank of Cleveland described the first business improvement it had witnessed in four years. Liquidity pressures had been relieved by a number of steps, as well. The RFC had begun making direct loans to embattled local governments.

The Federal Reserve had built its holdings of U.S. government securities to approximately $1.85 billion by August, $1 billion above its 1931 level. The gold drain also ceased, and foreign funds began to return to the United States. Foreign optimism improved considerably, especially in England, Germany, France, and Australia. Meetings among the European great powers to resolve their war debts and reparations promised to remove one of the largest constrictions on European trade and finance. An initial League of Nations survey on the world economy found cautious optimism in most countries.

The stock market dropped from nearly 80 on the DJII in early September to the low 70s for the last week of September, where it hovered until the week of October 3–8, when it dropped 10 points. In this one week, the names of RFC bank borrowers were publicized for the first time on the orders of House Speaker John Nance Garner; President Hoover made his Des Moines election speech in which he declared that the United States had been within a hair's breadth of going off the gold standard in February 1932; and the *Literary Digest* published its public opinion poll findings that voters favored Franklin Roosevelt over Hoover 50 to 40. Commodities dropped to new low prices at the same time. Wheat prices of 40¢ per bushel were the lowest on record.

The stock market did not recover from this fall during the rest of the year. Fear of Roosevelt's success was widespread up to the November 8th election because of his attacks on financial abuses and public utilities. His opening campaign speech in Columbus, Ohio, on August 20th offered a nine-point program in which every point was directed at securities issues, stock trading, bank operations, Federal Reserve lending, or public utilities. Roosevelt was portrayed in the press as demanding control of the stock and commodity exchanges. Banks' and brokers' market letters suggested that the market was held down by fear of Roosevelt's success, and E. F. Hutton even went on the radio in a broadcast paid for by the Republican Party to declare that electing Roosevelt would slow down economic recovery. Treasury Secretary Mills shrilly prophesied that Roosevelt threatened the economy.

The market rose very slightly after the presidential election, but then declined further after it became clear that there was to be no cooperation between Hoover and Roosevelt in the months until Roosevelt took over in March 1933. After the election, Roosevelt made it known that he was opposed to any new federal excise or income taxes to balance the budget, which put the prospect of balancing it out of reach. He also refused to cooperate with Hoover on European requests for a conference on war debts and reparations, insisting that Hoover bear the sole responsibility and then adding that he (Roosevelt) preferred ad hoc remedies negotiated individually with each country. Hoover, on the other hand, opposed Roosevelt's desire for a short December session of Congress, which would aid agricultural distress and repeal the Volstead Act, ending prohibition. In addition, Roosevelt waited until February to appoint his cabinet, which created a hiatus in the nation's power structure with no alternative centers of power to the "lame duck" secretaries of the Hoover Administration.

Two other crises were escalating as investors viewed the aftermath of the presidential election. Nevada closed all its banks November 2nd because of the failure of the Wingfield chain of 12 banks. Bank problems had become critical in Michigan, Ohio, Illinois, and Indiana as well.

New York City's finances had also reached a climax. The banks still held most of the city's last public bond offering in their inventories, and New York City's 4¼% bonds due in 1981 had dropped from $95 to $85 in three weeks.

The year 1932 closed with the DJII at 59 and investors in a high state of apprehension.

TECHNICAL ASPECTS OF THE MARKET—THE BROKERAGE BUSINESS CONTRACTS AS TRADING DRIES UP

The brokerage industry reached its nadir of the Depression in 1932. NYSE volume for the year was 35% of 1929 volume, and NYSE daily volume frequently dropped below 1 million shares, compared with the 5-million-share days in 1929. One day in June 1932, volume dropped to only 388,000 shares. The brokerage industry was reported to need annual volume of 700 million shares to operate profitably, even though the 1932 volume of 425 million shares equalled volume in 1925–26 and was 50% above years prior to 1925. (See Table A.21 in the Statistical Appendix.) Many firms did something similar to Goldman, Sachs, & Co. which asked its employees to report the bare minimum in salary they needed to live and then paid each employee the minimum. As a result, brokerage firm losses were reduced from $225 million in 1931 to $58 million in 1932.[6] Arbitrage profits were one of the few sources of income, particularly in maturing railroad bonds, which were usually paid off in a combination of cash and new bonds under directions from the RFC.

Trading volume on the Curb Exchange, where smaller, more speculative issues were listed, was only 57 million shares for all of 1932, compared with 476 million shares in 1929. The year 1932 was the worst year for the Curb Exchange in all its succeeding history, but the NYSE experienced lower volume in four of the succeeding seven years in the decade.

New issue business provided no alternative source of income to brokerage commissions. Corporate new issues were only $644 million, compared with over $10 billion in 1929. Fully half of 1932's new issues were refundings taking advantage of low interest rates. Municipal new issues were still $762 million, which was half of 1929–30 levels, the only market with any resemblance to its old activity levels.

In 1932 the brokerage industry contracted in the face of such manifest disinterest in its services. Member firms dropped to 621 in number, versus 665 at the peak in 1930, and offices dropped from 1,658 to 1,347. But NYSE seat prices reflected more of the realities. The peak seat price in 1932 was $185,000 and the low was $68,000, compared with a high price of $495,000 in 1929. Member borrowings to carry securities or margin accounts dropped to a low of $242 million in August, only 1.18% of the value of all NYSE stocks. This compared with borrowings of $8.5 billion in September 1929, when borrowings were 9.82% of the value of all NYSE stocks. (See Tables A.22 and A.25 in the Statistical Appendix.)

Selling pressure in the stock market was constant from financial institutions in trouble. Banks threatened with suspension invariably sold their liquid securities

335

tay afloat. Liquidators of closed banks sold the remaining stocks.
rmed with official consent to handle securities sales by bank liq-
number of casualty companies got into financial trouble, particularly
d, New York, and the Midwest, and sold their common stock holdings.
in Canada, one of the largest holders of U.S. common stocks (unlike
fe insurance companies, which were mostly forbidden by law to own
common stocks), sold heavily pursuant to a promise to Canadian Premier R. B.
Bennett to reduce its common equity holdings.

Short selling did not, on balance, create selling pressure on stocks. The short
interest on the NYSE declined from 2.8 million shares at the end of December
1931 to 1.9 million shares at the end of December 1932. September short interest
of 1.7 million shares was the lowest on record. Covering short sales provided
net buying interest in stocks during the year. During the year, the only significant
rise in the short interest was from 3.1 million shares to 3.9 million shares between
January 21st and February 10th, when the DJII dropped from 83 to 71. (See
Table A.23 in the Statistical Appendix.) Within days thereafter, a new NYSE
rule was enacted requiring that brokers obtain customer consent before lending
their stocks to short sellers. The margin requirement on short sales had been
raised to 33 1/3% in January. Both were technical efforts to limit short selling.

The public attitude toward the stock market was acutely negative by 1932 and
acted as a depressant on the market. At the end of January, the NYSE expelled
with some publicity Franklin V. Brodie, a specialist who had been crew captain
and varsity football center at Columbia University but who was now guilty of
buying stocks for his own account when he had orders on his books for customers
at the same price. Such self-dealing was symbolic of what the public suspected.
In March 1932 suspicion led the U.S. Senate to authorize an epochal investigation
into securities practices which ultimately led to the massive legal and structural
changes in the securities industry embodied in the Securities Act of 1933, the
Securities and Exchange Act of 1934, and the Glass-Steagall Act of 1933. As
the investigation began in 1932, there was wide publicity about pools formed
in 1928 and 1929 to manipulate stocks, about directors and officers speculating
against their own companies, about NYSE specialists trading for relatives, and
about banks giving bonuses to staff members for selling stocks owned by the
banks. In 1933 worse abuses would be revealed. Another 1932 Senate investigation into the marketing of foreign bonds revealed staggering levels of cupidity,
bribery, and distortion of facts by American underwriters. Securities affiliates
of the New York banks looked particularly bad, for they managed issues to pay
off their own loans even when bank officers advised that the issuer had little
prospect of repaying the bonds.

Negative public attitudes toward business and finance were stimulated by three
bankruptcies which received wide publicity during the first half of 1932. Beginning in January, the details of the Bank of United States collapse came before
the public when New York Superintendent of Banks Broderick went on trial for
his role in the debacle (for which he ultimately was justifiably acquitted). Ivar

Kreuger's suicide in March and the collapse of his companies attracted further attention, but nothing like that of the collapse of Middle West Utilities, run by Samuel Insull. Securities of Insull's companies had been sold directly to small investors by Insull's own securities firms and by the operating companies he controlled. His companies were numerous and widespread, as were their stockholders, so that the reverberations of his collapse permeated far into the public psyche. William Ward Foshay, a Minneapolis utility speculator who had a smaller system but one similar to Insull's, was sentenced to jail in March for his role in the collapse of his companies. The smell of fraud and self-dealing hung over all these men and tainted other businessmen.

Politicians embodied the public attitude against capital into law in the Tax Bill of 1932 by limiting tax deductions for capital losses to capital gains and initiating income taxes on dividends. However, it took Roosevelt to capture and guide the public's disgust. His first campaign speech did not have a single point that was not directed against the financial and business community. He, as much as anyone, raised the Crash to its symbolic position as the cause of the Depression. His proposals for controls over banks, stock trading, credit, public utilities, new issues, and foreign bond sales made it clear that substantial restrictive reform was in prospect for the securities industry.

SPECIFIC INDUSTRIES AND INDIVIDUAL STOCKS IN 1932

Data on individual companies can be found in Table A.1 in the Statistical Appendix. Table A.5 provides ratios for each company's high and low 1932 stock prices.

The Railroad Industry

The railroad industry was in extremis throughout 1932. Railroad revenues had dropped almost in half since 1929 (from $6.9 billion to $3.6 billion) and the industry registered a loss of $122 million despite the general rate increase authorized by the ICC in late 1931. The railroads reduced wages several times during the year, cut employees 18% (37% since 1929), reduced equipment purchases to $100 million, compared with $1 billion in each of 1929 and 1930, and cut dividends to $151 million, which was less than 40% of peak dividends.[7] The Atchison, Topeka & Santa Fe, the Canadian Pacific, the Pennsylvania, and the Southern Pacific among major railroads eliminated their dividends in 1932, following the elimination of dividends at the B&O and New York Central in 1931. The B&O even went into arrears on its preferred dividends. (See Table 11.1 for details on specific companies.)

The railroads were virtually unable to sell bonds in 1932, as only $61 million was raised publicly. Many railroads were threatened by bankruptcy. Thirteen railroads constituting 11,817 miles of track went into receivership—double the mileage in receivership in 1930 and 1931. Other railroads would have gone

Table 11.1
The Railroad Industry in 1932

	Price-earnings ratio		Market price as a % of book value		Dividend yield (%)		Low price as a % of 1929 high price	Return on equity (%)	Moody's bond ratings	Cash & equivalents ($ millions)
	High price	Low price	High price	Low price	High price	Low price				
Atchison, Topeka & Santa Fe	NM[a]	33	41	8	0	0	6	0.2	Aaa	22
Baltimore and Ohio	def.[b]	def.	15	3	0	0	3	def.	Aa	(22)[c]
Canadian Pacific	def.	def.	45	14	0	0	11	def.	Aa	15
Chesapeake and Ohio	10	3	64	20	7.81	25.64	14	6.1	Aaa	(4)
New York Central	def.	def.	23	5	0	0	3	def.	Aa	(68)
Norfolk & Western	12	5	65	28	5.93	14.04	20	5.5	Aaa	7
Pennsylvania	22	6	27	8	0	0	6	1.2	Aaa	49
Southern Pacific	def.	def.	17	3	0	0	4	def.	Aa	(7)
Union Pacific	13	4	44	13	6.32	21.43	9	3.5	Aaa	21
Averages	NM	NM	38	11	NM	NM	8	3.3	—	—

[a] NM = Not Meaningful.
[b] def. = Deficit.
[c] Brackets indicate short-term borrowing.

bankrupt had the RFC not swung into action in February as the lender of last resort for the industry. The Missouri Pacific, which had a history of endemic receiverships, sought RFC aid to pay off its New York bank lenders before the RFC was even open for business. The Missouri Pacific received $14.7 million in February 1932. Among the major railroads, the B&O, New York Central, Pennsylvania, Southern, Southern Pacific, and St. Louis–San Francisco received RFC loans in 1932 as the RFC authorized loans of $337 million to the railroad industry. (See Table A.32 in the Statistical Appendix.)

RFC loans to the railroads were made on the recommendation of the ICC, which remained ungenerous to the industry and its investors. The ICC insisted that RFC loans to the railroads for other than construction be used to refund maturing debt with exchange packages of cash and new debt—frequently 50% cash and 50% new debt. Arbitrageurs, rather than willing bondholders, usually made these exchanges work. Since the new bonds typically sold at sharp discounts, holders of maturing bonds took sharp losses. In a few desperate cases, the ICC insisted on reorganization before a railroad received a loan.

Railroad stocks were among the poorest valued in May and June 1932, when both stocks and the economy hit their low point for the Depression, at 8% of their highest 1929 prices and 11% of book value, compared with 12% and 49% for all stocks. There were many industries whose stocks averaged lower prices relative to their highest prices in 1929, but only paper and steel stocks had prices as low as 11% of book value. Investors with the courage to buy railroad stocks amid threatened default on their bonds and an economy in disarray got startling bargains. Chesapeake & Ohio and Union Pacific stocks yielded over 20% as the former maintained its dividend and the latter only dropped its dividend from $10.00 to $6.00. The Norfolk & Western yielded 14% after a dividend cut from $10.00 to $8.00.

The one ray of light for the railroads occurred in late July, when the ICC finally approved a plan for four eastern trunk lines built around the Pennsylvania, New York Central, C&O, and B&O railroads. The consolidation of the eastern railroads was expected to produce substantial operating economies.

The Operating Public Utility Industry

Operating utilities, particularly electric companies, came to the fore in 1932 as strong and dependable credits. The *New York Times* commented in August 1932, "The electric light and power industry has made a more favorable showing during the depression than any other industry." The industry's financial strength was formidable, compared with other industries. Industry revenues of $2.87 billion were slightly above 1929 revenues, and net income was still $343 million compared to $415 million in 1929. None of the major operating utilities followed here (see Table 11.2) had its bond ratings reduced during the year, and all the companies improved their cash liquidity. Utility bonds showed none of the acute credit fears apparent in the railroad bond market, and no utilities borrowed from

Table 11.2
The Operating Public Utility Industry in 1932

	Price-earnings ratio		Market price as a % of book value		Dividend yield (%)		Low price as a % of 1929 high price	Return on equity (%)	Moody's bond ratings	Cash & equivalents ($ millions)
	High price	Low price	High price	Low price	High price	Low price				
Commonwealth Edison	20	8	112	45	4.10	10.20	11	5.7	Aa	16
Consolidated Gas Co. of N.Y.	17	8	128	60	5.88	12.50	17	7.7	Aa	(12)[a]
Detroit Edison	23	10	106	47	4.90	11.10	14	4.5	A	7
Pacific Gas & Electric	18	8	123	57	5.41	11.75	17	7.0	Aa	18
Public Service of N.J.	17	8	140	65	5.33	11.43	20	8.2	Aa	14
Averages	19.0	8.4	122	55	5.12	11.40	16	6.6	—	—

[a] Brackets indicate short-term borrowing.

the RFC. Utility bonds became the clear industry of preference over railroad and industrial bonds. The unusual strength of the operating companies was vividly illustrated in midyear when, following the default of the Insull holding companies, which we shall discuss shortly, the principal Insull operating companies, Commonwealth Edison, Peoples Gas, and Public Service Co. of Northern Illinois, nonetheless were able to sell approximately $70 million of long-term bonds at rates between 6% and 7%.

The utility industry had significant problems, however. Industry dividends of $471 million exceeded the industry's net income. These high payout ratios were most common in holding company systems where strong subsidiaries were used to support weak ones, a practice which caused some commissions, led by Wisconsin, to forbid upstream dividends from operating companies to their holding companies. Such a mismatch between income and dividends could not be maintained long. Commonwealth Edison, Detroit Edison, and Public Service Corp. of New Jersey all cut their dividends during the year, and the industry was cutting back sharply in employees and construction spending. Full-time employees dropped from 437,000 to 384,000. Electric utility construction dropped from $597 million in 1931 to $285 million in 1932. The compression in construction budgets which was necessary was wrenching for many companies, and 54 utilities were put into receivership in 1932, although most were small transit companies, telephone companies, or holding companies. Small midwestern companies were particularly squeezed and got by paying suppliers in installments and scrounging secondhand equipment.[8]

Utility practices also became prominent issues in the presidential election, particularly for the public utility holding companies as a result of the Middle West Utilities bankruptcy and a critical Federal Power Commission report issued at the time. Roosevelt also strongly favored federal power generation at Niagara Falls, Muscle Shoals, and Boulder Dam, despite the considerable surplus in electric generating capacity due to the Depression. Local politicians, particularly Gifford Pinchot, Governor of Pennsylvania, made whipping posts of the utilities for their influence and profits. Oregon and Washington passed public power amendments to their constitutions.

The credit strength and respectable 6.6% return on equity in 1932 of the leading public utilities translated into stock values that were not much above average because of the problems of dividend reductions, construction cutbacks, and political attacks. The leading utility stocks were battered down to 16% of their highest 1929 prices and only 55% of book value, compared with 12% and 49% for all stocks. Utility dividend yields averaging 11.40% at their lowest prices were right in line with the yields on profitable companies' stocks in the tobacco, consumer products, food, and chemical industries.

It is interesting to note that at the lowest point in utility stock and bond prices in 1932 the stocks yielded 11.40%, while bonds of the same and comparably rated other utilities bore yields of only 5.80%. Of course, the stock investor had to worry about dividend cuts, but dividends averaged 96% of earnings for those leading companies, which was a relatively typical level and had already been cut to bring them into line with earnings. It appears that investor preference for bonds over stocks was so pronounced that no comparison with the returns on comparable stocks had any influence over investors' choices.

Holding and Investment Companies

The Public Utility Holding Companies

The public utility holding companies suffered an extended period of financial stress and low stock market valuations from 1932 into 1933 as dividends from their operating subsidiaries were reduced and their leverage worked in reverse. Public utility holding company stocks dropped to an average price that was only 4% of their highest 1929 prices and 26% of book value, which levels were roughly equalled again in 1933; Cities Service, Commonwealth & Southern, and IT&T eliminated their common stock dividends; and Cities Service, Columbia Gas & Electric, Electric Bond and Share, IT&T, and Middle West Utilities wrestled with large short-term debts. Middle West Utilities lost the battle and went into receivership in April 1932, throwing a pall over all other companies. (See Table 11.3 for details on specific companies.)

In some respects the valuations of public utility holding company stocks were surprising. Most of them still had positive earnings, electric and gas company revenues were barely down from 1929, and utility dividends in total were down only 25%. The principal subsidiaries of Columbia Gas & Electric, North American Co., Standard Gas & Electric, and United Gas Improvement were sustaining the impact of the Depression well. Yet the valuations of these companies' stocks were swept up in the problems of such companies as Electric Bond and Share or IT&T, which had significant foreign subsidiaries, or Middle West Utilities, which had heavily rural subsidiaries. The typical pattern in these troubled holding companies was that their subsidiaries went into arrears on their preferred stock dividends and eliminated their common stock dividends, thereby cutting off all cash flow to the holding companies, which had their own heavy debt and preferred stock fixed charges to cover. The companies had trouble raising money from the banks or the bond market, which had troubles of their own, so stockholders naturally feared that a wave of receiverships was likely and sold the public utility holding company stocks heavily.

Electric Bond and Share was an example of how foreign subsidiary problems and reduced subsidiary dividends could have an impact on even a fine company. Electric Bond and Share controlled and operated American & Foreign Power, American Power & Light, Electric Power & Light, and United Gas through significant stock holdings which were never 100% and were frequently much less, so that Electric Bond and Share was strictly dependent on dividend income. The first subsidiary in trouble was American & Foreign Power, whose Asian and South American subsidiaries were unable after 1931 to obtain foreign ex-

Table 11.3
The Public Utility Holding Companies in 1932

	Price-earnings ratio		Market price as a % of book value		Dividend yield (%)		Low price as a % of 1929 high price	Return on equity (%)	Moody's bond ratings	Cash & equivalents ($ millions)
	High price	Low price	High price	Low price	High price	Low price				
Cities Service	def.[a]	def.	89	16	0	0	2	def.	B	(58)[d]
Columbia Gas & Electric	22	4	111	22	4.76	23.53	3	5.1	Baa	(20)
Commonwealth & Southern	43	14	96	30	0	0	5	2.2	B pfd.	39
Electric Bond and Share	49	5	200	21	0	0	1	1.3	B pfd.	45
IT&T	def.	def.	43	7	0	0	2	def.	B	(42)
Middle West Utilities	NM[b]	NM	0	0	0	0	0	def.	NR[c]	(33)
North American	21	7	172	56	0	0	7	8.0	Baa	30
Standard Gas and Electric	59	13	33	7	5.71	26.23	3	0.6	Ba	19
United Gas Improvement	16	7	169	71	5.45	12.97	15	10.5	Aa pfd.	19
Averages	35.0	10.0	101	26	NM	NM	4	4.6	—	—

[a] def. = Deficit.
[b] NM = Not Meaningful.
[c] NR = Not Related
[d] Brackets indicate short-term borrowing.

change to service their foreign debts and dividend obligations. Local governments which controlled the companies' franchises also boldly refused to pay their bills. The situation became so stringent for American & Foreign Power that in April 1932 it eliminated its dividends on $160 million preferred stock owned by Electric Bond and Share. Electric Bond and Share had also advanced to the company $85 million in short-term loans which appeared of dubious value since the company had no access to foreign exchange to pay interest, and American & Foreign Power Co.'s public 5% debentures due in the year 2030 had sunk to a price of only $15.

The interruption of preferred dividends from American & Foreign Power in April 1932 was just the first of a series of such interruptions in 1932 for Electric Bond and Share. In July, United Gas missed the dividend on its second preferred stock, which placed that company in considerable peril since it had $21 million in short-term debt and an additional $26 million which it owed to Electric Bond & Share. In August, Electric Power & Light eliminated the dividend on its common stock, of which Electric Bond and Share owned 58%, and in September, American Power & Light eliminated the dividend on its common stock, of which Electric Bond and Share owned 31%. The market anticipated very serious problems at American Power & Light, which culminated in the elimination of preferred dividends in 1933 by all its principal subsidiaries—Florida Power & Light, Arkansas Power & Light, Mississippi Power & Light, New Orleans Public Service, Pacific Power & Light, and Portland Gas.

It was no wonder that Electric Bond and Share's stock sank to $1 2/3 and 21% of book value, versus its highest 1929 price of $189. It appears that the lack of cash flow from the subsidiaries would force the liquidation of the parent. Fortunately, Electric Bond and Share had short-term investments of $45 million and strong management, which enabled the company to weather the period.

By contrast, Middle West Utilities, which was run by Samuel Insull, and two related investment trusts, Insull Utilities Investments and Corporation Securities, were casualties of the cash flow squeeze, adjudicated into receivership in April 1932 because of overwhelming short-term debts. Middle West's stock sank to 12 1/2¢, compared with its highest 1929 price of $57, and in 1934 its charter expired for nonpayment of its franchise tax. Receivers took over the company and wrote off $206 million, which was two-thirds of the book value of the parent company's assets. Revenues of the parent company, which had been $18 million in 1931, shrank to $3.5 million in 1932—insufficient to pay interest on $75 million in debts.

Samuel Insull has been reviled for his role in Middle West Utilities and its investment trust affiliates and ensconced in financial folklore as a symbol of the complicated excesses of the holding companies in the 1920s. He has carried a taint of personal malfeasance because he fled to Europe to escape prosecution before what he considered an inflamed public, even though he returned in 1935, stood trial in three jurisdictions, and was exonerated of any criminal liability by each court. The collapse of Middle West Utilities undoubtedly had much to do with the passage of the Public Utilities Holding Company Act of 1935, which determined that the United States would have several hundred independent electric and gas utilities, each based on a geographically concentrated service territory. It is therefore worth getting the historical record straight on Insull, for the denouement of Middle West Utilities was part tragedy and part just deserts. As usual, there was good mixed with bad.

On the good side, Insull personally was a productive manager rather than a financial manipulator, which came to be his reputation. He started as Thomas Edison's private secretary. At 27, he had resuscitated the Electric Tube Co. and the Edison Machine Co. At 32, he declined the presidency of the newly formed General Electric Co. because of his antipathy to J. P. Morgan & Co. Instead, he became President of Commonwealth Edison in Chicago at a salary of $12,000 per year, compared with the $36,000 offered him at General Electric, and formed Commonwealth Edison into a fine company. Later, Insull retrieved Northern Illinois Public Service Co. from the brink of bankruptcy and turned it into a strong company. He also took over the management of the failing elevated railway system in Chicago at the request of the city.

In addition, Insull was technically productive. In partnership with General Electric in 1903, he built the first 5,000 kilowatt steam electric turbine, then one at 10,000 kilowatts, and by 1925 one at 175,000 kilowatts. He was the first major utility manager devoted to the central city generating plant, which firmly established the favorable economics of the electric utility industry while others were still committed to small turbines located throughout their service territories. He was also responsible for bringing the Pirelli cable to the United States, which substantially advanced electric transmission. On the economic side, Insull and his companies were ardent supporters of Chicago in a period when the city verged on bankruptcy with every payment it had to make. His companies advanced their property taxes and made direct loans to the city, and Insull worked to solve its problems. His companies worked in similar fashion in New England to restore the ailing local economies there. He also endowed the arts, particularly the opera, for which he built the Chicago Opera House.

At Middle West, Insull was a pioneer in bringing electric power service to rural America and making money at it long before the establishment of the Rural Electrification Administration under Roosevelt. Middle West Utilities was an exceptionally rural system serving 1.8 million customers in 5,300 communities in 36 states. *Moody's Public Utility Manual* described the system as including 239 operating utilities, 24 holding companies, and 13 non-utility companies. That sounds very complicated, but actually the principal companies were Central Illinois Public Service, Kentucky Utilities, Wisconsin Power & Light, Lake Superior District Power, Northwestern Public Service, Public Service Co. of Indiana, Northern Indiana Public Service, and Central & Southwest Utilities Co. With the exception of Northern Indiana Public Service, which serviced the Gary, Indiana, steel industry, these companies served a wide array of small towns and rural communities.

The problems of rural America had started to affect the finances of those companies before 1932. Central & Southwest had stopped paying cash dividends on its common stock in 1930 in anticipation of problems in its own subsidiaries, most of which cut their common stock dividends in 1931. There were no common stock dividends in 1931 from Arkansas-Missouri Power and United Public Service, which were lesser Middle West subsidiaries, and Midland United Co., which controlled Public Service Co. of Indiana, and Northern Indiana Public Service Co. never paid any dividends. In 1932 the rural economic situation was so acute that earnings of the major Middle West subsidiaries plummeted. Earnings at Central Illinois Public Service dropped from $1.1 million to $100,000; at Central & Southwest, earnings shifted from $2.2 million to a deficit of $400,000; Kentucky Utilities earnings dropped from $900,000 to $400,000; Mississippi Valley Utilities earnings of $1.7 million completely disappeared; Midland United earnings went from $2.4 million to a deficit of $1.6 million, and Wisconsin Power & Light earnings dropped from $700,000 to $200,000.

Such problems were not restricted to the Middle West system. Rural power companies generally had the same experience. Electric Bond and Share had problems with its Arkansas and Mississippi utilities. Commonwealth & Southern had sharp earnings declines at its Alabama Power, Georgia Power, and Consumers Power subsidiaries, which served rural areas. Even the North American Co., which was soundly run, got no common dividends after 1929 from its North American Light & Power Co. subsidiary, which served rural areas, and its preferred dividends were eliminated in 1932.

Despite the virtues of Samuel Insull and the operating utilities, the holding company superstructure of the Insull companies was quickly liquidated once it was placed into receivership, because the investment trusts, Insull Utilities Investments and Corporation Securities, had eliminated their net worth and had debts many times their remaining investment value, and because Middle West Utilities was seriously weakened by its investments in several companies that were not sound operating companies. Four Middle West subsidiaries went into receivership at about the same time—National Electric Power Co., Mississippi Valley Utilities Investment Co., United Public Service Co., and Commonwealth Light & Power Co.—in which Middle West had an investment of $100 million. In the following year, Midland United Co. and Kentucky Securities Corp., in which Middle West had an additional $50 million invested, went into receivership. These were not sound companies. National Electric Power, Commonwealth Light & Power, and United Public Service Co. were a mishmash of tiny gas, electric, ice, bus, and railroad companies in the Atlantic, Arkansas-Missouri, and the upper plains states, respectively, with no unified organization and no basic profitability. Many were not paying adequate returns when Middle West acquired them. Under depression conditions, they quickly began to lose money. Kentucky Securities Corp. and Mississippi Valley Utilities Investment Co. were absurd concoctions. The only substantial asset of Kentucky Securities Corp. was Lexington Utilities, serving Lexington, Kentucky, but it had a net worth of only

$300,000, versus a Middle West investment in Kentucky Securities of $9.6 million. The rest was ice, rail, and tiny electric and gas companies. Mississippi Valley Utilities Investment Co. was even worse. Out of total investments of $45 million, it had $39 million of investments which were not listed on any securities exchange and were without public markets. Midland United Co. at least had two sound operating subsidiaries, Public Service Co. of Indiana and Northern Indiana Public Service Co., but it too was burdened with weak investments. It had $20 million invested in money-losing railroads, $16 million of receivables from bankrupt companies elsewhere in the Middle West system, and $11 million of abandoned property which had not been written off.

Middle West realized virtually nothing out of its $150 million of investments in these companies. The $40 million invested in National Electric Power Co. was written off after Chase National Bank and Central Hanover Bank auctioned off the stock of the major operating subsidiaries of National Electric Power in 1932 and 1933 to pay off defaulted bank loans. Whatever subsidiaries the banks did not have as security for loans fell into the control of bondholders under court-approved reorganization plans. Mississippi Valley Utilities Investment Co. similarly returned none of the $37 million invested in it by Middle West. Mississippi Valley held $13 million in stock in North American Light & Power and Central & Southwest Utilities, which was now worth less than $1 million. It had $9 million invested in real estate and miscellaneous securities which were totally valueless, and bondholders took over the rest of its assets. Bondholders likewise took over the common stock of Commonwealth Light & Power. Kentucky Securities Corp. had no meaningful assets for anyone.

This wholesale destruction of asset values had a variety of causes. The least possible was realized when securities holdings were sold at the bottom of the Depression in 1932 and 1933. The Depression also revealed just how much junk there was in the Middle West companies that had no real value at any time. The Middle West companies had gone on a buying spree in which what they paid bore little relation to the underlying values. Kentucky Securities had paid 10 times book value for its utility holdings. In 1929, United Public Service Co. sold out to Middle West, which wanted it even though it made no profits. The National Electric Power subsidiaries were bought at premiums that bore no relation to their tiny operations and burden of railroad, bus, and ice company operations. It was as if Middle West was trying to put together utilities at any cost and of any type as part of a national competition, and then would rearrange them and sell off the poor assets afterward.

The high leverage of the Middle West system also acted to wipe out the common equity interest when the companies got in trouble. Mississippi Valley Utilities Investment Co. had $30 million of preferred and debt liabilities against its $45 million in investments. Midland United Co. had over $60 million of preferred and debt liabilities loaded onto $75 million of common equity. National Electric Power had debt and preferred stock liabilities of $507 million and only $45 million of common equity. Heavy leverage on weak companies led to a rush to liquidate by receivers and secured lenders who had no confidence in management and saw no prospect for an economic recovery restoring more reasonable values to the companies' real assets. The heavy leverage also led to contests among the receivers for the various companies to realize the most value for their companies, contests in which intercompany loans from Middle West Utilities got short shrift even though they were sizable in several cases.

Liquidation of Middle West was also hastened because the operating utility subsidiaries in unison eliminated their preferred and common stock dividends once Middle West was in receivership. Central & Southwest Co. even went so far as to rescind a preferred stock dividend which it had declared before Middle West went into receivership. Middle West's dividend revenues dropped from $14 million in 1931 to only $2.1 million in 1932. It was as if the subsidiaries abandoned the parent once its troubles had been institutionalized in the courts, and hoarded the maximum cash for themselves. This would have been unlikely in an industrial holding company, but a utility subsidiary has considerable independence because it sells securities on its own credit and relies on local regulation and politics to determine its rates and practices. This independence was magnified in the Middle West system because the parent rarely held 100% of the stock of its subsidiaries. Without the centrifugal forces of a viable parent company and the personality of Samuel Insull, the operating subsidiaries looked out for themselves.

The Middle West bankruptcy had a strong political impact. The company's stock had been widely distributed throughout the Midwest by direct company sales to small stockholders who abruptly found their investments totally valueless. Roosevelt naturally picked on the Middle West bankruptcy in his election campaign, since he blamed the Depression on stock market abuses and was in general fighting the utility companies.

The political attack on the public utility holding companies even had support from within the utility and financial communities, where for some time there had been growing concern over their unduly complicated financial structures and the excessive competition for properties. Harry Addinsell, President of Chase Harris Forbes, which was the largest underwriter of utility securities, gave great credibility to Roosevelt's criticisms by supporting them. In this atmosphere of default and political attack, one can understand why the stocks of the public utility holding companies dropped to only 4% of their highest 1929 prices and 26% of book value, even though many of the companies had solid finances and operating records.

The Investment Trusts

The investment trust stocks got about as low as they were going to go in 1931 when they dropped to prices generally less than 5% of their highest 1929 prices. (See Table 11.4 for details.) The stocks equalled these low levels in 1931, 1932, and 1933, and in periods of market recovery in 1932 and 1933 they rose only a few dollars above their lowest prices as investors generally shunned them.

Table 11.4
The Investment Trusts in 1932

	Price-earnings ratio		Market price as a % of book value		Dividend yield (%)		Low price as a % of 1929 high price	Return on equity (%)	Moody's bond ratings	Cash & equivalents ($ millions)
	High price	Low price	High price	Low price	High price	Low price				
Goldman Sachs Trading	def.[a]	def.	86	17	0	0	1	def.	NR[d]	(7)[e]
Lehman Corp.	def.	def.	90	53	4.67	7.74	23	def.	NR	8
Tri-Continental Corp.	def.	def.	NA	NA	0	0	3	def.	NR	5
United Corp.	32	8	45	11	2.86	11.43	3	1.4	NR	(12)
United Founders	NA[b]	NA	417	42	0	0	0	0	NR	(1)
Averages	NM[c]	NM	160	31	NM	NM	6	NM	—	—

[a] def. = Deficit.
[b] NA = Not Available.
[c] NM = Not Meaningful.
[d] NR = Not Rated.
[e] Brackets indicate short-term borrowing.

This depressed and inactive state allowed two interrelated trends to work extensively throughout 1932 and 1933. On the one hand, weaker trusts were unable to maintain adequate cash flow to service their preferred stock dividend requirements, which eliminated value in their common stocks. On the other hand, professional investors were able to buy up the securities of better trusts at substantial discounts to their underlying value. As usual, Goldman Sachs Trading Corp. was in the unfortunate vanguard of these trends. Its revenues dropped to only $500,000 in 1932, compared with $5 million in 1930, as 70% of its assets were tied up in American Trust Co. and Shenandoah Corp., which paid no dividends. Stockholder suits were filed against its leading directors, Walter Sachs, Sidney Weinberg, and Waddill Catchings, for wasting the company's assets and seeking to put the company into the hands of a receiver. The three men went on trial in August, which strengthened their resolve to get out of the investment trust business and to have Floyd Odlum of Atlas Corp. take control of Goldman Sachs Trading Corp. By year end Odlum had acquired 40% of Goldman Sachs Trading Corp. at dramatic discounts from book value.

Atlas had made a business out of such rescue missions, acquiring 18 trusts by the end of 1932, particularly those spawned by larger institutions which now wanted out of the business, such as Goldman Sachs, Chatham-Phenix National Bank & Trust, Jackson & Curtis, and Ungerleider & Co. This scavenging, combined with good management, enabled Atlas Corp. to increase its net asset value per share from $5 in 1929 to $7 in 1932, even while net assets per share of Goldman Sachs Trading Corp., Tri-Continental Corp., and United Founders declined almost 100%. Atlas' stock price actually sold at a substantial premium to net asset value. The price range of $4 1/4 to $11 3/8 for Atlas common in 1932 was up from 1931 and comparable to 1930. Atlas common reached an all-time high price of $18 5/8 in 1933. Thus, even while some fortunes were being destroyed in the investment trust field, others were being made.

Lehman Corp. was almost an exact contrast to Goldman Sachs Trading Corp. Lehman Corp. kept its revenues up at around $2.5 million on investments widely spread among government bonds and high quality stocks, compared with the concentrated Goldman Sachs investments, which paid no dividends. Lehman Corp.'s total absence of leverage allowed it to use liquid assets to repurchase its own stock at a discount from net asset value along the same lines as Atlas Corp's purchases. In June 1932, Lehman bought $5.4 million of its own stock at $35 when its net asset value was $47, having previously bought in $10 million of its stock at similar low points in June and October 1931. These purchases of almost one-third of the outstanding shares sharply raised the net asset values of the remaining Lehman Corp. stock. The combination of astute investments, no leverage, stock repurchases, and a $2.40 dividend (slightly reduced from $3.00 in 1931) led to a Lehman Corp. stock price at the lowest point in 1932 which was still 23% of its highest 1929 price, double the average for all stocks, and almost 8 times the average for its companion investment trusts.

Tri-Continental Corp. and United Founders Corp. were able to play modified versions of the Atlas-Lehman stock purchase theme. Tri-Continental bought in $3.5 million of its preferred stock at virtually half price, even though the dividend was still being paid, and United Founders bought in $4.6 million of subsidiary debentures at only $65 per $100 par value. These two companies were skirting the edge of discretion, however, as Tri-Continental's revenues were down to $2 million and four United Founders subsidiary trusts were in arrears on their preferred dividends.

During these maneuvers by the other investment trusts, J. P. Morgan's United Corp. remained stolid and unimaginative. Its revenues held up well at $15 million because 75% of its assets were invested in Columbia Gas & Electric, Niagara Hudson Power, and United Gas Improvement, which continued to pay dividends. But United Corp. took no advantage of this strength. It bought absolutely nothing— not even its own preference stock, which sold as low as $20 compared with its par value of $50—instead sticking motionlessly to the portfolio it had put together in 1929 and 1930. Its founders may have taken pride in United Corp.'s ability to pay a common stock dividend throughout 1932, but the company wasted its assets almost as much as Goldman Sachs did by failing to take advantage of them when the appropriate technique was evident all around it. United Corp. investors valued the company accordingly, at a low price only 3% of its highest 1929 price.

The Non-Utility Holding Companies

Alleghany Corp. and Transamerica Corp. reached such points of extremis in 1932 (see Table 11.5) that they were bailed out only by J. P. Morgan & Co. and the Reconstruction Finance Corporation. Alleghany Corp.'s situation was even similar to that of Middle West Utilities in that operating vision was combined with poor investments and excessive leverage. J. P. Morgan was simply more patient with the Van Sweringens than Central Hanover and Bankers Trust were with the Insulls.

Alleghany Corp. had eliminated its preferred stock dividend and taken losses of $12 million on securities sales in 1931 as the decline in the railroad industry forced the company into protective measures, but the further decline in the railroad industry in 1932 was more than the Van Sweringens or Alleghany could cope with. The Chesapeake Corp., through which Alleghany Corp. controlled the Chesapeake & Ohio Railroad, cut its dividend from $3.00 to $2.00 in July 1932, and the Missouri Pacific, which was the other principal Alleghany investment, eliminated its preferred dividends in the face of a 1932 loss of $10 million. The two cut Alleghany Corp. revenues $2 million, which it badly needed for interest on $80 million of debt. The market value of these and other railroad securities pledged by Alleghany Corp. to its bondholders also dropped drastically. The value of Chesapeake Corp. stock dropped from a high of $92 in 1929 to $4 7/8 in 1932, despite its $2.00 dividend. Missouri Pacific preferred stock, which had been as high as $149 in 1929, dropped to $2 1/2 in 1932, while its common stock dropped from $101 to $1 1/2, and its 5 1/2% bonds due in 1949,

Table 11.5
The Non-Utility Holding Companies in 1932

	Price-earnings ratio		Market price as a % of book value		Dividend yield (%)		Low price as a % of 1929 high price	Return on equity (%)	Moody's bond ratings	Cash & equivalents ($ millions)
	High price	Low price	High price	Low price	High price	Low price				
Alleghany Corp.	def.[a]	def.	23	2	0	0	1	def.	NR[c]	1
Transamerica	21	6	130	39	0	0	5	6.0	B	(13)[d]
Averages	NM[b]	NM	77	21	0	0	3	NM	—	—

[a] def. = Deficit.
[b] NM = Not Meaningful.
[c] NR = Not Rated.
[d] Brackets indicate short-term borrowing.

of which Alleghany Corp. held $11.2 million, dropped from $125 to $6 1/2. Lesser Alleghany investments, such as Erie Railroad common stock, dropped from $93½ to $2, and Pittston Co. common dropped from $23 to 50¢. Alleghany Corp. took a second $12 million loss in 1932, selling out its holdings in the Erie Railroad, New York, Chicago & St. Louis Railroad, and Père Marquette Railway, but it would have taken much larger losses if forced to sell out across the board, for at the end of the year its securities holdings had a market value of only $24 million, versus a book cost of approximately $200 million. In August 1932, trustees for the three Alleghany Corp. debenture issues impounded the income from all of the above securities pledged to debenture holders because the market value of the securities had fallen below the agreed limit of 150% of debentures outstanding. Fortunately the trustee was not allowed to sell the securities, for the values realized would have been miniscule. The outlook was nonetheless exceedingly bleak. The prices of the three debenture issues fell as low as $3 1/2 in anticipation that they would go into default and the collateral then be liquidated.

At the same time, the Van Sweringen brothers had $40 million in loans with J. P. Morgan and other New York banks secured by the brothers' controlling interest in Alleghany Corp., which was then worth less than $1 million at the 37 2/3¢ price for Alleghany Corp. common. The Van Sweringens were exceedingly lucky not to be sold out at this point, because it was difficult to construct a story for their recovery. They had tied up over $50 million of Alleghany Corp.'s funds in the Missouri Pacific Railroad, which was a very weak railroad. It had been through numerous bankruptcies, had a weak organization, had paid no common stock dividends in many years, was in arrears on its preferred stock dividends, and was the first corporation to borrow from the Reconstruction Finance Corporation, to which it was now heavily indebted.

By contrast, the Chesapeake & Ohio Railroad was a very fine one and maintained its common stock dividend throughout the Depression, but the Van Sweringens had piled so much leverage on top of this asset that its quality was highly diluted. The leverage went through three stages. At the first stage, Chesapeake Corp., which controlled the Chesapeake & Ohio, had $75 million of debt on $85 million of common equity; Alleghany Corp., which controlled Chesapeake Corp., had $147 million of debt and preferred stock on only $66 million of common equity, and the Van Sweringens had heaped $40 million of debt from J. P. Morgan on their controlling interest in Alleghany Corp. No wonder Alleghany preferred and common stocks both sold below $1 in 1932. With its bonds as low as $3 1/2, the stocks were considered worthless. These premonitions had not yet been translated into realities in 1932, however. J. P. Morgan was taking additional notes from the Van Sweringens for the interest on their loans and giving them room to maneuver.

Transamerica Corp. was getting room to maneuver also, but from the RFC. When the Giannini forces were victorious at the annual meeting on February 15, 1932, and took over the board of directors of both Transamerica and Bank of America, they gained a seriously weakened group of companies. Deposits at Bank of America had dropped from a peak of over $1 billion to $620 million, and the bank had borrowed over $135 million. On the same day as its annual meeting, it got the first RFC loan made to a bank, and it soon had borrowings of $61.5 million from the RFC. General Dawes, first President of the RFC, told A. P. Giannini in a February 1932 meeting that the RFC would provide $100 million if that was what it took to save the bank. He was close. Bank of America took $61.5 million directly and $30 million indirectly through Transamerica, secured by $65 million in mortgages which it bought from Bank of America.

Amid this turmoil and widespread discussions that Transamerica would be bankrupted, Transamerica's stock was reduced to approximately $2, which was 5% of its highest 1929 price. Giannini was able to restore health, however, cutting total RFC borrowings to $29 million by the end of 1932 and other borrowings to just $11 million, but most important, Bank of America deposits had risen from $620 million to $750 million by year end. The recovery carried Transamerica stock over $7, compared with its book value of $6, but the company remained highly subject to suspicions and rumors. Bank of America at year end was still the most illiquid of the big banks. In 1933, Transamerica's stock was back down to $2.

The Banks

The big banks were under great stress in 1932 as losses loomed on their foreign loans, domestic loans, stock market operations, and current operations. (See Table 11.6). Chase, Continental Illinois, First National Bank of Boston, First National Bank of Chicago, and National City Bank all reduced their dividends. Public opprobrium for the banks' role in creating the Depression reached an unprecedented pitch as populists like Huey Long and Father Coughlin attacked them as symbols of wealth. Bank stocks dropped to 9% of their highest 1929 prices, compared with 12% for all stocks, and to 60% of book value. Internally the banks had shifted attention sharply away from their stock prices to preserving their liquidity. The RFC was available as a lender of last resort, but borrowing from the RFC was considered disastrous for a major bank's reputation. Only Bank of America, a renegade among the big banks, borrowed from the RFC during 1932. The others stopped lending and called loans to build up their liquidity.

A measure of the liquidity of the big banks can be seen in Table 11.7, which shows how very liquid these banks were during 1932. The key point of comparison is column 6, indicating the percentage of total assets in highly liquid form, such as cash, call loans, acceptances, and U.S. government securities. The liquidity of many banks is understated because their call loans and acceptances could not be broken out of their total loans and discounts. Probably First National Bank of Chicago, Guaranty Trust Co., and Central Hanover Bank would have joined Bankers Trust and Irving Trust as the most liquid, with liquid assets

Table 11.6
The Banks in 1932

	Price-earnings ratio		Market price as a % of book value		Dividend yield (%)		Low price as a % of 1929 high price	Return on equity (%)	Moody's bond ratings	Cash & equivalents ($ millions)
	High price	Low price	High price	Low price	High price	Low price				
Bankers Trust	20	9	185	80	3.95	9.10	13	9.4	—	—
Central Hanover	NA[a]	NA	188	87	4.32	9.33	14	NA	—	—
Chase National	12	5	119	45	4.50	11.84	7	9.7	—	—
Continental Illinois	10	4	104	39	5.44	14.55	5	8.7	—	—
First National (Boston)	NA	NA	111	50	6.19	13.68	9	NA	—	—
First National (Chicago)	7	4	115	62	5.00	9.23	10	15.8	—	—
Guaranty Trust	14	6	119	53	5.59	12.50	13	8.5	—	—
Irving Trust	17	7	136	55	5.33	13.33	12	7.8	—	—
National City	20	8	181	67	3.46	9.38	4	9.7	—	—
Averages	14.3	6.1	140	60	4.38	10.29	9	9.9	—	—

[a] NA = Not Available.

Table 11.7
The Ten Leading Banks Ranked by Proportion of Liquid Assets (Column 6), December 31, 1932 ($ millions)

	Cash (1)	Call loans (2)	Bankers acceptances (3)	U.S. Treasuries (4)	Total liquid assets (1+2+3+4) (5)	% of total assets (6)	Total assets (7)
Bank of America	$ 64	NA[a]	NA	$170	$234	26.7%	$ 876
Chase National Bank	391	NA	$86	215	692	37.3	1,856
Continental Illinois	301	NA	NA	365	666	41.2	1,615
National City Bank	254	NA	0	78	332	41.6	798
First National Bank of Boston	160	36	9	107	312	48.2	647
Central Hanover	114	NA	NA	259	373	52.3	713
Guaranty Trust	198	NA	86	527	811	57.5	1,411
First National Bank of Chicago	240	NA	9	53	302	58.2	519
Bankers Trust	1,044	NA	29	319	452	59.2	763
Irving Trust	118	41	29	181	369	66.6	554

Source: Moody's Financial Manuals, 1933, 1934.

[a] NA = Not Available.

over 60% of total assets, had these other short-term assets been broken out. Rumors that at least one New York bank had liquid assets exceeding 80% of its funds in 1932 were probably true.

Loan losses and the liquidity squeeze created wide divergences among the leading banks' financial performances in 1932. Chase National Bank, Continental Illinois, and National City Bank, which had been the most aggressive banks, now led the industry down in dividend cuts, write-offs, and stock price declines. Both New York banks dropped their chief executives, Albert Wiggin and Charles Mitchell, because their personal qualities failed to fit the new demands of banking leaders.

Chase National Bank was harassed from every direction—foreign loans, stock market disasters, and municipal problems. The Chase had become the largest U.S. bank partly through its aggressive pursuit of foreign business, which now came back to haunt it. There was great concern in 1932 that loans in Germany and Eastern Europe would not be paid off and that the lending banks' capital would be threatened. (Everyone already knew South American loans would not pay off.) When Thomas Lamont of J. P. Morgan decried such speculation and claimed that the largest German loans were only $70 million at one New York bank, he was referring to Chase, which had $70 million of short-term loans in Germany. Lamont could not have soothed many worried depositors with his statement, since Chase had a net worth of only $259 million at the end of 1932.

There was no coincidence in the Federal Reserve's request to Albert Wiggin in 1931 to be Chairman of the "Standstill Committee," which sorted out Germany's short-term debts and required that they be gradually scaled down at the expense of Germany's reserves. The Chase's loans to Germany were $116 million at their peak; they were down to $67 million by the end of 1932. By comparison, the German loans of Guaranty Trust, Irving Trust, and Bankers Trust were down to $35 million, $26 million, and somewhere below $27 million, respectively, by the end of 1932.[9] Chase National Bank had equal problems from the results of its stock market activities. When the bank acquired the Harris Forbes companies in 1930, it appeared to be a great coup to capture one of the top four investment banking firms, but in 1932 the new company, Chase Harris Forbes, had to write down its capital from $95 million to $58 million. Chase took further stock market losses on General Theatres Equipment, which went bankrupt in 1932 owing Chase $19.7 million, and dragged down Pynchon & Co., stockbrokers, with it owing Chase an additional $11.9 million. Before Chase was finished with the General Theatres fiasco in all its ramifications, the bank lost almost $70 million.[10]

As if these associations were not bad enough, Chase was a leader with National City Bank in financing New York City as it approached default. Chase's municipal loans of $83 million were the largest of any bank, exceeded in percentage terms only by the Bank of America, which performed a leading lending role to municipalities throughout California. Fortunately the city's securities were not viewed as a default item, the city's problems being due to its political leaders rather than its underlying credit, as Charles Mitchell put it.

The impact of these problems on Chase was severe. During 1932 it cut its common stock dividend twice, from $4.00 to $2.25, and its liquid assets ratio at 38% of total assets was the second worst, next to Bank of America, which was already borrowing heavily from the Reconstruction Finance Corporation. Chase stock dropped to 7% of its 1929 high and to 45% of book value.

The Chase announced in December 1932 that Albert Wiggin would retire on January 10, 1933, shortly before reaching age 65. He appeared to be paying the price for the Chase's problems. It was the beginning of an unfortunate decline in public esteem for a man who had built a great institution and been called "the most popular banker in Wall Street." Wiggin was a big walrus of a man with a large, square head, sweeping mustaches, and weighing well over 200 pounds. In his three-piece suits with his hair slickly parted down the middle, he exuded the charm and the indifference of the rich and powerful.

Wiggin had become the largest Chase stockholder as he built the bank. He was also a figure on a national and international scale. Visitors to New York received by its mayor, Jimmy Walker, were apt to find Albert Wiggin in the car beside them as they rode down Fifth Avenue. As chairman of the Standstill Committee in 1931, he was arbiter over Germany's near-term fate as it tried to pay its debts. He organized Bankers Trust Co. with Henry P. Davison of J. P. Morgan & Co. and remained on the Bankers Trust board. His prestige was important in Chase's being able to attract the great Harris, Forbes organization which dominated utility finances to merge with Chase Securities, the bank's brokerage subsidiary. During the Fox Film debacle, William Fox reported the following Wiggin conversation with an emissary of President Hoover:

Mr. Wiggin told him to tell the President of the United States to please mind his own business and not interfere in what the bankers were doing in New York; they could take care of their own business; and he resented Mr. Hoover's interference in this matter.[11]

Wiggin later denied the story, but it was credible, given his power.

The ultimate decline in Wiggin's reputation occurred in 1933 when he was called before the Senate Committee on Banking and Currency and his personal finances were exposed in a broad web of self-dealing on Wiggin's part. Wiggin had set up several private corporations in Canada for income tax and estate purposes, and he used these corporations to trade on a large scale in Chase Bank stock. The trading was usually carried out in conjunction with Metpotan Securities, a Chase subsidiary. The result over five years from 1928 to 1932 was staggering. Trading aggregated over $860 million on both the buy and sell sides, from which Metpotan made $159,000, while Wiggin's three corporations made approximately $10.5 million.[12] A suspiciously large proportion of Chase Securities underwriting participations was split with Wiggin's Canadian corporations as well. Wiggin also appeared as a major beneficiary of inside information.

In June 1932, as Chairman of the Finance Committee of Brooklyn Manhattan Transit (BMT), which was then privately owned, he sold 26,400 BMT shares of his own and 50,000 held by Chase while Chase was analyzing a bank loan to BMT to meet a bond maturity that could not be publicly refunded. The bank loan was made, but on the precondition that dividends be eliminated. Following Wiggin's sales the stock dropped from $25 to $11.125 in four days.[13]

These activities all appeared worse than injudicious. There was a legitimate question whether Wiggin had acted criminally. The case was never filed against him, perhaps because the line between Chase as a public institution and his own creation was not clearly drawn at the time. Wiggin was so influential in the bank's growth and had so many outside corporate and stock market activities which brought business to Chase Bank that it appeared as if he was creating the business personally, rather than as the Chairman of the bank. He was not like the modern chief executive who rises to prominence and vast business connections because of his position in his bank and because he owes his influence to the bank.

Following his retirement in 1933, Wiggin was retained by Chase Bank at a salary of $100,000 per year, but this was rescinded following the Senate investigations. Winthrop W. Aldrich, a Rockefeller nephew who succeeded Wiggin as Chairman of Chase Bank, appeared at the Senate hearings to disavow Wiggin and express opposition to many of the policies he had followed.

Chase Bank's chief New York competitor was the National City Bank, which was doing little better than the Chase. Each bank had total assets at least double those of any other bank, except the Guaranty Trust Co., and each bank rivaled the other for foreign and stock market problems. National City Bank had $60 million in short-term loans in Germany, $15 million elsewhere in Europe, and $25 million in Cuba. It had even earned more in the foreign field from underwriting than had Chase—$25 million from 1926 to 1931, versus $13 million. J. P. Morgan had earned only $10 million, but on a much better quality business.

National City Co., the bank's securities affiliate, was badly hurt by the stock market. The securities affiliate wrote its net worth down from $55 million to $20 million in 1932. Its reputation was besmirched by the same committee that attacked Wiggin when it revealed that National City Co. had conducted large 1929 trading operations in the stock of Anaconda Copper, relieving the bank of its position when it knew of Anaconda's deteriorating profit position through Chairman Charles Mitchell, a director of the company.

Mitchell and National City Bank also became the symbol of the bankers dealing with New York City. He led the bankers' meetings with Mayor Walker, the Board of Estimate, and Controller Charles Berry. He was spokesman for the banks at City Council meetings when further loans were refused, and he was quoted in the newspapers on behalf of the banks demanding cuts in pay, welfare, and construction. When the time came to finance the city on a day-to-day basis through October and November, National City Bank and Chase National Bank provided the funds. Earlier in the year, the two banks led the syndicate which lent the city $151 million in direct loans and agreed to an additional $200 million through underwritten public offerings of notes. In November the two banks underwrote an 8-month note issue of $21.5 million for the city and found themselves stuck with half of it unsold.

At the end of 1932, National City Bank wrote down its net worth from $225 to $205 million and reduced the net worth of National City Co. by $35 million. The bank also followed Chase Bank in cutting its dividend twice, from $4.00 to $2.25. The dividends were identical to Chase's and were cut within one day of the cuts in the Chase dividends. The effect on National City stock was also parallel to that on the Chase's stock. National City stock dropped to 4% of its 1929 high. The stock had peaked at $580 per share in 1929 and now suffered at $24. In 1933 it would drop to $16. At $24 the stock was only 67% of book value and bore a dividend yield of 11.84%.

These ratios were about average for the big banks, which attests to the charm National City Bank still held despite its steep fall. But the bank was vulnerable too. There had been rumors in Paris during the year that National City was about to suspend deposits, a rumor few banks could weather in 1932. National City Bank deposits were also a high 9.92 times the bank's capital, compared with 7 times for the better banks and even 4 times for several banks. National City's liquid assets were a low 44% of total assets, as well. The bank was holding the line against the storms, but only barely.

The Chicago banks were in much worse condition than either Chase or National City Bank. Continental Illinois Bank & Trust and First National Bank of Chicago were keeping their doors open, but the banking disruption generally in Chicago was making life difficult for the two. In 1929 the number of Chicago banks had been reduced from 225 to 70 by mid-1932, when General Dawes' Central Republic Bank & Trust was temporarily closed, with $95 million in deposits. In the same week, 28 banks closed in Chicago. Continental Illinois and First Chicago participated in $10 million raised by Loop banks for Central Republic, but all would have capsized without the aid of the RFC, which lent $80 million. Both Continental Illinois and First Chicago had already been rocked by the default of Middle West Utilities and the collapse of the rest of the Insull holding company system. Both banks were heavily involved in loans to the City of Chicago and to Cook County as well, loans which were effectively frozen. Nor did the two banks have the strength to weather such shocks. Continental Illinois had deposits 16 times its capital. First Chicago had deposits 13 times its capital. Continental Illinois capital was sliced from $145 million in 1931 to $104 million in 1932 by loan write-offs. First Chicago's capital was cut from $52 million to a mere $45 million, which was only one-sixth the capital of the biggest banks. It also cut its dividend from $19.00 to $12.00, while the Continental Illinois cut its dividend from $16 to $8. With the two stocks knocked down to 19% and 5%, respectively, of their highest 1929 prices, one might have suspected the worst was over, but they both eliminated their dividends in 1933, became heavily dependent on the RFC for capital, and saw their stock prices drop a further 60%.

It was a marvel that both banks were supporting the Detroit and Cleveland banks at the end of 1932. Whether courage or imagination prevailed, Chicago was determined to remain the center of finance in the Midwest.

Bankers Trust, Central Hanover, and Guaranty Trust stood out in sharp contrast to the more troubled banks. These three banks did not reduce their dividends during the Depression, had the least loan write-offs, and were among the most liquid. They had not shared in the exuberance of the pre-Crash financial markets either. None of their people was called before the Senate Committee investigating stock exchange practices. The low point of the Depression for these banks occurred in 1932 rather than in 1933, even in the Bank Holiday, when their stocks were one-third higher than their lowest prices in 1932.

The Oil Industry

In 1932 the oil industry had a profit of $52 million, following losses of $45 million in 1931, as crude oil prices rose from an average of 93¢ per barrel to $1.01. This seems like a modest price rise, but it was from a low price of 68¢ per barrel in July 1931 to a high price of $1.07 per barrel in July 1932. The change was due to pro-rationing, which limited oil production, and to a 4¢ per gallon tariff on crude oil and gasoline, which eliminated imports after June 1932. The tariff was particularly significant since gasoline only cost 5 1/2¢ per gallon. However, oil sales, production, and employment, in contrast to prices, dropped to their lowest levels in the Depression.[14]

Despite the industry's return to profitability, none of the major companies had a return on equity as high as 3%. Shell Union Oil Corp. and The Texas Corp. still had losses, and Gulf, Phillips, Consolidated, Socony, and Standard Oil of New Jersey all operated at break-even. Gulf eliminated its dividend during the year, and Socony, Standard Oil of California, and The Texas Corp. reduced their dividends. (See Table 11.8.)

There were rumors that Royal Dutch Co., "Shell" Transport & Trading Co., its U.K. affiliate, and their joint venture, Batavian Petroleum Co., which controlled Shell Union Oil Corp. in the United States, were in financial distress. Sir Henri Deterding, Chairman of all of the companies except "Shell" Transport & Trading Co., resorted to the public media to deny the rumors, but they had a basis in fact. Shell Union Oil Corp. had not earned its interest payments since 1929, had little cash, and had stopped paying preferred dividends in September 1931. The parent companies had little cash, as well, even though they were profitable.

The international oil scene was still in turmoil and largely responsible for Shell's problems. There was nothing comparable to pro-rationing to reduce the oversupply of oil internationally, so price and market competition remained severe. Persian and Rumanian production reached new high levels during 1932, and while Russia's production slipped slightly it was still up 53% from 1929. Standard Oil of New Jersey in particular showed none of the compliance abroad

Table 11.8
The Oil Industry in 1932

	Price-earnings ratio		Market price as a % of book value		Dividend yield (%)		Low price as a % of 1929 high price	Return on equity (%)	Moody's bond ratings	Cash & equivalents ($ millions)
	High price	Low price	High price	Low price	High price	Low price				
Atlantic Refining	15	6	43	17	4.55	11.59	11	2.8	Aa	10
Gulf Oil of Pa.	NM[a]	38	66	34	0	0	11	0.9	A	17
Phillips Petroleum	43	11	26	6	0	0	4	0.6	Ba	(5)[d]
Shell Union Oil	def.[b]	def.	49	14	0	0	8	def.	Ba	14
Sinclair-Consolidated	NM	NM	50	22	0	0	9	0	Baa	39
Socony-Vacuum	71	31	44	19	3.33	7.62	11	0.6	NR[c]	79
Standard Oil (Calif.)	30	14	74	35	6.25	13.33	18	2.5	NR	14
Standard Oil (Ind.)	24	13	63	33	4.00	7.69	21	2.6	NR	88
Standard Oil (N.J.)	NM	NM	82	44	5.41	10.00	24	0	Aaa	179
Texas Corp.	def.	def.	47	24	5.56	10.81	13	def.	A	37
Averages	36.6	18.8	54	25	4.85	10.17	13	1.3	—	—

[a] NM = Not Meaningful.
[b] def. = Deficit.
[c] NR = Not Rated.
[d] Brackets indicate short-term borrowing.

which it showed at home, where it was a leader in the movement for pro-rationing. It acquired the foreign properties of Pan American Petroleum & Transport in 1932, which put it in direct competition with Shell in the Middle East and increased foreign production to over 63% of total Standard Oil production. New tankers were added to the fleet, and construction was begun on an oil pipeline in Mesopotamia. An international oil conference held at the Waldorf Astoria Hotel in New York to try to mitigate international competition in prices and markets broke up in hopeless disagreement in June 1932 after three weeks of wrangling.

The industry's problems also created opportunity, however. Standard Oil of New Jersey acquired the foreign properties of Pan American Petroleum & Transport from Standard Oil of Indiana for approximately $100 million in cash and stock. Sinclair Consolidated acquired Prairie Pipe Line Co. and Prairie Oil & Gas, bringing the Rockefellers into the resulting corporation, Consolidated Oil, as major stockholders. Standard Oil of California negotiated unsuccessfully to acquire the bankrupt Richfield Oil Co.

Oil stock values appeared dismal in the light of the industry's intense competition and the general economic difficulties. The leading oil stocks sank to only 13% of their highest 1929 prices and 25% of book value at the lowest point in 1932. Such values were among the worst for manufacturing industries.

The Chemical Industry

In 1932 the chemical industry had its worst year of the Depression by a considerable margin as sales declined to $2.2 billion from the industry's peak of $4.9 billion in 1930, employment dropped from 329,000 to 291,000, and profits dropped to $49 million, a 69% decline from 1929 for the leading companies and a return on equity of 7.5%. The profit decline would have been much worse, but the chemical companies were able to hold prices at 85% of their 1929 levels even though demand was only 45% of 1929 levels. Commercial Solvents, Du Pont, and Union Carbide cut their dividends, and only Monsanto earned its dividend even after the reductions.[15] (See Table 11.9 for data on specific companies.)

The chemical stocks shared the misfortune of stocks in general, even though the chemical companies were more profitable than most. Chemical stocks dropped to 14% of their highest 1929 prices and 71% of book value, compared with 12% and 49%, respectively, for all stocks. However, the chemical industry bade these low levels good-bye in 1932 and did dramatically better in 1933, when the lowest stock prices of the leading companies were 70% higher than the lowest prices in 1932 and every company had sharply improved earnings per share.

It is interesting to note the relative success of Du Pont and Allied Chemical at this point, because both companies maintained their financial strength under the most trying circumstances, yet their strategies were radically different. Du Pont was buoyed by its explosives business, from which it had made efforts to

Table 11.9
The Chemical Industry in 1932

	Price-earnings ratio		Market price as a % of book value		Dividend yield (%)		Low price as a % of 1929 high price	Return on equity (%)	Moody's bond ratings	Cash & equivalents ($ millions)
	High price	Low price	High price	Low price	High price	Low price				
Allied Chemical	24	12	122	60	6.82	13.95	12	5.0	A pfd.	100
Commercial Solvents	28	7	387	97	4.29	17.14	5	14.1	NR[a]	3
Dow Chemical	20	11	167	92	5.00	9.09	28	8.4	NR	1
E. I. Du Pont	33	12	176	65	3.33	9.09	10	5.3	Aa	63
Monsanto Chemical	13	5	103	43	4.03	9.62	16	8.0	A	2
Union Carbide	37	16	157	70	3.33	7.50	11	4.3	NR	11
Averages	25.8	10.5	185	71	4.47	11.07	14	7.5	—	—

[a] NR = Not Rated.

diversity in the 1920s. Explosives production declined only 30% from 219,390 short tons in 1929 to 153,000 short tons in 1931, its low point. In 1932, explosives production was back up to 214,707 short tons. The company was also aided by its dominant positions in various consumer areas into which it had diversified, such as rayon, leather cloth, and celluloid, where competition was less intense. Du Pont's strength derived as much from its investments in securities as it did from chemical operations, however.

Allied Chemical was likewise in strong product lines. It increased production of synthetic ammonia, which it alone produced in the United States, from 84,000 short tons in 1929 to 89,000 short tons in 1932 (it was as high as 135,000 short tons in 1930). Caustic soda and soda ash production, in which Allied Chemical was heavy, also declined less than other products, 25%–35%.[16]

At this point similarities ceased. Allied Chemical was conservative and secretive. No details of its sales or product lines were revealed to the public, nor the details or the income of its $100 million securities portfolio, despite pressure from the New York Stock Exchange. Allied made no effort to diversify beyond the heavy inorganic chemical and dye products of the five constituent companies which combined to form Allied Chemical in 1920. Its Chairman, Orlando Weber, had been a bicycle racing champion and automobile salesman, but had forsworn such demonstrative and voluble pursuits and became autocratic and withdrawn. He did not give speeches, or interviews, or public information on his company. The one outstanding mark made by the company was the production of synthetic ammonia for fertilizer in a new plant in New York.

Du Pont was in most respects the opposite of Allied Chemical, even termed "democratic" by one of its ten division directors. The company had long ceased to be a Du Pont family preserve, even though control of it was maintained through Christiana Securities, which held over 25% of the common stock and which was in turn controlled by Pierre, Irénée, and Lammot Du Pont. There were only seven Du Ponts on the board of directors out of a total of 36 directors. They were also outvoted on the executive and finance committees. At Du Pont a professional management structure had been developed comprised of corporate staff and ten operating divisions, with each division operating as an independent profit center. The divisions had been created through a combination of internal growth and acquisition in the last decade as the company sought to diversify beyond explosives. Not all the divisions were successful. Dye business in particular was poor. The company invested $43 million in dyes between the war and the mid-1930s before the division became profitable.[17] Nor could paints and lacquers, especially sales to the auto companies, have been particularly profitable in the 1930s. Nonetheless, the company knew the directions it wished to take, how to make its wishes effective, and had great staying power.

The Food Industry

The food industry reached its lowest level in the Depression in 1932 and substantially stayed there through 1933, but even with earnings down 45% in 1932 from their 1929 levels, the industry still earned a 12.4% return on equity (see Table 11.10). All the leading companies paid dividends, but six of these eight companies cut their dividends during 1932. With these dividend cuts behind them, the food stocks provide an insight into stock market valuations at the bottom of the Depression. The food stocks had dropped to 19% of their highest 1929 prices, compared with 12% for all stocks. The 12% yield and the average price-earnings ratio of 8 are particularly interesting since the companies had very little leverage and proven ability to adapt to the Depression.

The sales and profits of the leading food companies held up in direct relationship to the extent of the value added to their products and the strength of their brand names. Standard Brands, General Mills, National Biscuit, and General Foods, which had such household products as Chase & Sanborn Coffee, Wheaties, Shredded Wheat, and Jello, had the smallest profit declines and maintained returns on equity of 10%–28 1/2%, whereas those companies closer to commodities businesses, such as Borden, Pillsbury, and United Fruit, had returns on equity closer to 5%. This difference in product identity was particularly reflected in the companies' stock prices relative to book value. The lowest stock prices for the former companies were mostly well above book value, while for the latter they were mostly less than half of book value.

Standard Brands continued to pay a penalty for the speculation attendant on its origins. Volume in the stock during 1932 was still unusually high, at 40% of outstanding shares, and at the bottom of the market its yield of 12%, price-earnings ratio of 7, and price decline of 81% from the high in 1929 were all only average for the food stocks despite the company's spectacular 28 1/2% return on equity. The company's product line was unusually strong, with Fleischmann's Yeast, Chase & Sanborn Coffee, Royal jellies, Widlar's condiments, and Gillette's baking powder as its principal brand names. The credit markets gave the company its due recognition since Moody's rated its preferred stock to Aa, but there was no comparable recognition in the stock market.

The Mining Industry

The metal mining industry reached a dramatic nadir in 1932 as most of the industry closed down completely for half the year to work off inventories and await better metals prices. Anaconda, Phelps Dodge, and International Nickel closed almost all their mine and smelter operations by midyear, and the industry as a whole operated at approximately 25% of 1929 production levels. During 1932 only 50,000 people found full-time work in the industry, compared with 124,000 in 1929. Declining prices bedevilled the industry as base metals prices reached their lowest levels in the Depression. Copper prices dropped to 5 1/2¢

Table 11.10
The Food Industry in 1932

	Price-earnings ratio		Market price as a % of book value		Dividend yield (%)		Low price as a % of 1929 high price	Return on equity (%)	Moody's bond ratings	Cash & equivalents ($ millions)
	High price	Low price	High price	Low price	High price	Low price				
Borden	25	12	139	65	4.65	10.00	20	5.5	NR[a]	25
General Foods	21	10	373	182	4.88	10.00	24	17.8	NR	7
General Mills	12	7	125	70	6.00	10.71	31	10.3	Ba pfd.	6
National Biscuit	19	8	276	118	5.96	14.00	21	14.4	Aaa pfd.	31
National Dairy	17	7	238	108	6.45	14.29	16	14.5	Baa	26
Pillsbury	15	6	64	26	2.61	6.32	15	4.2	Baa	3
Standard Brands	16	7	450	209	5.56	11.94	19	28.5	Aa pfd.	22
United Fruit	16	5	60	19	6.25	20.00	6	3.7	NR	27
Averages	17.6	7.8	216	100	5.30	12.16	19	12.4	—	—

[a] NR = Not Rated.

per pound, versus 18¢ in 1929; lead prices were 2.9¢ per pound, versus 6 1/2¢ in 1929. The result of both price and production declines was a drop in sales for the metal mining industry from $1.2 billion in 1929 to only $238 million in 1932, and a net loss of $29 million.[18] Anaconda alone reported a $17 million loss, and only National Lead was able to report a profit. All the base metals companies eliminated their common stock dividends by 1932, and International Nickel even eliminated its preferred stock dividends. (See Table 11.11 for details on the industry.)

International trade and finance problems were an integral part of the metal mining industry's travails, for exports constituted approximately 50% of U.S. copper production, the principal U.S. mining commodity. U.S. copper production fell 75% from 1929 to 1932, and Chilean copper production (which was controlled by U.S. companies and virtually all exported) fell 66%, while the production of other major countries fell much less. Canada had increased copper production from 1929 levels by 1932; African production, principally from the Congo, had fallen only 18% from 1929; and European production was down only 14%. Protective measures enabled these smaller European, Canadian, and African producers to maintain relatively high output, while the U.S. corporations controlling two-thirds of world capacity in the United States and South America were forced to bear the brunt of the decline in world demand.[19]

Efforts were made to achieve a more even reduction in production worldwide through Copper Exporters, Inc., an association to control copper sales outside the United States. Major producers had agreed in December 1931 to operate at 26% of capacity, which was reduced to 20% in March 1932, but British and Belgian copper interests in the Congo refused to join the group. They flirted with joining it while they expanded their low-cost operations, until in June 1932 the association fell apart. Americans, led by International Nickel, quit to protest not receiving fair treatment, and at the same time a U.S. tariff of 4¢ a pound was imposed on copper imports, completely eliminating them. The industry was resolved on a worldwide fight to the finish with the lowest cost producers to be victors. Several weeks of negotiations at the Waldorf Astoria Hotel in New York in December 1932 were unproductive in restoring order to export marketing, just as a similar June meeting had been for the oil industry.

One can see in an industry such as metals mining a validation of Roosevelt's eventual economic nationalism. The results of dependence on international trade and efforts to negotiate sharing of markets had been disastrous for the U.S. economy.

The difficult situation in 1932 led to mining stocks reaching their low point in the Depression and levels of valuation comparable to the worst other industries. Common stocks of the base-metals-producing companies dropped to prices equal to only 7% of their highest 1929 prices and 18% of book value, which compared with industries such as holding companies, farm equipment, motion pictures, pulp and paper, railroads, and steel. The only high spot attributable in retrospect to 1932 was that it marked the bottom for the base metals companies. Sales and

Table 11.11
The Mining Industry in 1932

	Price-earnings ratio		Market price as a % of book value		Dividend yield (%)		Low price as a % of 1929 high price	Return on equity (%)	Moody's bond ratings	Cash & equivalents ($ millions)
	High price	Low price	High price	Low price	High price	Low price				
Alaska Juneau Gold	30	14	155	70	3.53	7.74	78	5.2	NR[c]	0
American Smelting	def.[a]	def.	64	12	0	0	4	def.	A	21
Anaconda Copper	def.	def.	35	5	0	0	2	def.	NR	(71)[d]
Homestake Mining	16	11	236	159	6.75	10.00	118	14.4	NR	11
International Nickel	def.	def.	144	39	0	0	5	def.	Ba pfd.	6
Kennecott Copper	def.	def.	70	19	0	0	5	def.	NR	15
National Lead	29	14	44	22	5.43	11.11	21	1.5	A pfd.	7
Phelps Dodge	def.	def.	34	11	0	0	5	def.	NR	9
Texas Gulf Sulphur	12	5	208	92	7.41	16.67	14	17.9	NR	4
Averages	NM[b]	NM	110	48	NM	NM	28	NM	—	—

[a] def. = Deficit.
[b] NM = Not Meaningful.
[c] NR = Not Rated.
[d] Brackets indicate short-term borrowing.

prices increased 50% in 1933, which made the industry profitable again. Every company had better income results in 1933, and their lowest stock prices in 1933 were almost 50% higher than in 1932.

The gold mining companies stood out from the base metal mining companies in 1932 as they had in 1931. Homestake Mining reported record earnings in 1932, and both Alaska Juneau and Homestake raised their dividends. Homestake's stock hit an historic high price of $163 in 1932, up 75% from its highest price in 1929, and while Alaska Juneau's stock did not hit a new high price, it too was up similarly from its highest 1929 price. The lowest 1932 stock prices in both cases were still close to their highest 1929 prices. It is interesting that the valuations of these gold mining stocks were based almost completely on anticipated changes in gold prices. Production was constant throughout the Depression at both companies, as were costs, with higher prices the only source of profit improvement. When this factor is combined with the relatively high price earnings ratios and market-to-book-value ratios for these companies, we get some insight into how confidently the stock market was betting on devaluation of the dollar in 1933.

The Motion Picture Companies

The collapse of the motion picture companies had been clear late in 1931 when individual theater subsidiaries of Fox Theatres and Warner Bros. had defaulted and RCA had been forced into recapitalizing RKO lest it default. But 1932 was the denouement for most of the companies, as sales dropped from $836 million to $611 million and the industry lost $86 million. In this case, the National Income and Products Accounts definition of losses, which amounted to $86 million, is better than Moody's definition, which was only $3 million. Financial reporting practices in the motion picture industry were notoriously weak. All the companies except Loew's were in some form of receivership, their debt ratings reduced to default levels and their stocks rendered valueless at $1 per share or less.[20] (See Table 11.12 for details on the industry.)

Paramount-Publix, the giant of the industry, with assets of $262 million, struggled to stay afloat in the face of a 1932 operating loss of $16 million and $113 million in debts. It sold its half interest in Columbia Broadcasting System back to William S. Paley for $5.2 million, sold 14 theaters in the South for cash, and discounted its films in progress to the banks for $13 million, but still it could not stay solvent. Like the other theater chains, it began defaulting on the debts of its subsidiary theaters, which were the least valuable. Its Balaban & Katz subsidiary missed interest payments in August 1932, and its Marks Brothers Theatres subsidiary missed interest payments in October 1932. Voluntary receivership followed in January 1933.

RKO went through a similar process, defaulting first on theater mortgages, then accepting voluntary receivership in January 1933. It had nine months operating losses of $5 million and no cash to service its $58 million in debts. An

Table 11.12
The Motion Picture Companies in 1932

	Price-earnings ratio		Market price as a % of book value		Dividend yield (%)		Low price as a % of 1929 high price	Return on equity (%)	Moody's bond ratings	Cash & equivalents ($ millions)
	High price	Low price	High price	Low price	High price	Low price				
Fox Film A	def.[a]	def.	45	8	0	0	1	def.	Caa	(8)[d]
Loew's	8	3	83	28	10.53	23.08	15	10.2	Ba	8
Paramount-Publix	def.	def.	30	4	0	0	2	def.	Ca	(17)
Radio-Keith-Orpheum	def.	def.	NA[c]	NA	0	0	NA	def.	Ca	(6)
Warner Bros. Pictures	def.	def.	30	4	0	0	1	def.	Caa	3
Averages	NM[b]	NM	48	12	NM	NM	5	NM	—	—

[a] def. = Deficit.
[b] NM = Not Meaningful.
[c] NA = Not Available.
[d] Brackets indicate short-term borrowing.

all-star New York board of directors was enmeshed in the embarrassment of bankruptcy, including P. D. Cravath, Arthur Lehman, Paul Mazur, David Sarnoff, Herbert Bayard Swope, Elisha Walker, and Owen D. Young. Their discomfiture must have been profound with David Sarnoff, Chairman of RCA, who ran RKO and had attracted them to the board of directors.

Warner Bros. did slightly better than the other companies above, despite losses of $14 million in 1932 and the elimination of preferred dividends. Its St. Louis subsidiary, Skouras Bros., went into receivership in November 1931, as did its Federal Theatres subsidiary in December 1932, but the parent company was still solvent. Warner Bros. low stock price of 50¢ in 1932 reflected the strong anticipation that the company would not survive, however.

Loew's contrasted dramatically with the plight of the other motion picture companies and was in no danger of default. Its $125 million in assets made it smaller than Paramount or Warner Bros., but in contrast to them its profits were almost $8 million, after $31 million in noncash charges for film amortization and depreciation. The company paid $6.5 million in dividends after a modest reduction from $4.00 to $3.00 per share, and still had $27 million in working capital and cash greater than all its current liabilities. The quality of film output from Loew's subsidiary, MGM, had much to do with its success, but MGM provided only about one-third of Loew's operating income and profits. Good management and a lower debt burden than the other theater companies were the rest of the story.

The Steel Industry

The steel industry had its worst year of the Depression in 1932 as sales and production dropped below one-quarter of levels in 1929 and losses amounted to $159 million. Employment was cut roughly to half of 1929's employment figure. This sustained low level of activity lasted from June 1932 through the first quarter of 1933 and was exacerbated by record low levels of export sales due to competition with steel from Russia, which was the largest producer outside the United States and which reached production levels 21% above those of 1929 in its effort to earn hard currency. Europe also kept up production at almost 3 times the level of the United States relative to 1929 by tough export competition.[21]

The steel stocks did poorly under such difficult circumstances (see Table 11.13). All the major companies lost money and eliminated their common stock dividends. Bethlehem Steel and Youngstown Sheet & Tube even eliminated their preferred dividends, as U.S. Steel would in early 1933, despite its cash holdings of over $100 million. The steel stocks dropped to low prices that were only 6% of their highest prices in 1929 and 10% of book value per share, abysmal valuations equalled only by farm equipment, pulp and paper, railroad, and holding company stocks. U.S. Steel remained the volume leader on the New York Stock Exchange, but in all other respects it was one of the worst stocks.

Steel industry results and stock prices in 1932 were much below those of 1933

Table 11.13
The Steel Industry in 1932

	Price-earnings ratio		Market price as a % of book value		Dividend yield (%)		Low price as a % of 1929 high price	Return on equity (%)	Moody's bond ratings	Cash & equivalents ($ millions)
	High price	Low price	High price	Low price	High price	Low price				
Bethlehem Steel	def.[a]	def.	23	5	0	0	5	def.	A	47
Inland Steel	def.	def.	57	20	0	0	9	def.	Baa	5
U.S. Steel	def.	def.	28	11	0	0	8	def.	Ba pfd.	106
Youngstown Sheet & Tube	def.	def.	33	5	0	0	3	def.	Baa	14
Averages	def.	def.	35	10	0	0	6	def.	—	—

[a] def. = Deficit.

because the economic upturn which began with Roosevelt affected the steel industry dramatically, but in fact the low level of production, exports, prices, profits, and employment persisted on a plateau from mid-1932 through March 1933.

The Automobile Manufacturers

The automobile industry also reached its lowest point in the Depression in 1932 as sales and production dropped to one-quarter of 1929's levels. The October and November production was only 10% of 1929 peaks. Industry losses amounted to $69 million for 1932. Employment was 299,999, versus 540,000 in 1929.[22]

All the auto companies, except Nash Motors, reported losses and reduced their dividends to either zero, as in the case of Hudson and Packard, or to $1.00, as in the case of Chrysler, General Motors, and Nash. Their stocks were uniformly pushed down to an average of 5% of their highest 1929 prices and 39% of book value, which were unusually low valuations for an industry which was transforming American life. (See Table 11.14 for details on each manufacturer.)

Ford Motor Co. in particular found 1932 a low point in both earnings and morale. The company introduced its new V-8 car in March 1932, but sales were so laggard that Ford's market share dropped to 24%, compared with its recent peak of 40% in 1930, and the company lost $70.8 million. Chrysler was suddenly challenging even Ford's number two position in the auto industry with a 17 1/2% market share based on its strong-selling and well-engineered Plymouth car.

Just as the V-8 car was being introduced, labor problems erupted at Ford in March 1932 in response to the prolonged downtime from August 1931 to March 1932 to prepare the new car and Ford's decision to cut its historic minimum wage of $7 per day to $4. On Monday, March 7th, thousands of workers marched to the gates of the River Rouge plant, Ford's 1,100-acre colossus of docks, foundries, and body, engine, and assembly plants, where they clashed with police, firemen, bullets, and tear gas. Four marchers died and 20 were wounded. The irony of men marching for jobs just as Ford was trying to introduce a new car was lost amid the strong emotions the battle created and the acute depression throughout southern Michigan.

The Consumer Products Companies

The Depression finally caught up with the consumer products companies in 1932 as most of the companies experienced their first sharp declines in sales and earnings. (See Table 11.15 for details on specific companies.) Colgate registered a loss, Kodak and Procter & Gamble had earnings declines of over 50%, and earnings of most of the other companies dropped approximately 30%. For many of the companies it was their first significant earnings decline since 1929. This decline also brought about dividend reductions at every company (except Gillette,

Table 11.14
The Automobile Manufacturers in 1932

	Price-earnings ratio		Market price as a % of book value		Dividend yield (%)		Low price as a % of 1929 high price	Return on equity (%)	Moody's bond ratings	Cash & equivalents ($ millions)
	High price	Low price	High price	Low price	High price	Low price				
Chrysler Corp.	def.[a]	def.	122	28	4.55	20.00	4	def.	NR[c]	43
General Motors	def.	def.	179	54	4.00	13.11	8	def.	Baa pfd.	173
Hudson Motor Car	def.	def.	57	14	0	0	3	def.	NR	4
Nash Motors	53	21	133	53	5.00	12.50	7	2.5	NR	32
Packard Motor Car	def.	def.	148	44	0	0	5	def.	NR	13
Averages	NM[b]	NM	128	39	2.71	9.12	5	NM	—	—

[a] def. = Deficit.
[b] NM = Not Meaningful.
[c] NR = Not Rated.

Table 11.15
The Consumer Products Companies in 1932

	Price-earnings ratio		Market price as a % of book value		Dividend yield (%)		Low price as a % of 1929 high price	Return on equity (%)	Moody's bond ratings	Cash & equivalents ($ millions)
	High price	Low price	High price	Low price	High price	Low price				
Coca-Cola	14	8	429	246	5.83	10.14	39	19.3	Baa pfd.	5
Colgate-Palmolive	def.[a]	def.	188	59	3.23	10.00	11	def.	B pfd.	13
Eastman-Kodak	35	14	157	63	3.41	8.57	13	4.5	Aaa pfd.	20
Gillette	12	5	259	108	4.17	10.00	7	21.1	Baa	7
International Shoe	24	11	200	91	4.55	10.00	26	8.2	Aaa pfd.	23
Lambert Co.	11	5	570	250	7.02	16.00	16	52.0	NR[b]	5
Procter & Gamble	34	16	307	145	5.12	11.00	20	10.2	Aaa	25
Wm. Wrigley Jr.	16	7	238	104	5.26	12.00	31	14.8	NR	25
Averages	21	9	294	133	4.82	10.96	20	18.6	—	—

[a] def. = Deficit.
[b] NR = Not Rated.

which went from zero to $1.00), and at Colgate, Kodak, and Lambert Co. the reductions were 50% or greater. Many of the companies had been increasing their dividends up to this point despite the Crash and the problems of 1930–31.

This change of fortunes brought the consumer products stocks down to low prices in 1932 which averaged 20% of their highest 1929 prices and 133% of book value, but these valuations were still attractive compared with stocks in general, which averaged 12% of their highest prices in 1929 and 49% of book value. All the companies paid dividends, and as a group they still averaged a return on equity of 18.6% which was second only to the tobacco industry.

However, these companies had not reached their bottom for the Depression in 1932. Unlike manufacturing companies, which recovered in 1933 as inventories were rebuilt, results of the consumer products companies followed consumer income, which declined further in 1933. Procter & Gamble, for example, had a 28% sales decline in 1933, and earnings at Gillette and Lambert Co. declined over 40%.

The Retailers

Retailers had their most difficult time in the Depression for a period stretching from mid-1932 until April 1933 as sales and profits declined to their lowest levels of the Depression. However, the division between S. S. Kresge, Macy's, J. C. Penney, and F. W. Woolworth, which still did well, and the other stores, which fared very poorly, remained, thereby making it more difficult to generalize about this industry than other industries. (See Table 11.16 for details on the industry.)

Financial results among the older department stores and mail order companies were uniform and dismal. The 40 public companies in these categories reported aggregate losses of $30 million.[23] Associated Dry Goods, Gimbel Brothers, Marshall Field, Montgomery Ward, and Sears Roebuck all reported losses, paid no dividends on their common stocks, and went into arrears on their preferred dividends during the year (except Sears, which had no preferred stock outstanding). Their stocks sank to low prices only 3 1/2% of their highest prices in 1929 and 14% of book value, among the worst valuations of any industry.

Circumstances were difficult for S. S. Kresge, R. H. Macy, J. C. Penney, and F. W. Woolworth as well. All of them reduced their dividends in the face of earnings declines averaging around 45%, but at least they still paid dividends, and while their stocks dropped to low prices equal to 13% of their highest 1929 prices and 75% of book value, these valuations compared well with the averages for all stocks of 12% and 49% respectively.

Because all sectors of the retail industry reported profits in 1933, the year 1932 appears as the low point for the industry; but sales recovery in 1933 was weak as the consumer sector lagged in the business recovery. Gimbel Brothers, S. S. Kresge, R. H. Macy, and F. W. Woolworth had virtually no sales gains in 1933. The earnings improvements came basically from reduced product and

Table 11.16
The Retailers in 1932

	Price-earnings ratio		Market price as a % of book value		Dividend yield (%)		Low price as a % of 1929 high price	Return on equity (%)	Moody's bond ratings	Cash & equivalents ($ millions)
	High price	Low price	High price	Low price	High price	Low price				
Associated Dry Goods	def.[a]	def.	48	13	0	0	4	def.	B pfd.	11
Gimbel Brothers	def.	def.	13	3	0	0	2	def.	Caa pfd.	7
S. S. Kresge	19	7	127	44	5.26	15.38	11	6.5	A	6
R. H. Macy	28	8	145	40	3.28	11.77	7	5.2	NR[c]	(2)[d]
Marshall Field	def.	def.	54	12	0	0	NA	def.	A	21
Montgomery Ward	def.	def.	71	15	0	0	2	def.	NR	28
J. C. Penney	22	8	233	87	6.00	16.15	12	10.2	A pfd.	23
Sears Roebuck	def.	def.	109	29	0	0	6	def.	NR	(26)
F. W. Woolworth	20	10	271	129	5.22	10.91	21	13.4	NR	20
Averages	22.2	8.3	119	41	NM[b]	NM	8	NM	—	—

[a] def. = Deficit.
[b] NM = Not Meaningful.
[c] NR = Not Rated.
[d] Brackets indicate short-term borrowing.

operating costs, which were relatively easy for these retailers with their rapid inventory turnover and unskilled employees.

The Tire Industry

From early 1932 to May 1933, the tire industry suffered an extended period of desperately low-level operations at approximately one-third of capacity, much like the other industries which were most deeply hurt by the Depression. This period marked the lowest point in the Depression for the tire industry and led to losses of $3 million in 1932, employment of only 110,000 people, versus 176,000 in 1929, and raw rubber prices of only 3¢ per pound, compared with over 20¢ in 1929 and $1 in 1925.[24]

The individual tire companies registered their lowest results in the Depression variously in 1932 and 1933, so that the two years blend into one extended low period that prevents us from singling out either year as the low point for the industry. (See Table 11.17 for details on 1932.) In 1932, Goodrich and Goodyear both had their largest losses and lowest stock prices, Goodyear eliminated its common stock dividends, and Goodrich's bond rating was reduced to Ba. Their stocks dropped to 4% and 2%, respectively, of their highest 1929 prices. Firestone realized its worst results the next year. The overall effect was stock prices averaging only 12% of their highest 1929 prices and 25% of book value, which made tire stocks among the lowest valued industries.

The Farm Equipment Industry

From spring 1932 through spring 1933, the farm equipment industry experienced its lowest level of operations in the Depression, at approximately one-quarter of its 1929 level of operations (see Table 11.18). In 1932, employment in farm equipment plants in Illinois, the center of the industry, averaged only 28% of 1929 employment. Export revenues were only 7 1/2% of 1929 levels. All the companies operated at profound deficits amounting to $30 million, which carried well into 1933, when losses still totalled $16 million, and which led International Harvester to cut its common stock dividend from $2.50 to $1.20 and Deere & Co. to cut its preferred stock dividend from 35¢ to 10¢. The J. I. Case preferred stock dividend was paid but was obviously very uncertain.[25]

The farm equipment stocks had similar low points in 1932 and early 1933, averaging 5% of their highest 1929 prices and only 14% of book value, which were equalled only by steel, pulp and paper, and railroad stocks among heavy industries. However, 1933 promised a profound reversal of these agricultural implement stock valuations when these stock prices rose sevenfold from their lowest 1932 levels as a result of Roosevelt's strong commitment to agricultural recovery.

Table 11.17
The Tire Industry in 1932

	Price-earnings ratio		Market price as a % of book value		Dividend yield (%)		Low price as a % of 1929 high price	Return on equity (%)	Moody's bond ratings	Cash & equivalents ($ millions)
	High price	Low price	High price	Low price	High price	Low price				
Firestone	18	10	70	41	5.26	9.09	30	3.9	B pfd.	15
B. F. Goodrich	def.[a]	def.	48	9	0	0	2	def.	Ba	16
Goodyear	def.	def.	182	25	0	0	4	def.	Baa	50
Averages	NM[b]	NM	100	25	NM	NM	12	NM	—	—

[a] def. = Deficit
[b] NM = Not Meaningful.

Table 11.18
The Farm Equipment Industry in 1932

	Price-earnings ratio		Market price as a % of book value		Dividend yield (%)		Low price as a % of 1929 high price	Return on equity (%)	Moody's bond ratings	Cash & equivalents ($ millions)
	High price	Low price	High price	Low price	High price	Low price				
J. I. Case	def.[a]	def.	44	11	0	0	4	def.	B pfd.	1
Deere & Co.	def.	def.	53	10	0	0	3	def.	B pfd.	(4)[c]
International Harvester	def.	def.	67	20	3.53	12.00	7	def.	Baa pfd.	57
Averages	def.	def.	55	14	NM[b]	NM	5	def.	—	—

[a] def. = Deficit.
[b] NM = Not Meaningful.
[c] Brackets indicate short-term borrowing.

The Tobacco Companies

In 1932 the tobacco companies (see Table 11.19) quite remarkably posted barely reduced profits of $106 million and a 20% return on equity, despite almost a 20% decline in cigarette production. These profits were due to a 50% drop in tobacco costs during the Depression and the general deflation in labor and other costs while finished cigarette prices continued to hold up remarkably well.[26]

The tobacco stocks had the best and most consistent valuations of any industry in these circumstances, with low stock prices that were still 35% of their highest 1929 prices and 116% of book value, compared with the averages for all stocks of 12% and 49%, respectively. None of the tobacco companies had reduced its dividends during the Depression, and insofar as the companies had bond ratings on their minimal amounts of debt, these ratings were Aaa.

The Pulp and Paper Industry

The pulp and paper industry had its worst year and was one of the most depressed industries in 1932 as its sales dropped to $1 billion, compared with $1.7 billion in 1929, and it operated at only 56% of capacity. (See Table 11.20 for data.) Employment was 108,000, versus 145,000 in 1929. Other industries operated at lower capacity, but the industry's loss of $24 million was unusually large for its modest size. The industry had gone critical earlier than 1932, as Crown Zellerbach and International Paper went into arrears on their preferred dividends in 1931 due to tough Canadian price competition and excessive debt leverage. Now, in 1932, the fear that the companies would default showed up in their Ba debt ratings and low stock prices of under $1 for many of the companies. The stocks of the leading pulp and paper companies at their lowest prices averaged only 5% of their highest 1929 prices and 8% of book value, one of the lowest valuations of any industry. Unfortunately, the industry's weak position vis-à-vis Canadian producers created little hope for improvement even if the economy improved.[27]

The Office Equipment Companies

The office equipment companies hit their lowest period in the Depression in 1932 as the industry registered losses of $400,000, its only loss year in the Depression, on sales of approximately one-third those of 1929. Office machines were one of the easiest spending reductions in the stringent business climate. IBM was able to maintain a 15% return on equity and its peak dividend rate of $6.00 per share, but Burroughs was forced to cut its dividend from $1.50 to 40¢ on break-even earnings, and National Cash Register and Remington Rand registered losses. The latter went into arrears on its preferred dividends. (See details in Table 11.21.)

Office equipment stocks dropped to 8% of their highest 1929 prices, below

Table 11.19
The Tobacco Companies in 1932

	Price-earnings ratio		Market price as a % of book value		Dividend yield (%)		Low price as a % of 1929 high price	Return on equity (%)	Moody's bond ratings	Cash & equivalents ($ millions)
	High price	Low price	High price	Low price	High price	Low price				
American Tobacco	10	5	223	105	6.90	14.63	35	22.0	Aaa	51
Liggett & Myers	10	5	174	84	7.58	15.63	30	18.2	Aaa	73
Reynolds Tobacco	12	8	235	159	7.50	11.11	41	19.8	NR[a]	60
Averages	10.7	6.0	211	116	7.33	13.79	35	20.0	—	—

[a] NR = Not Rated.

Table 11.20
The Pulp and Paper Industry in 1932

	Price-earnings ratio		Market price as a % of book value		Dividend yield (%)		Low price as a % of 1929 high price	Return on equity (%)	Moody's bond ratings	Cash & equivalents ($ millions)
	High price	Low price	High price	Low price	High price	Low price				
Crown Zellerbach	def.[a]	def.	29	9	0	0	4	def.	NR[d]	4
International Paper	NA[b]	NA	16	2	0	0	1	def.	Ba	(28)[e]
Kimberly-Clark	def.	def.	36	12	0	0	11	def.	Ba	2
Averages	NM[c]	NM	27	8	0	0	5	def.	—	—

[a] def. = Deficit.
[b] NA = Not Available.
[c] NM = Not Meaningful.
[d] NR = Not Rated.
[e] Brackets indicate short-term borrowing.

Table 11.21
The Office Equipment Companies in 1932

	Price-earnings ratio		Market price as a % of book value		Dividend yield (%)		Low price as a % of 1929 high price	Return on equity (%)	Moody's bond ratings	Cash & equivalents ($ millions)
	High price	Low price	High price	Low price	High price	Low price				
Burroughs Adding Machine	NM[a]	NM	217	104	3.08	6.40	6	2.2	NR[c]	15
IBM	13	6	195	88	5.13	11.32	21	15.0	NR	6
Remington Rand	def.[b]	def.	NM	NM	0	0	2	def.	Ba	6
National Cash Register A	def.	def.	94	31	0	0	4	def.	NR	5
Averages	NM	NM	169	74	2.74	5.91	8	8.6	—	

[a] NM = Not Meaningful.
[b] def. = Deficit.
[c] NR = Not Rated.

the average of 12% for all stocks, despite the modest loss the industry recorded, the growth inherent in office equipment technology, and the modest leverage and capital employed by the companies. In essence, the market treated them like capital equipment companies. Since this was hardly the case for such small equipment, the recovery in the stocks in 1933 and thereafter was dramatic.

Other Stocks

In 1932, General Electric and Westinghouse continued their unequal competition at sales levels barely one-third of sales in 1929. At this low point in the Depression both stocks were still market favorites, with General Electric the 6th most active stock on the NYSE and Westinghouse the 13th most active, but beyond that similarities ceased. (See Table 11.22 on GE and Westinghouse stocks.) The Depression markedly differentiated General Electric from Westinghouse. General Electric still made a modest profit, still paid a 40¢ per share dividend although it was down from $1.60 in 1931, kept its Aaa bond rating, and held $116 million in cash and investments. By contrast, Westinghouse had its second of three Depression years with large losses, eliminated its common stock dividend, had its preferred stock rating reduced to A, and held only $33 million in cash and investments. When, during 1932, the two companies were forced by the Justice Department into a consent decree which required them to eliminate their stockholdings in RCA as well as their board positions and manufacturing, sales, and patent agreements, General Electric promptly distributed its RCA stock with a market value of $26.5 million to its stockholders as an extra dividend, while Westinghouse sought a quid pro quo for all its RCA stock. Westinghouse offered its preferred stockholders a choice of their cash dividend or one half share of RCA stock, which distributed about one-third of its RCA stock, and ultimately sold the balance for cash.

The principal reflection in the stock market of these differences between General Electric and Westinghouse was their stock prices relative to book value, with General Electric's stock receiving 3 1/2 to 4 times the valuation of Westinghouse's stock. However, General Electric's superiority did not help it avoid a very low stock price equal to only 8% of its highest 1929 price and its lowest price in the Depression, due to the decline of two-thirds in its sales and production.

AT&T's stock remained surprisingly stable in 1932 in the face of a drop in earnings per share to $5.96 (see Table 11.22). The company earned only two-thirds of its longtime $9.00 per share dividend and had barely earned it in 1930 and 1931, but there was still enough confidence in the dividend that the stock dropped to only 23% of its highest 1929 price, compared with the average for all stocks of 12%, and to a yield of approximately 13%, which was in line with the most reliable other stocks. AT&T held over $200 million in cash, which helped this confidence.

Just as General Electric was solid and well run but not spectacular, so was American Can. It cut its dividend from $5.00 to $4.00 during 1932, as its earnings

Table 11.22
Other Stocks in 1932

	Price-earnings ratio		Market price as a % of book value		Dividend yield (%)		Low price as a % of 1929 high price	Return on equity (%)	Moody's bond ratings	Cash & equivalents ($ millions)
	High price	Low price	High price	Low price	High price	Low price				
American Can	23	9	130	53	5.41	13.33	16	5.7	A pfd.	14
AT&T	23	12	101	52	6.57	12.86	23	4.1	Aa	204
General Electric	63	21	236	77	1.54	4.71	8	3.7	Aaa	116
Radio Corp. of America	def.[a]	def.	59	22	0	0	5	def.	A pfd.	33
Westinghouse	def.	def.	NA[b]	NA	0	0	3	def.	Caa pfd.	26

[a] def. = Deficit.
[b] NA = Not Available.

declined even lower to $3.26, but this was the company's only dividend reduction in the Depression, and its earnings bounced back over 50% in 1933. With such stability and a 5.7% return on equity in 1932, it is somewhat surprising that American Can's stock dropped to 53% of book value, 16% of its highest 1929 price, and a yield of 13.33% at the lowest point in 1932 (see Table 11.22). These parameters were closer to the averages than one would expect for a well-above-average stock. Such valuations reflected the fear and illiquidity at the bottom of the 1932 market. There was more discrimination in 1933, when American Can's lowest price was two-thirds higher.

RCA had suffered a precipitous decline in sales between 1929 and 1931, from $177 million to $100 million, so it was severely taken aback in 1932 when sales declined much further to $66 million. There was little the company could do to cope with such a decline. It had a loss of $6.3 million, eliminated dividends on both its A and B preferred stocks, and renegotiated its Radio City lease at Rockefeller Center in exchange for 100,000 shares of common stock. But the company was too strapped to assist its 64%-owned motion picture subsidiary, RKO, which was rapidly heading for default on its bonds. Moody's reduced its rating on RCA preferred to Caa, suggesting that the parent's securities had also dropped into the speculative range. (See Table 11.22.)

During 1932, RCA was also cut adrift from the prominent patronage of GE and Westinghouse as the result of a consent decree between the parties and the Justice Department, which had fought RCA's 1930 deal with GE and Westinghouse on anti-trust grounds. The consent decree forced RCA to give up any exclusive licensing and patent rights with the two big companies, which in turn were forced to dispose of all their RCA stock and quit its board.

RCA's common stock dropped to 3% of its highest 1929 price during 1932, about equalling the low point it reached in 1931 and much below the average for all stocks of 12%. However, the preferred dividend arrears created a more depressing outlook for the common stock than in 1931, because there was no near-term prospect for any return to the common stockholder. Things were no better in 1933.

Summary

The year 1932 was the worst year of the Depression for most stocks as they dropped on average to 12% of their highest 1929 prices and only 49% of book value, but it was even worse than these averages in many industries which either defaulted or were barely saved. Actual defaults occurred only at Middle West Utilities and several of its related holding companies and among the subsidiaries of motion picture companies, but many railroads and numerous large banks, including the Bank of America, would have defaulted if the RFC had not become a lender of last resort. Many other industries did not default because they had little or no debt, but they created almost the same effect for common stockholders by becoming seriously in arrears on their preferred stock dividends, which had to be accumulated and eventually paid off before common stockholders could receive dividends again. Such preferred dividend problems were common among the trusts, holding companies, retailers, tire companies, pulp and paper companies, and office equipment companies, which drove their common stocks down to values that were frequently $1 or less. The stocks of the heavy industries such as steel, railroads, mining, automobiles, tires, farm equipment, and pulp and paper generally dropped to 5%–10% of their highest 1929 prices and 25% or less of book value, even if they did not have debt or preferred problems, because their level of business was so low that the outlook for future profits seemed hopeless. Most were either at 25% of capacity or closed down completely.

Even amid such economic disaster, however, a few islands of high profitability prevailed. The gold mining companies had record earnings and stocks which established new high prices 75% above their highest in 1929. The tobacco companies posted record profits too, with an average 20% return on equity, but their stocks were down to approximately one-third of their highest 1929 prices at the worst point in the market. Consumer products companies, food companies, chemical companies, and operating utilities still posted respectable returns on equity, as well, ranging from 18.6% to 6.6%, respectively, but stock prices in these industries were pushed far down with other stocks.

In many industries one or more companies stood out as exceptions to the applicable generalizations and established high patterns of excellence: the Chesapeake and Ohio and Norfolk & Western railroads, United Gas Improvement, Lehman Corp., Atlas Corp., Bankers Trust, Standard Brands, Loew's, F. W. Woolworth, Kimberly-Clark, IBM, and General Electric. They were unique tributes to good management.

NOTES

1. *Banking & Monetary Statistics*, p. 343.
2. Ibid., p. 371.
3. *Historical Statistics*, p. 1104.
4. *New York Times*, 6/1/32.
5. See Tables A.31 and A.32 in the Statistical Appendix.
6. *National Income Accounts*, p. 118.
7. Ibid., pp. 142, 102, 84; *Moody's Railroad Manual, 1934*, p. a18.
8. *New York Times*, 8/21/32; *National Income Accounts*, pp. 142, 128, 130, 103; *Moody's Utility Manual, 1934*, p. a23.
9. Bankers Trust had German loans of $27 million on 7/31/31 and $12 million on 12/31/33.
10. *Stock Exchange Practices*, part 4, pp. 3644–45.
11. Ibid., part 8, p. 3743.
12. Ibid., part 6, pp. 2835–75.
13. Ibid., p. 3025.
14. *National Income Accounts*, pp. 103, 126, 142; *Moody's Industrial Manual, 1933*, pp. a87; *1935*, p. a45.

15. *National Income Accounts*, pp. 103, 126, 142.

16. Product line information was obtained from *Moody's Industrial Manual, 1932*, p. a75.

17. L. F. Haber, *The Chemical Industry, 1900–1930*, Oxford: Clarendon Press, 1974, p. 315.

18. *National Income Accounts*, pp. 103, 142; *Moody's Industrial Manual, 1933*, pp. a77, a84, a85; *1935*, p. a45.

19. *Moody's Industrial Manual, 1933*, p. a78.

20. *National Income Accounts*, p. 142; *Moody's Industrial Manual, 1935*, p. a45.

21. *Moody's Industrial Manual, 1935*, p. a45; *National Income Accounts*, p. 142; *Moody's Industrial Manual, 1933*, pp. a93–a96.

22. *Moody's Industrial Manual*, 1933, pp. a71, a72; *1935*, p. a45; *National Income Accounts*, p. 102.

23. *Moody's Industrial Manual, 1935*, p. a45.

24. *National Income Accounts*, p. 102; *Moody's Industrial Manual, 1935*, pp. a25, a45.

25. *Moody's Industrial Manual, 1935*, pp. a2, a45.

26. Ibid., pp. a31, a32, a45; *National Income Accounts*, p. 142.

27. Ibid., pp. 102, 142; *Moody's Industrial Manual, 1935*, pp. a19, a45.

12

Bond Markets in 1932

BOND MARKETS IN GENERAL

Bond markets in 1932 were sharply divided between high quality and low quality credits because of the stress of economic conditions. High quality long-term bond rates dropped throughout most of the year to 3.35% on U.S. governments and 4.18% on Aaa utilities by the end of 1932, while interest rates on Baa rated utility and industrial bonds reached 10%–13% at the peak of the economic and financial crisis in the second quarter of 1932. Railroad bonds reached higher yields, and the ratings on most rail bonds were reduced by the bond rating agencies. By the end of 1932, however, low grade railroad and industrial bond yields were down from these peaks and had even dropped to yields 100–200 basis points below their yields in December 1931.

The municipal bond market accounted for almost half the year's new issues and was relatively stable until the last quarter of the year, when New York City's troubles erupted. The city had over $2 billion in debt outstanding, which suddenly dropped 20% in value, influencing the whole municipal market. Bond ratings were reduced for many states and cities which had been Aaa a few months previously. The municipal market ended 1932 in disarray, with many issues unable to obtain bids.

New issues of foreign bonds ceased in 1932, even for Canadian issuers, and Moody's reduced its ratings for 12 of the 31 countries followed in this study, after 23 ratings reductions in 1931. Eastern European bonds went into default in 1932 and traded below $30 most of the year, reflecting expectations that the defaults would be long-lasting. South American bonds mostly traded below $10 with no prospect of repayment. The bonds of many West European countries which had suffered declines of 20%–40% in the aftermath of the 1931 currency crisis recovered to approximately par, however, and the best foreign bonds, such as those of Switzerland, France, and the United Kingdom, traded close to the best corporate bond yields.

U.S. GOVERNMENT AND CORPORATE BOND MARKETS— HIGH GRADE BOND RATES DECLINE, BUT THERE IS A CRISIS IN LOW GRADE CORPORATE BONDS

The corporate bond market swung widely in 1932. Broadly speaking, prices rose enough in the first quarter to reduce yields 100–200 basis points on weak credits, then prices declined enough in the second quarter to raise yields 150–350 basis points. Prices finally rose again in the remaining two quarters to reduce yields 150–350 basis points. At the end of 1932, bonds of all ratings were generally at their highest prices of the year.

Two traditional precepts of the bond market were destroyed by these events in 1932. Confidence in rail bonds was destroyed by the rapid decline from Aaa to A, or even Baa, for most rail bond ratings. Railroads were revealed as the weakest and most volatile sector of the corporate bond market. Any expectation that bonds in the same industry or of the same rating would be treated the same in the market was also destroyed. There were unusually wide differences in prices and yields for what were earlier homogeneous groups, as investors drew their own conclusions about the security and prospects of individual companies and issues. This differentiation among issues (or disarray, depending on one's point of view) was one of the most characteristic features of the 1932 bond market.

One precept of the bond market was reenforced, however. The bond market performed its classic function of offering a reduced-risk investment despite the intervening hazards. The stronger Aaa and Aa corporate bonds which were able to maintain their ratings were surprisingly resilient against the extreme forces buffeting financial markets. These bonds fluctuated in price ranges only $1–$5 wider than in prior years. Indeed, the range was even narrower for Aaa and Aa utilities. More surprising was the recovery in prices of downgraded and weak bonds following the second-quarter crisis, so that investors had opportunities to sell their holdings at losses of only 10%–20%, compared with previous high prices. Such losses were minor, of course, in comparison to the losses in stock prices, which were still 75%–90%.

The First Quarter of 1932

Long-term interest rates on railroad bonds declined 100–200 basis points between December 1931 and March 1932 and somewhat less for utility and industrial bonds. Rail bond yields in December 1931 had varied from 7.36% on Aa bonds to 11.96% on Baa bonds (as expressed by Moody's indices for these bond classes), but these bond yields were down to 6.17% and 9.66% by the end of March. Utility bond yields, which had not risen to those available on rail bonds, did not recover as much and were 100–200 basis points below most rail bond yields in March 1932. U.S. bond yields declined from a peak of 4.26% in January 1932 to 3.92% by March.

The critical factors in this first-quarter bond market recovery were domestic rather than international. There was still an apparently innate human capacity for optimism which expressed itself in early projections for economic recovery during 1932. This optimism varied from Treasury Secretary Mellon's astringent variety, which led him to project a rise in industrial production of 15%, to the more ebullient *Wall Street Journal*, which predicted a 30% rise. A more important factor was the creation of the Reconstruction Finance Corporation, which began lending in February to railroads to cover bond maturities.

The pressure on the bond market from banks liquidating securities also appeared likely to be relieved by a number of factors. The Glass-Steagall Bill, passed by Congress during this first quarter, broadened the Federal Reserve's ability to lend to banks in trouble. Hoover and the Federal Reserve began a steady public relations campaign to stop both individual and bank hoarding which was expected to reduce runs on banks. Comptroller of the Currency John W. Pole ordered federal bank examiners to use the "intrinsic" value of all Aaa-Baa bonds in examinations of federally chartered banks, which is to say "par." Pole set up a pool managed by the New York Federal Reserve to liquidate the bonds of closed banks in a more orderly manner. He also eliminated the traditional March 31st "call" for bank financial statements to relieve the market of the pressures resulting from window dressing for the call date.

The corporate bond market in the first quarter also appears to have been influenced by the prospect of a massive $1.5 to $2 billion dollar tax increase to bring the federal budget into closer balance. Hoover favored a manufacturers excise tax to raise most of this amount, and there was considerable sentiment in Congress supporting him. John Nance Garner had just become Speaker of the House and almost simultaneously extracted from it a resolution to balance the budget. Even the most liberal politicians favored balancing the budget.

The bond market recovery in the first quarter had little to do with changes in basic interest rates and much to do with a change in the perceived ability of debtors to pay their bills—a contrast we shall observe to an even greater degree later in 1932. For example, U.S. government and Aaa bond yields declined less than 35 basis points in most cases in this period. Utility bonds rated from Baa to Aa and industrial bonds rated Aa changed hardly at all. No significant Federal Reserve open market purchases had begun to lower interest rates (as they would later in 1932), and short-term rates were relatively stable. U.S. Treasury bill rates only fell from 2.41% to 2.25% during the quarter. The change in bond yields was concentrated in the weaker rail and industrial issues, which had high possibilities of default earlier but which were now expected to benefit from an improving economy and the safety net provided by the RFC.

In short, bond interest rates declined in the first quarter because of a recovery in confidence.

The Crisis in Railroad Bonds

This confidence quickly faded as bond prices declined from April through June to new low prices paralleling the decline in common stock prices. Railroads bore the brunt of the decline in bond prices because of their large revenue and income losses and their total inability to refund the $300–$400 million in bond maturities they faced in 1932. For example, the 33 large railroad bond issues in this study suffered 13 rating changes downward and declined an average of 43% from their post-1929 high prices to their lowest prices in 1932. (See Tables A.7 and A.12 in the Statistical Appendix for price, yield, and rating data behind comments in this section.) Thirteen of these issues declined over 50% from their prior high prices. This dismal record occurred even though 24 of the 33 issues were rated Aaa in 1929. The record in smaller and lesser rated railroad issues was even worse. All the following railroads had bond issues which sold below $25, compared with prior high prices of $90 or more: the Baltimore and Ohio (3 issues); the Central Railroad of Georgia (3 issues); the Chicago, Rock Island & Pacific, the Missouri Pacific, and the New Orleans, Texas & Mexico railroads (13 issues combined); the Southern Railway (3 issues).

The bonds of the Wabash Railroad, which declared bankruptcy in December 1931, dropped to under $4, compared with high prices of $90–$103 previously. Four other major railroads—the Florida East Coast, the Mobile & Ohio, the Norfolk & Southern, and the Seaboard Airline—were also in default by mid-summer of 1932 on a total of $285 million in bonds.

The railroad bond market was highly erratic in this decline, and simple classifications based on bond ratings became meaningless. Yields on Aa rail bonds at their lowest prices ranged from 6% for the still highly regarded Chicago, Burlington & Quincy to 9 1/2% on several Aa rated Pennsylvania Railroad issues. Yields on A rated railroad bonds ranged from 6 1/8% to 10 5/8%, and among Baa rated issues the range was all the way from 8% to over 13%.

Even for a single railroad, the disparities in yields on various issues reached extremes out of all proportion to the relative risks of each issue. For example, the Pennsylvania Railroad had five bond issues, each over $40 million, on which yields at their low point in the spring crisis ranged from 5.49% to 13.81% after having been only 50 basis points apart in 1930. The security for these bonds differed, but they were all direct obligations of the Pennsylvania Railroad, which was a sound line earning its fixed charges, earning a profit, paying a dividend, and without short-term debt.

Only a few premier railroad bonds which retained their Aaa ratings avoided the extreme price declines common to most rail bonds. Senior debt of the Atchison, Topeka & Santa Fe Railroad, the New York Central & Hudson River Railroad, the Norfolk & Western Railroad, and the Pennsylvania Railroad retained this coveted status. Their highest bond yields were 5 1/8% to 5 1/2%.

The impact of railroad bond price declines was most significant on smaller banks. Federal Reserve member country banks owned $473 million in rail bonds in June 1932, which was over 50% of all the railroad bonds owned by member banks. Nonmember country banks probably held in excess of $500 million in railroad bonds, which was larger in proportion to their deposits.[1] Most country banks had invested heavily in bonds to obtain yields higher than those available on short-term securities.

Contrary to the impression engendered by Friedman and Schwartz, however, these banks sold relatively few bonds during the crisis in 1932. Corporate bond holdings of member country banks declined only $121 million (about 7%) in the first half of 1932, and the total corporate holdings of nonmember country banks appear to have declined approximately $200 million (about 10%). The heavy selling by country banks was in the fourth quarter of 1931, following the international crisis, rather than in the spring of 1932. We should add here that the selling activity of country banks appears to have been overrated by Friedman and Schwartz as a cause of the decline in bond prices throughout the Depression. Member country and nonmember country banks sold only $900 million in corporate investments between June 1929 and June 1932. Both categories of banks sold corporate investments more slowly than their deposits declined—18% versus 28% for member country banks, and 20% versus 42% for nonmember banks.[2]

Utility Bonds

Utility bonds which were rated Aaa or Aa showed little signs of the crisis in the railroad bond market, and yields on the various issues moved relatively closely together. Among the eight Aaa utility issues over $40 million studied here, their yields at their lowest prices ranged only between 4.92% and 5.51%. The Aa issue yields at their low prices ranged between 5.07% and 6.69%. (See Tables A.8 and A.13 in the Statistical Appendix for price, yield, and rating data behind comments in this section.)

Lesser rated utility bonds felt the crisis, however. The yields on six A rated utility bond issues over $40 million rose to an average of 7.19% in the second quarter. The yields on six Baa utility bond issues over $40 million rose to an average of 8.62%. Here again, however, yields within a rating category were more homogeneous, even when ratings were reduced, and there was little sign of the disarray evident in the railroad market.

The bond market in crisis revealed a marked investor preference for utility bonds over railroad bonds. A-rated rail bonds over $40 million in our study had average high yields of 8.19%, versus 7.55% on similar utility bonds; Baa rated rail bonds over $40 million had an average high yield of 12.40%, versus only 8.67% on similarly rated utilities.[3]

The preference for utility bonds enabled utilities to issue $540 million in securities during 1932, mostly for refundings, while railroads were able to issue a bare $60 million, mostly in exchange for maturing issues. Indeed, the ability of utilities to tap the market was quite remarkable. Commonwealth Edison Co., Peoples Gas Light & Coke Co., and Public Service Co. of Northern Illinois were all able to issue long-term bonds totalling $70 million at yields between 6% and 7% in August 1932, just shortly after their affiliated company, Middle West Utilities, had gone into bankruptcy.

Industrial Bonds

Industrial bond issues are hardly worthy of generalization during 1932, except in the Baa rating category. There were only two large Aaa issues—Standard Oil Co. (N.J.) 5% bonds due in 1946, and Standard Oil Co. (N.Y.) 4 1/2% bonds due in 1951. Their highest yields were 4.51% and 4.66%, respectively. Union Gulf Corp.'s 5% bonds due in 1950 were the only large Aa issue. Its highest yield was 4.92%. The five A rated large industrial issues bore yields ranging from 6.83% to 11.40%, and large Baa industrial issues ranged similarly from 6.74% to 12.11%. Yields in excess of 13%, comparable to Baa railroads, were available only on Ba rated industrial issues, such as General Steel Castings 5 1/2% bonds due in 1949, Pure Oil Co. 5 1/2% bonds due in 1940, and Shell Union Oil Co. 5% bonds due in 1947. (See Tables A.9 and A.14 in the Statistical Appendix for price, yield, and rating data behind comments in this section.)

The reader will note the wide yield variations on comparably rated industrial issues which reflected the same investor judgment as did railroad issues, namely, that the rating agencies were lagging behind events. Investors were making sharp judgments about which issuers would stay solvent, and investors paid up accordingly for those bonds but forced the other bonds to sharp discounts.

The losses during the second-quarter bond market crisis were much less on utility and industrial bonds than on railroad bonds. Among issues over $40 million, only seven utility issues and eight industrial issues rated Baa or higher dropped below $70, and only two of all these issues dropped below $50.

U.S. Government Bonds

The low point in government bonds was in January 1932, when the U.S. Treasury 4 1/4% bonds due in 1952 hit $99—down from a high price of $114 in 1931. Other long-term U.S. Treasury bonds were down $7–$8 at the same point. (See Table A.40 in the Statistical Appendix.) In the ensuing months, even when corporate bond prices declined in the second quarter, an opposite path was traced by U.S. government bonds. Their prices rose $1–$4 which reduced U.S. bond yields from an average of 3.92% in March 1932 to 3.76% in June. (See Table A.40 in the Statistical Appendix.) In April 1932, as we have already seen, the Federal Reserve began the most aggressive open market purchase program in its history, which expanded Federal Reserve holdings of U.S. government securities from $872 million at the end of March to $1,841 million at the end of July. During this period, the Federal Reserve bought $185 million of 1- to 5-year notes and $93 million of long-term bonds. The $744 million balance of Federal Reserve purchases was in U.S. securities under 1 year to maturity.[4]

The Federal Reserve publicly stated its policy during this open market purchase program and at one point in May even reassured the public that it intended to continue buying U.S. governments. Purchases finally came to a halt in August, after which Federal Reserve holdings of U.S. securities remained very stable at $1,850 million. U.S. bond yields remained relatively stable around 3.45% for the rest of the year, as well. The month-end yields on long-term U.S. bonds are outlined in Table 12.1.

This trend of U.S. bond prices reflected Federal Reserve open market purchases and investors' search for liquidity, but this judgment is simpler in retrospect than it was then, for other factors muddy this simple equation. For example, net new U.S. borrowing in 1932 exceeded $3 billion, and the federal budget deficit exceeded $2.5 billion, over one-half of federal expenditures. The social crisis which grew out of the economic crisis and expressed itself in the form of "Kingfish" Huey Long, Father Coughlin, Brownshirt gangs, the Bonus March on Washington, rising socialist and communist sympathies, and strikes and violence should also have affected the U.S. bond market negatively. Congress accurately reflected the apparent dichotomy between fiscal responsibility and ministering to the economic needs of the public and industry by refusing to pass a tax bill to raise $1.5 billion in new revenues during three months of debate. Banks and financial commentators repeatedly pointed to this delay and apparent irresponsibility as the principal cause of the weak bond and stock markets and lack of business confidence. If this was true, why did it not affect the U.S. bond market, where the results of a budget deficit would be most directly expressed?

The same question can be asked of Franklin Roosevelt's impact on the bond market. Roosevelt swept the Democratic primaries in New Hampshire, Minnesota, Georgia, Iowa, and Maine during March 1932, and the *New York Times* was calling him a "sure winner" for the Democratic nomination. It became clear that Roosevelt had an excellent opportunity to become President almost simultaneously with the April–June decline in bond and stock prices, yet again the U.S. government bond market where he would have his most direct impact remained unaffected.

The U.S. bond market should also have been affected by the sudden drain of U.S. gold reserves in the April–June quarter. Gold outflow exceeded $200 million in each of May and June 1932 after an apparent end to gold outflows in the prior two months. Only September and October 1931, during the Sterling Crisis, had equal gold reserve losses.

The Last Half of 1932

The corporate bond market recovered in the third quarter as quickly as it had declined in the second quarter, in line with improvement in the stock market and modest recovery in the economy. Moody's index of Baa railroad bond yields declined over 600 basis points to 8.15% by the end of September 1932, and yields declined roughly 300 basis points for A rated railroads, Baa rated utilities,

Table 12.1
Month-End Yields on U.S. Government Bonds, 1932 (percent)

January	February	March	April	May	June	July	August	September	October	November	December
4.26	4.11	3.92	3.68	3.76	3.76	3.58	3.45	3.42	3.43	3.45	3.35

Source: Banking & Monetary Statistics, p. 470.

and Baa rated industrials. Moody's indices for Aaa utility, industrial, and railroad bond yields declined roughly 50–100 basis points in the same quarter. New-issue business increased from less than $50 million per month in the first half of the year to $112 million in July and $133 million in August.

Railroad bonds and Baa utility bond prices began to weaken again in the fourth quarter, so that Moody's indices of their yields rose 50–100 basis points. At the same time, high grade industrial and utility bond prices continued to improve, which meant the two sectors of the market were again moving in different directions.

This last-half improvement in bond prices (except for rails and low grade utilities in the fourth quarter) reflected many factors. The economy began to improve noticeably, the RFC began loans to the states for relief and work projects, the Home Loan Banks began to operate, and Congress passed a $2.1 billion relief bill, which Hoover signed. One of the most important factors was a swing in insurance company cash flows. Their policy loans had risen to $3.5 billion— 18% of their investments—by mid-1932, up from $2.1 billion in 1929, but this trend reversed in the second half of 1932, so that by year end the insurance companies had become aggressive bond buyers. The Equitable Insurance Co. was buying utility issues on a massive scale, and it and other insurance companies were buying up whole new issues.[5]

It is surprising that such a strong bond market recovery occurred, because there were many contrary influences. Roosevelt was elected amid widespread brokerage commentary that his success would halt the economic recovery and provoke a new crisis in securities markets. The Federal Reserve halted its open market purchases after August, and Hoover tried to get its Chairman, Eugene Meyer, and other directors to hold Roosevelt hostage to their credit policies or resign en masse. Bank problems were obviously accelerating as well. Nevada closed its banks in November, and the Detroit banks' difficulties were becoming public knowledge as the Guardian Detroit Union Group reported a deficit, stopped dividends, and borrowed heavily from the Ford Motor Co., Edsel Ford, and the RFC. Banks closed in Oklahoma and Pittsburgh. New York City suddenly plunged into a major crisis as the municipal note and bond markets closed to it, and the banks refused to lend further to the city without a radical change in its budget. To make matters worse, England and France joined Germany in pressing for an end to war debt payments, and Roosevelt not only opposed any settlement of the war debts but also hinted that he might consider devaluing the U.S. dollar.

No economic rationale can be constructed to explain the bond market's second-half behavior, such as the decline in business investment and financing creating a shortage of bonds relative to the demand for them by savers. Such an argument would have applied even better in the second quarter of 1932, when bond prices were declining, and in any case, saving was also declining sharply on all fronts— individuals were using up their savings, business was losing money, and banks were reducing assets.

The only adequate explanation of the change in trend appears to be that the crisis in confidence of the second quarter was overcome, panic had run its course, and a safer view of the future prevailed. Two notable aspects of such a conclusion are that it supported the business community's emphasis on restoring confidence and that the restoration of confidence was apparent six months before the bank crisis of 1933. The bond market, like farmers, is never happy, but it closed out 1932 in much relieved condition and was on its way to a better 1933.

THE MUNICIPAL BOND MARKET SEPARATES SHARPLY INTO HIGH GRADE AND LOW GRADE CREDITS BECAUSE LOCAL GOVERNMENTS DEVELOP SEVERE FINANCIAL PROBLEMS FOR THE FIRST TIME IN THE DEPRESSION

State and local governments in urban, suburban, and rural locales across the nation began to experience widespread financial difficulties in 1932. Tax receipts at the state level fell in 1932 for the first time[6] and undoubtedly fell at city and town levels as well. Tax arrears skyrocketed in the large cities. Local governments also felt the effects of the Depression on their expenses, which tended to rise because of local responsibility for the welfare and sustenance of the unemployed.

Cities generally felt the effects of the Depression more than states, because the cities bore a heavier share of local government expenditures. Local governments spent $8.3 billion in 1932, compared with $4.4 billion spent by the federal government and only $2.4 billion spent by state governments. Local government expenditures had grown more too. They were up by 361% since 1913, compared with a 100% increase for state governments and only 13% for the federal government.[7] Financiers generally condemned cities for such expenditure growth, rather than the system for misplacing the burden of expenditures.

Reflecting these financial pressures on local governments, the municipal bond market in 1932 separated into two tiers of high grade and lower grade issues. The yield on Standard & Poor's high grade municipal bond index reached a peak of 5.03% in February 1932, as the market disruption caused by the international currency crisis carried over into 1932. After February, however, high-grade yields declined to a low of 4 3/4% in the last half of 1932. New York State, New Jersey, Missouri, and California, among the Aaa states with more than $100 million in outstanding debt, remained popular credits and had no difficulty selling bonds.

Municipal credits generally did not show the same degree of deterioration as corporate credits. Defaulted municipal issues, as of September 1, 1932, were only 1.8% of outstanding issues, compared with 19.4% of foreign issues, 14% of real estate issues, 7.2% of industrial issues, 5.4% of utility issues, and 3.5% of railroad issues. This record enabled municipalities to continue financing, and as a result they accounted for 49% of all new securities issues in 1932, compared with less than 20% in 1928–30.

The low grade tier of the municipal market experienced problems similar to the low grade tier of the corporate bond market, however. There were 25 bond rating reductions in 1932 among the 48 states and 20 largest cities, compared with 13 in 1931. Alabama, Arkansas, Chicago, Detroit, and Louisiana had been rated Aaa in 1930 but were now rated Baa, or even lost their ratings altogether, as in the case of Chicago and Louisiana. Mississippi, North Carolina, North Dakota, Philadelphia, South Carolina, South Dakota, and Tennessee dropped to an A rating. (See Table A.11 in the Statistical Appendix.) These bond rating reductions reflected underlying financial problems which were tied to declining incomes in the rural areas and rising welfare costs in the cities. States in the Southeast were especially affected. Much of Florida was in default. Ashville and Buncombe counties in North Carolina defaulted on a combined total of $50 million. Arkansas' road improvement districts were clearly going to default on what amounted to the highest per capita debt burden in the United States. Alabama, Tennessee, South Carolina, Louisiana, and Mississippi struggled with deficits and bond maturities which the market was unwilling to refund gracefully. Northern cities had similar problems. Chicago, Detroit, New York, Newark, and Philadelphia were unable to sell bonds much of the year and relied on the banking system instead.

The market reaction to these problems can be anticipated. Lower grade bond yields diverged considerably from high grade bond yields. Baa issues reached yields of 7–7 1/4%, and A rated issues reached yields of approximately 6 1/4%, compared with 5 1/4% on Aa issues and only 4 1/2% on Aaa issues. There was no secondary market throughout the year for Detroit and Michigan bonds, and there were various extended periods during the year when there was no secondary market for the bonds of Arkansas, Chicago, Louisiana, and North Carolina. At the worst point in the market, in January and February 1932, when the municipal bonds held by closed banks were being liquidated on a large scale, Salt Lake City, South Carolina, Elizabeth (New Jersey), Sacramento County (California), Newark (New Jersey), and Tennessee were unable to get bids on their competitive bond sales.

The problems of the cities were widely illustrated in New York City, which experienced a serious financial crisis in 1932. Over 1,150,000 persons were estimated to be unemployed in the city, and their ranks had been swelled by a quarter of a million persons who had migrated to the city from other states, seeking sustenance and opportunity. The city's debt had risen to over $2.1 billion, and its debt service requirements had doubled to over $200 million in the past ten years (see Table 12.2). Tax arrears had jumped to 19% of the 1931 tax levy and were expected to be higher in 1932. Revenues were expected to be further reduced by a record number of requests for lower tax assessments on city properties, to which the city broadly acceded with an across-the-board 7% cut in assessments later in the year. A drive to reopen the city's budget began in January 1932, as the budget deficit appeared likely to be in the area of $42–$44 million on a planned budget of $631 million.

The city also planned a capital budget of $108 million, for which it typically

Table 12.2
New York City Debt, 1922–1932 ($ millions)

	1922	1926	1927	1928	1929	1930	1931	1932
Outstanding debt	$1,293	1,566	1,661	1,762	1,859	1,969	2,128	2,246
Debt service requirements	$ 104	128	137	151	160	171	196	201

Source: New York Times, 12/1/32, p. 12.

borrowed from internal pension and sinking funds, and this program was also in trouble. It was too large in absolute terms, but it was also attacked by bankers and other financial observers because the revenue-producing operations it financed were not self-sustaining, particularly the subway, which had a politically sensitive 5¢ fare. Current expense items were also thought to be hidden in the capital budget, but it was too complicated to determine these clearly.

Perhaps the city's biggest problem was its mayor, Jimmy Walker. The sprightly Walker was handsome, affable, and a remarkable publicity symbol for the joys of New York City. He loved and frequented its theaters, restaurants, and women, opened the city to prominent visitors, and trumpeted its virtues abroad. Unfortunately, he was also disorganized, irresponsible, and trapped in the corrupt practices of Tammany Hall. Like his city, he was broke. He was also under intense attack from Judge Samuel Seabury, who had been specially commissioned by Governor Roosevelt to inquire into New York City Democratic Party corruption. Seabury's revelations of Walker's financial practices disclosed that the Mayor himself might be criminally liable. Unlike Walker, however, the city was fundamentally sound. Its wealth was so great that it accounted for approximately one-quarter of all federal Treasury receipts. Charles Mitchell of National City Bank later remarked that the city's difficulties were due to the policies it pursued rather than its credit.

The opening volley in the New York City crisis occurred in January, when Controller Charles W. Berry asked the banks for assistance in a $90 million loan which the bond market could not handle in normal competitive bidding fashion and which was necessary to meet city bond maturities of $55 million. The bankers, represented by Thomas Lamont of J. P. Morgan & Co. and Charles Mitchell, pressed Mayor Walker to cut the city budget and raise the 5¢ subway fare before they would underwrite the loan.

The bankers received a taste of the Mayor's attitude before they worked out an agreement when Walker condemned them publicly for "squeezing" the city and grinding the poor. Initially, he refused the bankers' demands until a federal loan, which he sought, was voted down in Congress. The banks, too, showed their mettle before reaching agreement on the loan when they lent the city only $12.5 million for 11 days at 6%, which the city combined with $15 million of its own cash to meet a bond maturity.

Price Waterhouse was brought in to review the city's records and advise the bankers. Under examination, the city's current loan requirements jumped from $90 million to $120 million and then to $150 million. Finally, a $351 million package to carry the city through the full year was worked out with 34 banks, which agreed to underwrite, at no profit, two 6% issues of $100 million each, due in 3–5 years, and to provide $151 million directly under a line of credit for contingency borrowing.

Mayor Walker had shelved plans for the midtown tunnel and deferred additional subway construction, totalling $110 million, before the $351 million agreement was reached, but the bankers were not impressed with these capital budget changes and demanded much more. The Board of Estimate gave the bankers a resolution promising financial retrenchment, a reduction in civic activities, and that the subway and other toll facilities would be put on a self-sustaining basis. Relief requirements of $20 million were cut to $10.5 million, new applications for home relief were refused, thousands of per diem city employees were put on a five-day week, and there was talk of a 25% cut in policemen's and firemen's pay or that 9,000 would be laid off.

The first installment of the $351 million was a public issue in January of $100 million in bonds due in 1935–37 at 5 3/4%. The issue was a great success, but the 5 3/4% interest rate compared with approximately 4 1/2% for high grade credits of comparable maturity and 3% on a $52 million 4-year New York Rapid Transit issue in 1931.

The budget dispute persisted in February and March despite the new credit agreement. Controller Berry estimated the deficit would still be $42 million and asked a halt in construction of $231 million in public works. Thirty civic groups joined with Berry to request a cut in civic salaries and an increase in the subway fare to 10¢. The Mayor and the Board of Estimate acceded to $213 million in construction budget cuts in March, and a second $100 million bond issue was made. However, Berry remained intensely critical of the Mayor in public for not making budget cuts beyond the construction program, accusing Walker of making all his cuts on paper. Berry, the Real Estate Board of New York, and the Fifth Avenue Association attacked the Mayor for failing to provide leadership and making no reductions in the city's operating costs; at the same time, Frank J. Taylor, City Commissioner of Welfare, claimed that the city's welfare program would collapse without $20 million more from June through November. True to his instincts, Walker cried that he could cut no more. With this reaction off his chest, he ordered his cabinet members to slash their budgets or quit.

The city borrowed under the $151 million bank line in July, and further budget cuts began. Summer school was eliminated, school repairs were stopped. The Mayor also sought a voluntary pay cut by city workers of one month's pay. A cut could not be forced on civic workers because most salary scales were mandated by New York State law. The city's position changed suddenly in September, when Mayor Walker resigned following arduous testimony exposing his personal affairs before Judge Seabury and Governor Roosevelt. It was found that Walker had gained over $250,000 in securities transactions which appeared to have been rigged to produce the profit, that his trip expenses abroad had been paid by benefactors, and that he had received loans and gifts exceeding $300,000. His brother, a doctor, was also exposed for receiving over $400,000 in fees split with him by doctors treating city employees.

Mayor Walker's successor, Joseph V. McKee, had been President of the Board of Estimate. He appeared to have honesty, courage, intelligence, and forthrightness—qualities necessary for the city's recovery. He immediately cut his own pay from $45,000 to $25,000 and limited the pay of his department heads to $12,000. His first budget request was for a reduction of $80 million on a budget of $425 million, exclusive of debt service. New York City bond prices jumped $3–$3 1/2 in the secondary markets, and bankers suggested that a long-term bond issue might be possible for the city.

Relations between McKee, Berry, and Tammany Hall began to deteriorate rapidly, however, and McKee was able to achieve little. When McKee proposed a 6% pay cut for civic employees, Berry attacked the plan in a bid for support for the coming mayoralty nomination. Berry suddenly was opposed to salary cuts and favored budget savings obtained by funding short-term subway debt, which would reduce debt service payments in the budget. He was joined by Tammany Hall members of the Board of Estimate whom McKee had previously attacked. This group was effectively able to place tentative budget preparations for 1933 in Berry's hands rather than McKee's. The resulting budget had only $6.7 million in cuts, with virtually no recognition of McKee's requested budget cuts.

The bond market took little time to evaluate this turn of events. New York City 4 1/4% bonds due in 1960–81, which had been selling around $95, dropped to $85 within three weeks. The bankers told Berry that they could provide no assistance in floating further loans until the politicians lived up to the promises of January 1932 to make substantial budget cuts. Charles Mitchell, speaking for National City Bank and the Chase National Bank, refused to co-manage a city bond issue unless budget economies of $75 million were realized. In his words, "There is no market today for New York City bonds." The Board of Estimate cut expenses $74.2 million and adopted a budget of $557.1 million, including debt service, but the bankers and citizens' watchdog groups remained dissatisfied, as only $17.8 million in real savings was effected.

A confrontation appeared to be brewing between the bankers and the politicians. When the banks refused the city $25 million to fund relief measures through the next six months, Al Smith warned of riots: "This thing is an insurance policy against possible riot and disorder." However, Chase National Bank and National City Bank did agree to see the city through the November elections in its financial requirements. The breaking point in the confrontation appeared to be December 15, 1932, when the city had its $151 million bank loan coming due, plus $52 million in bonds. Revenues were expected to be only $175 million in the period to December 15th, which left a shortfall of $28 million. The city also needed $200 million for operations between December and May until tax revenues came in again.

Berry tried to force the banks' hand in a contest of wills by postponing paying the city's bills, but by early December he gave in and recommended salary cuts, a new capital budget, and an increase in the subway fare to cover the pending $90 million subway deficit. New York's new Governor, Herbert Lehman, called a special session of the legislature to remove the mandatory wage laws for the city and to allow the city to reopen its budget. The Board of Estimate thereupon voted a $20 million reduction in salaries and wages for 1933. The bankers remained dissatisfied, and they obtained a second $20 million reduction in return for a $40 million loan and a promise to see the city through its critical December 15th obligations. Shortly thereafter, Comptroller Berry negotiated a $110 million loan for the city.

New York City was revealed to have several serious problems during this year of financial bargaining. Samuel Seabury uncovered massive corruption in the political structure of the city, most of which could be laid at the feet of Tammany Hall. Patronage was heavy in city employment, it affected pier leases and other city licenses, and construction contracts were given to the party faithful and on the basis of bribes and gifts. Aside from corruption, the city's records were in disarray. There was no credible data on city revenues or expenses, and Comptroller Berry's estimates of the city's cash needs were notoriously inaccurate. The city's need to borrow escalated by multiples of what was expected even within the month under discussion. Financial abuses were also opened up, such as selling city notes to the sinking funds set up for city bonds rather than purchasing outstanding bonds, and carrying tax arrears over from prior years as anticipated revenues in each succeeding year's budget. Professor Joseph Mc-Goldrick of Columbia University suggested that 1931 tax collections were $46 million below the budget estimate and that 1932 collections were $171 million below estimates. Property tax arrears were skyrocketing, of course, as commercial buildings defaulted and were foreclosed. The capital budget had also grown out of proportion, because projects which were supposed to be self-supporting were incurring deficits, and current overhead costs were being put into the capital budget. Finally, the city's debt load in absolute terms had become a problem, for the city's $2.25 billion in debts equalled the debts of the 47 other states.

The effects of the New York City crisis on its bonds were quite clear. New York City bonds traded at yields 1 1/2%–2% above New York State bonds during most of 1932 because of the city's financial problems. While New York State's bond prices rose steadily all year, New York City bonds traded at yields over 5% in December 1931 for the first time in a decade; they traded over 6% in July 1932, at the peak of the bankers' quarrels with Mayor Walker; they traded as low as 4 1/2% in September, when both stock and bond markets were at their best for the year and Mayor Walker had been replaced by Joseph McKee. But the city's bonds dropped again by over $10 per $100 in October and November, when it became clear that McKee did not have the support of his party and would get neither the Democratic nomination for Mayor nor City Council support for his budget. By the end of 1932 there was virtually no market for the city's bonds.

Other cities had problems similar to those of New York City. In Chicago there was a curious mixture of credit decline and legal tangles. The patronage and corruption of its gangland Mayor, Tony Cermak, was expressed in the quip "If Big Bill Thompson took Chicago for a ride, Tony Cermak would take it for a tour." As the Illinois legislature met in February, Chicago's delinquent taxes were $690 million, it was behind $45 million in civic employees' wages, and its teachers had been paid for only two months since April 1931. The legislature voted to adjourn without aid to Chicago, and Cermak threatened to nail shut the schools and City Hall. Some 500,000 persons were estimated to be destitute in Chicago, of which 120,000 were starving. Business had come to a stop. Suburban towns had declared business moratoriums, stopping all activities to prevent foreclosures from destroying the communities. In June 1932, Cook County actually defaulted on $1.7 million in interest and principal payments. Chicago's bonds dropped to prices which provided yields over 7%, and there was no market for a new Chicago bond issue on any terms. The city turned to the federal government, seeking a loan, but the bill was defeated in Congress even as it approved a $300 million program for local loans to be administered by the RFC.

Chicago's financial problem was related to a court fight in which property owners were successfully contesting the heavy taxes on real estate when there were no taxes on personal property. This conflict was resolved in July, when the presiding judge found in favor of the city's historic property tax practice and ordered tax sales on 600,000 realty parcels. Back taxes for 1928–30 poured in until they were virtually caught up by August. Pay arrears were caught up by September, except for teachers. The city had paid its outstanding tax warrants by the end of the year and was hoping for an A rating again in order to refund with long-term bonds a $15 million bond maturity. The prospects for this had already been reflected in the market, where Chicago's bonds had moved from $70 to $86, reducing the yield to 5.25%.

Detroit, by contrast, was a ravaged city crushed by the decline in the auto business. It had a $6 million deficit in its budget, $45 million in short-term debt, and bankers pressing it to balance the budget. Few other cities experienced a collapse in real estate values to the depths reached in Detroit. It was no coincidence that the first major statewide bank holiday occurred in Michigan. Detroit's tax collections were 36% delinquent. Some $50 million of its $60 million in tax collections went for debt service on over $400 million in debts, which the Common Council had voted as a prior lien on taxes in order to get Chicago and New York banks to renew $27 million in short-term debt. Civic employee salaries were cut 50% and everyone was put on a five-day week. Detroit was one of the first cities to experience labor violence when workers marched on Ford's River Rouge plant demanding jobs and guards opened fire on the men. A Communist protest rally at Arena Gardens attracted an overflow crowd of 6,000 people.

In July, Newark was unable to sell bonds to meet short-term debt maturities. Local institutions such as the Prudential Life, Mutual Benefit Life, Fidelity Union Trust, and National Newark & Essex Bank lent the city $6 million to prevent a default. The New York City banks ultimately rolled over the city's debts after sharp pay cuts, but in December, Newark still had to defer wages due police and firemen.

Westchester County had to cut wages 10% for a second time during the year. Nassau County was put under the control of a Bankers' Committee headed by

W. C. Potter, President of the Guaranty Trust Co. Atlantic City deferred wages due employees, and Philadelphia cut wages 22%.

New York State suffered a drop in revenues that forced it to sell its first tax anticipation notes since 1915, but it came through the year with its credit intact. Roosevelt doubled the state income tax to raise $76 million and cut the budget $21.5 million to $301 million, which created confidence in the state, despite a 1931 deficit of approximately $60 million. The state was able to borrow $50 million for one year in March at 3 1/2% with great success, and in December it sold $30 million in 50-year bonds at 3%. The state was strong enough to speed payments to New York City to assist it.

In the South, Tennessee was able to refund only a $12 million bond maturity through a negotiated sale at 5 3/4% worked out over two months of budget cuts and promises. South Carolina was unable to sell $5 million in bonds to meet a maturity and had to borrow from the banks. Mississippi was forced to institute a 2% sales tax to balance its budget. The new Governor of Arkansas, J. Marvin Futrell, campaigned on a promise to cut the state's budget 50% and to reduce its $200 million in debt, the largest per capita debt in the nation.

No city or state could sell bonds without the promise of a balanced budget. Even then, there was concern over cities' credits. The Massachusetts Public Utility Department refused to permit a bond sale by the Boston Metropolitan District with an 8-year non-call period and a call price of $105, even if it put the district temporarily in default until a new issue was sold callable in 5 years at $102 1/2. If political goals were coming into such conflict with financial requirements that default was an acceptable alternative, what could investors rely on?

Old habits had to give way in the crisis. Negotiated bond sales replaced competitive bids. Uncertainty was so great that few dealers would bid for any but the best bonds. Many bond sales were worked out only on a "best efforts" basis. Maturities of 1–5 years were sold frequently when long-term bonds could not be marketed, and serial bonds providing for orderly principal repayments each year replaced long-term bonds with a single maturity in which all principal was due at once.

The credit problems of municipal governments produced varying reactions in search of remedies. In Florida, the courts took relatively strong positions in support of bondholders. A special tax was levied in St. Petersburg for debt service, and tax receipts were split by the courts between debt service and city services in several cities. States changed their regulations on the financing of deficits, shifting from immediate budget balancing requirements to allow borrowing amortized over a few years. Loan limits related to budgets or property assessments were raised.

Budgets were cut everywhere, often by 30% or more. The American Society of Engineers estimated that $2 billion in public works were suspended. Layoffs were common, as were alternatives which maintained the work force, such as the five-day week, pay reductions, part-time work, forced vacations, and delayed paychecks. Many cities changed their annual tax collection practices to monthly or quarterly collections to avoid borrowing and paying interest but thereby passing the burden of raising money on to their constituents. The most troubled cities appealed to local businesses to pay their property taxes in advance. The same cities frequently came under the control of bankers' committees which lent the money to cover current deficits but took control of the city budget to assure repayment. It was a *sauve-qui-peut* environment.

Pressures built on the federal government during the year to come to the aid of local governments. Senate Leader Robinson wanted a $300 million federal bond issue to aid the states and cities, and $200 million for self-liquidating local government projects. Mayors of 28 cities joined to request a $5 billion bond issue for public works, proving they had not lost the imagination to spend, just the means. The first relief was in June, when Congress approved $300 million in RFC loans to the states. Thirty states asked for $200 million within the following month. New York State requested $50 million to raze and rebuild New York City's slums, and New York City asked for a further $120 million for the same purpose as well as for $50 million to finance construction of the Triborough Bridge. The RFC tended to parcel out its largesse in smaller amounts, however.

Illinois was first into the new honey pot when the RFC lent it $3 million on July 27, 1932, to supplement local relief. There was a flood of requests thereafter, and borrowings within the year by Arizona, Arkansas, Birmingham, Colorado, Florida, Idaho, Missouri, Montana, Newark, New York City, New York State, North Dakota, South Dakota, Utah, and West Virginia. The RFC also made its first self-liquidating municipal loan—$40 million—toward the $284 million water project of the Metropolitan Water District of Southern California.

But this limited aid was not enough. The low grade tier of the municipal bond market was still large and demoralized at the end of 1932.

THE FOREIGN BOND MARKET—THE INTERNATIONAL FINANCE SYSTEM CONTRACTS DUE TO TRADE BARRIERS, WAR DEBTS, DEFAULTS, AND LOSS OF CONFIDENCE

In 1932 the international events set in motion during the prior year were carried to their denouement. The value of world trade shrunk to approximately one-third of its 1929 level, crippling the debtor economies of Eastern Europe and South America. Trade barriers reached new heights as each country sought to preserve its own home market. England ended an historic era of free trade in August, following the Imperial Economic Conference in Canada, when it introduced a system of preferential tariffs on natural products to foster trade within the British Empire. Germany raised its tariffs 100% during the year in a futile effort to combat its foreign exchange problems, and thereby drove its imports down to the levels of 1898. Austria set import quotas for the same purpose. And the United States, which had begun the process in 1930 with the Smoot-Hawley

Tariff, applied tariffs to gasoline and oil imports which eliminated those two imports.

During 1932, arguments over the war debts and reparations created more of a problem for confidence in the economy than a financial problem. Congress extended the moratorium on war debts in December 1931 by sizable majorities, but because $11.2 billion of the original $13.8 billion remained to be paid, there was great uncertainty whether the United States would ultimately forgive the total, and the uncertainty created a corresponding burden on the budgets of the paying countries. In January, Chancellor Heinrich Bruening publicly repudiated Germany's obligation for reparations and made no provision in the 1932 budget for reparations payments. Italy proposed that all Europe repudiate its war debts in coordination and cancel reparations. France and England, in notes to the U.S. government, sought to renegotiate their war debts with the United States and in turn were willing to renegotiate Germany's reparations payments, but Treasury Secretary Mills refused a meeting on the subject. Hopes for a resolution of the problem were kindled in midyear when the European countries met in Lausanne, Switzerland, without the United States and agreed to end German reparations payments in return for $750 million in German bonds. The hope faded, however, when a "gentleman's agreement" was revealed conditioning the end to reparations on U.S. cancellation of Europe's war debts, which the United States refused to do.

As the December 1932 payment date approached, England and France petitioned the United States for a further extension of the moratorium on payments, and *The Economist*, England's respected financial weekly, recommended that England default on its obligations if the moratorium was refused. The timing of the issue fell uncomfortably into the interregnum between the Hoover and Roosevelt Administrations and into a disagreement between them on how to deal with the issue—Roosevelt preferring to deal individually with each debtor country to extract the best possible bargain. The moratorium was therefore not extended, and in December, France, Belgium, Hungary, and Poland defaulted on their war debts. England paid its installment, as due, in gold.

The impact of the war debts controversy on confidence in the economy was significant. Prominent bankers in the United States, such as Mitchell, Wiggin, and Lamont, considered the war debts to be the source of many current economic problems, as did many lesser financial figures. The Economic Committee of the League of Nations expressed the fear that there was no hope for trade renewal until credit relations were straightened out. Even trade unions called for cancelling the war debts.

Trade restrictions, the war debts, and the poor world economy combined to produce widely divergent bond prices for different foreign countries. The bonds of the best foreign credits, notably Canada, France, Switzerland, and the United Kingdom, were relatively stable. As the impact of the 1931 currency crisis wore off, prices of these countries' bonds recovered to within a few dollars of their best prices in prior years, and the yields on these bonds at their highest prices for 1932 were within 25–75 basis points of the yields on the very best domestic corporate issues—a relationship again close to the best bond market periods of prior years. The superiority of these four foreign issuers was reflected in other ways: their lowest yields ranged from 3.94% to 5.13%, compared with the Scandinavian countries at 5.75%–8.60% and other good foreign credits at over 7%; bonds of these four also showed the least variation against their 1931 bond price ranges, with the exception of Canada. There were stories behind each of these issuers.

The United Kingdom staged a dramatic recovery from the devaluation of sterling in 1931. The sterling exchange rate recovered from its lowest monthly average of approximately $3.37 in December 1931 to a high of $3.75 in April 1932.[8] After the drastic deficits and cutbacks of 1930–31, a budget surplus of $1.4 million was realized. All England's international borrowings from 1931 were prepaid by mid-1932, the bank rate was reduced in steps from 6% to 2%, and a complete refunding of the U.K. public debt was carried out at these lower rates. There was marked improvement in the export sectors of the U.K. economy, and for the first time in years there was a strong domestic new-issue bond market.

This strength was naturally reflected in the U.S. market for U.K bonds. Moody's maintained its Aaa rating on U.K. bonds, which traded in a price range between $107 and $90. (See Table A.15 in the Statistical Appendix for price and yield data on foreign bonds referred to in this section.) This high price provided the lowest yield in the foreign market and compared with the best prices of prior years.

Canada's bonds retained their premier position in the U.S. market, but not without some tremors. Canada, Ontario, Toronto, Quebec, and Montreal had all been downgraded from Aaa to Aa by *Moody's* in 1931, and Toronto and Montreal, as well as Nova Scotia, were further reduced to A ratings in 1932; New Brunswick had been reduced to A in 1931. By 1932, ratings were reduced to Baa on bonds of all the Western Canadian provinces, and British Columbia had to borrow $3.7 million from the federal government to meet U.S. debt service. The drop in the U.S. exchange rate for the Canadian dollar from $1.00 to approximately 82.75¢ in December 1931 was particularly disconcerting to investors. British Columbia, Montreal, and New Brunswick tried to float U.S. issues during the year without success, but Montreal and New Brunswick sold issues in Canada, thereby beginning the development of an indigenous Canadian market.

These negative influences were reflected in Canadian bond prices. Canada 4% bonds of 1960 sold as low as $71 in 1932, where the yield was 6.19%, the highest of the best foreign bonds; but the recovery in Canadian bonds was strong as the year progressed, and in line with the exchange rate, which improved to a peak of 91.25¢ in October. The high price of $92 for Canada 4% bonds due in 1960 provided a yield of only 4.51%, the lowest foreign yield except for on

U.K. bonds, which were of a much shorter maturity—1937. There was a 44% rise from the low price on these Canada bonds in 1931 to their high price in 1932, the best opportunity to make money in the high quality foreign issues.

France's bonds were made especially attractive by that country's strong foreign exchange position. Following its large losses in the devaluation of sterling, the Bank of France set a public policy of repatriating its reserves deposited abroad. Thereby France's gold reserves rose from $2.2 billion in mid-1931 to $3.3 billion by the end of 1932, principally because of withdrawals from the United States. The French franc exchange rate remained stable at 3.9¢, where it had been since 1926, but the strong upward pressure on it resulted in a rise to 6¢ in 1933. The prices of France's 7% external bonds due in 1949 ranged between $121 and $109 in 1932, which was little change from prior years.

Following the Sterling Crisis, Switzerland, like France, rapidly increased its gold reserves from approximately $125 million to over $500 million; its currency remained stable at approximately 19¢ per franc, where it had been since 1925 (and prior to World War I). However, this influx of capital into Switzerland forced the exchange rate for the Swiss franc up over 30¢ in 1933.[9] In this very favorable atmosphere, the prices of Switzerland's 5 1/2% external bonds due in 1946 were stable between $99 and $107 every year from 1929 to 1932, the narrowest price range of any foreign government bond. Even at the lowest prices in the 1932 market, Switzerland's yield of only 5.40% was as low as that on many of the best railroad bonds and within 30–40 basis points of the other best corporate bonds.

The bond prices of less creditworthy nations were more volatile in 1932, and their problems were reflected by Moody's, which reduced the bond ratings of Argentina, Denmark, Japan, and Norway in 1932. Austria's bond rating dropped from A to Ba, and Czechoslovakia's dropped from Baa to Ba. All Eastern Europe was rated Ba by the end of 1932. (See Table A.10 in the Statistical Appendix for ratings details on Canadian and other foreign governments.)

The Scandinavian countries were rocked by the collapse of the Kreuger empire. Ivar Kreuger, a Swede, had built an international business on loans and matches, trading loans to hard-pressed European countries for monopolies of their match markets. Like other bondholders, he found himself holding mostly worthless paper in 1932. Kreuger committed suicide in March 1932. His problems preceded 1932, however, for his empire was built on fraud, forged securities, and worthless loans. Mahler's Bank in Amsterdam had suspected as much in 1929 when it broke off its role as Kreuger's Dutch representative. Ernst & Ernst, accountants to his company, Kreuger & Toll, refused in 1929 to put their name to Kreuger & Toll's financial statements for a $50 million U.S. debenture offering managed by Lee, Higginson & Co. International Telephone & Telegraph confronted Kreuger directly with the accusation that he had falsified his balance sheets in 1929 after they had spent ten days going over his books in negotiations to buy Ericson Telephone Co. from him.

Prior to 1931, Kreuger had always been able to raise funds one way or another to keep his empire going, but the collapse of the credits of the many marginal countries to which he had lent, and the increased scrutiny of all credits, made further money-raising difficult for him. During the first quarter of 1932, he became desperate for funds and rushed between New York and Paris, scratching for loans of any size. He became a haggard, depressed, and desperate figure in the clubs and offices of the investment bankers. As suspicious financiers began to uncover his true position, Kreuger shot himself in his Paris apartment.

The principal impact of his death was in Sweden, where the stock exchange was closed and a private debt moratorium declared. Within days a Committee of Six investigating Kreuger & Toll, and Kreuger's own affairs, discovered the truth. They found asset values too low to liquidate profitably. It was eventually determined that Kreuger's estate had a deficit of $192 million, and Kreuger & Toll had liabilities of $48 million in excess of its assets. Shock pervaded Sweden, and the Banken Scandinivska Enskilda was severely shaken because Kreuger had a significant equity position in it as well as large loans from it. The bank survived, however, which is more than can be said for Kreuger's U.S. investment bankers, Lee Higginson & Co., who were owed $9 million by Kreuger & Toll. They closed later in 1932. Otherwise, the effects of Kreuger's demise were limited to the Scandinavian countries and to holders of his bonds, who never realized a cent.

The Kreuger debacle captured public attention, but a more important impact on bond prices was the foreign exchange weaknesses of the Scandinavian countries following the collapse of sterling. The currencies of all four Scandinavian countries declined throughout 1932, with a slight upturn in the spring—declines which reflected the relative international weakness of their respective economies. Their relative declines from September 1931 to December 1932 are outlined below:

Sweden	31.4%
Denmark	32.7%
Norway	33.5%
Finland	43.4%

These declines were mirrored in the relative yields of each country's bonds at their low prices, which were 5.74% for Sweden, 5.77% for Denmark, 6.08% for Norway, and 8.60% for Finland. Finland's bonds were particularly depressed because the Finnish Residential Mortgage Bank had to seek a moratorium on its foreign debt during 1932.

The middle-ranking credits rated Baa were the Argentine, Australia, Cuba, Czechoslovakia, Finland, Germany, Italy and Japan. The market prices for these countries' bonds had more variation than did other, better credits, as one would expect, but there was a surprising degree of similarity among these bonds at their highest prices late in 1932. The average yield for the group at this point was 7.80%, which was almost the same as in 1929 and 1930, and for six of the eight countries these yields varied between only 7% and 8 3/4%.

Italy's 7% bonds due in 1951 were the most stable of this group. They traded between $99 and $82, and the yield was only 9% at the lowest price. There was considerable financial appreciation for the discipline Mussolini imposed on Italy, summed up in the remark "At least he makes the trains run on time." Italy did not devalue its currency in 1931, either, and actually increased its exchange rate in 1933.

Cuba's 5 1/2% bonds, due in 1953, also did well, trading between $83 and $68, the latter price also producing a yield close to 9%. Cuba's credit was in a special position among underdeveloped countries because of the Platt Amendment in the Treaty of 1901, settling the Spanish-American War. That amendment not only limited Cuba's ability to incur debt but even gave the United States the right to intervene in the country to secure creditors' interests.

The most divergent price behavior in this Baa group occurred in the bonds of the Argentine, Germany, and Japan. The Argentine's 5% bonds due in 1945 dropped to $41, where the yield was almost 16%, reflecting defaults by Argentine local governments on almost $90 million of foreign debts. The Argentine's exchange rate declined from over 90¢ per peso in 1930 to 58¢ in 1932, and there was a steady decline in the country's gold reserves from over $600 million in 1929 to approximately $250 million in 1932, despite a restricted currency.

In 1932, Japan was already tracing a military pattern which Germany would soon copy. Japan invaded Manchuria in 1931 and then attacked Shanghai in 1932. Militarists had taken over the Cabinet in 1931 and devoted the country's resources to conquest with little regard for its financial impact. Gold reserves dropped from $425 million in 1931 to $214 million in early 1932, when foreign exchange controls were imposed. Japan went off gold in December 1931, and by December 1932 the yen had dropped from 49¢ to 21¢. Correspondingly, Moody's lowered the rating to Baa on Japan's 5 1/2% bonds due in 1965, which dropped as low as $43, where their yield was over 13%.

There were opportunities in 1932 for courageous speculators to make significant profits from the price movements in these middle grade credits. Australia's bonds rose over 150% from their lowest 1931 price of $35; Finland's bonds doubled in price from a low of $34 in 1931 to a high of $68 in 1932; bonds of Argentina rose 92 1/2% from their 1931 low price; Japan's rose by 72%; and Czechoslovakia's rose by approximately 50%. However, it is unlikely that speculators made major profits. Foreign bonds were sold mostly to individuals in amounts under $5,000 and experienced low trading volume. Knowledgeable institutions and individuals were too frightened by the financial destruction surrounding them to speculate in securities that did not have highly positive stories. As in so many crises, bond prices moved up and down on little volume, and most investors stuck with their investments.

Even bigger profits were potentially available in the low grade South American and East European bonds. Investors could have tripled their money in the bonds of Chile, Peru, Bolivia, Uruguay, Yugoslavia, and Berlin between their low and their high prices for 1931–32, but in this case investors would have needed more than triple the fortitude necessary in the medium grade foreign credits, for all these issuers were in severe financial distress. Chile, Peru, Bolivia, and Uruguay were in default. Chile's bonds traded between $15 and $3 1/2, Peru's between $10 and $3, Bolivia's between $10 and $3 1/4. Their fellow South American issuers traded little better. Rio de Janeiro bonds traded between $14 and $5, Rio Grande do Sul bonds traded between $12 and $4 1/2, and Mexico bonds traded between $5 and $2. Brazil bonds managed to trade as high as $25, and Uruguay and Buenos Aires bonds were unique, trading as high as $40 and $38, respectively.

The economies of these countries were ravaged by the declines in foreign trade and the prices of the export commodities, on which they relied for foreign exchange. Efforts to raise prices by restricting production were unavailing, and most South American countries were caught in a cycle of cutting government expenses, raising taxes, and seeking domestic loans in order to maintain government capital spending and some hope of sustaining their economies. The financial problems engendered social problems. Revolutions were endemic, as were border wars and internal revolts.

The circumstances among low grade European issuers were barely better. Germany looked like the best of these credits since its bonds had been rated Aa, even though they were now rated Baa, and Germany's industrial skills were well known, but by midyear the country appeared to be on the edge of revolution. Hitler was strong enough to give Hindenburg a serious challenge in the March elections for the presidency of the Republic. The reliability of the Army was put in question by the resignation of General Goerner, and the reliability of the government was put in question by Hindenburg's ouster of Chancellor Bruening—both in May 1932. There were regular weekend street riots between Nazis and Communists in which deaths were frequent, in July the Reich took over the government of Prussia and declared a state of emergency in Berlin, in September the military pushed the Republic to request the right to rearm, and the country's finances appeared to be collapsing. The Standstill Agreement on bank credits was extended for another year, but the Central Bank suggested that a moratorium on private debts abroad might also be necessary, as German gold reserves continued to decline. They dropped to $192 million at year end, compared with over $600 million in 1930. During 1932 the state of Saxony became the first German government to default on its U.S. debts, followed closely by the City of Heidelberg, which defaulted on a $10 million U.S. issue. Berlin was clearly expected to default, as its 6% bonds traded down to $15. Germany's 5 1/2% bonds due in 1965 hit a low price for 1932 of $24 in this pessimistic atmosphere, a price at which the yield on the bonds was no longer meaningful. The clear implication of such a price was default.

In 1932, Germany's 5 1/2% bonds due in 1965 recovered from $24 to a high price of $60 during the Lausanne Agreement, when it appeared that a solution to the reparations and war debts problems had been found. A price of $60 was much below the 1931 high price of $84, but it still represented an opportunity for a gain of almost 175% from the 1931 low price. Given the situation outlined above, it took a hardy speculator to gamble on this price change.

The bonds of East European issuers other than Germany presented less hope for recovery than did Germany's bonds. Hungary defaulted in 1932 after trying without success to arrange a standstill agreement similar to Germany's. Estimates of U.S. holdings of Hungarian short- and long-term debts varied between $200 and $300 million. Austria was forced into a "standstill agreement" on its debts in which it paid annual interest and 5% of its principal owing, and Vienna and other local governments defaulted outright, as did Greece and Bulgaria. Yugoslavia defaulted on its own debt and blocked foreign dinar payments by all its nationals. At the end of 1932, all of $289 million in loans sponsored by the League of Nations for the rebuilding of Europe after World War I was in default, except for issues by Danzig and Estonia.

We can sum up this detailed outline of foreign bond price behavior with two points: Western Europe's bonds recovered from the 1931 currency convulsion, and the yields on the best bonds even challenged Aaa corporate bond yields. However, East European and South American issuers' bonds hit new low prices in 1932 and suffered such social and economic dislocations that even hardy speculators were unwilling to bet on earning profits from the wide price gyrations of these bonds. Since the former countries did not need new funds and the latter could not obtain them, the new-issue market dried up. New issues during the whole year totalled only $66 million, of which a 1-year issue by Canada in September, at the height of the recovery in all markets, accounted for $60 million. Secondary market trading did continue, principally because banks alone sold $90 million in foreign bonds. The lack of buyers' appetite for these issues was transparently evident in the low prices to which foreign bonds were driven. Indeed, many of these bonds were repatriated by nationals who could make use of the issuer's domestic currency when foreign exchange payments were blocked.

The foreign bond debacle was essentially complete by the end of 1932, which makes this an appropriate point to raise the question of what guilt should be ascribed to the various parties to these issues. Support for exonerating most of the parties is ample. The League of Nations directly sponsored many loans to aid in rebuilding war-torn Europe, and this spirit spread to many European loans not directly sponsored by the League of Nations. Public works and utilities projects in Europe, financed by many issues, were a valid contribution to public well-being. There was widespread optimism in the 1920s that economic progress would continue. Exchange rates were stable. Trade was growing. Commodities prices were stable, and projects to develop further commodities supplies in South American countries seemed appropriate. There was no international conflict, and the Kellogg-Briand Peace Pact appeared to be evidence that countries would in the future negotiate their differences. Moody's recognized the broadly favorable outlook by rating most foreign bond issues somewhere between Aaa and A, which were investment-quality ratings.

German reparations and the European countries' war debts remained problems, but almost no one was able to foresee at this time that they would become critical components in the breakdown of the international financial system. The Dawes Plan and the Young Plan in the 1920s represented two constructive efforts to negotiate and resolve these problems, and this gave the world reasonable confidence.

There is also ample evidence which can lead us to apportion blame to the investment bankers who handled foreign bond issues. Ilse Mintz, in her *Deterioration in the Quality of Foreign Bond Issues in the United States, 1920–1930*, found that among 11 investment bankers one investment banker had no defaults among the many issues it managed, a second investment banker had only one default, and six investment bankers managed 70% of the bonds which went into default. Clearly, some firms were able to make credit judgments that protected investors. Two additional facts point to investment bankers' awareness of the incipient credit problems in, and investor resistance to, South American and East European bond issues: (1) The underwriting spreads which they charged, ranging from 4% up to as high as 10%, compared with 2%–3% on domestic issues, reflected the need to dramatically compensate salesmen to get the bonds sold; and (2) the bonds had to be sold disproportionately to small investors, as indicated by Dwight Morrow in his 1932 *Foreign Affairs* analysis of the German 5 1/2% bonds due in 1960, sold in 1930. Investors buying less than $5,000 of this issue accounted for 56% of its distribution. This widespread small retail distribution was further confirmed in the membership of the many foreign bondholders' protective committees subsequently formed. The 1932 Senate Finance Subcommittee investigation into the issuance of foreign bonds also showed that investment bankers made payoffs to foreign officials to get the assignment to manage issues, and in some cases made no effort to determine that the proceeds would be productively spent or that the means to service the debt existed. These latter cases should not be overemphasized, however. There are always unprincipled borrowers who have little intention of repaying their debts waiting to take advantage of a booming market that will not scrutinize their motives. This is particularly true of governments which can claim their sovereignty as an excuse for inhibiting investigation and responsible reporting. There are always intermediaries who will be their agents also.

The fundamental cause of the large volume of foreign issues in the United States was America's wealth. The United States had accumulated almost half the world's gold reserves and had an annual foreign trade surplus of approximately $1 billion. This wealth had to be recycled to other countries if the international financial system was to be maintained, and other countries would have had a rightful grievance against the United States if it had not been a willing international lender.

This was an historic opportunity to remove to New York a business that had been dominated by London for over a century. It was outside the American ethic to let such an opportunity go by. Once this is conceded, the clean record of two investment bankers having only one defaulted issue between them loses its relevance. It required that they manage only issues for Canada and Western Europe. A market cannot be won by dominating only the best issuers. This is a fine policy for one or two firms, but not for an industry. There are average and below average issuers who make up most of the market and for whom financing intermediaries should also exist. Economic elitism to the degree necessary to constrict all the investment bankers to the issuers represented by the two most successful investment bankers has never been a serious theme in U.S. economics or finance.

It was therefore quite within the rules of the game for investment bankers to use high sales commissions to distribute lesser quality bond issues to the American public, who in turn received higher interest rates for taking greater risks. The bankers acted in good faith that the loans would be repaid, which they evidenced by making large short-term loans themselves to the issuers. Investment bankers could not foresee the decline in commodities prices and trade in the 1930s, which exceeded anything in the century, the collapse of Germany's credit, or the subsequent rise of Nazism, which wiped out hopes for an East European financial recovery. Issuers, investors, and their intermediaries in the foreign bond market were all optimistic parties in a financial market that had an outcome which none of them could have foreseen.

SUMMARY OF 1932 FINANCIAL MARKETS

The overriding feature of 1932 was the economic decline both in the United States and abroad. Domestic unemployment of 36% at the worst point and a Gross National Product only half that of 1929 levied indelible hardships on people and businesses. These hardships were reflected in the collapse and reorganization of many businesses, the near immobilization of stock and bond markets in the months of May through July, and the federal government's efforts to stem the tide through the Reconstruction Finance Corporation, farm and real estate lending, and the Federal Reserve System's open market purchases. Abroad, the symptoms of the same hardships were a decline in foreign trade to one-third the 1929 level, higher tariffs, currency declines, and bond defaults throughout Eastern Europe and South America.

But this sweeping impression of Depression hardship must not obscure the considerable differences in the financial well-being of various sectors of the economy, various countries, and various financial markets. Indeed, companies in the same industry fared quite differently. There were companies, countries, and markets that collapsed permanently; there were others that approached the abyss but recovered; and there were a few who hardly felt the storm. Accordingly, investors had opportunities to lose their fortunes, make them, or simply preserve them if their foresight and nerves were sufficient.

First, let us recall the great differences in the profits and financial difficulties of various industries. Railroads led the collapse and lost permanently their leading credit standing with investors. Hotels and other commercial buildings which had frequently issued mortgage bonds to the public defaulted en masse because of declines in occupancy rates, frequently below 50%. Commodities industries suffered large losses, particularly nonferrous metal mining, coal mining, pulp and paper, and oil companies, although most of these companies did not have debts on which to default. Farmers were part of the commodities business, and they had debts which frequently wiped them out. Heavy industries also had substantial losses in 1932, especially automobiles, iron and steel, machinery and tools, tire and rubber, agricultural implements, and construction. Banks and other financial institutions had problems in direct relation to their involvement in loans to these industries.

These problems rarely led to bankruptcy or reorganization among the major corporations. A review of the companies in default in Moody's industrial, utility, railroad, and financial manuals for 1932 reveals lists of minor companies which are unknown now and were little known then, except locally. The few major companies which went into default were railroads or investment companies. Moody's data for 321 major industrial companies revealed that their holdings in cash and marketable securities declined only from $3 billion to $2.7 billion between 1929 and 1932.[10] The difference between large and small companies was also revealed in a Moody's survey of 1,099 companies, which indicated that they had a net income of $234 million, compared with a net loss of $2.8 billion for all corporations, large and small.

Numerous industries did not have losses, and several even maintained their profit levels. Cigarette companies actually earned $106 million in 1932, compared with $86 million in 1929. Can manufacturers, food, drug, grocery and variety store companies, and utilities all kept their net income at levels up to half their 1929 levels. The oil, chemical, publishing, and shoe industries earned profits, if not especially significant ones.

Just as there were differences in the profits or losses of various economic sectors, there were differences in how investors fared in the various financial markets. The undifferentiated impression of financial markets in 1932 is of horrifying losses. This was true in common stocks, which with few exceptions reached a midyear low point of 12% or less of their 1929 high prices. Bonds of East European and South American governments fell to approximately 10% of par value. Many railroad bonds, too, had great losses, but among the major issues which lost their top credit ratings the decline was to approximately 40% of par. Many depositors lost all or part of their money in small- and medium-sized banks which closed. A small proportion of municipal bonds went into default.

There were many financial markets where investors lost little, however. Many long-term bond prices were substantially even with their previous highest prices after the bond market recovery in the second half of 1932. U.S. government bond prices recovered to yields of 3 1/2%, compared with 3 1/4% in most of 1930 and 1931 and over 3 1/2% in 1929. Aaa utility bonds recovered to prices within $1 to $2 of their highest prices, set in 1931 before the currency crisis, as did the bonds of Standard Oil Co. (N.J.) and Standard Oil Co. (N.Y.). Aa utility bond prices recovered to within $2 to $5 of their highest 1931 prices, and many bonds of all ratings reached within $10 of their previous highest prices, including all the major Aa and A industrial bonds, all the major Aaa railroad bonds, and such foreign bonds as those of France, the Swiss Confederation, the United Kingdom, Belgium, Canada, Czechoslovakia, Italy, and Sweden. Most municipal bonds recovered to prices that were within $5 to $10 of their highest prices, set in 1931, except for bonds of the southern states, the Dakotas, and Chicago, Cleveland, Detroit and Philadelphia. If we take into account the 15% decline in the general price level in 1932, investors with slight dollar losses still had significant real wealth gains in these bonds.

Investors also had steady profits in the money market without waiting through steep price declines. U.S. Treasury bills, commercial paper, bankers acceptances, call loans, and time loans provided very low interest rates but excellent capital security. There were virtually no defaults in these areas, and consistent liquidity was available. In real terms the annual gains in this area exceeded 15%.

Thus, there was a broad gamut of fixed income investments in which investors maintained their capital and even had significant real returns, in contrast to the shocking losses in stocks, real estate, and foreign bonds of underdeveloped countries which are often considered symbolic of securities performance in this period.

NOTES

1. We do not have data on the railroad bond holdings of nonmember country banks, except that their corporate debt holdings were 30% of deposits, compared with 18% for member country banks, and exceeded country member banks' holdings in absolute terms ($2.28 billion versus $1.67 billion) on June 30, 1932. *Banking & Monetary Statistics*, pp. 99, 102.

2. Ibid., pp. 23, 102.

3. Moody's index of yields on Baa bonds confirms this railroad preference quite closely; however, Moody's index of yields on A rated bonds exaggerates the yields available on A rated railroad issues over $40 million, for which the average peak yield of 8.19% compares with the Moody's index yield of 10.10%.

4. *Banking & Monetary Statistics*, p. 343.

5. *New York Times*, 1/3/33.

6. *Statistical Abstract, 1939*, p. 216.

7. According to an Industrial Conference Board study quoted in the *New York Times*, 4/14/32, section 9, p. 1.

8. *Banking & Monetary Statistics*, p. 686.

9. Ibid., pp. 551, 680.

10. *Moody's Industrial Manual, 1934*, pp. a44–a47.

13

Political and Economic Influences on Securities Markets in 1933

Herbert Hoover's "lame duck" period in the presidency between Roosevelt's record victory in November and his inauguration in March 1933 marked one of the lowest points in the Depression for the economy, the banking system, securities prices, and morale. The inability of the two men to cooperate, particularly on financial matters such as war debts, the budget, the exchange value of the dollar, and commercial banking problems, culminated in the Bank Holiday, which was the first action of Roosevelt's administration and the psychological low point of the Depression. Securities and commodities markets were closed, along with the commercial banks.

Franklin Roosevelt ushered in a period of financial and economic experimentation in his First Hundred Days, the end of which marks the end of this study. He devalued the gold content of the dollar, abrogated all financial contracts payable in gold, prompted the Securities Act, which henceforth regulated new securities issues, signed the Glass-Steagall Act guaranteeing bank deposits, and created two federal agencies which became major participants in the financial markets—the Banks for Cooperatives and the Federal Savings and Loan Association System. In the economic area, his principal experiments were with the Agricultural Adjustment Act, the $500 million Wagner Relief Bill, the National Recovery Administration, which restrained competition and raised prices and wages, the creation of the Tennessee Valley Authority, and the creation of the Civilian Conservation Corps of 125,000 city unemployed set to work at reforestation for $1 a day.

There was a dramatic improvement in the economy and securities markets under Roosevelt. Commodities prices rose 100%, and wage rates rose for the first time in the decade under the stimuli of Roosevelt's measures and renewed optimism. The banks were reopened and their liquidity was restored. Stocks rose 100% or more between February and July, and bond prices rose significantly.

We know in retrospect that this was a turning point in U.S. history which led to new financial institutions and practices and to revivified securities markets. Investors appeared to recognize the change at the time, which is surprising in the light of the uncertainties they had endured.

HOOVER'S PERIOD AS A LAME DUCK CULMINATES IN THE BANK HOLIDAY AND IS FOLLOWED BY THE FINANCIAL AND ECONOMIC EXPERIMENTATION OF ROOSEVELT'S FIRST HUNDRED DAYS

Hoover and Roosevelt were so bitterly divided by different personalities, different social outlooks, and mutual efforts to gain political advantage against the other that the role of the federal government in the four months between Roosevelt's record victory and his inauguration was a disequilibrating one rather than a beneficial one. In November, Roosevelt made clear his intention of staying aloof from the decision-making process and from premature responsibility when the war debts controversy arose again as a result of British and French requests that their December payments be deferred and the whole matter be reexamined. Hoover and prominent New York bankers clearly favored a continuation of the war debts moratorium declared by Hoover in July 1931, and Hoover favored an extensive review of the problem besides, with a probable outcome that each country would be allowed to pay its debts in its own local currency, thereby preserving scarce gold reserves. While Roosevelt undertook not to hamper the review, he effectively scuttled it by proposing separate bargaining with each country and by stating in an article in *Cosmopolitan* magazine, "There is neither practicality nor honor in cancellation," a position which coincided with that of the Democratic leadership of the Senate.

Cooperation between the two Presidents worsened from that point on. In November, when Roosevelt requested a special session of Congress to permit beer and wine sales and to legislate agricultural relief, Hoover threatened to veto any such bills, and the Democratic Senate correspondingly threatened to veto any new administrative appointments that he made. The two Presidents' lack of cooperation became critical over the 1934 budget, which Hoover was preparing, entailing an $830 million cut in controllable expenditures and a new 2 1/4% excise tax on manufacturers. After some wavering Roosevelt opposed the 2 1/4% tax, except as a last resort, asking instead that Congress give the President blanket authority to cut costs. This ended Hoover's ability to tender a balanced budget, for the Congress was clearly looking to Roosevelt for guidance.

The evolving bank crisis also suffered from the failure of Hoover and Roosevelt to cooperate. Every state in the nation closed its banks between February 14th, when Governor William Comstock of Michigan closed that state's banks in a surprise weekend move, and March 4th, Roosevelt's Inauguration Day, when New York and Illinois banks finally closed. The political stalemate played a principal role in this fiasco by undermining confidence in the safety net provided for the banking system by the Reconstruction Finance Corporation.

Once in power, Roosevelt used the RFC's powers actively, but in the meantime, Bernard Baruch, one of Roosevelt's financial advisors, called RFC lending "money down a rat hole," and Senator Carter Glass, whom Roosevelt was seeking as Secretary of the Treasury, publicly suggested that the RFC be dissolved, even though the RFC was the lender of last resort for the entire financial system. Without it, there would clearly have been massive defaults. The array of financial institutions which had been forced to rely on the RFC was staggering. By December 31, 1932, loans had been authorized to 5,582 banks, 877 savings banks ("building and loan associations" in RFC terminology), 101 insurance companies, 85 mortgage loan companies, and 3 credit unions—a total of 6,648 institutions—for a total commitment by the RFC of over $1.25 billion. An additional $333 million had been committed to 62 railroads which were borrowing heavily from the banks.

For Roosevelt's own part, his antagonism toward banks, brokers, and business created uneasiness in financial circles. The intensity of this antagonism was illustrated in his inaugural speech, in which he proclaimed vitriolic, anti-business sentiments that were mellowed by his wonderful voice but still only passable in a crisis in which business was so weakened and despondent that it had lost all confidence.

Roosevelt's uncooperative position on the war debts and the 1934 budget, his role in causing a gold outflow, which we shall review later, his advisors' destructive attitudes toward the RFC, and his own antagonism toward the financial system were important factors among the causes of the bank crisis which culminated in a nationwide Bank Holiday on his first day in office. These factors had much to do with the timing of the bank crisis. Of course, the basic cause of the bank crisis was the destruction of bank asset values by the Depression, especially real estate asset values, but the federal government before and after the "lame duck" period played a constructive role in ameliorating the effects of the Depression on the banking system, whereas during this period Roosevelt exacerbated the problems and brought on the bank crisis. If he had handled the "lame duck" period differently, there would have been no Bank Holiday. We will see later in this chapter that the banking system was unusually liquid prior to the bank crisis and that recovery from it was unusually rapid, which further supports the point that the peculiar circumstances of Roosevelt's transition into power were the cause of the crisis.

Fortunately, Roosevelt's inauguration and the Hundred Days which followed reversed this destructive federal role in financial affairs. Roosevelt closed the banks across the nation, using powers under a Wartime Act of October 1917, then reopened them gradually, using conservators from the Comptroller of the Currency and equity injections from the RFC, both remedies having been organized previously by the U.S. Treasury and the Federal Reserve under Hoover but only passed in the Emergency Banking Act on March 9th by a special session of Congress. We will discuss the banking crisis at length later in this chapter.

Most of the measures undertaken during the Hundred Days gave heart to business and to financial markets, which rose sharply. A second Glass-Steagall Act within little more than a year was passed. This one was destined to become famous, for it provided a federal government guarantee on all bank deposits up to $2,500, eliminated interest on demand deposits, set margin limits on loans to carry securities, set the limit that one bank could lend to one creditor at 10% of the bank's capital, and split commercial banking and investment banking functions into two industries. Parenthetically, the guarantee of bank deposits, which was one of the most constructive financial acts of the Depression, was the work of Representative Steagall and Senator Vandenburg of Michigan, and was opposed by both Senator Glass and President Roosevelt.

The National Industrial Recovery Act was passed, embodying many of the ideas of Bernard Baruch, who had become one of Roosevelt's financial advisors. The act authorized $3.3 billion in public works and effectively suspended the anti-trust laws by authorizing executives of every industry to band together under the government's aegis to write industry codes of fair competition governing prices, wage rates, work practices, and operating capacities. The act also gave a stronger voice to unions, forced higher wages, and instituted a number of minor taxes, including the first income tax on corporate dividends and almost including an income tax on municipal bond interest. The National Recovery Administration was set up under Baruch's protégé, General Hugh Johnson, and within weeks numerous industry codes were in effect.

Further aid to business, directly or indirectly, was inherent in various other acts during the Hundred Days. The Home Owners Loan Act provided a federal guarantee to refinance mortgages on homes costing less than $20,000, which assisted both homeowners and their creditors. An executive order prohibiting interstate transportation of oil produced in contravention of state pro-rationing laws finally gave teeth to production restrictions in Texas and Oklahoma which were necessary to stop ruinous price-cutting in the oil industry. Beer and wine with an alcohol content up to 3.2% were authorized in the first breach in the Volstead Act, delighting drinkers, employees, and security holders in the beer industry, which quickly sprang to life.

Roosevelt's sympathy for the farmer led to substantial legislation affecting rural America. The Agricultural Adjustment Act provided for the withdrawal of farm land under production in return for federal cash payments, 4 1/2% refinancing of farm mortgages, and a promise of farm product price supports at a minimum of production cost. The Act also provided numerous measures to promote credit expansion, including presidential authority to devalue the gold content of the dollar by up to 60%, which we shall examine in more detail promptly, federal buying support for silver at 50¢ per ounce, and expansion of Federal Reserve credit. The impetus for credit expansion from the farm bloc could hardly have been more precisely identified than by writing these credit measures into a farm bill. The other major farm act of the period was the Farm Credit Act, which consolidated all farm lending programs under the administration of Henry Morganthau, Jr., authorized 12 Production Credit Corporations around the nation to help to finance farm production, and set up the Banks for Cooperatives.

The Reforestation Relief Act in particular caught the attention of contemporaries and subsequent historians. It set up the Civilian Conservation Corps of 125,000 unemployed city men to work for $1 per day under quasi-military conditions in the countryside and forests. The concept was a blend of the many things that made Roosevelt attractive—original, romantic, productive, and carried out against the opposition of his union supporters, who resented the low pay.

Roosevelt was equally bold in combining public relief spending and conventional thrift. Shortly after his inauguration, Senator Wagner's Federal Emergency Relief Bill passed Congress easily with Roosevelt's support, authorizing $500 million in public works and direct grants to the states, replacing the previous RFC self-liquidating loans to the states. At the same time, he instituted a variety of economy measures, such as a dramatic $400 million cut in veterans' disability benefits unrelated to service and a 15% cut in civil service salaries amounting to $125 million.

One piece of legislation which was sharply opposed by business interests was the Securities Act, even though the time had come for many of the measures it instituted. The Securities Act passed the House without debate and without a recorded vote. There were only two hours of debate on it in the Senate. The drastic declines in securities prices and the exposure of securities industry abuses by the Senate Banking and Currency Committee investigations into stock exchange practices created an atmosphere highly conducive to securities industry regulation.

The Securities Act required registration of all new securities offerings with the Federal Trade Commission (FTC), with the exception of local government issues, bank deposits, and commercial paper. Registration required use of a prospectus for an offering to provide full disclosure, such as details of the issuer's business, the purpose to which the funds were to be put, current financial statements and audits, prior transactions, large holders of the company's securities, the price to the public, and the commissions paid. Foreign government issuers were required to reveal their annual receipts and expenditures, the purposes of their financing, and their outstanding debts, finally breaching the sovereign defense of secrecy which foreign issuers frequently hid behind. The FTC was also given the authority to issue "stop" orders to halt any securities offerings which did not meet its registration requirements.

The securities industry complained vociferously about the Securities Act, principally because it established criminal and civil liability for all participants in an issue for all facets of it for up to two years after the discovery of any untrue statement or omission in the prospectus, or up to ten years after the date of issue. The liability for the total amount of an issue extended to directors, management, underwriters, accountants, lawyers, and any other experts playing a role in the prospectus. As F. H. Gordon, President of the Investment Banking

Association, said, "The bill imposes...an extreme degree of diligence, accuracy, and financial liability that is not only impracticable, but dangerous. Many responsible persons would refuse to assume it." Clarence Dillon, Senior Partner of Dillon, Read & Co., testified similarly before the Senate investigation into stock exchange practices. These liabilities reduced corporate financing to between $5 million and $25 million per month after a brief bulge of financing to beat implementation of the act.

The Tennessee Valley Act was the other major piece of legislation received with great hostility by business conservatives and the private electric utilities in the southern states covered by the act. Its social and industrial goals for this depressed area could hardly be faulted, however, and clearly some disposition of the government's power and nitrate plants built at Muscle Shoals during World War I was required. Senator George W. Norris of Nebraska had fought for the TVA solution for over a decade. That it passed now was due to Roosevelt's own interest in government hydroelectric development of the St. Lawrence Seaway and the widespread political opposition to electric utilities and their holding company superstructures.

Perhaps the most controversial step of the Hundred Days was Roosevelt's decision to devalue the international exchange rate of the dollar and abrogate the domestic use of gold. There were two steps to this process. On April 20, 1933, Roosevelt by executive order placed an embargo on gold exports, thereby freeing the exchange rate of the dollar to float vis-à-vis other currencies, and ordered all private gold holdings to be delivered to the Federal Reserve by May 1st. And in May, Roosevelt induced Congress to pass a joint resolution abrogating the gold clause in all private and government domestic financial contracts. The *Commercial & Financial Chronicle* said of these actions in its opening editorial, "The United States Government has the present week taken a step backward towards the darkness of the Middle Ages." Senator Glass called these steps acts of "national repudiation." Beforehand numerous bank presidents had made clear their sentiments that the gold standard was necessary for currency stability, economic and social stability, and international confidence, but there were prominent opposing views. J. P. Morgan told reporters: "I welcomed the reported action of the President and the Secretary of the Treasury in placing an embargo on gold exports. It has become evident that the effort to maintain the exchange value of the dollar at a premium as against depreciated foreign currencies was having a deflationary effect upon already severely deflated American prices and wages and employment." Charles Dawes and Melvin Traylor, Chicago bankers and politicians, supported Roosevelt too. John Maynard Keynes wrote in the summer issue of the *Yale Review* supporting the decision, saying, "The policy of national self-sufficiency, although not an ideal in itself or in the long run, is needed for the immediate future to guarantee each country its freedom while attempting to find a new mode of political economy." Both the stock and the commodities markets supported the decision by rising approximately 10% immediately on very heavy volume. Farmers and their spokesmen loved the devaluation. They had been urging it for some time as a means of expanding credit and raising prices.

The practical reason behind the devaluation of the dollar was to raise domestic commodities prices, which were just coming off their lowest levels in the century. Wheat, cotton, corn, copper, lead, and zinc, which were priced daily on international exchanges, suddenly rose in dollar terms by the amount of the dollar's devaluation, which was originally 10% and at one point in the summer was as much as 25%. Farm prices rose to their highest points since 1931. In a nation wrung out by deflation, these price rises were welcome relief.

Disconnecting gold and domestic credit conditions also made practical sense; otherwise the effort to raise domestic prices and economic activity might have led to a countervailing loss of gold and credit contraction. The United States was forced into a policy of self-sufficiency, as Keynes recommended, to compete with the preference systems being set up by England with the Commonwealth and Scandinavia, by France with its colonies, and by Germany with Eastern Europe. The United States had no alternative bilateral trade opportunity because foreign trade amounted to less than 5% of its Gross National Product.

Roosevelt's determination to follow a policy of economic isolation became manifestly clear at the International Monetary Conference held in London in the summer of 1933. No clear agenda was prescribed for the conference, but tariffs, war debts, wheat, gold, silver, and unemployment were topics which most countries wished to have discussed in an effort to find coordinated solutions. Roosevelt met with representatives of 11 major nations before the conference and had some kind of diplomatic connection with 42 others, but the conference foundered on a lack of agreement in advance. The French and English wanted to focus on renegotiating their war debts and on stabilizing the dollar's exchange rate, while the U.S. delegation was such a hodgepodge of interests that one suspects Roosevelt had decided in advance that the conference would be useless. Secretary of State Cordell Hull went to the conference seeking a tariff truce only to run headlong into Britain's aggressive efforts to complete bilateral trade preference arrangements with Scandinavia and similar French efforts with its colonies. A proposed 10% tariff cut which Hull surfaced was disavowed by Roosevelt, as was a proposal by "silverite" Senator Key Pittman from Nevada that precious metal cover for the world's currencies be reduced to 25%, and that in turn to 80% gold and 20% silver. Bernard Baruch was made the President's liaison with the U.S. delegation to keep things under control, and Raymond Moley and Herbert Swope shuttled back and forth between Washington and London with further injunctions. As if to illustrate that the American disarray was not unique, Dr. Alfred Hugenberg, the German Minister of Economics and Agriculture at the conference, proposed that Germany's African colonies be returned and that Germany be allowed to colonize Eastern Russia, only to be disavowed by his delegation, called home, and have his German National Battle Ring, a right-wing private armed force, suppressed. Roosevelt settled that the conference would be fruitless when he administered the conference a stinging personal rebuke for its preoccupation with the gold standard and turned down a tentative foreign exchange stabilization agreement worked out by Treasury aides at the conference. After Roosevelt's rebuke the conference broke up.

THE ECONOMY HITS A LOW POINT DURING THE BANK CRISIS COMPARABLE TO THE WORST IN 1932, BUT RECOVERS DRAMATICALLY DURING ROOSEVELT'S FIRST HUNDRED DAYS

The economy generally recovered from its low point in July 1932 until October 1932, when it began to decline again because of the financial and political uncertainties created in the "lame duck period" between Roosevelt's election as President in early November and his inauguration in early March. The decline in the economy carried through into March, when the Bank Holiday halted much business and set a low point in economic activity comparable to that reached in July 1932. The *Annalist*'s index of business activity hit a low point of 58.5 in March 1933, compared with its prior low point of 59.7 in July 1932 and its high point of 116.7 in July 1929.

In 1933 the Gross National Product reached its lowest point in the Depression at $55.6 billion, or 46% below 1929. In constant dollars this was 31 1/2% below 1929, but since all financial contracts were still pegged to 1929 prices, the current dollar number is as important as the constant dollar. The index of industrial production rose from 64 in 1932 to 76 in 1933, and inventory liquidation eased from $2.6 billion in 1932 to $1.4 billion as business picked up under Roosevelt. Other sectors of the economy continued to decline, however. Rentals dropped sharply, from $2.7 billion to $2 billion, and nonresidential construction dropped from $1.2 billion to $0.9 billion as the real estate industry continued in crisis. State and local governments also reduced their economic activity a further 10%, partly because of their dependence on real estate taxes. The service industries, which had been declining less than the general economy, also continued to decline an additional 10% in 1933. The net impact on workers was that although 27.7 million persons were employed, a 2% increase over 1932, total wages and salaries still dropped a further 5%, continuing to put pressure on the consumer sector of the economy. There was also pressure on labor relations as man-days lost due to strikes rose from a record 10 1/2 million in 1932 to 16.9 million in 1933.[1]

The dramatic business recovery which occurred in April through July as Roosevelt swung into action resulted in 1933 being a better year than 1932 for gross investment in the economy, business production, the number of persons employed, business profits, and reduced business failures. The positive change in the business outlook and rise in optimism halted the inventory liquidation which dominated 1932. Compared with 1932, business invested more, employed more people, and produced at higher capacity, even though final sales and the GNP were lower than 1932, because with inventory liquidation stopped due to the better outlook, production activity came more into line with final sales. Prices rose as inventory liquidation ceased, and this helped profits as well, so that corporations collectively lost only $435 million in 1933, compared with $2.7 billion in 1932. Business failures dropped too, from 31,822 with liabilities of $928 million in 1932 to 20,307 with liabilities of $503 million in 1933.[2]

The Bottom

The low point in the economy was perhaps more graphic in 1933 than in 1932 because the bank crisis stopped all financial activity, while in the rural areas farmers almost simultaneously brought recourse against them as debtors to a well-publicized halt and prepared for a national farm strike.

When the banks closed in many states during February and March, many businesses closed completely. It was difficult to transact business with most of a firm's cash tied up in closed banks. Suppliers were uncertain whether they would be paid, businesses did not know if their bank deposits would be available to them, consumers lacked cash and worried about their savings. In prior months, there had been a massive increase in the public's cash holdings, which kept some businesses open to some degree. Several North Carolina counties authorized businesses to issue scrip in place of small bills, a pattern repeated in Atlanta, Knoxville, Selma, and several Louisiana parishes. In Iowa and Nebraska new laws were passed to permit the operation of insolvent banks. Many cities issued their own scrip, such as Atlantic City, Hoboken, Evanston, and Homestead, Pennsylvania. But for many businesses it was easier simply to close up shop in the face of such extreme uncertainty, and some towns forced this on businesses by declaring business moratoriums as well as bank holidays. This was particularly true in Illinois and Indiana, where the banks were in disarray over a long period. This condition became progressively more widespread during February as state after state closed its banks.

The resulting low level of business activity in February and March 1933 was shocking. The steel industry nationwide operated at only 15% of capacity. The copper mining companies, which in 1932 had sought an agreement to operate at only 20% of capacity, now sought an accord to shut their mines completely for six months until inventories were in line with ultimate demand. Railroad freight revenues dropped to $2.2 million, their low point in the Depression and 10% lower than in July 1932. Machine tool orders for all of 1933, which depended on business expansion and investment, dropped to only half their 1932 volume and to a mere 5% of their 1929 volume. Supplies of capital equipment to the railroad industry, which had been virtually bankrupted by the Depression, were reduced to even lower levels since they operated only when the railroads expanded or replaced equipment. In all of 1933, there were only 63 locomotives, 2,861 freight cars, and 6 passenger cars manufactured in the United States, compared with 1929, when 1,161 locomotives, 93,965 freight cars and 1,436 passenger cars were manufactured. Automobile production averaged 100,000 cars per month, which was less than one-fifth of peak production in 1929. Building contracts dropped to half their level in 1932, which in itself had seemed impossibly low as building purchases and plans came to a virtual halt. In the oil production states, troops were used to shut down wells, and state officials sought a complete shutdown for 30 days. Even Western Electric Co., the production arm of the AT&T system, operated at only 15% of capacity in February.[3]

In the rural areas, farm income dropped to less than half that in the 1920s, and commodities prices were so low that it did not pay to plant crops or sustain livestock. Grain production, for which prices had averaged 44% of their pre-Crash prices, was particularly hard hit, dropping to only 61% of pre-Crash production. Relatively modest farm debts averaging $3,652 per farm loomed like insurmountable obligations because of the lack of farm cash flow, and creditors began to foreclose on farms on a massive scale until the farmers revolted against their plight and gained moratoriums on mortgage foreclosures.[4] At first, the revolt was personal and localized, such as when men armed with shotguns prevented bank or insurance company agents from entering a farm or from bidding at a foreclosure sale, as when 500 farmers in Kankakee, Illinois, stopped the Federal Joint Stock Land Bank's agents from foreclosing on several farms, or when a Chancery Court judge in Pike County, Mississippi, simply refused to order a foreclosure. But the revolt escalated into politics, such as when over 2,000 farmers marched on the Nebraska legislature, leading the Governor to issue a proclamation seeking an emergency suspension of farm mortgage sales. The Governor of Kentucky asked for a voluntary moratorium on foreclosures under similar pressure, and the Governor of Oklahoma issued an order prohibiting foreclosures. In Georgia the life insurance companies of the state voluntarily declared a moratorium on foreclosures on their farm real estate loans which were in arrears. The farm revolt soon carried into laws, such as in South Dakota, where a law was passed prohibiting all foreclosures for one year. Indiana declared a moratorium on tax sales for one year. Arkansas forbade mortgage sales for two years. Iowa allowed courts to give farmers relief from their debts for up to two years, and Wisconsin allowed similar relief for up to five years. North Dakota, Minnesota, Texas and West Virginia soon had similar laws.

Farm discontent was molded by Milo Reno, dynamic President of the Farmers Holiday Association, into a threat of a national farm strike on May 13th which would halt the movement of all farm goods if no farm relief was enacted. The threat was averted, however, when Congress passed the Farm Relief Bill and Roosevelt devalued the dollar, which caused the prices of farm commodities to rise dramatically.

The urban real estate market, in some respects the urban counterpart of farmers' problems, had no similar solution to its problems. Rental income declined a further 26% to only 37% of 1929. This is even more striking than other sectors' declines in income when we keep in mind that real estate owners' most important cost—their mortgage—had not changed over the period. As a result, real estate values plunged to their lowest levels in the Depression. During February and March there were daily auctions of foreclosed properties in New York City at which the properties were bought in routinely by the mortgage holders for the amount of their mortgages. The Pierre Hotel, one of the city's finest, was sold in this fashion. Nationwide, private purchases of real estate structures during 1933 amounted to only $1.5 billion, versus $2 billion in 1932 and $8.9 billion in 1929. The mortgage investments of major life insurance companies were approximately 25% in default. In the most heavily depressed cities, like Detroit and Cleveland, the real estate market had ceased to exist and banks with mortgage loans found their paper illiquid and almost worthless.[5]

The Turning Point

Once Roosevelt was in office, economic conditions changed dramatically in just a few months and securities and commodities prices quickly doubled. This change was partly due to the end of the banking crisis, partly due to the devaluation of the dollar, which helped to raise prices, and partly due to the confidence Roosevelt inspired in his own person and in the many changes embodied in legislation in his First Hundred Days. Steel production rose weekly from April through July until production was at 59% of capacity—triple the lowest levels of 1932. Rail freight revenues also rose monthly through the same period, as did building contracts, which were 4 times their 1933 low point by the fourth quarter of 1933. Automobile production doubled by the summer, and General Motors increased wages 5%.[6] Textile mills in South Carolina increased wages 10%–15%, as did coal companies for over 75,000 miners in Appalachia and a number of small companies. The *Guaranty Survey* described the last week of May as the best business rise since the start of the Depression, and the *Commercial & Financial Chronicle* described the second quarter of 1933 as a "recovery in trade and industry throughout the country on a scale probably never before witnessed." The *Annalist*'s index of business activity rose to 89.5 in July, versus a low point of 58.5 in March 1933 and a peak of 116.7 in July 1929. Roger Babson predicted that the nation would be back to normal in 12 months.

Further improvements took place after Congress passed the National Industrial Recovery Act (NRA) in August, allowing companies to coordinate prices, production, and competitive practices. General Electric Co. raised wages by $8 million and put non-office workers on a 36-hour week. Thirty-five builders in Atlantic City raised wages up to 100%. Fifteen garment manufacturing plants in Maryland reopened with a 50% wage increase and a 40-hour week. Oil producers and marketers finally got together, and oil prices rose to over $1 per barrel. Many industries were quick to agree on NRA codes of behavior.

Not all industries gained a quick recovery. Those related to railroad capital spending languished, as did the U.S. copper industry, despite a dramatic rise in the price of copper. Wheat prices rose to over $1.25 per bushel, but the markets for U.S. wheat showed no improvement because of the worldwide encouragement of domestic wheat production and Canada's displacement of U.S. wheat in Great

Britain under the Commonwealth system of trade preferences established in 1931. The coal industry showed no improvement in 1933 over its low level of production in 1932, and the retail trade generally only barely exceeded comparable period 1932 sales by the fourth quarter of 1933. The economy started to weaken again in the last quarter, as if to return to the low levels of 1932 and early 1933, but in fact the cycle had turned and the economy was to improve steadily all the way into 1937.[7]

PRICES BEGIN TO RISE FOR THE FIRST TIME IN THE DEPRESSION, DUE TO DEVALUATION OF THE DOLLAR AND THE CHANGE IN THE BUSINESS OUTLOOK

Most prices touched their lowest levels in the Depression between February and April 1933, during the bank crisis, as companies and individuals strained to gain cash and in many cases were reduced to bartering. The Wholesale Price Index dipped a further 4% from the end of 1932 to 62% of its pre-Crash level, and the Retail Food Price Index dropped a further 7% to 55% of its pre-Crash level. Farm prices were 37% and industrial commodities were approximately 25% of their pre-Crash levels. Economic activity had almost ceased in those areas of the economy where prices were most depressed.[8]

Prices began to rise immediately when Roosevelt took the nation off of the gold standard and devalued the dollar. Commodities prices were up 10% in April alone. This was to be expected with a 10% decline in the international value of the dollar, since many commodities were traded internationally. This had been a significant part of the thinking of farm interests and economists who had been behind the movement for devaluation. But the rise in prices most reflected understanding of Roosevelt's commitment to raise prices when he would go to the extreme of a premeditated, unforced devaluation. He was clearly willing to use the powers of government to this end on a previously unknown scale. By August there were in place under the National Industrial Recovery Act price, production, and marketing codes specifically directed to raising prices.

From March through September, prices rose every month under the stimulus of Roosevelt's various measures and the broad economic recovery. Wholesale prices generally were up 18%, but this broad measure concealed much more dramatic increases in general commodities prices. Moody's index of daily commodity prices rose 89%, led by rubber, which rose 203%; wheat, which rose 130%; softwood lumber, which rose 125%; oil, which rose 105%; and copper, which rose 84%. For a change, the trend of prices encouraged purchases and production for inventory. The heavy liquidation of inventories which characterized 1932 was reversed, and so was a 44-month trend of continually declining prices.[9]

The trend of price increases should not be exaggerated, however, as retail food prices rose only 20%, and prices for many goods continued to decline. In 1933 the GNP deflator for 1933 was still down 2%. Most durable goods prices were down approximately 12%, rents were down 14%, services were down 8%, and utilities rates declined. Those manufacturing industries which did experience price rises tended to be associated with commodities experiencing sharp price increases, such as oil and farm products, or related to new government public programs, such as construction and road building.[10]

THE BANKING SYSTEM, MONETARY POLICY, AND MONEY MARKETS—DOMESTIC AND FOREIGN DEPOSIT WITHDRAWALS RESULT IN THE BANK HOLIDAY OF MARCH 4, 1933, BUT RECOVERY IS QUICK WITH THE AID OF MANY NEW BANKING LAWS AND A SPIRIT OF RENEWED HOPE

The Crash initiated the Depression, and the Bank Holiday marked its bottom—two events like mileposts of this epoch—but while there was a certain inexorability about the Crash because of the high valuations placed on stocks and the heavy borrowing to buy them, there was no similar inevitability in conditions preceding the Bank Holiday. During the last months of 1932 and the first six weeks of 1933, interest rates were at their lowest sustained levels in U.S. history. Rates on 3- to 6-month Treasury notes and certificates averaged below .07%, and the average yields on bankers acceptances were below .50%. Call loans cost only 1%. The Federal Reserve was pursuing a policy of low interest rates that was a continuation of its dramatic policy change in March 1932, which led to Federal Reserve purchases of over $1 billion in U.S. Treasury securities. The January 1933 estimated excess reserves of member banks of over $600 million were the highest since this data began to be collected in 1929. Federal Reserve borrowings by weekly reporting banks in 101 cities averaged only $64 million in January.[11] Entering 1933, investments of all commercial banks were $15 billion, just short of the highest in history, even though deposits were only 70% of their historic peak.[12] U.S. government securities investments of weekly reporting banks in 101 cities had risen to over $5 billion, which was double their level at the time of the Crash, and at $5.5 billion, total investments of these larger banks were just short of a record. Their loans, other than on securities, were only $5.9 billion out of deposits of $21.4 billion.[13] This high proportion of liquid investments and low proportion of loans appeared to be ample liquidity for the worst contingencies. Foreign short-term deposits of approximately $750 million in New York banks (which held most foreign deposits) were covered by Federal Reserve gold holdings of over $4 billion.

Of course, all was not roses for the banking system. Nonmember and country banks were in serious trouble, as we saw in 1932; the RFC had lent almost $1 billion to 5,582 banks by December 31, 1932; member banks had no profits in 1932, but rather lost a quarter of a billion dollars; and banks in various cities, such as Detroit, Cleveland, Chicago and Indianapolis, which were particularly hard hit by the Depression, were in serious trouble. Nonetheless, the banking system appeared to be girded to meet the worst.

The first incident in the stream of events leading up to the Bank Holiday in March occurred on February 13th, when Governor Comstock of Michigan declared an eight-day bank holiday for 550 banks with $1.5 billion in deposits throughout Michigan because of the troubles of Detroit's leading banks, the Guardian National Bank of Commerce and the First National Bank of Detroit. This was the first instance of a major industrial state declaring a holiday, and the banks precipitating it were unusually large.

The Michigan bank holiday provides a case study in the problems of the banking system. In this case we are able to follow the expansionist attitudes of the 1920s and the effects on the banks of the stock market and real estate market collapses. But beyond these problems, the pivotal role of the Michigan bank holiday in the events leading up to the nationwide Bank Holiday in March enables us to look in on the interplay between banks and government as the crisis developed, and we thereby have an opportunity to judge whether these banks had to be closed or whether the U.S. government should have done more to keep them open. Indeed, Roosevelt may have hampered the RFC in lending to avert the bank crisis before he was inaugurated.

At the time of the Michigan bank holiday, there were two principal bank holding companies in Detroit. The Guardian Detroit Union Group (the Guardian Group), the smaller and weaker of the two, was based on the Guardian National Bank of Commerce and the Union Guardian Trust Co. The Detroit Banking Group, which was two-thirds again as large as the Guardian Group, was created to meet the aggressive plans of its smaller competitor and based on four banks which merged to become the First National Bank of Detroit.

The precursor of the Guardian Group began in June 1927, when the Guardian Detroit Bank was formed with the support of the Ford family and company in both capital and deposits. In May 1929 the Guardian Detroit Group was formed as a holding company over the bank to unite an investment banking affiliate with the bank and to begin acquiring Michigan banks.

Both purposes made good sense for management and the Michigan economy. There had been three years of intense and profitable stock market activity in which the expansion of the automobile industry had played a prominent role. New companies related to the auto industry had sprung up all over Michigan, and corresponding private wealth had also been created. Both needed the services of investment bankers, and local investment bankers would arguably better fill this role with their knowledge of both the people and their businesses than the New York investment bankers who had thus far dominated the activity.

There was also logic in acquiring other Michigan banks. The high failure rate among banks in the 1920s had convinced most observers that some form of branch banking was necessary to spread out both deposits and investments and to create economies of scale for sophisticated and well-capitalized management. There was a strong movement in Washington, with Senator Glass as its most evident spokesman and supported by the Federal Reserve, the U.S. Treasury Department, and the Comptroller of the Currency, to pass legislation for branch banking. The appeal of branch banking was particularly strong in Michigan, where bank branches were limited to one city but where the dynamism of automotive expansion had created a need for sharply expanded capital for factories, homes, public facilities, and the services that go with a rapid expansion in population. Until branch banking was legalized, group banking where banks in various cities were tied together through a holding company was the obvious intermediate step beyond single city banks.

Thus, the Guardian Group set out on a series of acquisitions which ultimately created a system of banks in 16 cities. The key merger in this chain was in December 1929, with the Union Commerce Corporation, another holding company with similar expansion plans, which brought the Union Guardian Trust and Keane, Higbie & Co., investment bankers, into the Guardian Group. They also brought a pack of trouble in the way of real estate loans and securities inventory into the group, but that story comes later. At the end of 1929, the Guardian Group appeared admirably positioned in Detroit commercial banking, in investment banking, and in regional banking, with the largest banks in 11 of 16 cities where they had bought banks.

The Detroit Bankers Co. was formed January 8, 1930, by four Detroit banks in an obvious reaction to the pace set by the Guardian Group. These banks were older and clearly more conservative than the Guardian Group, but they too saw the wisdom of a holding company system and spent over $7 million acquiring minority stock interests in ten outlying banks.[14]

Having seen the timing of the creation of these two bank holding companies, the reader can already guess that the first problems they confronted were in the stock market. These occurred in many ways. Numerous officers and employees in the Guardian Group borrowed to buy the company's stock during 1929. The stock rose to over $300 before the Crash, from approximately $120, where it had been for some time. The Crash eliminated these profits, however, and in December 1929 a group of directors joined together to guarantee a consolidated loan of $1.6 million with Bankers Trust Co. in New York to carry the "distress" securities of officers and employees. Banks in the Guardian Group had their own loans against Guardian Group shares, loans which the Guardian Group could not liquidate when they became under collateralized because of the pressure it would place on Guardian Group stock and the rumors it would create about the banks.

The directors of the Guardian Group got a harbinger of things to come in November 1929 when they were asked to bail out a sour underwriting of 25,000 shares of Guardian Group stock. The episode began earlier in 1929 when the Goldman Sachs Trading Corp. approached the original Union Guardian Trust Co. seeking to buy 30,000 of its shares at $130, versus the current market price of $120. This was ultimately worked out in an indirect fashion, and Goldman Sachs Trading Corp. made a handsome profit when the shares were traded on a one-for-one basis for Guardian Group shares and subsequently rose to over $300 per share. However, Guardian Group directors did not like this close association with a New York investment banking firm, which they feared would prejudice their chances of a significant investment banking business with various New York investment bankers. A first effort to get Sidney Weinberg of Goldman, Sachs & Co. to sell the stock was met only by indignation, but a second effort in mid-October 1929, as the vibration of the coming Crash began to be felt, produced an agreement whereby Goldman Sachs Trading Corp. would sell 25,000 shares at $184 when the market was $220. Weinberg got the best of this deal, for within days the market broke, and a selling group formed by the Guardian Group's investment banking subsidiaries to resell the stock was able to sell only 7,000 shares. In November, there was an appeal to the directors to buy the remaining stock at $184 for $3.4 million, even though the stock had dropped to $120. Edsel Ford put up $1.2 million, and others put up the balance to take this potential loss off the Guardian Group's hands.[15]

The Group's problems with the stock market grew as the Depression deepened. In October 1930 a group of 110 stockholders committed $4 million to support the Guardian Group's stock by buying it at $60 and then at $45, because the decline in the stock's price was unsettling depositors and creating rumors about the Group's condition. In December 1931, Edsel Ford, Henry Ford's oldest son, President of Ford Motor Co., and an early influence in forming the Guardian Group, lent $1 million in cash and $5 million in City of Detroit bonds to buttress the collateral of the investment banking subsidiaries on securities loans of $7.5 million from outside banks. At the end of 1931, when the Guardian Group raised its outside borrowing to $15 million, half of it to carry securities in inventory, Edsel Ford and Charles Mott, who was on the executive committee of General Motors, each guaranteed $2.5 million of the loans since the collateral was so weak. In March 1931 an advisory committee was set up from the Guardian Group board of directors to investigate the operations of the investment banking affiliates of the Group, and a separate examining committee for the main bank subsidiary looked into the potential for loan losses on securities loans. Both came to very negative conclusions. The former recommended that the investment banking subsidiaries of the Group be liquidated to pay off $5 million of loans with Group banks that were undercollateralized.[16] The latter committee found $3 million in potential losses on securities loans to bank officers and customers.[17]

When the Michigan bank holiday was declared, the Guardian Group's principal bank, the Guardian National Bank of Commerce, had $5.6 million in very slow loans to its investment banking affiliates against securities they had bought, $1.5 million in loans secured by almost worthless Guardian Group stock, and an unknown amount of slow or doubtful securities loans, compared with a net worth of only $15.2 million. Besides, the Guardian Group had $7.5 million in loans on securities it had taken over from its investment banking affiliates, and its directors had spent or loaned over $18 million supporting either Guardian Group loans or the Guardian Group stock.[18]

The other principal area of Detroit banking problems, besides the stock market, was in real estate loans. Real estate lending was not generally considered good banking practice, but as Robert O. Lord, President of the Guardian Group, told the Pecora Committee, "It was an inheritance of many years, and it was the practice in Detroit to loan on real estate, on homes." Wilson W. Mills, the Chairman of the First National Bank of Detroit, told the committee much the same thing:

Detroit had experienced probably the most rapid, phenomenal, and mushroom growth of industry of any community in the United States. Due to the automotive industry centralizing in Detroit, literally trainloads of people had been arriving daily to make their residences there. Schools had to be erected, churches established, and homes built for this influx of people, and the old banks were the only ones to do it.

Detroit's population had grown from 286,000 in 1900 to 1,569,000 in 1930, and the banks naturally played a prominent role in the residential, commercial, and industrial real estate expansion which went with such growth. That is not to say that the banks were cavalier in their real estate loans, however. The Detroit Clearing House Association required that the borrower pay off the principal within ten years.

The problem with real estate loans hit the Detroit banks in various ways. The Union Guardian Trust, which was part of the Guardian Group, was the most heavily committed to real estate, the weakest bank in the city, and the one whose closing precipitated the Michigan bank holiday. Compared with $50 million in deposits at the end of 1930, it had almost $30 million, directly or indirectly, invested in real estate. It began to flounder quickly in the Depression. The Guardian Group put in $4 million at the end of 1931 to remove weak real estate loans from the Union Guardian Trust Co., and still in May 1932 it became the first in Detroit to apply for a loan from the Reconstruction Finance Corporation when it sought $28 million to pay all its deposits, liquidate its real estate loans, and go out of the banking business except for handling trusts and estates. The RFC authorized loans of $15 million during 1930 to the Union Guardian Trust Co., and Ford Motor Co. lent a further $3.5 million at year end, but a deposit decline from $50 million at the end of 1930 to only $31 million at the end of 1932 turned Union Guardian Trust's real estate related assets into an illiquid 72% of its total assets, which finally forced it back to the RFC in January 1933, seeking enough loans to end its deposit business. At this depressed point in the market the RFC could only find assets in the Guardian Trust which would justify an additional $5 million in loans.

The real estate problems in the other Detroit banks were less severe but still a problem. The federal bank examiner's report of May 16, 1932, on the Guardian National Bank of Commerce said, "The real estate situation in the bank is serious, and at the present time it is very difficult to determine values of any Detroit property." Some 40 percent of the bank's capital was invested in real estate it had taken over from defaulted loans.[19] Within the Guardian Group as a whole approximately one-third of its total assets were in loans or investments related to real estate at the end of 1932.

The banks in the Detroit Bankers Co. had over 40% of their assets in real estate loans or investments at the end of 1932, although their emphasis on individual home mortgages had produced a more sound portfolio. Yet even in the area of home mortgages the experience of the First National Bank with a trusteed pool of $25 million residential mortgages against which participation certificates were sold revealed that $6.9 million went into default and $8.2 million was past due.[20]

No real estate lender could be even hopeful in Detroit at the end of 1932. Property values had declined over 40%, and there was little activity at these levels. There was no market whatsoever for large commercial buildings, and foreclosures on all types of property had become numerous. The city government was bankrupt and unable to provide services. Trade unionism, violence, and communism were making rapid inroads among the city's automobile workers. Father Coughlin, a Detroit Roman Catholic priest with a powerful radio presence, had developed a considerable radio audience by striking out bitterly against the banks and the financial system and recommending that people hold off paying their debts until an upward revaluation of the price of gold would raise wage and price levels so that the burden of existing debts would be reduced.

The Guardian Group approached the RFC on January 25, 1933, for a massive loan to relieve the burdens of its illiquid securities and real estate investments and rapidly declining deposits. The original request was for $43.5 million to cover all the deposits in the Union Guardian Trust Co. and to provide further liquidity for the Guardian National Bank of Commerce and a few of the Group's regional banks. The Ford Motor Co. was expected to subordinate to other depositors $7.5 million in deposits it held in the Union Guardian Trust to help with the bailout. The RFC offered $37.2 million on securities and loans with a face value of $61 million, provided an additional $6 million could be raised in new capital and $9 million in large deposits subordinated. President Hoover called the leaders of Chrysler, Ford, and General Motors to Washington during the first week of February to gain their support in the rescue mission, and Senator Couzens, the erratic senior senator from Michigan who had made his fortune with Henry Ford and then split with him, used the occasion to state that he would "shriek from the house tops" if further loans were made on the available collateral. Unfortunately, all the parties focussed on the Ford interests to play a major role in the rescue effort by subordinating their $7.5 million in Union Guardian Trust deposits. The Fords were also expected to contribute $2 million to capitalize a new mortgage company holding the Guardian Group's real estate loans and assets, to which the RFC would lend, as well as to share in contributing $4 million in new capital to Guardian Group banks. This was not illogical, since the Fords had approximately $30 million in deposits in Guardian Group banks, and the Guardian Group was indentified as "the Ford's bank," but Henry Ford clearly felt he was being victimized and refused, even withdrawing his son's offer to subordinate $7.5 million in Ford Motor Co. deposits. The Fords had already contributed or lent over $13 million to the Guardian Group to help with its problems, and Henry Ford claimed that it was now up to the federal government to save the banks in Detroit as they had the Dawes bank in Chicago. In Washington, there was an expressed feeling at the RFC that it was not up to them to bail out the Ford interests, and thus a two-party bluff of national consequences was deadlocked.

This deadlock produced a continuum of feverish activity in Detroit and Washington over the long weekend of Lincoln's Birthday, February 11–13, 1933. Meetings were held around the clock in Detroit, including representatives of the Guardian Group, the Detroit Bankers Co., Bankers Trust Co., First National Bank of Chicago, Continental Illinois Bank & Trust, Secretary of Commerce Roy D. Chapin, Undersecretary of the Treasury Arthur A. Ballantine, Chicago Federal Reserve Governor Eugene M. Stevens, and staffs of the RFC and Comptroller of the Currency. On Monday, February 13th, the board of directors of the RFC in Washington stayed in session until after 3:00 a.m. the next morning. But the RFC offered no more, the other industrialists waited on the Fords, and Henry Ford not only refused to subordinate his $7.5 million in deposits or contribute more capital but also threatened to withdraw $25 million in deposits from the First National Bank of Detroit if all the banks were not opened or closed together.

Finally, in the early morning of February 14th Governor Comstock was asked by the Detroit Clearing House Association to declare a bank holiday in Michigan. Not a cent had been raised for any of the banks in the negotiations, but it was expected that something would be worked out shortly and the banks reopened. In the meantime, the plight of the Detroit banks had been made known in such detail throughout the Detroit business community over the weekend that the holiday was expected to forestall deposit withdrawals by insiders, thereby protecting smaller depositors.

In the following two weeks both the Fords and the RFC were anxious to reopen the Detroit banks. The Fords offered to put up $11 million to recapitalize the two major Detroit banks, and Treasury Secretary Mills wanted massive RFC bank lending in order to forestall the Detroit crisis from spreading to banks in other major cities. In conjunction with the Ford offer, the RFC was prepared to lend $35 million to the Guardian National Bank of Commerce without additional capital being raised, and $100 million to the First National Bank of Detroit, if it could raise $20 million additional. At this point, Roosevelt, acting through William H. Woodin, his Secretary of the Treasury designate, instructed the RFC that any loans made prior to his taking office had to be on their own authority and responsibility. The First National Bank of Detroit was unable to raise the $20 million necessary, the RFC loans were not made, and the banks stayed closed.

The Guardian National Bank of Commerce, the Union Guardian Trust, and the First National Bank of Detroit never reopened. They were placed in the hands of a court-appointed liquidator in May 1933. A new bank, the National Bank of Detroit, was capitalized by General Motors and the RFC in April 1933 to take over the good assets and deposits of the closed banks. Edsel Ford also capitalized a new bank, the Manufacturers National Bank, which took over the good assets and deposits of the suburban Detroit banks in August 1933. The closed banks ultimately paid out 100% of their deposit liabilities, and the RFC ultimately authorized loans of $80 million to assist in liquidation of Guardian Group banks and $214 million for liquidation of the First National Bank of Detroit.[21]

One cannot resist raising judgmental questions about the roles of various participants in the Detroit bank holiday and its aftermath. Should more have been done to keep these banks open, and did Roosevelt somehow inhibit the RFC in this crisis? Many people questioned at the time whether the Detroit banks needed to be closed, such as Wilson W. Mills, Chairman of the Detroit Bankers Co., who said before the Pecora Committee,

Personally, I have no doubt whatsoever as to the solvency of the First National Bank at the time of the holiday....I believe that the First National Bank situation had become so inextricably tied up in the public and financial mind, and the official mind, with the Guardian Group situation that its own situation, its inherent ultimate soundness, and its ability to carry on in the service of the community and in the interest of its depositors, was entirely lost sight of.[22]

The answer was sought for the benefit of the Detroit public in grand jury proceedings instituted during the summer of 1933 and had a decided tone that the city had been victimized by outsiders.

Circumstantial evidence that more could have been done to keep these banks open was great. There never was an outright run on the Detroit banks by depositors. Saturday morning, February 11th, the last day they were open, was normal. Neither the Guardian National Bank of Commerce nor the First National Bank had a single dollar in RFC loans when they closed, and the former had $30 million in cash and U.S. government securities when it closed (28% of deposits),[23] while the latter had $85 million (23% of deposits).[24] The RFC ultimately lent both banks more to liquidate them than they were requesting to stay open, and it did so without the conditions that frustrated the original loan requests.

These are debating points, however, around the key issue of whether these major Detroit banks were solvent, for the RFC had no legislative power at that time to keep insolvent banks open. The Chief National Bank Examiner for the Federal Reserve District, Alfred P. Leybrun, who oversaw the regular RFC evaluation of the banks, was adamant afterward that they were insolvent, but Leybrun's testimony is highly suspect. He bore considerable criticism in Detroit for his role in the banks' closing and was clearly trying in later testimony to justify his actions. He never substantiated that the banks were insolvent. Various claims he made about the proportions of mortgages, real estate, slow or doubtful loans, and director loans to bank capital beg the question of whether the banks were insolvent or simply illiquid. Leybrun's judgments are called into further doubt by the intemperance of his remarks during negotiations for the original RFC loans, then during his testimony before the Pecora Committee, and by his tendency to write off as unacceptable whole areas of bank activity such as real estate lending, bank properties, loans to directors, and loans that were no longer fully collateralized. He even criticized the heavy reliance of the Detroit banks' debtors on the auto industry, as if that could have been avoided.

The obvious question is whether these banks had simply become illiquid. There had been an enormous decline in bank deposits in the last two years which had forced the banks to increase their liquid assets and reduce their regular loans as quickly as possible. The deposits of the Union Guardian Trust had declined from $50.1 million at the end of 1930 to $24 million when it closed. The Guardian National Bank of Commerce's deposits declined from $198 million on December 31, 1930, to approximately $108 million when it closed, and the First National Bank's deposits had declined from $555 million to $373 million when it closed.[25] Naturally, the remaining assets after a deposit drain on this scale were the least liquid.

There were several standards by which to judge whether the banks were solvent. The harshest standard was the liquidating value of assets judged at the time of the bank holiday. Even if this judgment was tempered by assuming gradual liquidation, it was still severe, with real estate prices down 30% from the 1920s and economic activity in Detroit near a standstill. A second standard was liquidating value after prices and the economy had been assumed to recover. This was a complete unknown, but there was wide recognition that values in 1932 and 1933 were unreasonably depressed. A third standard was to accept a bank as a going concern and make the assumption that loans and investments not already in default and honestly made would pay off even if they did so slowly. This last standard has the advantage that it also creates income to absorb losses on assets without affecting net worth. There is no question that banking policy today would call for the last standard to judge a bank portfolio, and that it made the most sense in Detroit for banks ground down to their least liquid assets in a community more severely hit by the Depression than any other major city in the country.

The banks' examiners applied the first standard, assuming gradual liquidation, to value the banks' assets, and the RFC offer of $37.2 million in February, 1933, to the Guardian Group was based exactly on the liquidating value of the loan assets, even if some of the liquidating values were generous.

We get quite a different outlook on the solvency of the Detroit banks if, as an example, we examine the depreciated book value of the assets of the Guardian National Bank of Commerce, piecing together the information we have on those assets. (See Table 13.1.) Approximately 40% of deposits were backed by cash, U.S. Treasury securities, and bonds. If we do not penalize slow loans on the basis that even the best were slow at this point in the Depression, the question becomes what capital loss should be assumed on doubtful loans of $18.7 million

Table 13.1

Balance Sheet for Guardian National Bank of Commerce, March 13, 1933 ($ millions)

		Assets		Liabilities	
	Cash	$16.4	Deposits	$108.1
	U.S. Treasury securities	14.1	Circulation	5.0
$1.5 decline in mkt. value $0.5 defaulted	Bonds	11.7	Other	3.8
$25.4 "slow" $18.7 "doubtful" of which $5.8 to securities affiliates $1.5 secured by GDUG stock	Loans	60.4		
$5.2 taken over by foreclosures	Mortgages	17.3	Net Worth	15.2
	Bank & other real estate	8.9		
	Other	3.5		
	TOTAL	$132.1	TOTAL	$132.1

Source: Moody's Financial Manual, 1934; Stock Exchange Practices, part 10, pp. 4622, 4634, 4647; bank examiner's report, December 7, 1932.

and foreclosed real estate of $5.2 million, versus the bank's net worth of $15.2 million. If business conditions recovered enough to get $9 million out of these two categories of loans, the Guardian National Bank of Commerce was solvent and justified the RFC loans it was seeking.

The same could not be said of the Guardian Detroit Union Group, the holding company, which had a $15 million loan from several banks and was almost completely without cash flow to service it, dividends from the bank subsidiaries having completely ceased. The Union Guardian Trust had no benefit of a large cash and securities position, having 72% of its assets in real estate and mortages, and so its solvency was more difficult to judge. But even if these collapsed, companies it was quite another story to close the Guardian National Bank of Commerce, which had deposits almost 4 times those of the Union Guardian Trust.

We do not have the same detail for the assets of the First National Bank of Detroit, but shortly after it was closed, bank examiners found that it had a net worth deficit of only $4 million on a liquidating basis, which assures that the bank was solvent on a "going concern" basis.

We do not have the same detail for the assets of the First National Bank of Detroit, but shortly after it was closed, bank examiners found that it had a net worth deficit of only $4 million on a liquidating basis, which assures that the bank was solvent on a "going concern" basis.

There appear to have been colossal misjudgments in the negotiations leading up to the Detroit bank holiday. The RFC set its demands much too high and tried to pin too much additional support for the banks on Henry Ford and the Detroit business community. The bank examiners were too heavily influenced against the banks by the boom mentality which had prevailed in their real estate and stock market lending activities, even though it could hardly have been avoided in Detroit in the 1920s. Insisting on covering all deposits 100% with RFC loans was also too demanding, since smaller loans might have exhausted depositors' demands for withdrawals.

The Ford interests were clearly balancing what they had to lose in deposits and capital in the Detroit banks with the additional capital they had to put up to keep the banks open. Total Ford deposits in the two groups of banks were approximately $50 million; in addition, they had original equity, loans, and guarantees in the Guardian Group with a book value of approximately $20 million, including over 50,000 shares of Guardian Group stock. The Fords were willing to put up a significant amount, as their $11 million offer of new capital to reopen the two main banks indicated, but Henry Ford expected in the negotiations before the bank holiday that the RFC would keep open the Detroit banks as it had the Dawes bank in Chicago without his help. He was wrong. It appears from Edsel Ford's testimony that he favored subordinating $7.5 million of Ford deposits in the Union Guardian Trust and that he placed the responsibility for not going further squarely on his father. By this time Henry Ford was strongly under the influence of Harry Bennett, a violent, demented, underworld figure who we know was in on the negotiations from a comment of Arthur Ballantine. Who knows what role Bennett played in Henry Ford's bluff.

Both sides expected that the bank holiday would be brief, but again they miscalculated. Roosevelt may have played an important role in this outcome. The RFC was prepared to lend $100 million to the First National Bank of Detroit and $35 million to the Guardian National Bank of Commerce to reopen them February 21st, and it was under heavy pressure from Treasury Secretary Mills to loan on a massive, nationwide scale to stop the crisis, when the RFC received word through Jesse Jones, a Democratic director later to become Chairman, that Roosevelt and Woodin wanted a discussion of the loans in New York before they were approved. The results of Secretary Mills' meeting with Secretary-designate Woodin were recorded in the February 23rd minutes of an RFC meeting as follows:

Mr. Woodin said that, while he would be glad to be kept informed of important developments, the problems now under consideration should be determined by the board in accordance with its own views and on its own responsibility.[26]

That was hardly a comment worthy of bringing a Treasury Secretary up to New York and holding up the efforts to solve a great crisis. What did Woodin really say? Again all the evidence is circumstantial. The Detroit loans were not made, and virtually no RFC loans were made during the ensuing two critical weeks until Roosevelt took office; Roosevelt's hostility toward the financial community had been fully demonstrated during the election campaign; and Woodin's guidance to Mills was similar to that given Hoover with respect to the war debts negotiations, where the clear intent was to scuttle the effort. It appears that either by active intervention or by creating doubts and then refusing to support a course of action, Roosevelt also scuttled the RFC's efforts to halt the bank crisis. It was an act of either incredible naiveté or incredible political cynicism.

The Michigan bank holiday immediately led to runs on banks in much of Ohio, especially Cleveland, and Indiana, especially Indianapolis. A nationwide banking panic developed during the two weeks beginning February 20th and February 27th which hit even the large New York City banks as both domestic and foreign depositors hurried to withdraw their funds. Domestic currency in circulation rose $1.5 billion to $7.25 billion as a result of domestic deposit withdrawals, and foreigners withdrew almost $300 million in gold. Weekly reporting banks in 101 cities lost over $4 billion in deposits in the two weeks, liquidated $750 million of their investments, and borrowed almost $1 billion from the Federal Reserve. New York City banks were particularly hard hit, borrowing from the Federal Reserve well over half of the $1 billion.

Financial markets were in turmoil. The Dow Jones Industrial Index dropped to 50, U.S. government bonds gave up all their gains since July 1932, and commodities prices hit a new postwar low. The Federal Reserve Bank of New York raised the discount rate from 2 1/2% to 3 1/2% and in five steps raised its buying rate for 91-day bankers acceptances from 1/2% to 3 5/8%. Call loan rates rose from 1% to almost 5%. The sterling exchange rate jumped from $3.40 to $3.46 1/2, and according to the *Commercial & Financial Chronicle*, ''Only active interference on the part of the London authorities prevents the rate from soaring.'' There was a 3% per annum premium on forward sterling, which created a heavy arbitrage flow of funds from New York to London despite the record low rate of 3/4% on 60 to 90-day bills in London.

Unlike 1907, when J. P. Morgan stemmed the Knickerbocker Bank Panic by lending freely, no private banks could stem this crisis. Everyone turned to government. There were meetings all day Friday, March 1st, in New York City between the Federal Reserve, New York's leading bankers, and Roosevelt's Secretary of the Treasury designate, William Woodin. Some $110 million of gold was earmarked by foreign bankers during the day, and over Thursday and Friday $700 million in currency was withdrawn. Stocks and commodities actually rose strongly on Friday in anticipation that Roosevelt would provide a solution to the bank crisis. At the urging of the New York Clearing House Association, Governor Herbert Lehman finally closed the New York banks at 4:20 a.m. Saturday morning so that they would not have to open for the usual half-day on

Saturday morning. Over $700 million in foreign deposits were expected to be presented for gold on Saturday morning had the banks not been closed. Illinois banks were also closed Saturday as a result of the same discussion that led Governor Lehman to close the New York banks. There were restrictions on bank deposit withdrawals in 31 states and the District of Columbia on Saturday, March 4th, as Franklin Roosevelt took the oath as President of the United States. Later in the day, after viewing a victory parade and attending a festive party, he took time out to sign a proclamation declaring a nationwide Bank Holiday under section 5(b) of the 1917 Emergency War Powers Act. Banks, stock exchanges, commodities exchanges, and the foreign exchange market were closed.

Roosevelt did not hesitate to condemn the banking community in his inaugural speech: "The rulers of the exchange of mankind's goods have failed, through their own stubbornness and their own incompetencies. Practices of the unscrupulous money changers stand indicted in the court of public opinion....They know the rules of a generation of self seekers." But Roosevelt had a greater role in causing the bank crisis than the bankers did. When a leading banker said the crisis was in Washington, not in New York, he was simply pointing out that political factors precipitated the bank crisis rather than economic ones. We have already seen that the banking system was more liquid as the bank crisis approached than at any previous point in its history, both in absolute and relative terms, and there had been a considerable economic recovery from the low point in the economy in the summer of 1932.

The bank crisis was principally the product of two factors: the inability of Hoover's administration to continue to cope with the impact of the Depression on the banking system during the "lame duck" period, and the irresponsible semi-public discussions of Roosevelt and his appointees before they were in power about taking the dollar off the gold standard.

The inability of the Hoover Administration to legislate or react effectively after the election was immediately clear when Hoover and Roosevelt could not agree on a response to European requests for a reduction in war debts, and it was emphasized further when the two could not agree on the necessary taxes to balance the budget, but the importance to the domestic financial system of this period without government leadership became obvious only when Governor Comstock closed the Michigan banks. The symbolism of this failure was graphic indeed. For the first time the RFC failed in its efforts to keep open a major bank. The Central Republic National Bank in Chicago had been kept open with larger loans when it was in worse trouble. Now, two banks controlled or heavily influenced by Henry Ford, one of the richest men in the United States and a personal friend of President Hoover, and in America's industrial heartland, where a bank holiday would have a widespread impact on jobs and the general economy, could not be kept open by RFC ministrations or political leverage over the Fords. As worried depositors in banks in other states withdrew their funds, and restrictions on deposits were imposed in state after state, the whole world suddenly realized that the Administration and the RFC had become ineffective. The lender of last resort for the banking system was in doubt. Frightened depositors lined up for cash, the only working substitute for bank deposits, which ballooned almost $2 billion from $5.4 billion on February 8th to $7.3 billion when the Bank Holiday was declared March 4th.[27] Since the banks paying out this cash got it from the Federal Reserve, their reserves were reduced almost $2 billion and much of their U.S. Treasury holdings was tied up as collateral with the Federal Reserve for loans.

As if the loss of the banking system's lender of last resort was not enough, Roosevelt and his advisors were clearly considering the possibility of taking the dollar off of the gold standard—in other words, devaluing it—which created an enormous incentive to turn dollar deposits into foreign currencies, whether the depositor was a foreigner or not. The public tip-off that Roosevelt was thinking along these lines came when Senator Glass turned down Roosevelt's offer to become Treasury Secretary because he would not give a commitment to maintain the value of the dollar. There were numerous less public indications of Roosevelt's thinking to those closer to events, however. Both Henry Wallace, the new Secretary of Agriculture designate, and George F. Warren of Cornell University, one of Roosevelt's closest agricultural advisors, openly favored devaluing the dollar. Roosevelt asked Gerard Swope, President of General Electric, what effects would follow from devaluing the dollar and was told "none." Roosevelt brought up the topic again at a business conference. By January 1933 the topic had become sufficiently public that Charles Mitchell felt constrained to speak out against devaluation at National City Bank's annual meeting.

The gold stock declined slowly at first, from $4,279 million on January 18, 1933, to $4,224 million on February 15, 1933, while discussion of going off the gold standard was muted, but the discussion became alarmingly public in the last week of February. Winthrop Aldrich, new chairman of the Chase National Bank, inveighed against the Roosevelt Administration's gold price plans in public testimony before the Senate Finance Subcommittee investigating stock exchange practices, as follows:

The shock to confidence at home and abroad of a deliberate breach of faith of the United States Government with respect to the gold standard of the present standard of value (meaning the present standard of weight and fineness) would be something we could not get over in years. . . . [It] would be an incredible shock to good faith everywhere. Excuse can be made for embarrassed countries like England for going off the gold standard that they couldn't help it, but no excuse can be made if we did it deliberately.[28]

Al Smith and Alexander Dana Noyes, financial editor of the *New York Times*, testified before the same committee against premeditated devaluation of the dollar and a conscious effort to inflate prices thereby.

The Hoover Administration tried strenuously to dampen speculation that Roosevelt planned to devalue the dollar and to get him to take a public position in this respect. In letters and during their transition meetings, Hoover personally asked Roosevelt for assurances on the dollar. Finally he wrote a public letter to the Republican National Committee opposing devaluation and calling for a sound currency, which was a highly political act but not an unreasonable one since he had received no assurances from Roosevelt and many rumors to the contrary. Someone needed to go on the public record against devaluation. Eugene Meyer, Governor of the Federal Reserve, and Treasury Secretary Mills tried privately to tie Roosevelt to a commitment not to devalue the dollar before they would authorize bond market purchases by the Federal Reserve to create reserves for the hard-pressed commercial banking system, but with no success.

The press carried these news items prominently, so that if the world did not know Roosevelt was considering devaluation it promptly found out. Foreign depositors rushed to get out of dollar deposits, which either they or the central banks receiving the new deposits quickly turned into gold "earmarked" for them at the Federal Reserve. No central bank was willingly going to take a passive position and risk foreign exchange losses on a large scale from devaluation, as France had when England devalued in 1931. As a result, the U.S. gold stock dropped a further $168 million by March 1st, another $100 million by March 3rd, and reports circulated that over $700 million would be presented for gold on March 4th, when the New York banks were closed by Governor Lehman. Even the New York banks were able to shift $66 million in assets abroad in the last two weeks before the Bank Holiday, despite the pressure from depositors to liquidate bank assets domestically.[29]

Hoover is frequently given tongue-in-cheek treatment by historians for his persistent demand of Roosevelt in this period that he assure the world of his commitment to a sound currency and to the gold standard, but Hoover had his finger on one of the key causes of the bank crisis. Loose talk by Roosevelt and his supporters about devaluing the dollar when they were still two to three months distant from the reins of power was naive and destructive. It led to foreign gold withdrawals of $300 million in February and the threat of massive withdrawals in March, which finally forced the New York banks to close. Hoover and the Federal Reserve were put in an impossible position. Once foreign and domestic depositors became fearful that their bank deposits would be either devalued or restricted (at worst, lost), there was no limit on what they could withdraw short of the banks' inability to pay. There was nothing the federal government could do to stop the runs on the banks. Hoover toyed with the idea of a federal guarantee of bank deposits and repeatedly asked the Federal Reserve for advice, but it gave him none since he was powerless to achieve any legislation affecting the situation. Roosevelt refused all requests from both Hoover and the Federal Reserve to give the reassurance to foreign depositors which he alone could give. Events were simply left to run their course until he got into office and took over the governing process.

Let us take a moment to look at the position of the banking system as it appeared on March 8, 1933, after Roosevelt had declared the Bank Holiday. Member bank reserves had dropped to $1.8 billion from $2.5 billion even though there was a net increase of almost $400 million in Federal Reserve securities purchases in the prior 2 1/2 weeks. The incremental reserves which should have been created by this expansion in Federal Reserve assets were more than offset since the first of the year by an increase in currency outstanding of almost $2 billion, a decline in the gold stock of almost $300 million, and an increase in nonmember deposits at the Federal Reserve of almost $100 million.[30]

The New York City banks' deposits had declined 28 1/2%, which was almost $2.4 billion, since the start of the year, when they were $8.3 billion. Banks outside New York City, which had been leaving deposits with the New York City banks as a form of reserves, withdrew $850 million, over half such deposits and one-third of all the New York City banks' withdrawals. The U.S. government and foreigners each withdrew over $100 million of deposits as well.

The New York City banks met these deposit withdrawals of almost $2.4 billion by borrowing $630 million from the Federal Reserve, allowing reserves to decline over $400 million, selling over $300 million in U.S. Treasury securities, and reducing loans for purposes other than carrying securities by approximately $400 million. This last category represented a squeeze on borrowers which was etched on the minds of its victims for a generation. These banks still held $3.3 billion of investments when the Bank Holiday was declared.[31]

The weekly reporting and therefore relatively large banks in 100 cities outside New York City had a 24% decline in deposits, amounting to $3.1 billion, between the beginning of 1933 and March 8th, compared with the 28 1/2% decline for the New York City banks. In both cases approximately 30% of the decline in deposits represented a decline in deposits from other banks. The banks outside New York City reacted somewhat differently from those in New York City to this deposit squeeze, reducing loans against securities by 17%, compared with a 5% rise in this category for the New York City banks, and resorting to the Federal Reserve for $456 million in borrowings, compared with $630 million borrowed by the New York City banks. The larger borrowing from the Federal Reserve by the New York City banks was due to the disproportionate reduction of reserves caused by foreign deposit withdrawals, since these deposits did not find their way back into the banking system, and by the relatively larger holdings of U.S. Treasury securities among the New York City banks, which they could pledge for Federal Reserve borrowings without using up all their flexibility (37% of deposits versus 24%).

We do not have data that provide a detailed picture of the position of country banks at the time of the Bank Holiday, but we can infer from data collected in the "call" of the Comptroller of the Currency on June 30th for bank financial statements that the country banks were in a worse position than the city banks. Almost 25% of all nonmember commercial banks opened on December 31, 1932, were still closed on June 30, 1933, and the deposits in nonmember banks had declined 26%, compared with 4% for the New York City banks and 9% for weekly reporting banks in 100 cities outside New York City. Member country banks deposits had declined 15%. The country banks cut back their loans sharply

in these six months—22% at member banks and 28% at nonmember banks—
but the most striking difference between these banks and the large banks was
the decline in investments of the former. They dropped 24% at nonmember banks
and 13% at country member banks, compared with minor changes at the city
banks.

It is helpful at this point to look also at the change in banking conditions
between October 1929 and June 1933. The impact of the Depression grew greater
in a progression from the New York City banks, which felt it least, to those
banks reporting weekly in 100 cities outside New York City, to the country
member banks, and last to the nonmember banks. Over this period the New
York City banks gained 2% more deposits, while other weekly reporting city
banks lost 23% of their deposits, country member banks lost 42% of their
deposits, and nonmember banks lost 59% of their deposits. All categories of
banks liquidated loans, ranging in the above order from a reduction of 41% by
the New York City banks to a reduction of 64% by the nonmember banks. Much
of these reductions was voluntary, of course, especially when loans were used
to carry securities. There was a sharp contrast in the investment patterns of these
banks, however. New York City banks more than doubled their investments as
their loans declined, and other weekly reporting banks increased their investments
36%, but country member banks were forced to reduce their investments 21%,
and nonmember banks reduced their investments 44%.

The resulting image of the banking system at the time of the Bank Holiday
and shortly thereafter is that while the country banks had suffered a sharp contraction in numbers, deposits, loans, and investments, the city banks had greatly
increased their investments both absolutely and relative to deposits, so that they
should have easily withstood the Depression had not political influences led to
both domestic and foreign runs on deposits when the U.S. government was in
no position to do anything to counter it.

Once Roosevelt was in office he was prepared to use the power of the federal
government to stabilize the banking system. On Saturday, March 4th, following
his inauguration, he invoked the War Powers Act of 1917 to declare a nationwide
Bank Holiday, closing all the commercial banks, the stock and commodities
exchanges, and the foreign exchange markets. Only limited banking activity was
allowed, such as new deposits in segregated accounts, cashing U.S. government
checks, trustee activities, exchanges of clearing house scrip, and limited withdrawals to buy food and similar necessities. Insurance and mortgage loan companies operating under New York law were also closed and prohibited from
paying dividends and making policyholder loans.

A special Sunday night session of Congress was called to consider the Emergency Banking Act, which was passed with only 35 minutes of debate and no
copies of the bill in members' hands. Roosevelt signed the bill the following
Thursday. The act authorized the RFC to borrow without limit and to buy
preferred stock in closed banks without collateral to help them reopen. The act
allowed bank notes to be issued up to 90% of collateral and the Federal Reserve

to make loans against any collateral, and it authorized the Comptroller of the Currency to appoint conservators who would authorize closed banks to reopen or oversee their liquidation. No deposit withdrawals were allowed for gold purchases, cash hoarding, or speculative foreign exchange purchases.

There was no longer a question of a President without authority. Simultaneously, banks were reopened, government influence over the financial markets was established, and rescue missions were put in place by the RFC. The New York City banks were opened one week after the Bank Holiday was declared with confidence that the $4.4 billion of liquid assets held in call loans, cash, federal reserves, and investments (mostly U.S. Treasuries) would cover the $7.5 billion they held in deposits. Fred Kent, a director of Bankers Trust Co. who had overseen World War I foreign exchange markets, was put in charge of the foreign exchange markets to make sure that currency speculation did not drain the New York banks of reserves. The only New York City Clearing House bank which did not open was the Harriman Bank & Trust, which J. P. Morgan & Co. refused to help despite a request from the Federal Reserve. The Harriman Bank's officers had been under criminal investigation since April 1932. It never reopened. The stronger banks all across the nation reopened in the following days with the approval of the Comptroller of the Currency.

The return of confidence was visible in the securities markets. The U.S. Treasury offered two new bond issues on March 13th—$400 million due August 15, 1933, at 4%, and $400 million due December 15, 1933, at 4 1/4%. Orders totalled $1.8 billion. The gold outflow was reversed as the United States gained over $325 million in gold in the week ending March 15th. Bank borrowing at the Federal Reserve dropped $180 million in the same week. During the next two weeks, short-term rates dropped 1%–2%. Bankers acceptance rates fell back to 2%, and call loan rates fell to 3%, as the Federal Reserve cut its buying rate for 90-day acceptances 3 times within five days. By the end of March, the public's cash hoard had dropped $1.2 billion to $6 billion and member bank borrowings at the Federal Reserve had dropped $1.4 billion to $559 million. Only the gold stock had not recovered, but it was still at $4 billion, which was an exceedingly strong position.[32] Stock, bond, and commodities prices rose dramatically throughout March following the Bank Holiday. Moody's daily index of staple commodities actually rose 6% from Friday, March 3rd, to Tuesday, March 7th, while the banks and markets were closed, anticipating Roosevelt's actions to restore the financial system. As the Guaranty Trust Co. remarked in its monthly *Survey* reviewing March, "Such an abrupt transition from panic to renewed hope probably has no parallel in financial history. . . . The very shock of the crisis seemed to bring a feeling akin to relief by removing the suspense and the vague dread that had existed so many months." The *Commercial & Financial Chronicle* remarked about the month of March, "Probably never. . .has such a gamut been run from paralyzing fear to renewed hope and encouragement."

The Roosevelt Administration strode forcefully into the markets despite the renewed optimism. The quarterly call by the Comptroller of the Currency for bank financial statements on March 31st was eliminated to avoid pressure on the markets as banks tried to windowdress "thin balance sheets." President Roosevelt announced the end of the gold standard on April 22nd, offering all those who failed to turn their gold into the Federal Reserve a maximum fine of $10,000 plus ten years in jail. In early May he introduced a joint resolution of Congress abrogating all gold contracts, and thereafter periodically set the gold value of the dollar at his whim. Eugene Meyer resigned on April 12th as Chairman of the Federal Reserve, and the Administration's influence over the Federal Reserve was soon made clear when in May the Treasury rather than the Federal Reserve announced a change in the Federal Reserve discount rate and that the Federal Reserve would resume buying U.S. Treasury securities. The Administration dominated the Federal Reserve in other ways as well, the most notable being the case of reopening the Bank of America, which San Francisco Federal Reserve Governor John U. Calkins opposed but which Secretary of the Treasury Woodin and Acting Comptroller of the Currency F. G. Awalt approved under considerable pressure from two Californians, Senator William Gibbs McAdoo and NRA Administrator General Hugh Johnson.

At the end of March, the RFC announced hurriedly prepared regulations governing RFC purchases of preferred stock in closed banks in order to help them reopen and by the end of June 1933 made preferred stock purchases or loans on preferred stock totalling $43 million. The National Bank of Detroit was opened April 1st in Detroit with $12.5 million in RFC funds and with Walter Chrysler and Alfred Sloane of General Motors on the board of directors. The new bank replaced the closed Guardian National Bank of Commerce and First National Bank of Detroit. The Hibernia National Bank and the National Bank of Commerce opened in New Orleans on May 27th with $0.5 million of RFC preferred stock funds each, replacing two permanently closed banks, the Hibernia Bank & Trust and the Canal Bank & Trust. The National City Bank opened in Cleveland on June 10th with $4 million in preferred stock investment from the RFC to create total capital of $10 million. The National City Bank replaced the Union Trust and Guardian Trust banks, which were liquidated with the help of a $43.6 million loan from the RFC and a $25 million loan from the new bank. By May 3rd, some 5,478 banks had been reopened, representing $26 billion in deposits, over 90% of all deposits. Slightly over 1,200 banks remained closed, most of which were small banks, with the exception of those in Baltimore, where the financial problems of several large insurance companies were keeping the banking situation precarious. Roger Babson, who had foreseen so many of the financial troubles between 1929 and 1933, suggested at the end of May that conditions might be back to normal within 12 months.

By midyear various legislative reforms were passed which added further stability to the markets—the Glass-Steagall Act, guaranteeing bank deposits and separating brokers and commercial bankers; the Securities Act, providing for federal regulation of new securities issues; and the National Recovery Act, to coordinate business competition and production.

Of course, not everything was quickly perfect within the financial infrastructure. Banks were slow to reopen in some states, and banks remained closed in Baltimore. At the end of April, Illinois still had 260 of its 704 banks closed, and Michigan had 121 of 436 banks closed. Some banks suffered further runs, such as the Westchester Trust Co. in mid-May, which had to declare a temporary bank holiday again. The Prudence Co., a leading New York mortgage loan company, went bankrupt in March despite $20 million in loans from the RFC, and at the same time the Globe & Rutgers Insurance Co., the third largest U.S. fire insurance company, had to seek court protection from its creditors and begin a year-long process of financial reorganization.

Nonetheless, it was clear by the end of 1933 that money market and banking conditions had recovered from the bank crisis. The Federal Reserve had increased its holdings of U.S. Treasury securities by $550 million (following the U.S. Treasury's announcement of a purchase program in mid-May), and this increased commercial banks' reserves so dramatically that they held record excess reserves of $815 million by the end of 1933. New low yields of 1/4% for bankers acceptances and 3/4% for call loans were established in September and October. Treasury notes and certificates with 3- to 6-month maturities dropped to yields averaging only .01% at approximately the same time.[33]

The banking system lost 3,400 banks which closed during the year and $3.4 billion in deposits (or approximately 10% of all deposits), but this was principally concentrated among nonmember and country member banks, which accounted for over 97% of the banks that did not reopen and 100% of the deposits lost. Weekly reporting banks in the nation's 101 larger cities ended the year with $8.7 billion of investments, which was slightly higher than they began the year with, and insignificant Federal Reserve borrowings.

A measure of the return to normalcy is provided by the return to normal public holdings of only $5.4 billion in currency, much below the $7.25 billion peak in March. A more striking measure of the changes which had taken place was evident in the rest of the decade, when bank suspensions approximated 50 per year, less than one-tenth the number of closings in the 1920s.[34]

NOTES

1. *National Income Accounts*, pp. 2, 4, 14, 102; *Statistical Abstract, 1939*, pp. 774, 347.

2. *National Income Accounts*, p. 126; *Statistical Abstract, 1939*, p. 307.

3. *Moody's Industrial Manual, 1935*, and *Moody's Railroad Manual, 1934*, blue insert pages on "The Nation's Basic Industries."

4. *Statistical Abstract, 1939*, pp. 639, 643, 625.

5. *National Income Accounts*, pp. 14, 80.

6. *Moody's Industrial Manual, 1935*, and *Moody's Railroad Manual, 1934*, blue insert pages on "The Nation's Basic Industries."

7. *Moody's Industrial Manual, 1935*, blue insert pages on "The Nation's Basic Industries."

8. *Statistical Abstract, 1939*, p. 315.

9. Ibid., p. 315; *Moody's Industrial Manual, 1935*, blue insert pages on "The Nation's Basic Industries."

10. *Statistical Abstract, 1939*, p. 315; *National Income Accounts*, p. 158.

11. *Banking & Monetary Statistics*, pp. 387. 147.

12. Ibid., p. 19.

13. Ibid., p. 146.

14. *Stock Exchange Practices*, part 12, p. 5102.

15. Ibid., part 10, pp. 4987–89.

16. Ibid., pp. 4620–21.

17. Ibid., part 9, pp. 4494–95.

18. Edsel Ford and C. Mott had each guaranteed $2.5 million, Edsel Ford had loaned $1 million in cash and $5 million in Detroit bonds, $4 million had been spent to support Guardian Group stock, and $3.4 million had gone to take over the stock bought from Goldman Sachs Trading Corp.

19. *Stock Exchange Practices*, part 9, p. 4507.

20. Ibid., part 11, pp. 5375–76.

21. Ibid., part 10, pp. 4754–56.

22. Ibid., part 12, p. 5489.

23. *Moody's Financial Manual, 1934*, p. 2369.

24. Ibid., p. 2368.

25. Deposits for the Guardian National Bank of Commerce on 12/31/30 were calculated by adding together the $124 million of the Guardian Detroit Bank and $74 million of the National Bank of Commerce which merged 12/31/31. See Moody's Financial Manual 1931, pp. 337, 1091. Deposits for the First National Bank-Detroit on 12/31/30 were calculated by adding together the $166 million of the First National Bank in Detroit and $345 million of the Peoples Wayne County Bank which merged 12/31/31, as well as the $44 million deposits of American State Bank of Detroit acquired in 1931. Redford State Savings Bank and Peoples State Bank of Redford were acquired in 1931, as well, but a record of their deposits is not available.

26. *Stock Exchange Practices*, part 10, pp. 4748–49.

27. *Banking & Monetary Statistics*, p. 387.

28. *Commercial & Financial Chronicle*, 3/4/33, p. 1438.

29. *Banking & Monetary Statistics*, p. 586.

30. Ibid., p. 387.

31. Ibid., pp. 178, 575.

32. Ibid., p. 387.

33. Ibid., pp. 387, 441, 445, 451, 460.

34. Ibid., p. 284.

14

The Stock Market in 1933

THE COURSE OF EVENTS—STOCK PRICES COME CLOSE TO THEIR LOW PRICES OF 1932 DURING THE BANK CRISIS, BUT MORE THAN DOUBLE DURING ROOSEVELT'S FIRST HUNDRED DAYS

One might have expected that the progression of the bank crisis and the quarrels between Roosevelt and Hoover would have produced a pronounced reaction in the stock market, but they did not. By the end of 1932 the stock market had been beaten down so far that it already had discounted just about the worst that could happen. The Dow Jones Industrial Index began the year at 59 and was still over 59 on February 11th. When the NYSE closed for the Bank Holiday, the Dow Jones Industrial Average was just below 54. Losses in the market had been so great that participation in it was at a low ebb. Daily trading volume since the start of the year averaged only 750,000 shares.

As the banks closed, there was no sign of a rush to raise cash in the market and no expansion of selling volume. Stocks were already so low that this should not be surprising. The Dow Jones Industrial, Railroad, and Utility indices were all at only 13% of their 1929 high points. The market prices of leading stocks averaged only 65% of book value, and dividend yields on the half of all stocks still paying a dividend averaged 8.70%, a real return of almost 20% when adjusted for deflation. These stock prices were within a hair's breadth of equalling the low points set in the summer of 1932.

Just as stock prices did not appear to be much influenced by the banking crisis, they were not much influenced by its resolution. The DJII closed at 62 on March 15th, the first day of trading on the NYSE since March 3rd, when the index was at 53. This was a 15% jump, which seems to belie the above assertion, but during the rest of March the DJII hovered in the mid 50s, which is exactly where it was through most of February as the bank crisis accelerated. The DJRI similarly stuck around its February level, and the DJUI actually declined 12% between March 4th, when the Bank Holiday was declared, and March 31st.

Roosevelt's subsequent decision to devalue the dollar had an explosive upward effect on stock prices and trading volume. The DJII jumped from 62 to 68 on April 19th on volume of 5.1 million shares, the day after gold export licenses were stopped and devaluation could be inferred. In the next three months the DJII rose to 90 in May, to almost 99 in June, and to almost 109 in July, with spectacular trading volume. Volume averaged over 5 million shares daily in June and July, with five days over 7 million shares and one over 9 million shares. The rise to 109 on the DJII represented a gain of 114% from the low point in the stock market just before the Bank Holiday. Leading stocks taken individually averaged a gain of 187% from their lowest prices to their highest prices for this period, and the previously most depressed stocks rose 300%–400%.

A radically new set of stock valuations was established. Stock prices for companies with meaningful earnings averaged 22.7 times 1933 earnings per share, compared with 10 times 1933 earnings in February. The 82 companies paying dividends had the yield on their stocks cut by the rise in prices from 8.70% at their lowest prices to an average of 3.60% now, although those with the steadiest dividend rates yielded 4 1/2% to 5 1/2%. Stock prices averaged 181% of book value, compared with only 65% in February. Stocks at their highest prices were back to 85% of their 1929 *low* prices, a significant amount of the attrition of the 1930s to make up in three months.

But traders and investors needed nerves of steel to enjoy these wonderful new prices and ride the market's upward movement. There were downward price movements in the course of the three-month rise which were quite unsettling. The DJII dropped from 96 to 88 between June 12th and 15th—the equivalent of 89 points on the current Dow Jones Industrial Index—then recovered all its lost ground by June 19th. Between July 18th and 21st, the market dropped from 108 to 88, some 200 points on today's Dow Jones Industrial Index, in three days. By August the index was back up to 105.

This sudden explosion of stock prices between April and July contains a clue to one of the mechanisms that produced the Depression and led the recovery from it—the independent trend of price levels. We have already seen from 1930 to 1932 that the decline in prices developed an internal momentum, particularly among staple commodities, which had its own severe feedback on economic conditions in terms of income, investment, inventories, and credit conditions. Roosevelt's decision to devalue the dollar on April 18th, which sparked the stock market boom the next day, suddenly marked the determination of his Administration to act directly and forcefully to raise price levels. The next sharp market rise occurred when Congress passed the Farm Bill, authorizing a 60% devaluation of the dollar on May 10th, and the DJII rose in two days to over 80 for the first time since March 1932. There were succeeding sharp market rises from May 22nd to May 27th, when Roosevelt induced Congress to pass a joint resolution abrogating the gold clause in all domestic financial contracts; from June 3rd to

June 12th, when the dollar dropped to its lowest levels in the foreign exchange markets since World War I; on June 19th, when Roosevelt made clear that the United States would not join in the World Monetary and Economic Conference effort to stabilize the dollar, from June 29th to July 3rd, when the National Recovery Act was passed; on August 17th, when the first NRA codes were filed for utilities, the construction trades, newspapers, canners, and the aviation industry setting work hours and wages; and August 25th, when the Federal Reserve increased its weekly U.S. Treasury purchases from the $10 million level to $35 million under NRA prompting to create easier credit. In all these cases there was a strong direct or indirect influence on price levels, and economic effects were secondary. As the *Commercial & Financial Chronicle* remarked in August, "When everything else fails, suggestions that the Administration intends to take active measures in the carrying out of the policy to which it stands committed act instantly as a stimulus to any flagging tendency in [stock and commodity] prices."

TECHNICAL ASPECTS OF THE MARKET—THE BROKERAGE INDUSTRY CONTINUES TO CONTRACT, BUT TRADING VOLUME AND MARGIN BORROWING RISE

The infrastructure of the securities industry continued to shrink in 1933. The number of member firms dropped to 610, which was the low point for the 1930s, and branch offices shrunk to 1,171 from 1,492 as recently as the end of 1931. Stock tickers dropped from 2,169 to 1,573 in the same period and would drop to 928 by 1938 as the brokerage industry progressively adapted to the loss of public interest in the stock and bond markets. The number of companies listed on the New York Stock Exchange also continued to decline to 788 from 831 in 1931. (See Tables A.24 and A.25 in the Statistical Appendix.)

The market process itself was under sharp criticism. The Senate Finance Subcommittee investigation into stock exchange practices brought a public glare to brokerage house practices which appeared slipshod and on the borderline of unethical, so the whole industry was cast in disrepute. Its leading light, Charles E. Mitchell, Chairman of National City Bank, was forced to resign and was tried for tax evasion, although he was subsequently acquitted. The Securities Act of 1933 was passed to place the brokerage industry under permanent strict surveillance. John G. Bennett, Jr., New York's Attorney General, attacked the Curb Exchange's trading practices.

Fortunately for the brokerage industry, these blows were countered by an increase in trading volume on the NYSE from 425 million shares in 1932 to 658 million shares in 1933, and from 57 million shares to 101 million shares on the Curb Exchange, as stock prices almost doubled. Stock exchange member borrowing rose from $300 million at the end of 1932 to $800 million at the end of 1933, although the large increase in stock prices kept this increase to only 2.4% of the market value of NYSE stocks, compared with 1.5% in December 1932.

The short interest declined all year from a peak of 1.9 million shares just before the Bank Holiday to only 700,000 shares by December. This modest short position was down from a recorded peak of 5.6 million shares in May 1931.[1]

The price of a seat on the NYSE, an infallible indicator of brokerage community expectations, rose from a low of $90,000 to $250,000, the best price since mid-1931.

SPECIFIC INDUSTRIES AND INDIVIDUAL STOCKS IN 1933

Most U.S. industries divided into those that were heavily depressed and those that were more stable and profitable between 1929 and 1933. The depressed group included such financially oriented industries as banks, holding companies, and investment trusts, as well as commodity-based industries such as mining (except for gold), pulp and paper, oil, and farm equipment. The common attributes of the stocks of these industries were the elimination of earnings and dividends, reduction in book values, and stock prices, which were still below book value after they recovered in 1933. The most stable and profitable industries were not capital intensive and generally had close contact with consumers. Tobacco companies and consumer products companies fared remarkably well, and so did food products companies, chemical companies, and many retailers. Their stocks sustained relatively high earnings, dividends, and prices relative to book value. During the 1933 recovery in stock prices, many of their stocks approached the levels of 1929, whereas stocks of the financial and commodities industries were lucky to exceed 25% of their highest 1929 prices.

The most capital intensive industries fell in between the poles of success and failure, with some, like operating utilities and telecommunications, maintaining stable revenues, profits, dividends, and work forces, while others, like railroads, auto manufacturers, and steel companies, had large losses, eliminated their dividends, and laid off almost half their work forces. The differences were largely a function of sales declines. While electric and gas utilities' sales declined only 3% between 1929 and 1933, sales of steel and autos declined over 75%.

Data on individual companies can be found in Table A.1 in the Statistical Appendix. Table A.6 provides ratios for each company's high and low 1933 stock prices.

The Railroad Industry

In 1933, railroad finances were much improved over 1932, thanks to the RFC (See Table 14.1.) Moody's reduced only three ratings on large railroad bond issues during the year, and railroad bonds generally yielded 1%–2% less during the bank crisis than they had at the low point in the bond market in 1932. This financial improvement was reflected in railroad stocks during the bank crisis, when they were still at prices averaging 88% higher than at their lowest prices

Table 14.1
The Railroad Industry in 1933

	Price-earnings ratio		Market price as a % of book value		Dividend yield (%)		Low price as a % of 1929 high price	Return on equity (%)	Moody's bond ratings	Cash & equivalents ($ millions)
	High price	Low price	High price	Low price	High price	Low price				
Atchison, Topeka & Santa Fe	def.ᵃ	def.	35	15	0	0	12	def.	Aaa	27
Baltimore and Ohio	def.	def.	27	6	0	0	6	def.	Aa	(22)ᶜ
Canadian Pacific	def.	def.	42	15	0	0	11	def.	Aa	29
Chesapeake and Ohio	13	7	96	49	5.71	11.20	36	7.2	Aaa	(4)
New York Central	def.	def.	40	9	0	0	5	def.	Aa	(69)
Norfolk & Western	12	7	84	53	4.52	7.21	38	7.3	Aaa	11
Pennsylvania	29	10	50	17	1.19	3.57	13	1.7	Aaa	29
Southern Pacific	def.	def.	20	6	0	0	7	def.	Aa	(21)
Union Pacific	17	8	61	28	4.55	9.84	20	3.7	Aaa	20
Averages	NMᵇ	NM	51	22	NM	NM	16	NM	—	—

ᵃ def. = Deficit.
ᵇ NM = Not Meaningful
ᶜ Brackets indicate short-term borrowing.

of 1932. Later in the summer of 1933, rail stocks rose an average of 213% above their 1933 low prices and 45% above their highest prices of 1932.

The underlying economics of the railroad industry reflected a more mixed pattern than its securities in 1933. Monthly railroad revenues began to exceed corresponding months of 1932 only in May. From May through September, revenues were up 10%–20% over the same months in 1932. For those watching the industry closely, the upturn was visible promptly in data on freight car loadings of grain, coal and coke, forest products, and ores. It was the first upturn in railroad volume since 1929.

But this change in fortunes was not enough to produce profits for 1933. Revenues were the same as 1932, and Moody's reported a $114 million loss for the industry, compared with $151 million in 1932. Nor did the improved situation prevent 1933 from being the worst year of the Depression for railroad receiverships. Eighteen railroads with over 21,000 miles of track went into receivership, with securities outstanding valued at $1.2 billion. This was twice the level of 1932 and the worst year on record since 1893. The two largest receiverships were the Missouri Pacific for $375 million on June 22nd and the Chicago, Rock Island & Pacific on November 22nd for $331 million—both after securities prices had recovered dramatically and when recovery appeared to be on its way.

This difficult economic situation for the industry led to a continued reduction in employees from 1,155,000 to 1,084,000 (41% below 1929) and kept equipment purchases at their 1932 level of $100 million, which was 10% of their 1929 level. There were only 10 locomotives and 6 passenger cars on order at the end of 1933.

The Emergency Railroad Transportation Act was passed in June 1933 to allow three regional groups of railroad executives to organize routes, track use, and equipment use in order to reduce costs, but the bill also contained employment guarantees to the unions; this eliminated most opportunities for savings. The bill had no effect on railroad finances, which were aided principally by the sharp business recovery of that summer.

Railroads presented a sorry picture in 1933 compared with 1929. Most of the railroads suffered losses or had insignificant earnings and had eliminated their dividends. Five large railroads had gone into receivership—the Seaboard Coast Line in 1930; the Wabash in 1931; the St. Louis & San Francisco in 1932; and the Missouri Pacific and Chicago, Rock Island in 1933. Railroad bonds had suffered massive ratings reductions, and most railroad stocks averaged approximately 15% of book value at their lowest 1933 prices, compared with 65% for stocks as a whole. The industry's back had been permanently broken. When the stock recovery came in 1933, most railroad stocks recovered to only 40% of book value, compared with 181% for all stocks.[2]

In 1933 the Chesapeake & Ohio and Norfolk & Western railroads continued to be exceptions to the general depression in the railroad industry because of their heavy coal traffic and advantageous long hauls. Both companies had returns on equity in excess of 7%, and in October the Chesapeake & Ohio even increased its annual dividend rate from $2.50 to $2.80 per share. The two stocks came closer to book value than any other railroad stocks in the 1933 recovery.

The Operating Public Utility Industry

Utilities experienced their worst year of the Depression in 1933, both in fact and psychologically. Earnings were down 18% to their lowest point in the Depression, as was employment,[3] and most of the companies cut their dividends again. Their stocks during the bank crisis dropped to the same levels as 1932, while most other stocks were still up over 30% from their lowest 1932 prices. Utility bonds were also under greater selling pressure than other industries in 1933. In the recovery, utility stock prices doubled while other stocks almost tripled. (See Table 14.2 for details on specific companies.)

The psychology of the industry, which had been a preferred industry earlier in the Depression, had also changed quite sharply, but the change was clearly not prompted by the industry's earnings, which represented a 5 1/2% return on equity while most U.S. industry operated at a loss. Investors' fears were for the future and over the political attacks to which the industry was subject. In the short run, political attacks were translated into lower rates and lower profits, but in the longer run government intrusion into the power-generating business brought fears of unmanageable surpluses of electric power. Federal hydroelectric power capacity expansions appeared to be dictated by political philosophy and the need to generate employment, rather than by the need for the resulting electric power. For example, the Grand Coulee Dam in its first phase was to have a capacity of 315,000 kilowatts, compared with a total existing capacity in its state of Oregon of only 336,000 kilowatts. The St. Lawrence Seaway project represented an addition of over 2 million kilowatts of capacity, from which annual production of approximately 11 billion kilowatt hours, compared with total sales in the Mid-Atlantic region of 20 billion kilowatt hours in 1933. In Nebraska, three separate public power developments, the Loup Power District, the Sutherland Project, and the Tri-Counties Project, threatened to create electric power capacity greater than the existing capacity of the state. What surplus power the Tennessee Valley Authority would create for the South was unknown but enormous, since Roosevelt was proposing to develop the entire Tennessee River Valley watershed.[4]

It is shocking to see the losses realized by investors in the stocks of operating utilities despite the financial strength of the industry. For example, at the peak of the market in 1933, the prices of operating utility stocks were still down 70% from their highest 1929 prices, even though earnings per share were down only 45% and dividends per share were down only 29%. And although utilities had not been particularly overvalued in 1929 and maintained their earnings and dividends better than other industries, this stock price decline of 70% compared with 58% for stocks in general. The most shocking example was probably Public Service of New Jersey, which had reduced its earnings and dividends by only 17% between 1929 and 1933, but its stock price had declined 60%. This was a

Table 14.2
The Operating Public Utility Industry in 1933

	Price-earnings ratio		Market price as a % of book value		Dividend yield (%)		Low price as a % of 1929 high price	Return on equity (%)	Moody's bond ratings	Cash & equivalents ($ millions)
	High price	*Low price*	*High price*	*Low price*	*High price*	*Low price*				
Commonwealth Edison	18	7	78	29	4.82	12.90	7	4.3	Aa	16
Consolidated Gas Co. of N.Y.	19	10	121	64	4.69	8.82	19	6.3	Aa	(12)[a]
Detroit Edison	19	10	80	42	4.35	8.33	12	4.2	Aa	7
Pacific Gas & Electric	22	10	110	52	6.25	13.33	15	5.1	Aa	16
Public Service of N.J.	17	10	136	79	4.91	8.48	24	7.8	Aa	15
Averages	19.0	9.4	105	53	5.00	10.37	15	5.5	—	—

[a] Brackets indicate short-term borrowing.

dramatic reversal of the preference expressed by investors for utility stocks in the prior years of the Depression.

Holding and Investment Companies

The holding and investment companies were among the most ravaged companies in the Depression. Many of their stocks sold for less than $1 at the lowest points in 1932 and 1933. The upturn in 1933 markets was therefore of particular benefit to them, since for once their leverage worked in their favor. Most of their stocks tripled, although this raised them only to approximately 16% of their highest 1929 prices, but several of the companies were saved from reorganization by the market's rise. For some of the companies, however, the stress had been too great and they were unable to benefit from the better conditions.

The Public Utility Holding Companies

The public utility holding companies could hardly have fared worse in 1933 than they did in 1932, when their stocks dropped to approximately 5% of their highest 1929 prices; in the bank crisis and under the threat of widespread public power growth, however, the utility holding company stocks declined to approximately the same level as 1932. Only United Gas Improvement was an exception from this widespread decline, but it was alone in the group in being able to maintain significant earnings and dividends. (See Table 14.3 on specific companies.)

Most of the companies carried significant troubles into 1933, and of course Middle West Utilities was far advanced in the process of liquidation. Columbia Gas & Electric and Standard Gas and Electric eliminated their regular dividends. Cities Service was clearly on the verge of losing its 25% interest in bankrupt Richfield Oil, because Cities Service was so loaded with long- and short-term debt that it could not even venture a reorganization proposal to the trustee in bankruptcy. American & Foreign Power was forced to turn to its parent, Electric Bond and Share, for an additional $10 million loan, taking it up to $35 million, in order to pay down its banks partially and get a further extension on its bank debt. There seemed to be little hope for the company, as all its foreign subsidiaries were either losing money or blocked from transferring profits. Currency devaluations cost the company a book loss of $10 million. Commonwealth & Southern was particularly threatened by the plans for the TVA. The two parties worked out a plan for the transfer of some assets, transmission cooperation, and power purchases, which was a good omen, but Commonwealth & Southern's stock sunk 23% below its 1932 low price, the only holding company whose stock dropped below its 1932 low price, because of investor fear that TVA power would create an unprofitable surplus in the region.[5]

The public utility holding company stocks tripled in the recovery following the bank crisis, but this still brought their stocks back to only 16% of their highest 1929 prices, and while the stocks appeared to be at or above book value

Table 14.3
The Public Utility Holding Companies in 1933

	Price-earnings ratio		Market price as a % of book value		Dividend yield (%)		Low price as a % of 1929 high price	Return on equity (%)	Moody's bond ratings	Cash & equivalents ($ millions)
	High price	Low price	High price	Low price	High price	Low price				
Cities Service	def.[a]	def.	78	19	0	0	2	def.	B	(43)[d]
Columbia Gas & Electric	NM[b]	18	147	47	1.79	5.56	6	2.7	Baa	(9)
Commonwealth & Southern	def.	def.	114	23	0	0	4	def.	B pfd.	34
Electric Bond and Share	NM	22	189	45	0	0	2	0.6	B pfd.	43
IT&T	NM	NM	59	14	0	0	3	0.3	B	(36)
Middle West Utilities	NM	NM	0	0	0	0	0	def.	NR[c]	(25)
North American	30	11	154	54	0	0	7	5.1	Baa	26
Standard Gas and Electric	def.	def.	23	5	0	0	2	def.	B	24
United Gas Improvement	20	11	208	117	4.80	8.57	23	10.3	Aa pfd.	20
Averages	NM	NM	108	36	NM	NM	5	3.8	—	—

[a] def. = Deficit.
[b] NM = Not Meaningful.
[c] NR = Not Rated.
[d] Brackets indicate short-term borrowing.

at these higher levels, it was only because their book values had been written down savagely. The recovery left public utility holding company stocks among the biggest losers in the Depression.

The Investment Trusts

In the general recovery in 1933, the prices of the investment trust stocks tripled, but the resulting prices were still so low relative to the 1929 values of these stocks that the recovery was not very meaningful. If we exclude Lehman Corp., the book values of the investment trust stocks had declined over 93% between 1929 and 1933, and even at their highest prices in 1933 these stocks were only 11% of their highest 1929 prices. None had meaningful earnings and none paid dividends. (See Table 14.4 for data on specific stocks.)

The rise in stock prices generally was a welcome benefit to the investment trusts because they held diversified stock portfolios, but for some companies the stress had been too great and they were unable to benefit from the better conditions. The hapless Goldman Sachs Trading Corp. cancelled its management contract with Goldman, Sachs & Co. near the bottom of the market in April 1933, and the name was changed to Pacific Eastern Corp. In September, Floyd Odlum bought a further 501,000 shares of Goldman Sachs Trading Corp., thereby gaining over 50% of the stock for his Atlas Corp. The portfolio he gained was made up mostly of stocks of minor companies which did not participate fully in the stock market recovery.

United Founders did not fare much better than Goldman Sachs Trading Corp. In May 1932, the United Founders portfolio had dropped to a value of 52¢ per share and at the end of 1933 was still only worth 63¢ per share, even though in 1933 the portfolio had been shifted from 21% industrial stocks to 47%, which should have created better than average profits.

Lehman Corp. remained a dramatic exception to the rest of the investment trusts and a hallmark of good investment management. Its book value per share at the end of 1933 was down only 12% from 1929, and its highest 1933 stock price was down only 41% from its highest price in 1929. Lehman Corp.'s respectable 6.2% return on equity permitted it to pay a $2.40 dividend, and its absence of leverage helped keep the stock relatively stable.

The Non-Utility Holding Companies

The improvements in market and economic conditions bailed Alleghany and Transamerica out of their troubles. (See Table 14.5 for specific details on these companies.) Alleghany was threatened with default on its three debenture issues, which were both secured by and serviced by the income from collateral securities, but both the income and market values of these securities rose, and Alleghany Corp. escaped the Depression with a default-like debt restructuring for only one of the three issues. This was reflected in their prices, which rose to approximately 10 times their 1932 low prices during 1933. Transamerica Corp.'s position also improved dramatically, in contrast to the embarrassment in 1932 of liquidating

Table 14.4
The Investment Trusts in 1933

	Price-earnings ratio		Market price as a % of book value		Dividend yield (%)		Low price as a % of 1929 high price	Return on equity (%)	Moody's bond ratings	Cash & equivalents ($ millions)
	High price	Low price	High price	Low price	High price	Low price				
Goldman Sachs Trading	def.[a]	def.	NA[c]	NA	0	0	1	def.	NR[d]	(4)[e]
Lehman Corp.	16	8	99	47	3.00	6.32	28	6.2	NR	4
Tri-Continental Corp.	def.	def.	700	220	0	0	5	def.	NR	2
United Corp.	NM[b]	17	375	100	0	0	5	0.8	NR	(5)
United Founders	NM	NM	480	80	0	0	1	0	NR	(1)
Averages	NM	NM	414	112	NM	NM	8	1.4	—	—

[a] def. = Deficit.
[b] NM = Not Meaningful.
[c] NA = Not Available.
[d] NR = Not Rated.
[e] Brackets indicate short-term borrowing.

Table 14.5
The Non-Utility Holding Companies in 1933

	Price-earnings ratio		Market price as a % of book value		Dividend yield (%)		Low price as a % of 1929 high price	Return on equity (%)	Moody's bond ratings	Cash & equivalents ($ millions)
	High price	Low price	High price	Low price	High price	Low price				
Alleghany Corp.	def.[a]	def.	52	5	0	0	2	def.	Ba	2
Transamerica	20	5	156	44	0	0	4	6.0	B	(7)[c]
Averages	NM[b]	NM	104	25	0	0	3	NM	—	—

[a] def. = Deficit.
[b] NM = Not Meaningful.
[c] Brackets indicate short-term borrowing.

several subsidiaries. Parent company revenues rose from $4 million to $8.6 million, and in January 1934, Transamerica was able to begin paying dividends again and the stock rose to approximately 4 times its 1932 and 1933 low prices.

Alleghany and Transamerica were saved from bankruptcy, but their stockholders were still far from recovering their 1929 values. The two stocks rose to only 14% of their highest 1929 prices in 1933, neither paid a dividend, and Transamerica's book value per share was down 88% from 1929.

The Banks

No bank escaped the Bank Holiday in March 1933, but this crisis sharply split the leading banks into those in trouble as a result of imprudent past practices and those which were solidly based. Conditions were worst for Chase National Bank and National City Bank in New York, and Continental Illinois and First National Bank in Chicago. (See Table 14.6 for data on specific banks.) Stocks of the former sank to two-thirds of their lowest prices in 1932, which was the bottom of the Depression for most stocks, and the chairmen of both banks were subjects of public opprobrium. Albert Wiggin of the Chase was humiliated by disclosures of his stock market and tax evasion practices before the Senate investigation into stock exchange practices and repudiated by his successor as Chairman, Winthrop Aldrich, who eliminated Wiggin's retainer with the bank and publicly condemned his management. Charles Mitchell, who had already resigned as Chairman of National City Bank, went to jury trial for evasion of taxes, and although he was found not guilty he suffered much adverse publicity.

There was harsh reality about equal to these two banks' poor publicity. The Chase wrote off $79 million in assets in 1933, plus an additional $48 million in February 1934, and it still held $32 million in German loans and $13 million in defaulted Cuban public works debt. The book value of Chase's stock had been reduced 54% between 1929 and 1933, and its dividend was reduced 58%. Even with the benefit of the market recovery during the First Hundred Days, Chase's stock recovered to only 13% of its highest 1929 price. National City Bank wrote down its assets by $120 million and suffered a book-value-per-share reduction of 59% between 1929 and 1933, but it outdid Chase by reducing its dividend 81% from 1929. The bank was seriously exposed to trouble by its high ratio of deposits, equal to almost 10 times its capital, when better banks had a ratio of only 7 times capital. The bank's troubles were reflected in its stock price, which recovered to merely 8% of its highest 1929 price during the Hundred Days.

Of the leading banks, the Chicago banks were in the most trouble. The Continental Illinois was the first to sell the RFC $50 million in preferred stock in November 1933, when it wrote off $73 million in assets and reduced its net worth to $38 million. This represented a 71% reduction in book value per share since 1929. When stockholders were offered a prior opportunity to buy the preferred stock, they subscribed for only $333 worth. First Chicago similarly

Table 14.6
The Banks in 1933

	Price-earnings ratio		Market price as a % of book value		Dividend yield (%)		Low price as a % of 1929 high price	Return on equity (%)	Moody's bond ratings	Cash & equivalents ($ millions)
	High price	Low price	High price	Low price	High price	Low price				
Bankers Trust	def.ᵃ	def.	221	129	4.00	6.82	17	def.	NRᶜ	—
Central Hanover	NAᵇ	NA	194	127	4.64	7.07	19	NA	NR	—
Chase National	11	5	127	53	4.08	9.69	6	11.4	NR	—
Continental Illinois	16	3	196	38	0	0	2	12.3	NR	—
First National (Boston)	NA	NA	95	54	5.71	10.00	9	NA	NR	—
First National (Chicago)	9	3	100	28	0	0	4	11.0	NR	—
Guaranty Trust	13	8	118	73	5.70	9.22	18	9.2	NR	—
Irving Trust	19	9	114	55	4.60	9.58	12	6.0	NR	—
National City	23	8	256	89	1.63	4.69	3	11.4	NR	—
Averages	15.2	6.0	158	72	3.37	6.34	10	10.2	—	—

ᵃ def. = Deficit.
ᵇ NA = Not Available.
ᶜ NR = Not Rated.

got $25 million from the RFC at the end of 1933 but did not incur a major write-off of assets.

Measures of the two banks' problems can be had in their deposit-to-capital ratios of 16.6 and 13.2, respectively, which were double those of the New York banks, and in the total elimination of the two Chicago banks' dividends. Their stocks sank to a mere one-third of their lowest 1932 prices and 2%–4% of their highest 1929 prices. Stocks of Continental Illinois and First Chicago rose during the Hundred Days to only 9% and 14%, respectively, of their highest 1929 prices.

The First National Bank of Chicago gained some solace within its problems, for in contrast to Continental Illinois, First Chicago's deposits increased from $460 million to $583 million in 1933. This was within striking distance of Continental Illinois' $630 million in deposits and was a tribute to the dynamic leadership of Melvin Traylor. As recently as 1929, First Chicago's deposits of $366 million had been only 42% of Continental Illinois' deposits of $872 million.

Bankers Trust, Central Hanover Bank, and Guaranty Trust stood in sharp contrast to the banks mentioned above. None of these three banks reduced its dividends during the Depression, and they suffered only modest (8%–22%) reductions in book value per share because of asset write-offs. Bankers Trust and Central Hanover had 1933 deposits 7 times capital, and Guaranty Trust's deposits were only 3.8 times capital. Such strength was reflected in their stocks, which during the bank crisis were still one-third above their lowest prices in 1932 and during the Hundred Days rose to 29% of their highest 1929 prices, compared with 11% for their troubled counterparts.

From this modest recovery by the stocks of the best banks to 29% of their highest 1929 prices, one can see that there were still fears about the banking system after President Roosevelt's reforms even though bank failures and runs were sharply and permanently reduced. The banking system still required significant remedial effort. Continental Illinois and First National Bank of Chicago sold preferred stock to the RFC late in 1933, the National City Bank sold $50 million preferred to the RFC in January 1934, and the Chase sold a similar $30 million of preferred in February 1934. In due course, all the leading banks except First National Bank of Boston issued preferred stock to the RFC under pressure from its Chairman, Jesse Jones, so that depositors would not be induced to switch out of borrowing banks when their names were published by the RFC. Bankers Trust, Central Hanover, and Irving Trust took only $5 million each and immediately relent it to the RFC. One can only go so far to help one's poor neighbors.

The Oil Industry

The oil industry began to recover in 1933, both because of the improved economy and because of the beginning of effective pro-rationing in Texas and Oklahoma, where prolific new fields were destroying the economics of oil pro-

duction. During 1933 martial law was imposed briefly in the two main fields—
East Texas and Oklahoma City—to enforce pro-rationing. And when Roosevelt
included in the National Recovery Act federal authority to halt the movement
between states of oil produced in contravention of state pro-rationing guidelines,
the power to restrict surplus production was finally realized. Price-cutting disappeared. Interior Secretary Harold Ickes had reported to the cabinet in May
that East Texas crude oil was selling for 4¢ a barrel, but crude oil prices averaged
$1.25 in the last quarter. Production was increased from 782 million barrels in
1932 to 892 million barrels in 1933, and employment in the industry rose 18%.
Sales rose from $397 million in 1932 to $515 million in 1933, and Moody's
reported a rise in profits for 40 oil companies from $52 million in 1932 to $80
million in 1933. To some extent the domestic oil situation was helped by an
excise tax imposed on imports in 1932 and an agreement between Interior Secretary Ickes and the principal oil companies that they would limit oil imports to
the average volume of the last six months of 1932. Oil imports in 1933 were
valued at only $26 million, compared with $61 million in 1932 and $146 million
in 1929.[6]

The improved situation in 1933 for the oil companies was not improved enough
to make them attractive investments. The leading companies averaged less than
a 3% return on equity, four of the companies had eliminated common dividends
by 1933, Standard Oil of New Jersey and Standard Oil of California halved their
dividends in 1933, and the other companies generally had reduced their dividends
by two-thirds by 1933. Only Standard Oil of California and Standard Oil of New
Jersey realized peak stock prices in 1933 which were above book value. (See
Table 14.7 for data on the industry.)

The industry still had its merits. Write-offs during 1929–33 were almost
nonexistent, and many of the companies had large cash positions, amounting to
$189 million at Standard Oil of New Jersey, $80 million at Socony-Vacuum,
and $75 million at Standard Oil of Indiana. The industry had very modest leverage
as well. In many respects the companies' stock prices performed close to the
averages, reaching 43% of their highest 1929 prices during the Hundred Days,
compared with the 42% average for all stocks. Still, one tends to expect better
results from an industry which was so large and powerful and which had a direct
link to the rapid growth of the automobile.

The Chemical Industry

The chemical industry remained a standout for profits in 1933, as the leading
companies averaged a 13.6% return on equity and even turned the year into one
of expansion, which was unique for 1933. (See Table 14.8 for data on specific
companies.) Production was up in most major chemicals—up 54% for sulphur,
38% for synthetic nitrogen, 33% for coal tar, 20% for fertilizer, and 16% for
caustic soda, explosives, soda ash, and sulfuric acid. Employment expanded by
10%. Industry profits rose from $49 million in 1932 to $83 million in 1933, and

Table 14.7
The Oil Industry in 1933

	Price-earnings ratio		Market price as a % of book value		Dividend yield (%)		Low price as a % of 1929 high price	Return on equity (%)	Moody's bond ratings	Cash & equivalents ($ millions)
	High price	Low price	High price	Low price	High price	Low price				
Atlantic Refining	13	5	63	24	3.03	8.08	16	4.7	A	13
Gulf Oil of Pa.	def.[a]	def.	93	36	0	0	11	def.	A	21
Phillips Petroleum	53	13	59	15	0	0	10	1.1	Baa	4
Shell Union Oil	def.	def.	68	24	0	0	13	def.	Ba	16
Sinclair-Consolidated	def.	def.	89	28	0	0	11	def.	Baa	34
Socony-Vacuum	24	8	63	22	2.06	5.83	13	2.6	Aaa	80
Standard Oil (Calif.)	NM[b]	NM	105	47	2.22	5.00	24	1.3	NR[c]	23
Standard Oil (Ind.)	30	15	85	43	2.94	5.88	27	2.8	NR	75
Standard Oil (N.J.)	49	24	107	51	2.08	4.35	28	2.2	Aaa	189
Texas Corp.	def.	def.	83	31	3.33	9.09	15	def.	A	37
Averages	NM	NM	82	32	1.57	3.82	17	2.5	—	—

[a] def. = Deficit.
[b] NM = Not Meaningful.
[c] NR = Not Rated.

Table 14.8
The Chemical Industry in 1933

	Price-earnings ratio		Market price as a % of book value		Dividend yield (%)		Low price as a % of 1929 high price	Return on equity (%)	Moody's bond ratings	Cash & equivalents ($ millions)
	High price	Low price	High price	Low price	High price	Low price				
Allied Chemical	28	13	214	100	3.95	8.45	20	7.7	Aa pfd.	100
Commercial Solvents	65	10	1,425	222	1.05	6.67	13	21.7	NR[a]	2
Dow Chemical	19	10	80	42	4.35	8.33	12	21.0	NR	1
E. I. Du Pont	33	11	291	97	2.86	8.59	14	8.9	Aa	77
Monsanto Chemical	16	5	252	76	2.41	8.00	31	15.6	Aa	2
Union Carbide	33	13	217	83	1.92	5.00	14	6.6	NR	18
Averages	32.3	10.3	413	103	2.76	7.51	17	13.6	—	—

[a] NR = Not Rated.

the profits of the leading companies expanded proportionately. Du Pont was positive enough about the future to acquire control of Remington Arms in May 1933 following two years of deficits reported by Remington. Commercial Solvents acquired chemical companies in Louisiana and California to position it better in the commercial alcohol business, which looked promising due to the end of Prohibition.

The strength of the chemical industry resulted in some fantastic stock valuations in the stock market recovery. Prices averaged 32 times earnings at their highest and 413% of book value. The small companies' stock prices came close to their highest 1929 prices, while the large companies' stocks were closer to the average for all stocks of 42% of 1929 high prices. Dividend yields dropped to 2.76% from 7.51% at the low point for 1933.

Commercial Solvents, which was always unique because of its small size and unusually high profitability, was further unique in 1933 because of its ideal position in alcohol production to benefit from the end of Prohibition. Its stock at its highest price was 65 times earnings. Commercial Solvents stock hit 81% of its 1929 high price and was up over 6 times from its 1933 low price.

Such stock price performances were all the more remarkable for stocks which had not been pushed very low in the bank crisis in the first place. The stocks of the three large companies had low prices in 1933 some 45% above their 1932 low prices and only barely dropped below book value.

The only blemish on the year for the industry was a bitter quarrel between Allied Chemical and the New York Stock Exchange in which the Exchange threatened to delist Allied Chemical's stock if the company did not improve its reporting to stockholders, in particular its accounting for over $90 million in investments and the purposes of its reserves. Wall Street professionals knew that, of the $90 million in investments, approximately $31 million was the company's own common and preferred stock which it had repurchased, only $21 million was U.S. Treasury securities, and $39 million was other securities. Allied Chemical tried to take a hard line with the Exchange but ultimately relented, revealing the above investments and a $40 million reserve for decline in their value from their purchase prices.

The Food Industry

During 1933 the division between the food processing companies and those with prominent brand products was further accentuated as the former experienced conditions even worse than 1932 while the latter came out of 1933 surprisingly close to their valuations at the peak of the boom in 1929. (See Table 14.9 for details on the industry.)

Among the processing companies, Borden's, General Mills, and National Dairy reported their lowest earnings of the Depression during 1933, and two of them cut their dividends. Moody's reported record low earnings for both bread and dairy products companies in 1933. The stocks of Borden's, National Dairy,

Table 14.9
The Food Industry in 1933

	Price-earnings ratio		Market price as a % of book value		Dividend yield (%)		Low price as a % of 1929 high price	Return on equity (%)	Moody's bond ratings	Cash & equivalents ($ millions)
	High price	Low price	High price	Low price	High price	Low price				
Borden	35	17	119	58	4.32	8.89	18	3.4	NR[a]	20
General Foods	19	10	333	175	4.50	8.57	26	18.2	NR	63
General Mills	20	10	178	90	4.23	8.33	40	8.9	Baa pfd.	51
National Biscuit	29	15	359	188	4.59	8.75	34	12.4	Aaa pfd.	21
National Dairy	26	11	217	92	4.62	10.91	13	8.4	Baa	23
Pillsbury	13	4	77	27	3.70	10.67	15	6.1	Baa	2
Standard Brands	33	12	950	350	2.63	7.14	31	28.8	Aaa pfd.	19
United Fruit	22	7	126	43	2.94	8.70	14	5.9	NR	37
Averages	24.6	10.8	295	128	3.94	9.00	24	11.5	—	—

[a] NR = Not Rated.

and Pillsbury sank to low prices below those of 1932 and to significantly below book value. At the low point in 1933, the processing companies' stocks averaged only 15% of their highest 1929 prices. Nor did the stocks recover particularly well in the Hundred Days as they rose to an average of 38% of their highest 1929 prices and 135% of book value.

The companies with prominent brand products had quite different results. The stock prices for General Foods, National Biscuit, and Standard Brands all came within 20% of their highest 1929 prices, which in real terms, allowing for the 22% decline in prices, were the equal of 1929's highest prices. Even during the worst of 1933 their stocks were still approximately twice book value, twelve times earnings per share, and up to two-thirds higher than their lowest 1932 prices, in contrast to the lower 1933 prices of the processing companies. The stocks of these branded products companies had some spectacular valuations in other respects as well. Their highest 1933 stock prices exceeded 3 times book value, approximately 20 or more times earnings per share, and a dividend yield around 4%. Investors obviously expected the 20% return on equity earned by these companies to expand even further in 1934.

Standard Brands closed out this period as one of the most spectacular companies in the nation, with an approximately 29% return on equity and a high stock price over 9 times book value and 33 times earnings per share. Moody's returned its preferred stock rating to Aaa during the year. The company's coffee, yeast, and baking powder product lines, which sustained earnings through the Depression, were supplemented in mid-1933 by commercial alcohol and gin, and sales of malt products were also expected to grow rapidly as the beer industry revived. The company's products were ideally positioned for the future.

The Mining Industry

The mining industry moved from a condition approaching rigor mortis in 1932 to tentative recovery in 1933 under the stimuli of higher prices and renewed industrial production. (See Table 14.10 for details.) President Roosevelt's devaluation of the dollar had considerable impact on prices, especially on gold prices, which rose from $20.67 an ounce to over $31 an ounce, but also on copper prices, which rose from 4 3/4¢ per pound to 8 1/2¢; zinc prices, which rose from 3¢ per pound to 5¢; and lead prices, which rose from 2 7/8¢ per pound to 4.35¢. Base metal mines all across the United States and Canada, which had been mothballed since mid-1932, opened again in May and June 1933. Moody's reported a 1933 net loss of $12 million for nine copper companies, a decided improvement from the $37 million net loss reported in 1932. Similar reports for companies mining other metals indicated 1933 profits of $17 million, versus a loss of $18 million in 1932.[7]

The mining recovery still remained heavily skewed toward foreign countries despite that U.S. mines were reopened. Overall domestic production and employment of mining companies in 1933 were unchanged from 1932, and pro-

Table 14.10
The Mining Industry in 1933

	Price-earnings ratio		Market price as a % of book value		Dividend yield (%)		Low price as a % of 1929 high price	Return on equity (%)	Moody's bond ratings	Cash & equivalents ($ millions)
	High price	Low price	High price	Low price	High price	Low price				
Alaska Juneau Gold	33	11	300	100	2.27	6.82	110	9.1	NR[c]	2
American Smelting	NM[a]	15	126	26	0	0	8	1.7	Aa	23
Anaconda Copper	def.[b]	def.	43	9	0	0	4	def.	NR	(70)[d]
Homestake Mining	19	7	508	201	4.56	11.72	156	27.7	NR	13
International Nickel	NM	13	230	68	0	0	9	5.3	Baa pfd.	16
Kennecott Copper	NM	NM	90	25	0	0	7	0.7	NR	21
National Lead	23	7	67	21	3.57	11.63	20	2.9	A pfd.	8
Phelps Dodge	def.	def.	54	13	0	0	6	def.	NR	8
Texas Gulf Sulphur	15	5	300	100	4.44	13.33	18	19.9	NR	9
Averages	NM	9.7	191	63	NM	NM	38	9.6	—	—

[a] NM = Not Meaningful.
[b] def. = Deficit.
[c] NR = Not Rated.
[d] Brackets indicate short-term borrowing.

duction of lead, zinc, and silver was down over twice as far from 1929 levels as was production in the rest of the world. Copper production in the United States was down 76% from 1929 levels, while production in the rest of the world was down only 11%. Domestic copper production in 1933 was actually down 12% to only 239,000 tons, versus 272,000 tons in 1932, while 1933 copper production was up 44% in Chile and Peru, 28% in Africa, 18% in Canada, and 12% in Europe.[8]

All the mining companies benefitted from higher metals prices, which not only allowed them to reopen mines but also created inventory profits. American Smelting's 1933 earnings, its first since 1930, were totally accounted for by inventory profits. The gold mining companies got an unusual earnings boost from higher gold prices, so that Moody's reported record 1933 earnings for nine gold mining companies of $32 million, versus $25 million in 1932 and $15 million in 1929. Homestake Mining, the largest U.S. gold miner, was able to report a 27.7% return on equity in 1933 as it doubled its earnings and increased its dividend over 50%.

The more pronounced recovery in mining activity outside the United States had a disproportionate effect on Kennecott Copper and International Nickel, which had large foreign production. In both cases, mineral production approximately doubled in 1933, while production at American Smelting, Anaconda, Phelps Dodge, and National Lead changed little.

The stocks of the mining companies presented a sorry picture at the bottom of the market in 1933 before prices and production recovered. Stock prices of the base metal producers averaged a mere 19% of book value and 11% of their highest 1929 prices. Only National Lead still paid a dividend. However, their stock prices were almost 50% higher than their lowest prices in 1932.

The recovery in mining conditions presented dramatic opportunities for stock profits. The stocks of base metals producers almost tripled, with copper producers rising the most. American Smelting stock quadrupled, and Anaconda stock nearly quadrupled. However, stocks of the U.S. producers still only averaged 75% of book value and 35% of their highest 1929 prices. Nor did any of the base metals producers have a respectable return on equity, and Anaconda and Phelps Dodge still were reporting deficits.

The gold mining stocks were alone among stocks of all industries—not just mining—in having dramatically better results in 1933 than in 1929. At their lowest points in 1933, the stocks of Alaska Juneau Gold Mining and Homestake Mining were still significantly above their highest 1929 prices, and at their highest prices their stocks were 230% and 300% higher, respectively, than they had been in 1929. Dividends had risen dramatically at both companies every year since 1930. Alaska Juneau stock was 3 times book value per share, and Homestake stock was over 5 times book value per share.

An interesting personal side note is provided by Alaska Juneau. Two of its principal stockholders were Bernard Baruch and Eugene Meyer, Chairman of the Federal Reserve Board of Governors under Hoover. They invested in the company during the 1920s but in 1933 were strongly opposed to Roosevelt's gold policies even while they reaped handsome rewards from it.

The Motion Picture Companies

The year 1933 was the low point in the motion picture industry, as movie sales dropped 11% to $546 million, compared with $831 million at their peak in 1931. Paramount and RKO followed the Fox companies into receivership early in the year. Even the redoubtable Loew's Corp. suffered a 50% decline in earnings from 1932, cut its dividend from $3.00 to $1.00, and watched its stock drop to 10% of its highest 1929 price. (See Table 14.11 for details on specific companies.)

The plight of the movie industry created despair in many respects. Most of the companies' stocks sank to $1 or less, making all comparisons with 1929 prices meaningless; their preferred stock and bond prices sank similarly. Paramount and RKO bonds and Warner Bros. preferred stock dropped below $10, suggesting default rather than any hope for reorganization of these companies. The Hollywood board members of these companies may have sloughed off such disasters, but at RKO there was an acutely embarrassed board of New York financiers.

But the seeds of recovery for the industry were already sprouting in 1933 despite the ragged performance of the industry's securities. The industry had earnings of $1.7 million in 1933, compared with a loss of $3 million in 1932, and Fox Film was able to come out of reorganization in April 1933 and earn $1.1 million for the year. Warner Bros. was able to earn $2.5 million in its fiscal year from August 1933 to August 1934, and Paramount was able to generate operating profits of $5.7 million in reorganization against an operating loss of $15.9 million in 1932. The production and distribution subsidiaries of most of the big companies were able to continue work without going into receivership, even while the parent holding companies, and particularly their real estate subsidiaries owning office buildings and theaters, were in default. The seeds of recovery were in these production and distribution subsidiaries, as was the "value added" of the industry.

A clue to this strength was apparent in the industry's employment figures, which dropped only 17% between 1930 and 1933 and were again up to record levels by 1935.[9] By the end of 1934 the industry was back to a break-even position. Only RKO was still left in reorganization. Debentures and preferred stocks which had appeared almost valueless in mid-1933 were moving back up toward their par values, and Fox Film Corp.'s debenture rating had even been upgraded to Baa. There was a sure sign of recovery when Floyd Odlum of Atlas Corp. swooped in for a bargain by optioning 25% of the stock of Fox Film.

Table 14.11
The Motion Picture Companies in 1933

	Price-earnings ratio		Market price as a % of book value		Dividend yield (%)		Low price as a % of 1929 high price	Return on equity (%)	Moody's bond ratings	Cash & equivalents ($ millions)
	High price	Low price	High price	Low price	High price	Low price				
Fox Film A	10	2	33	5	0	0	1	3.1	Ba	5
Loew's	16	4	80	18	2.70	11.76	10	5.1	Baa	11
Paramount-Publix	NA[a]	NA	NA	NA	NA	NA	NA	NA	Ca	NA
Radio-Keith-Orpheum	def.[b]	def.	NM[c]	NM	0	0	NM	def.	Ca	(5)[d]
Warner Bros. Pictures	def.	def.	70	8	0	0	1	def.	Caa	3
Averages	13.0	3.0	61	10	NM	NM	2	NM	—	—

[a] NA = Not Available.
[b] def. = Deficit.
[c] NM = Not Meaningful.
[d] Brackets indicate short-term borrowing.

The Steel Industry

The steel industry staged a dramatic recovery from April through August 1933 as steel ingot production tripled, largely because of a recovery in the auto industry. (See Table 14.12 for details on the industry in 1933.) Ingot production in July reached 3.2 million tons, the highest production since June 1930. Employment rose 168,000 to 917,000 people, representing 75% of the 1929 work force in the industry. Steel prices improved 5% during the year, which was remarkable since steel prices had dropped only 16% since 1929. Moody's reported that 44 steel companies lost $66 million in 1933, which was better than the $159 million they lost in 1932 but was nonetheless a sad economic performance.[10]

Steel production was also helped by a partial reversal of the loss of worldwide market share suffered by the U.S. steel industry since 1929. Under the stimulus of both arms buildup and devaluation of the dollar, steel exports surged from 0.6 million tons in 1932 to 1.4 million tons in 1933, while exports in the rest of the world actually declined. U.S. exports doubled again in 1934. The U.S. steel industry was still roughly twice as depressed in 1933 as the worldwide steel industry, however. U.S. steel production was down 58% from 1929 levels, compared with 31% in the rest of the world, and U.S. steel and iron exports were down 77% from 1929 levels, compared with 48% in the rest of the world.[11]

The recovery in steel production caused steel stock prices to rise 326% from their lowest 1933 prices, even though steel stocks were already up 38% from their lowest prices in 1932, but the continued losses in the industry and use of only one-third of its productive capacity kept the steel stocks badly depressed relative to any standard other than their previous low prices. Their highest prices in 1933 averaged only 57% of book value and 52% of their highest 1929 prices. None of the stocks paid dividends, and their price-earnings ratios were meaningless since they had no earnings. Inland Steel was alone in breaking even and equally alone in enjoying a high stock price that equalled its book value, but it was still down 60% from its highest 1929 price.

The Automobile Manufacturers

Monthly auto and truck production more than doubled in the First Hundred Days, and for the year as a whole production was up 50% from 1932 to over 2 million units. Moody's reported a swing in net income for 23 auto companies from a loss of $64 million in 1932 to a profit of $67 million in 1933. Chrysler, General Motors, and Packard swung from losses to profits, and Ford reduced its 1932 loss of $75 million to only $4 million in 1933.[12]

This turnaround in auto company profits made their stocks among the most dynamic in the market. (See Table 14.13 for details.) They had been depressed to only 7% of their 1929 high prices in the bank crisis, but as Chrysler recovered to earn 13.9% on its equity and to sell as many units as it had sold in 1929, its

Table 14.12
The Steel Industry in 1933

	Price-earnings ratio		Market price as a % of book value		Dividend yield (%)		Low price as a % of 1929 high price	Return on equity (%)	Moody's bond ratings	Cash & equivalents ($ millions)
	High price	*Low price*	*High price*	*Low price*	*High price*	*Low price*				
Bethlehem Steel	def.[a]	def.	40	8	0	0	7	def.	A	47
Inland Steel	NM[b]	NM	102	27	0	0	12	0.3	Baa	(2)[c]
U.S. Steel	def.	def.	38	13	0	0	9	def.	Baa pfd.	105
Youngstown Sheet & Tube	def.	def.	49	9	0	0	5	def.	Baa	14
Averages	def.	def.	57	14	0	0	8	NM	—	—

[a] def. = Deficit.
[b] NM = Not Meaningful.
[c] Brackets indicate short-term borrowing.

Table 14.13
The Automobile Manufacturers in 1933

	Price-earnings ratio		Market price as a % of book value		Dividend yield (%)		Low price as a % of 1929 high price	Return on equity (%)	Moody's bond ratings	Cash & equivalents ($ millions)
	High price	Low price	High price	Low price	High price	Low price				
Chrysler Corp.	21	3	290	39	1.72	12.90	6	13.9	NR[c]	37
General Motors	21	6	240	67	3.47	12.50	11	11.3	A pfd.	177
Hudson Motor Car	def.[a]	def.	89	17	0	0	3	def.	NR	3
Nash Motors	def.	def.	193	79	3.70	9.09	9	def.	NR	30
Packard Motor Car	NM[b]	NM	210	52	0	0	5	0	NR	15
Averages	NM	NM	204	51	1.78	6.90	7	NM	—	—

[a] def. = Deficit.
[b] NM = Not Meaningful.
[c] NR = Not Rated.

stock exploded, rising to over 7 1/2 times its 1933 low price, almost 3 times book value, and 21 times earnings. Chrysler's $1.00 per share dividend, which had looked so insecure in early 1933 that the stock yielded 13%, suddenly looked like it should be increased, and the stock at its highest price had a yield of only 1.72%.

General Motors was less spectacular than Chrysler in its recovery, but solid and impressive. It earned an 11.3% return on equity and increased its dividend from $1.00 to $1.25 per share, based on a 54% expansion in unit sales, three-quarters of which were Chevrolet sales. Its stock rose 350% from its 1933 low price and hit a high price 21 times earnings per share and 240% of book value.

The stocks of the other auto manufacturers rose dramatically as well, even though none of them was able to do better than break even in 1933. All the auto stocks averaged a price rise of over 350% to twice book value, although they were still only 29% of their highest 1929 stock prices.

The Consumer Products Companies

Since 1933 was a better year for business than consumers, the consumer products companies did not show the improvements over 1932 that other industries showed. (See Table 14.14 for details on specific companies.) Earnings per share changes for the consumer products companies were mixed as both Gillette and Lambert Co. experienced declines, and Coca-Cola, Colgate, Lambert, and Procter & Gamble reduced their dividends sharply. Return on equity for the group was down to 15.6% from 18.6% in 1932.

The resulting stock price performances for the group were almost exactly the same as for 1932 at both the lowest and highest levels. In both years stock prices averaged between 22% and 45% of their highest 1929 prices. The highest prices were 271% of book value and over 19 times earnings per share, which were among the most attractive valuations in the stock market, but the stocks only doubled during the First Hundred Days, while stocks in general rose 186%.

One usually thinks of consumer-based companies leading the way out of a recession or depression and their stocks behaving correspondingly. This was not so in 1933, when the stimulus to recovery came from the rise in basic products prices and the end of inventory liquidation.

The Retailers

Even though the retailers were dependent on the same flat consumer market as the consumer products companies, their stocks rose over 300% in 1933, making them one of the most profitable investments. (See Table 14.15 for details on specific retailers.) The difference was rooted in the much different prior results of the weaker retailers, compared with the consumer products companies. The older department stores and mail order companies reported deficits in 1932 of $30 million, and during the banking crisis their stocks dropped to only 10%

Table 14.14
The Consumer Products Companies in 1933

	Price-earnings ratio		Market price as a % of book value		Dividend yield (%)		Low price as a % of 1929 high price	Return on equity (%)	Moody's bond ratings	Cash & equivalents ($ millions)
	High price	Low price	High price	Low price	High price	Low price				
Coca-Cola	12	8	362	266	5.71	7.79	43	18.6	Baa pfd.	4
Colgate-Palmolive	def.ᵃ	def.	138	44	0	0	8	def.	B pfd.	13
Eastman-Kodak	22	11	148	75	3.33	6.52	17	6.8	Aaa pfd.	30
Gillette	19	7	222	85	5.25	13.77	5	11.1	Baa	7
International Shoe	22	9	243	104	3.57	8.33	31	11.5	NRᵇ	15
Lambert Co.	14	6	456	211	7.32	15.79	12	33.6	NR	3
Procter & Gamble	32	13	369	154	3.13	7.50	20	12.2	Aaa	28
Wm. Wrigley Jr.	15	9	228	140	5.26	8.57	43	15.2	NR	27
Averages	19.4	9.0	271	135	4.20	8.53	22	15.6	—	—

ᵃ def. = Deficit.
ᵇ NR = Not Rated.

Table 14.15
The Retailers in 1933

	Price-earnings ratio		Market price as a % of book value		Dividend yield (%)		Low price as a % of 1929 high price	Return on equity (%)	Moody's bond ratings	Cash & equivalents ($ millions)
	High price	Low price	High price	Low price	High price	Low price				
Associated Dry Goods	def.[a]	def.	91	16	0	0	5	def.	B pfd.	11
Gimbel Brothers	def.	def.	27	3	0	0	2	def.	B pfd.	4
S. S. Kresge	11	4	106	34	4.71	14.55	9	9.3	A	10
R. H. Macy	33	12	157	57	3.03	8.33	9	4.8	NR[d]	(1)[e]
Marshall Field	def.	def.	75	18	0	0	NA[c]	def.	A	10
Montgomery Ward	def.	def.	121	36	0	0	5	0.8	NR	25
J. C. Penney	10	3	280	95	2.14	6.32	18	28.0	A pfd.	9
Sears, Roebuck	20	6	131	36	0	0	7	6.5	NR	(32)
F. W. Woolworth	16	8	300	147	4.71	9.60	24	18.5	NR	22
Averages	18.0	6.6	143	49	NM[b]	NM	10	11.3	—	—

[a] def. = Deficit.
[b] NM = Not Meaningful.
[c] NA = Not Available.
[d] NR = Not Rated.
[e] Brackets indicate short-term borrowing.

of their highest 1929 prices and to 49% of their book values. Their recovery was therefore in the category of big gains by very depressed stocks, unlike the consumer products stocks, which never became that depressed.

The flat retail sales results for 1933 compared with 1932 masked two trends beneficial to the retailers. On the one hand, sales bottomed in April 1933 and moved steadily up thereafter; on the other hand, retailers got their costs tightly under control so that the recovery benefitted earnings. Montgomery Ward and Sears Roebuck moved back into the black. J. C. Penney increased earnings 250%, and all the other companies but R. H. Macy reduced their deficits or increased their earnings. These cost controls made 1933 less difficult than 1932, even in the bank crisis, so that retail stocks at their lowest prices in 1933 were still up one-third from their lowest prices in 1932.

The stock price gains of 1933 were far from restoring the retail industry to strength, however. The results of Woolworth and J. C. Penney, which earned 18 1/2% and 28% returns on equity, respectively, heavily influenced industry averages. Without these two companies, half the remainder had deficits, and the others had modest returns on equity. Montgomery Ward had gone through several years of losses and stringent cost-cutting under the new leadership of Sewell Avery. Sears Roebuck had developed financial problems related to its new home sales as homeowners defaulted on mortgages Sears had extended, which forced Sears to seek a moratorium on its responsibility to keep out of default $10 million in mortgages it had financed with Metropolitan Life. Sears announced it was going out of the home sales business. It was these companies with problems whose stocks rose the most in 1933. For example, Gimbel Brothers, which did not even make money in 1929, saw its stock rise 900% in 1933. Despite such increases, however, these retailers' stocks were back to only 25% of their highest 1929 prices (excluding J. C. Penney and Woolworth) and barely up to book value.

The Tire Industry

The tire industry in 1933 (see Table 14.16) reached a very low level of business. Production in March 1933 was 2 million tires, compared with 7 million per month at the peak in 1929, and crude rubber prices had dropped from 20¢ per pound in 1929 to 3¢ per pound in March 1933. The industry lost $13 million in 1932 and was on its way to a worse year in 1933. Goodrich and Goodyear had eliminated their common stock dividends and were in arrears on their pre-ferred stock dividends, and Firestone cut its common stock dividend from $1.00 to 40¢ per share.

The industry turned around sharply in the First Hundred Days. Monthly tire production surged to 6 million tires in June, compared with 7 million in 1929, and crude rubber prices almost tripled to 8¢ per pound. Sales in 1933 were $665 million, versus $595 million in 1932, and employment rose from 110,000 people to 124,000. The industry recorded a $9 million profit for the year, compared

Table 14.16
The Tire Industry in 1933

	Price-earnings ratio		Market price as a % of book value		Dividend yield (%)		Low price as a % of 1929 high price	Return on equity (%)	Moody's bond ratings	Cash & equivalents ($ millions)
	High price	Low price	High price	Low price	High price	Low price				
Firestone	def.[a]	def.	119	34	1.25	4.38	25	def.	Ba pfd.	17
B. F. Goodrich	NM[b]	17	85	12	0	0	3	0.7	Baa	12
Goodyear	def.	def.	209	40	0	0	6	def.	Baa	52
Averages	NM	NM	138	29	NM	NM	11	NM	—	—

[a] def. = Deficit.
[b] NM = Not Meaningful.

with 1932's loss of $13 million, helped by both the volume growth and the cost-cutting measures taken previously.

The tire company stocks, which had been down at 11% of their highest 1929 prices and only 29% of book value, surged 434% to over book value and their highest prices since 1930. The companies were so highly leveraged, with common equity ratios of only 22% to 45%, that the change in outlook for business had a dramatic effect on their stocks. The highest prices for tire stocks in 1933 averaged 35% of their highest 1929 prices, which was much closer to the average for all stocks of 42% than tire stocks had been for some time.

The Farm Equipment Industry

In 1933 the farm equipment industry (see Table 14.17) began a dramatic recovery under the impetus of much improved farm income following devaluation of the dollar. The industry had shrunk between 1929 and 1933 from 293 establishments with 42,000 employees to 170 establishments with 11,000 employees, but production and employment began a long-term secular uptrend in April 1933. This is well illustrated by the Illinois index of farm implement employment, which rose from a low point in March 1933 of 43 to 74 in December and 106 by May 1934.

Moody's reported that eight farm implement companies still lost $16 million in 1933, despite the improvement in business, but in 1934 they broke even. The industry had been down so far that it took a good deal of improvement to restore it to profitability.[13]

The farm implement stocks quadrupled in the First Hundred Days, compared with an average increase for all stocks of 186%; John Deere's stock rose over 700%. However, this rise in farm implement stocks barely brought them back to book value and to only 51% of their highest 1929 prices, for their recovery was from the depressed position of low prices equal to only 23% of book value and 7% of their highest 1929 prices. Both J. I. Case and Deere failed to pay their full preferred dividend obligations during 1933, and International Harvester cut its common stock dividend rate twice during 1933. Such actions had naturally been interpreted by investors as sign of considerable financial difficulty, and the stocks had declined accordingly.

The Tobacco Companies

The tobacco companies suffered their one difficult year of the Depression in 1933 as the profits of six cigarette companies followed by Moody's dipped from $106 million in 1932 to $59 million in 1933, even though production increased 8% to 112 billion cigarettes. (See Table 14.18 for specifics.) The culprits in this profit squeeze amid increased production were a 10% decline in sales and the Agricultural Adjustment Act, which raised tobacco prices from 10 1/2¢ to 13¢ per pound in 1933 while cigarette prices stayed stable.[14]

Table 14.17
The Farm Equipment Industry in 1933

	Price-earnings ratio		Market price as a % of book value		Dividend yield (%)		Low price as a % of 1929 high price	Return on equity (%)	Moody's bond ratings	Cash & equivalents ($ millions)
	High price	Low price	High price	Low price	High price	Low price				
J. I. Case	def.[a]	def.	76	23	0	0	7	def.	B pfd.	2
Deere & Co.	def.	def.	163	19	0	0	4	def.	B pfd.	4
International Harvester	def.	def.	90	27	1.30	4.29	10	def.	A pfd.	62
Averages	def.	def.	110	23	NM[b]	NM	7	def.	—	—

[a] def. = Deficit.
[b] NM = Not Meaningful.

Table 14.18
The Tobacco Companies in 1933

	Price-earnings ratio		Market price as a % of book value		Dividend yield (%)		Low price as a % of 1929 high price	Return on equity (%)	Moody's bond ratings	Cash & equivalents ($ millions)
	High price	*Low price*	*High price*	*Low price*	*High price*	*Low price*				
American Tobacco	30	16	253	136	5.49	10.20	42	8.2	Aaa	38
Liggett & Myers	20	10	265	132	5.10	10.20	46	12.9	Aaa	61
Reynolds Tobacco	33	17	338	169	5.56	11.11	41	10.1	NR[a]	49
Averages	27.7	14.3	285	146	5.38	10.50	43	10.4	—	—

[a] NR = Not Rated.

Earnings per share of the three major cigarette companies declined between 29% and 65% in 1933, and American Tobacco reduced its $6.00 dividend to $5.00. The companies' return on equity dropped to an average of 10.4% These results muted the recovery in tobacco stocks from their lowest 1933 prices to less than 100%, compared with the average of 186%.

However, the tobacco companies still constituted the outstanding stock investment of the Depression after gold stocks, for their highest 1933 prices averaged 84% of their highest 1929 prices, and the companies maintained their dividends throughout the Depression except for very modest changes.

The Pulp and Paper Industry

The paper stocks came back from the brink of being valueless in 1933. Crown Zellerbach stock had sold as low as $1, and International Paper & Power's stock was down to 50¢, but in the First Hundred Days they rebounded to $8 1/4 and $10, respectively, producing some of the largest gains of the year. Kimberly-Clark's stock, which had never been pushed as low as the stocks of these other companies, rebounded over 300%. (See Table 14.19 for specifics on the industry.)

These gains were not large in the perspective of how far the paper stocks had sunk, however. They had dropped to only 5% of their highest 1929 prices and 7% of book value during the bank crisis, the industry was still losing money, none of the companies paid dividends, Crown Zellerbach and International Paper both had substantial arrearages in preferred dividends which they would have to catch up, and International Paper's 6% gold bonds due in 1955 had sunk to a low price of $10, which suggested that default was imminent. As recovery began under President Roosevelt, paper sales for 1933 rose 16%, capacity use rose from 56% to 63%, and losses for 35 companies followed by Moody's were cut from $24 million in 1932 to only $5 million in 1933. The improvement in conditions had a terrific impact on the stocks of Crown Zellerbach and International Paper because of their unusual leverage. The former had 21% of its capital in the form of common stock, the latter had only 9%. However, the resulting stock prices for the industry were still only at one-half of book value and one-third of their highest 1929 prices. Canadian production and pricing were still overwhelming the industry, providing little hope for strong long-term recovery.[15]

The Office Equipment Companies

The office equipment companies (see Table 14.20) bounced back from a $400,000 loss in 1932 to earn $9 million in 1933, and their stocks rose an average of 264% in the Hundred Days, compared with an average of 186% for all stocks. Yet the office equipment companies ended the Depression in highly diverse manners. IBM had suffered only a modest decline in earnings, still had a 13%

Table 14.19
The Pulp and Paper Industry in 1933

	Price-earnings ratio		Market price as a % of book value		Dividend yield (%)		Low price as a % of 1929 high price	Return on equity (%)	Moody's bond ratings	Cash & equivalents ($ millions)
	High price	Low price	High price	Low price	High price	Low price				
Crown Zellerbach	NM[a]	NM	75	9	0	0	4	def.[c]	B	5
International Paper	NA[b]	NA	38	2	0	0	1	def.	Ba	(19)[d]
Kimberly-Clark	def.	def.	45	11	0	0	10	def.	Baa	2
Averages	NM	NM	53	7	0	0	5	def.	—	—

[a] NM = Not Meaningful.
[b] NA = Not Available.
[c] def. = Deficit.
[d] Brackets indicate short-term borrowing.

Table 14.20
The Office Equipment Companies in 1933

	Price-earnings ratio		Market price as a % of book value		Dividend yield (%)		Low price as a % of 1929 high price	Return on equity (%)	Moody's bond ratings	Cash & equivalents ($ millions)
	High price	Low price	High price	Low price	High price	Low price				
Burroughs Adding Machine	NM[a]	24	350	102	1.90	6.53	6	4.3	NR[c]	15
IBM	19	9	247	123	3.92	7.89	30	13.0	NR	2
Remington Rand	NM	NM	NM	NM	0	0	4	NM	Ba	5
National Cash Register A	def.[b]	def.	120	26	0	0	3	def.	NR	2
Averages	NM	16.5	239	84	1.94	4.81	11	8.7	—	—

[a] NM = Not Meaningful.
[b] def. = Deficit.
[c] NR = Not Rated.

return on equity, maintained its dividend, and had a high stock price in 1933 which was still 60% of its highest 1929 price. Burroughs was still profitable and paying dividends. By contrast, National Cash Register and Remington Rand broke even in 1933, despite substantial cost cutting efforts, and Remington Rand had substantial preferred dividend arrearages to catch up. Its high leverage, with only 16% of its capitalization made up by common stock, propelled its stock up by 335% in the 1933 recovery, but at this level the stock was still only 19% of its highest 1929 price, which was also the average for Burroughs, Remington Rand, and National Cash Register combined. Only IBM, at 60% of its highest 1929 stock price, had any claim within the industry to stable, high stock performance.

Other Stocks

The distinction between General Electric and Westinghouse remained sharp in 1933 (see Table 14.21). It was a poor year for electrical equipment manufacturers, with Moody's reporting profits of only $2 million for the industry, although that was better than 1932's net loss of $5 million. General Electric's sales declined in 1933 by $10 million to $137 million, and Westinghouse's sales declined $9 million to $68 million, largely because utility plant additions declined from $260 million in 1932 to $200 million in 1933. A sharp rise in consumer demand during the summer, which almost doubled refrigerator sales in May through October, was not enough to offset the decline in utilities' spending. General Electric still managed to report a profit amounting to a 3 1/2% return on equity in 1933, to pay a 40¢ dividend, and to maintain its large cash position of over $100 million, but Westinghouse reported losses nearly equal to its losses of $9 million in 1932 and saw its modest cash position slip $3 million lower even though it paid no common stock dividend.

These differing results were reflected in differing stock price performances. Westinghouse stock dropped to 6% of its 1929 high price and only 29% of book value in the bank crisis, while GE stock dropped to 11% of its 1929 high price and 100% of book value. They both rose to approximately 3 times their 1933 low price during the summer rally, but GE's high price was 30% of its 1929 high price and 273% of book value, compared with Westinghouse stock, which rose to only 20% of its 1929 high price and 89% of book value.

AT&T stock (see Table 14.21) sank to 64% of book value in March and to a yield of 10.34% because its $9.00 common stock dividend was not even reasonably near the company's 1933 earning power, which turned out to be $5.38 per share. The company kept its $9.00 dividend, however, cutting its construction budget to $107 million, versus $178 million in 1932 and $550 million in 1929, to conserve cash. The stock rose 50% during the summer to exactly 100% of book value, far below the averages of 186% and 181%, respectively, for all stocks, but it did reach 44% of its 1929 high price. The stock's

Table 14.21
Other Stocks in 1933

	Price-earnings ratio		Market price as a % of book value		Dividend yield (%)		Low price as a % of 1929 high price	Return on equity (%)	Moody's bond ratings	Cash & equivalents ($ millions)
	High price	Low price	High price	Low price	High price	Low price				
American Can	20	10	171	85	3.96	8.00	27	8.5	Aa pfd.	9
AT&T	25	16	100	64	6.67	10.34	28	4.0	Aa	219
General Electric	NM[a]	29	273	100	1.33	3.64	11	3.5	Aaa	112
Radio Corp. of America	def.[b]	def.	NM	NM	0	0	3	def.	Caa pfd.	20
Westinghouse	def.	def.	89	29	4.75	14.74	6	def.	A pfd.	33

[a] NM = Not Meaningful.
[b] def. = Deficit.

relatively high yield of 6.67% reflected some investor doubts about the possibility of earnings equal to the dividend.

American Can's earnings rebounded from $3.26 to $5.04 per share in 1933, and its preferred stock rating was raised back to Aa (see Table 14.21). Its common stock was 67% above its 1932 low price at its 1933 low point, and from there it doubled to 55% of its 1929 high price and 171% of book value during the summer rally.

RCA had as poor a year in 1933 as in 1932, despite the general recovery under Roosevelt (see Table 14.21). In 1933 RCA's sales were actually lower than in 1932, at $62 million versus $66 million, and the company again had a major loss, this time of $5.8 million. It was able to acquire DeForest Radio and Jenkins Television Corp. during the year and to make real progress on the development of television, but these events did little for the company's common stock. It sank to 3% of its highest 1929 price early in the year, and even though the stock was up 300% in the First Hundred Days, it was still up to only 10% of its 1929 peak.

Summary

All industries entered 1933 at depressed levels of activity and with depressed stock prices, although for stocks in general prices at their lowest point in the bank crisis of 1933 were 16% of their highest 1929 prices, versus 12% at the lowest point in 1932. Public utilities stocks were slightly lower in 1933 because of the political controversy over public power, and motion picture stocks were lower because three went into receivership. The worst valuations at this point were quite uniformly for the financial, motion picture, and commodities industry stocks, which were 2%–10% of their highest 1929 prices and less than 25% of book value, while the highest valuations were for gold mining stocks and consumer oriented stocks such as branded foods, consumer products, and tobacco, which were still over 125% of book value.

President Roosevelt's financial program produced a three-month rally in which stock prices rose an average of 186% to 42% of their highest 1929 prices and 181% of book value. The largest recoveries were in the stocks which were previously the most depressed, particularly the pulp and paper, motion picture, farm equipment, tire, and steel stocks, which rose over 400%. The financial stocks had larger recoveries than average but they still paid a heavy price for their excesses before the Crash as the highest stock prices for the banks, holding companies, and trusts averaged only approximately 16% of their highest 1929 prices. The heavy industries also continued to have low valuations as their highest stock prices averaged approximately 75% of book value. Most of the heavy industries continued to post losses in 1933, although they were sharply reduced, and by year end most companies were clearly on the road to profitability. These industries received substantial benefits from Roosevelt's decision to devalue the dollar as the steel and pulp and paper industries developed a renewed ability to meet price competition and the mining, oil, and farm equipment industries benefitted from substantially higher commodities prices.

The 1933 recovery brought some industry stocks back almost to their highest 1929 prices. Gold stocks were unique at new record prices over 250% above those in 1929. Stocks of the tobacco companies and branded food companies exceeded 80% of their highest 1929 prices, and the smaller chemical company stocks approached 100% of their highest 1929 prices. These companies, as well as the consumer products companies, had high stock prices exceeding 2 1/2 times book value. All these industries still had returns on equity exceeding 10%. It probably needs to be emphasized, however, that these industries which maintained their earnings, generally their dividends, and their stock price valuations so well through the Depression did not provide big stock gains in the recovery in 1933.

NOTES

1. *NYSE Year Book, 1938*, pp. 22, 72, 56, 59, 37; *1937*, p. 154. See also Tables A.21, A.22, and A.23 in the Statistical Appendix.

2. *Moody's Railroad Manual, 1934*, pp. a7, a11, a21, a23, a24; *National Income Accounts*, pp. 110, 126, 142.

3. *National Income Accounts*, pp. 126, 102.

4. *Moody's Public Utility Manual, 1934*, pp. a27–32; *National Income Accounts*, p. 126.

5. *Moody's Public Utility Manual, 1934*; pp. 522, 979, 2414.

6. H. F. Williamson et al., *The American Petroleum Industry, 1899–1959, the Age of Energy*, Evanston, Illinois: Northwestern University Press, 1963, p. 542; Frank Friedel, *Franklin D. Roosevelt, Launching the New Deal*, Boston: Little Brown and Company, 1973, p. 428; *Moody's Industrial Manual, 1934*, pp. a21, a43; *National Income Accounts*, pp. 102, 142.

7. *Moody's Industrial Manual, 1934*, pp. a10, a19; *1935*, p. a45.

8. Ibid., *1934*, p. a11; *National Income Accounts*, pp. 102, 142.

9. *National Income Accounts*, pp. 102, 126, 142.

10. *Moody's Industrial Manual, 1934*, pp. a30, a32; *1935*, p. a45; *National Income Accounts*, p. 102.

11. *Moody's Industrial Manual, 1935*, p. a30; *Moody's Industrial Manual, 1931*, p. xlv.

12. *Moody's Industrial Manual, 1934*, p. a4; *1935*, p. a45.

13. Ibid., *1935*, pp. a2, a45.

14. *Moody's Industrial Manual, 1935*, pp. a45, a32; *National Income Accounts*, p. 142.

15. *Moody's Industrial Manual, 1935*, pp. a45, a19; *National Income Accounts*, p. 142.

Bond Markets in 1933

BOND MARKETS IN GENERAL

The bond market went through a wide swing from crisis to recovery in 1933, much as it did in 1932, although the bond market in 1933 never reached the low point of 1932. U.S. Treasury securities in March and April 1933 had an average yield of 3.42%, which was equal to or below the average yield on U.S. Treasuries in every month but one during 1932.[1] The lowest 1933 prices for the three heavily traded U.S. Treasury issues followed in Table A.40 in the Statistical Appendix were $2 to $6 above their lowest 1932 prices. The prices of major corporate bonds at the time of the bank crisis were at their lowest levels for the year, but most remained $5–$10 above the lowest prices for the same issues in 1932. Nor did bonds of comparable ratings in 1933 show variations in yields as wide as in 1932, which in the earlier year was a sign of the disorganized state of the market. There were far fewer rating reductions in 1933 than in 1932, and two industrial bonds even had their ratings upgraded. It is somewhat surprising that the bond market was better in 1933 than in 1932, since the nationwide Bank Holiday of 1933 has been considered the culmination of the four-year financial crisis. In fact, the crisis in financial markets in February and March 1933 was a reaction to political developments at the time, as we have already noted, and the aftermath to the real financial shakeout which occurred in 1932.

The railroad sector of the bond market recovered quite impressively on a relative yield basis in 1933 after the beating it took in 1932, but this improvement was offset for investors by a relative deterioration in A and Baa rated utility bonds, reflecting widespread political antagonism toward electric utilities and the beginning of an active public power movement led by the TVA.

The municipal bond market had its worst year since 1921. Municipal interest rates peaked in May at an average of 5.27% for high grade bonds, compared with a peak of 5.03% in 1932. Some 27 municipal issuers had their bond ratings lowered during the year, versus 25 in 1932. A number of rural states and large industrial cities defaulted.

There was a recovery in bond prices generally through the summer of 1933, as there was in the stock market. Recoveries exceeded 30% in many lower grade railroad, utility, and industrial bond issues. Foreign bond issues which continued to be serviced in gold or at the exchange rate prevailing before Roosevelt devalued the dollar experienced massive price rises, particularly issues of the Republic of France and the Royal Dutch Co.

The recovery of corporate bond prices in 1933 did not generally restore them to the peak levels of 1930–31, however. Yields on bonds of similar rating categories were generally 1/8% to 1 1/8% higher in 1933 than in 1930–31 at the highest prices. Aaa corporate issues were generally $5 below their best 1930–31 prices, Aa corporate issues were $5–$10 below, A corporate issues were $5–$15 below, and Baa corporate issues were $10–$20 below. Foreign bonds fared worst in comparison with their previous best prices in 1929–32. West European and Canadian issues were down $5–$20, and many East European and South American issues were down $25–$75. These differences were quite irregular, however, depending on the circumstances of individual countries.

U.S. GOVERNMENT AND CORPORATE BOND MARKETS— ALL BOND PRICES DECLINE IN THE BANK CRISIS BUT THERE IS A GENERAL RECOVERY DURING PRESIDENT ROOSEVELT'S FIRST HUNDRED DAYS

The Bond Market During the Bank Crisis

As one would expect, bond prices dropped during the bank crisis, but surprisingly little compared to the attention the bank crisis has received from historians and not as far as they did in early 1932. For example, the yield on long-term U.S. Treasury bonds averaged only 3.42% in March, compared with the 4 1/4% peak yield in 1932, and the lowest 1933 price on the Treasury 3 1/2% bonds due in 1947 was $99 30/32, versus $94 2/32 in 1932. Short Treasury rates, however, rose by 1 3/4% as the Treasury issued 4 1/4% 9-month notes, and acceptance and call loan rates rose by 3%.[2]

It is arguable that there was no crisis at all in the corporate bond market. For example, even though railroad bond yields were at their highest for 1933 during the bank crisis, they were up only 1/8%-1/4% from their lowest yields in the prior three months, and yields on railroad bond of most ratings were down sharply from their yields at the end of 1932, as outlined in Table 15.1. The decline in railroad bond yields by comparison with the low point for railroad bond prices in the late spring of 1932 was even greater, as outlined in Table 15.2. Industrial bond yields rose only slightly in the bank crisis from their year-end yields, and were down significantly from spring 1932, as outlined in Table 15.3. A review of Tables A.12 and A.14 in the Statistical Appendix also reveals

Table 15.1
Changes in Yields on Railroad Bonds from December 1932 to April 1933

Bond ratings	Change in yields (basis points)
Aaa	5
Aa	(5)[a]
A	(54)
Baa	(51)

Source: Moody's Railroad Manual, 1972, pp. a50–a52.

[a] Parentheses indicate a decline in yields.

Table 15.2
Changes in Yields on Railroad Bonds from Spring 1932 to Spring 1933

Bond ratings	Change in yields (basis points)
Aaa	(77)[a]
Aa	(145)
A	(105)
Baa	(188)

Source: Table A.12 in the Statistical Appendix.

[a] Parentheses indicate a decline in yields.

Table 15.3
Changes in Yields on Industrial Bonds from Spring 1932 and from December 1932 to April 1933

Bond ratings	Change in yields since December 1932 (basis points)	Change in yields since spring 1932 (basis points)
Aaa	24	(32)[a]
Aa	16	(87)
A	23	(233)
Baa	60	(121)
Ba	20	(212)

Sources: Moody's Industrial Manual, 1974, pp. a50–a52, and Table A.14 in the Statistical Appendix.

[a] Parentheses indicate a decline in yields.

Table 15.4
Changes in Yields on Utility Bonds to Spring 1933

Bond ratings	Change in yields since December 1932 (basis points)	Changes in yields since spring 1932 (basis points)
Aaa	38	(26)
Aa	45	(13)
A	95	86
Baa	240	110

Sources: Moody's Utility Manual, 1974, pp. a6–a8, and Table A.13 in the Statistical Appendix.

that at the lowest bond prices in the bank crisis the yields on bond issues with Baa or lower ratings did not diverge as sharply from higher rated issues as they did in the late spring of 1932. This yield pattern suggests the absence of a crisis in the bond market during the bank crisis.

The same pattern was not true of yields on utility bonds. Their yields rose further than railroad and industrial bonds, and within the A and Baa rating categories they exceeded their highest 1932 yields by approximately 1% (see Table 15.4 and Table A.13 in the Statistical Appendix). The 1932 market preferences for utility bonds versus railroad bonds was suddenly reversed, but the problems in this one area of the corporate bond market do not justify describing the period as a crisis for corporate bonds in general.

It is surprising that the bank crisis did not produce a bond market crisis, because commercial banks sold long-term government and corporate bonds heavily in order to reinvest in shorter-term U.S. Treasury securities that were more liquid and could be discounted at the Federal Reserve banks. Total member bank selling between December 1932 and June 1933 call dates was $95 million in foreign bonds, $130 million in railroad bonds, $141 million in utility bonds, $243 million in industrial bonds, and $371 million in U.S. Treasury bonds, for a total of $980 million in bonds. Within these totals, country member banks sold $525 million of bonds. We can safely assume that nonmember country banks were selling bonds on at least a comparable scale. If we had comprehensive data for all banks on a weekly basis, it would undoubtedly show much heavier selling up to March 8th, as is found for weekly reporting banks, and then renewed buying as conditions improved. Most of the new buying power was deployed into $718 million in short-term U.S. Treasury bills and notes, however, and country member banks were able to reinvest only $111 million U.S. Treasury bills and notes compared to the $525 million in bonds which they sold.[3]

The Federal Reserve did little to ease this selling pressure, buying only $118 million of U.S. Treasury bonds between January 25, 1933, and March 8, 1933,[4] but the lack of a new-issue calendar helped the market to absorb the bank selling. During the first four months of 1933, new corporate and government bond issues totalled only $138 million, versus $620 million for the comparable four months in 1932 and \$2,028 million in 1931.[5] There was not a single new corporate bond issue in March 1933.

What accounted for the ability of the bond market to sustain bond prices so much better than it did during 1932 in the midst of the heavy bank selling and the psychological disequilibrium (at a minimum) caused by the bank crisis? We can respond in a general way that the other participants in the bond market besides the banks must have seen the bank crisis as an isolated circumstance which did not affect the economy and corporate creditworthiness in a fundamental way. More particularly, the critical financial point for life insurance companies had occurred in the late spring of 1932, and since then they had become large bond buyers, offsetting the selling by banks. Life insurance companies purchased \$350 million in additional bonds in 1933. (See Table A.37 in the Statistical Appendix.)

The Bond Market During and after President Roosevelt's First Hundred Days

Bond prices rose sharply during President Roosevelt's First Hundred Days, just as stock prices did. His public personality, decisive economic remedies in the form of increased RFC lending, the National Recovery Administration codes, the promise of higher prices for farm and business products, the strengthening of the commercial banking system, and the visible recovery in the economy raised bond prices for many reasons—corporate credits improved, confidence improved, and it was anticipated that the flow of investment funds would improve. Yields on U.S. Treasury bonds dropped from a high of 3.42% to 3.19% in September, close to the lowest yields on record registered in mid-1931, and corporate bond prices rocketed upward as if they were stocks. Price gains of \$20–\$30 were common, as yields for bonds rated A or less dropped by 2%–3%. Industrial bonds rated Ba averaged a decline in yield of 4.65%. At the highest point for corporate bond prices in August, the spread between Aaa and Baa rates had been reduced to approximately 1 1/2%, Baa rates were under 6%, and Ba rated industrial issues bore an average yield of only 6 5/8%. It was as if all the fear had suddenly gone out of the market. The change in corporate bond market conditions between March and August is summarized in Table 15.5.

Bond yields rose again in the fourth quarter in line with the decline in stock prices, but the rise was generally only 1/4%–3/8%. Utility bonds rated A and Baa were a marked exception to this generalization. In December, yields on these bonds rose to 7.22% and 10.12%, respectively, where they were close to their highest yields in the Depression. Railroad bonds rated Baa felt some of the same pressure, but their yield in December rose to only 7.43%. At this point, Baa railroad bond yields were 170 basis points over Baa industrial bond yields. Bond investors' preferences within these three groups had been completely reversed from what they were in the first half of 1931, when the bond market was at its highest prices of this study.

Table 15.5
Corporate Bond Market Changes from March 1933 to August 1933

Bond ratings	Average decline in yield (basis points)	Average rise in price	Average yield at August high price
Rails			
Aaa	65	$13.14	4.34%
Aa	157	18.67	4.88
A	198	24.00	4.88
Baa	415	32.22	5.85
Industrials			
Aaa	91	10.00	4.37
Aa	160	14.50	4.87
A	213	17.20	4.82[a]
Baa	274	23.14	5.66
Ba	465	26.75	6.62
Utilities			
Aaa	68	10.00	4.24
Aa	117	16.50	4.49
A	299	27.29	5.06
Baa	360	29.33	6.11

Sources: Tables A.12, A.13, and A.14 in the Statistical Appendix.

[a] Excluding Royal Dutch issues, which were expected to be payable at old exchange rates.

Railroad Bonds

Railroad bond prices recovered significantly in 1933 from the disorganized rout they had experienced in 1932. During the bank crisis, railroad bonds bore yields considerably below those of 1932—by 2.40% for Baa rail bonds. Variations in yields within a given bond rating, which are a good indicator of the stress and disorganization in a market sector, were cut at least in half throughout 1933, compared with 1932. During the late spring of 1932, for example, yields had varied by 3 1/2% for Aa railroad bonds and by 4 1/2% for A railroad bonds, whereas during the bank crisis these yields varied by only 1 1/2%.

Railroad bond prices in the recovery of the First Hundred Days showed a similar improvement versus 1932. Price gains from the highest prices of 1932 averaged approximately $4.00 for the issues rated from A to Aaa. Some issues showed remarkable gains, such as the various Pennsylvania Railroad issues which had been sold beyond reason in 1932, and in 1933 rose $22 to $30 from their low prices in the bank crisis. The Southern Railway's consolidated 5% issue due in 1994 rose over $40 from its low point in the bank crisis, as did the Cleveland, Cincinnati, Chicago & St. Louis Railway 4 1/2% issue due in 1977,

Table 15.6
Price Changes of Railroad Bonds, 1929–1933

Ratings in 1933	Change from high of 1932 to high of 1933	Change from high of 1929 to high of 1933
Aaa	$4.11	$ 2.88
Aa	4.33	(5.33)[a]
A	4.75	(6.67)
Baa	1.13	(15.11)

Source: Table A.12 in the Statistical Appendix.

[a]Parentheses indicate a decline in price.

and the Great Northern Railway 4 1/2% issue due in 1977. If one had been wise enough to buy rail bonds at the lowest prices of 1932, the gains at the high prices of 1933 would have averaged 34% for Aaa issues, 54% for Aa issues, 59% for A issues, and 101% for Baa issues. However, by comparison with 1929 high prices, all but those issues still rated Aaa showed a loss on average. The comparison is outlined in Table 15.6. In 1933 only three railroad bond issues had their ratings reduced by Moody's, compared with 22 reductions in 1932, but this left a sorry record for railroad bond rating reductions during the five years from 1929 to 1933 (see Table 15.7).

Table 15.7
Distribution of Railroad Bond Ratings for Issues over $40 Million,
1929 and 1933

	1929	1933
Aaa	24	9
Aa	9	6
A	0	9
Baa	1	9
Ba	0	1
	34	34

Source: Table A.7 in the Statistical Appendix.

Economic conditions could not have produced this greater calm than 1932 for railroad bonds because railroad revenues, freight car loadings, and pre-tax net income hit their lowest levels of the Depression during the first four months of 1933.[6] Rather, the improvement occurred because Congress and the ICC favored rationalization of the railroads into several major trunk systems and because the RFC lent almost $365 million to 62 railroads by March 31, 1933. The following railroads were the largest borrowers:[7]

Baltimore and Ohio	($ millions)
Pennsylvania	$65.4
Missouri Pacific	27.5
Chicago & Northwestern	23.1
St. Louis & Southwestern	21.0
N.Y., Chicago & St. Louis	18.1
New York Central	17.7
Southern	16.1
Wabash (in default)	14.8
Erie	14.8
	13.4

The railroads had made it through the worst of the Depression, but neither their public influence nor their credit would ever again reach the levels they had enjoyed before the Depression.

Public Utility Bonds

In 1933, public utility bonds split sharply into a group which maintained the preeminent position among corporate bonds that they established in 1931, and a typically lesser rated group which not only became the highest yielding sector of the market but also established yields in the second half of 1933 significantly in excess of its peak yields for 1932. Yields on utility issues rated Aaa and Aa at their highest were approximately 1/4% below their highest yields in 1932, and in the case of Aa bonds they were 3/4% below Aa rail bonds. There was no sign of disorganization in the market for these bonds, and they participated in the bond recovery of the Hundred Days such that Aaa utility bonds rose an average of $10 and Aa utility bonds an average of $16 1/2. There were larger recoveries of approximately $25 in the prices of bonds of Commonwealth Edison, Pennsylvania Power & Light, and Ohio Power. (See Tables A.8 and A.13 in the Statistical Appendix for data on prices, yields, and *Moody's* ratings.)

Lesser rated utility bonds had an opposite pattern. During the bank crisis the A and Baa rated utility bonds dropped approximately $30, to prices which averaged approximately $6 3/4 below their low prices of 1932. Unlike all other corporate bonds, these issues failed to recover to new high prices for the year during Roosevelt's Hundred Days, although they did recover much of their prior losses. Their recovery was short-lived, however. By December, yields on A and Baa rated public utility bonds had risen 1%–1 1/2% to 7 1/4% and 10%, respectively. Their prices were down close to their lowest prices of the year again. This price drop exceeded the decline in other corporate bond prices, which was quite modest.[8]

The decline in utility bond prices was prompted by New Deal legislation to set up the Tennessee Valley Authority and by a widespread political attack on investor-owned public utilities, both of which led to the first rate reductions by electric utilities in the Depression. The average revenue per kilowatt hour sold dropped from 2.88¢ to 2.69¢, with reductions in the South twice those of the northern states.[9] Rate reductions and uncertainty about the impact of the TVA on their business put acute pressure on the bonds of impacted utilities. For example, the yield on A rated bonds of Appalachian Power rose to 8 5/8% and of Georgia Power to 9 5/8%, while similarly rated Detroit Edison and New York Power & Light bonds yielded only 6 1/2%. In the Baa category, Alabama Power bonds dropped to a yield of 10 3/8% when Milwaukee Electric and American Gas & Electric bonds yielded only 8 1/2%. The Illinois companies were also severely affected. The yield on A rated bonds of Public Service of Northern Illinois was 8 5/8% at their low price, on a level with Appalachian Power mentioned above, and the yield on Baa rated Illinois Power & Light bonds was 12 5/8%, the highest of any large utility bond issue.

The emotional content of this differential price performance in A and Baa rated utility bonds was quite striking at variance with the economic substance of the industry. Not a single large utility bond issue had its rating reduced by Moody's, and no significant operating electric utility defaulted during the Depression. Electric power production in 1933 increased over 1932, particularly in the second half of 1933, when utility bonds were treated so differently by the market, and 1933 net income of gas and electric utilities of $186 million compared with a loss of $292 million for railroads and a loss of $123 million for durable goods manufacturers. Capital spending as well was under tight control at only $200 million for 1933, compared with $285 million in 1932 and over $900 million in 1930.[10]

On the whole, utility bonds did quite well both absolutely and in comparison with railroad bonds between 1929 and 1933. Based on their ratings at the end of this period, utility bond prices at their highs in 1933 compared with their highs in 1929, as follows:

Aaa	+ $5.00
Aa	+ 3.40
A	− 4.00
Baa	− 14.80

The distribution of public utility bond ratings for large issues remained much as it was in 1929 (see Table 15.8).

Industrial Bonds

Industrial bonds fared relatively well in 1933. Two large issues had their ratings raised (National Steel and American Smelting & Refining), and industrial bond yields in 1933 were lower than for railroad or utility bonds in most rating categories which was quite a unique change of investor preference. Based on Moody's bond yield indices of railroad, utility, and industrial bonds, industrial

Table 15.8
Distribution of Public Utility Bond Ratings for Issues over $40 Million,
1929 and 1933

	1929[a]	1933
Aaa	9	8
Aa	10	10
A	6	6
Baa	5	6
	30	30

Sources: Moody's Utility Manuals, 1930, 1934; Table A.8 in the Statistical Appendix.

[a] Large issues originating after 1929 are included in 1929 according to the ratings on prior smaller issues ranking *pari passu*.

bonds rated Aaa and Aa had yields in between utility and railroad bond yields, but after June, 1933, for these rating categories and throughout the year for A and Baa ratings, industrial bonds had the lowest yields. During much of the year, industrial bond yields were lower by only 1/4–1/2%, but when utility bond yields soared from September through December, yields on industrial bonds rated Baa were over 4% below Baa utility bond yields.

Generalizations about industrial issues rated Aaa or Aa are difficult since there were only two large issues in each category. The two Standard Oil issues in the Aaa category showed price variations almost exactly equal to the years 1929–32. (Price, yield, and rating information is drawn from Tables A.19 and A.14 in the Statistical Appendix.). A and Baa rated industrial bond issues were more representative and permit broader generalizations. Yields within these categories stayed relatively close together, indicating that there was little disorganization in these markets, as there had been in 1932. The low prices for these issues in the bank crisis were far above the lows of 1932 by $15 for the A issues and by $7.71 for Baa issues. Even the Ba issues had lows $11.25 above their 1932 low prices, although in this rating category there was considerable market disorganization in the bank crisis, with yields ranging from 8% to 13 3/4%.

There were significant price gains made in industrial bonds during the year. In the process of being upgraded to Aa, American Smelting & Refining bonds gained $22 from their 1933 low price. A-rated issues averaged a gain from their lowest prices of over $17, Baa issues gained over $23, and Ba issues gained almost $27. Four large issues related to the Royal Dutch–Shell group had gains of $33–$45, which reduced their yields abnormally because it appeared that as foreign issuers they might be forced to abide by their indenture commitments to pay in gold despite the U.S. devaluation and abrogation of gold contracts. A suit brought by Amsterdam brokers in the Court of Justice at The Hague to force gold payments was successful on only one of the four issues which was payable

Table 15.9
Distribution of Industrial Bond Ratings by Issues over $20 Million,
1929 and 1933

Bond ratings	1929[a]	1933
Aaa	6	2
Aa	3	2
A	4	5
Baa	4	7
Ba	3	4
	20	20

Sources: Moody's Industrial Manual, 1930, 1934; Table A.9 in the Statistical Appendix.

[a] Large issues originating after 1929 are included in 1929 according to the ratings on prior smaller issues ranking *pari passu*.

anyway in sterling, guilders, Swiss francs, or kronor, and so the suit gained nothing more than was already available.[11]

As a result of their strong 1933 market performance, industrial bond issues at their high prices compared well with their 1929 high prices, as follows:

Aaa	+ $2
Aa	− $2
A	+ $7
Baa	− $6
Ba	− $14

However, the distribution of industrial bond ratings in 1933 compared with 1929 revealed a considerable decline in ratings, however, as summarized in Table 15.9.

U.S. Treasury Bonds

U.S. treasury bonds in 1933 averaged a yield of 3.3%, which was 3/8% below the comparable yield in 1932 and generally reflects a less tumultuous year than 1932, despite the bank crisis. In January, when President Hoover was trying to force a balanced budget and a new sales tax on manufacturers on the lame duck Congress, the U.S. Treasury sold $277 million 5-year bonds at 2 5/8%, the lowest rate on record. Treasury yields were at their lowest level since the Sterling Crisis, and the Federal Reserve felt able to let its holdings of U.S. Treasury securities run down $165 million.

The bank crisis, of course, had a sharp impact on the Treasury market as weekly reporting member banks sold $568 million in U.S. Treasuries in the two weeks between February 22nd and March 8th to meet demands for cash, and the Federal Reserve bought virtually none of the offerings.[12] Long-term U.S. Treasury bonds lost $3 1/2 in the week of February 25th, and the average yield on long-term Treasuries in March and April rose 20 basis points to 3.42%, but this yield was still lower than for 11 of 12 months in 1932 and well below the high yield of 4 1/4% that year. Yields on short-term Treasury maturities rose much further. The new issue rate on Treasury bills in February had averaged less than 1/2%, but the U.S. Treasury was forced to pay 4% for 5 months and 4 1/4% for 9 months in an $800 million financing on March 13th.

The Treasury market dropped $3–$7 1/2, depending on the issue, in reaction to the Bank Holiday. (See Table A.40 in the Statistical Appendix.) But the market recovered quickly, and it can be seen from the modest movement in long-term rates and the Treasury's ability to sell $800 million on March 13th without any significant buying by the Federal Reserve that the reaction to the Bank Holiday was not great in the first place. Three- to 6-month Treasury yields were again down below 1/2% by April and below 1/8% in June through October.[13] Long-term treasury bond prices were back up within $1 of their highest January prices by June, and for the year as a whole the variation in long term U.S. Treasury bond prices was only one half that of 1932. In April the U.S. Treasury was able to sell $500 million in 2 7/8% 3-year bonds quite successfully as member banks began to rebuild their U.S. Treasury holdings. Weekly reporting banks were back up to their pre-crisis holdings by the end of May, and by December 1933 member bank U.S. Treasury holdings were $7.25 billion, compared with $6.5 billion at the end of 1932.[14]

In mid-May the Federal Reserve also began a program of open market purchases which carried on every week through November 15th, resulting in an increase of $595 million, equal to approximately one-third, in the Federal Reserve's U.S. Treasury holdings.[15]

The Treasury market paid virtually no attention to the U.S. government's rapidly expanding need for additional money from $1.78 billion in net new cash in the fiscal year ending June 30, 1933, to $2.9 billion in net new cash in fiscal 1934. President Hoover and his Treasury folk must have been grinding their teeth.[16]

Between 1929 and 1933, long-term U.S. Treasury bonds were an excellent way to preserve capital and even provided a little in the way of capital gains. The highest price in 1929 for the Treasury's 3 1/2% bonds due in 1947 was $100; in 1933 it was $103 20/32. Long-term Treasury bond prices were surprisingly stable through 1929–33, with the one exception, following the Sterling Crisis, when the Treasury 3 1/2% bonds due in 1947 dropped from almost $103 to $94. Otherwise the price range of these Treasury bonds from the Crash through 1933 was $96 to $103. (See Table A.40 in the Statistical Appendix.)

THE MUNICIPAL BOND MARKET HAS ITS WORST YEAR OF THE DEPRESSION DUE TO THE BURDEN OF WELFARE EXPENDITURES, WHICH PRODUCES NEW TAXES AND FEDERAL AID

The timing of events in the municipal bond market was different from that in the corporate and U.S. Treasury markets. The municipal bond market hit bottom in May rather than in March, its bottom was worse than in 1932, the underlying fundamentals were worse than in 1932, and the recovery during the Hundred Days was more subdued. By May, when the stock market was headed sharply higher, the municipal market was just reaching its low point, although in the subsequent recovery of the municipal market it reached its highest prices for the year in September at the same time as the stock and corporate bond markets.

The best municipal bonds bore yields of 3 1/8% to 3 1/2% in January 1933, and yields rose by approximately 3/4% in March through May as prices declined during the bank crisis. In some respects this bond price decline was sympathetic to the corporate bond market, for member banks sold no municipal bonds during the first half of 1933, while they were actually selling corporate bonds. Indeed, two of the prominent pressures on the municipal market were quite peculiar to it, namely, congressional efforts to remove the tax exemption on all government bonds, and other government efforts to amend municipal obligations to bondholders.

In February, Senator Cordell Hull of Tennessee, who was to become Secretary of State under Roosevelt, sponsored a Senate bill to remove the tax exemptions of both U.S. Treasury and municipal bonds. This proposal was successfully embodied in the Senate version of the National Industrial Recovery Act but removed in Conference Committee at the request of the Roosevelt Administration for the short-term goal of not disturbing a large U.S. Treasury financing when the market was still weak from the Bank Holiday.

The municipal market was much disconcerted in March and April by a Detroit-sponsored bill in the House of Representatives which would have given the courts the power to delay municipal debt payments up to ten years. The bill cleared the House Judiciary Committee but was defeated on April 15th.

Municipal bond prices in May 1933 were as low as in early 1932 for the high quality credits and worse than 1932 for the weakest credits. The best credits were states such as Pennsylvania, New York, Massachusetts, Kansas, California, Missouri, New Jersey, West Virginia, and Illinois, whose bonds bore yields of 3 3/4% to 4 1/2% at their lowest prices in May. These yields were almost exactly the same as the market's low point in 1932. The weakest issues were those of large cities and rural states, and here considerable extremes were reached. Yields were meaningless on many issues because of their financial troubles, and the prices for these issues were quoted by dealers as if near-term maturities were sure to be forcefully refunded into long-term maturities with the same holders.

For example, all of Miami's bonds, irrespective of coupons which ranged from 4 3/4% to 5 1/2% and maturities which ranged from 1935 to 1955, were quoted at $26. Louisiana bonds with maturities from 1934 to 1959 were uniformly quoted at $72, Detroit bonds with maturities from 1934 to 1951 were quoted at $45, and Philadelphia bonds due from 1939 to 1972 were quoted at $76. Bonds of Arkansas and Detroit were actually in default. North Carolina and Tennessee bonds yielded 7%, Chicago's bonds yielded 6 1/2%, New York City bonds yielded 6%, and Boston and Baltimore bonds yielded 5%. Many bonds were not quoted during May, and the volume of competitive bond sales which received no bids rose to record amounts. The *Commercial & Financial Chronicle* said, "Bids are so scarce that in the ordinary sense there is no municipal bond market. Dealers seem unwilling to buy for stock even at prices near or below the levels of June, 1932." Bonds of many prominent issues were quoted with spreads between bid and ask prices of $10, a differential of almost 1% in yield. (Table A.16 in the Statistical Appendix provides yields for representative municipal bonds.)

Municipal bond prices rose from their lowest point in May through September in line with the recovery in economic conditions and price rises in other securities markets. Most bonds rose enough in price to reduce yields 3/4% to 1% to their lowest yields for 1933. The lowest yields at this time, ranging from 3% to 3 1/4%, were on the bonds of New York State, Massachusetts, Maryland, New Hampshire, and Virginia. In a range of 3 3/8% to 3 3/4% were the bonds of California, Illinois, Missouri, Pennsylvania, Rhode Island, and Vermont. Many bonds of large cities bore yields in the 4%–5% range (Los Angeles, San Francisco, Chicago, Baltimore, Boston, Minneapolis, New York City, Philadelphia, and Milwaukee). Defaulted credits, such as Arkansas and Detroit, gained the most in this market rise as their yields declined approximately 4% to 9 1/2% and 10 7/8%, respectively, and distinction was made in the prices of issues with varying coupons and maturities as optimism grew that nearer-term issues might be paid off at least in part.

The market sold off again in the last two months of 1933, but only enough to raise yields approximately 1/2%. This decline was in line with other securities markets. The defaulted and highly problematical credits unfortunately sold off more than 1/2% in yield to approximately their lowest levels of the spring of 1933.

The wide swings in municipal bond prices, and their historic low prices in 1933, when those lows had been touched by corporate bonds in 1932, were a reflection of underlying problems in state and local government. A reflection of these problems can be seen in the bond ratings of the principal municipalities in Table A.11 in the Statistical Appendix. Ratings were reduced for 27 of these issuers, compared with 25 in 1932, and constituted the worst year of the Depression in this respect. The reader will remember that there were few corporate bond ratings reduced in 1933 and that several were even raised. Big cities and southern states dominated the ratings reductions. Moody's ratings were withdrawn on the bonds of Arkansas and Louisiana, Detroit's rating was reduced to an ignominious B, Alabama, Chicago, and South Carolina were reduced to Baa, and the balance of ratings reductions was to A. (See Table A.11 in the Statistical Appendix.)

In the southern states two problems converged—high debt burdens and loss of income due to the 40%–50% decline in agricultural revenues since 1930. All the states south of an area from North Carolina through Tennessee to Louisiana had per capita debts in excess of the national average and personal income far below it. Arkansas had the highest per capita debt in the nation and predictably defaulted on it in 1933. Georgia assumed $26.5 million of local road debts late in 1932, and Louisiana had delays in meeting debt service.

Outside this southern arc, the principal financial problem was relief expenditures. State and local government revenues nationwide declined to only $7.2 billion in 1933 from a peak of $7.8 billion in 1930, which in real terms was an increase of 13%, based on the price deflator for GNP. There had been a larger decline than the $600 million indicated in revenues from both individuals and corporations, especially business property taxes, which alone fell over $700 million between 1930 and 1933, but there was an offsetting increase in federal grants-in-aid of $400 million. These grants-in-aid skyrocketed under President Roosevelt from $500 million in 1933 to $1.6 billion in 1934. Nonetheless, state and local governments operated at a deficit of $69 million in 1933 and had an accumulated deficit on a national accounts basis of $1.9 billion since 1929. Every form of expenditure had been cut to cope with this financial problem, purchases of goods and services alone having been cut by $1.8 billion since 1930, except for relief payments, which rose almost $500 million during the period from a base of less than $100 million in 1929. The cumulative rise in relief payments from 1929 to 1933 was 62 1/2% of the accumulated deficit in the same period. If we add to relief payments the incremental interest in the period, most of which was on bond issues to finance relief payments, the proportion of the deficit accounted for rises to 83%.[17]

These macro-economic statistics masked two crucial differences between state and city governments. The relief burden was concentrated almost exclusively in the cities, whereas the ability to raise new tax revenues was concentrated in the states. General sales taxes were first introduced on a significant scale in 1933, especially in Illinois, Michigan, New York, and North Carolina, and amounted to $228 million in their first full year, 1934.[18] As a result of this dichotomy, the major cities had dramatic problems with revenue losses, relief expenditures, and the largest debt burdens. The paradox developed of state bonds in Michigan, Illinois, Massachusetts, New York, New Jersey, and Pennsylvania selling at low yields, while their major cities were in desperate straits and virtually unable to sell bonds.

The various states gave virtually no financial aid to their beleaguered cities and even hindered their efforts to raise revenues, as in New York City and Chicago. As a result, individual local governments dealt with the Depression with varying degrees of success, depending on such things as their outstanding debt, tax base, business conditions, social harmony, and administrative skill. These differences were reflected in their bonds, which sold at widely different yields, as illustrated by the following bond yields for New York State issuers at the end of 1933:

New York State	3.30%
Albany	3.60%
Binghamton	3.85%
Buffalo	4.20%
Syracuse	4.25%
Suffolk County	4.50%
Rochester	4.75%
Westchester County	5.00%
Port of New York (G.W. Bridge)	5.25%
New York City	5.73%
Hempstead	6.00%
Rye	6.00%
Yonkers	6.00%
Mamaroneck	7.50%

Detroit was in the worst trouble because of its reliance on the auto industry and the large amount of debt it had incurred to provide the public services for a 500% expansion in population since 1900. The 1933–34 budget dedicated 50% of its estimated $68 million in revenues to debt service and conspicuously excluded any provision to pay off $15 million in debt maturities during the fiscal year. Tax delinquencies were estimated to be 80%, having been 36% in 1932–33. The city was in an extreme cash bind, which led it to default on interest payments in February 1933. Its total debt of over $400 million, including short-term debt of $48 million to banks and local businesses and citizens, inhibited raising any further debt. The city tried issuing scrip to employees in lieu of paychecks, but it was refused at local stores and the effort floundered. After the city placed its final card on the table by arbitrarily moving to reduce interest rates on all its outstanding debts to a flat 3%, a refunding effort was agreed on whereby all bonds due in the next 10 years were extended to 30 years, short-term debt was extended at 4 1/2% to 1952 and 1962, and interest on all debt for the next two years was paid substantially with 3 1/4% bonds due in 1962. All back-tax collections and half of any revenue increases were committed to debt repayment to shorten these maturity extensions. The city's sole power in these negotiations was the clear perception that its back was right against the wall. Paradoxically, the refunding plan provided dramatic value-added to Detroit's bondholders even though it deferred and reduced bondholders' claims on the city. Once the refunding plan was settled, Detroit's bonds rose a sharp $25.

New York City's problems did not approach Detroit's, but the city was nonetheless in trouble. The city projected a $504 million budget, of which $40 million was for relief, down from a 1932 budget of $616 million. The city's bank borrowing ballooned to $140 million in April and then to $236 million in June because of slow tax payments and the city's inability to sell bonds. New York City's 4 1/2% bonds due in 1965, which served as a benchmark for the city's credit, had dropped in a free-fall from $97 1/2 in February to $78 in May with no market appetite for a new issue at any price.

The banks openly used their position as the city's only lenders to extract budget reductions, tax increases, and changes in financial policies. At the end of 1932, the New York State legislature had passed legislation allowing New York City to cut civil service salaries and reopen its budget, and under pressure from the banks Tammany Hall politicians had to agree to cut civil service wages, which in any case exceeded those of both New York State and the federal government.

Chicago's bonds performed much like New York City's, with the 4% issue due in 1950 falling from $89 in February to $73 in May, then rising to $88 in September and then dropping again to $80 in December. However, Chicago's problems were more complex than New York City's, even though Chicago's legal dispute over property taxes had been resolved and Cook County had cured its default on its interest payments by June 1933. The metropolitan Chicago governmental structure of seven major taxing units had obligations of $825 million, including bonds, tax warrants, unsatisfied sinking fund obligations, salaries in arrears, and bills outstanding.[19]

The financial problems of state and local governments had to be resolved on political ground rather than in the courts where corporate debts were settled, and the conflict between political constituencies and bondholders produced widely different results. A number of major issuers defaulted, such as Miami, Arkansas, Cook County, Atlantic City, and Detroit, but as we have already seen in the case of Detroit, default simply changed the basis of negotiations.

Refundings were one of the most common techniques for relieving financial stress. Detroit's refunding was achieved in a negotiated style. Arkansas Governor Marvin J. Futrell introduced the shotgun style, after Arkansas defaulted on $771,000 interest due on March 1, 1933. Futrell made no provision in the state budget for interest or principal payments on the $146 million of state and road improvement districts' debt; instead investors were offered 25-year 3% refunding bonds on which principal and interest would be paid. The state's 4 1/4% bonds due in 1958, which had been quoted at prices as high as $77 in January, dropped to $39 in May, and irate investors formed bondholder protection committees and threatened to sue. New York legal counsel and investment bankers paraded down to Little Rock to tell Futrell that he was breaching the covenants of the state's bond issues, attempting the impossible of refunding bonds with coupons of 4 1/2% –4 1/4% with a coupon of 3%, and that he was destroying the state's credit. But Futrell responded that 3% was better than nothing and that he did not care about

about the state's credit because he had the legislature pass a constitutional amendment prohibiting further state debt without a popular vote and limiting both taxes and spending. His logic won the day.

Other issuers undertook refundings with less conflict. New York City refunded its transit debt to relieve budget pressures. Toledo, which was in desperate straits, refunded $17 million in debts with 25% in cash and 75% in new bonds. Jackson, Mississippi, and Montana also had refunding programs.

RFC loans were another solution to state and city problems which achieved considerable political consensus. By the end of 1933, direct and indirect loans to 40 states and two territories were authorized amounting to $973 million and $361 million had been disbursed. (See Table A.33 in the Statistical Appendix.) For relief programs alone, Illinois got $45 million, Pennsylvania $30 million, Michigan $16 million, Ohio and New York $13 million each, and Wisconsin $12 million. When Tennessee could not get bids on a $10 million refunding issue of bonds, the RFC found an indirect way to lend the money through local banks. Even more important were self-liquidating loans by the RFC for projects that filled a public need and eased the relief burden by creating unskilled jobs, such as $110 million lent to build the Golden Gate and Oakland Bay bridges, and $75 million lent to build the Lincoln Tunnel between New York City and New Jersey. RFC loans were shortly replaced by massive federal grants-in-aid of $502 million in 1933 and $1.6 billion in 1934, channeled through the New Deal's ''alphabet agencies'' to aid local relief efforts.

There was resort to other remedies as well. Pay cuts were common in municipal government, as were layoffs, but less so than in private industry. It was more common to defer wages to civil servants, as in Chicago, Philadelphia, Atlantic City, and hundreds of smaller communities, or to pay employees with scrip, which was common. Philadelphia tried selling its own bonds to the public directly without investment bankers as intermediaries, and New York City actually hired 40 laid-off bond salesmen for the same purpose.

Physical conflict between financial and relief interests occurred in a few states. In Minnesota, the state's socialist governor, Floyd Olson, threatened the legislature with martial law and confiscation of wealth unless the legislature passed a relief bill, and in Georgia, Governor Eugene Talmadge declared martial law in July in the state capital and forcibly removed Captain J. W. Barnett from the Georgia Highway Board, where he was tying up $25 million that could be used for relief work.

The turmoil over municipal credits begat a long list of criticisms of municipal practices that had been acceptable in previous, less contentious times. The practical power of local governments to alter their commitments to bondholders was fundamental and quite startling, but besides that, critics claimed that municipal accounting practices were lax, employed shifting standards, lacked audits, and hid obligations that had accrued. Critics found municipal financial disclosures evasive and deceptive. Information on municipal activities was lacking on a wide scale. Local government systems were deemed inefficient, especially relative to the productivity standards of private business; politics and getting elected weighed too heavily in priorities and in decisions with significant financial implications; and outright graft was rampant. As we have already noted, there was widespread creditor opposition to the large-scale local government outlays for relief. Bondholders' grievances then were remarkably similar to their grievances today.

THE FOREIGN BOND MARKET REMAINS VOLATILE AND THIN AMID DEVALUATION OF THE DOLLAR, THE FAILURE OF THE WORLD ECONOMIC AND MONETARY CONFERENCE, AND RISING GERMAN AND JAPANESE AGGRESSION

International Events

The international system of trade and finance continued to be so sharply divided by national interests that recovery on a large scale remained impossible. Combined U.S. exports and imports of $3.1 billion in 1933 were barely up from 1932 and still only 32% of 1929's international trade volume.

Tariff and currency advantages were sought most notably by the United Kingdom. U.K. politicians and businessmen who were flush with the economic success of protective tariffs and the devaluation of sterling moved to gain further benefits in both areas. Following up on the success of Imperial Preference tariff arrangements with its previous colonies, the United Kingdom signed trade preference agreements with its historic trade partners, Sweden, Norway, Finland, and Iceland, during 1933. U.S. efforts to get European agreement to a short-term tariff truce in May 1933, while waiting to see whether the World Economic and Monetary Conference could stop the tariff wars, were rebuffed by the United Kingdom because of its momentum in the opposite direction. U.K. trade competition was also fostered by the tactics of the Exchange Equalization Fund, which made an effort to hold down the sterling exchange rate. The sterling-dollar exchange rate was approximately $3.25 at the end of 1932, compared with $4.85 prior to September 1931, but during 1933 a substantial sterling recovery set in, related both to Roosevelt's devaluation of the dollar and to Britain's improved finances. Sterling rose to over $3.50 in April and to over $4.00 in May, even though the Exchange Equalization Fund was selling substantial amounts of sterling to hold it down. Neville Chamberlain, Chancellor of the Exchequer, stated in April that British credit was "so fully restored that the Government is almost embarrassed by the amount of foreign money brought to London." Short-term U.K. interest rates were cut to record low levels of 1/4% to 1/2%, but still sterling rose until it averaged $5.15 in November— higher than it had been prior to September 1931. U.K. gold reserves rose to a record of over $925 million from under $600 million at the end of 1932. U.K. authorities were in a quandary whether to restore sterling to a fixed exchange rate, and if so whether to peg it to the old exchange rates of the French, Dutch,

Table 15.10
U.S. Dollar Exchange Rates with the Principal Developed Countries, 1933

	Rate as of February 1933	Rate as of December 1933	% Devaluation
Australia	$2.72	$4.07	50%
Austria	0.14	0.18	29
Belgium	0.14	0.22	57
Canada	0.84	1.01	20
Denmark	0.15	0.23	53
France	0.04	0.06	50
Germany	0.24	0.37	54
Italy	0.05	0.08	60
Japan	0.21	0.31	48
Netherlands	0.40	0.63	58
Norway	0.17	0.26	53
Sweden	0.18	0.26	44
Switzerland	0.19	0.30	58
United Kingdom	3.42	5.12	50
		Average	50

Source: Banking & Monetary Statistics, pp. 662–81.

and Swiss, who had remained on the gold standard, or to try for the trade and employment advantages of a lower exchange rate against the new, depreciated value of the dollar.

The United States competed on the tariff front and the currency front. In February 1933, President Hoover set the first tariff based on "American selling prices," whereby values of dutiable imports were set above their home country values. The first case was applied to rubber footwear.

We have already examined how President Roosevelt devalued the dollar, first by forbidding private gold holdings during the Bank Holiday, then in April by embargoing all public and private gold shipments under authorization from Congress to devalue the gold content of the dollar by up to 60%, and finally by annulling all public and private gold contracts attached to debts. The U.S. devaluation was surprisingly effective in the short run. The developed countries almost universally maintained their historic currency relationships and gold values, allowing the United States to devalue by 50%, as can be seen in Table 15.10.

On the face of it, this devaluation was a formidable trade advantage, but the estimated volume of U.S. exports remained unchanged. This was in part because tariff and other restrictions on international trade had become so widespread. Besides the U.K. tariff system, Canada had reduced tariffs reciprocally with France and had initiated "anti-dumping duties" which valued imports at prior exchange rates to assess tariffs. France had initiated a tariff system with its colonies similar to the U.K. system, Germany and Poland had initiated new tariffs, and the underdeveloped countries had become so hard-pressed that their foreign exchange was controlled and reserved for the barest necessities (excluding debt service in most cases). The other reason for the lack of change in U.S. exports was the rapid rise in U.S. prices, particularly commodities prices and foodstuffs, which were 40% of U.S. exports. Indeed, this rise in domestic prices was well articulated as the basic purpose behind devaluation of the dollar by most who favored it, including J. P. Morgan, Melvin Traylor (First National Bank of Chicago), the Committee for the Nation (which included the chief executives of many midwestern companies, General Robert E. Wood of Sears, Roebuck & Co. being the most notable), Agriculture Secretary Henry Wallace, and the farm block. We have already noted earlier the rise in stock prices following devaluation and the stock market's positive attention to rising prices.

Economic comment on this period gives too little attention to currency devaluation as a tool to raise domestic prices and overcome deflation, rather than as a tool of international trade competition. It is an indication of how far international trade had deteriorated that the economic response expected from devaluation was domestic rather than international.

Edward A. Filene, the Boston retailer, returning from a trip to Europe remarked, "...all European countries are headed for a regime of autarchy—that is, of economic isolation and intense nationalism, and America can do no better than to do likewise." The contrast in Table 15.11 between gold reserves of West European countries at the end of 1933 and at the end of 1930 points out how far the movement to autarchy had already gone in the financial arena, with each country seeking its own responses without reliance on international financial mechanisms.

There was a similar tale in the decline of the New York City banks' deposits from foreigners and other liabilities abroad between 1929 and 1933. This decline is outlined in Table 15.12.

Foreign securities issues in the United States declined over the period 1929 to 1933 in an even worse way, as follows:[20]

1929	$ 785 million
1930	1,146 million
1931	270 million
1932	67 million
1933	73 million

For a brief time in the spring of 1933 there was hope that the World Economic and Monetary Conference in London that summer would achieve international cooperation in trade restrictions, tariffs, exchange rates, public works, and renegotiation of Europe's war debts and that as a result international trade and finance would revive. Britain called the conference, but Roosevelt created hopes

Table 15.11
Gold Reserves of Major Countries at Year End, 1930 and 1933 ($ millions)

	12/31/30	12/31/33
Belgium	$ 191	$ 380
Canada	110	77
France	2,100	3,022
Germany	528	92
Italy	279	373
Netherlands	172	372
Norway	39	38
Sweden	65	100
Switzerland	138	387
United Kingdom	718	928
U.S.S.R.	249	416
United States	4,225	4,012

Source: Banking & Monetary Statistics, pp. 544–51.

that it could resolve matters by inviting leaders of the United Kingdom and France to Washington for prior discussion, then inviting representatives of 9 more countries and instructing U.S. embassies in 42 other countries to hold similar discussions.

Europe's war debts were a vital issue for the conference. Roosevelt had scuttled

Table 15.12
Foreign Liabilities of New York City Banks, 1929–1933 ($ millions)

	12/29	12/30	12/31	12/32	12/33
Creditor country					
France	924	799	549	71	27
Germany	205	161	41	30	18
Italy	157	111	33	40	12
Switzerland	105	222	66	78	12
United Kingdom	301	215	105	171	49
Other European	371	281	122	61	28
Canada	292	217	148	98	86
Latin America	188	130	103	122	97
Far East	49	38	69	44	43
All other	31	38	22	13	11
Total	2,672	2,355	1,303	746	392

Source: Banking & Monetary Statistics, pp. 574–76.

efforts to include the December 1932 payment in the moratorium on war debts by writing an article in *Cosmopolitan Magazine* in November 1932 against the moratorium and in favor of individual negotiations for repayment on a country-by-country basis. As a result, France, Belgium, and Poland defaulted unilaterally. The question was raised again for the June 15, 1933, payment. No progress was made, and France plus eight other countries defaulted. Italy paid $1 million of the $13.5 million it owed, Latvia paid 5% of what was due from it. The United Kingdom made a token payment of $10 million in silver on $76 million due. Finland paid what was due—$148,592. *The Economist* magazine had encouraged the U.K. government to default, and there was much sympathy among bankers on both sides of the Atlantic for this position. The June 1933 payment was the United Kingdom's last.

With the war debts issue resolved in this one-sided fashion, the divisive issue of the conference was currency exchange rates. Belgium, France, Holland, and Switzerland, which were still on the gold standard, were anxious to stabilize exchange rates, and the conference even reached momentary agreement in June on a currency stabilization scheme proposed by O. M. W. Sprague, a U.S. Treasury advisor, until Roosevelt placed the U.S. delegation on a tight leash by shuttling Raymond Moley and Herbert Bayard Swope back and forth between London and Washington as his personal emissaries. A U.S. offer for mutual tariff reductions of 10% was rebuffed by the French, in particular, whose Premier, Edouard Daladier, made currency stabilization a precondition for discussions on trade and fiscal policies. A feeling of despair settled over conference participants. In a syndicated newspaper article, Walter Lippmann predicted the conference's failure and criticized the countries involved for participating in a public conference on matters of such importance without prior agreements on what could be resolved. Roosevelt revealed again his instinct for both the jugular vein and publicity by delivering a stinging rebuke to the already despondent conference on July 8th for its preoccupation with foreign exchange rates rather than economic policies. He did not bother to get the help of advisors on the matter. He wrote the speech himself.

Two other matters disrupted the international scene in 1933—Hitler and Japan's invasion of China. Hitler's brutal and disruptive policies became clear around the world in 1933. In February he dissolved the Reichstag, forcing an election, and simultaneously curbed the socialists and threatened to rearm. Following a violent election campaign, capped by the burning of the Reichstag buildings, Hitler won a majority in the March 5th election and immediately revoked all constitutional rights and initiated a regime of repression. Hajalmar Schacht was put in charge of the Bundesbank again and placed an iron control over foreign exchange dealings. Jews were brutalized and outlawed from public positions, forcing Albert Einstein to depart Germany for the University of Madrid leaving behind his bank savings of $7,200. There were exhibitions of burning books at the universities, and opposition printing presses were smashed and closed. Senior ministers talked publicly of rearming Germany, and Nazis battling the Dolfuss Administration reduced Austria to chaos. There was a three-week period of internal confidence in which German stock prices rose 300%–400% following Hitler's election, but abroad there was fearful talk of another war with Germany as early as May 1933, American Jews held rallies to protest Nazi anti-Semitism, and Germany's 5 1/2% International bonds dropped to $38.

Germany's gold reserves dropped below $100 million under Schacht, compared with over $600 million in 1930, and Schacht's intention to operate under exchange controls rather than gold reserves was made clear when he nonetheless paid out $70 million in gold to liquidate Germany's debt to the U.S. Federal Reserve System rather than pay interest. A new "Standstill Conference" was called in June to arbitrate among Germany's creditors, with Albert Wiggin again representing short-term creditors and John Foster Dulles, senior partner of Sullivan & Cromwell, representing long-term lenders. A partial moratorium on both public and private foreign debt service was widely expected. The ultimate resolution on the negotiations was to continue full debt service on Dawes Plan German loans from the mid-1920s, to pay interest but not principal on the German International 5 1/2% bonds issued in 1930, and to dedicate foreign exchange earnings of the last six months of 1933 to paying interest or dividends on other foreign credits up to a maximum of 4%.

In 1933, Japan had less impact on international financial affairs than did Germany but was nonetheless an unpleasant harbinger of the direction of world affairs. Japan had forcefully invaded and taken over Manchuria, despite condemnation by the League of Nations, and in March 1933 the country showed its disdain for the League by withdrawing from membership. Japanese forces crossed the Great Wall of China in May, thus entering ancient Chinese territory and engaging in naked aggression.

Negative financial reactions to these activities were muted by rigid foreign exchange controls which kept Japanese gold reserves at just over $200 million, where they had been since the beginning of 1932. The dollar-yen exchange rate rose from 21¢ to 31¢ during the year because of U.S. exchange actions, but even 31¢ was a sharp decline from the 49¢ rate which had prevailed until December 1931. In any case, Japanese foreign trade was under strict government control and unable to respond to market influences. Japanese international bonds alone showed the free market impact of Japan's actions. The 5 1/2% issue due in 1965 dropped from $81 to an historic low price of $36 earlier in the year.

Foreign Bonds

Moody's reduced its ratings on bonds of eight major foreign issuers and the Canadian provinces of Ontario and Quebec during 1933, which provides a general measure of foreign bond market conditions compared with 1931 and 1932, when there were 33 and 17 ratings reductions, respectively. In 1933 the United Kingdom's bond rating was reduced to Aa so that no foreign Aaa bond issuers remained, and Belgium was reduced to A. Italy, however, was raised from a

Table 15.13
Average Yields at 1933 Low Prices for Large Bond Issues

Ratings	Rails	Utilities	Industrials	Foreign
Aaa	4.99%	4.92%	5.28%	—%
Aa	6.45	5.66	6.47	5.69
A	6.86	8.05	6.63	7.86
Baa	10.00	9.71	8.40	10.46

Sources: Tables A.7–A.10 and A.12–A.15 in the Statistical Appendix.

Baa to an A rating to reflect the efficiency achieved by Mussolini. (See Table A.10 in the Statistical Appendix.)

Foreign bond prices reflected a pattern similar to the changes in bond ratings. It was a difficult year, but not as bad as 1931 and 1932. During February and March, when pressure on the market was greatest because of member bank selling amounting to $95 million, bonds of the industrially developed countries reached low prices for the year which still averaged almost $15 above the lowest prices set in 1931 and 1932. The Aa rated bonds of Canada, France, Sweden, and the United Kingdom actually averaged lower yields in the early 1933 market drop than most comparably rated corporate issues, and the yields on A and Baa rated foreign issues compared very favorably with similar corporate issues (see Table 15.13).

The group of foreign bonds rated Ba, or lower, which included the bonds of Eastern Europe as well as those of South America, did not clearly fare better than in 1931 or 1932 because the issuers at their worst appeared to be in hopeless condition. In South America, a rating of Ba was a high one. Many South American countries were rated B or Caa by 1933. Aside from Cuba, no South American bond prices were higher than the 'teens at their low prices in 1933, and the bonds of Bolivia, Chile, Mexico, and Peru were all below $5. Austrian bonds, by contrast, had a low price of $42, Poland's had a low price of $59, and Germany's (which deserved a Ba rating) had a low price of $35. These East European bond prices were $15–$20 above the lowest prices of 1931 and 1932. (See Table A.15 in the Statistical Appendix.)

As prices and confidence recovered in 1933, these very low grade bonds provided the best opportunities for large price gains. The average gain in 1933 from low to high prices for large foreign issues rated Ba or lower was $18 1/2 or 169%. The gains in these bonds from the low prices of 1932 averaged $22.15 or 277%, but the reader must remember that half of these issues had low prices below $10. The price gains in the summer market recovery for foreign bonds rated between Aa and Baa were in line with the gains for corporate issues, except for several issues that were still payable in gold or foreign currencies which gained the holder the benefit of the U.S. dollar devaluation. Aa and A foreign bonds gained approximately $18 from their low prices, and Baa foreign bonds gained about $25.

Useful generalizations about foreign bonds rated Aa to Baa at their high prices in 1933 are difficult to make. The issues of Canada and Sweden, which were rated Aa and yielded between 4 1/2% and 4 7/8%, bore no yield premiums at all over corporate Aa issues, but A rated foreign issues at over 6% bore yields 1 1/4%–1 1/2% over A rated corporate issues. On the other hand, issues of Australia and the Argentine which were rated Baa earned no yield premium over Baa corporate issues at 5 7/8%, but Czechoslovakia's and Finland's issues of the same rating yielded almost 2% more than comparable corporate issues. Probably the best generalization is that investors valued the bonds of each country quite individually in light of its economy and external threats.

The bonds of France, Switzerland, and the United Kingdom provided unusual profit opportunities in 1933 because these governments continued to pay interest and principal either in gold or at the original rate of exchange for their local currency. Accordingly, France's 7% bonds due in 1949 rose from $113 to $173 because the French-U.S. exchange rate rose from 3.9¢ to 6.3¢ during the year, increasing both interest and principal by over 60% in dollar terms. United Kingdom 6 1/2% bonds due in 1937 rose from $102 to $125, where the yield would have been a negative 0.65% had not the value of sterling payments to service the debt risen by over 50% in dollar terms by the end of 1933.

Those countries in severe financial trouble tried to work out a variety of alternatives to paying their debts during 1933. Some, like Argentina and Colombia, rolled over maturing debts with U.S. commercial banks in an age-old pattern of waiting for something better to happen. Austria, Rumania, and Germany paid interest on some issues, deferring principal payments due. Greece and Bulgaria made partial payments, as did Germany on its debts incurred other than under the Dawes and Young plans, of 30%–50%, and placed the balance owing in local blocked accounts which earned interest. Salvador pledged 50% of its customs receipts to service foreign debts. Buenos Aires, Chile, and Yugoslavia placed local currency equal to debt service in local blocked accounts to earn interest, while the most desperate countries did not even do that. Bondholder committees were formed in virtually every such case to negotiate the best possible alternative for debt service, but invariably in such cases the bonds in question fell to prices that were purely speculative, usually below $20.

Some issuers found assistance from other governments. Canada and the United Kingdom lent Newfoundland money to pay its external debts, as did Canada alone to the province of British Columbia for the same purpose. The United Kingdom lent $5.5 million to Austria to keep it current. Germany notably refused to assist its local government issuers faced with default, much like the United States.

A comparison of the situation for foreign bondholders in 1929 and 1933 reveals one of the worst records for any class of securities, even though 1933 provided some recovery in foreign bond prices. Of 12 large foreign and Canadian bond

Table 15.14
Distribution of Bond Ratings on Large Foreign Issues, 1929 and 1933

Bond ratings	1929	1933
Non-Canadian ratings		
Aaa	7	0
Aa	5	4
A	8	5
Baa	8	7
Ba	2	7
B	0	3
Caa	0	3
Ca	0	1
Total	30	30
Canadian ratings		
Aaa	5	0
Aa	7	1
A	0	6
Baa	0	5
Total	12	12

Source: Table A.10 in the Statistical Appendix.

issues rated Aaa in 1929, none remained Aaa in 1933. Of 28 non-Canadian issues rated Baa or better in 1929, only 16 remained Baa or better in 1933. While none of 12 large Canadian issuers in 1929 was rated below Aa, by 1933 only one was rated that highly. The changes in ratings in all categories are outlined in Table 15.14.

Price losses on large foreign issues originally rated Aaa averaged only $1 from their high prices in 1929 to their high prices in 1933, even though every issue was reduced in rating, but all lesser rated large foreign issues fared much worse. Issues originally rated Aa averaged losses of $12 3/4 on the same basis, excluding the French issue, which was payable in gold. Issues originally rated A averaged losses of $38 3/8, although Italy's bonds showed a gain of $7. Issues rated Baa registered an average loss of $60 1/2, which illustrates the vulnerability of this rating applied to sovereign nations.

This poor experience was etched sufficiently on the public mind in 1933 that the Securities Act of 1933 had a specific section designed to force disclosure of foreign issuers' purposes and finances, irrespective of how that might infringe on their sovereignty, and the same act included provisions for creation of a Corporation of Foreign Securities Holders in order to defend U.S. bondholders' rights against defaulting governments.

SUMMARY OF 1933

The bank crisis in February and March 1933 was a most inauspicious way to begin the year, but in many respects it was caused by Roosevelt's tactics during the lame duck period and ended with his accession to power. Even though a large proportion of the nation's banks were closed in February and March, most areas of the economy and of the securities markets did not reach depths as low as they had been in May and June of 1932. Once Roosevelt took office and got passed a barrage of legislation in his First Hundred Days, strengthening the banks, devaluing the dollar, and creating an umbrella under the National Recovery Administration to raise prices and control competition, there was a dramatic improvement in the economy. Stock and bond prices exploded upward between April and August. Stock prices rose an average of 186% from their 1933 low prices. Yields on bonds rated A and Baa dropped 2%–3%. Only municipal bonds continued to deteriorate into the summer of 1933, and this was related to the problems cities had meeting welfare costs and raising new tax revenues.

After 3 1/2 years of a declining economy, declining stock prices, and persistent bond market problems as issuers' credits deteriorated, recovery in all respects was finally on its way.

NOTES

1. *Banking & Monetary Statistics*, p. 470.
2. Ibid., pp. 457, 470.
3. Ibid., pp. 76, 102.
4. Ibid., p. 387.
5. Ibid., p. 489. See also Tables A.26 and A.27 in the Statistical Appendix.
6. *Moody's Railroad Manual, 1934*, pp. a23, a24.
7. *Commercial & Financial Chronicle*, 4/1/33.
8. The large issues followed in this study produced yields in 1933 for A rated and Baa rated utility issues which were quite different from those indicated by Moody's, as follows:

Bond Ratings	Highest yields		Lowest yields	
	Moody's	Large issues	Moody's	Large issues
A	7.22	8.05	5.39	5.06
Baa	10.64	9.71	8.14	6.11

9. *Moody's Public Utility Manual, 1934*, p. a16.
10. Ibid., pp. a12, a13, a170–73; *National Income Accounts*, p. 126.
11. *Moody's Industrial Manual, 1934*, pp. 3206, 3208, 3210–11.
12. *Banking & Monetary Statistics*, pp. 146, 387.
13. Ibid., p. 460; see also Table A.18 in the Statistical Appendix.
14. Ibid., p. 174.
15. Ibid., p. 387.
16. *Statistical Abstract, 1939*, pp. 167–68.

17. *National Income Accounts*, pp. 54, 58.
18. Ibid., p. 54.
19. *Commercial & Financial Chronicle*, 4/29/33.
20. *Survey of Current Business*, February 1938 (reprinted as Table A.27 in the Statistical Appendix).

Summary and Conclusions

THE COURSE OF FINANCIAL EVENTS FROM 1929 TO 1933

Financial markets were so buffeted by the crosscurrents of political, social, and economic trends between 1929 and 1933 that a brief summary of the course of events may be helpful. Our opening focus is on stocks, which declined over 50% during the Crash between late October and mid-November. That the Crash was due to the reversal of speculative excesses appears unarguable. Valuations were extreme, with stock prices averaging 30 times earnings per share and 420% of book value when return on equity was only 16 1/2%. The speculative fervor had drawn funds away from the bond markets, which languished accordingly; from foreign countries, which hurt their currency reserves; and even from savings banks, which suffered their first deposit decline in years. The call loan market, which financed broker inventories and margin loans, was stretched out of all proportion to other money markets as it grew by over 165% in three years and paid interest rates almost double other money market instruments. Everyone was in the stock market, including foreigners, a greatly expanded number of brokerage salesmen, and many prominent commercial bankers who came to regret it. Stock trading volume tripled over three years, and the new issue volume of stocks increased over 700%.

The Crash did not occur in a void, of course, so there were other contributing factors besides the market's own excesses. The Federal Reserve had begun to tighten credit in 1928, so that the banking system was borrowing massive reserves by the time of the Crash and interest rates were high. Quite aside from monetary policy, small country banks were closing at the rate of 250–300 annually, which made many observers doubt the soundness of the U.S. financial structure. Some sectors of the U.S. economy had begun to decline as early as the spring of 1929, particularly construction, autos, and the farm economy. There were problems abroad, as well, for the English and German economic-financial systems were in trouble as a result of policies adopted in the restructuring following World War I, and the less developed countries were being thrown into disarray by declining commodities prices and political revolutions. These problems had been around for years, however, and could account for neither the heights nor the depths that stock prices reached.

The Crash was followed by a period of government activity that extended into the summer of 1930. President Hoover led an activist government policy to overcome the negative economic effects of the Crash. He was able to carry a $160 million cut in taxes quickly through Congress and to promote increases in both federal and local government public works spending. His Washington conferences of business, labor, and finance developed reassuring promises that private capital spending would increase in 1930. He promised a new tariff and a breakthrough in the consolidation of eastern railroads into five trunk lines, and he delivered on both promises. With Hoover's active support, the Federal Reserve quickly made clear that credit conditions would be eased, which they were through the summer of 1930. The Federal Reserve reduced its buying rate for acceptances 21 times from 4% to 1 3/4%, the lowest rate on record. Call loan rates dropped 500 basis points. Commercial bank borrowing from the Federal Reserve dropped to the lowest since 1918, and securities investments of commercial banks rose to a record high of $11 billion.

Easy money, government efforts, and the desire of human nature for well-being produced considerable optimism and a strong recovery in securities prices. In 1930, stocks recovered half their losses from the Crash, trading volume recovered to 5 million shares per day, which equalled the most exciting pre-Crash days, and the business of new securities issues recovered. The bond market also recovered from the neglect it suffered in pre-Crash 1929. Straight corporate bond issues without equity sweeteners were common again, foreign issuers found an active market for their new issues, and even holding companies and investment trusts found that they could sell straight bond issues.

The optimism of spring 1930 gave way to a severe decline in stock prices in June which pushed many stocks back to their lowest prices in 1929. Stocks declined less severely, but steadily, from September through December as well, so that by year end they were 25% lower than they had been at the worst point in the Crash. Bond prices dropped $5–$10 at the same time. There was no market for new issues of foreign bonds, even those of high quality, and many South American bonds dropped to prices between $30 and $50 as reorganizations of these foreign debts were discussed. Railroads also had problems issuing bonds, particularly the Erie, Missouri Pacific, and New York Central railroads. North Dakota, Arkansas, Mississippi, Cook County, and most Florida cities had similar problems issuing bonds, although municipal bond prices declined less than corporate and foreign bond prices. The tone of the bond markets was more of a problem than actual bond prices, for very few bond prices were lower than their lowest levels in 1929. The inability of so many issuers to sell new bond issues presaged problems for the future.

In the last half of 1930, many financial market participants showed signs of serious problems. J.P. Morgan & Co. and Kuhn, Loeb & Co. lost money in 1930 as a result of securities losses in the second half of the year. Kidder, Peabody & Co. and Pynchon & Co. had to be recapitalized by outsiders or they would have failed. Cyrus Eaton's Otis & Co. almost failed. Numerous smaller firms did fail. The commercial banks also had problems. Chase and National City banks had large write-offs. Manufacturers Trust eliminated its dividend and turned to the New York Clearing House Association to be rescued. The financial creations of Goldman, Sachs & Co. and the Van Sweringens began to topple from their short-term debts and declining asset values. The Guardian Detroit Union Group in Detroit had to be bailed out of its problems by the Ford family. W. C. Durant, who founded General Motors and rode the roller coaster of market success and failure since before World War I, was sold out by his broker for being undermargined for the last time. In December the Bank of United States failed, creating the largest bank failure in U.S. history.

The decline in securities prices in the second half of 1930 followed the trend in the economy for which there was no specific cause but rather a matrix of unfavorable events and trends. The Smoot-Hawley Tariff of June 1930, which raised U.S. tariffs to 44%, the highest in the world, is often cited as a root cause of the international trade war and decline in international trade which followed. The domestic economy never had recovered in 1930 to the degree anticipated, and in the second half of the year it turned sharply down. Real estate prices began a sickening slide. Railroads, consumer durables manufacturers, especially auto manufacturers, construction, steel, and mining industries were down the most in industry, but the decline was widespread as 2 1/4 million jobs were lost during the year. Individual income declined 25% and corporate income was down 40%. Wholesale and retail prices declined almost 15%, and business underwent a sharp inventory liquidation prompted by both declining prices and sales.

In the rural areas everything, including nature, conspired to create distress in 1930. The worst drought in U.S. history swept the plains states from North Dakota to Texas, creating a dust bowl in which nothing grew. Farm prices declined 29%, minimizing the value of whatever could be grown. And banks in farm communities closed at record rates as their loan assets based on real estate and farm products wasted away and their depositors shifted to the larger city banks. The bank closings even crept into larger cities, such as Omaha, Toledo, Detroit, and New York, where banks heavily involved in real estate lending were in serious trouble.

In Europe, events went critical in 1930 in both England and Germany. The political situation was disintegrating in England under the stress of a static economy and an unsustainable sterling foreign exchange rate. German politics had already disintegrated. Hitler was gaining strength rapidly, Hajalmar Schacht had resigned as President of the Reichsbank, the country's credit structure was collapsing, and Germany's foreign debts were unmanageable. Both countries demanded a reduction of their war debts and U.S. tariffs but were faced by an unyielding United States in both respects. Something had to give soon.

What gave was the European currency system in the summer of 1931. Co-operation among the European countries ceased after Germany and Austria announced their intention to form a customs union in March 1931. Under French prodding, the Austrian banking system collapsed in May when the Creditanstalt closed because of foreign deposit withdrawals. In June 1931, President Hoover was forced to defer the war debts due the United States from Europe because Germany could not make its payments. In July, the German banking system took a forced holiday of two months because both domestic and foreign liquidity were gone. In August, England struggled through international loans and domestic budget cuts to avoid devaluation because many of its banking assets were trapped, illiquid, in Germany and Austria. In September, England gave up a futile effort, devalued sterling by one-third, and introduced protective tariffs. Most of Europe followed her example. Immediately, a run on the U.S. dollar began, to which the Federal Reserve responded with higher interest rates and tighter credit.

The international trade and currency collapse of 1931 dealt a wide-ranging blow to the U.S. economy which exceeded the impact of either the Crash or the Bank Holiday of 1933. Prior to September, the economy had been stable at a low level, but beginning in September it plummeted to new low levels. The Gross National Product dropped so fast that for the year as a whole it was down 7.7%. International trade dropped 50%. Wholesale prices dropped 14%. Industry lost $870 million, which led to the elimination of a further 3 million jobs, a 25% unemployment rate, and frequent wage cuts of 10%–20%. The real estate market collapsed, as rents dropped by one-third and vacancy rates skyrocketed, making mortgages impossible to service. Commercial building foreclosures raged like an epidemic. Farm problems were even worse, as farm and other commodities prices dropped a further 30% from 1930 to the lowest levels in the century. The combination of drought and low prices made it worthless for many farmers to harvest their crops or take their livestock to market.

Prior to the international crisis, bank closings were much reduced because of very easy credit conditions. Interest rates and bank borrowings from the Federal Reserve were at record low levels. But after the collapse of sterling in September, banks began to fail at a record rate as the Federal Reserve tightened credit, foreigners withdrew $750 million in gold, and confidence within the United States dissipated. By year end a record 2,293 banks had failed, and while most of them were country banks outside the Federal Reserve System, there was still an alarming number of larger banks in trouble as banks failed or barely got bailed out in Los Angeles, Omaha, Chicago, Toledo, Pittsburgh, Philadelphia, Baltimore, New York, and Boston. Deposits dropped 10%. Banks of all sizes took record write-offs for losses on securities and real estate loans. Bank borrowings at the Federal Reserve rose from $223 million to $774 million, and currency hoarding shot up $900 million, draining the equivalent from bank reserves.

The Federal Reserve suddenly found itself in a dilemma, compared with its direct pursuit of easy credit in the two preceding years. The New York Federal Reserve wanted to intervene actively in the bond market, buying U.S. Treasury securities to expand bank reserves and raise bond prices, but the Federal Reserve Board in Washington took an opposite course by favoring high interest rates, which were the traditional response to a run on a nation's gold reserves, and voting against purchases of U.S. Treasuries. The New York Federal Reserve had on its side the obvious plight of the domestic economy and banking system. The Federal Reserve Board had more abstruse considerations on its side, such as the need to halt the run on the U.S. gold supply which had reached $750 million in six weeks, the need to retain the flexibility in the Federal Reserve's U.S. Treasury portfolio to assist in the financing of the $2.5 billion federal government deficit for 1932 and the $10.8 billion in U.S. Treasury debt maturities in the next two years, and the consideration of the attitudes of financial circles toward a still new and untried Federal Reserve system if its portfolio became overloaded with Treasury bonds it could not market. The result of this dilemma was that the Federal Reserve took no responsibility for the health of the banking system. At the end of the year the machinery was rapidly being put in place to create the Reconstruction Finance Corporation, which would take responsibility for the health of not only the banking system, but railroads and local government as well.

In this atmosphere of crisis, stock prices declined to their lowest levels since the Crash. The Dow Jones Industrial Index dropped to 74, which was down 62% from its highest point earlier in 1932 and down 80% from the peak of 381 in September 1929. Stocks in general dropped to 75% of book value, where their dividend yields (if they paid dividends) averaged almost 11%—over twice U.S. Treasury bond rates. Railroad stocks dropped to between 15% and 20% of book value as most of them eliminated their dividends, and 19 railroads declared bankruptcy. Stocks of more speculative companies dropped to less than 10% of their highest 1929 prices.

Bond prices dropped in parallel with stock prices, with losses of $30–$40 being commonplace even for good corporate and government credits. Ratings were reduced on 18 large railroad bond issues, 33 large foreign government bond issues, 8 large industrial bond issues, and 12 large municipal issues. Railroads again bore the brunt of the decline, as most large railroad bond issues dropped to prices between $50 and $60, endangering the net worth of many financial institutions. Railroad bonds rated Baa were in complete disarray, with yields ranging from 8% to 12%, and virtually no railroad was able to issue bonds. The railroad industry was permanently displaced from its position as the best credit to that of a sick industry. The prices of electric utility and industrial bonds rated A or better dropped $15–$20, which was much less than railroad bonds but still shocking for bondholders. Prices of Baa rated utility and industrial bonds dropped to between $60 and $70. Prices of high quality Scandinavian, Japanese, and Canadian bonds dropped to the same $60–$70 level, which turned out to be their lowest point in the Depression, and the prices of East European and South American bonds dropped to anywhere from $1 to $30 as most of these countries went into default. Municipal bond prices for cities such as Boston, Chicago, Detroit, St. Louis, New York, Cleveland, and Philadelphia dropped $20–$30, as well, under the pressure of declining tax revenues and rising welfare burdens. For the bonds of poor rural states, such as Arkansas, Louisiana, North Carolina, and South Dakota, the markets disappeared altogether from time to time.

For stocks and bonds of all types, the aftermath of the international currency crisis was the worst point in the Depression to date, far surpassing the Crash, when only stocks were affected, and the summer decline of 1930, when bond prices were still above the lowest levels in pre-Crash 1929.

Because of the profound collapse of the economy following the international crisis and tight money of 1931, the worst year of the Depression was 1932. Most measures of economic activity, such as the Gross National Product, National Income, and corporate sales, were down to half their 1929 levels in current dollar terms. International trade was only one-third of 1929 levels. Economic activity in capital intensive industries such as autos, steel, mining, machine tools, and construction was only one-quarter that of 1929.

Domestic problems were exacerbated by an almost complete cessation of international trade. Tariffs were raised 20% in the United Kingdom, Imperial Preference tariffs were established throughout the British Empire, Germany raised its tariffs 100% in a desperate effort to stay solvent, and most other countries began policies of autarchy designed to confine their economies to the home market. France, Switzerland, and the Netherlands began a focussed effort to turn in their international currency reserves for gold, which hampered international liquidity and justified the policies of autarchy.

There was widespread violence as industry lost $2.7 billion, cut wages and prices, and laid off workers so that nonfarm unemployment rose to 36%, and the number of people on relief rose to 18 million. There were riots at the Ford Motor Company's River Rouge plant in Detroit, hunger marches on Washington, 6,000 people in attendance at a Communist rally in New York City's Madison Square Garden; strikes increased 50% to 10 1/2 million man-days; and in the country farmers barricaded the roads and destroyed farm products in an effort to raise prices. The worst months of the year were April and May, which coincided with the lowest points in the securities markets.

The economic decline was accompanied by a liquidity squeeze among banks which had various asset problems. Their foreign loans were either in default or very slow due to "standstill agreements"; large urban real estate loans on commercial properties were valueless in many midwestern and West Coast cities and slow everywhere; farm and commodities loans had lost their collateral value;

small businesses had record defaults, and almost none could pay off their loans; and country bank bond holdings were reduced to half their book value by the decline in low grade bond prices. The Reconstruction Finance Corporation had to come to the aid of major banks in Baltimore, Philadelphia, Chicago, Detroit, Cleveland, and San Francisco. The first statewide bank holiday occurred in November in Nevada.

Depositors responded to such problems by hoarding currency, which rose from $4.3 billion to $5.3 billion, by shifting deposits into the Postal Savings System, which grew by $179 million to $785 million, by shifting deposits to the large, money-center banks, and by buying short-term U.S. Treasury securities even when the yield was negative, as it was in the fourth quarter of the year. Deposits outside New York City declined $3.25 billion, over 10%, and country member bank borrowings from the Federal Reserve rose to a record $556 million. Bank failures would have reached record proportions had it not been for the Reconstruction Finance Corporation, which approved loans totalling $736 million to 4,190 banks by July 1932 ($949 million by year end). The Federal Reserve made an effort to counter the deposit decline by buying almost $1 billion in U.S. Treasury securities in the open market between March and June 1932, but the reserves created thereby all went to the major New York City and Chicago banks, which were unwilling to lend them downstream to lesser banks. By year end, these major banks held anywhere from 40% to 60% of their assets in U.S. Treasury securities. In any case, the Federal Reserve could not be of much help since the U.S. Treasury and money market securities it could buy or discount were not the problem. Banks needed to mobilize frozen assets in real estate, business, commodities, foreign loans, and low grade bonds. Even the RFC was of only limited assistance in this respect, because it would lend only based on market values which were so depressed as to threaten the net worth of most banks.

Stock prices closely followed the trends in the economy and the banking system. The Dow Jones Industrial Index dropped to 41 on July 8, 1932, its lowest point in the Depression, down to 11% of its 1929 high. This low point was on a volume of only 720,000 shares and followed successive declines for 11 straight weeks from March into May. Stocks of every industry reached their lowest values at this time, unlike the bond market, where the timing of the lowest prices in the Depression was different for railroad, utility, municipal, and foreign bonds. During this low point for stocks, only 31 of the 142 stocks followed in this study maintained their 1931 dividend rate. The average stock price was at 49% of book value and yielded 12 1/2% if it paid a dividend at all. Stocks were also down a further 76% from their lowest point in the Crash. Price-earnings ratios averaged 9.7 but were meaningless.

At this point in the Depression the sharp negative images of the era's losers were established. Goldman Sachs Trading Corp. changed its name and sold out to Atlas Corp., and the Goldman Sachs partners fought a much publicized stockholder suit against them for wasting the assets of the Trading Corp. Ivar

Kreuger committed suicide, leaving behind him the biggest bankruptcy in history. Samuel Insull fled to Greece after his holding company, Middle West Utilities, went into bankruptcy. The Van Sweringens struggled publicly to keep afloat their holding company system for the Chesapeake & Ohio Railroad. Charles Mitchell of National City Bank of New York resigned his chairmanship amid a federal lawsuit for tax evasion and Senate committee exposure of his financial practices in the 1920s. Roosevelt's strident election campaign attacks on the brokers, bankers, and public utility holding company structures found a ready public ear in the midst of such financial disarray.

The domestic bond market reached its lowest prices to date in the summer of 1932 amid a flurry of reductions in bond ratings. Ratings were reduced for 12 countries, 5 Canadian provinces, 25 municipals, 13 railroads, 3 utilities, and 6 industrials followed in this study. But panic prices, which were in some sense analogous to the extremely low prices on common stocks, were only touched by Baa corporate bonds, which reached prices such that their yields were 7 1/2%–12%. Railroad bonds hit their lowest prices of the Depression by $4–$10, compared with 1931 or 1933, with Baa railroad bonds generally dropping to prices of $30 and $40. Industrial bonds rated Baa similarly hit their lowest prices of the Depression. Utility bonds did not hit their lowest prices until 1933, whereas foreign bonds had already hit their lowest prices in 1931 (except for South American bonds in default, which had prices so low as to be meaningless— under $10). Municipal bonds also hit their lowest prices to date by $10–$15, as the low grade sector of that market came to a halt. New York City began its financial crisis, Mayor Jimmy Walker was forced to resign, and the banks began to set budget conditions for new loans. Cook County defaulted. Most major cities were in arrears on employees' salaries, salaries were cut 25%–50% everywhere, and Detroit tried to survive pledging $50 million of its $60 million in revenues for debt service. All the southern states had great difficulty selling even short-term bonds. The RFC provided some help by authorizing $313 million in state and local government loans, but municipal bond problems were just beginning in earnest and would be significantly worse in 1933.

Many of the institutional changes of the Depression were also wrought in 1932. The Reconstruction Finance Corporation was set up in January with authority to lend $1.5 billion to railroads and banks. The Federal Intermediate Credit Banks were set up to aid farm cooperatives and farm lenders. The Federal Home Loan Bank Board was established, creating a widespread federal savings and loan industry which was fundamental to preserving home ownership when homes would otherwise have been foreclosed because of mortgage arrears. The Senate began committee hearings into stock exchange practices and foreign bond issues, hearings which led to the Securities Act of 1933, the founding of the Securities and Exchange Commission, Federal Reserve control over stock margin requirements, and the Glass-Steagall Act, which separated commercial and investment banking. In Texas and Oklahoma, oil pro-rationing finally began.

The postscript to the economic hardship of 1932 was the bank crisis of February and March 1933, which provided a climactic end to the downdrift in economic affairs and securities markets, just as the Crash in 1929 was a climactic beginning. The bank crisis began on February 14, 1933, when Governor Comstock of Michigan closed all the Michigan banks for a "holiday" of one week in order to save the banks in the Guardian Detroit Union Group and its stronger neighbor, the Detroit Bankers Co. By March 4th, less than three weeks later, 31 states had declared bank holidays, and in the early morning of Saturday, March 4th, Roosevelt's Inauguration Day, the banks in New York City and Chicago closed. Roosevelt's first act as President that day was to declare a national Bank Holiday, closing every bank in the nation. Banks began to reopen on March 8th, but with deposit withdrawals restricted to personal and business necessities. By March 29th, some 12,800 of the 18,000 banks in the nation were open, but many of those open still had deposit restrictions, and all of them had been inspected and approved by the federal government. Foreign exchange transactions for all banks were restricted and supervised in New York by Fred Kent, a retired director of Bankers Trust, who had absolute powers of control, as he had in World War I.

The immediate cause of the nationwide Bank Holiday was rooted in Roosevelt's mishandling of the lame-duck period between his election in November and his inauguration in March, although the ultimate reason the banks were all forced to close was that values had collapsed behind their assets in corporate and foreign bonds, stocks, and loans for real estate, commodities, and general business. Roosevelt hamstrung the federal government in this period just when it needed the strength to deal with problems. The budget disagreement was a public example of the inability to make federal decisions as Roosevelt wavered on whether to approve a 2 1/4 percent federal excise tax. His unwillingness to take a position on resolution of the war debts problem was in the same vein. So was his insistence on a special session of Congress to deal with farm problems. The Michigan bank holiday made manifest that this federal stalemate applied to the banking system, and thereupon depositors and banks alike all tried to save themselves. Currency in circulation shot up $1.8 billion to $7.25 billion between February 8th and March 8th, draining the equivalent from bank reserves. Interbank deposits among banks in 101 cities dropped $1.2 billion as banks lost faith in each other. Banks called loans, especially real estate and general business loans, in an effort to stay liquid.

This domestic run on the banks was compounded by a similar loss of foreign depositors anticipating a devaluation of the dollar. Roosevelt and his associates carelessly discussed their devaluation ideas before they had the means either to implement them or to forestall foreign reactions. Devaluation became a public debate, and foreigners began to convert deposits into gold. Between February 8th and March 4th, the United States lost $300 million in gold, with $110 million of that lost on Friday, March 4th, and $700 million in additional gold demanded for Saturday, when the banks closed.

These combined domestic and foreign deposit withdrawals squeezed all banks without distinction, including the New York City banks. The Federal Reserve made a considerable effort to offset the reserve loss, which amounted to over $2.1 billion between February 8th and March 4th, by discounting $1.2 billion in bills and buying almost $500 million in U.S. Treasury securities. For banks in the 101 weekly reporting cities, $1.1 billion of their $1.3 billion in reserves were borrowed, and in New York City, Federal Reserve borrowings of $632 million actually exceeded reserves of $618 million.

With its discount powers limited mostly to U.S. Treasuries, there was a limit to what the Federal Reserve could do. The real responsibility for sustaining the banking system had been lodged with the Reconstruction Finance Corporation, which failed to keep the Michigan banks open and hardly tried to keep banks in other states open. The RFC approved only $286 million in loans to banks between December 31, 1932, and March 31, 1933, compared with $220 million in June 1932 alone. Here Roosevelt hamstrung the government in a more subtle but destructive way. The virulent attacks he had made during the election campaign on the whole financial infrastructure of the nation were suddenly made manifest in the paralysis of the RFC. Given Roosevelt's attitude toward business, doubts were widespread that the RFC would do much to help the banks.

The economy declined in conjunction with the bank crisis in part because it was difficult to do business with the banks closed in many states. Machine tool orders for February–April 1933 dropped to half their 1932 level and one-twentieth their 1929 level. Retail trade touched its lowest point in the Depression, as did the *Annalist* index of economic activity. Monthly railroad revenues were the lowest in the Depression in February 1933. Construction contracts were only one-half of the 1932 level, and U.S. Steel's orders reached a record low, which left the company operating at only 15% of capacity in March, 1933. The copper mining industry was trying to get all U.S. mines to close completely for 6 months. In many cities, local business simply shut down with the banks for a week or two.

Stock prices dropped to 50.16 on the Dow Jones Industrial Index on February 27, at which point the average stock was approximately 16% of its highest 1929 price, 65% of book value, and, if it had any earnings and dividends, 10.3 times earnings and yielding 8.7%. This low stock price level was marginally higher than the lowest point for stocks in 1932. The bank stocks dropped to their lowest prices of the Depression.

Bond prices also fell in the bank crisis, as U.S. Treasury bond rates rose from 3.22% at the beginning of the year to 3.42% in March, and Aaa railroad and utility bond yields rose to approximately 5%. But unlike stocks, however, there was a considerable distance between the lowest prices of the bond market in 1932 and those during the bank crisis, particularly for railroad bonds. The comparative railroad bond yields are outlined below for the worst points in the market in both years. (See Tables A.7 and A.12 in the Statistical Appendix.)

	1932	1933
Aaa	5.81%	4.99%
Aa	7.65	6.45
A	8.19	6.86
Baa	12.40	10.00

The differences in bond prices between the two crisis points were $10–$20 for numerous issues. The differences were on a similar scale for industrial and most foreign bond issues, with the exception of South American issues.

Utility and municipal bonds were an exception to this generalization. Utility bonds rated A or lower fell to lower prices than in 1932 by $5–$10, which was enough to raise their yields by approximately 100 basis points over the highest yields available in 1932. This greater decline was a reflection of Roosevelt's sharp attacks on public utility holding companies and his support for public power. Prices of municipal bonds rated A or lower declined $5–$10 beyond their lowest prices in 1932, raising yields 50–100 basis points on the bonds of major cities and most plains and southern states. Changes in municipal bond ratings told much of the story, as 27 states and major cities had their bond ratings reduced—the most in the Depression. Tax revenue losses and welfare burdens were simply crushing the cities and the farm states. There were only eight reductions in foreign bond ratings, all but one of which applied to South American countries; two Canadian issuers had their ratings reduced; three railroad ratings were reduced; there were no utility rating reductions; and two industrial ratings were increased.

There was, in fact, an air of unreality about the bank crisis. We see part of that in the bond market's reaction, which was less severe than in 1932. In the stock market, prices were very low, but the volume of trading was so slight that few were affected by the low prices. The various state bank holidays and business moratoriums also served to mitigate the impact of the bank crisis on securities prices, credits, and business obligations. It had occurred when the worst in the economy was past and when bank reserves and investments were at record high levels. Nor was there anything anyone could do about the runs on the banks. Everyone had to simply sit and wait.

Roosevelt's accession to power and his actions in the subsequent Hundred Days had a tonic effect on the economy. Above all, Roosevelt focussed on raising prices. The deflationary cycle of prices had become self-generating and very destructive, creating inventory losses for business, delays in production as business hesitated to add to inventories or to plant and equipment, drastic revenue reductions for farm and other commodities producers, and an impossible situation for farm, commercial, and real estate debtors who had to pay off obligations incurred at totally different price levels.

Now the process reversed. Lumber prices doubled, copper prices rose 75%, zinc prices rose 65%, lead prices rose 43%, cotton prices rose 60%, crude oil prices rose 75%, scrap steel prices rose 70%. Wages rose too.

Roosevelt raised prices in various ways. Devaluation of the dollar immediately raised the prices of all international commodities. The National Industrial Recovery Act provided a legal framework under which both government and business acted together to raise prices without fear of anti-trust punishment. On the farm scene, the Agricultural Adjustment Administration focussed on raising and sustaining farm prices. The whole atmosphere changed from the Hoover emphasis on the bond and money markets and on financial institutions to direct action on prices and incomes. This included myriad decisions such as enforcing crude oil pro-rationing across state lines, pushing the Federal Reserve to buy over $600 million in U.S. Treasury securities until both bank reserves and excess reserves were at records, and even new union laws that helped sustain prices.

Roosevelt did have to focus on financial institutions, however, because of the Bank Holiday. The RFC was empowered to invest in preferred stock of any bank, which at last broke the vicious circle of lending to banks only on the current, much depreciated, value of their assets. The combination of President Roosevelt's embargo on gold ownership and control over foreign exchange transactions, Comptroller of the Currency inspection of banks' finances, and RFC capital advances, permitted most of the major banks to reopen. In due course, federal deposit insurance further eased the banking situation. The Glass-Steagall Act separating commercial and investment banking and the Securities Act of 1933 completed Roosevelt's early financial reforms.

The dynamic recovery in the economy between April and July 1933 was not particularly related to these financial reforms, or even to the resolution of the bank crisis, but rather to Roosevelt's impact on prices and confidence. The degree of recovery was almost inconceivable to those battered by over three years of downdrift. The *Annalist* index of economic activity rose from 58.5 in March to 90 in July. Steel industry activity rose to 50% of capacity as output tripled by July. By December, construction contracts quadrupled. Automobile production doubled March levels by June. Rail revenues rose 37%. Retail sales rose 50%.

In due course, the macro-economic statistics for 1933 would indicate a year very similar to 1932. For example, the GNP in 1933 was $55.6 billion, versus $58 billion in 1932, and Personal Income was $47 billion, versus $50 billion in 1932, but there was a radical shift in trend that began in the second quarter of 1933. Within the similar GNP figures for 1932 and 1933 was a pronounced shift in 1933 to more business gross investment and more production as inventories were restored. Corporate profits improved to $435 million in 1933, versus a loss of $2.7 billion in 1932, and business failures dropped from approximately 32,000 in 1932 to 20,000 in 1933. The pain was not over, but the patient was mending fast. The year 1933 was one of dramatic recovery which is only obscured in the macro-economic numbers because of the disastrous first four months caused by the bank crisis.

The change in trend under Roosevelt was abrupt and unmistakable in the securities markets. The average stock rose 186% between February and August, which brought stock prices back to 42% of their highest prices in 1929. The average stock price was 181% of book value and 22.7 times earnings per share, which indicated high expectations for profit recovery. Some of the most depressed stocks tripled, such as holding companies, investment companies, and paper, tire, steel, and farm equipment manufacturers, and so did stocks in some of the most dynamic industries, such as chemicals and business machines. New York Stock Exchange volume increased fivefold to over 5 million shares per day through June and July—shades of 1929.

The bond market had an explosive rise that reduced yields 50–100 basis points for Aaa and Aa bonds and 300 basis points or more for Baa and many A rated bonds. Baa railroad bond prices gained over $30 as their average yield dropped from 10% to under 6%. Industrial bonds rated Baa gained $25–$30, and many A rated utility bonds gained as much as $35, after having been under unusual price pressure earlier. Some Baa rated foreign bonds rose as much as $45. Municipal bond rates also dropped 100–300 basis points, depending on the credit, and while municipal issuers' problems carried on for some time, the market improvement was enough to give hope for a bright resolution even to issuers such as Detroit, Cleveland, Chicago, New York, Tennessee, South Carolina, and Louisiana.

The financial markets had made up their minds that the Depression was over.

CONCLUSIONS ABOUT STOCKS

1. The simplest conclusion about stocks between 1929 and 1933 is that everyone lost. There was no way to pick stocks which rose against the trend. At the peak of the recovery in 1933, the average stock was back to only 42% of its highest 1929 price, and only three stocks were above their highest prices in 1929—Alaska Juneau Gold Mining, Homestake Mining, and Monsanto Chemical. Dow Chemical, National Biscuit, and Owens-Illinois Glass Co. were virtually right at their highest 1929 prices. Of course, results were even worse at the bottom of the stock market in 1932, when stock prices averaged only 12% of their highest 1929 prices. At that low point, only Homestake Mining's stock was above its highest 1929 price, and only four other stocks exceeded even one-third of their highest 1929 prices.

Nor were there any companies that had improved financial results between 1929 and 1933, with the exception of gold mining companies, which increased both earnings and dividends. Homestake Mining's earnings increased 379% and its dividends increased 143%. Every other company had a decline in earnings per share during this period, with the very best companies, such as Coca-Cola, A&P, and IBM experiencing declines of only 10%–15%. The tobacco companies came the closest to improved earnings per share, which they were able to maintain through 1932, until rising tobacco prices in 1933 sharply cut cigarette profit margins.

Nor could the stock investor choose stocks which at least provided dividend increases, other than gold stocks. There were eight other stocks which paid higher dividends in 1933 than in 1929—Central Hanover Trust, Chesapeake and Ohio Railroad, Coca-Cola, A&P, Guaranty Trust, IBM, Lehman Corp., and Monsanto Chemical—but six of these increases occurred in 1930 and the other two occurred only after the recovery began in 1933. We should note, however, that 23 companies maintained their 1929 dividend rates throughout 1929 to 1933 and that this meant a substantial rise in real income to their stockholders due to the sharp decline in general prices. Here was the one redeeming feature of stock ownership.

2. Despite the general ravages of the Depression, individual corporate management skills made significant differences in companies' financial results and in their stocks. If we compare similar companies in similar circumstances, we find wide ranges in earnings, dividends, and financial stability, ranging all the way from growth on one hand to bankruptcy on the other. The Chesapeake and Ohio and the Norfolk & Western railroads stood out for their stable dividends, while other railroads eliminated theirs. J. C. Penney kept paying a dividend and had a return on equity at least double that of Sears and Montgomery Ward. General Electric had positive earnings every year, while Westinghouse lost money from 1931 through 1933. Lehman Corp. paid a dividend of no less than $2.40 from 1930 to 1933, and its stock dropped to only one-quarter of its highest 1929 price, whereas no other investment trust maintained a dividend or held its stock above 5% of its highest 1929 price. Woolworth maintained its dividend and had twice the return on equity of Kresge, which halved its dividend and its earnings. Loew's completely outclassed the other film companies—Paramount, RKO, and Warner Bros.—by reporting significant earnings and dividends while they went bankrupt. Every year but 1933, Procter & Gamble paid higher dividends than in 1929 and averaged a return on equity of 19%, while Colgate-Palmolive eliminated its dividend entirely and had two years of losses. United Gas Improvement excelled among the public utility holding companies, maintaining its 1929 dividend and earnings throughout the period while the other public utility holding companies paid no dividends at all, and only North American Co. also had a meaningful return on equity. Among department stores in New York City, Gimbel Brothers had a loss every year and a stock price as low as 75¢ (book value was $28 per share), while Macy's earned at least $2 per share each year, paid dividends ranging from $2 to $3, and had a low stock price of $17 (book value was $42 per share). Inland Steel stood out in a lousy industry by reporting only one year of losses, while Bethlehem Steel, U.S. Steel, and Youngstown Sheet & Tube lost money from 1931 through 1933. IBM was already a glamour stock in every sense, with a $6.00 dividend which it maintained from 1930 through 1933 and a return on equity of 16 1/2% through that period, compared with

Remington Rand, which made virtually nothing from 1930 to 1933, and Burroughs, which earned only a 3% return on equity in 1932 and 1933. The list of companies which excelled among their peers could be made longer, but the point is already well enough buttressed—good management made a big difference in the face of adversity.

3. Those investors who had the courage to speculate had their best opportunities among weaker companies. Surprisingly few companies went bankrupt—only Middle West Utilities, Paramount, RKO, and Warner Bros. among those studied here—and among the strongest and stablest companies, stock prices went down less and rose less. In the recovery of 1933, stocks which were up over 400% were those that had been pushed down the furthest—holding and investment companies, such as Alleghany Corp., International Paper & Power, Commonwealth & Southern, and United Founders; heavy industry, such as Armour & Co., Deere, American Smelting, Bethlehem Steel, Caterpillar, and Youngstown Sheet & Tube; and companies tied to automobiles, such as Chrysler, B. F. Goodrich, Goodyear, and Hudson Motor Car. Some companies that had come close to bankruptcy or were in reorganization had stock recoveries on this scale, such as Gimbel Brothers and Warner Bros.

4. The worst stock results between 1929 and 1933 were registered by financially oriented companies. There were 32 stocks that at their highest prices in 1933 were still 20% or less of their highest 1929 prices. Nineteen of these were financially oriented. Holding company stocks which were still below 20% of their highest 1929 prices included Alleghany Corp., Cities Service, Columbia Gas & Electric, Commonwealth & Southern, Electric Bond and Share, IT&T, Middle West Utilities, North American Co., Standard Gas and Electric, and Transamerica Corp. Investment company stocks below the same parameter included Goldman Sachs Trading Corp., Tri-Continental Corp., United Corp., and United Founders. Among the bank stocks still below 20% of their highest 1929 prices were Chase National, Continental Illinois, First National Bank of Boston, First National Bank of Chicago, and National City Bank of New York. Just as financial markets reacted in wider swings than the economy during the Depression, financial stocks suffered more than stocks in the basic manufacturing and distribution industries.

The other industry which performed particularly poorly was the entertainment industry. The stocks of Paramount, RCA, RKO, and Warner Bros. also failed to recover beyond 20% of their highest 1929 prices. Somehow a myth has developed that Depression crowds anxious for escape sustained the movie business. This was not remotely true, as Fox Films, Paramount, RKO, and Warner Bros. were all forced into financial reorganization because they defaulted on their debts. The Depression public lost much of its disposable income and therefore eliminated nonnecessities, including the movies.

The other stocks which did not recover beyond 20% of their highest 1929 prices were a random selection due to individual circumstances, including Alcoa,

Anaconda, Commonwealth Edison (which suffered from the fallout of the Insull empire's collapse), Gillette Safety Razor, Gimbel Brothers (which deserved it), Hudson Motor Car, Montgomery Ward, Westinghouse, and Remington Rand.

5. The best stock results between 1929 and 1933 were registered by gold and tobacco stocks. Gold stocks were the only group to exceed their 1929 results in all respects—earnings, dividends, and stock prices. Gold mining companies benefitted from a double whammy—a decline in costs due to the general deflation and a precipitous increase in product prices due to the devaluation of the dollar. The tobacco companies benefited from the general deflation and a 50% decline in tobacco prices, while cigarette consumption declined only 7% cumulatively from 1929 to 1933. Thus, the tobacco companies from 1929 to 1932 had stable earnings, stable dividends, and returns on equity in the range of 20%. The tobacco stocks appropriately recovered to 84% of their highest 1929 prices in the 1933 rally.

The only other industry which came close to the tobacco and gold mining industries was small chemicals, which included Commercial Solvents, Dow Chemical, Monsanto Chemical, and a close neighbor, Owens-Illinois Glass. The stocks of these four companies recovered to 95% of their highest 1929 prices in the 1933 rally as their earnings rebounded to levels in excess of 1929 (except for Commercial Solvents). These companies achieved this favorable record only in 1933, however, as their earnings and dividends had fluctuated through a wide range between 1929 and 1932, and the companies' returns on equity were by and large modest. The larger chemical companies, such as Du Pont, Allied Chemical, and Union Carbide, were fine companies but not exceptional.

6. To complete our attention to stocks in this volume we will leave the reader with a comparison of the average parameters for stocks at their highest prices in 1929 and their lowest prices in 1932:

	1929	1932
Price-earnings ratios	30	10
Market-to-book-value ratios	420%	49%
Return on equity	16.5%	8.4%
Dividend yield	3.0%	12.5%
Dividend paying stocks	134	88

In 1932, out of 142 companies fourteen still paid dividends at their 1929 rate, another nine were higher, and the average change was a reduction of 51%.

CONCLUSIONS ABOUT BONDS

1. The most important general conclusion about corporate and foreign bonds must be that they preserved their value well despite the vicissitudes of the Depression, despite massive reductions in bond ratings, and despite large losses

in South American bonds. All but four of the corporate bonds rated A or better at the end of 1933 (which includes 57 of the 83 large issues followed in this study) recovered to high prices in 1933 within $10 of their highest 1929 prices. For all corporate bonds rated A or better averaged collectively, their highest prices in 1933 represented a recovery to exactly their highest prices of 1929. Indeed, most utility and industrial bond issues reached higher prices in 1933 than in 1929, as did most Aaa railroad bonds. This represented a sweeping maintenance of value since many of these bond issues had their ratings reduced, all the companies suffered significant diminution in earnings, and many companies had deficits. If we take into account the 22% increase in the value of the dollar between 1929 and 1933 due to deflation, the price performance of these bonds turns into a gain in real terms of approximately 22%. On all these bonds, income of 4% to 5% was sustained as well.

All but one of the foreign bond issues rated A or better in 1933 recovered to within $10 of their highest 1929 prices, even though every issue had its rating reduced at least once. France's gold 7% bonds of 1949 rose to $173 from a high price of $114 in 1929 because of their gold value.

Investors in high grade bonds during the Depression had no loss in principal value plus 4%–5% in interest payments, compared with an average loss in value for stocks of 58% and a 50% reduction in dividend income (which was only 3% to begin with at the highest prices in 1929).

These bonds also performed well in the intervening period between 1929 and 1933, compared with stocks. Here we will use 1929 high and low prices as benchmarks, as if 1929 were a normative year. At its lowest price in the Depression, the average corporate and foreign bond was approximately 27% below its highest price in 1929, which loss was offset by the increase in the value of the dollar due to deflation, and compared with a decline in stocks of approximately 88%. In the Depression, bonds had the further advantage over stocks that bonds presented a potential for profit in 1930 and 1931 beyond the highest prices of 1929. The average bond rated A or better reached a peak price in these two years which was 4.6% above its highest 1929 price. By comparison, the highest stock prices in 1930 averaged only 75% of 1929, and highest prices in 1931 averaged only 51% of 1929.

Corporate bonds which were rated Baa in 1933 fared significantly less well between 1929 and 1933 than those rated A, and these Baa bonds were a sizable group, including 22 issues (26 if Ba industrials are included) of the 83 large issues studied here. These Baa bonds were still down over 13% from their highest 1929 prices at their highest prices in 1933, compared with equivalence between the two years for A or better bonds. These Baa bonds also dropped much further at the worst points in the market in 1932 and 1933 than did A or better bonds— 47% versus 27%. We can see in this decline why the equity of many financial institutions was threatened with extinction if they held large low grade bond portfolios.

The moral of this Baa story cannot be simply not to buy Baa corporate bonds, because the issues examined here were only Baa in retrospect. Some 14 of the 22 Baa corporate issues in 1933 were previously rated A or higher, and one Aaa rated railroad issue dropped below Baa.

We must keep in perspective, however, that Baa corporate bonds were still quite a favorable investment throughout the Depression. While Baa bond prices in 1933 were 13% below their highest prices, the price level had declined 22% in the same period, producing a real return of 9%; in addition, the investor had regular interest coupon payments of 4%–5%. Investors also had a modest opportunity for profit in 1930 and 1931 when Baa bond issues were up over 3% from their highest 1929 prices. Both the overall return from 1929 to 1933 and the intermediate profit opportunity were much better than the massive destruction of capital and income in the stock market.

It should be noted explicitly that there were no defaults among large corporate bond issues, and no issues where value was permanently reduced more than $20, compared with their highest prices in 1929.

2. The ultimate safety of even Baa corporate bond investments did not carry over into the Baa sector of the foreign government bond market. Twelve of the large foreign bond issues dropped to ratings below Baa during the Depression, and even at their highest prices in 1933 were still down almost 60% from their highest 1929 prices. At the lowest point in the market, these bonds were down 77% from their highest 1929 prices. Nor was there an opportunity in 1930 or 1931 to get out of these bonds at a profit. The price deterioration was steady beginning relatively early in 1930.

This destruction of bond values occurred principally in South American and East European issues, whereas foreign bonds which were able to sustain Baa ratings, such as issues of Australia, Czechoslovakia, Finland, and Japan, maintained their value more in line with the pattern for Baa corporate issues. The highest prices for these Baa foreign issues in 1933 were down only 9% from their highest prices in 1929, after suffering a decline of over 55% in the worst markets. The moral for the investor in foreign bonds was to avoid investments in the underdeveloped countries.

3. Between 1929 and 1933, high grade municipal bonds were the preeminent investment, but low grade municipal bonds performed more like Baa corporate bonds. Unfortunately, in the municipal market the low grade sector in this timespan included A rated bonds, which meant 21 of the 48 issues followed here were low grade.

Let us follow the high grade municipal bonds first. The high grade municipal issuers were predominantly states, because the welfare burden was destroying the cities' credit ratings. There were only four cities among the 27 Aa and Aaa municipal issues followed in this study. The highest prices in 1933 on high grade bonds averaged $12 higher, or 80 basis points lower in yield, than the highest prices in 1929, and the lowest prices in 1932 and 1933 averaged only $6 1/2 (or 41 basis points) below the highest prices in 1929. In virtually every year of the Depression, there were also opportunities to sell most of these bonds at higher prices than in 1929. These bonds also consistently received interest coupon payments of 4%–4 1/2%. Municipal bonds rated Aaa and Aa therefore represented the most attractive investment in the Depression. In absolute terms, they offered price appreciation of 12% plus interest between 1929 and 1933, with a minimum of price volatility. Adjusted for the 22% decline in the price level in these years, the real return on these bonds was approximately 50% over four years, compared with high grade corporate bonds which had a real return of approximately 40% over four years.

The municipal issuers rated A or lower were principally large cities, and states from the South or the dust bowl area. All were under considerable financial pressure. An A rating in this market for issuers of the size followed in this study was a low and troublesome rating which meant the issuer had difficulty selling long-term debt. Bonds of the cities rated A or Baa had high prices in 1933 which were down approximately $9 (60 basis points) from their highest prices in 1929. State bonds with the same ratings were down approximately $11 1/2 (79 basis points) from their highest 1929 prices. In both cases this was a better performance than Baa corporate bonds, which in 1933 were down 13% from their highest 1929 prices. Both these municipal categories also declined less than Baa corporate bonds in the worst market periods, declining approximately 25% (just over 200 basis points), compared with 47% for the latter.

If we adjust for the price level decline (GNP price deflator) of 22% between 1929 and 1933, the difference of 25% between the highest prices in 1929 and 1933 for A and Baa municipals becomes a loss of 3%, which when added to the approximate 4% interest coupon payments becomes a total return of 13% over four years. Thus even these poorer-performing municipal bonds provided a real return on investment between 1929 and 1933.

Aside from the generalizations above, there was a considerable destruction of principal values in the bonds of Miami, Detroit, Arkansas, and Louisiana. Bonds of these issuers were all reduced to ratings below Baa. The highest prices for these bonds in 1933 were still 40% below their highest prices in 1929, and at their lowest prices these bonds were down 59% from their highest prices in 1929. There frequently was no market for these bonds in 1932 and 1933, so we must qualify the general attractiveness of municipal bonds between 1929 and 1933 to take account of these unfavorable investments. The reader will remember that in the corporate bond market there were only two issues which dropped below the Baa rating, and they still recovered to respectable prices in 1933. These four municipal issuers had debt outstanding of over $700 million and therefore were a significant blight on the municipal bond record.

4. Between 1929 and 1933, money market securities such as Treasury bills, bankers acceptances, commercial paper, and call loans offered a positive return without the risks of fluctuating principal values that accompanied all types of bonds. However, money market returns were barely better than holding cash, for the average returns from 1929 to 1933 were only 1.1% on 3- to 6-month Treasury notes, 1 1/2% on bankers acceptances, 2.7% on commercial paper,

and 2% on call loans. In fact, the most representative of these rates was that for Treasury notes, since banks dominated investment in the other money market vehicles, and only U.S. Treasury obligations were in large supply. At the low return earned on Treasury notes, the motivation of investors was safety as much as income. The significant real return from money market investments was preservation of capital as prices declined 22% between 1929 and 1933. Of course, the same return accrued to cash holdings.

5. U.S. Treasury bond prices rose $4 1/2–$7 between September 1929 and the summer of 1933, providing among the best returns in the 1929–33 period. The total return for the four years from the approximately 4% current coupon yield on Treasury bonds each year plus a capital gain of approximately 5% was 20%–22%. Adjusted for a 22% decline in prices (GNP implicit price deflator), the total return over four years was 42%–44%.

There were opportunities for even greater gains in Treasury bonds in the intervening period between 1929 and 1933. The highest long-term Treasury bond prices occurred in May and June 1931 when yields dropped to 3.13%. These prices were $5–$6 above the average Treasury bond prices in September 1929, in sharp contrast to the DJII, which was down 49% from September 1929 at its highest point in 1931.

Holding Treasury bonds from 1929 through 1933 was not a strategy free of all risk and concern for investors. Treasury bond prices dropped $7–$14, depending on the issue selected, between June 1931 and January 1932 in the wake of the international currency crisis, and Treasury bonds had average annual price fluctuations during the Depression of $4 1/2–$9, depending on the issue selected (See Table A.40.) These fluctuations were particularly meaningful to financial intermediaries and to dealers who had to distribute the heavy volume of new Treasury issues resulting from the budget deficit.

6. Between 1929 and 1933, railroad bonds suffered a reversal in credit standing which was not paralleled in other industries and which was particularly hard on the financial system because of the $11.8 billion in railroad bonds outstanding. Among the 33 large railroad bond issues, there were 34 separate ratings reductions between 1929 and 1933, compared with only 2 reductions among the 30 large utility issues. Prices of railroad bonds with 1933 ratings of A or better dropped 34% in 1932 and 1933 from their highest prices in 1929, compared with only 18% for utilities. And yields on rail bonds became higher than comparably rated utility bonds by anywhere from 1/8% to 1%, after having been the preferred corporate bond for many years.

The deterioration in railroad credit is understated by these arithmetic parameters, since without the direct aid of the Reconstruction Finance Corporation many of the major railroads would have defaulted. Public utilities received no help from the RFC.

7. Bond market yields showed surprisingly little sensitivity to real returns due to price level changes. While the price level (GNP implicit price deflator) declined 22% between 1929 and 1933, yields on corporate bonds rated A or better were

essentially unchanged, and in the intervening years between 1929 and 1933, yields rose rather than declined. This was even true of Aaa utility bonds, which suffered almost no fears of default or even of ratings reductions. Between 1929 and 1933, Aaa utility bond yields at all stages of the market were encompassed between 4 1/2% and 5 1/4%. Treasury bond yields in the same period fluctuated between only 3–1/4% and 4–1/4%. The yields of lesser rated corporate bonds actually rose as deflation increased, even though prices of these bonds almost completely recovered in 1933. Bond interest rates were affected more by available savings and by investors' needs for liquidity than by the real returns available.

The financial system in general adapted poorly to changes in price levels, whether we are referring to bank loans or bonds. Lenders were unwilling to adjust the debts due to them for the severe price level changes, and interest rates could not be said to have declined at all. Creditors accordingly had to bear debt burdens much greater in real terms than they had bargained for. In the real estate, farm, and commodities businesses, and eventually in many rural states, these debt burdens bankrupted the debtors. Thus, the financial system stuck to its practices as price levels changed, and the economy was required to adapt.

THE MINOR ROLE OF MONETARY POLICY IN THE DEPRESSION

1. The cumulative severity of the Depression was the result of a series of shocks. These began with the collapse of the stock market in the Crash, which was a symptom of the overconfidence and overexpansion which existed in the economy. Successive shocks were the decline in the economy and in prices in 1930, the international currency crisis in 1931 and its aftermath in 1932, and the bank crisis in 1933. There was no direct link among these events. Had the international currency system been handled differently following World War I, the Depression might have ended in 1930. If Roosevelt had been more cautious and cooperative in the lame duck period there would have been no bank crisis, and recovery from the low level of economic activity in 1932 would have begun earlier.

2. Price level changes had an important impact on economic activity and cannot be treated as simply a dependent variable resulting from changes in economic and credit conditions. Price level changes had a momentum of their own which, once in motion, was difficult to reverse. Inventories, real investment, profits, and asset values were profoundly affected by price level changes. The impetuses for price level changes came from many directions: foreign devaluations, lack of demand in commodities markets, business competition, business efforts to cut costs, forced liquidations, anticipatory withholding of purchasing power, lack of purchasing power, and farmers' needs for a minimum sustaining cash flow.

The securities markets were much affected by these price changes. They made bonds an attractive investment, but the same price changes made stocks a poor investment because stocks represented the owners of real goods which depreciated and the debtors who had greater burdens. Since bond markets did not change with price level changes, the bond markets represented one of the principal instruments through which the burden of deflation was imposed on the economy.

It was one of Roosevelt's signal achievements that he was able to reverse the deflationary momentum of the Depression through devaluation, the National Industrial Recovery Act, the Agricultural Adjustment Act, and many other isolated actions.

3. It is difficult to unduly blame the Federal Reserve for its conduct of financial activities or for the depth of the Depression. The Federal Reserve was not held responsible before the Depression for the health of the myriad small banks in the banking system. There was widespread recognition that the U.S. banking industry was too fragmented, and a move to national branch banking as a remedy was widely supported. The need to give some institution responsibility for sustaining the banks became clear after the international currency crisis, but it was the Reconstruction Finance Corporation that was given this responsibility, not the Federal Reserve System.

The Federal Reserve's basic credit responsibility was to provide reserves to the banking system, and its tool to expand the credit system was open market purchases of securities, which it used to considerable degree and with appropriate timing. The Federal Reserve purchased $666 million in bills and Treasury securities between August 7, 1929, and December 3, 1929, as the stock market weakened, expanding its holdings by 281%. In 1931, between July 29th and October 21st, it purchased $751 million in securities, expanding its holdings 101% even though it lost $700 million in gold reserves as the international currency crisis developed. In 1932, between April 6th and July 6th, as the economy reached its nadir, the Federal Reserve bought $935 million in securities, expanding its holdings 99%. In 1933, between February 15th and March 8th—just three weeks as the bank crisis developed—the Federal Reserve bought $458 million in securities, expanding its holdings 25%. Thus, Federal Reserve securities holdings had expanded to $2.2 billion on March 1, 1933, just before the Bank Holiday, from $0.4 billion in September 1929, just before the Crash, even though business activity had declined 50% and price levels had declined 22%. This expansion occurred in spite of the fact that Federal Reserve securities holdings had never exceeded $1 billion at any prior time in the 1920s. In the same period, from September 1929 to December 1933, investments of weekly reporting banks in 101 cities rose from $5.4 billion to $8.6 billion, with the only break in trend occurring between October 1931 and April 1932, when investments dropped from $7.8 billion to $7 billion. Outside New York City there was a similar decline in investments, from $5.2 billion to $4.6 billion.

The Federal Reserve has been criticized with respect to its actions in 1930, when the economy declined sharply, banks failed in large numbers, and the Federal Reserve did not make open market purchases of securities. Any such criticism relies on the Federal Reserve's taking responsibility for the health of the many small banks which failed, for the larger banks were not in trouble. Their investments expanded consistently from $5.5 billion in January 1930 to $6.8 billion in December 1930. There is no justification for assigning the responsibility for small banks to the Federal Reserve in hindsight, however, when neither the Federal Reserve nor informed observers assumed it at the time and when Congress assigned the responsibility to the RFC 18 months later.

The one point at which both the economy and the investments of weekly reporting banks in 101 cities declined without the Federal Reserve making securities purchases to offset the decline was between October 1931 and April 1932. The Federal Reserve had made significant purchases between July and October 1931, but it stopped after gold losses reached $700 million. At this point, the Federal Reserve was constrained in its purchases by inadequate free gold to back its currency issue, and not until the law was changed in April 1932 to allow the Federal Reserve to use U.S. Treasury bonds to back its currency issue was the Federal Reserve able to resume securities purchases, which it did heartily. Some criticism of the degree of the Federal Reserve's abstention from securities purchases may be valid at this point, but the basic constraint of law on its activity must be accepted.

4. If the Federal Reserve did its job correctly in the Depression, the obvious implication is that monetary policy could not have been more effective in countering the Depression. An underlying theme of this volume has been to outline the principal factors affecting securities markets in order to place in perspective the minor role that was available for monetary policy.

Monetary policy could do nothing to affect the disruptive shocks to the economic system of the Crash in 1929, which was due to speculative excess; or the shocks of the international currency crisis, which was a heritage of World War I; or the shocks of the bank crisis, which was due to Roosevelt's inept handling of the devaluation of the dollar and his immobilization of the RFC. Even if monetary policy could have had some impact on these events, there were more direct ways to prevent these shocks, ways which simply were not taken.

We must therefore make the distinction between monetary policy as preventive medicine and curative medicine. It could not stop the shocks to the economic system, but could it have cured the ills which developed? This is a meaningful distinction, since it recognizes that the Depression trends were in place and that monetary policy might have reversed them—not that monetary policy could have prevented the trends from developing.

Nonetheless, when we seek to explain how monetary policy might have cured the Depression, no convincing paths occur. The first result of expansionary monetary policy is to create additional bank reserves that will expand credit in the banking system. But this did occur without any noticeable impact on the course of the Depression. Reserves of all member banks expanded from $2.4 billion on June 29, 1929, to $2.5 billion on December 31, 1932, even though total deposits declined from $35.9 billion to $28.7 billion. In this period bank reserves expanded by over 30% relative to deposits, to a record in both absolute and proportional terms. The only quarter-to-quarter drop of significance in these reserves was in the fourth quarter of 1931 following the devaluation of sterling, when reserves dropped from $2.3 billion to $2 billion, but this decline only reduced reserves from 7% of deposits to slightly under 6 1/2% of deposits—not the stuff depressions are made of.[1]

The second result of expansionary monetary policy is for surplus bank reserves to be translated into investments in securities that represent either loans to new issuers or cash transfers to sellers, who can now employ the cash in direct economic activities which constitute incremental economic production. Again, this did occur without any noticeable impact on the course of the Depression. Investments of member banks grew from $10.1 billion in June 1929 to $12.3 billion on December 31, 1932, which represented an expansion of 52.7% relative to deposits and an even greater expansion of 105.9% relative to loans. Again the only quarter-to-quarter drop of significance in these investments was in the quarter following the devaluation of sterling, when investments dropped from $12.2 billion to $11.3 billion, but in this instance the proportion of investments to both deposits and loans held constant.

Friedman and Schwartz have argued in *The Great Contraction* that a more expansionary monetary policy would have so reduced yields on U.S. Treasury securities that banks would have purchased low grade corporate bonds, thereby buoying their prices and reducing the asset deterioration which current holders of these bonds suffered. This is a difficult argument to accept on many counts, first because banks did buy corporate bonds in direct proportion to their growth in investments between June 1929 and June 1931, which includes the key period of 1930, when Friedman and Schwartz identify a bank crisis in which monetary policy was not sufficiently expansive. After September 1931 it is difficult to see what would have induced banks to buy corporate bonds. Their holdings dropped from $2.1 billion on June 30, 1931, to $1.7 billion on December 31, 1932, even while their U.S. Treasury and municipal investments expanded by $1.3 billion.[2] This diversion of funds occurred from corporate bonds to government bonds even though Baa corporate bond rates rose to 8 1/2% on utility bonds and over 12% on railroad bonds compared with under 4% on U.S. Treasury bonds. This was the widest spread on record between rates on these securities. If buying was not induced at these rate spreads, it is difficult to suggest that some realistic higher spread would have induced buying. In fact, between September 1931 and December 1932, banks liquidated 4% of their long-term U.S. Treasury bonds and increased their holdings of shorter maturity U.S. Treasury bills and notes by 90%, even though yields on these latter securities probably averaged under 1%.[3] There would have been little logic for banks to have bought low grade long-term railroad bonds (which had the principal price deterioration) in 1932 while both the banks and the railroads had their economic future in question and both were relying on the RFC to save their industries from massive defaults. The low level of economic activity had too great an impact on both industries for banks to consider buying low grade railroad bonds under the stimulation of easier monetary policy. The banks wanted short-term liquid U.S. Treasury investments, which made the only sense under the circumstances.

The third result of expansionary monetary policy is for surplus bank investments to cause easier loan policies so that economic activity is quickened. This failed to happen even though bank reserves and investments grew between 1929 and 1932. Loans unrelated to securities or to other banks, which is to say loans on real estate and for business, declined from $14.8 billion in June 1929 to $8.8 billion in December 1932. Whether banks would have been induced to ease their loan requirements and whether such easing would have had much impact on the course of the Depression is highly speculative. In the real estate area, which went through unusual stringency with masses of foreclosures and sharply reduced prices, bank loans were only reduced from $3.2 billion in June 1929 to $2.9 billion in December 1932, which suggests that credit availability was not a root cause of real estate distress and in turn that credit availability would not have led to real estate expansion as long as the fundamental ills remained.

But what about other areas of the economy? Railroads sought credit from the banks and were refused, which forced the railroads to seek loans from the RFC. But the railroads' needs were principally to refund bond maturities. The railroads were not seeking incremental borrowings to expand investments. Their direction was quite the opposite—because of the decline in freight revenues, they eliminated investments. Nor could simple credit availability have turned this trend, for the railroads had to maintain minimum earnings coverages of their interest and rental expenses to keep their bonds as legal investments for fiduciaries, and any increment in borrowing charges threatened these coverages.

Other large businesses did not have a recognizable appetite for incremental bank borrowings. Among the other major nonfinancial corporations in this study, only seven had significant bank debt, even though most of them could have obtained it, and their cash and equivalents stayed quite stable, despite sharply reduced sales and capital spending. Moody's found for 321 industrial corporations that between 1929 and 1932 their cash and marketable securities only declined from $3 billion to $2.7 billion and that their ratio of current assets to current liabilities rose from 4.9 to 6.4.[4] These companies had the means to expand. They simply did not want to do so because of economic conditions. Smaller businesses, and especially farmers, may very well have wished to expand their activity, but they were constrained by the availability of credit; however, it is most unlikely that greater availability of reserves would have led banks to expand such credit. Farmers in particular had become very adverse risks because of the decline in farm products prices, the large surpluses of farm products, and the impact of the drought. What is more, farm loans had become difficult to collect on as farmers banded together and used force to prevent foreclosures and property sales. Small businesses as well had become inordinately risky under the economic circumstances.

A slightly different situation prevailed with respect to loans from one bank to another. These loans increased rather than decreased, following the devaluation of sterling in September 1931 from $457 million in June 1931 to $790 million in December 1931. Thereafter, they declined steadily to $444 million in December 1932. Friedman and Schwartz have argued that more expansive monetary policy would have induced more loans to failing banks, which in turn would have led to more loans by the recipients to end users of the capital. It is difficult to see why these failing banks would have acted differently from other banks. They therefore would have used the loan proceeds to build up their liquidity rather than to make loans. But be that as it may, why would banks in surplus lend to banks in trouble? Banks in trouble had already sold or pledged their liquid securities, and the RFC had invariably lent a high percentage of the market value of less liquid assets, including real estate. What remained for other banks to lend on? They surely would not have lent more on illiquid assets than the RFC, which was infused with a public purpose and had no earnings or liquidity requirements. The traditionally conservative lending practices of banks suggest that they would have been dissatisfied with the merits of loans to failing banks irrespective of the lending banks' liquidity.

The only other bank loans which might have been induced by a more expansive monetary policy were loans against securities. For weekly reporting banks in 101 cities, these loans declined from $8.2 billion in November 1929 to $3.7 billion in April 1933. Both brokers and nonbrokers liquidated these loans, with brokers loans dropping from $2 billion to $0.5 billion, and nonbrokers loans dropping from $6.2 billion to $3.2 billion. The elimination of so much purchasing power had a significant negative effect on securities prices. These loans have little relevance for monetary policy, however. Higher securities prices would have been nice, but they would have had no direct impact on the economy, and just how much higher they would have been remains uncertain in view of the very negative economic and international events which determined the general course of the markets. When stock prices tripled in 1933 under the impetus of Roosevelt's new programs, loans on securities played a minor role by expanding by less than 10%. Nor is there any evidence that securities loans were restricted by banks. On the contrary, investors wisely wanted to reduce their investments in stocks, in particular, which was evident in the decline in New York Stock Exchange volume to under 1 million shares per day and in investors' failure to respond to a reduction in brokers' margin requirements to only 25% in 1930. When the stock market recovered between 1931 and 1933, the banks were willing to meet the demand for expanded securities loans from the New York brokers, increasing these loans 16%, 44%, and 210% at points in 1931, 1932, and 1933, respectively.[5]

There is a *non sequitur* in all of the arguments for expanded loans resulting from a more expansionary monetary policy—these loans created liabilities for the banks, corporations, farmers, real estate operators, small businessmen, or investors involved, whereas their problems and concerns were with the asset side of their balance sheet. Their loans had defaulted or become illiquid, their inventory values had declined, their farm products prices were too low, their rents had declined, their products went unsold, or their securities declined in value, and borrowing money to incur more of these problems was absurd. On the contrary, as prices declined, the real cost of borrowing became so high that borrowing was a source of financial problems rather than a cure for them.

Even if we cannot trace how a more expansive monetary policy would have influenced loan levels and the economy, there is an argument that price levels are nonetheless somehow determined by money supply. Since price trends were an important independent influence on the economy during the Depression, we must explore the possible relationship between prices and money supply. Unfortunately, one cannot find a meaningful relationship. For example, if we look at the period from just before the Crash to just before the Sterling Crisis, from June 1929 to June 1931, demand deposits plus currency (M_1) declined 8.1%, and all deposits plus currency (M_2) declined 6.4%, while wholesale prices declined 24.3% and farm prices 39.4%. Then from June 1931 to June 1933, demand deposits plus currency (M_1) declined 19% and all deposits plus currency (M_2) declined 27.3%, while wholesale prices declined only 10.9% and farm prices declined 17.4%.[6] What direct relationship can we establish between money supply and prices when in one two-year period prices decline 3 to 6 times as much as money supply (depending on the definitions), then in an immediately following two-year period, prices decline half as much or equal to the decline in money supply (depending on the definitions)?

The lack of influence had by monetary policy on the economy can be seen when recovery finally arrived under Roosevelt. Stock prices almost tripled, low grade bond prices doubled, wholesale and farm prices rose 18% and 45%, respectively, and the index of production rose 50% between March and August 1933. But at the same time, money supply, whether defined to include all deposits or just demand deposits, was lower than December 1932 in both June and December 1933. Bank loans were reduced on almost every front. Total bank loans were $15.2 billion in December 1932, $12.9 billion in June 1933, and $12.8 billion in December 1933. Real estate loans and loans to other banks declined on every call date from December 1932 to December 1933, and other loans, excluding loans on securities, declined from $6 billion in December 1932 to $4.9 billion in June 1933 and $5 billion in December 1933. Bank reserves did expand in 1933 beyond the level of December 1932, and in particular rose 36.7% between March 1933 and December 1933, but these incremental reserves went totally into adding U.S. Treasury investments.[7] Thus, the recovery in the economy, prices, and securities prices received little or no impetus from monetary policy, even though the bank crisis had much to do with the decline in the economy in February through April. The banking system did great harm to the economy and financial markets when it was not functioning at all, but once the system was functioning again, external stimuli orchestrated by President Roosevelt became the determining forces affecting the economy and financial markets.

The final trends in this period illustrate clearly the determining role of social, political, and economic events on the course of financial markets, rather than some elusive influence exerted by the financial system over the course of the economy. That has been the theme of this volume.

NOTES

1. *Banking & Monetary Statistics*, pp. 73–74.
2. Ibid., pp. 76–77.
3. Ibid., pp. 77, 460.
4. *Moody's Industrial Manual, 1934*, p. a44.
5. *Banking & Monetary Statistics*, pp. 142–46.
6. *Monetary Statistics*, pp. 24–28; *Statistical Abstract, 1939*, p. 315.
7. *Statistical Abstract, 1939*, p. 315; *Banking & Monetary Statistics*, pp. 77, 460; *Monetary Statistics*, pp. 28–29.

Statistical Appendix

A NOTE ON STATISTICAL SOURCES

The Statistical Appendix provides general statistics on financial markets helpful for their serious study between 1929 and 1933; however, there has been no effort, except in a few cases, to duplicate the information available in the U.S. Government's publications, *Historical Statistics of the United States Colonial Times to 1970* and *National Income and Product Accounts of the United States, 1929–1965*, or in the Federal Reserve's comprehensive book, *Banking and Monetary Statistics. Historical Statistics of the United States* provides in-depth statistical series on social factors, federal and local government budgets, prices, and some business matters. *National Income and Products Accounts of the United States, 1929–1965* provides thorough general economic data and much specific data on separate industries' sales, profits, taxes, dividends, and employment. *Banking and Monetary Statistics* is an irreplaceable source of data on the commercial banking system and international exchange rates and reserves.

Excellent information on individual corporations and governments is available in the various contemporary Moody's manuals for industrials, railroads, public utilities, banks and financial companies, and governments.

CONTENTS

TABLE A.1
Summary Financial Statistics for Leading Stocks, 1929–1933 (a)

	Earnings (loss) per share (b)					Price range per share (c)				
	1929	1930	1931	1932	1933	1929	1930	1931	1932	1933
Alaska Juneau Gold Mining Co.	$ 0.71	$ 0.57	$ 0.74	$ 0.57	$ 1.00	$ 10–4 1/4	$9 1/8–4 1/2	$ 20–7	$ 17–7 1/4	$ 33–11
Alleghany Corp.	0.53	0.14	(2.40)(f)	(2.82)	(0.32)	57–17	35–5 3/4	13–1 1/8	3 5/8–3/8	8 1/4–7/8
Allied Chemical & Dye Corp.	12.60	9.77	6.74	3.62	5.50	355–197	343–170	183–64	88–43	152–71
Aluminum Company of America	11.19	1.93	(2.88)	(7.59)	(4.88)	540–146	356–141	224–48	90–22	96–37
American Can Co.	8.02	8.08	5.11	3.26	5.04	185–86	157–105	130–58	74–10	101–50
American Radiator & Standard Sanitary Corp.	1.94	0.60	(0.02)	(0.62)	(0.10)	55–28	40–15	21–5	12–3	19–4 5/8
American Smelting and Refining Co.	10.02	3.76	(2.09)	(5.04)	0.72	130–62	80–38	59–18	27–5 1/8	54–11
American Telephone & Telegraph Co.	15.22	10.26	9.44	5.96	5.38	310–193	274–170	202–112	137–70	135–87
American Tobacco Co.	5.77	8.56	9.08	8.46	3.00	116–80	132–99	129–61	87–41	91–49
Anaconda Copper Mining Co.	7.83	2.07	(0.37)	(1.94)	(0.79)	140–67	82–25	43–9	19–3	21–5
Armour and Co. A	0.20	(1.05)	6.47	(3.05)	(0.10)	18–5 1/2	8 1/8–2 3/4	4 1/2–3/4	2 3/4–5/8	7 3/4–1 1/8
Associated Dry Goods Corp.	3.41	2.01	(2.27)	(5.59)	(1.76)	71–25	51–19	30–5 3/4	11–3	20–3 1/2
Atchison, Topeka & Santa Fe Railway Co.	22.69	12.86	6.96	0.55	(1.03)	299–195	243–168	203–79	94–18	80–35
The Atlantic Refining Co.	6.20	1.02	0.19	1.45	2.46	78–30	51–17	24–8 5/8	22–8 5/8	33–12
Baltimore and Ohio Railroad Co.	10.31	7.44	0.56	(3.31)	(0.84)	145–105	122–55	88–14	12–3 3/4	38–8 1/4
Bankers Trust Co.	5.10	4.70	3.05	3.85	(3.84)	258–105	180–94	124–50	76–33	75–44
Bethlehem Steel Co.	11.01	5.26	(2.12)	(8.11)	(4.77)	141–78	110–47	70–17	30–7	49–10
Borden Co.	5.50	5.12	3.82	1.71	1.06	102–53	90–60	77–35	43–20	37–18
Burroughs Adding Machine Co.	2.34	1.50	0.81	0.23	0.26	97–29	52–18	32–10	11–6 1/4	21–6 1/8
Canadian Pacific Railway Co.	2.85	2.55	0.68	(0.33)	(0.21)	68–46	57–35	45–11	23–7 1/4	21–7 1/2
J. I. Case Co.	13.75	9.67	(8.35)	(17.37)	(14.66)	467–130	363–84	132–33	66–17	104–31
Caterpillar Tractor Co.	6.16	4.63	0.72	(0.86)	0.16	90–45	80–22	53–10	15–4 3/4	30–5 1/2
Central Hanover Bank & Trust Co.	NA(h)	NA	NA	NA	NA	525–265	410–192	277–108	162–75	151–99
The Chase National Bank	4.60	NA	5.17	5.06	3.42	285–135	180–76	110–25	50–19	38–16
The Chesapeake and Ohio Railway Co.	5.42	4.46	3.49	3.07	3.69	70–40	51–32	47–23	32–9 3/4	49–25
Chrysler Corp.	4.94	0.05	0.33	(2.58)	2.78	135–26	43–14	26–12	22–5	58–7 3/4
Cities Service Co.	0.99	1.48	0.50	(0.11)	def.(j)	68–20	44–13	21–5	6 7/8–1 1/4	6 1/4–1 1/2
The Coca-Cola Co.	10.25	11.15	11.82	8.68	8.82	179–101	191–133	170–98	120–69	105–74
Colgate-Palmolive-Peet Co.	4.03	3.76	3.12	(0.74)	(0.57)	90–40	65–44	51–24	32–10	22–7
Columbia Gas & Electric Corp.	3.12	1.76	1.42	0.96	0.51	140–52	87–31	46–12	21–4 1/4	28–9
Commercial Solvents Corp.	1.51	1.07	0.84	0.51	0.88	70–23	38–14	22–6 5/8	14–3 1/2	57–9
Commonwealth Edison Co.	12.83	12.65	10.12	6.24	4.56	450–202	336–217	257–109	122–49	83–31
The Commonwealth & Southern Corp.	0.70	0.60	0.40	0.12	(0.02)	32–10	20–7 1/2	12–3	5 1/8–1 5/8	6 1/8–1 1/4
Consolidated Gas Co. of New York	4.75	5.06	4.94	4.08	3.32	183–80	137–78	110–57	68–32	64–34
Continental Can Co.	5.02	5.04	3.27	2.78	4.31	92–41	72–44	63–30	41–18	78–35
Continental Illinois Nat'l Bank & Trust Co.	27.25	20.77	19.09	15.41	6.17	1040–635	770–170	416–115	147–55	98–19
Corn Products Refining Co.	5.75	4.87	3.54	2.77	2.87	126–70	111–65	87–36	55–25	91–45
Crown Zellerbach Corp.	1.43	(0.11)	(0.29)	(0.91)	0.04	25–16	19–4 1/4	1 7/8–1 1/8	2 7/8–7/8	8 1/4–1
The Curtis Publishing Co.	8.46	7.12	3.29	(0.41)	(2.64)	132–100	126–85	100–20	31–7	32–6 1/2
Deere & Co.	13.72	6.07	(1.78)	(6.80)	(6.03)	128–62	163–29	45–8 1/2	19–3 1/2	49–5 3/4
The Detroit Edison Co.	11.16	8.75	8.98	5.21	4.83	385–151	256–161	195–110	122–54	92–48
Dow Chemical Co.	4.08	3.44	2.95	1.99	5.35	80–60	100–49	51–30	40–22	78–30
E. I. Du Pont de Nemours & Co.	7.09	4.64	4.27	1.81	2.95	231–80	145–81	107–50	60–22	96–32
Eastman Kodak Co.	9.57	8.84	5.78	2.52	4.13	625–150	255–142	186–77	88–35	90–46
Electric Bond and Share Co.	1.97	2.43	1.15	0.33	0.15	190–50	118–37	61–8 3/4	16–1 2/3	14–3 1/3
The Firestone Tire & Rubber Co.	2.74	(0.65)	1.26	1.07	(0.21)	62–25	33–15	22–13	19–11	32–9 1/8
The First National Bank of Boston	NA	NA	NA	NA	NA	214–113	133–65	86–31	42–19	35–20
The First National Bank of Chicago	32.96	24.29	19.56	32.98	19.36	2390–640	830–460	516–227	240–130	176–50
Fox Film Corp. A	10.26	4.06	(1.60)	(3.65)	0.48	106–19	57–16	38–2 1/2	5 7/8–1	4 7/8–3/4
General Electric Co.	2.35	2.00	1.33	0.41	0.38	101–42	95–42	55–23	26–8 1/2	30–11
General Foods Corp.	3.68	3.63	3.44	1.97	2.10	82–35	61–44	56–28	41–20	40–21
General Mills Corp.	4.83	3.71	3.93	4.13	3.56	89–50	59–60	50–29	50–28	71–36
General Motors Corp.	5.49	3.25	2.01	(0.21)	1.70	92–34	54–12	48–21	25–7 5/8	36–10
The Gillette Safety Razor Co.	5.18	3.46	1.22	1.96	1.04	143–80	106–18	39–9	24–10	20–7 5/8
Gimbel Brothers, Inc.	(0.52)	(0.87)	(2.98)	(5.81)	(1.82)	48–11	21–4 1/4	7 7/8–1 3/4	3 3/4–7/8	7 5/8–3/4
Goldman Sachs Trading Corp.	0.94	0.63	0.13	(0.02)	NA	121–32	47–4 3/8	11–1 3/4	5–1	4 7/8–1 1/2
The B. F. Goodrich Co.	4.87	(9.08)	(9.40)	(7.46)	0.18	106–30	59–16	21–2 3/8	12–2 1/4	22–3
The Goodyear Tire & Rubber Co.	9.34	3.16	0.04	(4.24)	(0.79)	155–60	97–35	53–14	40–5 1/2	48–9 1/4
Great Atlantic & Pacific Tea Co. of Amer.	11.72	13.86	13.40	10.02	8.94	494–162	260–155	260–130	168–103	187–115
Guaranty Trust Co. of New York	29.10	25.34	6.13	25.48	27.29	1205–490	860–406	566–248	348–160	351–217
Gulf Oil Corp. of Pennsylvania	9.83	2.35	(5.23)	0.60	(2.51)	209–115	167–59	76–26	45–33	62–34
Homestake Mining Co.	4.16	5.94	9.70	9.94	19.94	93–65	83–72	138–81	163–110	373–145
Hudson Motor Car Co.	7.36	0.20	(1.25)	(3.40)	(2.76)	94–30	63–18	36–7 3/4	12–2 7/8	16–3
Ingersoll-Rand Co.	10.50	4.72	(0.32)	(3.17)	(0.17)	224–120	239–147	182–26	45–15	78–19
Inland Steel Co.	9.76	5.42	1.05	(2.77)	0.14	113–71	98–50	71–20	28–10	46–12
International Business Machines Corp.	10.92	11.42	10.97	9.01	8.05	255–109	197–131	180–92	117–53	153–76
International Harvester Co.	7.11	4.55	(1.03)	(3.14)	(1.79)	142–65	116–45	61–22	34–10	46–14
International Nickel Co. of Canada, Ltd.	1.47	0.67	0.22	(0.14)	(0.53)	73–25	44–13	20–7	13–3 1/2	23–6 3/4
International Paper & Power Co. A	NA	NA	NA	NA	NA	44–20	31–5 1/2	10–1 7/8	4 3/8–1/2	10–1/2
International Shoe Co.	4.37	3.26	2.61	1.80	2.59	78–54	62–48	54–37	44–20	56–24
International Telephone & Telegraph Co.	2.95	2.07	1.20	(0.61)	0.11	149–53	77–18	39–7 1/8	16–2 5/8	22–5 1/8
Irving Trust Co.	2.61	1.93	1.62	1.72	1.33	102–45	75–28	43–15	30–12	25–12
Kennecott Copper Corp.	5.55	1.66	0.41	(0.68)	0.21	105–49	63–20	32–10	19–5	26–7 1/8
Kimberly-Clark Corp.	6.54	4.99	2.33	(0.02)	(0.32)	57–45	59–38	41–14	20–6 1/2	25–5 7/8
S. S. Kresge Co.	2.68	1.90	1.69	0.98	1.50	58–28	37–26	30–15	19–6 5/8	17–5 1/2
The Lambert Co.	10.04	9.52	8.20	5.02	2.98	157–80	113–71	88–40	57–25	41–19
Lehman Corp.	NA	0.49	(7.36)	(24.99)	5.04	136–63	97–52	64–35	52–31	80–38
Liggett & Myers Tobacco Co.	7.82	7.15	6.87	6.85	4.04	106–80	114–77	91–39	66–32	98–49
Loew's Inc.	7.28	9.11	7.27	4.67	2.34	85–32	96–42	64–62	38–13	37–8 1/2
R. H. Macy & Co.	6.70	4.76	3.61	2.18	2.01	256–110	159–82	106–50	61–17	66–24
Marshall Field & Co.	5.02	1.82	(5.16)	(7.19)	(1.41)	NA	48–24	33–9 1/2	14–3	18–4 1/4
Middle West Utilities Co.	0.63	1.08	0.86	(0.44)	NA	57–20	38–15	25–4 3/4	7–1/8	7/8–1/16
Monsanto Chemical Co.	2.88	1.71	2.99	2.37	5.14	81–47	64–18	29–16	31–13	83–25
Montgomery Ward & Co.	2.60	0.22	(2.25)	(1.59)	0.18	157–43	50–15	29–7	17–3 1/2	29–8 5/8

TABLE A.1 (continued)

Book value per share (d)					Year-end capitalization ($millions)		Debt/preferred/common ratios as % of capitalization		Cash and equivalents (short term debt) ($millions) (e)				
1929	1930	1931	1932	1933	1929	1933	1929	1933	1929	1930	1931	1932	1933
$ 10	$ 11	$ 11	$ 11	$ 11	17	15	7/-/93	-/-/100	0	0	0	0	2
21	21	19	16	16	211	198	27/27/46	38/32/30	(27)	(17)	(7)	1	2
95	94	74	72	71	210	246	-/16/84	-/19/81	87	87	94	100	100
23	24	21	16	15	204	220	18/67/15	17/72/11	27(g)	27	30	27	26
50	53	53	57	59	174	165	-/25/75	-/24/76	22	16	6	14	9
16	15	15	12	12	137	179	6/3/91	7/5/88	28	25	21	21	16
66	57	48	42	43	181	192	19/26/55	21/39/40	23	25	22	21	23
150	153	150	144	135	3800	3493	33/3/64	27/3/70	71	419	289	204	219
31	33	36	39	36	280	254	-/21/79	-/19/81	35(g)	29(g)	40(g)	51(g)	38
61	60	58	55	54	578	637	11/-/89	18/-/82	(35)	(48)	(62)	(71)	(70)
37	36	30	29	31	341	431	36/30/34	29/34/37	22	9	33	36	16
30	30	28	23	22	41	48	14/36/50	12/49/39	9	8	9	11	11
230	233	231	230	227	985	990	32/13/55	31/13/56	38	34	20	22	27
54	52	51	51	52	144	145	10/-/90	10/-/90	13	11	6	10	13
146	144	141	139	139	1055	982	51/6/43	62/5/33	(19)	(23)	(43)	(22)	(22)
43	45	40	34	34	85	107	5.63 (d)	7.19 (d)	-	-	-	-	-
144	139	135	128	124	611	735	25/14/61	20/15/65	118	55	50	47	47
35	35	32	31	31	137	142	4/-/96	2/-/98	11	17	25	25	20
7	7	6.50	6	6	29	34	-/-/100	-/-/100	17	19	17	15	15
50	49	53	51	50	1318	1265	32/9/59	39/10/51	70	39	24	15	29
170	178	167	149	136	39	46	-/28/72	-/33/67	(1)	(4)	(2)	1	2
23	22	20	19	19	40	49	12/-/88	13/-/87	(6)	4	8	8	6
100	103	95	86	78	82	105	5.72	7.92	-	-	-	-	-
65	63	47	42	30	207	360(i)	5.19	6.47	-	-	-	-	-
41	48	49	50	51	600	480	40/-/60	36/-/64	7	10	3	(4)	(4)
26	26	26	18	20	122	191	26/-/74	33/-/67	39	42	50	43	37
9	9	8	8	8	1040	895	41/26/33	45/23/32	(60)	(92)	(69)	(58)	(43)
23	25	27	28	29	58	51	-/10/90	-/9/91	7	10	8	5	4
20	22	20	17	16	56	55	-/26/74	-/44/56	7	7	15	13	13
28	20	19	19	19	555	500	23/29/48	31/30/39	(8)	(67)	(44)	(20)	(0)
4.74	3.89	3.71	3.62	4.06	11	11	-/-/100	-/-/100	6	5	5	3	2
136	134	133	109	106	347	303	39/-/61	53/-/47	20	20	14	16	21
6.60	5.65	5.21	5.35	5.35	1240	1025	45/33/22	39/30/31	53	41	42	39	34
53	53	53	53	53	1212	1038	23/18/59	33/17/50	(9)	(66)	(59)	(12)	(11)
43	46	46	42	44	77	80	-/6/94	-/-/100	16	13	9	13	9
211	233	193	141	50	88	145	6.02	16.64	-	-	-	-	-
34	35	35	34	35	115	122	2/20/78	2/22/76	41	42	36	39	40
14	14	11	10	11	96	110	32/43/25	30/49/21	(1)	(6)	(1)	4	5
13	13	13	9	10	46	52	-/27/73	-/19/81	35	36	34	24	24
46	50	46	36	30	60	71	3/44/53	-/52/48	(2)	(5)	(7)	(4)	4
126	118	116	115	115	280	260	42/-/58	48/-/52	(8)	4	5	7	7
20	22	24	24	27	22	19	18/16/66	9/14/77	1	NA	(1)	1	1
35	40	38	34	33	352	392	-/29/71	-/25/75	34	63	69	63	77
63	65	50	56	61	135	141	-/4/96	-/4/96	50	36	23	20	30
81	39	11	8	7.40	540	930	-/12/88	-/27/73	93	52	33	45	43
31	29	26	27	27	119	156	15/38/47	16/39/45	30	12	15	15	17
53	43	40	38	37	72	80	6.52	7.40	-	-	-	-	-
313	316	289	256	176	44	52	7.09	13.24	-	-	-	-	-
59	41	37	13	15	39	106	49/-/51	10/-/90	(41)	(1)	(8)	(8)	5
14	13	12	11	11	341	396	1/-/99	1/-/99	124	142	122	116	112
13	12	12	11	12	61	63	-/-/100	-/-/100	9	13	13	7	11
36	36	39	40	40	49	51	6/33/61	-/45/55	(3)	13	11	6	7
18	18	17	14	15	871	953	-/14/86	-/22/78	127	179	205	173	177
24	16	8	9	9	26	54	-/-/100	19/9/72	11	10	9	7	7
34	37	25	30	20	74	85	35/22/43	40/22/38	4	6	6	7	4
41	12	7	6	NA	34	249	6/-/94	NA	(15)	(10)	(10)	(7)	(4)
57	35	33	25	26	104	150	38/22/40	38/28/34	(24)	10	21	16	12
38	36	27	22	23	171	202	5/39/56	34/44/22	42	37	37	50	52
45	53	60	63	65	160	119	-/22/78	-/16/84	41	73	91	99	97
325	330	317	310	298	268	293	3.40	3.40	-	-	-	-	-
74	75	68	68	67	406	401	16/-/84	25/-/75	27	28	14	17	21
97	67	69	69	72	19	25	-/-/100	-/-/100	5	6	8	11	13
38	32	27	21	18	27	59	-/-/100	4/-/96	17	14	9	4	3
46	46	41	36	35	36	50	-/5/95	-/7/93	16	19	12	11	12
55	56	53	49	45	96	95	31/-/69	44/-/56	15	11	12	5	(2)
55	58	60	60	62	44	37	8/-/92	-/-/100	4	4	5	6	2
54	53	53	51	51	296	305	-/26/74	-/28/72	26	30	46	57	62
7	10	9	9	10	179	168	5/16/79	4/16/80	17	10	3	6	16
33	32	32	28	26	727	640	49/38/13	52/39/9	14	(26)	(36)	(28)	(19)
25	26	24	22	23	75	105	-/10/90	-/-/100	27	28	21	23	15
46	44	45	37	37	468	450	30/9/61	42/8/50	(23)	(21)	(44)	(42)	(36)
27	27	25	22	22	108	134	4.95	3.84	-	-	-	-	-
33	30	29	27	29	207	308	1/-/99	1/-/99	47	26	20	15	21
56	56	55	55	55	44	44	14/23/63	17/22/61	3	1	2	2	2
15	15	15	15	16	103	102	18/2/80	22/2/76	4	11	2	6	10
8	11	11	10	9	6	8	-/-/100	-/-/100	4	5	5	5	3
92	74	57	58	81	58	100	-/-/100	-/-/100	33	17	21	8	4
33	34	36	38	37	168	143	24/16/60	17/13/70	(7)	33	48	73	61
38	45	48	46	46	117	111	35/18/47	25/15/60	10	8	6	8	11
49	47	44	42	42	87	77	9/-/91	9/10/81	4	2	(4)	(2)	(1)
39	39	32	26	24	91	122	33/26/41	28/33/39	(5)	17	16	21	10
13	13	10	0	0	88	222	-/24/76	-/35/65	(1)	(18)	(29)	(33)	(25)
32	31	33	30	33	11	15	15/-/85	9/-/91	2	2	2	2	2
33	30	30	24	24	133	174	-/12/88	2/15/83	38	28	34	28	25

TABLE A.1 (continued)

	Earnings (loss) per share (b)					Price range per share (c)				
	1929	1930	1931	1932	1933	1929	1930	1931	1932	1933
The Nash Motors Co.	$ 6.59	$ 2.78	$ 1.76	$ 0.38	$(0.44)	$119-40	$ 59-21	$ 41-15	$ 20-8	$ 27-11
National Biscuit Co.	3.28	3.41	2.86	2.44	2.11	95-56	93-69	84-36	47-20	62-32
National Cash Register Co. A	5.25	2.26	0.52	(2.09)	(0.36)	149-59	84-28	40-7 1/8	19-6 1/4	24-5 1/8
The National City Bank of New York	4.83	3.88	3.32	3.18	2.02	580-180	258-80	110-34	65-24	46-16
National Dairy Products Corp.	4.04	4.10	3.47	1.88	1.01	87-36	62-35	51-20	31-14	26-11
National Lead Co.	25.49	7.58	5.48	3.15	6.11	210-129	190-114	132-79	92-45	140-43
The New York Central Railroad Co.	16.69	7.21	0.49	(3.66)	(1.08)	257-160	193-105	132-25	37-8 3/4	59-14
Norfolk & Western Railway Co.	29.14	22.06	14.51	11.42	15.33	290-191	265-182	217-106	135-57	177-111
The North American Co.	5.03	4.53	3.41	2.01	1.22	187-67	133-57	90-26	43-14	37-13
Otis Elevator Co.	3.99	3.44	2.01	(0.04)	(1.43)	113-49	80-48	59-16	23-9	25-10
Owens-Illinois Glass Co.	4.80	2.45	2.45	1.62	4.86	99-43	61-32	40-20	42-12	97-32
Pacific Gas & Electric Co.	3.52	3.07	2.79	2.10	1.48	99-42	75-41	55-30	37-17	32-15
Packard Motor Car Co.	1.68	0.60	(0.19)	(0.45)	0.01	33-13	23-7	12-4	5-1 1/2	7-1 3/4
Paramount-Publix Corp.	5.79	5.90	2.01	(4.94)	NA	76-35	77-35	50-5 1/2	11 1/2-1 1/2	NA
J. C. Penney Co.	4.66	2.88	3.13	1.57	5.51	105-66	80-28	45-27	35-13	56-19
The Pennsylvania Railroad Co.	8.83	5.29	1.51	1.03	1.46	110-73	87-53	64-16	23-6 1/2	42-14
Phelps Dodge Corp.	2.69	(2.73)	(0.94)	(0.92)	(0.31)	80-31	44-20	26-5 7/8	12-3 7/8	19-4 1/2
Phillips Petroleum Co.	5.19	0.71	(1.34)	0.19	0.36	47-24	45-12	17-4	8 1/8-2	19-4 3/4
Pillsbury Flour Mills, Inc.	5.12	4.05	3.60	1.51	2.11	64-30	38-25	37-20	23-9 1/2	27-9 3/8
Pittsburgh Plate Glass Co.	5.39	2.18	1.01	(0.03)	1.87	76-49	59-33	43-17	21-12	40-13
The Procter & Gamble Co.	2.97	3.34	3.37	1.26	1.52	98-43	79-53	71-36	43-20	48-20
Public Service Corp. of New Jersey	3.93	3.92	3.82	3.46	3.26	138-54	124-65	97-49	60-28	57-33
Pullman Inc.	5.24	4.37	0.62	(1.00)	(0.70)	99-73	89-47	59-15	28-11	58-18
Radio Corp. of America	1.58	0.02	(0.34)	(0.51)	(0.47)	115-26	69-11	28-5	14-3	12-3
Radio-Keith-Orpheum Corp.	0.92	1.45	(1.87)	(4.18)	(1.31)	47-12	50-14	25-1	1/4	1
Remington Rand, Inc.	3.51	0.11	(3.32)	(2.96)	0.01	58-20	47-14	20-1 7/8	7 1/2-1	11-2 1/2
R. J. Reynolds Tobacco Co. B	3.22	3.43	3.64	3.36	1.62	66-39	59-40	55-33	40-27	54-27
Safeway Stores, Inc.	8.68	4.81	5.68	4.22	4.11	195-90	122-39	70-39	59-30	62-28
Sears, Roebuck and Co.	6.62	3.01	2.47	(0.53)	2.35	181-80	101-43	63-30	37-10	47-13
Shell Union Oil Corp.	1.26	(0.56)	(2.23)	(0.12)	(0.49)	32-19	26-8 1/4	10-2 1/2	8 3/4-2 1/2	11 5/8-4
Sinclair Consolidated Oil Corp.	2.82	1.77	(1.63)	0.02	(0.05)	45-21	32-10	16-4	9-4	16-5
Socony-Vacuum Oil Co.	2.23	0.92	(0.13)	(0.17)	0.71	48-32	40-20	26-8 3/8	12-5 1/4	12-6
Southern Pacific Co.	12.74	8.24	1.92	(1.53)	(1.32)	158-105	127-88	110-27	38-6 1/2	39-11
Standard Brands, Inc.	1.37	1.22	1.08	1.14	1.15	45-20	29-14	21-11	18-8 3/8	38-14
Standard Gas and Electric Co.	6.59	6.04	4.02	0.59	(1.73)	244-74	129-53	88-25	35-7 5/8	23-5 1/8
Standard Oil Co. of California	3.63	2.88	1.11	1.07	0.58	88-52	75-42	52-23	32-15	45-20
Standard Oil Co. (Indiana)	4.66	2.73	1.04	1.04	1.12	63-43	60-30	39-14	25-13	34-17
Standard Oil Co. (New Jersey)	4.76	1.65	(0.34)	0.01	0.97	83-48	85-44	53-26	37-20	48-23
Swift & Co.	2.18	2.08	0.11	(0.89)	1.72	36-31	35-27	31-14	19-7	25-7
The Texas Corp	4.91	1.53	(1.01)	(0.22)	(0.05)	72-50	61-28	36-10	18-9 1/4	30-11
Texas Gulf Sulphur Co.	6.40	5.50	3.52	2.33	2.93	85-43	67-40	56-20	27-12	45-15
The Timken Roller Bearing Co.	5.88	3.12	1.07	(0.20)	0.90	139-59	89-40	59-17	23-7 3/4	36-14
Transamerica Corp.	3.23	0.78	0.26	0.34	0.48	67-20	47-10	18-2	7 1/8-2 1/4	9 3/8-2 5/8
Tri-Continental Corp.	NA	(1.19)	(4.86)	(2.85)	(1.40)	57-10	20-5 5/8	12-2	5 1/2-1 1/2	8 3/4-2 3/4
Union Carbide & Carbon Corp.	3.94	3.12	2.00	0.98	1.58	140-59	106-53	72-27	36-16	52-20
Union Pacific Railroad Co.	20.37	15.63	9.93	7.49	7.92	298-200	243-167	205-70	95-28	132-61
United Aircraft & Transport Corp.	4.51	1.24	1.05	0.53	0.56	162-31	99-18	39-10	34-6 1/2	47-17
The United Corp.	0.49	0.78	0.76	0.44	0.24	76-19	52-14	31-7 1/2	14-3 1/2	15-4
United Founders Corp.	3.54	0.89	0.13	NA	NA	76-25	44-6	10-1 1/8	3 1/8-5/16	3-1/2
United Fruit Co.	6.78	4.24	2.32	1.95	3.16	159-99	105-47	68-18	32-10	68-23
The United Gas Improvement Co.	1.55	1.54	1.46	1.36	1.23	62-22	49-24	38-15	22-9 1/4	25-14
United States Gypsum Co.	5.33	4.15	2.48	0.86	1.00	92-35	58-31	50-15	27-11	54-18
United States Steel Corp.	21.14	9.12	(1.39)	(11.08)	(7.09)	262-150	199-134	152-36	53-21	68-23
Warner Bros. Pictures, Inc.	1.77	(2.19)	(3.81)	(1.76)	(0.75)	67-30	80-10	20-1 1/8	4 1/2-1/2	9 1/8-1
Westinghouse Electric & Manufacturing Co.	10.36	4.49	(1.52)	(3.55)	(3.45)	293-100	202-88	108-23	44-16	59-19
F. W. Woolworth Co.	3.66	3.56	4.24	2.27	3.14	104-52	72-52	73-35	46-22	51-25
Wm. Wrigley Jr. Co.	5.80	6.15	5.07	3.55	3.76	81-65	81-65	80-46	57-25	57-35
The Youngstown Sheet & Tube Co.	17.28	5.17	(6.55)	(11.75)	(7.64)	344-91	150-70	78-12	28-4	38-7 1/8

TABLE A.1 (continued)

Book value per share (d)					Year-end capitalization ($millions)		Debt/preferred/ common ratios as % of capitalization		Cash and equivalents (short term debt) ($millions) (e)				
1929	1930	1931	1932	1933	1929	1933	1929	1933	1929	1930	1931	1932	1933
$ 20	$ 18	$ 17	$ 15	$ 14	54	38	-/-/100	-/-/100	42	38	37	32	30
16	16	16	17	17	118	118	-/21/79	-/21/79	23	25	29	31	21
29	28	27	20	20	46	33	-/-/100	-/-/100	1	2	4	5	3
44	41	36	33	18	240	159	6.90	9.92	-	-	-	-	-
16	15	14	13	12	160	178	30/7/63	39/6/55	21	20	24	26	23
212	212	212	207	209	87	87	-/40/60	-/40/60	8	10	10	7	8
165	159	155	150	148	1428	1408	46/-/54	47/-/53	(22)	(25)	(59)	(68)	(69)
201	212	208	207	210	432	421	29/5/66	24/5/71	6	5	4	7	11
32	34	32	35	24	760	597	49/26/25	53/28/19	14	(24)	(11)	30	26
21	22	21	20	18	46	39	-/14/86	-/17/83	8	12	15	12	11
35	33	33	32	37	44	45	11/18/71	-/-/100	5	5	5	7	3
30	30	30	30	29	409	624	51/12/28	48/21/31	20	12	15	18	16
4.61	4.33	3.68	3.38	3.34	66	49	-/-/100	-/-/100	18	19	14	13	15
47	50	48	38	NA	215	NA	38/-/62	NA	6	7	(13)	(17)	NA
18	16	17	15	20	67	60	-/30/70	-/17/83	7	12	14	23	9
91	87	83	84	84	1590	1690	37/-/63	35/-/65	34	53	41	49	29
60	49	36	35	35	118	181	-/-/100	-/-/100	18	13	9	9	8
39	36	35	31	32	139	160	26/-/74	18/-/82	6	(12)	(13)	(5)	4
34	36	37	36	35	30	40	38/-/62	26/-/74	(4)	(6)	2	3	2
43	43	42	37	39	96	83	-/-/100	-/-/100	13	10	8	11	10
11	14	15	14	13	99	119	11/15/74	9/16/75	9	16	15	25	28
44	45	44	42	42	564	595	37/21/42	34/27/39	1	11	13	14	15
86	84	79	73	69	282	260	-/-/100	-/-/100	66	68	63	40	38
6.89	6.50	Nil	Nil	Nil	106	84	30/22/39	9/48/43	32	16	25	26	30
19	24	20	6	Nil	80	42	41/14/45	96/4/-	3	4	(6)	(6)	(5)
6 1/2	5	1 1/2	Nil	Nil	65	42	34/28/38	42/42/16	8	7	7	6	5
15	16	16	17	16	152	157	-/-/100	-/-/100	18	33	44	60	49
43	42	36	36	38	39	45	1/27/72	-/33/67	6	3	7	6	8
40	41	40	34	36	224	213	-/-/100	-/-/100	(31)	(17)	(12)	(26)	(32)
22	19	18	18	17	406	356	30/9/61	23/11/66	8	7	14	14	16
50	48	18	18	18	374	265	23/2/75	20/4/76	17	36	44	39	34
31	32	27	27	27	645	930	16/-/84	9/-/91	(3)	45	64	79	80
223	225	231	227	191	2040	2088	39/-/61	40/-/60	28	30	27	(7)	(21)
4	4	4	4	4	68	57	-/21/79	-/12/88	32	25	20	22	19
109	108	109	106	102	957	1048	50/31/19	47/31/22	23	23	18	19	24
46	33	44	43	42	575	541	-/-/100	-/-/100	27	16	14	14	23
38	40	39	39	40	648	623	-/-/100	1/-/99	123	80	89	88	75
49	47	48	45	45	1354	1330	13/-/87	14/-/86	242	226	280	179	189
38	38	37	35	36	313	265	27/-/73	18/-/82	(30)	(9)	45	56	49
45	44	40	38	36	568	463	22/-/78	23/-/77	78	63	44	37	37
11	12	13	13	15	28	37	-/-/100	-/-/100	5	6	5	4	9
20	20	18	17	17	46	50	-/-/100	-/-/100	14	14	14	14	14
50	47	5 1/2	6	6	1166	150	-/-/100	5/-/95	4	6	(21)	(13)	7
16	10	1/8	Nil	1 1/4	75	51	-/58/42	15/14/71	20	8	8	5	2
30	30	24	23	24	291	233	3/2/95	4/3/93	68	46	22	11	18
219	224	220	217	216	969	940	40/10/50	38/11/51	16	20	17	21	20
14	14	14	14	10	37	30	-/32/68	-/-/100	16	14	18	16	9
Nil	28	9	9	4	412	582	-/22/78	-/21/79	18	(15)	(13)	(12)	(5)
31	9	2 1/4	3/4	5/8	217	108	19/8/73	27/15/58	(10)	(12)	(3)	(1)	(1)
78	70	65	53	54	195	163	8/-/92	8/-/92	24	23	26	27	37
15	14	14	13	12	670	680	37/16/47	39/16/45	36	(31)	20	19	20
47	50	50	42	42	61	57	-/12/88	-/14/86	6	8	11	13	13
204	206	199	188	181	2052	1978	6/18/76	6/18/76	191	188	145	106	105
22	25	22	15	13	144	153	49/10/41	60/4/36	5	5	4	3	3
87	87	81	74	66	230	173	-/2/98	-/2/98	29	32	33	33	27
16	17	17	17	17	162	173	3/-/97	3/-/97	6	17	23	20	22
21	23	24	24	25	48	57	-/-/100	-/-/100	22	25	27	25	27
109	109	97	85	77	214	196	34/7/59	45/8/47	13	5	14	14	14

TABLE A.1 (continued)

	Year end per share dividend rates (k)					Return on year-end equity (%) (l)				
	1929	1930	1931	1932	1933	1929	1930	1931	1932	1933
Alaska Juneau Gold Mining Co.	$ 0	$ 0.40	$ 0.50	$ 0.60	$ 0.75	7.1	5.2	6.7	5.2	9.1
Alleghany Corp.	0	0	0	0	0	2.5	NM(o)	def.	def.	def.
Allied Chemical & Dye Corp.	6.00	6.00	6.00	6.00	6.00	13.3	10.4	9.1	5.0	7.7
Aluminum Company of America	0	0	0	0	0	49.4	8.0	def.	def.	def.
American Can Co.	5.00	5.00	5.00	4.00	4.00	16.0	15.2	9.6	5.7	8.5
American Radiator & Standard Sanitary Corp.	1.50	1.00	0.60	0	0	12.1	4.0	def.	def.	def.
American Smelting and Refining Co.	4.00	4.00	1.50	0	0	15.2	6.6	def.	def.	1.7
American Telephone & Telegraph Co.	9.00	9.00	9.00	9.00	9.00	10.1	6.7	6.3	4.1	4.0
American Tobacco Co.	5.00	5.00	6.00	6.00	5.00	18.8	25.9	25.2	22.0	8.2
Anaconda Copper Mining Co.	7.00	2.50	0	0	0	12.8	3.5	def.	def.	def.
Armour and Co. A	0	0	0	0	0	0.5	def.	def.	def.	def.
Associated Dry Goods Corp.	2.50	2.50	1.00	0	0	11.2	6.7	def.	def.	def.
Atchison, Topeka & Santa Fe Railway Co.	10.00	10.00	10.00	0	0	9.9	5.5	3.0	0.2	def.
The Atlantic Refining Co.	2.00	2.00	1.00	1.00	1.00	11.5	2.0	0.3	2.8	4.7
Baltimore and Ohio Railroad Co.	7.00	7.00	0	0	0	7.1	5.2	0.4	def.	def.
Bankers Trust Co.	3.00	3.00	3.00	3.00	3.00	10.9	10.4	7.6	9.4	def.
Bethlehem Steel Co.	6.00	6.00	2.00	0	0	7.6	3.8	def.	def.	def.
Borden Co.	3.00	3.00	3.00	2.00	1.60	15.9	14.6	11.9	5.5	3.4
Burroughs Adding Machine Co.	1.80	1.00	1.50	0.40	0.40	33.4	22.0	27.8	2.2	4.3
Canadian Pacific Railway Co.	2.50	2.50	1.25	0	0	6.6	6.2	1.7	def.	def.
J. I. Case Co.	6.00	6.00	0	0	0	8.1	5.4	def.	def.	def.
Caterpillar Tractor Co.	3.00	4.00	2.00	0.50	0.50	27.0	20.6	3.6	def.	0.8
Central Hanover Bank & Trust Co.	6.00	7.00	7.00	7.00	7.00	NA	NA	NA	NA	NA
The Chase National Bank	3.70	4.00	4.00	2.25	1.55	7.1	NA	11.0	9.7	11.4
The Chesapeake and Ohio Railway Co.	2.50	2.50	2.50	2.50	2.80	14.3	9.3	7.1	6.1	7.2
Chrysler Corp.	3.00	1.00	1.00	1.00	1.00(q)	19.0	0.2	1.3	def.	13.9
Cities Service Co.	0.30	0.30	0.30	0	0	11.6	17.1	6.2	def.	def.
The Coca-Cola Co.	4.00	6.00	8.00	7.00	6.00	25.2	24.2	25.6	19.3	18.6
Colgate-Palmolive-Peet Co.	2.00	2.50	2.50	1.00	0	19.8	17.5	15.3	def.	def.
Columbia Gas & Electric Corp.	2.00	2.00	1.50	1.00	0.50(q)	11.1	8.8	7.5	5.1	2.7
Commercial Solvents Corp.	1.00	1.00	1.00	0.60	0.60	31.9	27.6	22.6	14.1	21.7
Commonwealth Edison Co.	8.00	8.00	8.00	5.00	4.00	9.4	9.4	7.6	5.7	4.3
The Commonwealth & Southern Corp.	0	0.60	0.30	0	0	10.6	10.6	7.6	2.2	def.
Consolidated Gas Co. of New York	4.00	4.00	4.00	4.00	3.00	9.0	9.5	9.0	7.7	6.3
Continental Can Co.	2.50	2.50	2.50	2.00	2.50	11.6	11.0	7.1	6.7	9.8
Continental Illinois National Bank & Trust Co.	16.00	16.00	16.00	8.00	0	13.4	9.3	8.3	8.7	12.3
Corn Products Refining Co.	4.00	4.25	4.00	3.00	3.00	17.0	14.0	10.2	8.0	11.1
Crown Zellerbach Corp.	1.00	1.00	0	0	0	10.4	def.	def.	def.	def.
The Curtis Publishing Co.	7.00	7.00	4.00	0	0	63.9	53.3	25.7	def.	def.
Deere & Co.	1.20	1.20	0	0	0	29.6	12.2	def.	def.	def.
The Detroit Edison Co.	8.00	8.00	8.00	6.00	4.00	8.9	7.4	7.7	4.5	4.2
Dow Chemical Co.	2.00	2.00	2.00	2.00	2.00	17.5	15.6	12.5	8.4	21.0
E. I. Du Pont de Nemours & Co.	5.20	4.70	4.00	2.75	2.75	22.2	11.6	11.2	5.3	8.9
Eastman Kodak Co.	8.00	8.00	8.00	3.00	3.00	15.2	13.5	10.0	4.5	6.8
Electric Bond and Share Co.	0	0	0	0	0	3.3	4.1	4.3	1.3	0.6
The Firestone Tire & Rubber Co.	1.60	1.00	1.00	1.00	0.40	8.9	def.	4.8	3.9	def.
The First National Bank of Boston	3.20	3.20	3.20	2.60	2.00	NA	NA	NA	NA	NA
The First National Bank of Chicago	20.00	18.00	18.00	12.00	0	10.5	10.4	9.2	15.8	11.0
Fox Film Corp. A	1.00	1.00	0	0	0	17.5	6.4	def.	def.	3.1
General Electric Co.	1.00	1.60	1.60	0.40	0.40	16.8	15.9	11.1	3.7	3.5
General Foods Corp.	3.00	3.00	3.00	2.00	1.80	28.7	30.2	19.5	17.8	18.2
General Mills Inc.	3.50	3.00	3.00	3.00	3.00	12.8	9.8	10.1	10.3	8.9
General Motors Corp.	3.60	3.30	3.00	1.00	1.25	30.5	18.1	11.8	def.	11.3
The Gillette Safety Razor Co.	5.00	4.00	0	1.00	1.05	18.4	21.6	14.7	21.1	11.1
Gimbel Brothers, Inc.	0	0	0	0	0	def.	def.	def.	def.	def.
Goldman Sachs Trading Corp.	0	0	0	0	0	2.3	5.1	1.8	def.	def.
The B. F. Goodrich Co.	4.00	0	0	0	0	8.5	def.	def.	def.	0.7
The Goodyear Tire & Rubber Co.	5.00	5.00	3.00	0	0	24.6	8.8	NM	def.	def.
Great Atlantic & Pacific Tea Co. of America	5.00	6.00	7.00	7.00	7.00	26.4	26.1	22.5	16.0	13.8
Guaranty Trust Co. of New York	19.00	20.00	20.00	20.00	20.00	9.0	7.7	1.9	8.5	9.2
Gulf Oil Corp. of Pennsylvania	1.50	1.50	1.50	0	0	13.2	3.1	def.	0.9	def.
Homestake Mining Co.	7.00	7.00	9.80	11.00	17.00	4.3	8.9	14.1	14.4	27.7
Hudson Motor Car Co.	5.00	3.00	1.00	0	0	19.4	0.6	def.	def.	def.
Ingersoll-Rand Co.	7.00	6.00	4.00	2.00	1.50	22.9	10.3	def.	def.	def.
Inland Steel Co.	3.50	4.00	2.00	0	0	17.8	9.6	2.0	def.	0.3
International Business Machines Corp.	5.00	6.00	6.00	6.00	6.00	19.6	19.7	18.2	15.0	13.0
International Harvester Co.	2.50	2.50	2.50	1.20	0.60	13.2	8.6	def.	def.	def.
International Nickel Co. of Canada, Ltd.	0.90	1.00	0.20	0	0	21.0	6.9	2.3	def.	5.3
International Paper & Power Co. A	2.40	0	0	0	0	def.	def.	def.	def.	def.
International Shoe Co.	3.00	3.00	3.00	2.00	2.00	17.2	12.7	11.0	8.2	11.5
International Telephone & Telegraph Corp.	2.00	2.00	0.60	0	0	6.4	4.7	2.7	def.	0.3
Irving Trust Co.	1.60	1.60	1.60	1.60	1.15	9.7	7.1	6.5	7.8	6.0
Kennecott Copper Corp.	5.00	2.00	0.50	0	0	16.8	5.5	1.4	def.	0.7
Kimberly-Clark Corp.	3.00	2.50	2.50	0	0	11.6	8.9	4.1	def.	def.
S. S. Kresge Co.	1.60	1.60	1.60	1.00	0.80	18.1	12.6	11.2	6.5	9.3
The Lambert Co.	8.00	8.00	8.00	4.00	3.00	132.6	89.4	76.8	52.0	33.6
Lehman Corp.	0	3.00	3.00	2.40	2.40	NA	0.1	def.	def.	6.2
Liggett & Myers Tobacco Co.	5.00	5.00	5.00	5.00	5.00	23.8	21.1	19.2	18.2	12.9
Loew's Inc.	3.25	4.00	4.00	3.00	1.00	19.2	20.2	15.1	10.2	5.1
R. H. Macy & Co.	3.00	3.00	2.75	2.00	2.00	13.8	10.2	8.2	5.2	4.8
Marshall Field & Co.	NA	2.50	2.50	0	0	12.8	4.6	def.	def.	def.
Middle West Utilities Co.	0.70	0	0	0	0	5.0	8.6	8.3	def.	def.
Monsanto Chemical Co.	1.25	1.25	1.25	1.25	2.00	9.0	5.6	8.9	8.0	15.6
Montgomery Ward & Co.	3.00	0	0	0	0	7.9	def.	def.	def.	0.8

Moody's bond ratings (m)					12/31/29 Market valuation		
1929	1930	1931	1932	1933	Year-end shares o/s (millions)	1929 closing price (e)	Market value ($ millions)
Caa	NR[(n)]	NR	NR	NR	1.4	$ 8	11
Baa	Ba	Ba	NR	Ba	4.2	24	101
Aa pfd	Aa pfd	Aa pfd	A pfd	Aa pfd	2.2	265	583
Aa	Aa	A	Baa	Baa	1.5	290	435
Aa pfd	Aa pfd	A pfd	A pfd	Aa pfd	2.5	123	306
Aaa	Aaa pfd	A pfd	A pfd	A pfd	10.2	32	321
Aa	Aa	A	A	A	1.8	73	131
Aaa	Aaa	Aa	Aa	Aa	13.2	223	2,937
Aaa	Aaa	Aaa	Aaa	Aaa	2.3	97	223
NR	NR	NR	NR	NR	8.8	75	660
A	A	Ba	Ba	Baa	2.0	5 5/8	11
Baa pfd	Baa pfd	Ba pfd	B pfd	B pfd	0.6	29	17
Aaa	Aaa	Aaa	Aaa	Aaa	2.4	224	537
Aaa	Aaa	Aa	Aa	A	2.7	38	102
Aaa	Aaa	Aaa	Aa	Aa	2.5	117	291
NR	NR	NR	NR	NR	2.5	134	335
Aa	Aa	A	A	A	3.2	95	303
NR	NR	NR	NR	NR	3.7	67	246
NR	NR	NR	NR	NR	5.0	46	230
Aaa	Aaa	Aa	Aa	Aa	3.0	190	570
Baa pfd	Baa pfd	B pfd	B pfd	B pfd	0.2	196	39
A	A	Baa	Ba	NR	1.9	198	376
NR	NR	NR	NR	NR	1.1	313	344
NR	NR	NR	NR	NR	5.3	154	816
Aaa	Aaa	Aaa	Aaa	Aaa	1.5	202	303
NR	NR	NR	NR	NR	4.5	37	164
Ba	Ba	B	B	B	28.9	27	765
Baa pfd	Baa pfd	Baa pfd	Baa pfd	Baa pfd	1.0	134	134
A pfd	A pfd	Baa pfd	B pfd	B pfd	2.0	52	104
A	A	Baa	Baa	Baa	8.5	75	637
NR	NR	NR	NR	NR	2.4	31	74
Aaa	Aa	Aa	Aa	Aa	1.4	242	338
A pfd	Baa pfd	Ba pfd	B pfd	B pfd	34.0	14	459
Aaa	Aaa	Aa	Aa	Aa	11.5	100	1,151
NR	NR	NR	NR	NR	1.7	52	88
NR	NR	NR	NR	NR	0.8	680	544
Aaa	Aaa	Aaa	Aaa	Aa pfd	2.5	92	230
Baa	Ba	B	NR	B	2.0	18	36
A pfd	Baa pfd	Ba pfd	B pfd	Ba pfd	1.8	115	207
Baa pfd	Baa pfd	B pfd	B pfd	B pfd	0.9	460	414
Aaa	Aaa	A	A	Aa	1.2	204	244
NR	NR	NR	NR	NR	0.6	66	40
Aa	Aa	Aa	Aa	Aa	10.3	117	1,205
Aaa pfd	Aaa pfd	Aaa pfd	Aaa pfd	Aaa pfd	2.3	178	409
Aa pfd	A pfd	B pfd	B pfd	B pfd	13.5	86	1,155
Baa pfd	B pfd	B pfd	B pfd	Ba pfd	2.2	27	59
NR	NR	NR	NR	NR	2.2	113	248
NR	NR	NR	NR	NR	0.3	695	208
Ba	Ba	Caa	Caa	Ba	0.9	22	20
Aaa	Aaa	Aaa	Aaa	Aaa	7.2	244	1,753
NR	NR	NR	NR	NR	5.3	50	265
Ba pfd-	Ba pfd	Ba pfd	Ba pfd	Baa pfd	0.7	41	28
Aa pfd	A pfd	A pfd	Baa pfd	A pfd	43.5	41	1,761
NR	Baa	Baa	Baa	Baa	2.2	103	226
B pfd	B pfd	B pfd	Caa pfd	B pfd	1.0	13	13
NR	NR	NR	NR	NR	5.6	39	216
A	Baa	Baa	Ba	Baa	1.1	42	46
A	Baa	Baa	Baa	Baa	1.4	62	87
Aaa pfd	Aaa pfd	Aaa pfd	Aaa pfd	Aaa pfd	2.1	238	500
NR	NR	NR	NR	NR	0.9	675	607
Aaa	Aaa	Aa	A	A	4.5	138	621
NR	NR	NR	NR	NR	0.25	80	20
NR	NR	NR	NR	NR	1.6	58	92
Aaa pfd	Aaa pfd	A pfd	Baa pfd	A pfd	1.0	155	155
Aa	Aa	A	Baa	Baa	1.2	73	87
Aa	Aa	Aa	NR	NR	0.6	162	97
Aa pfd	Aa pfd	A pfd	Baa pfd	A pfd	4.4	81	356
A pfd	A pfd	Ba pfd	Ba pfd	Baa pfd	13.8	33	458
Baa	Baa	Ba	Ba	Ba	2.5[(r)]	28	70
Aa pfd	Aaa pfd	Aaa pfd	Aaa pfd	NR	3.8	61	231
A	Baa	B	B	B	5.9	75	441
NR	NR	NR	NR	NR	4.6	53	243
NR	NR	NR	NR	NR	9.4	59	549
A	A	Baa	Baa	Baa	0.5	49	24
Aaa pfd	Aaa	Aa	A	A	5.5	34	187
NR	NR	NR	NR	NR	0.7	97	67
NR	NR	NR	NR	NR	1.0	75	75
Aaa	Aaa	Aaa	Aaa	Aaa	2.6	97	252
Baa	Baa	Ba	Ba	Baa	1.4	43	60
NR	NR	NR	NR	NR	1.3	145	188
A	A	A	A	A	1.4	50[(s)]	70
Ba	Ba	NR	NR	NR	13.4	27	358
Baa	A	A	A	Aa	0.4	49	19
NR	NR	NR	NR	NR	4.6	49	224

TABLE A.1 (continued)

	Year end per share dividend rates (k)					Return on year-end equity (%) (l)				
	1929	1930	1931	1932	1933	1929	1930	1931	1932	1933
The Nash Motors Co.	$ 6.00	$ 4.00	$ 2.00	$ 1.00	$ 1.00	32.6	15.6	10.6	2.5	def.
National Biscuit Co.	3.75	3.30	2.80	2.80	2.80	20.5	21.3	17.9	14.4	12.4
National Cash Register Co. A	4.00	4.00	0	0	0	18.4	8.0	1.9	def.	def.
The National City Bank of New York	4.00	4.00	4.00	2.25	0.75	7.1	NA	11.0	9.7	11.4
National Dairy Products Corp.	2.00	2.60	2.60	2.00	1.20	21.3	21.6	19.3	14.5	8.4
National Lead Co.	5.00	8.00	5.25	5.00	5.00	12.0	3.6	2.6	1.5	2.9
The New York Central Railroad Co.	8.00	8.00	0	0	0	10.1	4.5	0.3	def.	def.
Norfolk & Western Railway Co.	8.00	10.00	10.00	8.00	8.00	14.5	10.4	6.7	5.5	7.3
The North American Co.	0	0	0	0	0	15.7	13.3	10.7	8.0	5.1
Otis Elevator Co.	1.50	2.50	2.50	1.00	0.60	18.9	15.7	9.4	def.	def.
Owens-Illinois Glass Co.	4.50	3.00	2.00	2.00	3.00	13.7	7.4	7.4	5.1	13.1
Pacific Gas & Electric Co.	2.00	2.00	2.00	2.00	2.00	11.7	10.2	9.3	7.0	5.1
Packard Motor Car Co.	1.10	0.60	0.40	0	0	36.4	13.9	def.	def.	0
Paramount-Publix Corp.	3.00	4.00	0	0	0	12.3	11.8	4.2	def.	NA
J. C. Penney Co.	7.00	5.50	2.40	2.10	1.20	25.5	17.9	18.2	10.2	28.0
The Pennsylvania Railroad Co.	4.00	4.00	2.00	0	0.50(q)	9.7	6.1	1.8	1.2	1.7
Phelps Dodge Corp.	3.00	2.00	0	0	0	4.5	def.	def.	def.	1.1
Phillips Petroleum Co.	2.00	2.00	0	0	0	13.2	2.0	def.	0.6	1.1
Pillsbury Flour Mills, Inc.	2.00	2.00	2.00	1.60	1.00	15.0	11.4	9.7	4.2	6.1
Pittsburgh Plate Glass Co.	3.00	2.00	1.00	1.00	1.00	12.7	5.1	2.4	def.	4.8
The Procter & Gamble Co.	2.00	2.20	2.40	2.20	1.50	26.0	23.6	22.8	10.2	12.2
Public Service Corp. of New Jersey	3.40	3.40	3.40	3.20	2.80	8.9	8.7	8.7	8.2	7.8
Pullman Inc.	4.00	4.00	3.00	3.00	3.00	6.1	5.2	0.8	def.	def.
Radio Corp. of America	0	0	0	0	0	22.9	0	def.	def.	def.
Radio-Keith-Orpheum Corp.	0	0	0	0	0	7.6	def.	def.	def.	def.
Remington Rand, Inc.	0	1.60	0	0	0	53.3	2.3	def.	def.	NM
R. J. Reynolds Tobacco Co. B	3.00	3.00	3.00	3.00	3.00	21.5	21.4	22.8	19.8	10.1
Safeway Stores Inc.	3.00	5.00	5.00	3.00	3.00	20.2	11.5	15.6	11.7	11.0
Sears, Roebuck and Co.	2.50	2.50	2.50	0	0	16.6	7.3	6.2	def.	6.5
Shell Union Oil Corp.	1.40	0	0	0	0	5.7	def.	def.	def.	def.
Sinclair Consolidated Oil Corp.	2.00	1.00	0	0	0	5.6	3.7	def.	0	def.
Socony-Vacuum Oil Co.	1.60	1.60	1.00	0.40	0.35(q)	7.2	2.9	def.	0.6	2.6
Southern Pacific Co.	6.00	6.00	4.00	0	0	5.7	3.7	0.8	def.	def.
Standard Brands, Inc.	1.50	1.20	1.20	1.00	1.00	34.3	30.3	28.4	28.5	28.8
Standard Gas and Electric Co.	3.50	3.50	3.50	2.00	0	6.0	5.6	3.7	0.6	def.
Standard Oil Co. of California	2.50	2.50	2.00	1.00	1.00	7.9	6.5	2.5	2.5	1.3
Standard Oil Co. (Indiana)	3.25	2.50	1.00	1.00	1.00	12.1	6.9	2.6	2.6	2.8
Standard Oil Co. (New Jersey)	2.00	2.00	2.00	2.00	1.00	9.7	3.5	0.7	0	2.2
Swift & Co.	2.00	2.00	2.00	0	0	5.8	5.5	0.3	def.	4.7
The Texas Corp.	3.00	3.00	2.00	1.00	1.00	10.9	3.5	def.	def.	def.
Texas Gulf Sulphur Co.	4.00	4.00	3.00	2.00	2.00	58.6	44.3	27.7	17.9	19.9
The Timken Roller Bearing Co.	3.00	3.00	2.00	1.00	0.60	29.5	15.8	5.9	def.	5.3
Transamerica Corp.	1.60	1.00	0	0	0	4.5	1.7	4.6	6.0	8.0
Tri-Continental Corp.	0	0	0	0	0	NA	def.	def.	def.	def.
Union Carbide & Carbon Corp.	2.60	2.60	2.60	1.20	1.00	13.1	10.4	8.3	4.3	6.6
Union Pacific Railroad Co.	10.00	10.00	10.00	6.00	6.00	9.3	7.0	4.5	3.5	3.7
United Aircraft & Transport Corp.	0	0	0	0	0	32.2	8.9	7.5	3.8	NA
The United Corp.	0	0.50	0.75	0.40	0	1.3	2.4	2.5	1.4	0.8
United Founders Corp.	0	0	0	0	0	8.6	9.9	5.8	0	0
United Fruit Co.	4.00	4.00	3.00	2.00	2.00	8.7	6.1	3.6	3.7	5.9
The United Gas Improvement Co.	1.20	1.30	1.20	1.20	1.20	10.3	11.0	10.4	10.5	10.3
United States Gypsum Co.	1.60	2.10	1.60	1.00	1.00	11.4	8.4	5.0	2.1	2.4
United States Steel Corp.	8.00	7.00	4.00	0	0	10.4	4.7	def.	def.	def.
Warner Bros. Pictures, Inc.	4.00	3.00	0	0	0	8.0	def.	def.	def.	def.
Westinghouse Electric & Manufacturing Co.	4.00	5.00	2.50	0	0	11.9	5.2	def.	def.	def.
F. W. Woolworth Co.	2.40	2.40	4.40	2.40	2.40	22.9	20.9	24.9	13.4	18.5
Wm. Wrigley Jr. Co.	4.00	4.00	4.00	3.00	3.00	27.7	26.6	21.2	14.8	15.2
The Youngstown Sheet & Tube Co.	5.00	5.00	0	0	0	15.9	4.8	def.	def.	def.
Averages						16.49%	11.63%	10.19%	8.42%	8.50%
Number of Companies						136	125	102	80	88

Sources: Moody's Industrial Manuals 1930-1935, Moody's Utility Manuals 1930-1935, Moody's Railroad Manuals 1930-1935, Moody's Financial Manuals 1930-1935.

Notes:

(a) Fiscal year data is included in the prior year for fiscal years ending before June 30 and in the current year when the fiscal year ends after June 30.

(b) All per share data is adjusted for stock splits, but not for minor stock dividends, and is as first reported, ignoring restatements of earnings. Earnings per share frequently ignore large writeoffs made directly against net worth and not flowed through the income statement.

(c) Stock prices are rounded to the nearest dollar except when below $10.00.

(d) Book values per share and debt-equity ratios are usually as reported, but occasional adjustments have been made for declines in the market values of securities held where the change in book value is significant and the information is available. Financial corporations are most affected by these adjustments, and, therefore, the data for them is the least consistent herein. Deposit-to-capital ratios are listed for banks rather than capitalization ratios.

(e) Companies for which cash and equivalents are indicated had no short-term debt except in a few cases in which minor amounts of short-term debt were netted against cash and equivalents. Companies which had short-term debt are indicated by brackets. They had cash as well, but it was ignored on the assumption that it was working cash.

(f) Brackets indicate a loss.

(g) Estimate.

(h) NA = not available.

(i) Includes Equitable Trust Co. and Interstate Trust Co. which were merged into the Chase National Bank in May, 1930.

TABLE A.1 (continued)

	Moody's bond ratings (2)				12/31/29 Market valuation		
1929	1930	1931	1932	1933	shares o/s (millions)	1929 closing price (c)	Market value ($ millions)
NR	NR	NR	NR	NR	2.7	$ 54	145
Aaa pfd	Aaa pfd	Aaa pfd	Aaa pfd	Aaa pfd	2.4	180	431
NR	NR	NR	NR	NR	1.6	77	122
NR	NR	NR	NR	NR	5.5	211	1,160
A	A	A	Baa	Baa	5.1	49	248
A pfd	A pfd	A pfd	A pfd	A pfd	0.3	134	40
Aaa	Aaa	Aa	Aa	Aa	4.6	170	782
Aaa	Aaa	Aaa	Aaa	Aaa	1.4	227	317
A pfd	A	Baa	Baa	Baa	5.6	98	548
A pfd	Aa pfd	Aa pfd	A pfd	B pfd	0.5	69	34
A	A	A	NR	NR	0.8	53	42
Aa	Aa	Aa	Aa	Aa	3.8	53	199
NR	NR	NR	NR	NR	15.0	16	245
Baa	Baa	B	Ca	Ca	2.7	51	137
A pfd	A pfd	A pfd	A pfd	A pfd	2.4	75	180
Aaa	Aaa	Aaa	Aaa	Aaa	11.5	74	653
NR	NR	NR	NR	NR	2.0	39	78
A	Baa	Ba	Ba	Baa	2.5	35	87
Baa	Baa	Baa	Baa	Baa	0.5	35	17
NR	NR	NR	NR	NR	2.2	54	119
Aaa	Aaa	Aaa	Aaa	Aaa	6.4	54	345
Aa	Aa	Aa	Aa	Aa	5.4	83	450
NR	NR	NR	NR	NR	3.4	85	287
A pfd	Baa pfd	Baa pfd	Caa pfd	Caa pfd	6.6	44	290
NR	NR	NR	Ca	Ca	1.8	20	36
Baa	Ba	Ba	Ba	Ba	1.3	27	35
NR	NR	NR	NR	NR	9.0	50	446
Baa pfd	Baa pfd	Baa pfd	Baa pfd	Baa pfd	0.6	115	69
NR	NR	NR	NR	NR	4.6	89	410
A	Ba	Ba	Ba	Ba	13.1	23	306
Baa	Baa	Baa	Baa	Baa	5.5	24	134
Aaa	Aaa	NR	NR	Aaa	17.4	33	580
Aaa	Aaa	Aaa	Aa	Aa	3.7	124	458
Aa pfd	Aa pfd	Aa pfd	Aa pfd	Aaa pfd	12.5	27	339
Baa	Ba	Ba	Ba	B	1.6	119	190
NR	NR	NR	NR	NR	12.8	61	782
NR	NR	NR	NR	NR	2.2	54	119
Aaa	Aaa	Aaa	Aaa	Aaa	25.4	66	1,679
Aa	Aa	Aa	Aa	Aa	6.0	34	204
Aa	Aa	A	A	A	9.9	56	555
NR	NR	NR	NR	NR	2.5	55	137
NR	NR	NR	NR	NR	2.4	78	187
NR	Baa	B	B	B	23.4	42	979
NR	NR	NR	NR	NR	2.0	13	26
NR	NR	NR	NR	NR	9.2	79	726
Aaa	Aaa	Aaa	Aaa	Aaa	2.2	216	475
Ba pfd	Ba pfd	Ba pfd	Ba pfd	NR	1.8	47	85
NR	NR	NR	NR	NR	7.3	32	235
NR	NR	NR	NR	NR	3.9	37	144
NR	NR	NR	NR	NR	2.6	104	269
Aa pfd	Aa pfd	Aa pfd	Aa pfd	Aa pfd	20.5	34	686
A pfd	A pfd	A pfd	A pfd	A pfd	1.1	40	44
Aaa pfd	Aaa pfd	Baa pfd	Ba pfd	Baa pfd	8.5	171	1,453
Baa	B	Caa	Caa	Caa	2.6	41	105
Aaa pfd	Aaa pfd	Aa pfd	A pfd	A pfd	2.6	145	375
NR	NR	NR	NR	NR	9.8	71	692
NR	NR	NR	NR	NR	2.0	68	136
Aa	A	Baa	Baa	Baa	1.2	110	132
							$ 49,791

Notes: (continued)

(j) def. = deficit.

(k) Per share data is adjusted for stock splits but not for minor stock dividends.

(l) No adjustment to earnings has been made in return on equity calculations for write-offs taken directly against net worth and not flowed through the income statement. Thus, earnings are over-stated in numerous instances. Nor has adjustment been made to reported equity for changes in the values of securities portfolios.

(m) Moody's bond ratings for each year are as reported in the Moody's manuals for the subsequent year. Moody's describes its ratings as follows:

Aaa bonds "...meet the highest tests in asset value, earning power and stability..."

Aa bonds "...fall one scale lower than those of very highest grade lien in the test of asset value, earning power and stability, they always rank well in the high grade field and frequently the difference in their statistical rating from that of the highest grade is but slight. Sometimes certain non-statistical factors so qualify their position as to lower the final rating slightly."

A bonds "...are entirely sound obligations of representative companies but, lacking the higher degree of protection obtainable in bonds of Aaa or Aa grades, they are more likely to reflect changing conditions by price fluctuations."

Baa bonds "...generally make a good showing in the tests of asset value, earning power and stability, but they warrant more discrimination than those of higher rating. Many unseasoned issues of strong companies are given this rating as well as the junior bonds of large corporations with several funded obligations. Occasionally a Baa bond represents an issue of a representative corporation, where the outlook is uncertain and a once prime investment while still sound has acquired a speculative tinge."

(continued)

(m) (continued)

Ba bonds "...always have some characteristic of uncertainty...sometimes they are fairly typical issues of small companies subject to the limitations of that group. In other cases they are clearly dominated by uncertainties such as violent fluctuations in earnings or declining trends."

B bonds "...are characterized by speculative features...frequently their asset value is somewhat uncertain, their earning power is weak or of a fluctuating character and their stability is comparatively poor."

Caa bonds "usually have a decidedly poor statistical standing and fall short of requirements such as asset value, earning power and stability. Bonds in default or in an uncertain position for a long period frequently receive this rating.

Ca bonds "...are still lower in standing than those defined before...In some cases bonds awaiting reorganization are given this rating..."

C bonds "...are not to be classed as investments at all as they seldom possess other than speculative value..."

Source: Moody's Public Utilities 1933, pp. viii - ix.

(n) NR = not rated.

(o) NM = not meaningful.

(p) pfd = preferred stock rating as no debt rating is available.

(q) Irregular dividend paid at year-end.

(r) Includes class A, B, and C shares.

(s) February, 1930, initial public offering price.

TABLE A.2
Ratios for Leading Stocks - 1929 (a)

	Price-earnings ratio		Market price as % year-end book value		% Yield	
	High price	Low price	High price	Low price	High price	Low price
Alaska Juneau Gold Mining Co.	14	6	100	43	0	0
Alleghany Corp.	108	32	271	81	0	0
Allied Chemical & Dye Corp.	28	16	374	207	1.69	3.05
Aluminum Company of America	48	13	2348	635	0	0
American Can Co.	23	11	370	156	2.70	5.80
American Radiator & Standard Sanitary Corp.	28	15	344	175	2.73	5.35
American Smelting and Refining Co.	13	6	197	94	3.08	6.45
American Telephone & Telegraph Co.	20	13	207	129	2.90	4.65
American Tobacco Co.	20	14	374	258	4.31	6.25
Anaconda Copper Mining Co.	18	9	230	110	5.00	10.40
Armour & Co. A	90	28	49	15	0	0
Associated Dry Goods Corp.	21	7	237	83	3.52	10.00
Atchison, Topeka & Santa Fe Railway Co.	13	9	130	85	3.34	5.13
The Atlantic Refining Co.	13	5	144	56	2.56	6.67
Baltimore and Ohio Railroad Co.	14	10	99	72	4.83	6.65
Bankers Trust Co.	31	21	367	244	1.90	2.86
Bethlehem Steel Co.	13	7	98	54	4.26	7.70
Borden Co.	19	10	291	151	2.45	5.66
Burroughs Adding Machine Co.	42	12	1386	414	1.86	6.21
Canadian Pacific Railway Co.	24	16	136	92	3.68	5.40
J. I. Case Co.	34	9	275	77	1.28	4.60
Caterpillar Tractor Co.	15	7	391	196	3.33	6.67
Central Hanover Bank & Trust Co.	NA(f)	NA	525	265	1.14	2.26
The Chase National Bank	62	29	438	208	1.30	2.74
The Chesapeake and Ohio Railway Co.	13	7	184	106	3.57	6.52
Chrysler Corp.	27	5	519	100	2.22	11.55
Cities Service Co.	69	20	782	235	0.44	1.50
The Coca-Cola Co.	17	10	778	439	2.23	3.96
Colgate-Palmolive-Peet Co.	22	10	450	200	2.22	5.00
Columbia Gas & Electric Corp.	45	17	500	185	1.43	3.85
Commercial Solvents Corp.	46	13	1477	425	1.43	5.00
Commonwealth Edison Co.	35	16	331	149	1.78	3.96
The Commonwealth & Southern Corp.	46	15	485	155	0	0
Consolidated Gas Co. of New York	39	17	345	151	2.19	5.00
Continental Can Co.	18	8	214	95	2.72	6.10
Continental Illinois National Bank & Trust Co.	38	23	493	301	1.54	2.52
Corn Products Refining Co.	22	12	371	206	3.17	5.71
Crown Zellerbach Corp.	17	11	179	114	4.00	6.25
The Curtis Publishing Co.	16	12	1015	769	5.30	7.00
Deere & Co.	9	5	278	135	0.94	1.61
The Detroit Edison Co.	35	14	306	120	2.08	5.30
Dow Chemical Co.	20	15	400	300	2.50	3.33
E. I. Du Pont de Nemours & Co.	33	11	660	250	2.52	6.50
Eastman Kodak Co.	28	16	421	238	3.02	5.33
Electric Bond and Share Co.	96	25	233	62	0	0
The Firestone Tire & Rubber Co.	23	9	200	81	2.58	6.40
The First National Bank of Boston	NA	NA	404	213	1.50	2.83
The First National Bank of Chicago	39	19	412	204	1.55	3.13
Fox Film Corp. A	10	2	180	32	0.94	5.26
General Electric Co.	43	18	718	300	1.19	2.85
General Foods Corp.	22	10	631	269	3.66	8.57
General Mills, Inc.	18	10	234	132	3.93	7.00
General Motors Corp.	17	6	511	190	3.91	10.75
The Gillette Safety Razor Co.	28	15	596	350	3.50	6.25
Gimbel Brothers, Inc.	def.(g)	def.	126	29	0	0
Goldman Sachs Trading Corp.	129	34	295	78	0	0
The B. F. Goodrich Corp.	22	8	186	67	3.77	10.53
The Goodyear Tire & Rubber Co.	17	6	408	158	3.23	8.33
Great Atlantic & Pacific Tea Co. of America	42	14	1098	360	1.01	3.09
Guaranty Trust Co. of New York	41	17	371	151	1.58	3.88
Gulf Oil Corp. of Pennsylvania	21	12	282	155	0.72	1.30
Homestake Mining Co.	22	16	96	67	7.53	10.77
Hudson Motor Car Co.	13	5	247	100	5.32	13.16
Ingersoll-Rand Co.	21	11	487	261	3.13	5.83
Inland Steel Co.	12	7	205	129	3.10	4.93
International Business Machines Corp.	23	10	464	198	1.96	4.59
International Harvester Co.	20	9	263	120	1.76	3.85
International Nickel Co. of Canada, Ltd.	50	17	1043	352	1.23	3.60
International Paper & Power Co. A	NA	NA	133	62	5.45	12.00
International Shoe Co.	18	12	312	216	3.85	5.56
International Telephone & Telegraph Corp.	51	18	324	115	1.34	3.75
Irving Trust Co.	39	17	378	167	1.57	3.56
Kennecott Copper Corp.	19	9	318	149	4.76	10.20
Kimberly-Clark Corp.	9	7	102	80	5.26	6.67
S. S. Kresge Co.	22	10	387	187	2.76	5.71
The Lambert Co.	16	8	1963	1000	5.10	10.00
Lehman Corp.	NA	NA	149	69	0	0
Liggett & Myers Tobacco Co.	14	10	321	242	4.72	6.25
Loew's Inc.	12	4	224	84	3.82	10.20
R. H. Macy & Co.	38	16	522	224	1.17	2.73
Marshall Field & Co.	NA	NA	NA	NA	NA	NA
Middle West Utilities Co.	91	32	456	160	1.23	3.50
Monsanto Chemical Co.	28	16	253	147	1.54	2.66
Montgomery Ward & Co.	60	16	476	129	1.91	7.05

TABLE A.2 (continued)

Year-end Dividend payout ratio (%)	1929 low price as % 1929 high price	1929 closing price (b)	1929 closing price as % 1929 low price	1929 closing price as % 1929 high price	1929 volume (b) as % outstanding shares
0	43	$ 8	188	80	90
0	30	24	141	42	301
48	55	265	135	75	44
0	27	290	199	54	7
62	47	123	143	66	545
78	51	32	114	58	48
40	48	73	118	56	233
59	62	223	116	72	39
87	69	97	121	84	24
90	48	75	112	54	210
0	31	8 5/8	102	31	66
73	35	29	116	41	234
44	65	224	115	75	52
32	38	38	127	49	270
68	72	117	111	81	148
59	41	134	128	52	NA
55	56	95	122	67	412
55	52	678	126	66	30
77	30	46	159	47	21
88	68	48	104	71	45(c)
44	28	198	152	42	164
49	50	57	127	63	1
NA	50	313	118	60	NA
80	47	154	114	54	NA
46	57	51	128	73	47
61	19	37	142	27	328
30	29	27	133	40	70
39	56	134	133	75	35
50	44	52	130	58	6
64	37	75	144	54	133
67	32	31	135	44	96
62	45	242	120	54	15(d)
0	32	14	137	44	13(e)
84	44	100	125	55	130
50	45	52	127	57	255
58	61	680	107	65	NA
70	56	92	131	73	91
70	64	18	113	72	2
83	76	115	115	87	3
9	48	92	148	72	5
72	39	204	135	53	11
49	75	66	110	83	1
73	35	117	146	51	24
84	57	178	119	67	45
0	26	86	171	45	83
58	40	27	108	44	1
NA	53	113	100	53	NA
61	50	695	109	54	NA
10	18	22	116	21	458
51	42	62	148	61	100
82	43	48	137	59	98
72	56	50	100	56	63
65	36	41	121	45	68
113	56	103	129	72	82
0	23	13	118	27	56
0	26	39	121	32	64(e)
81	36	42	111	40	161
54	39	62	103	40	278
43	33	238	147	48	1
65	41	675	138	56	NA
15	55	138	120	66	98
168	70	80	123	86	10
69	40	58	153	62	199
67	54	155	129	69	8
36	63	73	103	65	32
46	43	162	149	64	48
35	46	81	125	57	46
61	35	34	136	47	126(c)
NA	45	28	140	64	25
69	69	61	113	78	2
68	36	75	142	50	178
61	44	53	118	52	NA
90	47	59	120	56	122
46	79	49	109	86	19
60	48	34	121	59	12
80	51	97	121	62	238(e)
0	46	75	119	55	70
64	75	97	121	92	41
45	38	43	134	51	171
45	43	145	132	57	41
NA	NA	NA	NA	NA	NA
111	35	27	134	47	92(d)
43	58	49	104	60	157
115	27	49	114	31	318

TABLE A.2 (continued)

	Price-earnings ratio		Market price as % year-end book value		% Yield	
	High price	Low price	High price	Low price	High price	Low price
The Nash Motors Co.	18	6	595	200	5.04	15.00
National Biscuit Co.	29	17	594	350	3.95	6.70
The National City Bank of New York	120	37	1318	409	0.69	2.22
National Dairy Products Corp.	22	9	458	225	2.30	5.55
National Lead Co.	8	5	99	61	2.38	3.88
The New York Central Railroad Co.	15	10	156	97	3.11	5.00
Norfolk & Western Railway Co.	10	7	144	95	2.76	4.19
The North American Co.	37	13	584	210	0	0
Otis Elevator Co.	35	12	538	233	1.33	3.06
Owens-Illinois Glass Co.	21	9	283	123	4.55	10.47
Pacific Gas & Electric Co.	28	12	330	140	2.02	4.76
Packard Motor Car Co.	20	8	716	282	3.33	8.45
Paramount-Publix Corp.	13	6	200	75	3.95	8.55
J. C. Penney Co.	23	14	583	367	6.67	10.61
The Pennsylvania Railroad Co.	13	8	121	80	3.64	5.50
Phelps Dodge Corp.	30	12	133	52	3.75	9.68
Phillips Petroleum Co.	9	5	121	62	4.26	8.33
Pillsbury Flour Mills, Inc.	13	6	188	88	3.13	6.67
Pittsburgh Plate Glass Co.	14	9	177	114	3.95	6.12
Procter & Gamble Co.	33	14	891	391	2.04	4.65
Public Service Corp. of New Jersey	35	14	314	123	2.46	6.30
Pullman Inc.	19	14	115	85	4.04	5.48
Radio Corp. of America	73	17	1669	377	0	0
Radio-Keith-Orpheum Corp.	32	8	247	63	0	0
Remington Rand, Inc.	17	6	892	308	0	0
R. J. Reynolds Tobacco Co. B	21	12	440	260	4.55	7.70
Safeway Stores, Inc.	22	10	453	209	1.54	3.33
Sears, Roebuck and Co.	27	12	453	200	1.38	3.15
Shell Union Oil Corp.	25	15	145	86	4.38	7.37
Sinclair Consolidated Oil Corp.	16	7	90	42	4.44	9.50
Socony-Vacuum Oil Co.	22	14	155	103	3.33	5.00
Southern Pacific Co.	12	8	71	47	3.80	5.70
Standard Brands, Inc.	33	15	1125	462	3.33	7.50
Standard Gas and Electric Co.	37	11	224	68	1.43	4.73
Standard Oil Co. of California	23	14	178	113	3.05	4.81
Standard Oil Co. (Indiana)	14	9	166	113	5.16	7.56
Standard Oil Co. (New Jersey)	17	10	169	98	2.41	4.15
Swift & Co.	16	14	95	82	5.55	6.45
The Texas Corp.	15	10	160	111	4.17	6.00
Texas Gulf Sulphur Co.	14	7	773	391	4.71	9.30
The Timken Roller Bearing Co.	24	10	695	295	2.16	5.08
Transamerica Corp.	21	6	1345	402	2.39	8.00
Tri-Continental Corp.	NA	NA	356	63	0	0
Union Carbide & Carbon Corp.	36	15	467	197	1.86	4.40
Union Pacific Railroad Co.	15	10	136	91	3.36	5.00
United Aircraft & Transport Corp.	36	7	1157	222	0	0
The United Corp.	155	39	205	51	0	0
United Founders Corp.	22	7	245	81	0	0
United Fruit Co.	24	15	204	127	2.52	4.04
The United Gas Improvement Co.	40	14	413	147	1.94	5.45
United States Gypsum Co.	17	7	196	74	1.74	4.57
United States Steel Corp.	12	7	128	74	3.05	5.30
Warner Bros. Pictures, Inc.	38	17	295	136	6.15	13.35
Westinghouse Electric & Manufacturing Co.	28	10	337	115	1.71	4.00
F. W. Woolworth Co.	28	14	650	325	2.31	4.60
Wm. Wrigley Jr. Co.	14	11	386	310	4.94	6.15
The Youngstown Sheet & Tube Co.	20	5	316	83	1.45	5.49
Averages	29.8	12.4	420%	181%	2.96%	5.96%
Number of Companies	135	135	141	141	124	124

Notes:
(a) All data except 1929 closing price and volume come from "Summary Financial Statistics for Leading Stocks, 1929-1933."

(b) From the New York Times 12/31/29.

(c) Includes volume on Canadian Stock Exchange.

(d) Includes volume on the Chicago Stock Exchange and the Curb Exchange.

TABLE A.2 (continued)

Year-end Dividend payout ratio (%)	1929 low price as % 1929 high price	1929 closing price (b)	1929 closing price as % 1929 low price	1929 closing price as % 1929 high price	1929 volume (b) as % outstanding shares
91	34	$ 54	135	45	114
114	59	72	129	76	45
83	31	211	117	36	NA
50	42	49	163	75	61
20	61	134	104	64	89
48	62	170	106	66	70
27	66	227	119	78	25
0	36	98	146	52	61
38	43	69	141	61	34
94	43	53	123	54	1
57	42	53	126	54	44
65	40	16	123	48	43
52	46	51	146	67	240
150	63	75	114	71	2
45	66	74	101	67	33
112	39	39	126	49	21
39	51	35	146	74	57
39	47	35	117	55	110
56	64	54	110	71	1
67	44	54	126	55	35
87	39	83	154	60	137
76	74	85	116	86	71
0	23	44	169	38	635
0	26	20	167	43	382
0	34	27	135	47	328
93	59	50	129	76	27
35	46	115	128	59	159
38	44	89	111	49	89
111	59	23	121	72	17
71	47	24	114	53	204
72	67	33	103	69	41
47	67	124	118	78	22
110	45	27	135	68	46(e)
53	30	119	161	49	280
69	63	61	117	74	28
70	68	54	126	86	22
42	58	66	138	80	56
92	86	34	110	94	4
61	69	56	112	78	48
63	51	5	128	65	162
51	42	78	132	56	102
50	30	42	209	63	26(h)
0	18	13	130	23	115(e)
66	42	79	134	56	56
49	67	216	108	72	32
0	19	67	152	29	310
0	25	32	168	42	197
0	33	37	148	49	NA
59	62	104	105	65	23
77	35	34	155	55	54
38	30	40	114	43	16
38	57	171	114	65	239
444	47	41	137	63	162
48	34	145	145	49	30
66	50	71	137	68	25
69	80	68	105	84	10
29	26	110	121	32	4
66%	48%		159%	59%	105%
121	141		140	140	128

Notes: (continued)

(e)   Less than a full year of trading because listed after January 1, 1929.

(f)   NA = not available.

(g)   def. = deficit.

(h)   Includes volume on the Los Angeles, San Francisco, and Curb stock exchanges.

	Price-earnings ratio		Market price as % year-end book value		% Yield	
	High price	Low price	High price	Low price	High price	Low price
Alaska Juneau Gold Mining Co.	16	8	91	45	4.40	8.90
Alleghany Corp.	NM[b]	NM	167	27	0	0
Allied Chemical & Dye Corp.	35	17	370	183	1.75	3.53
Aluminum Company of America	NM	NM	1483	588	0	0
American Can Co.	19	13	314	210	3.20	4.75
American Radiator & Standard Sanitary Corp.	67	25	250	94	2.50	6.65
American Smelting and Refining Co.	21	10	140	67	5.00	10.53
American Telephone & Telegraph Co.	27	17	266	165	3.30	5.30
American Tobacco Co.	15	12	400	300	3.79	5.05
Anaconda Copper Mining Co.	40	12	135	41	3.05	10.00
Armour & Co. A	def.[c]	def.	23	8	0	0
Associated Dry Goods Corp.	25	9	170	63	4.90	13.16
Atchison Topeka & Santa Fe Railway Co.	19	13	104	72	4.12	5.95
The Atlantic Refining Co.	50	17	98	33	3.92	11.76
Baltimore and Ohio Railroad Co.	16	7	83	38	5.70	12.90
Bankers Trust Co.	38	20	400	210	1.65	3.20
Bethlehem Steel Co.	21	9	76	33	5.45	12.75
Borden Co.	18	12	258	172	3.33	5.00
Burroughs Adding Machine Co.	35	12	745	257	1.92	5.56
Canadian Pacific Railway Co.	22	14	133	81	4.40	7.15
J. I. Case Co.	38	9	225	49	1.65	7.15
Caterpillar Tractor Co.	17	5	364	100	5.00	18.18
Central Hanover Bank & Trust Co.	NA[d]	NA	400	186	1.70	3.65
The Chase National Bank	NA	NA	285	120	2.22	5.25
The Chesapeake and Ohio Railway Co.	11	7	134	84	4.90	7.80
Chrysler Corp.	NM	NM	165	54	2.30	7.15
Cities Service Co.	30	9	520	152	0.68	2.31
The Coca-Cola Co.	17	12	764	532	3.14	4.51
Colgate-Palmolive-Peet Co.	17	12	295	200	3.85	5.68
Columbia Gas and Electric Corp.	49	18	310	111	2.30	6.45
Commercial Solvents Corp.	36	13	800	295	2.65	7.15
Commonwealth Edison Co.	27	17	251	152	2.38	3.69
The Commonwealth and Southern Corp.	33	13	304	114	3.00	8.00
Consolidated Gas Co. of New York	27	15	260	148	2.90	5.15
Continental Can Co.	14	9	157	96	3.47	5.68
Continental Illinois National Bank & Trust Co.	37	18	345	166	2.08	4.32
Corn Products Refining Co.	23	13	317	186	3.83	6.54
Crown Zellerbach Corp.	def.	def.	136	30	5.26	28.53
The Curtis Publishing Co.	18	12	969	654	5.56	8.24
Deere & Co.	27	5	326	58	0.74	4.14
The Detroit Edison Co.	29	18	217	136	3.13	4.97
Dow Chemical Co.	29	14	455	223	2.00	4.08
E. I. Du Pont de Nemours & Co.	31	18	454	253	3.25	5.80
Eastman Kodak Co.	29	16	392	218	3.14	5.63
Electric Bond and Share Co.	49	15	NA	NA	0	0
The Firestone Tire & Rubber Co.	def.	def.	114	52	3.03	6.67
The First National Bank of Boston	NA	NA	310	151	2.40	4.90
The First National Bank of Chicago	34	19	263	146	2.15	3.90
Fox Film Corp. A	14	4	139	39	1.75	6.25
General Electric Co.	48	21	680	300	1.25	2.85
General Foods Corp.	17	12	508	367	4.92	6.82
General Mills, Inc.	16	11	155	105	5.08	7.50
General Motors Corp.	17	10	300	178	5.56	9.38
The Gillette Safety Razor Co.	31	5	460	78	3.80	22.20
Gimbel Brothers, Inc.	def.	def.	57	11	0	0
Goldman Sachs Trading Corp.	NM	NM	379	35	0	0
The B. F. Goodrich Corp.	def.	def.	169	46	0	0
The Goodyear Tire & Rubber Co.	31	11	269	97	5.15	14.29
Great Atlantic & Pacific Tea Co. of America	19	11	491	292	2.31	3.87
Guaranty Trust Co. of New York	34	16	260	123	2.33	4.93
Gulf Oil Corp. of Pennsylvania	71	25	223	79	0.90	2.54
Homestake Mining Co.	14	12	124	107	8.43	9.72
Hudson Motor Car Co.	NM	NM	197	56	4.76	16.67
Ingersoll-Rand Co.	51	31	520	320	2.51	4.08
Inland Steel Co.	18	11	175	104	4.08	6.90
International Business Machines Corp.	17	11	340	226	3.05	4.58
International Harvester Co.	25	10	215	83	2.15	5.55
International Nickel Co. of Canada, Ltd.	66	19	630	185	2.05	6.95
International Paper & Power Co. A	NA	NA	97	17	0	0
International Shoe Co.	19	15	238	185	4.84	6.25
International Telephone & Telegraph Corp.	37	9	167	39	2.60	11.10
Irving Trust Co.	39	15	279	104	2.15	5.70
Kennecott Copper Corp.	38	12	191	61	3.20	10.00
Kimberly-Clark Corp.	12	8	105	68	4.24	6.58
S. S. Kresge Co.	19	14	247	173	4.32	6.15
The Lambert Co.	12	7	1027	645	7.08	11.27
Lehman Corp.	NM	NM	131	70	3.09	5.77
Liggett & Myers Tobacco Co.	16	11	335	226	4.39	6.49
Loew's Inc.	11	5	252	110	4.15	9.50
R.H. Macy & Co.	33	17	338	174	1.89	3.66
Marshall Field & Co.	26	13	123	62	5.21	10.42
Middle West Utilities Co.	NM	NM	302	119	0	0
Monsanto Chemical Co.	37	11	206	58	1.95	6.94
Montgomery Ward & Co.	def.	def.	152	45	0	0

TABLE A.3 (continued)

Year-end dividend payout ratio (%)	1930 low price as % 1930 high price	1930 low price as % 1929 high price	1930 high price as % 1929 low price	1930 high price as % 1929 high price	1930 low price as % 1929 low price
70	49	45	215	91	106
0	16	10	206	61	34
61	50	48	175	97	86
0	40	26	244	66	97
62	67	57	183	85	122
167	38	27	143	73	54
106	48	29	129	62	61
88	62	55	142	88	88
58	75	85	165	114	124
121	30	18	122	59	37
0	34	15	148	45	50
124	37	27	204	72	76
78	69	56	125	81	86
196	33	22	170	65	57
94	45	38	116	84	52
64	52	36	171	70	90
114	43	33	141	78	60
59	67	59	170	88	113
67	35	19	180	54	62
98	61	52	124	84	76
62	23	18	280	78	65
86	28	24	178	89	49
NA	47	37	155	78	72
NA	42	27	133	63	56
56	63	46	127	73	80
NM	33	10	165	32	54
20	30	19	220	65	65
54	70	74	189	107	132
66	68	49	163	72	110
114	36	22	167	62	60
93	37	20	165	54	61
63	65	48	166	75	107
100	37	23	195	63	75
79	57	43	171	75	98
50	61	48	176	78	107
77	48	36	12	74	58
87	59	52	159	88	93
def.	22	17	119	76	27
98	67	64	126	95	85
20	18	23	263	127	47
91	63	42	170	66	107
58	49	61	167	125	82
101	56	35	181	63	101
90	56	54	170	96	95
0	31	20	236	62	74
def.	45	41	132	89	60
NA	49	30	118	62	58
74	55	36	130	64	72
25	28	15	300	54	84
80	44	42	226	94	100
83	72	54	174	74	126
81	68	45	118	66	80
102	59	35	159	59	94
116	17	13	132	74	23
0	20	9	191	44	39
0	9	4	147	39	14
0	27	15	155	56	42
158	36	23	162	63	58
43	60	31	160	53	96
79	47	34	175	71	83
64	35	28	145	80	51
118	87	77	128	89	111
NM	29	19	166	67	47
127	62	66	199	107	123
74	59	51	138	87	82
53	66	51	191	77	122
55	39	32	178	82	69
149	30	18	176	60	52
0	18	13	155	70	28
92	77	62	115	79	89
97	23	12	145	52	34
83	37	27	167	74	62
120	32	19	129	60	41
50	64	67	131	104	84
84	70	45	132	64	93
84	63	45	141	72	89
612	54	38	154	71	83
70	68	73	143	108	96
44	44	49	300	113	131
63	52	32	145	62	75
137	50	NA	NA	NA	NA
0	39	26	190	67	75
73	28	22	136	79	38
0	30	10	117	32	35

TABLE A.3 (continued)

	Price-earnings ratio		Market price as % year-end book value		% Yield	
	High price	Low price	High price	Low price	High price	Low price
The Nash Motors Co.	21	8	328	117	6.78	19.05
National Biscuit Co.	27	20	580	430	3.55	4.78
National Cash Register Co. A	37	12	300	100	4.96	14.29
The National City Bank of New York	67	21	630	195	1.55	5.00
National Dairy Products Corp.	15	9	326	184	4.20	7.45
National Lead Co.	25	15	90	54	4.21	7.02
The New York Central Railroad Co.	27	15	117	64	4.15	7.60
Norfolk & Western Railway Co.	12	8	125	86	3.77	5.49
The North American Co.	29	13	420	180	0	0
Otis Elevator Co.	23	14	364	218	3.13	5.21
Owens-Illinois Glass Co.	25	13	185	97	4.92	9.38
Pacific Gas & Electric Co.	24	13	250	137	2.67	4.88
Packard Motor Car Co.	38	12	500	152	2.60	8.55
Paramount-Publix Corp.	13	6	163	75	5.20	11.40
J.C. Penney Co.	28	10	500	175	6.88	19.64
The Pennsylvania Railroad Co.	16	10	96	58	4.60	7.55
Phelps Dodge Corp.	def.	def.	90	41	4.55	10.00
Phillips Petroleum Co.	63	17	125	33	4.44	16.67
Pillsbury Flour Mills, Inc.	9	6	106	69	5.26	8.00
Pittsburgh Plate Glass Co.	27	15	137	77	3.39	6.06
Procter & Gamble Co.	24	16	564	379	2.78	4.15
Public Service Corp. of New Jersey	32	17	276	144	2.75	5.20
Pullman Inc.	20	11	104	55	4.49	8.51
Radio Corp. of America	NM	NM	1062	169	0	0
Radio-Keith-Orpheum Corp.	def.	def.	263	74	0	0
Remington Rand, Inc.	NM	NM	940	280	3.40	11.43
R. J. Reynolds Tobacco Co. B	17	12	390	268	5.10	7.50
Safeway Stores, Inc.	25	8	290	93	4.10	12.82
Sears, Roebuck and Co.	34	14	251	107	2.50	5.80
Shell Union Oil Corp.	def.	def.	118	24	0	0
Sinclair Consolidated Oil Corp.	18	6	64	20	3.10	10.00
Socony-Vacuum Oil Co.	44	22	129	65	4.00	8.00
Southern Pacific Co.	15	11	57	39	4.70	6.80
Standard Brands, Inc.	24	12	725	350	4.15	8.55
Standard Gas and Electric Co.	21	9	119	49	2.71	6.60
Standard Oil Co. of California	26	15	164	92	3.33	5.95
Standard Oil Co. (Indiana)	22	11	150	75	4.17	8.34
Standard Oil Co. (New Jersey)	52	27	174	90	2.35	4.55
Swift & Co.	17	13	92	71	5.71	7.41
The Texas Corp.	40	18	135	62	4.92	10.71
Texas Gulf Sulphur Co.	12	7	558	333	5.97	10.00
The Timken Roller Bearing Co.	29	13	445	200	3.37	7.50
Transamerica Corp.	60	13	100	21	2.13	10.00
Tri-Continental Corp.	def.	def.	199	56	0	0
Union Carbide & Carbon Corp.	34	17	353	177	2.45	4.91
Union Pacific Railroad Co.	16	11	108	75	4.12	5.99
United Aircraft & Transport Corp.	80	15	705	129	0	0
The United Corp.	67	18	185	50	1.00	3.60
United Founders Corp.	49	7	489	67	0	0
United Fruit Co.	25	11	150	67	3.81	8.51
The United Gas Improvement Co.	32	16	350	171	2.65	5.40
United States Gypsum Co.	14	7	116	62	3.62	6.77
United States Steel Corp.	22	15	98	66	3.50	5.20
Warner Bros. Pictures, Inc.	def.	def.	445	57	3.75	30.00
Westinghouse Electric & Manufacturing Co.	45	20	232	101	2.50	5.70
F.W. Woolworth Co.	20	15	450	325	3.30	4.60
W.M. Wrigley Jr. Co.	13	11	352	283	4.94	6.15
The Youngstown Sheet & Tube Co.	29	14	138	64	3.33	7.14
Averages	28.6	13.1	302%	139%	3.56%	7.75%
Number of Companies	118	118	141	141	125	125

Notes: (a) All data come from Table A.1 "Summary Financial Statistics for Leading Stocks, 1929-1933."
(b) NM = not meaningful
(c) def. = deficit
(d) NA = not available.

TABLE A.3 (continued)

Year-end dividend payout ratio (%)	1930 low price as % 1930 high price	1930 low price as % 1929 high price	1930 high price as % 1929 low price	1930 high price as % 1929 high price	1930 low price as % 1929 low price
143	36	18	148	50	53
97	74	73	166	98	123
177	33	19	142	56	47
103	31	14	143	44	44
63	57	40	172	71	97
106	60	54	147	90	88
111	54	41	120	75	66
45	69	63	139	91	95
0	43	30	198	71	85
73	60	42	163	71	98
122	52	32	142	62	74
65	55	41	179	76	98
100	30	21	177	70	54
68	45	46	220	101	100
191	35	27	121	76	42
76	61	48	119	79	73
def.	45	25	142	55	65
282	27	26	188	96	50
49	66	39	127	59	83
92	56	43	120	78	67
66	67	54	184	81	123
87	52	47	230	90	120
92	53	46	122	90	64
0	16	10	265	60	42
0	28	30	417	106	117
NM	30	24	235	81	70
87	68	61	151	89	103
104	32	20	136	63	43
83	43	24	126	56	54
0	32	26	137	81	43
56	31	22	152	71	48
174	50	42	125	83	63
73	69	56	121	80	84
98	48	31	145	64	70
58	41	22	174	53	72
87	56	51	144	91	81
92	50	48	140	95	70
121	52	53	177	102	92
96	77	75	113	97	87
196	46	39	122	85	56
73	60	47	156	79	93
96	45	29	151	64	68
128	21	15	235	70	50
0	28	10	200	35	56
83	50	38	180	76	90
64	69	56	122	82	84
0	18	11	320	61	58
64	38	18	274	68	74
0	14	8	176	58	24
94	45	30	106	66	47
84	49	39	223	79	109
51	53	34	166	63	90
77	67	51	133	76	89
def.	12	15	267	123	33
46	44	30	202	69	88
67	72	50	138	69	100
65	80	80	125	100	100
97	47	48	170	103	80
94%	46%	36%	167%	75%	75%
115	142	141	141	141	141

TABLE A.4
Ratios for Leading Stocks - 1931(a)

	Price-earnings ratio		Market price as % year-end book value		% Yield	
	High price	Low price	High price	Low price	High price	Low price
Alaska Juneau Gold Mining Co.	27	10	182	64	2.50	7.14
Alleghany Corp.	def.[(b)]	def.	68	6	0	0
Allied Chemical & Dye Corp.	27	10	195	68	3.28	9.38
Aluminum Company of America	def.	def.	1067	229	0	0
American Can Co.	25	11	245	109	3.85	8.62
American Radiator & Standard Sanitary Corp.	def.	def.	140	33	2.86	12.00
American Smelting and Refining Co.	def.	def.	123	38	2.54	8.33
American Telephone & Telegraph Co.	21	12	132	73	4.46	8.04
American Tobacco Co.	14	7	358	169	4.65	9.84
Anaconda Copper Mining Co.	def.	def.	74	16	0	0
Armour & Co. A	def.	def.	15	3	0	0
Associated Dry Goods Corp.	def.	def.	107	21	3.33	17.39
Atchison Topeka & Santa Fe Railway Co.	29	11	88	34	4.93	12.66
The Atlantic Refining Co.	NM[(c)]	NM	47	17	4.17	11.59
Baltimore and Ohio Railroad Co.	NM	NM	61	10	0	0
Bankers Trust Co.	41	16	310	125	2.42	6.00
Bethlehem Steel Co.	def.	def.	52	13	2.86	11.76
Borden Co.	20	9	220	100	3.90	8.57
Burroughs Adding Machine Co.	18	6	469	146	4.69	15.00
Canadian Pacific Railway Co.	NM	16	113	27	2.78	11.36
J. I. Case Co.	def.	def.	74	19	0	0
Caterpillar Tractor Co.	NM	14	265	50	3.77	20.00
Central Hanover Bank & Trust Co.	NA	NA	269	105	2.53	6.48
The Chase National Bank	21	5	175	40	3.64	16.00
The Chesapeake and Ohio Railway Co.	14	7	98	48	5.32	10.87
Chrysler Corp.	NM	NM	100	46	3.85	8.33
Cities Service Co.	42	10	259	62	1.43	6.00
The Coca-Cola Co.	14	8	630	363	4.71	8.16
Colgate-Palmolive-Peet Co.	16	8	255	120	4.90	10.42
Columbia Gas & Electric Corp.	32	9	242	63	3.26	12.50
Commercial Solvents Corp.	26	8	567	171	4.55	15.09
Commonwealth Edison Co.	25	11	193	82	3.11	7.34
The Commonwealth & Southern Corp.	30	8	212	53	2.50	10.00
Consolidated Gas Co. of New York	22	12	200	104	3.64	7.02
Continental Can Co.	19	9	137	65	3.97	8.33
Continental Illinois National Bank & Trust Co.	22	6	216	60	3.85	13.91
Corn Products Refining Co.	25	10	249	103	4.60	11.11
Crown Zellerbach Corp.	def.	def.	17	10	0	0
The Curtis Publishing Co.	30	6	769	154	4.00	20.00
Deere & Co.	def.	def.	98	18	0	0
The Detroit Edison Co.	22	12	168	95	4.10	7.27
Dow Chemical Co.	17	10	213	125	3.92	6.67
E. I. Du Pont de Nemours & Co.	25	12	268	125	3.74	8.00
Eastman Kodak Co.	32	13	321	133	4.30	10.39
Electric Bond and Share Co.	NM	8	103	15	0	0
The Firestone Tire & Rubber Co.	17	10	85	50	4.55	7.69
The First National Bank of Boston	NA	NA	200	72	3.72	10.32
The First National Bank of Chicago	26	12	163	72	3.49	7.93
Fox Film Corp. A	def.	def.	113	20	0	0
General Electric Co.	41	18	448	187	2.91	6.96
General Foods Corp.	16	8	467	233	5.36	10.71
General Mills, Inc.	13	7	128	74	6.00	10.34
General Motors Corp.	24	10	282	124	6.25	14.29
The Gillette Safety Razor Co.	37	7	244	56	0	0
Gimbel Brothers, Inc.	def.	def.	23	5	0	0
Goldman Sachs Trading Corp.	NM	NM	156	25	0	0
The B. F. Goodrich Corp.	def.	def.	64	10	0	0
The Goodyear Tire & Rubber Co.	NM	NM	196	52	5.66	21.43
Great Atlantic & Pacific Tea Co. of America	19	10	433	217	2.69	5.38
Guaranty Trust Co. of New York	NM	NM	172	75	3.53	8.06
Gulf Oil Corp. of Pennsylvania	def.	def.	112	38	1.97	5.77
Homestake Mining Co.	14	8	200	117	7.10	12.10
Hudson Motor Car Co.	def.	def.	96	29	3.85	12.90
Ingersoll-Rand Co.	def.	def.	444	63	2.20	15.38
Inland Steel Co.	68	19	134	38	2.82	10.00
International Business Machines Corp.	16	8	300	153	3.33	6.52
International Harvester Co.	def.	def.	115	42	4.10	11.36
International Nickel Co. of Canada, Ltd.	NM	NM	212	74	1.00	2.86
International Paper & Power Co. A	NA	NA	32	6	0	0
International Shoe Co.	21	14	225	154	5.56	8.11
International Telephone & Telegraph Corp.	33	6	87	16	1.54	8.42
Irving Trust Co.	27	9	159	56	3.72	10.67
Kennecott Copper Corp.	NM	NM	110	34	1.56	5.00
Kimberly-Clark Corp.	18	6	73	25	6.10	17.86
S. S. Kresge Co.	18	9	200	100	5.33	10.67
The Lambert Co.	11	5	800	364	9.09	20.00
Lehman Corp.	def.	def.	121	61	4.35	8.57
Liggett & Myers Tobacco Co.	13	6	253	108	5.49	12.82
Loew's Inc.	9	3	142	53	6.25	16.67
R. H. Macy & Co.	29	14	241	114	2.59	5.50
Marshall Field & Co.	def.	def.	103	30	7.58	26.32
Middle West Utilities Co.	29	6	240	46	0	0
Monsanto Chemical Co.	10	5	88	48	4.31	7.81
Montgomery Ward & Co.	def.	def.	97	23	0	0

TABLE A.4 (continued)

Year-end dividend payout ratio (%)	1931 low price as % 1931 high price	1931 low price as % 1929 high price	1931 high price as % 1929 low price	1931 high price as % 1929 high price	1931 low price as % 1929 low price
68	35	70	471	200	165
0	9	2	76	23	7
89	35	18	93	52	32
0	21	9	153	41	33
98	45	31	151	70	67
def.	24	9	75	38	18
def.	31	14	95	45	29
95	55	36	105	65	58
66	47	53	161	111	76
0	21	6	64	31	13
0	17	4	82	25	14
def.	19	8	120	42	23
144	39	26	104	68	41
526	36	11	73	31	29
0	16	10	84	61	13
98	40	19	118	48	48
def.	24	12	90	50	22
79	45	34	145	75	66
185	31	10	110	33	34
184	24	16	98	66	24
0	25	7	102	28	25
278	19	11	118	59	22
NA[d]	39	21	104	53	41
77	23	9	81	39	19
72	49	33	118	67	58
303	46	9	100	19	46
60	24	7	104	31	25
68	58	55	168	95	97
80	47	27	128	57	60
106	26	9	88	33	23
119	30	9	96	31	29
79	42	24	127	57	54
75	25	9	117	38	29
81	52	31	138	60	71
76	48	33	154	68	73
84	27	11	66	40	18
113	41	29	124	69	51
0	60	5	12	8	7
122	20	15	100	76	20
0	19	7	73	35	14
89	56	29	129	51	73
47	59	38	85	64	50
94	47	22	134	46	63
138	41	29	124	70	51
0	14	5	122	32	18
79	59	35	88	59	52
NA	36	14	76	40	27
92	44	18	81	40	35
0	7	2	200	36	13
120	42	23	131	54	55
87	50	34	160	68	80
76	58	33	100	56	58
149	44	23	141	52	62
0	23	6	49	27	11
0	22	4	72	116	16
0	16	1	34	9	5
0	16	3	55	20	9
def.	26	9	88	34	23
52	50	26	160	53	80
326	44	21	116	47	51
def.	34	12	66	36	23
101	59	87	212	148	125
def.	30	8	68	28	20
def.	14	12	152	81	22
190	28	18	100	63	28
55	51	36	165	71	84
def.	36	15	94	43	34
91	35	10	80	27	28
0	18	4	51	23	9
115	69	47	100	69	69
50	18	5	74	26	13
99	35	15	96	42	33
122	31	10	65	30	20
107	34	25	91	92	31
95	50	26	107	52	54
98	45	25	110	56	50
def.	51	26	110	51	56
73	43	37	114	86	49
55	38	28	200	75	75
69	47	20	96	41	45
def.	29	NA	NA	NA	NA
0	19	8	125	44	24
42	55	20	62	36	34
0	24	4	67	18	16

TABLE A.4 (continued)

	Price-earnings ratio		Market price as % year-end book value		% Yield	
	High price	Low price	High price	Low price	High price	Low price
The Nash Motors Co.	23	9	241	88	4.88	13.33
National Biscuit Co.	29	13	525	225	3.33	7.78
National Cash Register Co. A	NM	14	148	26	0	0
The National City Bank of New York	33	10	306	94	3.64	11.76
National Dairy Products Corp.	15	6	283	111	5.10	13.00
National Lead Co.	24	14	62	37	3.98	6.65
The New York Central Railroad Co.	NM	NM	83	16	0	0
Norfolk & Western Railway Co.	15	7	104	51	4.61	9.43
The North American Co.	26	8	265	76	0	0
Otis Elevator Co.	29	8	281	76	4.24	15.63
Owens-Illinois Glass Co.	16	8	121	61	5.00	10.00
Pacific Gas & Electric Co.	20	11	183	100	3.64	6.67
Packard Motor Car Co.	def.	def.	326	109	3.33	10.00
Paramount-Publix Corp.	25	3	104	11	0	0
J. C. Penney Co.	14	9	265	159	5.33	8.89
The Pennsylvania Railroad Co.	NM	11	74	18	3.13	12.50
Phelps Dodge Corp.	def.	def.	72	16	0	0
Phillips Petroleum Co.	def.	def.	49	11	0	0
Pillsbury Flour Mills, Inc.	9	5	100	54	5.41	10.00
Pittsburgh Plate Glass Co.	43	17	102	40	2.33	5.88
Procter & Gamble Co.	21	11	473	240	3.38	6.67
Public Service Corp. of New Jersey	25	13	220	111	3.51	6.94
Pullman Inc.	NM	NM	70	18	5.08	20.00
Radio Corp. of America	def.	def.	NM	NM	0	0
Radio-Keith-Orpheum Corp.	def.	def.	125	5	0	0
Remington Rand, Inc.	def.	def.	1333	125	0	0
R. J. Reynolds Tobacco Co. B	15	9	344	206	5.45	9.10
Safeway Stores, Inc.	12	7	194	108	7.14	12.82
Sears, Roebuck and Co.	26	12	154	73	3.97	8.33
Shell Union Oil Corp.	def.	def.	53	13	0	0
Sinclair Consolidated Oil Corp.	def.	def.	89	22	0	0
Socony-Vacuum Oil Co.	def.	def.	81	26	3.85	11.94
Southern Pacific Co.	57	14	48	12	3.64	14.81
Standard Brands, Inc.	19	10	553	289	5.71	10.91
Standard Gas and Electric Co.	22	6	81	23	3.98	14.00
Standard Oil Co. of California	47	21	118	52	4.81	10.87
Standard Oil Co. (Indiana)	38	13	100	36	2.56	7.14
Standard Oil Co. (New Jersey)	def.	def.	110	54	3.77	7.69
Swift & Co.	NM	NM	84	38	6.45	14.29
The Texas Corp.	def.	def.	82	23	5.56	20.00
Texas Gulf Sulphur Co.	16	6	431	154	5.36	15.00
The Timken Roller Bearing Co.	55	16	328	94	3.39	11.76
Transamerica Corp.	NM	8	NA	NA	0	0
Tri-Continental Corp.	def.	def.	NM	NM	0	0
Union Carbide & Carbon Corp.	36	14	300	113	3.61	9.63
Union Pacific Railroad Co.	21	7	93	32	4.88	14.29
United Aircraft & Transport Corp.	38	10	279	71	0	0
The United Corp.	41	10	97	24	2.42	10.00
United Founders Corp.	NM	NM	446	61	0	0
United Fruit Co.	29	8	97	26	4.41	16.27
The United Gas Improvement Co.	26	10	271	107	3.16	8.00
United States Gypsum Co.	20	6	100	30	3.70	10.67
United States Steel Corp.	def.	def.	96	23	2.63	11.11
Warner Bros. Pictures, Inc.	def.	def.	80	9	0	0
Westinghouse Electric & Manufacturing Co.	def.	def.	133	27	2.31	11.36
F. W. Woolworth Co.	17	8	429	206	6.03	12.57
Wm. Wrigley Jr. Co.	16	9	333	192	5.00	8.70
The Youngstown Sheet & Tube Co.	def.	def.	80	12	0	0
Averages	24.8	9.7	212	75	4.08	10.89
Number of Companies	84	89	139	139	108	108

Notes: (a) All data come from Table A. 1 "Summary Financial Statistics for Leading Stocks, 1929-1933."
          (b) def. = deficit.
          (c) NM = not meaningful.
          (d) NA = not available.

TABLE A.4 (continued)

Year-end dividend payout ratio (%)	1931 low price as % 1931 high price	1931 low price as % 1929 high price	1931 high price as % 1929 low price	1931 high price as % 1929 high price	1931 low price as % 1929 low price
114	37	13	103	34	38
98	43	38	150	88	64
0	18	5	68	27	12
120	31	6	61	19	19
75	39	23	142	62	56
96	60	38	102	63	61
0	19	10	83	51	16
69	49	37	114	75	55
0	29	14	134	48	39
124	27	14	120	52	33
82	50	20	93	40	47
72	55	30	131	55	71
def.	33	12	92	36	31
0	11	7	143	66	16
77	60	26	68	43	36
132	25	15	88	58	22
0	23	7	84	33	19
0	29	9	71	36	17
56	54	31	123	58	67
99	40	22	88	57	35
71	51	37	165	72	84
89	51	36	180	70	91
484	25	15	81	59	21
0	18	4	108	24	19
0	4	2	208	53	8
0	9	3	100	34	9
82	60	50	141	83	85
88	56	20	78	36	43
101	48	17	79	35	38
0	25	8	53	31	13
0	25	9	76	36	19
def.	31	17	81	54	26
208	25	17	105	70	26
111	52	24	105	47	55
87	28	10	119	36	34
225	44	28	100	63	44
96	36	22	91	62	33
def.	49	31	110	64	54
NM	45	39	100	86	45
def.	28	14	72	50	20
85	36	24	130	66	47
187	29	12	100	42	29
0	11	3	90	27	10
0	17	4	120	21	20
130	38	19	122	51	46
101	34	23	103	69	35
0	26	6	126	24	32
99	25	10	163	41	39
0	14	2	40	13	6
129	26	11	69	43	18
82	39	24	173	61	68
15	30	16	143	54	43
def.	24	14	101	58	24
0	11	3	67	30	7
def.	20	8	108	37	22
104	48	34	140	70	67
79	58	57	123	99	72
0	15	8	89	53	14
107	35	19	108	51	39
88	142	141	141	141	141

TABLE A.5
Ratios for Leading Stocks - 1932(a)

	Price-earnings ratio		Market price as % year-end book value		% Yield	
	High price	Low price	High price	Low price	High price	Low price
Alaska Juneau Gold Mining Co.	30	14	155	70	3.53	7.74
Alleghany Corp.	def.(b)	def.	23	2	0	0
Allied Chemical & Dye Corp.	24	12	122	60	6.82	13.95
Aluminum Company of America	def.	def.	563	138	4.44	18.18
American Can Co.	23	9	130	55	5.41	13.33
American Radiator & Standard Sanitary Corp.	def.	def.	100	25	0	0
American Smelting and Refining Co.	def.	def.	64	12	0	0
American Telephone & Telegraph Co.	23	12	101	52	6.57	12.86
American Tobacco Co.	10	5	223	105	6.90	14.63
Anaconda Copper Mining Co.	def.	def.	35	5	0	0
Armour & Co. A	def.	def.	9	2	0	0
Associated Dry Goods Corp.	def.	def.	48	13	0	0
Atchison, Topeka & Santa Fe Railway Co.	NM(c)	33	41	8	0	0
The Atlantic Refining Co.	15	6	43	17	4.55	11.59
Baltimore and Ohio Railroad Co.	def.	def.	15	3	0	0
Bankers Trust Co.	20	9	185	80	3.95	9.10
Bethlehem Steel Co.	def.	def.	23	5	0	0
Borden Co.	25	12	139	65	4.65	10.00
Burroughs Adding Machine Co.	NM	NM	217	104	3.08	6.40
Canadian Pacific Railway Co.	def.	def.	45	14	0	0
J. I. Case Co.	def.	def.	44	11	0	0
Caterpillar Tractor Co.	def.	def.	79	23	3.33	11.43
Central Hanover Bank & Trust Co.	NA(d)	NA	188	87	4.32	9.33
The Chase National Bank	12	5	119	45	4.50	11.84
The Chesapeake and Ohio Railway Co.	10	3	64	20	7.81	25.64
Chrysler Corp.	def.	def.	122	28	4.55	20.00
Cities Service Co.	def.	def.	89	16	0	0
The Coca-Cola Co.	14	8	429	246	5.83	10.14
Colgate-Palmolive-Peet Co.	def.	def.	188	59	3.23	10.00
Columbia Gas & Electric Corp.	22	4	111	22	4.76	23.53
Commercial Solvents Corp.	28	7	387	97	4.29	17.14
Commonwealth Edison Co.	20	8	112	45	4.10	10.20
The Commonwealth & Southern Corp.	43	14	96	30	0	0
Consolidated Gas Co. of New York	17	8	128	60	5.88	12.50
Continental Can Co.	15	6	98	43	4.88	11.11
Continental Illinois National Bank & Trust Co.	10	4	104	39	5.44	14.55
Corn Products Refining Co.	20	9	162	74	5.45	12.00
Crown Zellerbach Corp.	def.	def.	29	9	0	0
The Curtis Publishing Co.	def.	def.	344	78	0	0
Deere & Co.	def.	def.	53	10	0	0
The Detroit Edison Co.	23	10	106	47	4.90	11.10
Dow Chemical Co.	20	11	167	92	5.00	9.09
E.I. Du Pont de Nemours & Co.	33	12	176	65	3.33	9.09
Eastman Kodak Co.	35	14	157	63	3.41	8.57
Electric Bond and Share Co.	49	5	200	21	0	0
The Firestone Tire & Rubber Co.	18	10	70	41	5.26	9.09
The First National Bank of Boston	NA	NA	111	50	6.19	13.68
The First National Bank of Chicago	7	4	115	62	5.00	9.23
Fox Film Corp. A	def.	def.	45	8	0	0
General Electric Co.	63	21	236	77	1.54	4.71
General Foods Corp.	21	10	373	182	4.88	10.00
General Mills, Inc.	12	7	125	70	6.00	10.71
General Motors Corp.	def.	def.	179	54	4.00	13.11
The Gillette Safety Razor Co.	12	5	259	108	4.17	10.00
Gimbel Brothers, Inc.	def.	def.	13	3	0	0
Goldman Sachs Trading Corp.	def.	def.	86	17	0	0
The B. F. Goodrich Corp.	def.	def.	48	9	0	0
The Goodyear Tire & Rubber Co.	def.	def.	182	25	0	0
Great Atlantic & Pacific Tea Co. of America	17	10	267	163	4.17	6.80
Guaranty Trust Co. of New York	14	6	119	53	5.59	12.50
Gulf Oil Corp. of Pennsylvania	NM	38	66	34	0	0
Homestake Mining Co.	16	11	236	159	6.75	10.00
Hudson Motor Car Co.	def.	def.	57	14	0	0
Ingersoll-Rand Co.	def.	def.	125	42	4.44	13.33
Inland Steel Co.	def.	def.	57	20	0	0
International Business Machines Corp.	13	6	195	88	5.13	11.32
International Harvester Co.	def.	def.	67	20	3.53	12.00
International Nickel Co. of Canada, Ltd.	def.	def.	144	39	0	0
International Paper & Power Co. A	NA	NA	16	2	0	0
International Shoe Co.	24	11	200	91	4.55	10.00
International Telephone & Telegraph Corp.	def.	def.	43	7	0	0
Irving Trust Co.	17	7	136	55	5.33	13.33
Kennecott Copper Corp.	def.	def.	70	19	0	0
Kimberly-Clark Corp.	def.	def.	36	12	0	0
S. S. Kresge Co.	19	7	127	44	5.26	15.38
The Lambert Co.	11	5	570	250	7.02	15.38
Lehman Corp.	def.	def.	90	53	4.67	7.74
Liggett & Myers Tobacco Co.	10	5	174	84	7.58	15.63
Loew's Inc.	8	3	83	28	10.53	23.08
R. H. Macy & Co.	28	8	145	40	3.28	11.77
Marshall Field & Co.	def.	def.	54	12	0	0
Middle West Utilities Co.	NA	NA	NM	NM	NA	NA
Monsanto Chemical Co.	13	5	103	43	4.03	9.62
Montgomery Ward & Co.	def.	def.	71	15	0	0

TABLE A.5 (continued)

Year-end dividend payout ratio (%)	1932 low price as % 1932 high price	1932 low price as % 1929 high price	1932 high price as % 1929 low price	1932 high price as % 1929 high price	1932 low price as % 1929 low price
105	46	78	400	170	182
0	10	1	21	6	2
166	49	12	45	25	22
def.	24	4	62	17	15
123	41	16	86	40	35
0	25	5	43	22	11
0	19	4	44	21	8
151	51	23	71	44	36
71	47	35	109	75	51
0	16	2	28	14	4
0	23	3	50	15	11
0	27	4	44	15	12
0	19	6	48	31	9
69	39	11	73	28	29
0	18	3	20	14	4
78	43	13	72	29	31
0	23	5	38	21	9
117	47	20	81	42	38
308	48	6	45	13	22
0	32	11	50	34	16
0	26	4	51	14	13
def.	29	5	33	17	10
NA	46	14	61	31	28
55	38	7	37	18	14
81	30	14	80	46	24
def.	23	4	85	16	19
0	18	2	34	10	6
81	58	39	119	67	68
def.	31	11	80	36	25
104	20	3	40	15	8
118	25	5	61	20	15
80	40	11	60	27	24
0	32	5	50	16	16
98	47	17	85	37	40
72	44	20	100	45	44
104	37	5	23	14	9
108	45	20	79	44	36
0	30	4	18	12	5
0	23	5	31	23	7
0	18	3	31	15	6
115	44	14	81	32	36
100	55	28	67	50	37
152	37	10	75	26	25
84	40	13	59	33	23
0	10	1	32	8	3
93	58	30	76	51	44
NA	45	9	37	20	17
36	54	10	38	19	20
0	17	1	31	6	5
98	33	8	62	26	20
102	49	24	117	50	57
73	56	31	100	56	56
def.	31	8	74	27	22
51	42	7	30	17	13
0	23	2	34	8	8
0	20	1	16	4	3
0	19	2	32	11	6
0	14	4	67	26	9
70	61	21	104	34	64
78	45	13	73	30	33
0	51	11	39	22	20
111	67	118	251	175	169
0	24	3	32	13	8
def.	33	7	38	20	13
0	36	9	39	25	14
67	45	21	107	46	49
def.	29	7	52	24	15
0	27	5	52	18	14
0	11	1	22	10	3
111	45	26	81	56	37
0	16	2	30	11	5
93	40	12	67	27	27
0	26	5	39	18	10
0	33	11	44	35	14
102	35	11	68	33	24
80	44	16	71	36	31
def.	60	23	83	38	49
73	48	30	83	62	40
64	34	15	119	45	41
92	28	7	55	24	15
0	21	NA	NA	NA	NA
0	2	0	35	12	1
53	42	16	66	38	28
0	21	2	40	11	8

TABLE A.5 (continued)

	Price-earnings ratio		Market price as % year-end book value		% Yield	
	High price	Low price	High price	Low price	High price	Low price
The Nash Motors Co.	53	21	133	53	5.00	12.50
National Biscuit Co.	19	8	276	118	5.96	14.00
National Cash Register Co. A	def.	def.	95	31	0	0
The National City Bank of New York	20	8	181	67	3.46	9.38
National Dairy Products Corp.	17	7	238	108	6.45	14.29
National Lead Co.	29	14	44	22	5.43	11.11
The New York Central Railroad Co.	def.	def.	23	5	0	0
Norfolk & Western Railway Co.	12	5	65	28	5.93	14.04
The North American Co.	21	7	172	56	0	0
Otis Elevator Co.	def.	def.	115	45	4.35	11.11
Owens-Illinois Glass Co.	26	7	131	38	4.76	16.67
Pacific Gas & Electric Co.	18	8	123	57	5.41	11.75
Packard Motor Car Co.	def.	def.	148	44	0	0
Paramount-Publix Corp.	def.	def.	30	4	0	0
J. C. Penney Co.	22	8	233	87	6.00	16.15
The Pennsylvania Railroad Co.	22	6	27	8	0	0
Phelps Dodge Corp.	def.	def.	34	11	0	0
Phillips Petroleum Co.	43	11	26	6	0	0
Pillsbury Flour Mills, Inc.	15	6	64	26	2.61	6.32
Pittsburgh Plate Glass Co.	def.	def.	57	32	4.76	8.33
Procter & Gamble Co.	34	16	307	143	5.12	11.00
Public Service Corp. of New Jersey	17	8	140	65	5.33	11.43
Pullman Inc.	def.	def.	38	15	10.71	27.27
Radio Corp. of America	def.	def.	NA	NA	0	0
Radio-Keith-Orpheum Corp.	def.	def.	NA	NA	0	0
Remington Rand, Inc.	def.	def.	NM	NM	0	0
R. J. Reynolds Tobacco Co. B	12	8	235	159	7.50	11.11
Safeway Stores, Inc.	14	7	164	83	5.08	10.00
Sears, Roebuck & Co.	def.	def.	109	29	0	0
Shell Union Oil Corp.	def.	def.	49	14	0	0
Sinclair Consolidated Oil Corp.	NM	NM	50	22	0	0
Socony-Vacuum Oil Co.	71	31	44	19	3.33	7.62
Southern Pacific Co.	def.	def.	17	3	0	0
Standard Brands, Inc.	16	7	450	209	5.56	11.94
Standard Gas and Electric Co.	59	13	33	7	5.71	26.23
Standard Oil Co. of California	30	14	74	35	6.25	13.33
Standard Oil Co. (Indiana)	24	13	63	33	4.00	7.69
Standard Oil Co. (New Jersey)	NM	NM	82	44	5.41	10.00
Swift & Co.	def.	def.	54	20	0	0
The Texas Corp.	def.	def.	47	24	5.56	10.81
Texas Gulf Sulphur Co.	12	5	208	92	7.41	16.67
The Timken Roller Bearing Co.	def.	def.	135	45	4.35	12.90
Transamerica Corp.	21	6	130	39	0	0
Tri-Continental Corp.	def.	def.	NA	NA	0	0
Union Carbide & Carbon Corp.	37	16	157	70	3.33	7.50
Union Pacific Railroad Co.	13	4	44	13	6.32	21.43
United Aircraft & Transport Corp.	64	12	243	46	0	0
The United Corp.	32	8	45	11	2.86	11.43
United Founders Corp.	NA	NA	417	42	0	0
United Fruit Co.	16	5	60	19	6.25	20.00
The United Gas Improvement Co.	16	7	169	71	5.45	12.97
United States Gypsum Co.	31	13	64	26	5.93	14.55
United States Steel Corp.	def.	def.	28	11	0	0
Warner Bros. Pictures, Inc.	def.	def.	30	4	0	0
Westinghouse Electric & Manufacturing Co.	def.	def.	59	22	0	0
F. W. Woolworth Co.	20	10	271	129	5.22	10.91
Wm. Wrigley Jr. Co.	16	7	238	104	5.26	12.00
The Youngstown Sheet & Tube Co.	def.	def.	33	5	0	0
Averages	23.4	9.7	126	49	5.05	12.45
Number of Companies	75	77	137	137	85	85

Notes: (a)   All data come from Table A.1 "Summary Financial Statistics for Leading Stocks, 1929-1933."
           (b)   def. = deficit.
           (c)   NM = not meaningful.
           (d)   NA = not available.

TABLE A.5 (continued)

Year-end dividend payout ratio (%)	1932 low price as % 1932 high price	1932 low price as % 1929 high price	1932 high price as % 1929 low price	1932 high price as % 1929 high price	1932 low price as % 1929 low price
263	40	7	50	17	20
115	43	21	84	49	36
0	33	4	32	13	11
71	37	4	36	11	13
106	45	16	86	36	39
159	49	21	71	44	35
0	24	3	23	14	5
70	42	20	71	47	30
0	33	7	64	23	21
def.	39	8	47	20	18
123	29	12	98	42	28
95	46	17	88	37	40
0	30	5	38	15	12
0	13	2	33	15	4
134	37	12	53	33	20
0	28	6	32	21	9
0	32	5	39	15	13
0	25	4	34	17	8
48	41	15	77	36	31
def.	57	16	43	28	24
175	47	20	100	44	47
92	47	20	111	43	52
def.	39	11	38	28	15
0	21	3	54	12	12
0	NA	NA	NA	1	2
0	13	2	38	13	5
89	68	41	103	61	69
71	51	15	66	30	33
0	27	6	46	20	13
0	29	8	46	27	13
0	44	9	43	20	19
235	44	11	38	24	16
0	17	4	36	24	6
88	47	19	90	47	42
339	22	3	47	14	10
187	47	18	62	36	29
96	52	21	58	40	30
NM	54	24	77	45	42
0	37	19	61	53	23
def.	51	13	36	25	19
88	44	14	63	32	28
def.	34	6	39	17	13
0	30	3	36	11	11
0	27	3	55	10	15
122	44	11	61	26	27
80	29	9	48	32	14
0	19	4	110	21	21
91	25	5	74	18	18
0	10	0	13	4	1
103	31	6	32	20	10
88	42	15	100	35	42
186	41	12	77	29	31
0	40	8	35	20	14
0	11	1	15	7	2
0	36	5	44	15	16
106	48	21	88	44	42
85	44	31	88	70	38
0	14	3	32	19	5
109	35	12	61	29	24
69	141	140	140	141	141

TABLE A.6
Ratios for Leading Stocks - 1933(a)

	Price-earnings ratio		Market price as % year-end book value		% Yield	
	High price	Low price	High price	Low price	High price	Low price
Alaska Juneau Gold Mining Co.	33	11	300	100	2.27	6.82
Alleghany Corp.	def.(b)	def.	52	5	0	0
Allied Chemical & Dye Corp.	28	13	214	100	3.95	8.45
Aluminum Company of America	def.	def.	640	247	0	0
American Can Co.	20	10	171	85	3.96	8.00
American Radiator & Standard Sanitary Corp.	def.	def.	158	39	0	0
American Smelting and Refining Co.	NM(c)	15	126	26	0	0
American Telephone & Telegraph Co.	25	16	100	64	6.67	10.34
American Tobacco Co.	30	16	253	136	5.49	10.20
Anaconda Copper Mining Co.	def.	def.	43	9	0	0
Armour & Co. A	def.	def.	15	3	0	0
Associated Dry Goods Corp.	def.	def.	91	16	0	0
Atchison, Topeka & Santa Fe Railway Co.	def.	def.	35	15	0	0
The Atlantic Refining Co.	13	5	63	24	3.03	8.08
Baltimore and Ohio Railroad Co.	def.	def.	27	6	0	0
Bankers Trust Co.	def.	def.	221	129	4.00	6.82
Bethlehem Steel Co.	def.	def.	40	8	0	0
Borden Co.	35	17	119	58	4.32	8.89
Burroughs Adding Machine Co.	NM	24	350	102	1.90	6.53
Canadian Pacific Railway Co.	def.	def.	42	15	0	0
J. I. Case Co.	def.	def.	76	23	0	0
Caterpillar Tractor Co.	NM	NM	158	29	1.67	9.09
Central Hanover Bank & Trust Co.	NA(d)	NA	194	127	4.64	7.07
The Chase National Bank	11	5	127	53	4.08	9.69
The Chesapeake and Ohio Railway Co.	13	7	96	49	5.71	11.20
Chrysler Corp.	21	3	290	39	1.72	12.90
Cities Service Co.	def.	def.	78	19	0	0
The Coca-Cola Co.	12	8	362	266	5.71	7.79
Colgate-Palmolive-Peet Co.	def.	def.	138	44	0	0
Columbia Gas & Electric Corp.	NM	18	147	47	1.79	5.56
Commercial Solvents Corp.	65	10	1425	222	1.05	6.67
Commonwealth Edison Co.	18	7	78	29	4.82	12.90
The Commonwealth & Southern Corp.	def.	def.	114	23	0	0
Consolidated Gas Co. of New York	19	10	121	64	4.69	8.82
Continental Can Co.	18	8	177	80	3.21	7.14
Continental Illinois National Bank & Trust Co.	16	3	196	38	0	0
Corn Products Refining Co.	24	12	260	129	3.30	6.67
Crown Zellerbach Corp.	NM	NM	75	9	0	0
The Curtis Publishing Co.	def.	def.	320	65	0	0
Deere & Co.	def.	def.	163	19	0	0
The Detroit Edison Co.	19	10	80	42	4.35	8.33
Dow Chemical Co.	15	6	289	111	2.56	6.67
E. I. Du Pont de Nemours & Co.	33	11	291	97	2.86	8.59
Eastman Kodak Co.	22	11	148	75	3.33	6.52
Electric Bond and Share Co.	NM	22	189	45	0	0
The Firestone Tire & Rubber Co.	def.	def.	119	34	1.25	4.38
The First National Bank of Boston	NA	NA	95	54	5.71	10.00
The First National Bank of Chicago	9	3	100	28	0	0
Fox Film Corp. A	10	2	33	5	0	0
General Electric Co.	NM	29	273	100	1.33	3.64
General Foods Corp.	19	10	333	175	4.50	8.57
General Mills, Inc.	20	10	178	90	4.23	8.33
General Motors Corp.	21	6	240	67	3.47	12.50
The Gillette Safety Razor Co.	19	7	222	85	5.25	13.77
Gimbel Brothers, Inc.	def.	def.	27	3	0	0
Goldman Sachs Trading Corp.	def.	def.	NA	NA	0	0
The B. F. Goodrich Corp.	NM	17	85	12	0	0
The Goodyear Tire & Rubber Co.	def.	def.	209	40	0	0
Great Atlantic & Pacific Tea Co. of America	20	13	280	177	3.85	6.09
Guaranty Trust Co. of New York	13	8	118	73	5.70	9.22
Gulf Oil Corp. of Pennsylvania	def.	def.	93	36	0	0
Homestake Mining Co.	19	7	518	201	4.56	11.77
Hudson Motor Car Co.	def.	def.	89	77	0	0
Ingersoll-Rand Co.	def.	def.	223	54	1.92	7.89
Inland Steel Co.	NM	NM	102	27	0	0
International Business Machines Corp.	19	9	247	123	3.92	7.89
International Harvester Co.	def.	def.	90	27	1.30	4.29
International Nickel Co. of Canada, Ltd.	NM	13	230	68	0	0
International Paper & Power Co. A	NA	NA	38	2	0	0
International Shoe Co.	22	9	243	104	3.57	8.33
International Telephone & Telegraph Corp.	NM	NM	59	14	0	0
Irving Trust Co.	19	9	114	55	4.60	9.58
Kennecott Copper Corp.	NM	NM	90	25	0	0
Kimberly-Clark Corp.	def.	def.	45	11	3.20	13.62
S. S. Kresge Co.	11	4	106	34	4.71	14.55
The Lambert Co.	14	6	456	211	7.32	15.79
Lehman Corp.	16	8	99	47	3.00	6.32
Liggett & Myers Tobacco Co.	20	10	265	132	5.10	10.20
Loew's Inc.	16	4	80	18	2.70	11.76
R. H. Macy & Co.	33	12	157	57	3.03	8.33
Marshall Field & Co.	def.	def.	75	18	0	0
Middle West Utilities Co.	NA	NA	NM	NM	0	0
Monsanto Chemical Co.	16	5	252	76	2.41	8.00
Montgomery Ward & Co.	NM	NM	121	36	0	0

TABLE A.6 (continued)

Year-end dividend payout ratio (%)	1933 low price as % 1933 high price	1933 low price as % 1929 high price	1933 high price as % 1929 low price	1933 high price as % 1929 high price	1933 low price as % 1929 low price
75	33	110	776	330	259
0	11	2	49	14	5
109	47	20	77	43	36
0	39	7	66	18	25
79	50	27	117	55	58
0	24	8	68	35	17
0	20	8	87	42	18
167	64	28	70	44	45
167	54	42	114	78	61
0	22	4	34	16	7
0	15	6	141	43	20
0	18	5	80	28	14
0	44	12	41	27	18
41	38	16	110	42	41
0	22	6	36	26	8
def.	59	17	71	29	42
0	20	7	63	35	13
151	49	18	7	36	34
154	29	6	72	22	21
0	36	11	46	31	16
0	30	7	80	22	24
313	18	6	67	33	12
NA	66	19	57	29	37
45	42	6	28	13	12
76	51	36	123	70	63
36	13	6	223	43	30
0	24	2	31	9	8
68	73	43	104	59	76
0	32	8	55	24	18
98	32	6	54	20	17
68	16	13	248	81	39
88	37	7	41	18	15
0	20	4	63	19	13
90	53	19	80	35	43
58	45	38	190	85	85
0	19	2	15	9	3
78	49	36	130	72	64
0	12	4	52	33	6
0	20	5	32	24	7
0	12	4	79	38	10
83	52	12	61	24	32
37	38	38	130	98	50
93	33	14	120	42	40
73	51	17	60	34	31
0	24	2	28	7	7
def.	29	25	128	86	37
NA	57	9	31	16	18
0	28	4	28	14	8
0	15	1	26	5	4
105	37	11	71	30	26
67	53	26	114	49	60
84	51	40	142	80	72
74	28	11	106	39	29
101	38	5	25	14	10
0	10	2	7	16	7
0	31	1	15	4	5
0	14	3	58	21	8
0	19	6	80	31	15
78	63	23	112	37	71
73	62	18	72	29	44
0	38	11	54	30	21
85	39	156	574	401	223
0	19	3	42	17	8
def.	24	8	53	35	16
0	26	12	65	41	17
75	50	30	140	60	70
def.	30	10	71	32	22
0	29	9	92	32	27
0	5	1	50	23	3
77	43	31	104	72	44
0	23	3	42	15	10
86	48	12	56	25	26
0	28	7	53	25	15
def.	24	10	56	44	13
53	32	9	61	29	20
101	46	12	51	26	24
48	48	28	127	59	6
103	50	46	123	92	61
43	23	10	116	44	27
100	36	9	60	26	22
0	24	NA	NA	NA	NA
0	NM	0	4	2	0
39	30	31	177	102	53
0	30	5	67	18	20

TABLE A.6 (continued)

	Price-earnings ratio		Market price as % year-end book value		% Yield	
	High price	Low price	High price	Low price	High price	Low price
The Nash Motors Co.	def.	def.	193	79	3.70	9.09
National Biscuit Co.	29	15	359	188	4.59	8.75
National Cash Register Co. A	def.	def.	120	26	0	0
The National City Bank of New York	23	8	256	89	1.63	4.69
National Dairy Products Corp.	26	11	217	92	4.62	10.91
National Lead Co.	23	7	67	21	3.57	11.63
The New York Central Railroad Co.	def.	def.	40	9	0	0
Norfolk & Western Railway Co.	12	7	84	53	4.52	7.21
The North American Co.	30	11	154	54	0	0
Otis Elevator Co.	def.	def.	139	56	2.40	6.00
Owens-Illinois Glass Co.	20	7	262	86	3.09	9.38
Pacific Gas & Electric Co.	22	10	110	52	6.25	13.33
Packard Motor Car Co.	NM	NM	210	52	0	0
Paramount-Publix Corp.	NA	NA	NA	NA	NA	NA
J. C. Penney Co.	10	3	280	95	2.14	6.32
The Pennsylvania Railroad Co.	29	10	50	17	1.19	3.57
Phelps Dodge Corp.	def.	def.	54	13	0	0
Phillips Petroleum Co.	53	13	59	15	0	0
Pillsbury Flour Mills, Inc.	13	4	77	27	3.70	10.67
Pittsburgh Plate Glass Co.	21	7	103	33	2.50	7.69
Procter & Gamble Co.	32	13	369	154	3.13	7.50
Public Service Corp. of New Jersey	17	10	136	79	4.91	8.48
Pullman Inc.	def.	def.	84	26	5.17	16.67
Radio Corp. of America	def.	def.	NM	NM	0	0
Radio-Keith-Orpheum Corp.	def.	def.	NM	NM	0	0
Remington Rand, Inc.	NM	NM	NM	NM	0	0
R. J. Reynolds Tobacco Corp. B	33	17	338	169	5.56	11.11
Safeway Stores, Inc.	15	7	163	74	4.84	10.71
Sears, Roebuck and Co.	20	6	131	36	0	0
Shell Union Oil Corp.	def.	def.	68	24	0	0
Sinclair Consolidated Oil Corp.	def.	def.	89	28	0	0
Socony-Vacuum Oil Co.	24	8	63	22	2.06	5.83
Southern Pacific Co.	def.	def.	20	6	0	0
Standard Brands, Inc.	33	12	950	350	2.63	7.14
Standard Gas and Electric Co.	def.	def.	23	5	0	0
Standard Oil Co. of California	NM	NM	105	47	2.22	5.00
Standard Oil Co. (Indiana)	30	15	85	43	2.94	5.88
Standard Oil Co. (New Jersey)	49	24	107	51	2.08	4.35
Swift & Co.	15	4	69	19	0	0
The Texas Corp.	def.	def.	83	31	3.33	9.09
Texas Gulf Sulphur Co.	15	5	300	100	4.44	13.33
The Timken Roller Bearing Co.	40	16	212	82	1.67	4.29
Transamerica Corp.	20	5	156	44	0	0
Tri-Continental Corp.	def.	def.	700	220	0	0
Union Carbide & Carbon Corp.	33	13	217	83	1.92	5.00
Union Pacific Railroad Co.	17	8	61	28	4.55	9.84
United Aircraft & Transport Corp.	NM	30	470	170	0	0
The United Corp.	NM	17	375	100	0	0
United Founders Corp.	NM	NM	480	80	0	0
United Fruit Co.	22	7	126	43	2.94	8.70
The United Gas Improvement Co.	20	11	208	117	4.80	8.57
United States Gypsum Co.	54	18	129	43	1.85	5.56
United States Steel Corp.	def.	def.	38	13	0	0
Warner Bros. Pictures, Inc.	def.	def.	70	8	0	0
Westinghouse Electric & Manufacturing Co.	def.	def.	89	29	4.75	14.74
F. W. Woolworth Co.	16	8	300	147	4.71	9.60
Wm. Wrigley Jr. Co.	15	9	228	140	5.26	8.57
The Youngstown Sheet & Tube Co.	def.	def.	49	9	0	0
Averages	22.7	10.3	181	65	3.63	8.70
Number of Companies	73	82	136	136	82	82

Notes: (a) All data come from Table A.1 "Summary Financial Statistics for Leading Stocks, 1929-1933."
       (b) def. = deficit.
       (c) NM = not meaningful.
       (d) NA = not available.

TABLE A.6 (continued)

Year-end dividend payout ratio (%)	1933 low price as % 1933 high price	1933 low price as % 1929 high price	1933 high price as % 1929 low price	1933 high price as % 1929 high price	1933 low price as % 1929 low price
def.	41	9	68	23	28
133	52	34	109	64	57
0	21	3	41	16	9
36	35	3	26	8	9
119	42	13	72	30	31
82	31	20	109	67	33
0	24	5	37	23	9
52	63	38	93	61	58
0	35	7	55	20	19
def.	40	9	51	22	20
62	33	32	226	98	74
135	47	15	76	32	36
0	25	5	54	21	13
NA	NA	NA	NA	NA	NA
22	34	18	85	53	29
34	33	13	58	38	19
0	24	6	61	24	15
0	25	10	79	40	20
47	35	15	90	42	31
53	33	17	82	53	27
99	42	20	112	49	47
86	58	24	106	41	61
def.	31	18	79	58	25
0	25	3	46	10	12
0	NM	NM	NM	NM	NM
0	23	4	55	19	13
185	50	41	138	82	69
73	45	14	69	32	31
0	28	7	59	26	16
0	34	13	61	36	21
0	31	11	76	36	24
49	35	13	53	35	19
0	28	7	37	25	10
87	37	31	190	84	70
0	22	2	31	9	7
172	44	24	87	55	38
89	50	27	79	54	40
103	48	28	100	58	48
0	28	19	81	69	23
def.	37	15	60	42	22
68	33	18	105	53	35
67	39	10	61	26	24
0	28	4	47	14	13
0	31	5	88	15	28
63	38	14	88	37	34
76	46	20	66	44	31
0	36	10	152	29	55
0	27	5	79	20	21
0	17	1	12	4	2
63	34	14	68	43	23
98	56	23	114	40	64
100	33	20	154	59	51
0	34	9	45	26	15
0	11	1	30	14	3
def.	32	6	59	20	19
76	49	24	98	49	48
80	61	43	88	70	54
0	19	5	43	26	8
82	35	16	85	42	31
70	139	139	139	139	139

TABLE A.7

Moody's Ratings for Railroad Bond Issues over $40 Million Maturing after December 31, 1950   1929–1933

Issues	1929	1930	1931	1932	1933
1. Atchison, Topeka & Santa Fe general 4% due 1995	Aaa	Aaa	Aaa	Aaa	Aaa
2. Atchison, Topeka & Santa Fe adjusted 4% due 1995	Aaa	Aaa	Aaa	Aaa	Aaa
3. Atlantic Coast Line first consolidated 4% due 1952	Aaa	Aaa	Aa	A	A
4. Central Pacific guaranteed 5% due 1960	Aa	Aa	Baa	Baa	Ba
5. Central Railroad of New Jersey 5% due 1987	Aaa	Aaa	A	A	A
6. Chesapeake and Ohio general 4½% due 1992	Aaa	Aaa	Aaa	Aaa	Aaa
7. Chicago, Burlington & Quincy general 4% due 1958	Aaa	Aaa	Aaa	Aa	Aa
8. Chicago, Burlington & Quincy first and refunding 5% due 1971 "A"	Aaa	Aaa	Aa	A	A
9. Chicago, Milwaukee & St. Paul first 4% due 1989 "A"	Aa	Aa	A	A	Baa
10. Chicago, Rock Island & Pacific general 4% due 1988	Aaa	Aaa	Aa	Baa	Baa
11. Chicago & West Indiana consolidated 4% due 1952	Aa	Aa	Aa	Aa	Aa
12. Cleveland, Cincinnati, Chicago & St. Louis refunding 4½% due 1977 "E"	Aa	Aa	Baa	Baa	Baa
13. Great Northern general 4½% due 1977 "E"	Aa	Aa	Baa	Baa	Baa
14. Lake Shore & Michigan Southern 3½% due 1997	Aaa	Aaa	Aaa	Aaa	Aaa
15. New York Central consolidated 4% due 1998	Aaa	Aaa	A	A	A
16. New York Central & Hudson River 3½% due 1997	Aaa	Aaa	Aaa	Aaa	Aaa
17. Norfolk and Western first consolidated 4% due 1996	Aaa	Aaa	Aaa	Aaa	Aaa

Issues	1929	1930	1931	1932	1933
18. Northern Pacific prior lien 4% due 1997	Aaa	Aaa	Aaa	Aa	Aa
19. Northern Pacific general lien 3% due 2017	Aaa	Aaa	Aa	A	A
20. Northern Pacific refunding 6% due 2047 "B"	Aa	Aa	Baa	Baa	Baa
21. Oregon-Washington Railroad & Navigation Co first and refunding 4% due 1961	Aaa	Aaa	Aaa	Aaa	Aaa
22. Pennsylvania Railroad consolidated 4½% due 1960	Aaa	Aaa	Aaa	Aaa	Aaa
23. Pennsylvania Railroad general 4½% due 1965 "A"	Aaa	Aaa	Aaa	Aa	Aa
24. Pennsylvania Railroad general 5% due 1968 "B"	Aaa	Aaa	Aaa	Aa	Aa
25. Pennsylvania Railroad secured 5% due 1964	Aaa	Aaa	Aa	A	A
26. Pennsylvania Railroad debenture 4½% due 1970	–	Aa	A	Baa	Baa
27. Reading general and refunding 4½% due 1997 "A"	Aa	Aa	A	A	A
28. Southern Pacific Oregon Lines first 4½% due 1977	Aaa	Aaa	Aa	Baa	Baa
29. Southern Pacific first refunding 4% due 1955	Aaa	Aaa	Aa	Baa	Baa
30. Southern Railroad first consolidated 5% due 1994	Aaa	Aaa	Aa	A	A
31. Union Pacific first lien and refunding 4% due 2008	Aaa	Aaa	Aaa	Aaa	Aaa
32. Virginian first 5% due 1962	Aa	Aa	Aa	Aa	Aa
33. West Shore first 4% due 2361	Aaa	Aaa	Aa	Aa	A
34. Western Maryland first 4% due 1952	Baa	Baa	Baa	Baa	Baa
Ratings reductions	–	0	18	13	3

TABLE A.8

Moody's Ratings for Public Utility Bond Issues over $40 Million Maturing after December 31, 1950 1929–1933

Issues	1929	1930	1931	1932	1933
1. Alabama Power first and refunding 4½% due 1967	A	A	A	Baa	Baa
2. American Gas & Electric debenture 5% due 2028	Baa	Baa	Baa	Baa	Baa
3. American Telephone & Telegraph debenture 5% due 1960	Aa	Aa	Aa	Aa	Aa
4. American Telephone & Telegraph debenture 5% due 1965	-	Aa	Aa	Aa	Aa
5. Appalachian Electric Power first and refunding 5% due 1956	A	A	A	A	A
6. Bell Telephone of Pennsylvania first and refunding 5% due 1960	Aaa	Aaa	Aaa	Aa	Aa
7. Columbia Gas & Electric debenture 5% due 1952	Baa	Baa	Baa	Baa	Baa
8. Columbia Gas & Electric debenture 5% due 1961	-	-	Baa	Baa	Baa
9. Commonwealth Edison first 4% due 1981 "F"	-	-	Aa	Aa	Aa
10. Consolidated Gas of New York debenture 4½% due 1951	-	-	Aa	Aa	Aa
11. Consumers Power first 4% due 1958	Aaa	Aaa	Aaa	Aaa	Aaa
12. Detroit Edison general and refunding 4½% due 1961 "D"	-	-	Aa	A	A
13. Duke Power first and refunding 4½% due 1967	Aa	Aa	Aa	Aa	Aa
14. Duquesne Light first 4½% due 1967 "A"	Aaa	Aaa	Aaa	Aaa	Aaa
15. Georgia Power first and refunding 5% due 1967	A	A	A	A	A
16. Illinois Bell Telephone first and refunding 5% due 1956 "A"	Aaa	Aaa	Aaa	Aaa	Aaa
17. Illinois Power & Light first and refunding 5% due 1956 "C"	Baa	Baa	Baa	Baa	Baa
18. Milwaukee Electric Railway & Light first 5% due 1961 "B"	Baa	Baa	Baa	Baa	Baa

Issues	1929	1930	1931	1932	1933
19. Illinois Bell Telephone first and refunding 5% due 1956 "A"	Aaa	Aaa	Aaa	Aaa	Aaa
20. New York Power & Light first 4½% due 1967	A	A	A	A	A
21. Ohio Power first and refunding 4½% due 1956 "D"	Aa	Aa	Aa	Aa	Aa
22. Pacific Gas & Electric first and refunding 5½% due 1952 "C"	Aa	Aa	Aa	Aa	Aa
23. Pacific Gas & Electric first and refunding 4½% due 1960 "F"	-	Aa	Aa	Aa	Aa
24. Pennsylvania Power & Light first 4½% due 1981	-	-	Aa	Aa	Aa
25. Philadelphia Co. secured 5% due 1967 "A"	A	A	A	A	A
26. Philadelphia Electric first and refunding 4% due 1971	-	-	Aaa	Aaa	Aaa
27. Public Service of Northern Illinois 4½% due 1981 "F"	-	-	A	A	A
28. Public Service Electric & Gas first and refunding 4½% due 1967	Aaa	Aaa	Aaa	Aaa	Aaa
29. Southern California Edison refunding 5% due 1951	Aaa	Aaa	Aaa	Aaa	Aaa
30. Southwestern Bell Telephone first and refunding 5% due 1954 "A"	Aaa	Aaa	Aaa	Aaa	Aaa
Ratings reductions	-	0	0	3	0

TABLE A.9

Moody's Ratings for Industrial Bond Issues over $20 Million Maturing after December 31, 1939 1929–1933

Issues	1929	1930	1931	1932	1933
1. Aluminum Company of America 5% due 1952	Aa	Aa	A	Baa	Baa
2. American Smelting & Refining first 5% due 1947	Aa	Aa	A	A	Aa
3. Batavian Petroleum 4½% due 1942	Aaa	Aaa	A	A	A
4. General Steel Castings 5½% due 1949	Baa	Ba	Ba	Ba	Ba
5. Goodyear Tire & Rubber first collateral 5% due 1957	Baa	Baa	Baa	Baa	Baa
6. Gulf Oil of Pennsylvania debenture 5% due 1947	Aaa	Aaa	Aa	A	A
7. Inland Steel first 4½% due 1978 "A"	Aa	Aa	A	Baa	Baa
8. Koppers Gas & Coke 5½% due 1950	–	Baa	Baa	Baa	Baa
9. National Dairy Products 5¼% due 1948	A	A	A	Baa	Baa
10. National Steel first collateral 5% due 1956	–	–	Baa	Baa	A
11. Pittsburgh Coal 6% due 1949	Ba	Ba	B	B	B
12. Pure Oil 5½% due 1940	–	Baa	Baa	Ba	Ba
13. Royal Dutch debenture 4% due 1945 "A"	–	Aaa	A	A	A
14. Shell Pipe Line debenture 5% due 1952	A	A	Baa	Baa	Baa
15. Shell Union Oil 5% due 1947	A	Ba	Ba	Ba	Ba
16. Standard Oil (N.J.) debenture 5% due 1946	Aaa	Aaa	Aaa	Aaa	Aaa
17. Standard Oil (N.Y.) debenture 4½% due 1951	Aaa	Aaa	Aaa	Aaa	Aaa
18. Swift 5% due 1946	–	A	A	A	A

TABLE A.9 (continued)

Issues	1929	1930	1931	1932	1933
19. Union Gulf collateral 5% due 1950	–	Aaa	Aaa	Aa	Aa
20. Youngstown Sheet & Tube first 5% due 1978 "A"	A	A	Baa	Baa	Baa
Ratings reductions	–	2	8	6	0

TABLE A.10

Moody's Ratings for Foreign and Canadian Government Bond Issues[a] 1929–1933

Foreign Governments	1929	1930	1931	1932	1933
1. Argentina	Aa	Aa	A	Baa	Baa
2. Australia	Aaa	Aa	Baa	Baa	Baa
3. Austria	–	A	A	Ba	Ba
4. Belgium	Aa	Aa	Aa	Aa	A
5. Bolivia	Baa	Ba	B	B	Caa
6. Brazil	Baa	Ba	B	B	B
7. Bulgaria	Baa	Baa	Ba	B	B
8. Chile	A	A	B	B	Caa
9. Columbia	Baa	Baa	Ba	Ba	Ba
10. Cuba	A	A	Baa	Baa	ba
11. Czechoslovakia	A	A	Baa	Baa	Baa
12. Denmark	Aaa	Aaa	Aa	A	A
13. Finland	A	A	Baa	Baa	Baa
14. France	Aa	Aa	Aa	Aa	Aa
15. Germany	Aa	Aa	Baa	Baa	Baa
16. Hungary	Baa	Baa	Ba	B	Ba/B
17. Italy	A	A	Baa	Baa	A
18. Japan	Aa	Aa	A	Baa	Baa
19. Mexico	Ba/B[b]	Ba/B	Caa/Ca	Caa/Ca	Ca
20. Netherlands	Aaa	Aaa	A	A	A
21. Norway	Aaa	Aaa	Aa	A	A
22. Peru	A/Baa	Baa	B	B	Caa
23. Poland	Baa/Ba	Baa	Baa	Ba	Ba
24. Rumania	Baa	Baa	Ba	Ba/B	B/Caa
25. Spain	Baa	Baa	Baa	Ba	Ba
26. Sweden	Aaa	Aaa	Aa	Aa	Aa

TABLE A.10 (continued)

Foreign Governments	1929	1930	1931	1932	1933
27. Swiss Confederation	Aaa	Aaa	Aa	Aa	Aa
28. United Kingdom	Aaa	Aaa	Aaa	Aaa	Aa
29. Uruguay	A	A	Baa	Ba/B	Ba/B
30. Venezuela	Baa	Ba	Baa	Baa	Baa
31. Yugoslavia	Ba	Ba	Ba	B	B
Ratings Reductions	–	5	23	12	8

Canadian Governments					
1. Alberta	Aa	Aa	Baa	Baa	Baa
2. British Columbia	Aa	Aa	Aa	Baa	Baa
3. Canada	Aaa	Aaa	Aa	Aa	Aa
4. Manitoba	Aa	Aa	Baa	Baa	Baa
5. Montreal	Aaa	Aaa	Aa	A	A
6. New Brunswick	Aa	Aa	A	A	A
7. Nova Scotia	Aa	Aa	Aa	A	A
8. Ontario	Aaa	Aaa	Aa	Aa	A
9. Prince Edward Island	Aa	Aa	A	Baa	Baa
10. Quebec	Aaa	Aaa	Aa	Aa	A
11. Saskatchewan	Aa	Aa	Baa	Baa	Baa
12. Toronto	Aaa	Aaa	Aa	A	A
Ratings Reductions	–	0	10	5	2

Source: Ratings are from Moody's Government Manuals published in the year following that indicated.

Notes: (a)   Ratings apply to external, dollar denominated issues wherever possible.

(b)   Split ratings indicate more than one external issue with different ratings due to different security for the bonds.

TABLE A.11

Moody's Ratings for Bond Issues of States and Cities with Populations over 500,000 1929-1933

Issuer	Total Debt Outstanding[a] ($ millions)	1929	1930	1931	1932	1933
Alabama	60	Aaa	Aaa	Aa	Baa	Baa
Arizona	2	Aaa	Aaa	Aa	Aa	Aa
Arkansas	160	Aaa	Aaa	A	Baa	NR[b]
Baltimore	174	Aaa	Aaa	Aaa	Aaa	Aa
Boston	125	Aaa	Aaa	Aaa	Aa	A
Buffalo	97	Aaa	Aaa	Aaa	Aa	Aaa
California	137	Aaa	Aaa	Aaa	Aaa	Aa
Chicago	426	Aaa	Aaa	NR	NR	Baa
Cleveland	125	Aaa	Aaa	Aaa	Aa	A
Colorado	7	Aaa	Aaa	Aaa	Aaa	Aaa
Connecticut	13	Aaa	Aaa	Aaa	Aaa	Aaa
Delaware	3	Aaa	Aaa	Aaa	Aaa	Aaa
Detroit	394	Aaa	Aa	Aa	Baa	B
Florida	0	No Debt				
Georgia	4	Aaa	Aaa	Aa	Aa	A
Idaho	$	Aaa	Aaa	Aa	Aa	Aa
Indiana	0	Aaa	Aaa	Aaa	No Debt	
Illinois	208	Aaa	Aaa	Aaa	Aa	Aa
Iowa	12	Aaa	Aaa	Aaa	Aa	Aa
Kansas	22	Aaa	Aaa	Aaa	Aaa	Aa
Kentucky	0	Aaa	Aaa	Aaa	No Debt	
Los Angeles	231	Aaa	Aaa	Aa	Aa	A
Louisiana	127	Aaa	Aaa	Aa	NR	NR
Maine	30	Aaa	Aaa	Aaa	Aaa	Aa
Maryland	35	Aaa	Aaa	Aaa	Aaa	Aa
Massachusetts	115	Aaa	Aaa	Aaa	Aaa	Aaa
Miami	30	Baa	NR	NR	B	Caa
Michigan	83	Aaa	Aaa	Aaa	Aa	A
Milwaukee	47	Aaa	Aaa	Aaa	Aa	A
Minneapolis	59	Aaa	Aaa	Aaa	Aaa	Aa
Minnesota	114	Aaa	Aaa	Aaa	Aa	Aa
Mississippi	39	Aaa	Aaa	A	A	A
Missouri	111	Aaa	Aaa	Aaa	Aaa	A
Montana	5	Aaa	Aaa	Aaa	Aa	A
Nebraska	0	No Debt				
Nevada	0	Aaa	Aaa	No Debt		
New Hampshire	7	Aaa	Aaa	Aaa	Aaa	Aa
New Jersey	164	Aaa	Aaa	Aaa	Aaa	Aa
New Mexico	11	Aaa	Aaa	Aaa	Aa	A

TABLE A.11 (continued)

Issuer	Total Debt Outstanding(a) ($ millions)	1929	1930	1931	1932	1933
New York	437	Aaa	Aaa	Aaa	Aaa	Aaa
New York City	2071	Aaa	Aaa	Aaa	Aa	A
North Carolina	172	Aaa	Aaa	Aaa	A	A
North Dakota	41	Aa	Aa	Aa	A	A
Ohio	1	Aaa	Aaa	Aaa	NR	NR
Oklahoma	14	Aaa	Aaa	Aaa	NR	NR
Oregon	54	Aaa	Aaa	Aaa	Aa	A
Pennsylvania	87	Aaa	Aaa	Aaa	Aaa	Aaa
Philadelphia	449	Aaa	Aaa	Aa	A	A
Pittsburgh	61	Aaa	Aaa	Aaa	Aa	Aa
Rhode Island	21	Aaa	Aaa	Aaa	Aaa	Aa
St. Louis	70	Aaa	Aaa	Aaa	Aaa	Aa
San Francisco	159	Aaa	Aaa	Aaa	Aaa	Aa
South Carolina	35	Aaa	Aaa	Aa	A	Baa
South Dakota	50	Aa	Aa	Aa	A	Baa
Tennessee	88	Aaa	Aaa	Aa	A	A
Texas	0	Aaa	Aaa	No Debt		
Utah	10	Aaa	Aaa	Aaa	Aa	Aa
Vermont	8	Aaa	Aaa	Aaa	Aaa	Aaa
Virginia	21	Aaa	Aaa	Aaa	Aaa	Aa
Washington	12	Aaa	Aaa	Aaa	Aaa	NR
West Virginia	87	Aaa	Aaa	Aaa	Aaa	Aa
Wisconsin	0	Aaa	Aaa	No Debt		
Wyoming	4	Aaa	Aaa	Aaa	Aa	Aa
Ratings Reductions		-	1	12	25	27

Source: Ratings are from Moody's Governments Manuals published in the year following that indicated.

Notes: (a) Debt outstanding is as reported in Moody's Governments Manual 1934.
(b) NR = not rated.

TABLE A.12

Price and Yield Ranges for Railroad Bond Issues over $40 Million Maturing after December 31, 1950 1929-1933

Issues	1929	1930	1931	1932	1933
1. Atchison, Topeka & Santa Fe general 4% due 1995	$95-90(a) 4.23%-4.47(b)	$99-92 4.04%-4.37	$101-82 3.96%-4.93	$95-75 4.23%-5.40	$97-83 4.13%-4.87
2. Atchison, Topeka & Santa Fe adjusted 4% due 1995	93-85 4.32-4.75	95-87 4.23-4.63	98-78 4.09-5.19	89-65 4.53-6.23	89-75 4.53-5.40
3. Atlantic Coast Line first consolidated 4% due 1952	95-88 4.35-4.87	97-88 4.21-4.90	98-76 4.14-6.03	85-60 5.22-8.06	92-66 4.64-7.35
4. Central Pacific guaranteed 5% due 1960	104-99 4.75-5.06	106-100 4.63-5.00	105-61 4.68-8.71	79-31 6.67-17.08	80-45 6.60-11.80
5. Central Railroad of New Jersey 5% due 1987	110-104 4.51-4.80	115-106 4.29-4.70	115-93 4.29-5.40	98-75 5.11-6.73	102-82 4.89-6.15
6. Chesapeake and Ohio general 4½% due 1992	100-93 4.50-4.86	106-97 4.23-4.65	107-77 4.18-5.90	100-70 4.50-6.49	108-101 4.14-4.45
7. Chicago, Burlington & Quincy general 4% due 1958	94-88 4.37-4.71	98-92 4.12-4.51	100-82 4.00-5.26	93-74 4.96-5.98	96-78 4.26-5.65
8. Chicago, Burlington & Quincy first and refunding 5% due 1971 "A"	107-101 4.62-4.96	111-103 4.42-4.83	111-90 4.43-4.63	100-68 5.00-7.55	101-76 4.94-6.76
9. Chicago, Milwaukee & St. Paul first 4% due 1989 "A"	87-80 4.64-5.07	88-77 4.59-5.27	88-50 4.59-8.08	71-42 5.73-9.59	73-38 5.58-10.58

TABLE A.12 (continued)

Issues	1929	1930	1931	1932	1933
10. Chicago, Rock Island & Pacific general 4% due 1988	92-82 4.38%-4.94	$91-86 4.43%-4.71	$96-63 4.18%-6.45	$80-51 5.08%-7.94	$71-42 5.74%-9.60
11. Chicago & West Indiana consolidated 4% due 1952	89-83 4.74-5.29	94-84 4.43-5.23	92-55 4.60-8.70	76-55 6.09-8.83	81-60 5.64-8.19
12. Cleveland, Cincinnati, Chicago & St. Louis refunding 4½% due 1977 "E"	101-91 4.45-5.00	103-94 4.35-3.82	102-50 4.40-9.15	71-28 6.50-16.11	78-37 5.91-12.27
13. Great Northern general 4 1/2% due 1977 "E"	97-92 4.66-4.94	101-93 4.45-4.88	100-56 4.50-8.20	75-38 6.14-11.95	74-34 6.24-13.32
14. Lake Shore & Michigan Southern 3½% due 1997	82-76 4.32-4.67	86-79 4.12-4.49	87-70 4.07-5.08	80-66 4.44-5.39	87-72 4.07-4.95
15. New York Central consolidated 4% due 1998	91-84 4.42-4.80	98-88 4.09-4.58	98-60 4.09-6.72	81-56 4.99-7.20	84-58 4.81-6.96
16. New York Central & Hudson River 3½% due 1997	82-76 4.32-4.67	87-78 4.07-4.55	87-69 4.07-5.16	79-67 4.50-5.31	84-69 4.23-5.16
17. Norfolk and Western first consolidated 4% due 1996	93-88 4.32-4.58	98-91 4.09-4.42	101-84 3.96-4.81	100-79 4.00-5.12	101-87 3.96-4.64
18. Northern Pacific prior lien 4% due 1997	92-84 4.37-4.80	97-89 4.13-4.52	97-74 4.13-5.46	87-65 4.63-6.22	85-75 4.75-5.39
19. Northern Pacific general lien 3% due 2047	68-62 4.42-4.85	71-64 4.24-4.70	70-47 4.30-6.39	65-49 4.63-6.13	62-48 4.85-6.26

TABLE A.12 (continued)

Issues	1929	1930	1931	1932	1933
20. Northern Pacific refunding 6% due 2047 "B"	$114-109 5.26%-5.50	$115-109 5.22%-5.50	$114-71 5.26%-8.45	$91-45 6.59%-13.33	$93-60 6.45%-10.00
21. Oregon-Washington Railroad & Navigation Co. first and refunding 4% due 1961	91-84 4.54-5.01	96-88 4.23-4.74	98-68 4.12-6.42	84-61 5.06-7.23	90-75 4.64-5.82
22. Pennsylvania Railroad consolidated 4½% due 1960	102-97 4.38-4.68	106-100 4.15-4.50	107-90 4.09-5.17	103-87 4.31-5.41	106-95 4.13-4.83
23. Pennsylvania Railroad general 4½% due 1965 "A"	100-94 4.50-4.85	105-98 4.23-4.62	105-66 4.22-7.19	88-50 5.27-9.47	95-73 4.81-6.67
24. Pennsylvania Railroad general 5% due 1968 "B"	109-102 4.51-4.88	112-106 4.35-4.66	111-77 4.40-6.69	94-55 5.38-9.38	101-78 4.94-6.62
25. Pennsylvania Railroad secured 5% due 1964	105-100 4.71-5.00	106-99 4.65-5.04	106-59 4.64-7.57	90-53 5.68-9.68	98-73 5.13-7.18
26. Pennsylvania Railroad debenture 4½% due 1970	-	101-91 4.45-5.02	99-55 4.55-8.47	75-33 6.22-13.81	86-56 5.38-8.37
27. Reading Co. general and refunding 4½% due 1997 "A"	100-93 450-4.85	103-96 4.36-4.70	103-68 4.36-6.66	86-57 5.26-7.93	95-76 4.75-5.92
28. Southern Pacific Oregon Lines first 4½% due 1977	99-93 4.55-4.88	103-95 4.35-4.77	102-70 4.40-6.58	85-48 5.39-9.53	80-53 5.75-8.68

TABLE A.12 (continued)

Issues	1929	1930	1931	1932	1933
29. Southern Pacific first refunding 4% due 1955	$93-87 4.46%-4.89	$98-$91 4.13%-4.61	$98-73 4.13%-6.17	$87-50 4.95%-9.31	$84-60 5.23%-7.85
30. Southern Railroad first consolidated consolidated 5% due 1994	110-104 4.52-4.80	112-103 4.43-4.85	111-67 4.48-7.50	87-47 5.77-10.66	96-55 5.22-9.12
31. Union Pacific first lien and refunding 4% due 2008	92-85 4.36-4.73	98-89 4.09-4.51	99-68 4.04-5.91	89-70 4.51-5.75	94-78 4.27-5.16
32. Virginian first 5% due 1962	108-100 4.35-5.00	110-101 4.11-4.96	108-78 4.52-6.69	96-70 5.27-7.54	102-84 4.87-6.19
33. West Shore first 4% due 2361	90-83 4.44-4.82	95-86 4.21-4.65	94-61 4.26-6.56	79-65 5.06-6.15	86-88 4.65-6.06
34. Western Maryland first 4% due 1952	82-73 5.37-6.22	89-74 4.83-6.18	84-39 5.27-12.03	67-38 7.12-12.50	74-53 6.38-9.33

TABLE A.12 (continued)

	1929	1930	1931	1932	1933
Average yields – Aaa bonds(c)	4.43-4.80	4.23-4.65	4.10-5.63	4.45-5.81	4.23-5.03
Number of Aaa bonds	24	24	13	9	9
Average yields – Aa bonds(c)	4.69-5.09	4.51-5.04	4.37-6.75	5.17-7.65	4.88-6.45
Number of Aa bonds	8	9	11	7	6
Average yields – A bonds(c)	–	–	4.38-7.07	5.27-8.19	4.88-6.86
Number of A bonds	–	–	5	9	9
Average yields – Baa bonds(c)	5.37-6.22	4.82-6.18	4.82-9.31	6.07-12.40	8.56-10.00
Number of Baa bonds	1	1	5	9	9

Source: Moody's Railroad Manual 1934.

Notes:
(a) Quotes above $10 are rounded off to the nearest dollar.
(b) Yields are calculated assuming purchase and maturity at mid-year.
(c) Ratings are as shown in Moody's Railroad Manual for the following year i.e. 1932 Manual = 1931 rating.

TABLE A.13

Price and Yield Ranges for Public Utility Bond Issues over $40 Million Maturing after December 31, 1950   1929–1933

Issues	1929	1930	1931	1932	1933
1. Alabama Power first and refunding 4¼% due 1967	$97-90(a) 4.67%-5.10(b)	$100-93 4.50%-4.91	$100-79 4.50%-5.92	$85-70 5.47%-6.74	$82-45 5.70%-10.42
2. American Gas & Electric debenture 5% due 2028	98-91 5.10-5.50	101-94 4.95-5.32	101-73 4.95-6.85	91-63 5.50-7.94	92-64 5.44-7.82
3. American Telephone & Telegraph debenture 5% due 1960	105-100 4.69-5.00	108-100 4.51-5.00	110-94 4.39-5.41	106-92 4.62-5.57	108-93 4.49-5.50
4. American Telephone & Telegraph debenture 5% due 1965	-	108-100 4.54-5.00	110-94 4.305.39	107-92 4.59-5.53	107-93 4.58-5.47
5. Appalachian Electric Power first and refunding 5% due 1956	100-93 5.00-5.50	103-95 4.80-5.36	101-84 4.73-6.28	95-72 5.37-7.54	97-$\overline{64}$ 5.32-8.62
6. Bell Telephone of Pennsylvania first and refunding 5% due 1960	108-103 4.52-4.81	113-104 4.23-4.75	115-100 4.11-5.00	110-99 4.38-5.07	111-102 4.31-4.87
7. Columbia Gas & Electric debenture 5% due 1952	101-97 4.93-5.23	104-99 4.71-5.08	101-72 4.92-7.71	89-60 5.95-9.51	89-60 5.96-9.63
8. Columbia Gas & Electric debenture 5% due 1961	-	-	100-63 5.00-8.39	88-58 5.83-9.15	88-58 5.88-9.20

TABLE A.13 (continued)

Issues	1929	1930	1931	1932	1933
9. Commonwealth Edison first 4% due 1981 "F"	-	-	$95-76 4.24%-5.39	$90-69 4.51%-5.96	$94-70 4.30%-5.88
10. Consolidated Gas Company of New York debenture 4½% due 1951	-	-	108-90 4.20-5.32	101-87 4.42-5.62	102-87 4.34-5.66
11. Consumers Power first 4½% due 1958	96 ask 4.76	103-91 4.31-5.11	105-90 4.19-5.19	103-88 4.31-5.365	105-88 4.18-5.38
12. Detroit Edison general and refunding 4½% due 1961 "D"	-	-	106-89 4.15-5.23	98-87 4.63-5.39	100-75 4.50-6.44
13. Duke Power first and refunding 4½% due 1967	99-96 4.56-4.73	103-95 4.34-4.79	105-99 4.23-4.56	100-85 4.50-5.47	102-85 4.39-5.48
14. Duquesne Light first 4½% due 1967 "A"	101-96 4.45-4.73	104-96 4.28-5.73	106-93 4.18-4.92	105-93 4.23-4.92	105-97 4.22-4.68
15. Georgia Power first and refunding 5% due 1967	99-94 5.00-5.37	103-94 4.83-5.38	104-76 4.77-6.79	90-63 5.66-8.24	91-54 5.59-9.61
16. Illinois Bell Telephone first and refunding 5% due 1956 "A"	105-101 4.67-4.96	107-103 4.54-4.80	108-100 4.47-5.00	107-97 4.52-5.27	108-106 4.44-4.58
17. Illinois Power & Light first and refunding 5% due 1956 "C"	97-92 5.21-5.58	100-92 5.00-5.59	99-67 5.07-8.10	83-49 6.48-11.13	71-43 7.81-12.68
18. Milwaukee Electric Railway & Light first 5% due 1961 "B"	102-97 4.88-5.19	104-97 4.75-5.20	105-84 4.69-6.18	95-73 5.34-7.24	87-63 5.96-8.48

TABLE A.13 (continued)

Issues	1929	1930	1931	1932	1933
19. New England Telephone & Telegraph first 4½% due 1961 "B"	$101-96 4.44%-4.74	$105-98 4.21%-4.62	$108-93 4.04%-4.95	$105-91 4.20%-5.10	$108-97 4.02%-4.69
20. New York Power & Light first 4½% due 1967	95-88 4.79-5.23	98-90 4.61-5.10	101-80 4.44-5.84	97-73 4.67-6.45	99-73 4.56-6.47
21. Ohio Power first and refunding 4½% due 1956 "D"	95-89 4.83-5.27	100-91 4.50-5.13	102-85 4.37-5.62	97-74 4.71-6.69	100-81 4.50-6.04
22. Pacific Gas & Electric first and refunding 5½% due 1952 "C"	104-103 5.20-5.27	106-104 5.05-5.19	107-98 4.96-5.66	107-95 4.94-5.93	107-95 4.93-5.94
23. Pacific Gas & Electric first and refunding 4½% due 1960 "F"	-	99-95 4.56-4.82	103-85 4.32-5.55	100-82 4.50-5.81	102-83 4.37-5.75
24. Pennsylvania Power & Light first 4½% due 1981	-	-	100-80 4.50-5.72	95-73 4.76-6.28	97-76 4.66-6.04
25. Philadelphia Co. secured 5% due 1967 "A"	100-96 5.00-5.24	103-96 4.83-5.25	104-80 4.77-6.43	90-68 5.66-7.63	91-61 5.59-8.53
26. Philadelphia Electric first refunding 4% due 1971	-	-	100-81 4.00-5.12	100-83 4.00-4.99	100-89 4.00-4.62
27. Public Service Co. of Northern Illinois 4½% due 1981 "F"	-	-	100-75 4.51-6.11	88-58 5.18-7.89	93-53 4.88-8.63

TABLE A.13 (continued)

	1929	1930	1931	1932	1933
28. Public Service Electric & Gas first and refunding 4½% due 1967	$100-97 4.50%-4.79	$103-95 4.34%-4.79	$106-94 4.18%-4.85	$104-91 4.28%-5.05	$106-97 4.17%-4.68
29. Southern California Edison refunding 5% due 1951	103-97 4.78-5.23	106-100 4.55-5.00	106-97 4.54-5.24	105-94 4.60-5.51	106-92 4.51-5.72
30. Southwestern Bell Telephone first and refunding 5% due 1954 "A"	105-101 4.66-4.95	107-103 4.52-4.79	108-98 4.44-5.15	107-97 4.50-5.23	108-100 4.41-5.00
Average Yields - Aaa bonds(c) Number of Aaa bonds	4.60-4.87 8	4.37-4.82 8	4.24-5.04 9	4.33-5.18 8	4.24-4.92 8
Average Yields - Aa bonds(c) Number of Aa bonds	4.82-5.07 4	4.58-4.98 6	4.37-5.39 10	4.60-5.80 10	4.49-5.66 10
Average Yields - A bonds(c) Number of A bonds	4.90-5.29 5	4.72-5.20 5	4.62-6.63 6	5.20-7.19 6	5.00-8.05 6
Average Yields - Baa bonds(c) Number of Baa bonds	5.03-5.38 4	4.85-5.30 4	4.93-7.45 5	5.75-8.62 6	6.11-9.71 6

Source: Moody's Utility Manual 1934.

Notes:
(a)   Quotes above $10 are rounded off to the nearest dollar.
(b)   Yields are calculated assuming purchase and maturity at mid-year.
(c)   Ratings are as shown in Moody's Utility Manual for the following year.   i.e. 1932 manual = 1931 rating.

TABLE A.14

Price and Yield Ranges for Industrial Bond Issues over $20 Million Maturing after December 31, 1939   1929-1933

Issues	1929	1930	1931	1932	1933
1. Aluminum Company of America 5% due 1952	$104-100(a) 4.71%-5.00(b)	$105-100 4.64%-5.00	$106-93 4.55%-5.57	$100-81 5.00%-6.74	$99-80 5.08%-6.91
2. American Smelting & Refining first 5% due 1947	102-98 4.83-5.17	104-100 4.66-5.00	104-86 4.64-6.41	96-73 5.39-8.15	100-78 5.00-7.58
3. Batavian Petroleum 4½% due 1942	95-90 5.03-5.19	96-92 4.95-5.48	97-73 4.86-8.29	94-71 5.28-8.95	104-90 3.97-5.95
4. General Steel Castings 5½% due 1949	106-89 4.93-6.49	106-89 5.01-6.52	96-59 5.86-10.67	74-38 8.40-16.44	85-47 7.08-13.79
5. Goodyear Tire & Rubber first collateral 5% due 1957	95-85 5.35-6.13	96-83 5.28-6.32	93-64 5.51-8.44	88-62 5.93-8.78	92-68 5.61-8.03
6. Gulf Oil of Pennsylvania debenture 5% due 1947	102-99 4.83-5.09	104-99 4.66-5.09	104-86 4.64-6.41	100-83 5.00-6.83	102-92 4.80-5.84
7. Inland Steel first 4½% due 1978 "A"	94-90 4.82-5.25	99-91 4.55-5.00	98-73 4.60-6.30	88-60 5.19-7.67	90-66 5.07-6.99

TABLE A.14 (continued)

Issues	1929	1930	1931	1932	1933
8. Koppers Gas & Coke 5¼% due 1950	-	$104-100 5.18%-5.50	$104-69 5.17%-8.91	$91-52 6.35%-12.11	$88-72 6.69%-8.68
9. National Dairy Products 5¼ due 1948	99-92 5.33-5.96	101-95 5.16-5.70	103-84 4.99-6.86	96-72 5.63-8.48	96-75 5.65-8.17
10. National Steel first collateral 5% due 1956	-	-	99-68 5.07-7.97	85-60 6.21-9.14	96-69 5.30-7.96
11. Pittsburgh Coal 6% due 1949	-	103-96 5.74-6.37	99-74 6.09-8.93	90-68 7.02-9.94	98-82 6.20-8.02
12. Pure Oil 5½% due 1940	-	100-87 5.59-7.36	94-62 6.39-12.71	85-60 8.08-13.96	90-64 7.35-13.65
13. Royal Dutch debenture 4% due 1945 "A"	-	92-86 4.75-5.37	93-66 4.69-8.11	88-65 5.29-8.50	104-83 3.59-6.01
14. Shell Pipe Line debenture 5% due 1952	98-91 5.15-5.71	98-81 5.15-6.66	93-60 5.57-9.40	87-57 6.14-10.02	93-69 5.60-8.26
15. Shell Union Oil 5% due 1947	99-92 5.09-5.72	98-71 5.18-8.19	88-57 6.19-10.66	86-47 6.47-13.20	92-65 5.84-9.60
16. Standard Oil (N.J.) debenture 5% due 1946	104-100 4.66-5.00	105-101 4.51-4.95	106-99 4.45-5.10	105-99 4.51-5.10	106-100 4.39-5.00
17. Standard Oil (N.Y.) debenture 4½% due 1951	100-92 4.50-5.11	101-95 4.43-4.88	101-83 4.42-5.97	98-82 4.66-6.11	102-88 4.34-5.56

TABLE A.14 (continued)

Issues	1929	1930	1931	1932	1933
18. Swift & Co. 5% due 1940	-	$101-99 4.87%-5.13	$103-89 4.59%-6.64	$95-67 5.79%-11.40	$101-87 4.83%-7.41
19. Union Gulf Corp. collateral 5% due 1950	-	102-99 4.84-5.08	103-90 4.76-5.86	101-84 4.92-6.52	103-96 4.74-5.36
20. Youngstown Sheet & Tube first 5% due 1978 "A"	101-99 4.95-5.06	105-100 4.74-5.00	104-45 4.79-11.19	75-44 6.78-11.45	86-52 5.89-9.74
Average Yields - Aaa bonds(c)	4.76-5.20	4.69-5.14	4.54-5.64	4.59-5.61	4.37-5.28
Number of Aaa bonds	4	6	3	2	2
Average Yields - Aa bonds(c)	4.79-5.07	4.62-5.00	4.64-6.41	4.92-6.52	4.87-6.47
Number of Aa bonds	3	3	1	1	2
Average Yields - A bonds(c)	5.14-5.58	4.98-5.62	4.71-6.88	5.32-8.77	4.50-6.63
Number of A bonds	3	4	7	5	5
Average Yields - Baa bonds(c)	5.14-6.31	5.32-6.39	5.42-9.77	5.89-9.30	5.66-8.40
Number of Baa bonds	2	3	6	8	7
Average Yields - Ba bonds(c)	--	5.31-7.03	6.05-10.09	7.49-13.39	6.62-11.27
Number of Ba bonds	--	3	3	4	4

TABLE A.14 (continued)

Source: Moody's Industrial Manual 1934.

Notes:

(a) Quotes above $10 are rounded off to the nearest dollar.

(b) Yields are calculated assuming purchase and maturity at mid-year.

(c) Ratings are as shown in Moody's Industrial Manual for the following year. i.e. 1932 Manual = 1931 rating.

TABLE A. 15
Price and Yield Ranges for Representative Foreign Bond Issues in U.S. Dollars 1929-1933

Issues	1929	1930	1931	1932	1933
1. Argentine gold 5% due 1949 ($27.0)(a)	$93-85(b) / 5.59%-6.33(c)	$93-82 / 5.60%-6.69	$88-40 / 6.30%-15.72	$67-41 / 9.46%-15.84	$92-50 / 5.94%-13.54
2. Australia gold 5% due 1952/1955 ($73.3)	97-90 / 5.21-5.75	94-70 / 5.44-7.73	76-35 / 7.10-15.16	89-47 / 5.88-11.68	90-71 / 5.81-7.77
3. Austria gold 7% due 1957 ($23.1)	—	95-87 / 7.43-8.20	98-35 / 7.14-20.25	55-20 / 13.19-NM(d)	65-42 / 11.24-17.13
4. Belgium gold 6% due 1955 ($34.6)	102-98 / 5.85-6.16	106-100 / 5.55-6.00	105-72 / 5.62-8.83	100-80 / 6.00-7.90	98-78 / 6.17-7.18
5. Berlin gold 6% due 1958 ($13.9)	93-81 / 6.54-7.64	94-64 / 6.47-9.78	84-14 / 7.37-NM	48-15 / 13.05-NM	57-24 / 11.13-NM
6. Bolivia external refunding 8% due 1947 ($22.1)	104-87 / 7.59-9.52	100-35 / 8.00-23.84	55-6 1/2 / 15.79-NM	10-3 1/4 / NM-NM	15-4 / NM-NM
7. Brazil 8% due 1941 ($31.4)	97-65 / 8.40-14.14	89-46 / 9.64-20.56	71-13 / 13.33-NM	25-14 / NM-NM	39-16 / 26.94-NM

TABLE A.15 (continued)

Issues	1929	1930	1931	1932	1933
8. City of Buenos Aires 6% due 1961 ($38.9)	$94-83 6.45%-7.39	$91-62 6.69%-9.99	$84-20 7.32%-NM	$38-17 16.09%-NM	$43-16 14.35%-NM
9. Canada 4% due 1960 ($100.0)	-	96-95 4.24-4.30	97-64 4.18-6.88	92-71 4.51-6.19	93-79 4.45-5.50
10. Chile 6% due 1961 ($44.2)	94-86 6.45-7.11	97-70 6.45-8.85	86-9 1/4 7.14-NM	15-3 1/2 NM-NM	17-4 7/8 NM-NM
11. Cuba external sinking fund gold 5½% due 1951 "A" ($11.7)	107-98 5.00-5.65	102-97 5.35-5.74	99-70 5.58-8.55	83-66 7.06-9.18	84-61 7.00-10.06
12. Czechoslovakia gold 8% due 1951 "A" ($11.7)	11-106 7.01-7.44	112-109 6.91-7.16	111-80 6.97-10.39	101-68 7.89-12.42	99-86 8.11-9.65
13. Denmark 4½% due 1962 ($51.9)	92-85 5.00-5.49	95-91 4.81-5.07	100-51 4.50-9.38	82-47 5.77-10.19	77-58 6.22-8.38
14. Finland gold 5½% due 1958 ($13.7)	92-83 6.09-6.86	92-73 6.10-7.91	89-34 6.36-16.62	68-35 8.60-16.24	77-54 7.56-10.89
15. France gold 7% due 1949 ($66.7)	114-106 5.81-6.46	121-112 5.24-6.94	122-109 5.12-6.17	121-109 5.13-6.14	173-113 1.75-5.75
16. Germany International 5½% due 1965 ($98.3)	-	91-68 6.13-8.33	84-22 6.70-NM	60-24 8.76-NM	64-35 8.92-15.93

TABLE A.15 (continued)

Issues	1929	1930	1931	1932	1933
17. Italy Gold 7% due 1951 ($84.6)	$98-92 7.18%-7.76	$101-89 6.91%-8.10	$101-79 6.90%-9.34	$99-82 7.10%-8.99	$105-85 6.52%-8.66
18. Japan 5½% due 1965 ($71.0)	–	100-90 5.50-6.20	99-69 5.57-8.23	74-43 7.68-13.06	81-36 6.99-15.51
19. Mexico gold 4% due 1945 ($50.7)	13-10 NM-NM	22-9 NM-NM	12-2 NM-NM	5-2 NM-NM	8-3 NM-NM
20. Norway 5% due 1963 ($30.0)	98-92 5.13-6.52	85-63 6.06-8.29	102-60 4.88-8.74	85-63 6.08-8.36	93-73 5.48-7.21
21. Peru 6% due 1960 ($48.4)	90-68 6.78-9.11	84-33 7.32-18.37	40-5 1/4 15.32-NM	10-3 NM-NM	14-3 1/2 NM-NM
22. Poland gold 8% due 1950 ($23.1)	99-81 8.10-10.21	98-70 8.21-11.98	90-32 9.12-25.27	65-44 13.11-19.12	74-59 11.52-14.58
23. City of Rio Grande do Sul 6% due 1968 ($23.0)	92-65 6.57-9.38	80-35 7.62-17.70	56-7 1/2 10.89-NM	12-4 1/2 NM-NM	31-8 1/4 19.42-NM
24. Rio de Janeiro 6% due 1953 ($29.5)	96-68 6.35-9.37	85-43 7.36-14.72	68-7 1/2 10.17-NM	14-5 NM-NM	26-6 1/2 NM-NM
25. Sweden gold 5½% due 1954 ($30.0)	106-101 5.07-5.43	107-103 5.10-5.28	107-68 4.99-8.75	97-75 5.74-7.92	110-88 4.75-6.56
26. Swiss Confederation 5½% due 1946 ($30.0)	105-100 5.06-5.50	106-103 4.95-5.22	107-99 4.84-5.55	106-101 4.90-5.40	NA(e)

TABLE A.15 (continued)

Issues	1929	1930	1931	1932	1933
27. United Kingdom 5½% due 1937 ($136.3)	$105-101 4.74%-5.34	$106-103 4.49%-4.99	$109-88 3.81%-8.06	$107-90 3.94%-7.96	$125-102 (0.65)%-4.94
28. Uruguay gold 6% due 1960 ($27.7)	100-92 6.00-6.61	100-70 6.00-8.87	89-21 6.88-NM	40-20 15.37-NM	40-16 15.43-NM
29. Yugoslavia 7% due 1962 ($28.9)	89-71 7.95-10.03	88-75 8.05-9.50	85-29 8.36-NM	45-14 15.76-NM	24-13 NM-NM
Average Yields - Aaa bonds Number of Aaa bonds	5.04-5.51 6	4.93-5.53 6	3.81-8.06 1	3.94-7.96 1	–
Average Yields - Aa bonds Number of Aa bonds	5.75-6.32 3	5.58-6.82 6	4.88-7.76 7	5.76-6.71 5	2.58-5.69 4
Average Yields - A bonds Number of A bonds	6.41-7.50 10	6.48-8.29 9	6.34-14.74 3	5.93-9.28 2	6.10-7.86 4
Average Yields - Baa bonds Number of Baa bonds	7.61-10.81 4	7.63-15.03 3	6.99-14.27 9-6(f)	7.80-12.49 8-7	7.22-12.21 6
Average Yields - Ba or lower bonds Number of Ba or lower bonds	7.95-10.03 1	8.33-17.78 4	11.05-NM 8	14.43-19.12 6-1	14.63-13.92 8-3

616

TABLE A.15 (continued)

Source: Moody's Government Manual 1934.

Notes:
(a) Amounts outstanding are in millions as reported in Moody's Governments Manual 1934.
(b) Quotes above $10 are rounded off to the nearest dollar.
(c) Yields are calculated assuming purchase and maturity at mid-year.
(d) Yields at prices below $30 are treated as not meaningful and indicated by NM.
(e) NA = not available.
(f) Numbers of issues for Baa or lower bonds are shown for both high and low yields because yields on bonds with prices below $30 were not calculated.

TABLE A.16

Representative Municipal Bond Interest Rates 1929–1933

Issuer	Total debt(a) ($millions)	1929 High %	1929 Low %	1930 High %	1930 Low %	1931 High %	1931 Low %	1932 High %	1932 Low %	1933 High %	1933 Low %
Alabama	60	4.50(b)	4.25	4.95	4.10	5.00	4.00	6.00	5.00	6.50	5.00
Arkansas	160	4.80	4.40	4.85	4.35	5.00(c)	4.60	6.90	6.10	14.68(d)	7.36
California	137	4.40	4.10	4.15	3.85	4.10	3.55	4.40	3.75	4.40	3.75
Los Angeles	231	4.65	4.30	4.50	4.00	4.40	3.90	5.50	4.40	5.75	4.60
San Francisco	159	4.60	4.30	4.50	4.05	4.50	4.00	5.00	4.35	5.15	4.30
Connecticut	13	4.10	3.95	4.10	4.10	4.00	3.30	4.00	3.50	3.50	2.00
Delaware	3	4.35	4.15	4.20	3.90	4.25	3.60	4.25	3.50	3.75	3.50
Miami	30	5.75	5.00	6.25	5.50	10.85	8.35	NM(e)	11.00	$23bid(f)	$40bid
Georgia	4	4.25	3.90	4.10	3.75	3.80	3.50	4.00	3.75	3.80	3.25
Idaho	4	4.75	4.25	4.75	4.30	4.50	4.10	4.50	4.25	5.50	4.25
Illinois	208	4.50	4.10	4.20	3.90	4.50	3.50	5.0	3.90	4.50	3.70
Chicago	426	4.60	4.20	4.40	4.00	6.50	4.05	6.50	5.20	7.04	5.14
Iowa	12	4.30	4.10	4.25	3.90	4.15	3.60	4.60	4.00	4.35	3.00
Kansas	22	4.40	4.10	4.20	3.90	4.00	3.60	4.50	3.75	4.00	3.75
Louisiana	127	4.80	4.30	4.80	4.40	5.00(c)	4.25	6.25	5.50	9.00	6.00
Maine	30	4.25	4.00	4.15	3.85	3.90	3.50	4.20	3.60	4.25	3.30

TABLE A.16 (continued)

Issuer	Total debt(a) ($millions)	1929 High %	1929 Low %	1930 High %	1930 Low %	1931 High %	1931 Low %	1932 High %	1932 Low %	1933 High %	1933 Low %
Maryland	35	4.25	4.00	4.15	3.80	4.10	3.45	4.75	3.50	4.00	3.00
Baltimore	174	4.25	4.15	4.15	3.85	4.30	3.65	4.90	3.95	5.00	3.90
Massachusetts	115	4.10	3.95	4.00	3.80	4.35	3.50	4.50	3.65	4.10	3.00
Boston	125	4.15	3.95	4.00	3.85	4.60	3.60	5.00	4.30	5.50	4.25
Michigan	83	4.30	4.15	4.40	4.00	(c)	3.60	(c)	(c)	5.25	4.10
Detroit	394	4.50	4.20	4.50	4.10	5.00(c)	4.05	(c)	(c)	16.42	11.55
Minnesota	114	4.40	4.00	4.15	3.90	4.00	3.50	4.50	4.00	4.35	3.70
Minneapolis	59	4.50	4.15	4.40	3.90	4.15	3.50	4.70	4.90	5.00	3.90
Mississippi	39	4.70	4.30	4.60	4.20	5.00	4.20	6.25	5.00	6.00	6.00
Missouri	111	4.35	4.10	4.20	3.90	4.40	3.50	4.60	3.75	4.25	3.40
St. Louis	70	4.45	4.10	4.20	3.95	4.50	3.50	4.80	3.70	4.30	3.60
Montana	5	4.90	4.30	4.60	4.25	4.75	4.05	4.80	4.40	4.90	4.50
New Hampshire	7	4.20	4.10	4.10	3.90	4.20	3.75	4.20(c)	3.70	4.05	3.20
New Jersey	164	4.35	4.15	4.30	3.90	4.20	3.40	4.40	3.80	4.30	3.50
New Mexico	11	5.00	4.50	4.70	4.40	4.60	4.10	4.90	4.40	7.33	5.25

TABLE A.16 (continued)

Issuer	Total debt(a) ($millions)	1929 High %	1929 Low %	1930 High %	1930 Low %	1931 High %	1931 Low %	1932 High %	1932 Low %	1933 High %	1933 Low %
New York	437	4.00	3.90	4.00	3.60	4.00	3.35	3.95	3.25	3.95	3.30
New York City	2071	4.30	4.10	4.30	3.95	5.25	3.80	5.40	4.55	6.20	4.80
North Carolina	172	4.50	4.15	4.35	3.95	(c)	3.85	5.60	4.75	6.50	4.90
North Dakota	41	4.90	4.50	4.90	4.10	4.75	4.10	5.25	4.75	6.00	5.25
Ohio(g)	6	5.00	4.50	4.50	3.75	5.50	3.00	6.50	5.50	NA(h)	NA
Cleveland	125	4.50	4.15	4.30	3.80	5.00	3.80	5.50	4.75	8.10(i)	5.00
Oklahoma	1	4.50	4.00	4.40	4.00	4.00	4.00	3.90	3.90	3.90	3.90
Oregon	54	4.40	4.10	4.30	4.00	4.00	3.75	4.35	4.15	5.75	4.15
Pennsylvania	87	4.00	3.90	3.95	3.85	3.85	3.50	3.85	3.70	3.50	2.90
Philadelphia	449	4.10	4.00	4.05	4.00	4.75	3.80	5.50	4.75	6.05	4.80
Rhode Island	21	4.30	4.00	4.25	3.95	4.25	3.55	4.35	3.60	4.00	3.40
South Carolina	35	4.35	4.15	4.35	4.10	4.20	4.05	5.80	4.15	7.00	5.50
South Dakota	50	4.60	4.25	4.50	4.10	(c)	4.00	6.00(c)	5.75	8.00	6.00
Tennessee	88	4.60	4.35	4.50	4.00	5.75	3.95	5.75	5.00	7.00	5.10

TABLE A.16 (continued)

Issuer	Total debt(a) ($millions)	1929 High %	1929 Low %	1930 High %	1930 Low %	1931 High %	1931 Low %	1932 High %	1932 Low %	1933 High %	1933 Low %
Utah	10	4.40	4.20	4.30	4.00	4.50	3.60	3.60	3.50	4.25	3.40
Vermont	8	4.10	4.00	4.10	3.75	4.50	3.65	4.50(c)	3.65	3.90	3.40
Virginia 3%/91(j)	21	4.25	4.05	4.15	3.70	3.70	3.25	3.80	3.35	3.45	3.10
Washington	5	4.25	4.15	4.80	4.80	(c)	(c)	(c)	(c)	4.25	3.90
West Virginia	87	4.40	4.05	4.20	3.75	4.50	3.50	4.70	3.70	4.35	3.60
Milwaukee	47	4.60	4.20	4.45	3.90	4.20	3.60	4.60	4.00	5.50	4.50

TABLE A.16 (continued)

Source: The Bank and Quotation Record, published monthly by The Commercial & Financial Chronicle.

Notes: (a)   As reported in Moody's Governments Manual 1934.

(b)   Yields shown are for the longest term issues with the closest coupons to market rates and indicate the levels at which business was generally transacted during a month. A single issue could not be followed because most issues were too small to be consistently quoted and representative.

(c)   At points during the year there were no quotes for these bonds due to uncertainties about their creditworthiness.

(d)   Arkansas defaulted in August, 1933, and its bonds traded flat thereafter on a current yield basis, i.e. all 5% bonds had one price, irrespective of maturity. This yield is for 4½% bonds due in 1951.

(e)   NM = not meaningful.

(f)   All Miami bonds, irrespective of coupon or maturity, traded at the same price.

(g)   Ohio quotes are based on notes due in 1932.

(h)   NA = not available.

(i)   Cleveland bonds traded flat on a current yield basis in December, 1933. i.e. all 5% bonds had one price, irrespective of maturity. The 8.10% yield is for 4½% bonds due in 1953.

(j)   Virginia quotes are based on a single 3% issue due in 1991.

TABLE A.17

Short-Term Open Market Interest Rates   1927-1934 weekly

| | Prevailing rates on– | | | Average rate on New York Stock Exchange call loans | |
	Prime com- mercial paper 4 to 6 months	Prime bankers' accept- ances 90 days	New York Stock Exchange time loans 90 days	New	Renewal
1927					
January 1	4.50%	3.75%	4.69%	5.57%	5.60%
January 8	4.38	3.75	4.56	4.75	4.85
January 15	4.25	3.63	4.50	4.12	4.15
January 22	4.25	3.69	4.50	4.23	4.35
January 29	4.13	3.69	4.50	4.00	4.00
February 5	4.13	3.69	4.44	4.00	4.00
February 12	4.13	3.63	4.44	4.00	4.00
February 19	4.00	3.75	4.38	4.02	4.00
February 26	4.00	3.75	4.38	4.12	4.00
March 5	4.00	3.69	4.44	4.16	4.20
March 12	4.13	3.63	4.44	4.00	4.00
March 19	4.13	3.63	4.44	3.93	4.00
March 26	4.13	3.63	4.44	4.23	4.20
April 2	4.13	3.63	4.50	4.47	4.40
April 9	4.13	3.63	4.50	4.18	4.15
April 16	4.13	3.63	4.50	4.48	4.44
April 23	4.13	3.63	4.50	4.02	4.10
April 30	4.13	3.63	4.38	4.14	4.40
May 7	4.13	3.63	4.38	4.15	4.20
May 14	4.13	3.63	4.38	4.25	4.15
May 21	4.13	3.63	4.38	4.16	4.25
May 28	4.13	3.63	4.44	4.47	4.40
June 4	4.25	3.63	4.50	4.50	4.50
June 11	4.25	3.63	4.50	4.19	4.35
June 18	4.25	3.63	4.50	4.03	4.19
June 25	4.25	3.00	4.50	4.00	4.00
July 2	6.25	3.09	4.63	4.71	4.80
July 9	4.25	3.63	4.50	4.15	4.25
July 16	4.25	3.63	4.50	4.60	4.00
July 23	4.25	3.56	4.44	3.31	3.95
July 30	4.25	3.38	4.38	3.73	3.85
August 6	4.13	3.13	4.38	3.66	3.93
August 13	4.00	3.13	4.25	3.75	3.75
August 20	4.00	3.13	4.25	3.60	3.65
August 27	4.00	3.13	4.00	3.50	3.50

TABLE A.17 (continued)

	Prevailing rates on—			Average rate on New York Stock Exchange call loans	
	Prime commercial paper 4 to 6 months	Prime bankers' accept- ances 90 days	New York Stock Exchange time loans 90 days	New	Renewal
September 3	4.00%	3.13%	4.00%	3.50%	3.50%
September 10	4.00	3.13	4.13	3.59	3.50
September 17	4.00	3.13	4.13	3.94	3.85
September 34	4.00	3.13	4.23	3.99	3.95
October 1	4.00	3.13	4.25	3.92	4.00
October 8	4.00	3.19	4.25	4.18	4.20
October 15	4.00	3.25	4.38	4.10	4.00
October 22	4.00	3.25	4.38	4.75	3.90
October 29	4.00	3.25	4.25	3.50	3.50
November 5	4.00	3.25	4.25	3.61	3.70
November 12	4.00	3.25	4.19	3.50	3.50
November 19	4.00	3.25	4.19	3.50	3.50
November 26	4.00	3.25	4.13	3.50	3.50
December 3	4.00	3.25	4.13	4.27	4.10
December 10	4.00	3.25	4.25	4.08	4.20
December 17	4.00	3.25	4.19	4.00	4.00
December 24	4.00	3.25	4.19	4.36	4.20
December 31	4.00	3.25	4.25	5.48	5.38
1928					
January 7	4.00	3.25	4.25	4.57	4.88
January 14	3.88	3.38	4.31	4.20	4.20
January 21	4.00	3.38	4.44	3.85	4.10
January 28	4.00	3.38	4.44	3.82	3.70
February 4	4.00	3.50	4.44	4.45	4.55
February 11	4.00	3.50	4.56	4.34	4.40
February 18	4.00	3.50	4.56	4.42	4.44
February 25	4.00	3.50	4.56	4.21	4.25
March 3	4.00	3.50	4.56	4.42	4.45
March 10	4.13	3.50	4.56	4.25	4.25
March 17	4.13	3.50	4.63	4.50	4.50
March 24	4.13	3.50	4.63	4.45	4.45
March 31	4.13	3.50	4.69	4.73	4.65
April 7	4.25	3.69	4.81	5.20	5.00
April 14	4.25	3.75	4.94	5.39	5.45
April 21	4.38	4.88	5.00	4.71	4.90
April 28	4.50	3.88	5.00	4.98	4.95

TABLE A.17 (continued)

	Prevailing rates on—			Average rate on New York Stock Exchange call loans	
	Prime commercial paper 4 to 6 months	Prime bankers' acceptances 90 days	New York Stock Exchange time loans 90 days	New	Renewal
May 5	4.50%	3.88%	5.00%	5.25%	5.30%
May 12	4.50	3.88	5.00	5.67	5.60
May 19	4.50	3.88	5.00	5.67	5.60
May 26	4.63	4.06	5.50	6.00	6.00
June 2	4.63	4.06	5.50	6.10	6.00
June 9	4.63	4.00	5.69	6.09	6.10
June 16	4.75	4.00	5.75	5.80	5.80
June 23	4.88	4.06	5.75	6.21	6.00
June 30	4.88	4.13	5.94	7.20	7.00
July 7	4.88	4.13	5.88	6.59	6.75
July 14	5.13	6.25	5.88	6.55	6.40
July 21	5.13	4.38	6.00	5.44	5.80
July 28	5.25	4.50	6.00	5.50	5.50
August 4	5.25	4.73	6.00	6.77	6.60
August 11	5.38	4.63	6.25	6.91	6.50
August 18	5.38	4.63	6.38	6.27	6.60
August 25	5.38	4.63	6.50	7.05	6.80
September 1	5.50	4.63	6.50	7.45	7.40
September 8	5.63	4.50	6.50	7.69	7.50
September 15	5.63	4.50	7.00	7.39	7.40
September 22	5.50	4.50	7.38	7.65	7.30
September 29	5.50	4.50	7.38	6.93	6.90
October 6	5.50	4.50	7.25	7.70	7.50
October 13	5.50	4.50	7.13	6.42	6.50
October 20	5.50	4.50	7.00	7.06	7.00
October 27	5.50	4.50	6.94	6.85	6.30
November 3	5.50	4.50	6.94	7.83	7.50
November 10	5.50	4.50	7.00	6.25	6.38
November 17	5.28	4.50	6.68	6.20	6.20
November 24	5.38	4.50	6.94	6.50	6.50
December 1	5.28	4.50	7.00	8.39	7.38
December 8	5.38	4.50	7.13	9.87	8.80
December 15	5.38	4.50	7.75	7.25	8.00
December 22	5.38	4.50	7.75	7.26	7.20
December 29	5.38	4.50	7.75	10.83	10.00

TABLE A.17 (continued)

	Prevailing rates on—			Average rate on New York Stock Exchange call loans	
	Prime commercial paper 4 to 6 months	Prime bankers' acceptances 90 days	New York Stock Exchange time loans 90 days	New	Renewal
1929					
January 5	5.38%	4.50%	7.63%	9.37%	10.50%
January 12	5.38	4.75	7.75	6.61	6.60
January 19	5.38	4.75	7.75	7.27	7.20
January 26	5.50	5.00	7.75	6.00	6.00
February 2	5.50	5.00	7.63	7.10	6.60
February 9	5.50	5.00	7.63	7.05	6.60
February 16	5.50	5.13	7.75	7.42	7.13
February 23	5.63	5.25	7.75	6.61	7.00
March 2	5.63	5.25	7.75	8.65	7.70
March 9	5.75	5.25	7.75	9.90	8.80
March 16	5.75	5.25	7.88	7.32	7.40
March 23	5.88	5.38	8.00	8.97	8.40
March 30	5.88	5.54	8.00	14.40	12.75
April 6	5.88	5.50	9.00	10.12	10.00
April 13	6.00	5.50	9.00	8.48	8.00
April 20	6.00	5.50	8.75	7.91	7.90
April 27	6.00	5.38	8.38	9.95	8.00
May 4	6.00	5.38	8.50	11.33	11.40
May 11	6.00	5.50	8.75	11.83	12.40
May 18	6.00	5.50	8.88	9.40	9.20
May 25	6.00	5.50	9.00	6.48	6.60
June 1	6.00	5.50	8.88	6.00	6.00
June 8	6.00	5.50	8.38	6.96	6.80
June 15	6.00	5.50	8.25	7.56	7.60
June 22	6.00	5.50	8.00	7.00	7.00
June 29	6.00	5.50	7.88	9.79	9.40
July 6	6.00	5.31	7.50	11.05	11.00
July 13	6.00	5.13	7.50	8.88	8.60
July 20	6.00	5.13	7.75	9.56	9.80
July 27	6.00	5.13	8.13	8.18	7.60
August 3	6.00	5.13	8.75	10.26	9.80
August 10	6.00	5.13	8.88	9.11	9.60
August 17	6.13	5.13	8.88	7.13	7.40
August 24	6.13	5.13	8.88	6.76	7.00
August 31	6.13	5.13	8.88	8.54	8.20

TABLE A.17 (continued)

	Prevailing rates on–			Average rate on New York Stock Exchange call loans	
	Prime commercial paper 4 to 6 months	Prime bankers' acceptances 90 days	New York Stock Exchange time loans 90 days	New	Renewal
September 7	6.13%	5.13%	8.88%	8.65%	9.00%
September 14	6.25	5.13	8.88	8.09	8.20
September 21	6.25	5.13	9.00	8.48	8.40
September 28	6.25	5.13	9.13	9.03	8.40
October 5	6.25	5.13	9.13	8.08	8.20
October 12	6.25	5.13	8.63	5.63	6.20
October 19	6.25	5.13	7.75	6.28	6.40
October 26	6.25	4.94	7.25	5.35	6.00
November 2	6.13	4.63	6.00	5.94	5.80
November 9	5.88	4.63	6.00	6.00	6.00
November 16	5.88	4.38	5.75	5.90	5.90
November 23	5.63	3.81	5.25	4.86	5.00
November 30	5.38	3.81	4.88	4.50	4.50
December 7	5.13	3.81	4.63	4.50	4.50
December 14	5.00	3.88	4.88	4.50	4.50
December 21	5.00	3.88	4.88	4.56	4.50
December 28	5.00	4.00	4.98	5.64	5.50
1930					
January 4	5.00	3.94	4.88	5.96	6.00
January 11	5.00	3.88	4.75	4.25	4.60
January 18	4.88	4.00	4.69	4.24	4.50
January 25	4.88	4.00	4.75	4.06	4.50
February 1	4.88	4.00	4.63	4.12	4.40
February 8	4.88	3.81	4.88	4.22	4.40
February 15	4.63	3.75	4.69	4.19	4.00
February 22	4.63	3.75	4.75	4.40	4.40
March 1	4.63	3.75	4.63	4.28	4.40
March 8	4.63	3.54	4.50	3.84	4.00
March 15	4.50	3.25	4.25	3.54	3.90
March 22	4.00	2.81	3.88	2.97	3.00
March 29	3.88	2.63	4.00	3.78	3.80
April 5	3.86	2.86	4.60	4.00	4.60
April 12	3.88	2.88	4.25	3.67	4.00
April 19	3.88	2.94	4.25	3.83	4.00
April 26	3.86	3.00	4.13	3.54	4.60

TABLE A.17 (continued)

	Prevailing rates on–			Average rate on New York Stock Exchange call loans	
	Prime commercial paper 4 to 6 months	Prime bankers' acceptances 90 days	New York Stock Exchange time loans 90 days	New	Renewal
May 4	6.00%	5.38%	8.50%	11.33%	11.40%
May 11	6.00	5.50	8.75	11.83	12.40
May 18	6.00	5.50	8.88	9.40	9.20
May 25	6.00	5.50	9.00	6.48	6.60
June 1	6.00	5.50	8.88	6.00	6.00
June 8	6.00	5.50	8.38	6.96	6.80
June 15	6.00	5.50	8.25	7.56	7.60
June 22	6.00	5.50	8.00	7.00	7.00
June 29	6.00	5.50	7.88	9.79	9.40
July 6	6.00	5.31	7.50	11.05	11.00
July 13	6.00	5.13	7.50	8.88	8.60
July 20	6.00	5.13	7.75	9.56	9.80
July 27	6.00	5.13	8.13	8.18	7.60
August 3	6.00	5.13	8.75	10.26	9.80
August 10	6.00	5.13	8.88	9.11	9.60
August 17	6.13	5.13	8.88	7.13	7.40
August 24	6.13	5.13	8.88	6.76	7.00
August 31	6.13	5.13	8.88	8.54	8.20
September 7	6.13	5.13	8.88	8.65	9.00
September 14	6.25	5.13	8.88	8.09	8.20
September 21	6.25	5.13	9.00	8.48	8.40
September 21	6.25	5.13	9.00	8.48	8.40
September 28	6.25	5.13	9.13	9.03	8.40
October 5	6.25	5.13	9113	8.08	8.20
October 12	6.25	5.13	8.63	5.63	6.20
October 19	6.25	5.13	7.75	6.28	6.40
October 26	6.25	4.94	7.25	5.35	6.00
November 2	6.13	4.63	6.00	5.94	5.80
November 9	5.88	4.63	6.00	6.00	6.00
November 16	5.88	4.38	5.75	5.90	5.90
November 23	5.63	3.81	5.25	4.86	5.00
November 30	5.38	3.81	4.98	4.50	4.50
December 7	5.13	3.81	4.63	4.50	4.50
December 14	5.00	3.88	4.98	4.50	4.50
December 21	5.00	3.88	4.88	4.56	4.50
December 28	5.00	4.00	4.98	5.64	5.50

TABLE A.17 (continued)

	Prevailing rates on–			Average rate on New York Stock Exchange call loans	
	Prime commercial paper 4 to 6 months	Prime bankers' acceptances 90 days	New York Stock Exchange time loans 90 days	New	Renewal
1931					
January 3	2.88%	1.88%	1.36%	2.94%	3.13%
January 10	2.88	1.75	2.38	1.50	1.50
January 17	2.88	1.63	2.25	1.50	1.50
January 24	2.88	1.50	1.88	1.50	1.50
January 31	2.75	1.44	1.88	1.50	1.50
February 7	2.63	1.38	1.86	1.50	1.50
February 14	2.63	1.25	1.88	1.50	1.50
February 21	2.50	1.50	2.13	1.50	1.50
February 29	2.50	1.50	2.13	1.50	1.50
March 7	2.50	1.50	2.13	1.58	1.50
March 14	2.50	1.50	2.25	1.67	1.70
March 21	2.50	1.50	2.13	1.41	1.50
March 28	2.50	1.50	1.86	1.58	1.50
April 4	2.38	1.50	1.86	1.53	1.50
April 11	2.38	1.50	2.13	1.74	1.60
April 18	2.38	1.50	2.13	1.54	1.50
April 25	2.38	1.44	1.86	1.50	1.50
May 2	2.38	1.25	1.88	1.50	1.50
May 9	2.38	1.19	1.88	1.40	1.50
May 16	2.25	1.06	1.75	1.38	1.30
May 23	2.13	.86	1.63	1.50	1.50
May 30	2.13	.86	1.63	1.50	1.50
June 6	2.13	.86	1.63	1.50	1.50
June 13	2.00	.86	1.38	1.50	1.50
June 20	2.00	.88	1.38	1.50	1.58
June 27	2.00	.86	1.63	1.50	1.50
July 4	2.60	.88	1.63	1.50	1.50
July 11	2.00	.88	1.36	1.50	1.50
July 18	2.00	.88	1.36	1.50	1.50
July 25	3.00	.88'	1.36	1.50	1.50
August 1	2.00	.88	1.36	1.50	1.50
August 8	2.00	.88	1.36	1.50	1.50
August 15	2.00	.88	1.36	1.50	1.50
August 22	3.00	.88	1.36	1.50	1.50
August 29	3.00	.88	1.36	1.50	1.50

TABLE A.17 (continued)

	Prevailing rates on–			Average rate on New York Stock Exchange call loans	
	Prime com- mercial paper 4 to 6 months	Prime bankers' accept- ances 90 days	New York Stock Exchange time loans 90 days	New	Renewal
September 5	2.00%	.88%	1.36%	1.50%	1.50%
September 12	2.00	.88	1.50	1.50	1.50
September 19	2.00	.88	1.50	1.50	1.50
September 26	2.00	1.06	1.75	1.50	1.50
October 3	2.60	1.25	2.25	1.50	1.50
October 10	3.25	1.25	2.50	1.53	1.50
October 17	3.38	2.75	3.00	2.13	2.13
October 24	4.00	3.26	3.75	2.50	2.50
October 31	4.00	3.25	3.75	2.50	2.50
November 7	4.00	3.25	3.75	2.50	2.50
November 14	4.13	3.00	3.75	2.50	2.50
November 21	3.00	2.00	3.25	2.50	2.50
November 28	3.06	2.94	3.25	2.50	2.50
December 5	3.98	3.00	3.25	2.50	2.50
December 12	3.98	3.00	3.25	2.55	2.50
December 19	3.98	3.00	3.25	2.55	2.50
December 26	3.98	3.00	3.50	3.60	3.60
1932					
January 2	3.86	3.60	3.50	3.21	3.12
January 9	3.86	3.60	3.75	3.94	3.10
January 16	3.86	2.94	3.75	2.50	2.50
January 23	3.86	2.75	3.63	3.50	2.50
January 30	3.86	2.75	3.63	2.50	2.50
February 6	3.86	2.75	3.63	2.50	2.50
February 13	3.86	2.81	3.63	2.50	2.50
February 20	3.86	2.81	3.63	2.50	2.50
February 27	3.86	3.75	3.63	2.50	2.50
March 5	3.63	2.63	3.36	2.50	2.50
March 12	3.63	2.63	3.25	2.50	2.50
March 19	3.63	2.50	3.25	2.50	2.50
March 26	3.63	2.36	2.86	2.50	2.50
April 2	3.63	2.38	2.86	2.50	2.50
April 9	3.63	2.13	2.98	2.50	2.50
April 16	3.63	1.50	2.75	2.50	2.50
April 23	3.36	1.60	3.13	2.50	2.50
April 30	3.36	.88	3.00	2.50	2.50

TABLE A.17 (continued)

	Prevailing rates on—			Average rate on New York Stock Exchange call loans	
	Prime commercial paper 4 to 6 months	Prime bankers' acceptances 90 days	New York Stock Exchange time loans 90 days	New	Renewal
May 7	3.36%	1.00%	1.86%	2.50%	2.50%
May 14	3.13	1.60	1.75	2.50	2.50
May 21	3.00	.86	1.50	2.50	2.50
May 28	2.88	.86	1.50	2.50	2.50
June 4	2.88	.86	1.50	2.50	2.50
June 11	2.75	.86	1.50	2.50	2.50
June 18	2.63	.86	1.50	2.50	2.50
June 25	2.63	.86	1.50	2.50	2.50
July 2	2.63	.81	1.50	2.50	2.50
July 9	2.63	.75	1.50	2.25	2.25
July 16	2.50	.75	1.50	2.00	2.00
July 23	2.50	.75	1.36	2.00	2.00
July 30	2.50	.75	1.36	2.00	2.00
August 6	2.36	.75	1.38	2.00	2.00
August 13	2.25	.75	1.38	2.50	2.50
August 20	2.13	.75	1.38	2.00	2.00
August 27	2.13	.75	1.38	2.00	2.00
September 3	2.13	.75	1.36	2.00	2.00
September 10	2.13	.75	1.36	2.00	2.00
September 17	2.13	.75	1.36	2.00	2.00
September 24	2.13	.75	1.36	2.00	2.00
October 1	2.13	.75	1.13	3.00	2.00
October 8	2.13	.75	1.13	2.00	2.00
October 15	1.88	.63	1.00	1.50	1.50
October 22	1.88	.50	.88	1.00	1.00
October 29	1.88	.50	.63	1.00	1.00
November 5	1.88	.50	.75	1.00	1.00
November 12	1.63	.50	.50	1.00	1.00
November 19	1.63	.50	.50	1.00	1.00
November 26	1.63	.50	.50	1.00	1.00
December 3	1.63	.50	.50	1.00	1.00
December 10	1.63	.38	.50	1.00	1.00
December 17	1.50	.38	.50	1.00	1.00
December 24	1.38	.38	.50	1.00	1.00
December 31	1.38	.38	.50	1.00	1.00

TABLE A.17 (continued)

	Prevailing rates on—			Average rate on New York Stock Exchange call loans	
	Prime com-mercial paper 4 to 6 months	Prime bankers' accept-ances 90 days	New York Stock Exchange time loans 90 days	New	Renewal
1933					
January 7	1.38%	.38%	.50%	1.00%	1.00%
January 14	1.38	.38	.50	1.00	1.00
January 21	1.38	.38	.50	1.00	1.00
January 28	1.38	.26	.50	1.00	1.00
February 4	1.38	.25	.50	1.00	1.00
February 11	1.38	.25	.50	1.00	1.00
February 18	1.38	.44	.50	1.00	1.00
February 25	1.38	.63	1.13	1.00	1.00
March 4	1.38	3.25	3.00	2.06	1.00
March 11	(a)	(a)	(a)	(a)	(a)
March 18	4.25	3.25	4.25	4.31	4.75
March 25	3.25	2.60	2.75	3.00	3.10
April 1	3.13	2.00	2.25	3.60	3.60
April 8	3.00	1.50	1.50	1.91	3.10
April 15	2.75	.86	1.00	1.25	1.38
April 22	2.25	.54	1.25	1.00	1.00
April 29	2.25	.50	1.25	1.00	1.00
May 6	2.25	.50	1.00	1.00	1.00
May 13	2.13	.50	1.13	1.00	1.00
May 20	2.13	.50	1.13	1.00	1.00
May 27	2.13	.50	1.13	1.00	1.00
June 3	2.00	.44	.86	1.00	1.00
June 10	1.86	.38	.88	1.00	1.00
June 17	1.86	.38	1.00	1.00	1.00
June 24	1.63	.36	.88	1.00	1.00
July 1	1.63	.38	.63	1.00	1.00
July 8	1.63	.38	.75	1.00	1.00
July 15	1.63	.80	1.13	1.00	1.00
July 22	1.50	.50	1.38	1.00	1.00
July 29	1.50	.50	1.36	1.00	1.00
August 5	1.50	.50	1.36	1.00	1.00
August 12	1.50	.50	1.13	1.00	1.00
August 19	1.50	.50	1.13	1.00	1.00
August 26	1.50	.44	1.00	1.00	1.00

TABLE A.17 (continued)

	Prevailing rates on–			Average rate on New York Stock Exchange call loans	
	Prime commercial paper 4 to 6 months	Prime bankers' acceptances 90 days	New York Stock Exchange time loans 90 days	New	Renewal
September 2	1.50%	.31%	.86%	.85%	.85%
September 9	1.50	.25	.63	.75	.75
September 16	1.38	.25	.63	.75	.75
September 23	1.25	.25	.69	.75	.75
September 30	1.25	.25	.69	.75	.75
October 7	1.25	.25	.69	.75	.75
October 14	1.25	.25	.69	.75	.75
October 21	1.25	.25	.69	.75	.75
October 28	1.25	.25	.69	.75	.75
November 4	1.25	.25	.69	.75	.75
November 11	1.25	.31	.69	.75	.75
November 18	1.25	.38	.88	.75	.75
November 25	1.25	.50	.88	.75	.75
December 2	1.36	.50	.75	.75	.75
December 9	1.36	.63	1.60	.82	.80
December 16	1.36	.63	1.13	1.60	1.00
December 23	1.50	.63	1.13	1.00	1.00
December 30	1.50	.63	1.00	1.00	1.00
1934					
January 6	1.50	.50	1.00	1.00	1.00
January 13	1.50	.50	1.13	1.00	1.00
January 20	1.50	.50	1.13	1.00	1.00
January 27	1.38	.50	1.13	1.00	1.00
February 3	1.38	.50	1.13	1.00	1.00
February 10	1.38	.50	.88	1.00	1.00
February 17	1.38	.50	.88	1.00	1.00
February 24	1.38	.50	.88	1.00	1.00
March 3	1.38	.50	.88	1.00	1.00
March 10	1.25	.38	.88	1.00	1.00
March 17	1.25	.25	.88	1.00	1.00
March 24	1.13	.25	.88	1.00	1.00
March 31	1.13	.25	.88	1.00	1.00
April 7	1.13	.25	.88	1.00	1.00
April 14	1.00	.19	.88	1.00	1.00
April 21	1.00	.19	.88	1.00	1.00
April 28	1.00	.19	.88	1.00	1.00

TABLE A.17 (continued)

	Prevailing rates on–			Average rate on New York Stock Exchange call loans	
	Prime com- mercial paper 4 to 6 months	Prime bankers' accept- ances 90 days	New York Stock Exchange time loans 90 days	New	Renewal
May 5	1.00%	.19%	.88%	1.00%	1.00%
May 12	1.00	.19	.88	1.00	1.00
May 19	1.00	.19	.88	1.00	1.00
May 26	1.00	.19	.88	1.00	1.00
June 2	1.00	.19	.88	1.00	1.00
June 9	1.00	.19	.88	1.00	1.00
June 16	.88	.19	.88	1.00	1.00
June 23	.88	.19	.88	1.00	1.00
June 30	.88	.19	.88	1.00	1.00
July 7	.88	.19	.88	1.00	1.00
July 14	.88	.19	.88	1.00	1.00
July 21	.88	.19	.88	1.00	1.00
July 28	.88	.19	.88	1.00	1.00
August 4	.88	.19	.88	1.00	1.00
August 11	.88	.19	.88	1.00	1.00
August 18	.88	.19	.88	1.00	1.00
August 25	.88	.19	.88	1.00	1.00
September 1	.88	.19	.88	1.00	1.00
September 8	.88	.19	.88	1.00	1.00
September 15	.88	.19	.88	1.00	1.00
September 22	.88	.19	.88	1.00	1.00
September 29	.88	.19	.88	1.00	1.00
October 6	.88	.19	.88	1.00	1.00
October 13	.88	.19	.88	1.00	1.00
October 20	.88	.19	.88	1.00	1.00
October 27	.88	.16	.88	1.00	1.00
November 3	.88	.13	.88	1.00	1.00
November 10	.88	.13	.88	1.00	1.00
November 17	.88	.13	.88	1.00	1.00
November 24	.88	.13	.88	1.00	1.00
December 1	.88	.13	.88	1.00	1.00
December 8	.88	.13	.88	1.00	1.00
December 15	.88	.13	.88	1.00	1.00
December 22	.88	.13	.88	1.00	1.00
December 29	.88	.13	.88	1.00	1.00

Source: Banking & Monetary Statistics, pp. 455–458.
Notes: (a) Bank Holiday.

TABLE A.18

Yields on 3-6 Month Treasury Notes and on Treasury Bills 1920-1941 (monthly)
(Averages of daily rates except where otherwise indicated. Per cent per annum)

3- to 6-month Treasury notes and certificates

Year	Jan	Feb	Mar	Apr	May	June	July	Aug	Sept	Oct	Nov	Dec	Yearly average
1920	4.50	4.50	4.75	5.25	5.50	5.75	5.81	5.83	5.81	5.75	5.75	5.88	5.42
1921	5.67	5.30	5.38	5.20	5.16	4.99	4.60	4.75	4.75	4.21	4.03	3.90	4.83
1922	3.90	3.81	3.55	3.21	3.25	3.25	3.30	3.13	3.34	3.71	3.66	3.65	3.47
1923	3.66	3.65	4.12	4.13	3.95	3.84	3.91	3.86	4.01	4.22	3.94	3.88	3.93
1924	3.76	3.54	3.57	3.38	2.99	2.44	1.92	1.90	2.14	2.41	2.58	2.57	2.77
1925	2.61	2.62	2.78	2.78	2.73	2.86	3.06	3.01	3.17	3.53	3.65	3.51	3.03
1926	3.49	3.18	3.14	3.08	3.17	2.93	3.11	3.27	3.42	3.58	3.35	3.07	3.23
1927	3.23	3.29	3.20	3.39	3.33	3.07	2.96	2.70	2.68	3.08	3.04	3.17	3.10
1928	3.31	3.33	3.27	3.62	3.90	3.92	4.12	4.36	4.57	4.70	4.26	4.26	3.97
1929	4.66	4.39	4.60	4.80	5.09	4.80	4.55	4.70	4.58	4.37	3.47	3.03	4.42
1930	3.39	3.36	2.05	3.00	2.41	1.89	1.83	1.53	1.77	1.74	1.40	1.48	2.23
1931	1.24	1.06	1.38	1.49	.88	.55	.41	.42	.45	1.70	1.77	2.41	1.15
1932	2.48	2.42	2.35	1.11	.31	.34	.22	.14	.03	neg.	neg.	.04	.78
1933	.07	.01	1.34	.45	.29	.07	.19	.01	.04	.09	.22	.29	.26

TABLE A.18 (continued)

Treasury bills (average rate on new issues offered within period)

Year	Jan	Feb	Mar	Apr	May	June	July	Aug	Sept	Oct	Nov	Dec	Yearly average
1929	--	--	--	--	--	--	--	--	--	--	--	3.276	--
1930	--	3.306	--	2.933	2.544	--	--	1.960	--	--	1.726	--	--
1931	.949	1.207	1.465	1.313	1.014	.631	.485	.598	1.217	2.468	2.225	3.253	1.402
1932	2.681	2.655	2.079	.767	.428	.408	.417	.440	.233	.176	.181	.065	.879
1933	.207	.485	2.289	.565	.418	.267	.367	.211	.102	.157	.419	.695	.515
1934	.670	.628	.273	.179	.138	.070	.072	.198	.270	.208	.217	.143	.256
1935	.136	.114	.154	.169	.145	.128	.065	.101	.214	.189	.135	.069	.137
1936	.099	.081	.113	.099	.182	.226	.141	.182	.155	.132	.095	.209	.143
1937	.360	.384	.583	.696	.647	.561	.492	.519	.530	.343	.145	.104	.447
1938	.099	.084	.074	.083	.027	.023	.053	.047	.096	.023	.024	.007	.053
1939	.002	.004	.005	.019	.006	.006	.017	.058	.101	.028	.018	.010	.023
1940	neg.(a)	.004	neg.	.003	.042	.071	.009	.019	.021	neg.	.003	neg.	.014
1941	neg.	.034	.089	.092	.082	.089	.097	.108	.055	.049	.242	.298	.103

Source: Banking & Monetary Statistics, p. 460.
Notes: (a) neg. = negative.

TABLE A.19

Dow Jones Stock Indices (month ends)
1929–1933

1929	Industrials	Railroads	Utilities
January	317.51	158.54	97.92
February	317.41	155.49	96.12
March	308.85	150.90	95.24
April	319.29	152.03	97.53
May	296.76	152.08	93.73
June	333.79	161.68	118.50
July	347.70	173.43	126.12
August	380.33	188.76	140.41
September	343.45	173.78	139.61
October	273.51	159.82	95.34
November	238.95	145.89	82.63
December	248.48	144.72	88.27
1929 high	381.17 (September)	189.11 (September)	144.61 (September)
1929 low	198.69 (November)	128.07 (November)	64.72 (November)

1930			
January	267.14	148.86	92.09
February	271.11	152.34	100.50
March	286.10	157.28	106.13
April	279.23	145.08	105.15
May	275.07	143.86	102.95
June	226.34	128.00	82.79
July	233.99	130.95	86.46
August	240.42	131.28	86.76
September	204.90	121.67	75.91
October	183.35	112.50	67.73
November	183.39	105.54	64.10
December	164.58	96.58	60.80
1930 high	294.07 (April)	157.94 (March)	108.62 (April)
1930 low	157.51 (December)	91.65 (December)	55.14 (December)

TABLE A.19 (continued)

1931	Industrials	Railroads	Utilities
January	167.55	108.18	62.41
February	189.66	109.49	71.61
March	172.36	96.88	67.54
April	151.19	88.14	60.20
May	128.46	72.06	52.35
June	150.18	84.36	60.37
July	135.39	73.44	55.86
August	139.41	68.18	57.33
September	96.61	53.59	37.91
October	105.43	52.19	40.51
November	93.87	40.84	37.06
December	77.90	33.63	31.41
1931 high	194.36 (February)	111.58 (February)	73.40 (March)
1931 low	73.79 (December)	31.42 (December)	30.55 (December)

1932			
January	76.19	37.02	30.61
February	81.44	36.29	33.25
March	73.28	29.57	28.60
April	56.11	21.44	24.22
May	44.74	14.30	17.74
June	42.84	13.43	17.08
July	54.26	21.74	22.79
August	73.16	36.53	33.10
September	17.56	34.61	31.61
October	61.90	28.01	27.45
November	56.35	25.04	26.08
December	59.93	25.90	27.50
1932 high	88.78 (March)	41.30 (January)	35.92 (March)
1932 low	41.22 (July)	13.23 (July)	16.53 (July)

TABLE A.19 (continued)

1933	Industrials	Railroads	Utilities
January	60.90	28.92	26.69
February	51.39	24.08	21.68
March	55.40	25.54	19.33
April	77.66	32.37	25.09
May	88.11	42.42	29.50
June	98.14	48.60	34.35
July	90.77	45.46	29.99
August	102.41	52.46	30.86
September	94.82	40.95	25.61
October	88.16	35.94	23.08
November	98.14	38.18	23.45
December	99.90	40.80	23.29
1933 high	108.67 (July)	56.33 (July)	37.73 (July)
1933 low	50.16 (February)	23.43 (February)	19.33 (March, April)

Source: The Dow Jones Averages 1885 - 1980,
Homewood, Illinois: Dow Jones Irwin, 1981.

TABLE A.20

VALUES OF ALL NYSE LISTED COMMON STOCKS BY INDUSTRIES AS OF SEPTEMBER 1, 1929

Name of Group	Total market value (a)
Automobile Industry	$5,928,351,213
Finance Industry	$2,045,495,341
Chemical Industry	$6,751,526,695
Building Industry	$746,799,525
Electrical Equipment Industry	$5,012,946,283
Food Industry	$3,657,635,440
Farm Machinery Industry	$697,801,544
Machinery & Metal Industry	$697,801,544
Amusement Industry	$868,629,761
Land–Realty–Hotel Industry	$177,694,457
Mining Industry (excluding Iron)	$2,856,152,362
Petroleum Industry	$7,412,416,734
Paper & Publishing Industry	$588,723,865
Retail Merchandising Industry	$4,972,704,395
Railroad Industry	$11,013,844,835
Steel–Iron–Iron Mining–Coke Industry	$3,522,613,129
Textile Industry	$291,103,077
Airplanes–Airlines–Airports	$695,994,594
Gas & Electric Utilities (Operating)	$5,145,432,664
Gas & Electric Holding Co's	4,331,108,778
Communications	5,058,875,539
Other Utilities	252,137,783
Utilities Industry	$14,787,554,764
Business & Office Equipment Industry	$839,960,457
Shipping Services Industry	$68,296,988

TABLE A.20 (continued)

Name of Group	Total market value (a)
Ship Building & Operating Industry	$75,337,160
Garment Industry	$72,046,836
Leather & Boot Industry	$96,957,821
Tobacco Industry	$1,562,343,527
Rubber Tire & Goods Industry	$291,557,281
U.S. Companies Operating Abroad	$2,433,102,503
Miscellaneous Businesses	$99,315,087
United States Companies – All (b)	$80,358,326,623
Foreign Stocks – All	$1,756,319,383
All Stocks	$82,114,646,006

Sources: New York Times, Sept. 21, 1929, p. 26.
N.Y.S.E. Bulletin, April, 1930.

Notes: (a)   Common stock values are calculated by subtracting from the values for all stocks listed, as calculated by the NYSE, the value of preferred stocks for the corresponding industries as of April 1, 1930, the first date for which the preferred stock totals were available separately. The industry calculations were first available for 9/1/29 and first published in the detail on page 3 of this table in the NYSE Bulletin, April, 1930.

(b)   Includes Canada and Cuba.

TABLE A.20 (continued)

VALUES OF ALL NYSE LISTED COMMON STOCKS BY INDUSTRIES AS OF JULY 1, 1932

Name of Group		No. of companies	No. of issues[b]	Total shares listed[a]	Total market value
			COMMON STOCKS		
Automobile & Truck Mfg.		22	22	83,188,432	$ 459,921,940
Automobile Acces. Mfg.		35	35	22,554,367	84,378,001
Automobile Industry	Total	57	57	105,742,799	544,299,941
Bank and Trust		7	7	31,026,064	$ 249,300,576
Investment Trust		18	16	15,219,296	55,771,210
Insurance		4	4	3,935,526	29,721,506
Miscellaneous Financial		4	3	4,083,969	29,457,305
Finance Industry	Total	33	30	54,264,855	364,250,597
Heavy Chemical		29	29	46,594,587	$815,411,741
Light Chemical		5	5	3,165,053	96,049,708
Fertilizer		5	5	2,168,264	2,821,780
Glass		3	5	3,304,261	28,120,043
Drug & Cosmetics		9	9	7,393,085	52,073,513
Chemical Industry	Total	51	51	62,625,532	994,476,785
Building Materials		16	17	11,363,772	$ 59,838,687
Engineering & Construction		6	5	3,548,676	11,762,845
Building Industry	Total	22	22	14,912,448	71,601,532
Heavy Electrical Equipment		4	4	33,702,078	$ 330,923,600
Light Electrical Equip. incl. Household Equip't		7	9	2,636,609	6,404,935
Electrical Equipment Industry	Total	11	13	36,338,687	337,328,535
Meats & Fish		7	7	5,982,394	$ 24,219,153
Milk & Milk Products		6	7	12,283,133	190,454,654
Flour, Cereals, Bread		11	12	14,428,079	209,849,467
Sugar (U.S.A. only)		3	3	2,611,777	16,313,611
Mineral Water & Drinks		4	4	1,952,747	124,036,895
Foods, Groceries, Canning		10	10	22,831,174	331,237,113
Confections & Fruits		6	6	4,863,324	87,259,154
Food Industry	Total	47	49	64,952,628	983,370,047
Farm Machinery Industry	Total	7	6	8,086,516	$ 65,848,523
Light Machinery & Metal Products		41	45	35,369,919	$ 253,370,324
Heavy Machinery & Metal Products		16	17	9,332,849	49,502,221
Machinery & Metal Industry	Total	58	62	44,702,768	302,872,545
Radio Set-Phonograph-Piano Mfrs.		3	3	3,726,108	$ 3,012,324
Motion Pictures		8	6	9,313,991	28,557,261
Theatres		6	4	4,636,461	7,998,261
Amusement Industry	Total	17	13	17,676,560	39,567,776
Land-Realty-Hotel Industry	Total	6	6	4,713,324	$ 22,348,314
Coal Mining		13	13	5,998,007	$ 13,579,742
Copper Mining		15	15	41,829,650	194,920,171
Non-Cuprous Metal Mining (excluding Iron)		12	12	9,220,453	81,012,561
Mining Industry (excluding Iron)	Total	40	40	57,048,110	289,512,474
Petroleum & Natural Gas		42	44	177,043,520	$ 1,632,780,823
Petroleum & Natural Gas Holding Co's		1	1	1,235,823	2,317,168
Petroleum Industry	Total	43	45	178,279,343	1,635,097,991
Paper & Card Board Mfrs.		13	14	9,081,494	$ 15,952,488
Printing & Publishing		8	8	4,718,181	27,573,559
Paper & Publishing Industry	Total	21	22	13,799,675	43,526,047
Chain Store & Restaurants		32	32	42,848,744	$ 590,980,041
Department Stores		25	23	12,597,524	68,612,305
Mail Order Houses		3	3	9,739,269	69,270,149
Miscellaneous Distributors		6	9	2,770,353	29,757,334
Retail Merchandising Industry	Total	66	67	67,955,890	758,619,829
Railroads		85	79	74,833,796	$ 965,345,143
Railroad Holding & Investment Co's		2	2	5,952,292	11,074,999
Railroad Equipment		15	15	14,096,394	123,336,190
Railroad Industry	Total	102	96	94,882,482	1,099,756,332
Steel-Iron-Iron Mining-Coke Industry	Total	36	32	31,664,669	$ 325,355,270
Silk & Rayon		15	13	4,714,635	$ 22,378,381
Cotton		6	5	3,192,391	13,846,355
Wool-Worsted-Carpet-Rug Mfrs.		7	6	2,086,493	8,421,759
Textile Industry	Total	28	24	9,993,519	44,646,495
Airplanes-Airlines-Airports	Total	8	8	16,746,169	$ 46,749,092
Gas & Electric Utilities (Operating)		20	13	62,691,674	$ 1,105,825,709
Gas & Electric Holding Co's		15	15	85,512,014	579,159,355
Communications		8	6	34,712,898	1,597,284,599
Traction Co's		9	9	3,608,248	21,368,477
Omnibus Operaters		3	3	1,085,340	4,237,345
Express Co's		4	4	2,736,762	19,866,024
Water & Central Heating Utilities		3	1	307,500	4,689,375
Utilities Industry	Total	62	51	190,654,436	3,332,430,884
Business & Office Equipment Industry	Total	8	8	10,236,053	$ 103,110,014
Shipping Services Industry	Total	5	6	1,862,457	$ 3,679,512

TABLE A.20 (continued)

Name of Group		No. of companies	COMMON STOCKS No. of issues[b]	Total shares listed	Total market value
Ship Building & Operating Industry	Total	7	7	3,252,915	$ 6,090,368
Garment Industry	Total	6	5	1,151,228	$ 3,556,481
Leather & Boot Industry	Total	11	10	6,157,305	$ 137,205,427
Tobacco Industry	Total	18	20	23,714,819	$ 739,107,279
Rubber Tire & Goods Industry	Total	8	9	9,680,245	$ 40,118,922
	Utilities	3	3	8,591,038	$ 24,279,898
	Railroads	3	3	345,000	236,550
United States Companies	Sugar	6	6	3,540,187	15,858,188
Operating in Colonial	Fruits	2	2	3,673,179	39,181,073
Possessions and in	Mining	4	4	10,314,540	20,409,287
Foreign Countries	Petroleum	1	1	330,000	123,750
	Miscellaneous	4	4	2,060,381	3,788,021
U.S. Companies Operating Abroad[c]	Total	23	23	28,854,325	103,876,767
Miscellaneous Businesses	Total	7	7	3,445,379	$ 21,198,820
United States Companies-All	Total	808	789	1,163,395,136	$12,459,602,599
European Companies	Total	12	10	2,220,455	$ 11,646,080
North Amer. (Incl. West Indian) Companies	Total	11	9	33,994,242	$ 229,009,205
Foreign Stocks-All[d]	Total	23	19	36,214,697	$ 240,655,285
U.S. Stocks-All	Total	808	789	1,163,395,136	$12,459,602,599
All Stocks	Total	831	808	1,199,609,833	$12,700,257,884

Source: NYSE Bulletin, July, 1932.

Notes:
(a) Shares listed are taken at the close of the NYSE on the last trading day of the preceding month.

(b) Number of issues is less than the number of companies whenever a company had only preferred stock listed.

(c) "U.S. Companies Operating Abroad" are those companies incorporated in the United States which largely confine their industrial activities within U.S. colonial possessions and/or foreign countries.

(d) "Foreign Stocks" are those issued by companies incorporated in foreign countries (including Canada and Cuba).

VALUES OF ALL NYSE LISTED COMMON STOCKS
AS OF MARCH 1, 1933

		COMMON STOCKS		
Name of Group		No. of companies	No. of issues(b)	Total shares listed(a)	Total market value
Automobile & Truck Mfg		21	21	83,921,930	$ 591,546,478
Automobile Acces. Mfg		35	34	21,493,013	97,213,173
Automobile Industry	Total	56	55	105,414,943	688,759,651
Bank and Trust		7	7	30,245,981	$ 375,012,953
Investment Trust		17	15	12,471,591	68,342,900
Insurance		4	4	3,935,526	45,836,838
Miscellaneous Financial		4	3	4,083,979	44,784,199
Finance Industry	Total	32	29	50,737,077	533,976,890
Heavy Chemical		29	29	46,496,249	$ 1,100,838,197
Light Chemical		5	5	3,165,053	125,880,187
Fertilizer		5	5	2,170,740	4,168,882
Glass		3	3	3,359,261	44,549,395
Drug & Cosmetics		9	9	7,455,856	60,850,992
Chemical Industry	Total	51	51	62,647,159	1,336,287,653
Building Materials		16	17	11,363,912	$ 73,817,054
Engineering & Construction		6	5	3,548,731	15,037,658
Building Industry	Total	22	22	14,912,643	88,854,712
Heavy Electrical Equipment		4	4	33,702,083	$ 425,393,788
Light Electrical Equip't		7	9	2,637,709	8,048,272
Electrical Equipment Industry	Total	11	13	36,339,792	433,442,060
Meats & Fish		6	6	5,732,394	$ 25,003,271
Milk & Milk Products		6	7	12,291,310	156,339,974
Flour, Cereal, Bread		11	12	13,976,499	278,319,622
Sugar (U.S.A. Co's only)		3	3	2,611,777	28,531,999
Mineral Water & Drinks		4	4	1,951,289	117,615,223
Foods, Groceries, Canning		10	10	22,904,694	468,278,756
Confections & Fruits		6	6	4,863,324	104,894,567
Food Industry	Total	46	48	64,331,287	1,178,943,412
Farm Machinery Industry	Total	7	6	8,086,516	$ 83,046,857
Light Machinery & Metal Products		42	45	35,370,442	$ 359,711,538
Heavy Machinery & Metal Products		15	16	9,236,852	54,917,554
Machinery & Metal Industry	Total	57	61	44,607,294	414,629,092
Radio Set-Phonograph-Piano Mfrs		3	3	3,739,807	$ 3,221,279
Motion Pictures		8	6	9,319,327	28,002,066
Theatres		5	4	4,655,898	3,977,192
Amusement Industry	Total	16	13	17,715,032	35,200,537
Land-Realty-Hotel Industry	Total	6	6	4,710,416	$ 20,371,681
Coal Mining		14	14	6,068,295	$ 16,208,001
Copper Mining		15	15	41,954,231	262,896,026
Non-Cuprous Metal Mining (excluding Iron)		12	12	9,570,635	106,162,707
Mining Industry (excluding Iron)	Total	41	41	57,593,161	385,266,734
Petroleum & Natural Gas		43	45	180,876,669	$ 1,822,184,702
Petroleum & Natural Gas Holding Co's.		-	-	-	-
Petroleum Industry	Total	43	45	180,876,669	1,822,184,702
Paper & Card Board Mfrs.		12	13	8,931,500	$ 16,631,957
Printing & Publishing		8	8	4,711,281	29,308,846
Paper & Publishing Industry	Total	20	21	13,642,781	45,940,803
Chain Stores & Restaurants		30	32	37,496,898	$ 677,902,161
Department Stores		25	23	13,034,033	89,567,201
Mail Order Houses		3	3	9,739,269	113,321,652
Miscellaneous Distributors		5	8	2,585,353	19,109,228
Retail Merchandising Industry	Total	63	66	62,855,553	899,900,242
Railroads		84	78	74,862,951	$ 1,725,087,124
Railroad Holding & Investment Co's		3	2	5,952,292	32,948,467
Railroad Equipment		14	15	14,096,411	172,775,243
Railroad Industry	Total	101	95	94,911,654	1,930,810,834
Steel, Iron, Iron Mining, Coke Industry	Total	36	32	31,664,669	$ 385,733,103
Silk & Rayon		15	13	4,765,032	$ 30,048,411
Cotton		6	5	3,192,391	17,826,080
Wool-Worsted-Carpet-Rug Mfrs.		7	6	2,086,493	10,978,840
Textile Industry	Total	28	24	10,043,916	58,853,331
Airplanes-Airlines-Airports	Total	7	7	16,524,445	$ 91,783,941
Gas & Electric Utilities		19	12	62,121,135	$ 1,425,048,788
Gas & Electric Holding Co's		16	16	86,558,718	695,279,179
Communications		8	6	34,713,860	1,995,902,776
Traction		9	9	3,608,262	27,788,709
Omnibus Operaters		3	3	1,067,773	4,145,927
Express Co's		4	4	2,736,762	22,866,572
Water & Central Heating Utilities		3	1	307,500	5,150,625
Utilities Industry	Total	62	51	191,114,010	4,176,182,576
Business & Office Equipment Industry	Total	8	8	10,474,053	$ 114,439,245
Shipping Services Industry	Total	5	6	1,862,557	$ 3,873,790

TABLE A.20 (continued)

Name of Group		No. of companies	No. of issues[b]	COMMON STOCKS Total shares listed	COMMON STOCKS Total market value
Ship Building & Operating Industry	Total	7	7	3,252,915	$ 7,622,786
Garment Industry	Total	6	5	1,151,229	$ 4,293,230
Leather & Boot Industry	Total	10	10	6,157,428	$ 119,428,499
Tobacco Industry	Total	18	20	23,672,103	$ 835,562,763
Rubber Tire & Goods Industry	Total	7	7	7,646,469	$ 47,102,274
United States Companies Operating in Colonial Possessions and in Foreign Countries	Utilities	3	3	8,691,338	$ 43,242,902
	Railroads	3	3	345,300	569,347
	Sugar	6	6	3,540,187	26,498,129
	Fruits	1	1	2,924,995	74,952,997
	Mining	4	4	10,307,190	43,066,309
	Petroleum	1	1	330,000	123,750
	Miscellaneous	4	4	2,060,381	6,207,717
U.S. Companies Operating Abroad[c]	Total	22	22	28,199,391	194,661,151
Miscellaneous Businesses	Total	7	7	3,441,495	$ 24,697,999
United States Companies-All	Total	795	778	1,154,586,657	$15,961,890,548
European Companies	Total	10	9	2,181,055	$ 13,307,920
North Amer. (Incl. West Indian) Companies	Total	10	8	32,904,178	$ 293,214,089
Foreign Stocks-All[d]	Total	20	17	35,085,233	$ 306,522,009
U.S. Stocks-All	Total	795	778	1,154,586,657	$15,961,890,548
All Stocks	Total	815	795	1,189,671,890	$16,268,412,557

Source: NYSE Bulletin, March, 1933.

Notes: (a)   Shares listed are taken at the close of the NYSE on the last trading day of the preceding month.

      (b)   Number of issues is less than the number of companies whenever a company had only preferred stock listed.

      (c)   "United States Companies Operating Abroad" are those companies incorporated in the United States which largely confine their industrial activities within U. S. colonial possessions and/or foreign countries.

      (d)   "Foreign Stocks" are those issued by companies incorporated in foreign countries (including Canada and Cuba).

TABLE A.21

NYSE Monthly Trading Volume 1900–1941 (millions of shares)

Year	Jan	Feb	Mar	Apr	May	June	July	Aug	Sept	Oct	Nov	Dec	Total
1900	10	10	15	15	9	7	6	4	5	11	24	23	139
1901	30	22	27	42	35	20	16	11	14	14	18	17	265
1902	15	13	12	26	14	8	16	14	21	16	17	16	187
1903	16	11	15	12	12	15	15	14	11	13	11	15	159
1904	12	9	11	8	5	5	12	12	19	33	32	28	187
1905	21	25	29	29	20	12	13	20	16	18	27	30	261
1906	39	22	19	24	24	20	16	32	26	21	19	20	282
1907	23	16	32	19	16	10	13	15	12	17	10	12	195
1908	16	10	16	11	21	9	14	19	17	14	25	22	195
1909	17	12	13	19	17	20	13	24	20	22	18	17	212
1910	24	16	15	14	12	16	14	10	8	13	11	10	164
1911	10	10	7	5	11	10	5	15	17	11	15	9	126
1912	11	7	14	16	14	7	7	9	10	14	10	12	131
1913	9	7	7	8	5	10	5	6	8	7	4	7	83
1914	10	6	6	7	5	4	8	(a)	(a)	(a)	(a)	2	47
1915	5	4	8	21	13	11	14	20	18	27	17	14	172
1916	16	12	15	13	16	13	9	14	30	28	34	32	233
1917	16	14	19	14	20	19	13	12	14	17	15	13	185
1918	13	11	8	7	21	12	8	7	8	20	15	12	143
1919	12	12	21	29	35	34	35	24	24	37	30	25	318
1920	20	22	29	28	17	9	13	14	15	14	22	24	228

TABLE A.21 (continued)

Year	Jan	Feb	Mar	Apr	May	June	July	Aug	Sept	Oct	Nov	Dec	Total
1921	16	10	16	16	17	18	9	11	13	13	15	18	173
1922	15	16	23	31	30	25	15	18	22	26	21	20	261
1923	20	23	26	20	23	20	13	13	15	16	23	25	236
1924	27	21	18	18	14	17	24	23	18	18	42	44	284
1925	42	33	39	25	37	31	33	33	37	55	50	43	460
1926	39	36	52	31	23	38	37	45	37	40	31	42	452
1927	35	45	50	50	47	48	39	51	52	51	52	63	582
1928	58	47	86	82	85	65	39	69	92	100	116	93	931
1929	111	78	106	83	91	70	93	96	100	142	72	84	1,125
1930	62	69	97	111	78	77	48	40	54	65	52	59	811
1931	43	64	66	54	47	59	34	25	51	48	37	50	577
1932	34	32	33	31	23	23	23	83	67	29	23	23	425
1933	19	19	20	53	104	126	120	42	43	39	34	35	655
1934	55	57	30	30	25	17	21	17	13	16	21	24	324
1935	19	14	16	22	30	22	29	43	35	47	57	46	382
1936	67	61	51	40	21	21	35	27	31	44	50	49	497
1937	59	50	50	35	19	16	21	17	34	51	29	28	409
1938	24	15	23	17	14	24	39	21	24	42	28	27	297
1939	25	14	25	20	13	12	18	17	57	24	19	18	262
1940	16	13	16	27	39	16	7	8	12	14	21	18	208

Source: Banking & Monetary Statistics, p. 485.
Notes: (a) NYSE closed.

TABLE A.22

Collateralized[a] Borrowing by NYSE Members 1927–1934 (monthly)

		Member Borrowings[b]	Market Values All Listed Stocks[c]	Ratio %
1927				
Jan.	1	$3,292,860,255	$38,376,162,138	8.58
Feb.	1	3,138,786,338	38,602,044,866	8.13
Mar.	1	3,256,459,379	39,966,306,016	8.14
Apr.	1	3,289,781,174	40,126,835,948	8.19
May	1	3,341,209,847	40,507,450,825	8.24
June	1	3,457,869,029	42,529,863,513	8.13
July	1	3,568,966,843	41,963,647,182	8.50
Aug.	1	3,641,695,290	44,909,464,478	8.10
Sept.	1	3,673,891,333	45,531,368,411	8.06
Oct.	1	3,914,627,570	47,609,636,595	8.22
Nov.	1	3,946,137,374	46,028,970,485	8.57
Dec.	1	4,091,836,303	48,526,525,537	8.43
1928				
Jan.	1	$4,432,907,321	$49,736,350,946	8.91
Feb.	1	4,420,352,541	49,145,011,528	8.99
Mar.	1	4,322,578,914	48,484,707,019	8.91
Apr.	1	4,640,174,172	52,371,329,870	8.86
May	1	4,907,782,599	54,818,925,860	8.95
June	1	5,274,046,281	55,735,456,606	9.46
July	1	4,898,351,487	52,930,378,356	9.25
Aug.	1	4,837,347,579	53,728,776,349	9.00
Sept.	1	5,051,437,405	57,385,881,463	8.80
Oct.	1	5,513,639,685	59,332,123,511	9.29
Nov.	1	5,879,721,062	61,075,813,465	9.62
Dec.	1	6,391,644,264	66,113,255,317	9.66
1929				
Jan.	1	$6,439,740,511	$67,478,138,151	9.54
Feb.	1	6,735,164,241	71,114,287,624	9.47
Mar.	1	6,678,545,917	71,871,889,789	9.29
Apr.	1	6,804,457,408	69,770,122,189	9.75
May	1	6,774,930,395	73,718,875,840	9.19
June	1	$6,665,137,925	$70,921,426,187	9.40
July	1	7,071,221,274	77,264,128,909	9.15
Aug.	1	7,473,794,294	81,569,046,497	9.16
Sept.	1	7,881,619,426	89,668,276,854	8.79
Oct.	1	8,549,383,979	87,082,472,079	9.82
Nov.	1	6,108,824,868	71,759,485,710	8.51
Dec.	1	4,016,598,769	63,589,338,823	6.32

TABLE A.22 (continued)

		Member Borrowings(b)	Market Values All Listed Stocks(c)	Ratio %
1930				
Jan.	1	$3,989,510,273	$64,707,878,131	6.17
Feb.	1	3,984,768,065	69,008,836,529	5.77
Mar.	1	4,167,588,352	70,806,703,327	5.89
Apr.	1	4,656,302,339	76,075,447,459	6.12
May	1	5,063,131,359	75,304,607,812	6.72
June	1	4,747,831,912	75,018,855,283	6.33
July	1	3,727,711,289	63,892,327,059	5.83
Aug.	1	3,689,482,297	67,221,337,495	5.49
Sept.	1	3,598,633,069	67,721,086,999	5.31
Oct.	1	3,481,452,761	60,143,183,105	5.79
Nov.	1	2,556,124,087	55,025,710,617	4.65
Dec.	1	2,162,249,002	53,311,859,703	4.06
1931				
Jan.	1	$1,893,612,890	$49,019,878,459	3.86
Feb.	1	1,720,345,318	52,061,956,709	3.30
Mar.	1	1,839,756,058	57,054,766,481	3.22
Apr.	1	1,908,810,494	53,336,394,495	3.58
May	1	1,651,128,124	48,569,988,485	3.40
June	1	1,434,683,650	42,533,985,679	3.37
July	1	1,391,324,922	47,417,147,581	2.93
Aug.	1	1,344,092,754	44,422,740,446	3.03
Sept.	1	1,354,067,358	44,587,026,110	3.04
Oct.	1	1,044,407,879	32,327,037,441	3.23
Nov.	1	796,268,768	34,246,649,501	2.33
Dec.	1	730,151,908	31,105,267,133	2.35
1932				
Jan.	1	$587,159,813	$26,693,836,532	2.20
Feb.	1	512,017,942	26,377,647,814	1.94
Mar.	1	524,663,758	27,585,989,257	1.90
Apr.	1	533,103,059	24,501,826,280	2.18
May	1	379,016,662	20,319,088,631	1.87
June	1	300,397,222	16,141,061,080	1.86
July	1	243,574,295	15,633,479,577	1.56
Aug.	1	241,599,943	20,494,759,465	1.18
Sept.	1	331,699,320	27,782,501,806	1.19
Oct.	1	379,801,584	26,734,828,668	1.42
Nov.	1	324,702,198	23,440,661,828	1.39
Dec.	1	337,612,558	22,259,137,174	1.52

TABLE A.22 (continued)

	Member Borrowings[b]	Market Values All Listed Stocks[c]	Ratio %
1933			
Jan. 1	$346,804,658	$22,767,636,718	1.52
Feb. 1	359,341,058	23,073,194,091	1.56
Mar. 1	359,957,056	19,700,985,961	1.83
Apr. 1	310,961,581	19,914,893,399	1.56
May 1	322,492,188	26,815,110,054	1.20
June 1	528,509,438	32,473,061,395	1.63
July 1	780,386,120	36,348,747,926	2.15
Aug. 1	916,243,934	33,143,545,382	2.76
Sept. 1	917,215,274	36,669,889,331	2.50
Oct. 1	896,597,531	32,729,938,196	2.74
Nov. 1	776,182,033	30,117,833,982	2.58
Dec. 1	789,229,539	32,542,456,452	2.43
1934			
Jan. 1	$845,132,524	$33,094,751,244	2.55
Feb. 1	903,074,507	37,364,990,391	2.42
Mar. 1	938,010,227	36,657,646,692	2.56
Apr. 1	981,353,947	36,699,914,685	2.67
May 1	1,088,226,358	36,432,143,818	2.99
June 1	1,016,386,686	33,816,513,632	3.00
July 1	1,082,240,126	34,439,993,735	3.14
Aug. 1	923,055,826	30,752,107,676	3.00
Sept. 1	874,207,876	32,618,130,662	2.68
Oct. 1	831,529,447	32,319,514,504	2.57
Nov. 1	827,033,416	31,613,348,531	2.62
Dec. 1	831,115,348	33,888,023,435	2.45

Notes: (a) Collateral is not limited to NYSE stocks.
(b) Borrowing by New York City NYSE members only.
(c) Listed stocks include preferred stocks.

Source: New York Stock Exchange Yearbook 1938, p. 61.

TABLE A.23

New York Stock Exchange Short Interest 1931–1936
(reporting periods vary)

1931	Number of shares in total short interest	1931	Number of shares in total short interest	1932	Number of shares in total short interest
May 25[a]	5,589,700	Nov. 9	2,897,874	Jan. 14	3,064,761
June 4	4,948,260	Nov. 10	2,925,417	Jan. 15	3,068,026
June 17	4,384,474	Nov. 11	2,988,446	Jan. 18	3,064,761
June 26	3,978,149	Nov. 12	3,020,601	Jan. 19	3,069,649
July 3	3,634,261	Nov. 13	3,013,807	Jan. 20	3,136,766
July 10	3,770,569	Nov. 16	3,104,185	Jan. 21	3,145,087
July 17	3,645,982	Nov. 17	3,131,796	Jan. 22	3,171,568
July 24	3,718,218	Nov. 18	3,237,159	Jan. 25	3,266,739
July 31	4,038,850	Nov. 19	3,364,776	Jan. 26	3,327,471
Aug. 7	4,374,200	Nov. 20	3,429,535	Jan. 27	3,277,702
Aug. 14	4,342,500	Nov. 23	3,537,787	Jan. 28	3,463,342
Aug. 21	4,271,800	Nov. 24	3,584,161	Jan. 29	3,536,207
Aug. 28	4,408,100	Nov. 25	3,568,538	Feb. 1	3,600,265
Sept. 4	4,338,000	Nov. 27	3,690,795	Feb. 2	3,636,435
Sept. 11	4,480,400	Nov. 30	3,745,642	Feb. 3	3,688,934
Sept. 18	4,241,300	Dec. 1	3,667,067	Feb. 4	3,685,682
Sept. 21*	3,961,300	Dec. 2	3,665,152	Feb. 5	3,700,119
Sept. 22	3,162,813	Dec. 3	3,736,577	Feb. 8	3,754,942
Sept. 23	2,831,128	Dec. 4	3,662,800	Feb. 9	3,842,241
Sept. 24	2,949,412	Dec. 7	3,594,468	Feb. 10	3,931,885
Sept. 25	2,987,385	Dec. 8	3,553,345	Feb. 11	3,965,142
Sept. 28	2,985,088	Dec. 9	3,594,720	Feb. 15	3,437,833
Sept. 29	3,063,203	Dec. 10	3,767,235	Feb. 16	3,363,727
Sept. 30	3,036,928	Dec. 11	3,698,320	Feb. 17	3,234,068
Oct. 1	2,814,935	Dec. 14	3,559,707	Feb. 18	3,177,712
Oct. 2	2,643,170	Dec. 15	3,404,039	Feb. 19	3,192,702
Oct. 5	2,612,414	Dec. 16	3,181,031	Feb. 23	2,996,691
Oct. 6	2,597,898	Dec. 17	3,138,802	Feb. 24	2,964,016
Oct. 7	2,173,800	Dec. 18	3,134,456	Feb. 26	3,049,978
Oct. 8	2,243,535	Dec. 21	2,909,672	Feb. 29	3,081,194
Oct. 9	2,163,771	Dec. 22	2,874,224	Mar. 1	3,102,876
Oct. 13	2,182,197	Dec. 23	2,862,146	Mar. 2	3,098,316
Oct. 14	2,254,370	Dec. 24	2,891,885	Mar. 3	3,018,470
Oct. 15	2,254,676	Dec. 28	2,888,854	Mar. 4	3,100,862
Oct. 16	2,246,874	Dec. 29	2,888,648	Mar. 7	3,096,178
Oct. 19	2,241,968	Dec. 30	2,858,928	Mar. 8	3,131,776
Oct. 20	2,239,700	Dec. 31	2,842,072	Mar. 9	3,164,725
Oct. 21	2,239,200			Mar. 10	3,163,532
Oct. 22	2,243,327	**1932**		Mar. 11	3,133,629
Oct. 23	2,300,320			Mar. 14	3,107,484
Oct. 26	2,374,059	Jan. 4	2,962,127	Mar. 15	3,131,159
Oct. 27	2,440,169	Jan. 5	3,122,915	Mar. 16	3,162,712
Oct. 28	2,540,943	Jan. 6	3,092,929	Mar. 17	3,240,304
Oct. 29	2,652,127	Jan. 7	3,087,616	Mar. 18	3,242,247
Oct. 30	2,676,649	Jan. 8	3,072,601	Mar. 21	3,465,818
Nov. 2	2,764,959	Jan. 11	3,076,399	Mar. 22	3,422,258
Nov. 4	2,816,934	Jan. 12	3,137,369	Mar. 23	3,560,231
Nov. 5	2,846,236	Jan. 13	3,152,366	Mar. 24	3,479,756

TABLE A.23 (continued)

1932	Number of shares in total short interest	1932	Number of shares in total short interest	1932	Number of shares in total short interest
Mar. 28	3,427,664	June 8	2,135,307	Aug. 19	1,813,742
Mar. 29	3,315,913	June 9	2,189,292	Aug. 22	1,831,109
Mar. 30	3,305,253	June 10	2,217,345	Aug. 23	1,797,619
Mar. 31	3,299,268	June 13	2,056,245	Aug. 24	1,796,150
Apr. 1	3,279,398	June 14	2,050,523	Aug. 25	1,865,055
Apr. 4	3,189,596	June 15	2,039,699	Aug. 26	1,878,810
Apr. 5	3,059,658	June 16	2,003,604	Aug. 29	1,838,205
Apr. 6	3,063,927	June 17	2,016,125	Aug. 30	1,961,550
Apr. 7	2,849,895	June 20	2,000,211	Aug. 31	1,968,643
Apr. 8	2,626,399	June 21	2,011,943	Sept. 1	1,934,647
Apr. 9	2,605,831	June 22	2,054,574	Sept. 2	1,988,871
Apr. 11	2,469,087	June 23	2,088,812	Sept. 6	1,944,056
Apr. 12	2,405,319	June 24	2,087,312	Sept. 7	2,023,342
Apr. 13	2,355,297	June 27	2,089,312	Sept. 8	1,999,958
Apr. 14	2,348,174	June 28	2,102,983	Sept. 9	2,042,222
Apr. 15	2,323,738	June 29	2,101,693	Sept. 12	1,987,905
Apr. 18	2,346,486	June 30	2,100,528	Sept. 13	1,887,021
Apr. 19	2,379,468	July 1	2,131,783	Sept. 14	1,709,868
Apr. 20	2,450,863	July 5	2,097,983	Sept. 15	1,716,886
Apr. 21	2,510,209	July 6	2,127,371	Sept. 16	1,657,096
Apr. 22	2,537,193	July 7	2,152,611	Sept. 19	1,758,515
Apr. 25	2,619,701	July 8	2,145,778	Sept. 26	1,746,216
Apr. 26	2,603,078	July 11	2,232,722	Oct. 3	1,800,886
Apr. 27	2,573,355	July 12	2,202,640	Oct. 10	1,876,496
Apr. 28	2,668,698	July 13	2,221,002	Oct. 17	1,798,059
Apr. 29	2,720,183	July 14	2,218,830	Oct. 24	1,884,826
May 2	2,758,161	July 15	2,217,553	Oct. 31	1,839,939
May 3	2,783,880	July 18	2,222,884	Nov. 7	1,859,381
May 4	2,829,042	July 19	2,263,168	Nov. 14	1,819,947
May 5	2,728,820	July 20	2,282,786	Nov. 21	1,847,078
May 6	2,731,311	July 21	2,282,058	Nov. 28	1,862,804
May 9	2,633,278	July 22	2,258,061	Dec. 5	1,874,181
May 10	2,624,640	July 25	2,276,870	Dec. 12	1,825,043
May 11	2,607,622	July 26	2,273,612	Dec. 19	1,888,306
May 12	2,601,568	July 27	2,341,507	Dec. 27	1,874,541
May 13	2,601,628	July 28	2,331,711		
May 16	2,639,086	July 29	2,259,349	**1933**	
May 17	2,575,871	Aug. 1	2,181,599		
May 18	2,597,783	Aug. 2	2,156,531	Jan. 3	1,796,976
May 19	2,601,148	Aug. 3	2,176,258	Jan. 9	1,740,304
May 20	2,546,748	Aug. 4	2,151,840	Jan. 16	1,783,538
May 23	2,496,579	Aug. 5	2,060,722	Jan. 23	1,829,702
May 24	2,468,827	Aug. 8	1,817,583	Jan. 30	1,845,047
May 25	2,457,742	Aug. 9	1,807,270	Feb. 6	1,886,279
May 27	2,194,942	Aug. 10	1,842,255	Feb. 14	1,894,632
May 31	2,140,560	Aug. 11	1,807,363	Feb. 20	1,877,043
June 1	2,060,633	Aug. 12	1,821,978	Feb. 27	1,654,221
June 2	2,040,989	Aug. 15	1,703,344	Mar. 3	1,464,063
June 3	2,025,812	Aug. 16	1,745,816	Mar. 14	1,343,901
June 6	2,050,566	Aug. 17	1,730,605	Mar. 20	1,358,265
June 7	2,094,459	Aug. 18	1,836,253	Mar. 27	1,430,349

TABLE A.23 (continued)

1933	Number of shares in total short interest	1936	Number of shares in total short interest
Apr. 3	1,464,874	June 30	1,138,358
Apr. 10	1,446,336	July 31	996,399
Apr. 17	1,438,139	Aug. 31	974,338
Apr. 24	1,427,696	Sept. 30	1,011,670
May 1	1,415,330	Oct. 30	1,066,184
May 8	1,457,114	Nov. 30	1,230,579
May 15	1,523,257	Dec. 31	1,136,814
May 22	1,610,893		
May 29	1,419,854	**1937**	
June 5	1,476,183		
June 30	1,417,637	Jan. 29	1,314,840
July 31	972,613	Feb. 26	1,435,022
Aug. 31	901,999	Mar. 31	1,199,064
Sept. 29	875,000	Apr. 30	1,012,186
Oct. 31	779,220	May 28	1,049,964
Nov. 29	793,888	June 30	944,957
Dec. 29	712,868	July 30	1,007,736
		Aug. 31	966,935
		Sept. 30	967,593
1934		Oct. 29	1,214,082
		Nov. 30	1,184,215
Jan. 31	1,030,083	Dec. 31	1,051,870
Feb. 28	970,494		
Mar. 29	929,495	**1938**	
Apr. 30	910,742		
May 31	741,038	Jan. 31	1,228,005
June 29	717,241	Feb. 28	1,142,482
July 31	723,161	Mar. 31	1,097,858
Aug. 31	826,911	Apr. 29	1,384,113
Sept. 28	869,415	May 31	1,343,573
Oct. 31	882,397	June 30	1,050,164
Nov. 30	796,575	July 29	833,663
Dec. 31	714,234	Aug. 31	729,480
		Sept. 30	588,345
1935		Oct. 28	669,530
		Nov. 29	587,314
Jan. 31	764,854	Dec. 30	500,961
Feb. 28	741,513		
Mar. 29	760,678		
Apr. 30	772,230		
May 31	768,199		
June 28	840,537		
July 31	870,813		
Aug. 30	998,872		
Sept. 30	913,620		
Oct. 31	930,219		
Nov. 29	1,032,788		
Dec. 31	927,028		
1936			
Jan. 31	1,103,399		
Feb. 28	1,246,715		
Mar. 31	1,175,351		
Apr. 30	1,132,817		
May 29	1,117,059		

Source: New York Stock Exchange Yearbook 1938, p. 56.

Notes: (a) Reports began in May, 1931.

TABLE A.24

New York Stock Exchange Listed Issues   1914–1939 (Annually)

Year	Stocks	Bonds	Total
1914	511	1,082	1,593
1915	511	1,096	1,607
1916	540	1,149	1,689
1917	613	1,171	1,784
1918	627	1,102	1,729
1919	612	1,131	1,743
1920	691	1,114	1,805
1921	756	1,115	1,871
1922	792	1,156	1,948
1923	778	1,234	2,012
1924	889	1,262	2,151
1925	927	1,332	2,259
1926	1,043	1,367	2,410
1927	1,081	1,420	2,501
1928	1,097	1,491	2,588
1929	1,176	1,534	2,710
1930	1,293	1,543	2,836
1931	1,308	1,607	2,915
1932	1,278	1,601	2,879
1933	1,237	1,549	2,786
1934	1,209	1,568	2,777
1935	1,187	1,540	2,727
1936	1,185	1,463	2,648
1937	1,212	1,409	2,621
1938	1,259	1,376	2,635
1939	1,237	1,393	2,630

Source: New York Stock Exchange Yearbook 1938, p. 60.

TABLE A.25

New York Stock Exchange Member Data

Year	New York City Members	Firms	Out-of-town Members	Firms	Total Members	Firms
1900	975	421	125	100	1,100	521
1910	1,004	489	96	92	1,100	581
1920	979	447	121	116	1,100	563
1930	1,200	541	130	124	1,330	665
1931	1,237	540	112	109	1,349	649
1932	1,264	530	93	91	1,357	621
1933	1,288	529	87	81	1,375	610
1934	1,286	499[a]	89	122[a]	1,375	621
1935	1,280	496	95	125	1,375	621
1936	1,278	509	97	135	1,375	644
1937	1,277	512	98	135	1,375	647
1938	1,275	513	100	139	1,375	652
1939	1,258	485	101	142	1,375	627

*Classification revised.

Year	Offices in New York	Offices Out-of-town	Total
1900	83	93	176
1910	188	367	555
1920	107	555	662
1930	294	1,364	1,658
1931	252	1,240	1,492
1932	208	1,139	1,347
1933	186	985	1,171
1934	191	1,024	1,215
1935	149	944	1,093
1936	152	940	1,092
1937	175	1,007	1,182
1938	179	1,006	1,185
1939	154	926	1,080

TABLE A.25 (continued)

New York Stock Exchange Seat Prices

Year	High	Low
1918	$ 60,000	$ 45,000
1919	110,000	60,000
1920	115,000	85,000
1921	100,000	77,500
1922	100,000	86,000
1923	100,000	76,000
1924	101,000	76,000
1925	150,000	99,000
1926	175,000	133,000
1927	305,000	170,000
1928	595,000	290,000
1929(b)	625,000	550,000
1929(c)	495,000	350,000
1930	480,000	205,000
1931	322,000	125,000
1932	185,000	68,000
1933	250,000	90,000
1934	190,000	70,000
1935	140,000	65,000
1936	174,000	89,000
1937	134,000	61,000
1938	85,000	51,000

Source: New York Stock Exchange Yearbook 1938, pp. 22, 25.

Notes: (a)   Classification revised
            (b)   To Feb. 18, 1929.
            (c)   Ex-rights.

TABLE A.26

U. S. Corporate Capital Flotations by Industry Type 1924–1937 ($ millions) (monthly)

Year and month	Total (new capital and refunding)	New Capital Total	Indus-trial	Invest. trusts, trading, holding, etc.	Lands, build-ings, etc.	Public utilities	Rail-roads	Misc.
1924								
January	305	277	57		17	113	72	17
February	266	228	66		14	92	51	6
March	266	255	99		22	90	35	9
April	276	250	38		29	116	53	14
May	496	447	61		27	277	71	11
June	316	253	14		16	95	106	21
July	279	233	31		29	104	51	18
August	288	195	33		19	72	39	32
September	312	273	37		42	60	127	7
October	418	362	66		32	113	107	44
November	243	235	63		39	75	52	5
December	373	314	112		47	118	15	23
Totals[a]	3,839	3,322	677		333	1,326	780	207
Monthly averages	320	277	56		28	110	65	17
1925								
January	509	413	105	15	51	199	17	26
February	504	450	94	0	36	201	87	33
March	353	282	52	0	57	121	37	16
April	483	411	222	0	59	76	33	21
May	296	261	51	0	40	100	48	21
June	379	312	25	0	114	111	20	42
July	398	323	99	0	62	78	57	27
August	241	212	45	0	34	95	19	19
September	311	294	50	0	55	129	14	47
October	371	301	85	0	81	92	15	28
November	376	366	111	0	65	115	6	67
December	518	475	129	0	62	164	25	94
Totals	4,738	4,101	1,068	15	715	1,481	380	441
Monthly averages	395	342	89	1	60	123	32	37
1926								
January	615	546	196	35	56	179	32	47
February	414	381	155	2	42	131	23	28
March	480	443	187	2	54	122	32	47
April	443	332	59	6	50	136	37	43
May	454	442	52	0	49	267	18	56
June	472	379	64	6	93	141	38	36
July	474	415	82	0	75	190	31	37
August	243	176	35	0	52	48	15	26
September	329	283	93	0	48	41	62	39
October	350	277	72	1	73	104	9	16
November	595	331	86	9	51	130	15	40
December	429	353	94	10	66	108	35	41
Totals	5,300	4,357	1,175	71	709	1,598	346	457
Monthly averages	442	363	98	6	59	133	29	38
1927								
January	613	510	176	20	73	215	6	19
February	786	541	111	22	50	262	55	41
March	495	393	67	1	57	139	56	74
April	522	390	119	10	53	132	33	42
May	719	453	111	28	40	161	68	45
June	708	538	170	18	59	130	111	50
July	371	342	73	3	49	109	13	94
August	444	278	60	12	36	77	75	18
September	457	378	83	10	45	153	10	76
October	735	575	120	13	71	200	33	139
November	618	404	118	15	42	120	17	93
December	852	589	45	21	56	367	31	68
Totals	7,319	5,391	1,254	175	630	2,065	506	760
Monthly averages	610	449	105	15	53	172	42	63

		Refunding				
Total	Indus-trial	Invest. trusts, trading, holding, etc.	Lands, build-ings, etc.	Public utilities	Rail-roads	Misc.
28	7		0	20	0	0
37	17		0	14	7	0
12	7		1	3	0	1
26	5		0	18	2	0
49	4		0	2	43	0
63	0		0	50	13	0
46	11		0	20	15	0
93	13		0	3	77	0
39	4		0	31	4	1
57	23		0	21	0	12
8	0		0	7	1	0
59	37		1	15	0	6
516	129		2	204	161	21
43	11		0	17	13	2
95	57		3	21	6	6
53	19		4	5	25	1
70	7		4	50	2	7
71	8		2	7	54	0
35	11		0	23	0	1
68	15		2	30	17	3
75	36		2	30	8	0
29	10		3	16	0	0
16	14		0	2	0	0
70	22		15	18	14	2
11	2		2	6	0	0
43	1		0	18	10	15
637	203		37	229	134	34
53	17		3	19	11	3
69	26		2	26	15	0
33	14		0	17	0	1
37	20		2	16	0	0
111	2		3	80	25	0
12	3		2	8	0	0
93	15		1	73	2	1
60	16		8	22	10	3
67	42		1	21	0	3
45	22		0	5	0	18
74	21		7	42	3	1
265	218		0	31	13	2
76	35		0	29	9	4
943	435		27	370	77	34
79	36		2	31	6	3
103	1		1	95	3	3
245	42		6	113	77	7
102	16		2	49	34	1
132	19		4	64	25	19
266	107		2	94	62	1
169	20		16	25	94	15
29	17		0	6	1	5
166	31		2	24	109	1
79	9		0	47	10	13
160	36		3	112	0	9
214	71		1	132	0	11
263	52		2	150	43	17
1,928	419		38	912	457	101
161	35		3	76	38	8

TABLE A.26 (continued)

Year and month	Total (new capital and refunding)	New Capital						
		Total	Industrial	Invest. trusts, trading, holding, etc.	Lands, buildings, etc.	Public utilities	Railroads	Misc.
1928								
January	588	423	90	51	77	139	33	33
February	626	425	85	16	48	150	27	100
March	766	405	96	42	49	97	51	71
April	842	493	79	32	77	192	34	79
May	782	608	141	109	75	134	5	144
June	831	614	134	32	59	304	0	85
July	324	285	74	13	61	58	18	62
August	201	183	29	3	29	92	14	16
September	428	391	92	10	45	192	0	53
October	659	603	103	88	81	197	46	88
November	767	709	216	112	73	98	58	152
December	1,003	941	247	278	43	161	79	132
Totals	7,818	6,080	1,386	787	716	1,811	364	1,015
Monthly averages	651	507	115	66	60	151	30	85
1929								
January	971	828	184	277	66	131	49	122
February	976	853	165	239	118	178	5	149
March	941	882	232	180	77	264	21	108
April	721	587	161	82	34	114	75	121
May	1,314	923	235	78	49	230	97	234
June	641	625	149	72	40	128	91	145
July	863	804	123	221	41	295	22	102
August	788	763	92	454	36	91	1	90
September	1,508	1,201	238	529	7	236	12	179
October	757	724	242	79	24	96	57	226
November	202	187	52	3	17	26	58	30
December	345	262	25	9	13	144	57	14
Totals	10,026	8,639	1,897	2,222	520	1,932	547	1,521
Monthly averages	836	720	158	185	43	161	46	127
1930								
January	702	629	36	63	28	473	7	21
February	496	469	145	16	18	163	104	22
March	646	631	124	2	17	225	214	49
April	680	628	226	62	64	126	139	11
May	927	864	196	2	8	570	60	28
June	513	445	122	4	15	163	121	21
July	429	402	42	10	22	221	55	53
August	190	122	61	0	3	47	1	9
September	347	285	10	70	16	115	71	2
October	214	151	68	3	9	58	5	8
November	142	138	15	0	15	90	4	14
December	188	181	17	0	30	116	14	4
Totals	5,473	4,944	1,061	233	245	2,365	797	244
Monthly averages	456	412	88	19	20	197	66	20
1931								
January	581	400	70	0	6	199	122	3
February	88	74	2	2	6	55	8	1
March	401	269	81	0	4	62	111	11
April	457	267	66	0	8	157	4	33
May	251	169	5	0	10	131	22	1
June	253	131	8	0	4	112	6	1
July	156	115	11	1	2	100	0	1
August	52	46	10	0	3	22	12	0
September	176	156	4	0	67	31	52	3
October	18	17	2	1	9	2	0	3
November	70	50	1	0	6	35	8	0
December	86	67	12	0	5	42	0	8
Totals	2,589	1,763	272	4	129	949	346	64
Monthly averages	216	147	23	0	11	79	29	5

TABLE A.26 (continued)

		Refunding				
Total	Industrial	Invest. trusts, trading, holding, etc.	Lands, buildings, etc.	Public utilities	Railroads	Misc.
165	42	0	2	66	45	10
201	30	0	0	113	49	9
361	51	0	25	136	142	6
349	62	1	20	189	61	17
174	27	0	8	108	23	9
217	77	3	15	70	42	10
39	34	0	3	0	1	1
19	4	0	1	6	0	8
37	6	0	13	10	0	8
55	36	0	5	12	0	2
59	36	0	1	9	0	14
62	28	0	0	31	0	2
1,738	431	4	93	751	364	96
145	36	0	8	63	30	8
143	75	0	3	45	13	7
122	34	0	0	75	7	7
58	4	0	0	53	0	1
134	36	0	0	14	84	0
391	263	0	0	113	8	7
16	2	2	0	12	0	0
59	23	0	0	25	5	6
25	1	0	0	18	0	6
307	93	0	0	144	69	0
33	26	0	0	6	0	1
15	5	0	2	0	8	0
83	0	0	0	6	76	0
1,387	563	2	7	511	271	35
116	47	0	1	43	23	3
73	1	0	0	19	53	0
28	4	0	0	9	14	0
15	2	0	0	4	9	1
51	7	0	0	5	39	0
63	28	0	0	35	0	1
27	0	0	0	9	58	0
26	5	0	0	14	8	0
68	27	0	0	1	40	0
62	0	0	0	57	5	0
63	12	0	0	47	0	4
4	0	0	0	0	4	0
7	5	0	0	1	0	1
529	91	0	1	201	229	7
44	8	0	0	17	19	1
181	1	0	2	125	53	0
14	1	0	0	9	4	0
132	3	0	0	40	89	1
189	36	1	0	148	2	2
81	1	0	1	79	1	0
122	3	0	0	108	10	0
41	4	0	0	3C	0	0
6	0	0	0	6	0	0
20	1	0	0	11	8	0
1	0	0	1	0	u	0
20	0	0	0	16	4	0
19	8	0	0	11	0	0
826	58	1	4	590	171	3
69	5	0	0	49	14	0

TABLE A.26 (continued)

	Total (new capital and refunding)	Total	Industrial	Invest. trusts, trading, holding, etc.	Lands, buildings, etc.	Public utilities	Railroads	Misc.
Year and month								
1932								
January	48	47	2	0	1	43	0	0
February	45	39	0	0	3	30	4	2
March	57	48	0	0	2	42	3	1
April	48	15	0	0	1	13	0	2
May	22	7	0	0	0	7	0	0
June	29	4	0	0	0	4	0	0
July	112	63	1	0	0	61	0	0
August	133	26	1	0	0	15	4	6
September	11	7	0	0	1	6	0	0
October	67	48	4	0	0	45	0	0
November	42	11	1	1	0	7	2	0
December	29	10	8	0	1	1	0	1
Totals	644	325	17	1	8	274	13	12
Monthly averages	54	27	1	0	1	23	1	1
1933								
January	65	22	3	0	0	7	12	0
February	38	1	0	0	1	0	0	0
March	5	3	3	0	0	0	0	0
April	36	17	1	0	0	16	0	0
May	16	4	3	0	0	1	0	0
June	60	12	9	0	0	3	0	0
July	96	53	45	1	0	7	0	0
August	14	14	14	0	0	0	0	0
September	27	9	9	0	0	0	0	0
October	3	3	3	0	0	0	0	0
November	7	7	7	0	0	0	0	0
December	16	16	15	0	0	0	0	0
Totals	382	161	112	1	1	34	12	0
Monthly averages	32	13	9	0	0	3	1	0
1934								
January	7	6	6	0	0	0	0	0
February	15	13	1	0	0	12	0	0
March	26	14	5	0	0	2	6	0
April	88	28	5	0	0	0	23	0
May	32	29	3	0	0	8	18	0
June	33	9	0	0	0	0	0	9
July	146	20	2	0	0	11	7	0
August	18	8	1	0	0	6	1	0
September	17	7	1	0	0	3	1	2
October	31	0	0	0	0	0	0	0
November	30	8	1	0	0	6	1	0
December	47	35	1	19	0	0	15	0
Totals	491	178	26	19	0	49	73	11
Monthly averages	41	15	2	2	0	4	6	1
1935								
January	8	5	3	0	0	3	0	0
February	30	6	6	0	0	1	0	0
March	120	8	0	0	0	7	1	0
April	156	22	15	0	1	0	6	0
May	126	45	30	0	0	0	15	0
June	129	14	8	0	0	1	5	0
July	542	55	20	0	0	9	1	25
August	210	30	11	0	0	3	15	0
September	276	45	16	0	1	19	9	0
October	252	73	60	0	0	11	0	2
November	251	33	4	0	0	29	0	0
December	167	67	41	2	0	0	21	3
Totals	2,267	404	214	2	2	84	73	30
Monthly averages	189	34	18	0	0	7	6	2

New Capital

TABLE A.26 (continued)

		Refunding				
Total	Indus-trial	Invest. trusts, trading, holding, etc.	Lands, build-ings, etc.	Public utilities	Rail-roads	Misc.
2	0	0	0	2	0	0
6	0	0	0	5	1	0
9	0	0	0	9	0	0
33	0	0	0	33	0	0
15	0	0	0	15	0	0
25	0	0	0	16	9	0
49	0	0	0	49	0	0
107	0	0	0	85	23	0
4	0	0	0	4	0	0
19	3	0	0	16	0	0
31	0	0	0	31	0	0
18	1	0	0	2	15	0
319	4	0	0	266	48	0
27	0	0	0	22	4	0
42	4	0	0	38	0	0
36	0	0	0	0	36	0
2	0	0	0	2	0	0
18	2	0	0	12	5	0
12	6	0	0	6	0	0
48	6	0	0	0	42	0
43	42	0	0	0	1	0
0	0	0	0	0	0	0
18	14	0	0	0	4	0
0	0	0	0	0	0	0
0	0	0	0	0	0	0
1	0	0	0	1	0	0
221	74	0	0	59	88	0
18	6	0	0	5	7	0
2	0	0	0	2	0	0
2	2	0	0	0	0	0
13	0	0	0	13	0	0
59	0	0	0	6	54	0
3	3	0	0	0	0	0
24	0	0	0	4	20	0
126	0	0	0	33	93	0
10	10	0	0	0	0	0
10	0	0	0	10	0	0
31	9	0	0	20	2	0
22	0	0	0	22	0	0
12	3	0	0	1	8	0
313	27	0	0	110	176	0
26	2	0	0	9	15	0
2	2	0	0	0	0	0
23	3	0	0	10	8	3
112	45	0	0	51	16	0
134	6	0	0	84	21	22
82	57	0	0	20	6	0
115	20	0	0	88	8	0
487	153	0	0	329	0	4
180	81	0	6	32	58	3
231	78	0	0	145	8	0
179	6	4	0	170	0	0
217	29	0	1	188	0	0
101	14	0	0	83	0	3
1,864	493	4	6	1,200	124	36
155	41	0	1	100	10	3

TABLE A.26 (continued)

Year and month	Total (new capital and refunding)	Total	Industrial	New Capital Invest. trusts, trading, holding, etc.	Lands, buildings, etc.	Public utilities	Railroads	Misc.
1936								
January	274	73	41	0	0	2	31	0
February	195	13	9	0	2	0	0	3
March	595	59	25	0	0	27	6	1
April	688	128	55	0	0	15	55	3
May	305	38	28	5	0	3	0	1
June	528	152	42	0	2	16	81	11
July	294	70	30	7	1	10	5	17
August	232	171	9	0	0	2	40	120
September	250	75	62	0	0	0	4	8
October	381	110	53	0	5	6	9	37
November	264	109	50	0	0	8	10	42
December	626	218	70	1	3	36	27	81
Totals	4,632	1,215	472	13	12	124	267	326
Monthly averages	386	101	39	1	1	10	22	27
1937								
January	300	96	58	0	0	8	7	23
February	392	152	66	0	3	8	63	12
March	320	139	41	0	1	13	71	13
April	165	78	31	0	1	3	80	14
May	169	77	41	0	1	7	25	3
June	418	269	177	0	9	25	12	55
July	139	82	47	0	0	30	3	2
August	107	51	24	0	0	4	3	19
September	152	113	99	0	0	12	1	0
October	136	67	27	0	2	32	5	0
November	37	2	19	0	0	6	0	2
December	57	43	28	0	0	7	5	3
Totals	2,393	1,194	659	0	10	153	225	146
Monthly averages	183	99	55	0	1	13	19	12

TABLE A.26 (continued)

		Refunding				
Total	Indus-trial	Invest. trusts, trading, holding, etc.	Lands, build-ings, etc.	Public utilities	Rail-roads	Misc.
201	110	0	0	27	64	0
181	29	0	3	135	0	14
536	77	0	0	234	218	8
560	182	0	0	301	67	10
267	106	0	0	113	49	0
376	158	0	0	169	26	23
225	19	0	1	140	45	20
62	7	0	1	42	12	0
175	26	0	4	121	26	4
272	11	0	2	259	0	0
155	41	0	0	102	7	5
408	19	0	0	359	22	7
3,417	785	0	12	2,002	529	89
285	65	0	1	167	44	7
204	72	0	1	71	52	8
240	74	0	15	144	6	1
181	15	0	0	148	3	14
87	36	0	0	7	41	3
92	39	0	0	51	0	3
149	12	0	3	131	3	1
57	56	0	0	0	0	0
56	4	0	2	47	3	0
39	39	0	0	0	0	0
70	0	0	2	51	16	0
10	9	0	0	1	0	0
14	0	0	0	11	0	0
1,199	356	0	23	665	125	30
100	30	0	2	55	10	2

Source: <u>Survey of Current Business</u>, May 1938, pp. 18-20.

TABLE A.27
U.S. Corporate and Government Capital Flotations by Type of Issue   1924-1937 (monthly) ($ millions)

Year and month	Total new capital and refund- ing	New capital total	Do- mestic total	Corp- orate total	Long term	Short term	Pre- ferred stocks	Com- mon stocks	Farm loan and other govern- ment agencies	Muni- cipal, States, etc.	Foreign total	Corp- orate	Govern- ment	United States posses- sions
1924														
January	548	476	438	271	188	19	15	49	69	99	38	6	32	0
February	538	410	326	227	138	31	12	47	5	94	84	1	80	3
March	370	357	355	253	166	32	5	50	2	100	2	2	1	0
April	494	465	384	249	171	33	29	16	4	131	81	1	78	2
May	631	580	570	447	190	9	41	207	6	117	10	0	9	1
June	620	555	534	249	180	40	16	13	44	241	21	4	17	0
July	434	386	288	159	97	24	31	7	14	115	98	74	24	0
August	455	331	265	157	115	8	19	16	1	107	66	38	28	0
September	579	510	346	215	163	14	32	7	10	121	164	58	106	0
October	690	632	432	326	220	27	55	23	15	91	200	36	164	0
November	431	422	308	228	145	28	9	46	7	73	113	8	104	2
December	561	469	341	248	151	11	55	31	2	90	128	66	61	1
Totals	6,352	5,593	4,588	3,029	1,924	276	318	511	179	1,380	1,005	293	703	9
Monthly averages	529	466	382	252	160	23	26	43	15	115	84	24	59	1
1925														
January	696	598	533	363	251	44	43	25	37	133	65	50	12	3
February	666	575	461	374	254	24	41	55	9	77	114	76	38	0
March	506	427	363	243	148	14	66	14	12	108	64	39	25	0
April	627	531	470	375	219	20	106	29	6	89	61	37	23	1
May	533	494	473	250	178	6	31	35	36	187	20	11	9	0
June	673	564	428	288	189	10	38	50	2	138	136	24	112	0
July	696	576	415	280	162	11	44	62	3	132	161	43	118	0
August	404	301	266	186	124	7	22	33	1	80	35	26	9	0
September	496	468	379	263	173	19	44	28	5	112	89	31	57	0
October	506	426	340	258	126	16	72	43	8	74	86	43	40	9
November	590	575	393	321	165	12	38	107	6	66	181	44	137	1
December	731	687	604	404	241	37	48	78	44	157	83	71	11	1
Totals	7,126	6,220	5,125	3,605	2,231	221	594	558	169	1,352	1,095	496	590	9
Monthly averages	594	518	427	300	186	18	50	47	14	113	91	41	49	1
1926														
January	732	652	567	493	301	43	78	71	5	68	85	53	27	6
February	638	561	499	324	173	28	75	48	4	171	61	57	4	0
March	653	611	561	416	218	24	104	70	29	115	51	27	24	0
April	639	523	396	285	228	27	20	9	2	109	127	47	80	0
May	666	652	555	415	208	27	24	157	4	136	97	26	70	2
June	725	583	472	307	236	18	31	23	30	135	111	72	88	1
July	582	522	411	317	212	11	27	68	6	89	111	98	13	0
August	353	285	216	141	108	9	12	12	4	71	69	35	34	0
September	542	493	360	223	164	13	22	24	2	136	132	60	72	0
October	580	487	373	270	213	15	32	10	1	102	114	6	106	2
November	699	432	332	259	146	21	38	54	4	69	100	72	28	0
December	622	543	447	305	212	13	47	33	0	142	96	49	48	0
Totals	7,430	6,344	5,189	3,754	2,418	249	509	578	91	1,344	1,156	603	542	10
Monthly averages	619	529	432	313	201	21	42	48	8	112	96	50	45	1
1927														
January	941	781	669	442	336	11	54	42	24	203	111	68	42	1
February	942	696	607	526	255	12	174	85	4	76	89	15	75	0
March	672	568	452	361	243	13	21	85	4	87	116	32	84	0
April	907	671	455	314	222	11	48	34	13	128	216	76	140	1
May	962	693	636	421	268	22	71	59	3	213	57	32	24	0
June	926	753	639	482	334	37	51	60	2	155	114	56	54	3
July	484	453	364	278	184	21	47	26	1	85	89	64	26	0
August	617	450	339	248	139	29	32	48	0	91	111	30	81	0
September	634	541	419	302	185	4	50	63	4	114	122	77	45	0
October	1,034	857	595	446	325	26	73	23	32	117	261	129	130	2
November	773	555	376	279	157	14	65	42	1	97	179	125	50	3
December	1,040	773	666	558	314	20	190	34	0	109	107	31	75	1
Totals	9,934	7,791	6,219	4,657	2,962	221	874	600	87	1,475	1,573	734	827	11
Monthly averages	828	649	518	388	247	18	73	50	7	123	131	61	69	1
1928														
January	775	583	447	347	208	16	64	58	2	98	136	76	59	1
February	884	625	522	390	241	22	86	41	2	130	103	35	68	0
March	984	619	484	356	183	16	109	47	2	126	135	49	86	0
April	1,060	692	572	449	228	13	74	134	0	123	120	45	75	0
May	1,047	870	622	466	195	18	121	133	4	152	248	142	103	3
June	1,038	803	603	456	146	7	70	233	27	121	199	158	40	2
July	447	407	354	273	87	14	78	95	1	80	53	11	41	0
August	270	251	250	182	76	46	16	44	0	68	1	1	0	0
September	543	501	395	329	174	7	56	91	2	64	106	63	44	0
October	800	745	656	557	192	6	144	214	1	99	88	47	42	0
November	970	910	839	654	241	20	135	258	15	170	71	55	16	0
December	1,173	1,110	1,045	889	205	26	195	463	8	148	65	52	13	0
Totals	9,992	8,114	6,789	5,346	2,175	210	1,149	1,812	64	1,379	1,325	734	586	6
Monthly averages	833	676	566	446	181	18	96	151	5	115	110	61	49	1

	Domestic								Foreign			
		Corporate					Farm loan and other government agencies	Municipal, states, etc.				United States possessions
			Bonds and notes		Preferred stocks	Common stocks						
Refunding total	Domestic total	Corporate total	Long term	Short term					Foreign total	Corporate	Government	
72	29	28	26	0	0	2	0	1	43	0	43	0
128	20	19	12	7	0	0	0	0	108	18	90	0
13	13	12	9	0	2	0	0	1	0	0	0	0
29	28	26	16	1	6	3	0	2	1	0	1	0
52	49	49	48	1	0	0	0	1	3	0	3	0
65	65	63	44	17	2	0	0	2	0	0	0	0
48	48	46	41	3	2	0	0	2	0	0	0	0
124	94	93	89	0	3	1	0	1	30	0	30	0
70	43	39	26	2	11	0	0	4	27	0	27	0
57	57	57	47	10	0	0	0	1	0	0	0	0
10	6	5	3	0	0	1	0	2	3	3	0	0
93	59	56	34	20	1	2	0	3	33	3	30	0
759	511	492	396	60	28	8	0	19	248	25	234	0
63	43	41	33	5	2	1	0	2	21	2	19	0
98	88	85	20	62	2	1	0	3	10	10	0	0
92	52	48	44	3	0	1	0	3	40	5	35	0
79	76	70	70	0	0	0	3	3	3	0	3	0
96	79	69	66	0	2	1	5	6	17	3	14	0
39	39	35	25	1	0	9	1	3	0	0	0	0
110	69	68	48	2	2	16	0	2	40	0	40	0
120	93	75	32	9	25	9	6	13	27	0	27	0
103	33	29	19	0	0	9	0	4	70	0	70	0
28	20	16	11	2	1	2	0	4	8	0	8	0
81	81	70	61	4	2	3	5	5	0	0	0	0
15	12	11	5	1	5	0	0	1	4	0	4	0
45	43	41	34	3	4	0	0	1	2	2	0	0
906	685	618	436	87	43	52	20	48	221	20	201	0
75	57	51	36	7	4	4	2	4	18	2	17	0
80	65	63	57	0	4	3	0	2	14	5	9	0
77	26	25	23	0	0	2	0	1	52	8	40	0
42	39	37	35	1	1	0	0	2	3	0	3	0
116	101	99	81	17	1	0	0	2	15	12	3	0
14	14	12	10	2	0	0	0	2	0	0	0	0
141	133	88	86	2	0	0	40	5	8	6	6	0
60	54	54	35	12	1	5	0	1	6	6	0	0
68	57	56	53	0	3	1	0	1	11	11	0	0
50	36	35	32	2	0	2	0	1	13	10	3	0
93	45	44	30	2	12	0	0	1	48	30	18	0
266	266	264	176	1	1	86	0	2	0	0	0	0
79	44	41	24	6	11	0	0	3	35	35	0	0
1,086	881	820	641	45	34	99	40	22	205	123	82	0
91	73	68	53	4	3	8	3	2	17	10	7	0
160	107	103	89	0	3	11	0	4	54	0	54	0
246	246	245	219	7	10	9	0	1	0	0	0	0
103	103	102	91	2	9	0	0	1	0	0	0	0
236	231	132	113	0	12	7	93	7	5	0	5	0
269	269	266	248	17	0	0	0	3	0	0	0	0
173	141	137	91	1	3	41	0	4	33	33	0	0
31	24	23	15	1	7	0	0	1	6	6	0	0
168	168	166	79	13	74	0	0	1	0	0	0	0
92	79	75	72	1	3	0	0	4	14	4	10	0
178	135	133	70	31	32	0	0	1	43	26	17	0
219	209	205	200	0	5	0	0	4	9	9	0	0
267	266	263	217	9	23	15	0	2	2	0	0	2
2,143	1,978	1,850	1,504	82	180	84	93	35	165	78	85	2
179	165	154	125	7	15	7	8	3	14	7	7	0
192	157	155	130	1	16	9	0	2	35	10	25	0
260	196	192	160	19	1	11	0	4	64	10	54	0
365	365	361	253	10	85	13	0	4	0	0	0	0
368	321	314	240	0	14	60	0	7	47	35	12	0
177	165	162	104	4	51	3	0	3	13	13	0	0
235	152	143	37	0	63	43	0	9	83	74	9	0
40	40	39	9	1	2	26	0	1	0	0	0	0
20	20	19	3	3	5	8	0	1	0	0	0	0
42	39	37	24	0	0	13	0	2	3	0	3	0
56	49	48	12	10	6	20	0	1	7	7	0	0
60	57	56	8	2	4	43	0	1	2	2	0	0
63	59	58	18	4	2	33	0	1	4	4	0	0
1,877	1,620	1,584	999	54	248	282	0	36	258	154	104	0
156	135	132	83	5	21	24	0	3	21	13	9	0

TABLE A.27 (continued)

Year and month	Total new capital and refunding	New capital total	Domestic total	Corporate total	Bonds and notes Long term	Bonds and notes Short term	Preferred stocks	Common stocks	Farm loan and other government agencies	Municipal, States, etc.	Foreign total	Corporate	Government	United States possessions
1929														
January	1,066	918	878	804	250	11	106	438	0	74	40	24	16	0
February	1,058	934	869	800	152	19	250	378	0	68	66	53	11	1
March	1,057	997	772	668	223	7	132	306	0	104	225	214	10	0
April	817	678	662	571	160	29	95	287	0	91	16	16	0	0
May	1,513	1,121	1,074	899	298	25	98	478	0	175	47	24	23	0
June	802	785	613	463	91	22	114	236	0	150	172	162	10	1
July	948	888	852	768	136	8	145	479	0	84	35	35	0	0
August	884	859	838	757	89	7	235	426	0	81	21	6	15	0
September	1,617	1,309	1,301	1,201	224	16	171	858	0	99	8	0	8	0
October	881	847	794	676	224	10	148	293	0	118	53	48	5	0
November	298	281	246	163	9	32	4	118	0	84	35	24	9	2
December	651	566	521	232	85	19	18	109	0	289	45	30	14	1
Totals	11,592	10,183	9,420	8,002	1,873	205	1,517	4,407	0	1,418	763	637	120	5
Monthly averages	966	827	785	667	156	17	126	367	0	118	64	53	10	0
1930														
January	827	750	719	611	436	48	4	122	0	108	31	18	11	2
February	626	596	470	389	224	14	21	128	2	80	126	81	45	0
March	822	799	658	516	368	25	55	68	20	123	141	115	26	0
April	960	905	731	582	251	70	100	161	0	149	175	47	127	1
May	1,181	1,108	988	847	375	65	51	356	1	140	119	17	101	1
June	781	709	533	378	156	69	75	78	8	148	176	68	103	6
July	586	554	475	367	241	56	51	20	0	107	80	35	45	0
August	291	205	166	83	35	9	12	27	0	83	39	38	1	0
September	497	378	375	284	178	44	26	35	15	76	3	1	3	0
October	445	377	278	127	85	20	12	10	0	151	100	24	76	0
November	269	257	247	136	55	62	3	15	26	85	10	2	8	0
December	394	384	364	164	54	39	1	70	15	184	21	16	3	1
Totals	7,677	7,023	6,004	4,483	2,460	520	412	1,091	87	1,434	1,020	461	448	10
Monthly averages	640	585	500	374	205	43	34	91	7	120	85	38	46	1
1931														
January	649	467	335	280	218	17	27	19	6	49	132	120	12	0
February	221	206	201	74	41	6	8	19	9	118	4	0	4	0
March	701	566	553	260	218	32	7	3	15	279	13	10	4	0
April	591	387	370	267	111	55	36	66	0	102	18	0	18	0
May	428	344	334	161	102	30	16	13	0	173	10	8	2	0
June	402	251	225	108	84	17	3	3	0	119	27	25	1	0
July	268	223	223	115	22	91	0	2	15	93	0	0	0	0
August	127	120	120	46	21	13	10	2	0	74	0	0	0	0
September	314	271	221	106	77	18	8	5	0	114	51	50	0	1
October	46	45	45	17	14	0	2	2	12	16	0	0	0	1
November	131	110	110	50	19	8	1	23	6	54	0	0	0	0
December	145	124	123	67	25	3	0	39	12	44	1	0	0	1
Totals	4,023	3,116	2,860	1,551	951	289	116	195	75	1,235	255	213	41	2
Monthly averages	335	260	238	129	79	24	10	16	6	103	21	18	3	0
1932														
January	199	185	185	47	41	1	4	0	0	138	0	0	0	0
February	95	74	74	39	28	7	2	2	0	35	0	0	0	0
March	192	162	162	48	42	5	0	1	5	109	0	0	0	0
April	143	71	71	15	14	1	0	0	25	31	0	0	0	0
May	125	91	91	7	5	2	0	0	0	84	0	0	0	0
June	148	84	84	4	4	0	0	0	0	80	0	0	0	0
July	156	105	105	63	62	0	0	1	16	27	0	0	0	0
August	173	62	60	26	15	9	1	1	0	34	2	0	2	0
September	139	89	69	7	6	0	0	0	4	58	20	0	20	0
October	124	100	96	48	40	6	1	1	9	38	4	0	4	0
November	77	45	44	11	8	1	0	2	5	29	1	0	0	1
December	160	125	125	10	5	1	1	3	13	101	0	0	0	0
Totals	1,730	1,192	1,165	325	271	34	10	10	77	762	27	0	26	1
Monthly averages	144	99	97	27	23	3	1	1	6	64	2	0	2	0
1933														
January	110	65	65	22	18	1	3	1	9	33	0	0	0	0
February	57	20	20	1	1	0	0	0	1	17	0	0	0	0
March	19	17	17	3	0	0	1	2	0	13	0	0	0	0
April	46	26	26	17	0	16	0	9	0	9	0	0	0	0
May	60	44	44	4	1	0	0	3	0	40	0	0	0	0
June	224	109	109	12	3	0	1	8	0	97	0	0	0	0
July	163	118	116	53	0	0	7	46	35	29	1	0	0	0
August	56	46	46	15	0	0	4	10	0	32	0	0	0	0
September	95	64	64	9	0	0	0	9	18	37	0	0	0	0
October	59	58	58	3	0	0	0	3	0	55	0	0	0	0
November	89	87	87	7	0	0	0	6	0	80	0	0	0	0
December	76	57	57	16	0	0	0	15	0	41	0	0	0	0
Totals	1,054	710	708	161	24	17	15	105	64	483	2	0	0	1
Monthly averages	88	59	59	13	2	1	1	9	5	40	0	0	0	0

TABLE A.27 (continued)

		Refunding										
		Domestic							**Foreign**			
		Corporate					Farm loan and other government agencies	Municipal, states, etc.				
			Bonds and notes									
Refunding total	Domestic total	Corporate total	Long term	Short term	Preferred stocks	Common stocks			Foreign total	Corporate	Government	United States possessions
148	145	143	57	5	22	59	0	2	4	0	4	0
124	122	120	77	0	28	15	0	1	2	2	0	0
60	60	58	51	3	0	4	0	2	0	0	0	0
139	135	134	86	12	2	34	0	1	4	0	4	0
392	392	391	103	1	39	247	0	2	0	0	0	0
17	6	6	0	0	1	4	0	1	10	10	0	0
60	60	59	15	21	0	23	0	1	0	0	0	0
25	25	25	16	1	0	9	0	0	0	0	0	0
308	307	307	70	0	57	180	0	1	1	0	1	0
34	34	33	5	0	27	1	0	1	0	0	0	0
17	16	15	9	2	0	5	0	1	1	0	1	0
85	85	83	6	0	0	76	0	2	0	0	0	0
1,409	**1,387**	**1,374**	**496**	**46**	**178**	**655**	**0**	**11**	**22**	**12**	**10**	**0**
117	116	115	41	4	15	55	0	1	2	1	1	0
77	57	55	44	11	0	0	0	2	20	18	2	0
30	29	28	21	6	0	1	0	1	1	0	1	0
22	18	15	10	5	0	0	0	3	4	0	4	0
55	51	47	46	1	0	0	0	3	4	4	0	0
73	68	63	26	28	0	10	0	5	6	0	6	0
71	51	47	42	3	0	3	0	4	20	20	0	0
32	32	26	21	5	0	0	0	5	0	0	0	0
86	83	68	67	0	1	0	0	15	3	0	3	0
118	62	57	50	7	0	0	0	4	57	5	52	0
68	60	55	16	30	8	1	0	5	8	8	0	0
12	7	4	4	0	0	0	0	3	5	0	5	0
9	9	7	2	5	0	0	0	3	0	0	0	0
654	**527**	**474**	**351**	**100**	**9**	**14**	**0**	**53**	**127**	**55**	**72**	**0**
54	44	40	29	8	1	1	0	4	11	5	6	0
182	182	181	175	6	0	0	0	1	0	0	0	0
15	15	14	7	7	0	0	0	1	0	0	0	0
135	130	129	127	3	0	0	0	1	5	3	2	0
204	202	187	155	33	0	0	11	4	2	2	0	0
84	84	81	49	1	31	0	0	2	0	0	0	0
151	144	122	104	18	0	0	20	2	8	0	8	0
45	45	41	30	10	0	0	0	4	0	0	0	0
7	7	6	5	1	0	0	0	1	0	0	0	0
43	43	20	9	10	1	0	20	3	0	0	0	0
1	1	1	0	1	0	0	0	0	0	0	0	0
21	21	20	16	4	0	0	0	0	0	0	0	0
21	21	19	0	19	0	0	0	1	0	0	0	0
907	**893**	**821**	**677**	**111**	**32**	**0**	**51**	**21**	**15**	**5**	**10**	**0**
76	74	68	56	9	3	0	4	2	1	0	1	0
14	14	2	0	2	0	0	13	0	0	0	0	0
21	21	6	2	4	0	0	15	1	0	0	0	0
29	29	9	7	0	0	2	20	0	0	0	0	0
72	72	33	2	31	0	0	0	39	0	0	0	0
34	34	15	7	8	0	0	15	4	0	0	0	0
64	64	25	10	15	0	0	30	9	0	0	0	0
50	50	49	11	39	0	0	0	1	0	0	0	0
111	111	107	56	51	0	0	0	4	0	0	0	0
50	10	4	4	0	0	0	0	6	40	0	40	0
24	24	19	3	15	0	2	0	5	0	0	0	0
32	32	31	31	0	0	0	0	1	0	0	0	0
35	35	18	2	16	0	0	0	17	0	0	0	0
538	**498**	**319**	**135**	**180**	**0**	**3**	**93**	**87**	**40**	**0**	**40**	**0**
45	42	27	11	15	0	0	8	7	3	0	3	0
45	45	42	32	11	0	0	0	3	0	0	0	0
37	37	36	32	5	0	0	0	1	0	0	0	0
3	3	2	0	0	0	2	0	1	0	0	0	0
21	19	17	6	11	0	0	0	2	2	2	0	0
17	17	12	0	12	0	0	0	5	0	0	0	0
114	54	48	42	6	0	0	0	6	60	0	60	0
45	45	43	0	13	0	30	0	2	0	0	0	0
10	10	0	0	0	0	0	0	10	0	0	0	0
31	31	18	4	14	0	0	12	1	0	0	0	0
1	1	0	0	0	0	0	0	1	0	0	0	0
2	2	0	0	0	0	0	0	2	0	0	0	0
19	19	1	0	1	0	0	14	4	0	0	0	0
344	**283**	**219**	**115**	**72**	**0**	**32**	**26**	**37**	**62**	**2**	**60**	**0**
29	24	18	10	6	0	3	2	3	5	0	5	0

TABLE A.27 (continued)

| | | | | New Capital | | | | | | | | | | |
| | | | Domestic | | | | | | | | Foreign | | | |
Year and month	Total new capital and refunding	New capital total	Domestic total	Corporate total	Corporate — Bonds and notes, Long term	Short term	Preferred stocks	Common stocks	Farm loan and other government agencies	Municipal, states, etc.	Foreign total	Corporate	Government	United States possessions
1934														
January	91	48	48	6	0	0	0	6	5	37	0	0	0	0
February	89	81	81	13	0	12	0	1	7	61	0	0	0	0
March	149	99	99	14	9	0	1	3	3	83	0	0	0	0
April	239	141	141	28	23	1	0	4	15	98	0	0	0	0
May	144	100	100	29	26	0	1	2	13	58	0	0	0	0
June	307	119	119	9	0	0	0	9	12	98	0	0	0	0
July	376	214	214	20	0	18	0	2	105	88	0	0	0	0
August	260	180	180	8	8	0	0	0	153	19	0	0	0	0
September	71	39	39	7	4	1	0	2	0	32	0	0	0	0
October	157	122	122	0	0	0	0	0	83	38	0	0	0	0
November	142	104	104	8	8	0	0	0	10	86	0	0	0	0
December	187	139	139	35	34	0	0	1	0	104	0	0	0	0
Totals	2,212	1,386	1,386	178	112	32	3	31	405	803	0	0	0	0
Monthly averages	184	116	116	15	9	3	0	3	34	67	0	0	0	0
1935														
January	142	93	92	5	1	2	1	1	6	81	0	0	0	0
February	96	50	50	7	7	0	0	0	0	44	0	0	0	0
March	290	105	105	8	8	0	0	0	0	97	0	0	0	0
April	507	90	90	22	11	6	5	0	4	64	0	0	0	0
May	472	82	82	45	39	0	1	5	0	37	0	0	0	0
June	513	55	55	14	14	0	0	0	0	42	0	0	0	0
July	645	127	127	55	27	0	26	2	0	72	0	0	0	0
August	437	148	148	30	29	0	0	0	85	33	0	0	0	0
September	437	173	173	45	42	0	0	3	0	128	0	0	0	0
October	368	148	147	73	70	0	2	1	15	59	1	0	0	1
November	382	120	118	33	30	0	3	0	0	85	2	0	0	2
December	462	221	221	67	45	3	17	2	40	114	0	0	0	0
Totals	4,752	1,412	1,409	404	323	11	54	15	150	855	3	0	0	3
Monthly averages	396	118	117	34	27	1	5	1	13	71	0	0	0	0
1936														
January	412	124	116	65	60	1	2	2	0	51	8	8	0	0
February	303	107	107	13	4	0	4	6	4	90	0	0	0	0
March	767	128	128	59	45	1	2	11	11	58	0	0	0	0
April	1,003	176	176	128	87	15	2	24	0	48	0	0	0	0
May	420	112	112	38	13	0	2	22	6	68	0	0	0	0
June	733	218	217	152	121	2	19	10	1	64	1	0	0	1
July	339	103	103	70	39	0	7	23	0	33	0	0	0	0
August	409	178	178	171	146	0	14	10	0	46	0	0	0	0
September	409	178	178	75	60	0	7	19	0	103	1	0	3	1
October	466	188	173	95	60	0	13	22	0	78	15	15	0	0
November	381	158	158	109	96	1	6	6	0	49	0	0	0	0
December	726	266	266	218	96	4	11	108	0	48	0	0	0	0
Totals	6,254	1,973	1,949	1,192	816	23	90	262	22	735	25	23	3	2
Monthly averages	521	164	162	99	68	2	7	22	2	61	2	2	0	0
1937														
January	618	244	244	96	63	2	21	10	0	147	0	0	0	0
February	559	190	190	152	92	4	3	53	4	34	0	0	0	0
March	384	187	187	139	99	0	18	23	0	47	0	0	0	0
April	317	159	159	78	38	0	11	29	11	70	0	0	0	0
May	265	149	149	77	46	0	7	24	29	44	0	0	0	0
June	560	360	360	269	150	37	61	21	0	91	0	0	0	0
July	341	248	248	82	40	0	36	6	89	77	0	0	0	0
August	187	79	79	51	34	0	3	13	0	28	0	0	0	0
September	224	157	154	87	87	0	15	10	0	41	3	0	3	0
October	203	96	93	67	46	0	20	1	0	27	3	0	0	3
November	137	95	95	27	22	0	1	4	25	43	0	0	0	0
December	164	122	122	43	26	1	9	7	0	79	1	0	0	1
Totals	3,960	2,085	2,078	1,194	744	45	204	201	157	727	7	0	3	4
Monthly averages	330	174	173	99	62	4	17	17	13	61	1	0	0	0

Compiled by The Commercial & Financial Chronicle
Source: Survey of Current Business, February, 1938, pp. 16-21, with corrections from Survey of Current Business, April, 1938.

TABLE A.27 (continued)

			Domestic						Foreign			
		Corporate					Farm loan and other government agencies	Municipal, states, etc.				United States possessions
			Bonds and notes		Preferred stocks	Common stocks						
Refunding total	Domestic total	Corporate total	Long term	Short term					Foreign total	Corporate	Government	
43	43	2	2	0	0	0	23	18	0	0	0	0
8	8	2	2	0	0	0	2	4	0	0	0	0
50	50	13	13	0	0	0	22	15	0	0	0	0
98	97	58	58	0	0	0	30	9	1	1	0	0
44	44	3	0	3	0	0	20	21	0	0	0	0
189	189	24	4	20	0	0	147	17	0	0	0	0
162	162	125	50	76	0	0	30	6	0	0	0	0
79	29	10	4	7	0	0	11	8	50	0	50	0
32	32	10	10	0	0	0	13	9	0	0	0	0
35	35	31	2	29	0	0	0	4	0	0	0	0
38	28	22	22	0	0	0	0	6	10	0	10	0
48	48	12	9	3	0	0	18	17	0	0	0	0
826	765	312	175	137	0	0	317	136	61	1	60	0
69	64	26	15	11	0	0	26	11	5	0	5	0
49	49	2	1	2	0	0	30	16	0	0	0	0
46	46	23	10	13	0	0	13	10	0	0	0	0
185	185	112	112	0	0	0	20	53	0	0	0	0
418	418	134	112	3	19	0	192	92	0	0	0	0
391	391	82	76	6	0	0	267	42	0	0	0	0
457	457	115	115	0	0	0	319	23	0	0	0	0
517	513	487	472	10	5	0	11	16	4	0	0	4
289	213	180	151	5	24	0	0	33	76	0	76	0
265	265	231	229	1	1	0	13	21	0	0	0	0
220	216	179	164	0	16	0	24	13	4	0	0	4
262	262	217	216	0	1	0	17	28	0	0	0	0
241	201	101	85	0	3	12	81	19	40	0	40	0
3,340	3,216	1,864	1,743	39	69	12	987	365	124	0	116	8
278	268	155	145	3	6	1	82	30	10	0	10	1
288	240	201	183	17	0	0	0	38	48	0	48	0
196	196	181	162	8	11	1	6	8	0	0	0	0
639	616	536	524	1	11	0	9	71	24	0	24	0
827	765	530	485	7	37	2	199	37	62	30	32	0
308	308	267	252	0	12	4	4	37	0	0	0	0
516	514	376	325	1	47	3	93	45	2	0	0	2
236	236	225	220	2	2	1	2	9	0	0	0	0
80	80	62	55	0	6	0	8	11	0	0	0	0
231	231	175	156	0	19	1	0	56	0	0	0	0
278	278	272	249	0	18	4	1	5	0	0	0	0
223	199	155	145	0	7	3	28	16	24	0	24	0
459	459	408	391	4	12	1	3	49	0	0	0	0
4,281	4,123	3,387	3,147	40	181	20	353	382	158	30	127	2
357	344	282	262	3	15	2	29	32	13	2	11	0
374	289	204	81	7	116	0	26	60	85	0	85	0
370	271	240	155	1	28	56	21	9	99	0	99	0
199	197	181	162	0	15	4	4	12	0	0	0	0
158	123	87	69	0	5	13	22	14	35	0	35	0
116	116	92	71	0	20	1	16	8	0	0	0	0
200	200	149	125	14	10	1	30	21	0	0	0	0
93	93	57	20	0	28	9	29	8	0	0	0	0
109	109	56	35	16	3	2	27	25	0	0	0	0
67	67	39	0	0	38	1	20	7	0	0	0	0
107	106	70	70	0	0	0	34	2	1	0	0	2
42	42	10	9	1	0	0	27	4	0	0	0	0
42	42	14	5	9	0	0	23	5	0	0	0	0
1,875	1,655	1,199	802	47	264	87	280	175	221	0	219	2
156	138	100	67	4	22	7	23	15	18	0	18	0

TABLE A.28

Number of Bank Suspensions   1921-1936 (monthly)

All Banks

Month	Totals 1921-1936	1921	1922	1923	1924	1925	1926	1927	1928	1929	1930	1931	1932	1933	1934	1935	1936
January	1,620	63	57	35	152	100	71	135	56	58	90	198	342	236	23	3	1
February	951	29	42	36	90	62	51	80	48	70	87	76	119	150	6	0	5
March	4,163	45	30	46	69	42	53	75	64	52	80	86	45	3,460	4	3	9
April	686	42	32	31	72	45	57	48	47	40	90	64	74	30	5	4	5
May	693	40	29	29	80	55	66	46	30	66	59	91	82	12	1	2	5
June	795	21	19	30	52	37	81	40	29	79	87	167	151	11	5	4	2
July	743	30	12	48	45	27	142	35	24	67	64	93	132	12	3	5	4
August	616	36	24	52	35	19	49	26	20	18	67	158	85	22	2	1	2
September	757	29	19	53	34	28	42	36	20	37	67	305	67	13	1	3	3
October	1,185	57	26	71	40	53	87	51	41	41	71	522	102	17	3	1	2
November	1,205	63	34	102	48	77	154	42	77	70	256	175	93	8	2	3	1
December	1,529	50	42	113	58	73	123	55	42	61	352	358	161	29	2	5	5
Totals	14,943	505	366	646	775	618	976	669	498	659	1,350	2,293	1,453	4,000	57	34	44

National Banks

Month	Totals 1921-1936	1921	1922	1923	1924	1925	1926	1927	1928	1929	1930	1931	1932	1933	1934	1935	1936
January	252	7	6	4	27	24	7	18	7	4	9	20	74	44	0	1	0
February	171	2	10	6	20	15	8	14	6	13	18	15	24	20	0	0	0
March	1,120	4	1	5	14	6	5	11	7	6	8	18	7	1,028	0	0	0
April	83	5	3	5	10	12	5	5	5	3	5	17	6	2	0	0	0
May	100	4	3	4	8	10	9	10	5	6	2	24	14	1	0	0	0
June	131	1	2	6	7	3	13	7	1	9	10	26	44	1	0	1	0
July	82	2	2	5	6	3	4	2	1	7	9	16	20	3	1	1	0
August	94	4	3	7	5	3	8	4	4	2	8	29	17	0	0	0	0
September	97	2	2	6	2	4	6	2	3	3	7	46	12	1	0	1	0
October	198	7	7	7	8	10	15	7	2	4	10	100	20	1	0	0	0
November	167	7	3	19	9	10	25	5	8	1	26	35	19	0	0	0	0
December	224	7	7	16	6	18	18	6	8	6	49	63	19	0	0	0	1
Totals	2,719	52	49	90	122	118	123	91	57	64	161	409	276	1,101	1	4	1

State Member Banks

Month	Totals 1921-1936	1921	1922	1923	1924	1925	1926	1927	1928	1929	1930	1931	1932	1933	1934	1935	1936
January	78	2	1	3	12	8	4	8	1	2	4	5	13	15	0	0	0
February	39	1	0	1	6	2	2	2	4	2	1	5	6	7	0	0	0
March	175	1	3	5	3	1	1	5	3	1	1	1	0	150	0	0	0
April	20	0			1	2	1	4	1	1	2	3	5	0	0	0	0
May	21	1	0	3	0	4	1	3	0	1	0	2	6	0	0	0	0
June	27	1	1	1	1	2	3	1	1	1	1	10	4	0	0	0	0
July	16	2	1	2	1	0	1	0	1	2	0	2	4	0	0	0	0
August	21	1	0	1	1	1	0	1	0	1	1	12	2	0	0	0	0
September	31	1	0	0	0	1	1	4	1	0	2	16	4	1	0	0	0
October	47	4	2	3	1	3	5	2	1	1	0	25	0	0	0	0	0
November	50	2	2	7	5	1	6	1	1	4	7	8	6	0	0	0	0
December	67	3	4	6	7	3	10	—	2	1	8	18	5	1	0	0	0
Totals	592	19	13	32	38	28	35	31	16	17	27	107	55	174	0	0	0

Nonmember Banks, other than Private and Mutual Savings Banks

Month	Totals 1921-1936	1921	1922	1923	1924	1925	1926	1927	1928	1929	1930	1931	1932	1933	1934	1935	1936
January	1,223	48	49	26	109	61	58	105	44	52	72	164	248	164	20	2	1
February	702	23	31	28	55	41	39	62	38	52	68	52	86	118	4	0	5
March	2,733	33	24	33	48	33	47	57	51	31	69	63	33	2,198	1	3	9
April	542	32	27	23	59	30	50	34	38	35	80	41	54	28	2	4	5
May	534	31	24	19	70	33	51	32	24	57	53	61	60	11	1	2	5
June	599	18	11	20	40	30	60	29	26	67	53	126	100	10	4	3	2
July	609	23	7	38	35	23	135	33	21	58	46	68	105	7	2	4	4
August	470	27	19	43	26	14	40	21	15	15	52	110	63	21	2	1	1
September	599	24	16	46	32	22	34	29	14	32	52	231	51	10	1	2	3
October	892	43	15	59	28	37	58	37	38	35	57	384	81	14	3	1	2
November	951	52	28	75	33	62	105	34	67	63	220	130	68	8	2	3	1
December	1,179	36	30	91	43	47	89	41	30	50	282	267	136	27	1	5	4
Totals	11,033	390	281	501	578	433	766	514	406	547	1,104	1,697	1,085	2,616	43	30	42

Private Banks

Month	Totals 1921-1936	1921	1922	1923	1924	1925	1926	1927	1928	1929	1930	1931	1932	1933	1934	1935	1936
January	67	6	1	2	4	7	2	4	4	0	5	9	7	13	3	0	0
February	39	3	1	1	9	4	2	2	0	3	0	4	3	5	2	0	0
March	135	7	2	3	4	2	0	2	3	14	2	4	5	84	3	0	0
April	41	5	2	3	2	1	1	5	3	1	3	3	9	0	3	0	0
May	38	4	2	3	2	8	5	1	1	2	4	4	2		0	0	0
June	38	1	5	3	4	2	5	3	1	2	3	5	3	0	1	0	0
July	36	3	2	3	3	1	2	0	1	0	9	7	3	2	0	0	0
August	31	4	2	1	3	1	1	0	1	0	6	7	3	1	0	0	1
September	30	2	1	1	0	1	1	1	2	2	6	12	0	1	0	0	0
October	48	3	2	2	3	3	9	5	0	1	4	13	1	2	0	0	0
November	37	2	1	1	1	4	18	2	1	2	3	2	0	0	0	0	0
December	59	4	2	0	2	5	6	8	2	4	13	10	1	1	1	0	0
Totals	599	44	23	23	37	39	52	33	19	31	58	80	37	109	13	0	1

Source: Federal Reserve Bulletin, September, 1937, pp. 907-908.

TABLE A.29
Deposits of Suspended Banks ($ millions)   1921-1936 (monthly)

All Banks

Month	Total 1921-1936	1921	1922	1923	1924	1925	1926	1927	1928	1929	1930	1931	1932	1933	1934	1935	1936
January	678	23	13	6	48	27	14	31	12	18	27	76	219	133	32	1	0
February	348	22	17	6	24	16	12	26	18	24	32	34	52	62	1	.	1
March	3,480	15	12	14	14	10	10	33	17	9	23	34	11	3,276	0	1	1
April	227	7	7	9	17	15	14	13	9	10	32	42	32	19	1	0	1
May	252	11	8	7	29	16	14	13	7	16	19	43	34	33	0	0	1
June	531	17	3	11	8	10	??	10	11	25	58	190	133	22	1	1	0
July	307	10	2	13	16	6	45	12	8	61	30	41	49	11	0	1	2
August	329	8	5	16	7	2	10	18	6	7	23	180	30	19	0	0	0
September	353	5	3	9	6	9	13	9	9	10	22	234	14	7	0	5	1
October	628	14	4	15	10	14	17	14	8	12	20	471	20	6	0	0	3
November	472	16	7	21	11	20	41	10	28	22	180	68	43	2	0	0	0
December	907	25	10	24	19	22	42	10	11	15	372	277	71	7	0	1	2
Total	8,512	172	91	150	210	168	260	199	142	231	837	1,690	706	3,597	37	10	11

National Banks

Month	Total 1921-1936	1921	1922	1923	1924	1925	1926	1927	1928	1929	1930	1931	1932	1933	1934	1935	1936
January	186	3	2	1	13	9	3	5	2	10	3	15	63	56	0	0	0
February	91	2	4	2	9	5	4	7	4	4	14	6	17	16	0	0	0
March	1,568	1	1	4	6	3	1	5	2	2	7	11	4	1,521	0	0	0
April	51	2	0	1	4	6	1	4	2	1	3	19	3	4	0	0	0
May	57	2	2	1	9	6	3	6	2	4	1	12	6	1	0	0	0
June	119	0	2	3	3	2	4	2	2	4	15	31	42	8	0	0	0
July	64	0	1	2	8	2	1	2	0	9	11	7	18	3	0	0	0
August	69	1	1	5	3	1	2	8	2	0	3	32	11	0	0	0	0
September	103	1	0	2	0	3	3	1	3	1	1	79	3	1	0	5	0
October	150	4	2	2	3	6	5	2	0	4	3	111	6	0	0	0	0
November	161	3	2	6	3	5	11	1	13	0	63	28	26	0	0	0	0
December	184	2	4	6	4	9	6	1	4	2	43	87	13	0	0	0	1
Total	2,804	21	20	34	65	56	44	46	36	42	170	439	214	1,611	0	5	1

State Member Banks

Month	Total 1921-1936	1921	1922	1923	1924	1925	1926	1927	1928	1929	1930	1931	1932	1933	1934	1935	1936
January	55	1	0	1	5	3	1	5	1	1	5	7	11	14	0	0	0
February	37	1		1	4	0	0	1	6	0	0	8	8	7	0	0	0
March	771	0	6	1	0	0	0	2	1	0	1	0	0	760	0	0	0
April	20	0	0	0	0	1	2	2	0	0	0	0	2	12	0	0	0
May	14	1	0	2	0	3	1	1	0	1	0	0	5	1	0	0	0
June	63	11	0	0	0	0	0	1	3	0	0	0	39	8	0	0	0
July	18	2	0	0	0	0	0	0	0	0	11	0	2	2	0	0	0
August	56	0	0	1	0	0	0	0	0	0	1	1	53	1	0	0	0
September	37	0	0	0	0	1	1	1	1	0	1	0	30	2	2	0	0
October	124	1	0	1	0	0	1	2	0	0	0	0	117	0	0	0	0
November	53	0	0	3	1	1	5	2	1	2	32	4	0	3	0	0	0
December	216	1	0	3	3	1	10	0	0	1	164	26	7	0	0	0	0
Total	1,464	17	7	13	14	10	23	18	10	16	202	294	55	783			

Nonmember Banks, other than Private and Mutual Savings Banks

Month	Total 1921-1936	1921	1922	1923	1924	1925	1926	1927	1928	1929	1930	1931	1932	1933	1934	1935	1936
January	428	18	10	4	29	14	10	20	8	8	18	52	143	61	31	1	0
February	297	16	13	4	9	10	8	18	9	20	18	18	25	38	1	0	1
March	1,124	12	5	9	8	6	9	25	13	7	15	23	5	985	0	1	1
April	149	5	7	8	12	7	10	6	6	9	27	19	16	15	1	0	1
May	174	8	6	3	19	5	10	6	4	11	18	25	26	32	0	0	1
June	339	6	1	8	5	7	24	5	9	16	40	119	82	14	1	1	0
July	217	8	1	10	7	4	43	10	7	41	17	29	28	7	0	0	2
August	198	6	3	11	3	1	8	9	3	6	18	94	17	19	0	0	0
September	208	3	3	7	6	6	9	8	4	8	19	121	9	4	0	0	1
October	343	8	2	11	7	8	8	9	7	8	16	237	14	5	0	0	3
November	249	12	5	127	14	22	7	15	20	84	35	14	2	0	0	0	
December	497	21	6	15	13	11	24	8	6	13	159	162	50	7	0	1	1
Total	4,134	125	62	101	124	95	184	132	93	165	449	936	429	1,189	35	5	11

Private Banks

Month	Total 1921-1936	1921	1922	1923	1924	1925	1926	1927	1928	1929	1930	1931	1932	1933	1934	1935	1936
January	9	0	0	0	0	1	0	0	0	0	1	2	1	1	1	0	0
February	14	4	1	0	3	1	0	0	0	0	0	2	1	1	0	0	0
March	17	2	0	0	1	1	0	0	0	1	0	0	2	10	2	0	0
April	7	0	0	0	1	1	0	1	0	0	2	1	1	0	0	0	0
May	6	0	0	0	0	0	1	0	0	0	0	0	0	0	0	0	0
June	10	0	0	0	0	0	0	0	0	5	2	1	0	0	0	0	0
July	8	0	0	1	1	0	1	0	1	0	1	2	1	0	0	0	0
August	6	0	0	0	1	9	0	0	0	0	2	2	1	0	0	0	0
September	5	0	0	0	0	0	0	0	1	1	1	3	0	0	0	0	0
October	11	1	0	0	0	0	2	1	0	0	0	6	0	0	0	0	0
November	8	1	0	0	0	1	4	1	0	0	1	0	0	0	0	0	0
December	10	0	0	0	0	0	1	0	0	0	6	2	0	0	0	0	0
Total	111	9	2	2	8	8	9	4	3	8	15	21	8	13	1	0	0

Source: _Federal Reserve Bulletin_, September, 1937, pp. 909-910.

TABLE A.30

Reconstruction Finance Corporation Loans
February, 1932[a]–1933 (monthly)

($ millions)

Month	Amount authorized	Amount disbursed	Amount repaid	Amount outstanding
1932				
February	$ 92	$ 71	$ 0	$ 71
March	142	121	9	183
April	229	156	7	332
May	199	159	16	475
June	388	298	49	724
July	171	171	35	861
August	189	146	35	972
September	138	72	45	999
October	162	138	48	1,089
November	97	61	27	1,123
December	129	132	29	1,225
Totals	1,936	1,525	300	1,225
1933				
January	143	118	32	1,311
February	283	199	36	1,474
March	218	180	56	1,598
April	163	117	40	1,675
May	142	196	47	1,824
June	154	124	95	1,853
July	201	115	113	1,855
August	58	83	74	1,865
September	45	39	62	1,843
October	522	49	70	1,829
November	382	186	51	1,957
December	492	370	68	2,259
Totals	2,802	1,776	743	2,259

Source: Report of the Reconstruction Finance Corporation, Fourth Quarter, 1933, p. 22.

Notes: (a) The first loans were in February, 1932.

TABLE A.31

Reconstruction Finance Corporation Loans to Banks and Trust Companies
February, 1932[a]–1933 (monthly)
($ millions)

Month	Amount authorized	Amount disbursed	Amount repaid	Amount outstanding
1932				
February	$ 45	$ 40	$ 0	$ 40
March	109	86	8	118
April	152	112	7	223
May	113	108	13	319
June	220	152	45	426
July	97	104	28	502
August	88	78	31	548
September	30	27	40	535
October	22	81	40	575
November	23	20	22	573
December	51	43	21	595
Totals	949	851	256	595
1933				
January	56	43	26	612
February	132	78	21	669
March	99	63	41	691
April	63	24	28	687
May	55	88	38	737
June	39	12	75	674
July	101	66	68	672
August	34	52	35	689
September	22	16	28	677
October	103	15	31	661
November	41	50	25	686
December	111	71	46	711
Totals	857	579	462	711

TABLE A.31 (continued)

Additional Amounts[b] under the Emergency Banking Act of March 9, 1933 (monthly)

($ millions)

Month	Amount authorized	Amount disbursed	Amount repaid	Amount outstanding
1933				
March	$15	$13	0	$13
April	8	8	0	21
May	17	5	0	26
June	8	18	0	44
July	15	8	0	52
August	3	8	0	59
September	4	4	0	63
October	31	3	0	66
November	90	44	0	110
December	313	154	0	264
Totals	504	264	0	264

Notes: (a) The first loans were in February, 1932.
   (b) Additional amounts include preferred stock purchased, loans against preferred stock, and capital notes purchased.

Source: Report of the Reconstruction Finance Corporation, Fourth Quarter, 1933, pp. 23, 32.

TABLE A.32

Reconstruction Finance Corporation Loans to Railroads February, 1932[a]–1933 (monthly)

($ millions)

Month	Amount authorized	Amount disbursed	Amount repaid	Amount out-standing
1932				
February	$47	$31	$ 0	$31
March	14	25	1	55
April	38	19	0	74
May	61	16	3	87
June	54	55	2	139
July	16	28	3	165
August	13	42	0	205
September	21	13	0	220
October	26	25	2	243
November	38	9	0	249
December	9	23	0	272
Total	337	284	12	272
1933				
January	3	8	0	280
February	19	25	8	296
March	5	15	0	311
April	12	12	0	323
May	23	18	0	341
June	7	18	5	354
July	0	1	24	331
August	4	0	0	371
September	0	1	0	332
October	0	5	6	330
November	1	3	0	333
December	0	4	0	337
Total	74	110	45	337

Source: Report of the Reconstruction Finance Corporation, Fourth Quarter, 1933, pp. 28, 29.

Notes: (a) The first loans were in February, 1932.

TABLE A.33

Reconstruction Finance Corporation Loans under the Emergency Relief and Construction Act of 1932 — mostly to State and Local Governments July, 1932[a]–1933 (monthly)

($ millions)

Month	Amount authorized	Amount disbursed	Amount repaid	Amount outstanding
1932				
July	$ 3	$ 0	$ 0	$ 0
August	64	4	0	4
September	73	10	0	14
October	103	17	0	31
November	23	22	0	53
December	47	44	0	97
Total	313	97	0	97[b]
1933				
January	59	43	0	140
February	73	40	0	180
March	47	44	0	224
April	54	47	0	271
May	14	55	1	325
June	26	6	0	331
July	53	11	0	342
August	0	6	1	347
September	2	7	1	353
October	253	8	0	361
November	154	37	1	397
December	0	40	1	437
Total	737	345	5	437[c]

Source: Report of the Reconstruction Finance Corporation, Fourth Quarter, 1933, p. 30.

Notes: (a) The first loans were in August, 1932.
(b) Includes $1 million for agriculture.
(c) Includes $75 million for agriculture.

TABLE A.34

Reconstruction Finance Corporation Loans by
Type of Borrower
1932–1933

($ millions)

	Amount outstanding December 31, 1932	Amount outstanding December 31, 1933
Banks and trust companies	$595	$976
Railroads	272	337
State and local governments	96	362
Building & loan associations	84	66
Insurance companies	62	61
Mortgage loan companies	77	178
Credit unions	0	1
Agricultural agencies and other agricultural purposes (a)	38	265
Other	1	13
Totals	1,225	2,259

Notes: (a) includes the following loans:

Federal Land Banks	19	142
Joint Stock Land Banks	2	14
Federal Intermediate Credit Banks	0	0
Agricultural Credit Corporations	2	2
Regional Agricultural Credit Corporations	5	30
Livestock Credit Corporations	8	2
Processors and distributors	0	0
Financing exports of agricultural surplus	0	7
Financing agricultural commodities and livestock	1	68
Agric. Adjustment Act of 1933	0	0

Source: Report of the Reconstruction Finance Corporation, Fourth Quarter, 1932, pp. 20–33.

TABLE A.35

Changes in the Gold Stock of the United States
1925–1938 (monthly)

($ millions)

Year and month	Gold stock (end of period)	Increase in gold stock	Domestic gold prod'n	Net gold import	Ear-marked gold decrease or increase (-)	Gold under earmark (end of period)
1925						
January	4,136	-76.6	(a)	-68.5	- .8	46.0
February	4,077	-53.5		-47.0	-6.4	47.4
March	4,052	-23.2		-17.8	-9.3	54.2
April	4,055	3.6		-12.7	14.9	39.4
May	4,070	11.5		-2.0	16.0	26.6
June	4,073	3.4		-2.3	5.1	21.6
July	4,060	5.5		5.8	-3.1	25.5
August	4,095	12.6		2.7	11.6	16.7
September	4,095	-1.2		-2.7	1.5	15.8
October	4,120	25.9		22.7	2.9	13.0
November	4,110	-10.0		-13.9	2.0	11.0
December	4,112	2.0		1.2	-2.0	13.0
1926						
January	4,125	12.2		16.3	-6.0	19.0
February	4,136	11.5		21.6	-11.0	30.0
March	4,155	18.4		39.2	-23.0	53.0
April	4,151	-3.4		-4.8	0	53.0
May	4,146	-4.8		-6.4	0	53.0
June	4,160	14.0		15.5	- .6	53.6
July	4,184	23.7		14.8	4.0	49.6
August	4,186	2.0		-17.8	19.2	30.4
September	4,179	-7.4		-7.1	-2.4	32.8
October	4,186	7.7		7.7	0	32.8
November	4,190	3.2		9.0	-7.5	40.3
December	4,205	15.4		9.8	1.0	39.3
1927						
January	4,277	72.3		44.5	19.5	19.8
February	4,299	21.3		19.9	3.2	16.6
March	4,310	11.1		10.8	-1.5	18.1
April	4,323	12.9		11.9	-1.0	19.1
May	4,321	-1.4		31.7	(b)-35.5	114.1
June	4,300	-20.9		12.8	(b)-36.7	114.6
July	4,293	-7.5		8.9	(b)-23.1	114.4
August	4,301	8.5		6.4	-2.5	116.9
September	4,284	-17.5		-11.5	-9.0	125.9
October	4,254	-30.2		-8.6	-25.0	150.9
November	4,164	-89.7		-53.2	-40.0	190.9
December	4,092	-71.7		-67.4	-8.5	199.4

TABLE A.35 (continued)

Year and month	Gold stock (end of period)	Increase in gold stock	Domestic gold prod'n	Net gold import	Ear-marked gold decrease or increase (–)	Gold under earmark (end of period)
1928						
January	4,086	-6.0		-13.8	5.5	193.9
February	4,075	-11.2		-11.1	2.9	191.1
March	4,018	-57.6		-94.9	35.8	155.3
April	3,979	-38.7		-91.2	45.7	109.5
May	3,873	-105.7		-81.7	-26.5	136.1
June	3,822	-51.0		-79.9	30.1	106.0
July	3,826	3.4		-63.9	60.9	45.1
August	3,836	10.3		.7	5.9	39.1
September	3,838	2.1		.5	-1.2	40.3
October	3,855	17.3		13.3	1.2	39.1
November	3,841	-14.0		6.7	-25.0	64.1
December	3,854	13.2		23.3	-15.8	79.9
1929						
January	3,840	-14.4		47.2	-65.0	144.9
February	3,866	26.4		25.5	0	144.9
March	3,901	34.4		24.8	7.5	137.4
April	3,973	72.4		23.1	48.6	88.8
May	4,014	40.6		23.6	16.1	72.7
June	4,037	23.4		30.2	-7.5	80.2
July	4,054	16.3		34.7	-22.0	102.2
August	4,073	18.9		18.4	-1.0	103.2
September	4,085	12.1		17.6	-6.6	109.8
October	4,099	14.4		17.5	-4.5	114.3
November	4,080	-19.2		-23.2	1.0	113.3
December	3,997	-82.9		-64.4	-22.0	135.3
1930						
January	4,004	6.8		4.0	.5	134.8
February	4,066	61.9		60.0	0	134.8
March	4,136	70.2		55.5	15.0	119.8
April	4,204	68.5		65.7	.5	119.3
May	4,230	25.9		23.5	2.0	117.3
June	4,248	17.6		13.9	2.0	115.3
July	4,230	-18.4		-19.6	-3.0	118.3
August	4,214	-15.5		-19.6	0	118.3
September	4,224	10.2		2.5	4.0	114.3
October	4,248	23.3		26.4	-6.1	120.4
November	4,284	36.8		35.2	-2.1	122.5
December	4,306	22.1		32.7	-15.2	137.7

TABLE A.35 (continued)

Year and month	Gold stock (end of period)	Increase in gold stock	Domestic gold prod'n	Net gold import	Earmarked gold decrease or increase (−)	Gold under earmark (end of period)
1931						
January	4,356	49.4		34.4	11.9	125.8
February	4,378	22.0		16.1	2.5	123.3
March	4,410	32.0		25.6	3.0	120.3
April	4,439	28.7		49.5	−7.5	127.8
May	4,511	72.4		49.6	4.0	123.8
June	4,669	158.0		63.8	92.3	31.5
July	4,662	−6.6		19.5	−29.7	61.2
August	4,708	45.7		57.5	−16.0	77.2
September	4,454	−254.3		20.6	−279.1	356.3
October	4,005	−448.4		−337.7	−107.6	463.9
November	4,127	122.0		89.4	28.3	435.8
December	4,173	45.8		56.9	−22.9	458.5
1932						
January	4,129	−44.2	3.4	−73.0	25.4	433.1
February	4,067	−62.3	3.3	−90.6	26.4	406.8
March	4,103	36.0	3.2	−24.7	58.3	348.5
April	4,080	−23.1	3.2	−30.2	4.0	344.5
May	3,865	−214.1	3.8	−195.5	−22.1	366.7
June	3,632	−233.9	3.9	−206.0	−28.8	395.4
July	3,687	58.0	2.2	−3.4	56.2	339.2
August	3,801	111.7	4.7	6.1	100.5	238.7
September	3,906	104.8	4.7	27.9	72.3	166.4
October	3,977	70.8	5.0	20.6	45.8	120.6
November	4,053	75.6	4.3	21.7	48.6	72.1
December	4,226	173.5	4.3	100.9	(b)71.0	73.7
1933						
January	4,266	40.0	3.9	128.5	(b)−91.5	92.6
February	4,093	−173.4	2.8	8.9	−178.3	270.8
March	3,995	−97.2	4.8	−13.1	−100.1	370.9
April	4,025	29.5	3.5	−10.0	33.7	337.2
May	4,028	3.6	3.2	−21.1	22.1	315.1
June	4,031	2.2	2.7	−3.2	3.5	311.6
July	4,033	2.7	3.2	−83.9	84.5	227.1
August	4,041	7.5	3.2	−80.4	79.5	147.6
September	4,037	−3.8	5.3	−56.7	49.3	98.3
October	4,036	−.7	4.8	−32.4	26.9	71.5
November	4,036	−.1	4.6	−.8	.6	70.9
December	4,036	−.5	5.1	−9.1	11.8	59.1

TABLE A.35 (continued)

Year and month	Gold stock (end of period)	Increase in gold stock	Domestic gold prod'n	Net gold import	Earmarked gold decrease or increase (-)	Gold under earmark (end of period)
1934						
January	(c)4,033	-2.1	4.4	-2.8	12.2	46.9
February	7,438	3,405.0	5.7	452.6	68.7	10.7
March	7,694	256.1	7.4	237.3	-.8	11.5
April	7,757	62.2	7.5	54.7	-1.1	12.7
May	7,779	22.4	8.1	33.6	.5	12.2
June	7,856	77.1	7.4	63.7	1.0	11.2
July	7,931	74.4	8.5	52.3	.6	10.6
August	7,978	47.4	7.4	37.2	-1.1	11.7
September	7,978	.4	9.5	-18.7	2.4	9.3
October	8,002	23.5	10.2	10.8	.3	9.0
November	8,132	129.9	7.9	120.9	-.1	9.1
December	8,238	106.2	8.8	92.1	.1	9.0
1935						
January	8,391	153.3	7.6	149.4	1.1	7.9
February	8,327	135.3	6.6	122.8	.2	7.6
March	8,567	40.4	8.0	13.0	-.7	8.3
April	8,710	143.4	7.8	148.6	-2.3	10.6
May	8,858	148.1	8.6	140.0	-1.5	12.1
June	9,116	257.1	8.6	230.4	1.0	11.1
July	9,144	27.9	10.2	16.2	-.4	11.6
August	9,203	59.5	10.0	46.0	1.8	9.8
September	9,368	165.0	10.7	156.7	1.0	8.8
October	9,693	325.2	11.5	315.3	-1.9	10.6
November	9,920	226.7	9.5	210.6	.6	10.1
December	10,125	205.2	11.5	190.0	1.3	8.8
1936						
January	10,182	57.2	9.2	45.6	-1.7	10.5
February	10,167	-15.5	8.4	-16.6	-9.5	20.1
March	10,184	17.2	9.6	5.5	1.0	19.1
April	10,225	41.0	9.6	28.1	-.2	19.2
May	10,402	176.7	10.4	170.0	-3.2	22.5
June	10,608	206.6	10.0	277.8	-24.8	47.3
July	10,648	39.2	12.8	15.4	2.3	45.0
August	10,716	68.4	13.1	67.5	-11.9	56.9
September	10,845	129.0	12.1	171.8	-28.8	85.7
October	11,045	199.7	13.8	218.8	-11.3	97.0
November	11,184	139.6	11.8	75.8	3.0	94.0
December	11,258	73.3	10.9	57.0	-.7	94.7

TABLE A.35 (continued)

Year and month	Gold stock (end of period)	Increase in gold stock	Domestic gold prod'n	Net gold import	Ear- marked gold decrease or increase (-)	Gold under earmark (end of period)
1937						
January	11,358	100.1	9.6	121.3	-48.3	143.0
February	11,436	78.2	8.3	120.3	-8.0	151.0
March	11,574	137.9	10.8	154.3	-.4	151.4
April	11,799	225.6	9.2	215.8	7.2	144.2
May	11,990	191.1	12.4	155.4	26.2	118.0
June	12,318	327.8	11.2	262.0	-15.9	133.9
July	12,446	127.3	12.7	175.4	-35.5	169.4
August	12,567	121.6	16.9	104.8	-5.3	174.7
September	12,741	174.3	12.2	145.5	9.3	165.4
October	12,803	62.0	14.9	90.5	-8.0	173.4
November	12,774	-29.3	13.8	22.1	-20.1	193.6
December	12,760	-14.0	11.9	18.0	-101.6	295.1
1938						
January	12,756	-4.6	11.0	2.1	-1.1	296.2
February	12,776	20.7	10.0	8.0	-18.2	314.4
March	12,795	18.5	10.7	52.9	-.6	315.0
April	12,869	74.3	10.6	71.1	-1.2	316.2
May	12,919	49.8	11.5	52.8	-53.9	370.2
June	12,963	44.2	9.6	55.3	-15.5	385.7
July	13,017	54.5	14.2	63.8	-20.9	406.6
August	13,136	118.3	14.7	166.0	-28.8	435.4
September	13,760	623.8	14.1	520.9	-13.3	448.6
October	14,065	305.0	13.5	562.4	-110.2	558.8
November	14,312	247.5	15.5	177.8	-7.4	566.2
December	14,512	199.6	13.3	240.5	-62.4	628.6

Source: Banking and Monetary Statistics, p. 537.

Notes: (a) Data for gold production begins in 1932.
     (b) Includes adjustments for changes in gold held abroad by the Federal Reserve banks.
     (c) Gold valued at $20.67 per fine ounce through January, 1934, and $35.00 thereafter.

TABLE A.36

Net Public and Private Debt by Major Sectors
1916 to 1940 (year end)

($ billions)

Year	Total public and private	Total public	Federal[a]	State and local	Total private	Corporate Total corporate	Corporate Long[b] term	Corporate Short[b] term
1940	189.8	61.2	44.8	16.4	128.6	75.6	43.7	31.9
1939	183.3	59.0	42.6	16.4	124.3	73.5	44.4	29.2
1938	179.9	56.6	40.5	16.1	123.3	73.3	44.8	28.5
1937	182.2	55.3	39.2	16.1	126.9	75.8	43.5	32.3
1936	180.6	53.9	37.7	16.2	126.7	76.1	42.5	33.5
1935	175.0	50.5	34.4	16.1	124.5	74.8	43.6	31.2
1934	171.6	46.3	30.4	15.9	125.3	75.5	44.6	30.9
1933	168.5	40.6	24.3	16.3	127.9	76.9	47.9	29.0
1932	175.0	37.9	21.3	16.6	137.1	80.0	49.2	30.8
1931	182.9	34.5	18.5	16.0	148.4	83.5	50.3	33.2
1930	192.3	31.2	16.5	14.7	161.1	89.3	51.1	38.2
1929	191.9	30.1	16.5	13.6	161.8	88.9	47.3	41.6
1928	186.3	30.2	17.5	12.7	156.1	86.1	–	–
1927	177.9	30.3	18.2	12.1	147.6	81.2	–	–
1926	169.2	30.3	19.2	11.1	138.9	76.2	–	–

TABLE A.36 (continued)

Year	Total individual and non-corporate	Farm[e]		Nonfarm mtge		Other nonfarm		
		Production	Mortgage	1- to 4-family	Multi-family resid'l. & com'l.	Commercial	Financial[d]	Consumer
1940	53.0	2.6	6.5	16.5	9.6	4.3	5.2	8.3
1939	50.8	2.2	6.6	15.5	9.5	3.8	6.0	7.2
1938	50.0	2.2	6.8	15.0	9.5		10.1	6.4
1937	51.1	1.6	7.0	14.7	9.6		11.3	6.9
1936	50.6	1.4	7.2	14.6	9.8		11.2	6.4
1935	49.7	1.5	7.4	14.7	10.1		10.8	5.2
1934	49.8	1.3	7.6	14.8	10.7		11.2	4.2
1933	51.0	1.4	7.7	14.6	11.7		11.7	3.9
1932	57.1	1.6	8.5	15.8	13.2		14.0	4.0
1931	64.9	2.0	9.1	17.2	13.7		17.6	5.3
1930	71.8	2.4	9.4	17.9	14.1		21.6	6.4
1929	72.9	2.6	9.6	18.0	13.2		22.4	7.1
1928	70.0	2.7	9.8		29.6		21.6	6.3
1927	66.4	2.6	9.8		26.9		21.8	5.3
1926	62.7	2.6	9.7		24.0		21.2	5.2

TABLE A.36 (continued)

Year	Total public and private	Total public	Federal[a]	State and local	Total private	Total corporate	Corporate Long[b] term	Short[b] term
1925	162.9	30.6	20.3	10.3	132.3	72.7		
1924	153.4	30.4	21.0	9.4	123.0	67.2		
1923	146.7	30.4	21.8	8.6	116.3	62.6		
1922	140.2	30.7	22.8	7.9	109.5	58.6		
1921	136.3	30.1	23.1	7.0	106.2	57.0		
1920	135.7	29.9	23.7	6.2	105.8	57.7		
1919	128.3	31.1	25.6	5.5	97.2	53.3		
1918	117.5	26.0	20.9	5.1	91.5	47.0		
1917	94.5	12.1	7.3	4.8	82.4	43.7		
1916	82.2	5.7	1.2	4.5	76.5	40.2		

Source: Historical Statistics, p. 989.

Notes:
(a)   Debt held by the public as shown in The Budget of the United States Government, Fiscal Year 1974.
(b)   Long term debt has a maturity of 1 year or more, short term debt less than 1 year.
(c)   Farmers' financial and consumer debt is included in the nonfarm categories.
(d)   Debt owed to banks for purchasing or carrying securities, customers' debt to brokers, and debt owed to life insurance companies by policyholders.

TABLE A.36 (continued)

Year	Total individual and non-corporate	Farm[c]		Nonfarm mtge		Other nonfarm		
		Production	Mortgage	1- to 4-family	Multi family resid'l com'l	Commercial	Financial[d]	Consumer
1925	59.6	2.8	9.7		21.3	21.1		4.7
1924	55.8	2.7	9.9		18.6	20.6		4.0
1923	53.7	3.0	10.7		16.3	20.0		3.7
1922	50.9	3.1	10.8		14.1	19.7		3.2
1921	49.2	3.3	10.7		12.8	19.4		3.0
1920	48.1	3.9	10.2		11.7	19.3		3.0
1919	43.9	3.5	8.4		10.1	19.3		2.6
1918	44.5	2.7	7.1		9.6		25.1	
1917	38.7	2.5	6.5		9.3		20.4	
1916	36.3	2.0	5.8		8.4		20.1	

TABLE A.37

Assets of U.S. Life Insurance Companies
1921–1940

($ millions)

Year	Total	Bonds	Stocks	Mortgages	Real Estate	Other(a)	Net rate of interest earned on assets (%)
1940	30,802	17,092	605	5,972	2,065	5,068	3.45
1939	29,243	15,734	587	5,683	2,139	5,100	3.54
1938	27,755	14,473	586	5,445	2,179	5,072	3.59
1937	26,249	13,272	558	5,230	2,192	4,997	3.69
1936	24,874	11,869	615	5,128	2,149	5,113	3.71
1935	23,216	10,041	583	5,357	1,990	5,245	3.70
1934	21,844	8,533	482	5,875	1,693	5,261	3.92
1933	20,896	7,189	487	6,701	1,267	5,252	4.25
1932	20,754	6,843	574	7,336	935	5,066	4.65
1931	20,160	6,806	567	7,673	684	4,430	4.93
1930	18,880	6,431	519	7,598	548	3,784	5.05
1929	17,482	6,001	416	7,316	464	3,285	5.05
1928	15,961	5,655	285	6,778	403	2,840	5.05
1927	14,392	5,146	145	6,200	351	2,550	5.05
1926	12,940	4,653	125	5,580	303	2,279	5.09
1925	11,538	4,333	81	4,808	266	2,050	5.11
1924	10,394	4,034	64	4,175	239	1,882	5.17
1923	9,455	3,783	57	3,662	243	1,710	5.18
1922	8,652	3,656	56	3,122	197	1,621	5.12
1921	7,936	3,390	69	2,792	186	1,499	5.02

Source: Historical Statistics, p. 1060.
Notes: (a) Includes policy loans.

TABLE A.38

Summary of the Federal Administrative Budget
1916–1939

($ millions)

Fiscal year	Budget receipts (a)	Budget expenditures (b)	Surplus or deficit (c) (-)	Total public debt (d)
1939	4,979,066	8,841,224	-3,862,158	40,439,532
1938	5,588,012	6,764,628	-1,176,617	37,164,740
1937	4,955,613	7,733,033	-2,777,421	36,424,614
1936	3,997,059	8,421,608	-4,424,549	33,778,543
1935	3,705,956	6,497,008	-2,791,052	28,700,893
1934	3,014,970	6,644,602	-3,629,632	27,053,141
1933	1,996,844	4,598,496	-2,601,652	22,538,673
1932	1,923,892	4,659,182	-2,735,290	19,487,002
1931	3,115,557	3,577,434	-461,877	16,801,281
1930	4,057,884	3,320,211	737,673	16,185,310
1929	3,861,589	3,127,199	734,391	16,931,088
1928	3,900,329	2,961,245	939,083	17,604,293
1927	4,012,794	2,857,429	1,155,365	18,511,907
1926	3,795,108	2,929,964	865,144	19,643,216
1925	3,640,805	2,923,762	717,043	20,516,194
1924	3,871,214	2,907,847	963,367	21,250,813
1923	3,852,795	3,140,287	712,508	22,349,707
1922	4,025,901	3,289,404	736,496	22,963,382
1921	5,570,790	5,061,785	509,005	23,977,451
1920	6,648,898	6,357,677	291,222	24,299,321
1919	5,130,042	18,492,665	-13,362,623	25,484,506
1918	3,645,240	12,677,359	-9,032,120	12,455,225
1917	1,100,500	1,953,857	-853,357	2,975,619
1916	761,445	712,967	48,478	1,225,146

Source: Historical Statistics, p. 1104.

Notes: (a) Excludes receipts from borrowing.
(b) Excludes debt repayment.
(c) Receipts compared with expenditures.
(d) As of end of period.

TABLE A.39

Federal Income Tax Rates
1913–1939

Income Year	First bracket			Top bracket	
	Rate		Income	Rate	Income over
1936-1939	4	%	$4,000	79%	$5,000,000
1934-1935	4		4,000	63	1,000,000
1932-1933	4		4,000	63	1,000,000
1930-1931	1 1/8		4,000	25	100,000
1929	3/8		4,000	24	100,000
1925-1928	1 1/8		4,000	25	100,000
1924	1 1/2		4,000	46	500,000
1923	3		4,000	56	200,000
1922	4		4,000	56	200,000
1921	4		4,000	73	1,000,000
1919-1920	4		4,000	73	1,000,000
1918	6		4,000	77	1,000,000
1917	2		2,000	67	2,000,000
1916	2		20,000	15	2,000,000
1913-1915	1		20,000	7	500,000

Source: Historical Statistics, p. 1095.

TABLE A.40

Representative U.S. Treasury Bond Prices[a] and Yields 1929-1933 (monthly)

	1929					
	4th Liberty 4 1/4% - 1938		1st Liberty 3 1/2% - 1947		Treasury 4 1/4% - 1952	
	Low Price	High Price	Low Price	High Price	Low Price	High Price
January	$99.31 -	100.12	$98.30 -	99.31	$110.0 -	111.26
	4.26% -	4.20	3.58% -	3.50	3.61% -	3.50
February	99.24 -	100.3	97.12 -	99.23	108.5 -	110.14
	4.28 -	4.24	3.70 -	3.52	3.72 -	3.58
March	98.17 -	100.0	97.4 -	98.26	105.0 -	108.13
	4.46 -	4.25	3.72 -	3.59	3.92 -	3.70
April	98.26 -	99.30	97.6 -	98.12	106.3 -	109.20
	4.42 -	4.26	3.72 -	3.62	3.85 -	3.63
May	98.15 -	99.20	96.6 -	98.3	105.22 -	109.10
	4.46 -	4.30	3.79 -	3.64	3.88 -	3.65
June	98.19 -	99.14	96.0 -	96.18	106.4 -	107.21
	4.44 -	4.32	3.80 -	3.76	3.85 -	3.75
July	98.21 -	100.0	96.11 -	97.16	107.2 -	108.26
	4.44 -	4.25	3.78 -	3.69	3.79 -	3.68
August	98.10 -	99.6	96.20 -	97.17	106.3 -	107.13
	4.48 -	4.36	3.75 -	3.69	3.85 -	3.77
September	98.12 -	99.7	97.6 -	98.0	106.10 -	107.0
	4.48 -	4.36	3.72 -	3.65	3.84 -	3.79
October	98.11 -	99.27	96.12 -	98.10	106.12 -	110.23
	4.48 -	4.28	3.78 -	3.63	3.83 -	3.56
November	99.23 -	101.1	97.0 -	99.3	111.0 -	112.23
	4.28 -	4.08	3.73 -	3.57	3.55 -	3.45
December	101.2 -	102.0	99.0 -	100.0	111.0 -	112.30
	4.08 -	3.98	3.58 -	3.50	3.55 -	3.44
High - Low	$98.10 -	102.0	$96.0 -	100.0	$105.0 -	112.30
	4.48 -	3.98	3.80 -	3.50	3.92 -	3.44
Dates	8/10 -	12/11	6/20 -	12/6	3/13 -	12/13
Price Range	$3.22		$4.00		$7.30	

TABLE A.40 (continued)

	4th Liberty 4 1/4% – 1938		1st Liberty 3 1/2% – 1947		Treasury 4 1/4% – 1952	
	Low Price	High Price	Low Price	High Price	Low Price	High Price
January	$100.23 – 4.14% –	101.11 4.06	$98.26 – 3.59% –	99.18 3.53	$109.24 – 3.59% –	111.15 3.50
February	100.30 – 4.12 –	101.13 4.04	99.0 – 3.58 –	99.28 3.51	110.5 – 3.58 –	111.13 3.50
March	101.8 – 4.06 –	102.16 3.88	99.19 – 3.53 –	100.3 3.49	111.8 – 3.51 –	113.14 3.38
April	101.13 – 4.04 –	101.31 3.96	100.0 – 3.50 –	100.19 3.45	110.28 – 3.53 –	111.24 3.48
May	101.24 – 4.00 –	102.10 3.92	100.1 – 3.50 –	100.13 3.47	111.8 – 3.51 –	112.22 3.42
June	102.8 – 3.92 –	102.29 3.84	100.9 – 3.48 –	101.4 3.41	112.16 – 3.44 –	113.4 3.40
July	102.24 – 3.84 –	103.3 3.80	100.25 – 3.44 –	101.3 3.41	112.11 – 3.44 –	113.3 3.40
August	102.12 – 3.90 –	103.6 3.79	100.27 – 3.43 –	101.3 3.41	112.10 – 3.44 –	112.31 3.41
September	102.27 – 3.84 –	103.16 3.74	100.30 – 3.42 –	101.7 3.40	112.15 – 3.43 –	113.6 3.39
October	103.9 – 3.77 –	103.20 3.73	101.1 – 3.41 –	101.10 3.40	112.17 – 3.43 –	113.6 3.39
November	103.14 – 3.75 –	103.27 3.70	101.1 – 3.41 –	102.0 3.34	113.3 – 3.40 –	113.10 3.38
December	103.14 – 3.75 –	103.25 3.71	101.21 – 3.37 –	102.0 3.34	111.30 – 3.47 –	113.9 3.38
High – Low	$100.23 – 4.14 –	103.27 3.70	$98.26 – 3.59 –	102.0 3.34	$109.24 – 3.60 –	113.14 3.38
Dates	1/22 –	11/24	1/22 –	11/28	1/29 –	3/20
Price Range	$3.04		$3.06		$3.22	

TABLE A.40 (continued)

1931

	4th Liberty 4 1/4% – 1938		1st Liberty 3 1/2% – 1947		Treasury 4 1/4% – 1952	
	Low Price	High Price	Low Price	High Price	Low Price	High Price
January	$102.24 – 3.80% –	104.4 3.58	$100.23 – 3.44% –	102.9 3.32	$110.10 – 3.55% –	113.8 3.36
February	102.29 – 3.78 –	103.30 3.61	100.20 – 3.45 –	101.23 3.36	109.24 – 3.59 –	112.12 3.42
March	103.15 – 3.69 –	103.29 3.61	101.12 – 3.39 –	101.27 3.35	110.20 – 3.53 –	112.11 3.42
April	103.22 – 3.65 –	104.5 3.57	101.22 – 3.36 –	101.30 3.34	111.22 – 3.46 –	112.15 3.41
May	104.0 – 3.60 –	105.5 3.42	101.27 – 3.35 –	102.23 3.28	112.10 – 3.42 –	114.3 3.31
June	104.22 – 3.49 –	105.1 3.44	102.16 – 3.30 –	102.21 3.29	113.2 – 3.38 –	114.8 3.30
July	104.21 – 3.50 –	105.0 3.44	102.15 – 3.30 –	102.23 3.28	112.20 – 3.40 –	113.20 3.34
August	104.23 – 3.49 –	104.29 3.46	102.7 – 3.32 –	102.20 3.29	112.0 – 3.44 –	112.16 3.41
September	101.31 – 3.93 –	104.29 3.46	101.9 – 3.40 –	102.10 3.32	108.21 – 3.66 –	112.16 3.41
October	100.0 – 4.25 –	102.30 3.77	98.13 – 3.63 –	101.18 3.37	101.28 – 4.12 –	109.20 3.59
November	100.23 – 4.14 –	102.0 3.92	99.12 – 3.55 –	100.16 3.46	104.7 – 3.95 –	107.28 3.71
December	98.15 – 4.51 –	101.6 4.05	97.9 – 3.73 –	100.0 3.50	100.2 – 4.25 –	104.28 3.91
High – Low	$98.15 – 4.51 –	105.5 3.92	$97.9 – 3.73 –	102.23 3.28	$100.2 – 4.25 –	114.8 3.30
Dates	12/30 –	5/19	12/18 –	5/20	12/29 –	6/2
Price range	$6.22		$5.14		$14.6	

	1932					
	4th Liberty **4 1/4% – 1938**		**1st Liberty** **3 1/2% – 1947**		**Treasury** **4 1/4% – 1952**	
	Low Price	**High Price**	**Low Price**	**High Price**	**Low Price**	**High Price**
January	$98.8 – 99.26		$94.2 – 97.29		$98.30 – 102.19	
	4.59% – 4.29		4.03% – 3.68		4.33% – 4.06	
February	98.29 – 100.15		94.6 – 98.11		100.1 – 103.16	
	4.47 – 4.16		4.02 – 3.64		4.25 – 3.99	
March	100.0 – 101.0		97.30 – 100.7		102.14 – 103.20	
	4.25 – 4.06		3.68 – 3.48		4.07 – 3.98	
April	101.16 – 102.26		100.0 – 101.2		102.28 – 106.13	
	3.97 – 3.73		3.50 – 3.41		4.04 – 3.79	
May	101.24 – 102.25		99.30 – 101.2		101.16 – 106.4	
	3.92 – 3.73		3.51 – 3.41		4.14 – 3.81	
June	101.29 – 102.26		99.30 – 101.6		102.0 – 105.11	
	3.90 – 3.73		3.51 – 3.40		4.10 – 3.86	
July	102.17 – 103.0		101.2 – 101.12		104.26 – 107.4	
	3.77 – 3.69		3.41 – 3.38		3.90 – 3.73	
August	102.25 – 103.8		100.20 – 101.6		106.22 – 107.18	
	3.73 – 3.64		3.45 – 3.40		3.77 – 3.71	
September	103.0 – 103.24		100.12 – 101.15		107.14 – 108.28	
	3.69 – 3.55		3.47 – 3.37		3.72 – 3.62	
October	103.8 – 103.24		101.11 – 101.25		106.31 – 108.17	
	3.64 – 3.55		3.38 – 3.35		3.75 – 3.64	
November	103.1 – 103.20		101.10 – 101.28		107.0 – 108.4	
	3.69 – 3.57		3.38 – 3.35		3.75 – 3.66	
December	103.15 – 104.8		101.26 – 102.6		107.29 – 110.0	
	3.60 – 3.46		3.35 – 3.31		3.68 – 3.55	
High – Low	$98.8 – 104.8		$94.2 – 102.26		$98.30 – 110.0	
	4.59 – 3.46		4.03 – 3.31		4.33 – 3.55	
Dates	1/12 – 12/27		1/26 – 12/22		1/12 – 12/27	
Price range	$6.00		$8.24		$11.02	

TABLE A.40 (continued)

1933

	4th Liberty 4 1/4% – 1938		1st Liberty 3 1/2% – 1947		Treasury 4 1/4% – 1952	
	Low Price	High Price	Low Price	High Price	Low Price	High Price
January	$103.4 3.56%	103.30 3.39	$102.9 3.30%	103.20 3.18	$109.17 3.56%	111.0 3.46
February	100.30 4.04	103.19 3.46	100.0 3.50	103.18 3.18	105.15 3.84	111.4 3.45
March	100.12 4.17	102.9 3.75	99.30 3.51	101.24 3.34	103.14 3.99.0	109.5 3.58
April	101.17 3.91	103.10 3.52	100.0 3.50	102.6 3.30	105.3 3.87	108.20 3.62
May	102.11 3.73	103.8 3.54	100.23 3.43	102.24 3.25	107.2 3.73	109.22 3.55
June	102.28 3.62	103.8 3.54	102.0 3.32	103.1 3.23	109.10 3.57	100.8 3.51
July	102.21 3.67	103.1 3.52	102.17 3.27	102.28 3.24	109.26 3.54	110.12 3.50
August	102.16 3.70	102.30 3.60	102.15 3.28	102.23 3.25	109.26 3.54	110.28 3.46
September	102.16 3.70	103.10 3.52	102.0 3.32	102.31 3.24	110.0 3.52	111.3 3.45
October	102.29 3.62	103.31 3.39	102.1 3.32	102.28 3.24	109.22 3.55	110.17 3.49
November	100.30 4.04	103.3 3.50	99.0 3.59	102.4 3.31	104.10 3.95	109.30 3.53
December	101.11 3.95	101.30 3.82	99.29 3.51	100.20 3.43	105.20 3.83	106.24 3.75
High – Low	$100.12 4.17	103.30 3.39	$99.0 3.59	103.20 3.18	$103.14 3.99.0	111.4 3.45
Dates	3/3	1/4	11/10	1/26	3/3	2/2
Price Range	$3.18		$4.20		$7.22	

Source: Prices are from The Commercial and Financial Chronicle, monthly, 1929-1933.
Notes: (a) Prices are quoted in 1/32nds of a dollar per $100. i.e. 99.31 = 99 31/32.

TABLE A.41
Money Supply 1920 - 1940 (monthy)
($billions)

									Consolidated totals				
	Currency held by the public	Deposits adjusted, commercial banks			Deposits at		S & L shares	M_1 (Cols. 1 + 2)	M_2 (Cols. 8 + 3)	Duplications betw. col. 9 and cols. 5 + 6	M_3 (Cols. 9+5 +6 – 10)	Duplications betw. cols. 11 and 7	M_4 (Cols. 11 + 7 –12)
Date		Demand	Time	Total	Mut. sav. banks	Post. sav. syst.							
	(1)	(2)	(3)	(4)	(5)	(6)	(7)	(8)	(9)	(10)	(11)	(12)	(13)
1920													
Jan.	4.20	19.28	10.49	29.77	4.96	0.16		23.48	33.97	0.35	38.74		
Feb.	4.33	19.50	10.66	30.16	4.99	0.16		23.83	34.49	0.35	39.29		
Mar.	4.40	19.73	10.87	30.60	5.03	0.16		24.13	35.00	0.35	39.84		
Apr.	4.44	19.57	11.01	30.58	5.07	0.16		24.01	35.02	0.35	39.99		
May	4.44	19.53	11.10	30.63	5.11	0.16		23.97	35.07	0.35	39.99		
June	4.49	19.33	11.24	30.57	5.15	0.16		23.82	35.06	0.35	40.02		
July	4.53	19.28	11.24	30.52	5.18	0.16		23.81	35.05	0.34	40.05		
Aug.	4.60	19.16	11.34	30.50	5.22	0.16		23.76	35.10	0.33	40.15		
Sept.	4.65	19.07	11.37	30.44	5.27	0.16		23.72	35.09	0.32	40.20		
Oct.	4.68	18.87	11.38	30.25	5.30	0.16		23.55	34.93	0.32	40.07		
Nov.	4.56	18.57	11.41	29.98	5.33	0.16		23.13	34.54	0.31	39.72		
Dec.	4.51	18.85	11.46	30.31	5.36	0.16	1.74	23.36	34.82	0.30	40.04	0.06	41.72
1921													
Jan.	4.34	18.35	11.52	29.87	5.39	0.16		22.69	34.21	0.29	39.47		
Feb.	4.30	18.18	11.45	29.63	5.41	0.16		22.48	33.93	0.28	39.22		
Mar.	4.24	17.72	11.41	29.13	5.43	0.16		21.96	33.37	0.28	38.68		
Apr.	4.18	17.45	11.38	28.83	5.45	0.16		21.63	33.01	0.27	38.35		
May	4.15	17.43	11.34	28.77	5.47	0.16		21.58	32.92	0.26	38.29		
June	4.07	17.09	11.30	28.39	5.49	0.15		21.16	32.46	0.25	37.85		
July	4.01	16.92	11.22	28.14	5.50	0.15		20.93	32.15	0.26	37.54		
Aug.	3.96	17.03	11.25	28.28	5.52	0.15		20.99	32.24	0.26	37.65		
Sept.	3.93	16.82	11.23	28.05	5.53	0.15		20.75	31.98	0.26	37.40		
Oct.	3.83	17.04	11.32	28.36	5.54	0.15		20.87	32.19	0.26	37.62		
Nov.	3.77	17.15	11.32	28.47	5.56	0.15		20.92	32.24	0.26	37.69		
Dec.	3.76	17.10	11.30	28.40	5.57	0.14	1.96	20.86	32.16	0.26	37.61	0.07	39.50
1922													
Jan.	3.64	17.03	11.26	28.29	5.60	0.14		20.67	31.93	0.26	37.41		
Feb.	3.64	17.22	11.44	28.66	5.62	0.14		20.86	32.30	0.26	37.80		
Mar.	3.66	17.24	11.54	28.78	5.65	0.14		20.90	32.44	0.27	37.96		
Apr.	3.66	17.78	11.69	29.47	5.66	0.14		21.44	33.13	0.27	38.66		
May	3.64	17.98	11.78	29.76	5.67	0.14		21.62	33.40	0.27	38.94		
June	3.66	18.18	12.07	30.25	5.68	0.14		21.84	33.91	0.27	39.46		
July	3.64	18.31	12.33	30.64	5.72	0.14		21.95	34.28	0.27	39.87		
Aug.	3.69	18.26	12.52	30.78	5.76	0.14		21.95	34.47	0.27	40.10		
Sept.	3.75	18.51	12.50	31.01	5.80	0.13		22.26	34.76	0.27	40.42		
Oct.	3.75	18.59	12.66	31.25	5.85	0.13		22.34	35.00	0.27	40.71		
Nov.	3.77	18.53	12.70	31.23	5.88	0.13		22.30	35.00	0.27	40.74		
Dec.	3.81	19.25	12.91	32.16	5.92	0.13	2.22	23.06	35.97	0.27	41.75	0.08	43.89
1923													
Jan.	3.76	19.16	12.95	32.11	5.97	0.13		22.92	35.87	0.27	41.70		
Feb.	3.82	19.19	13.10	32.29	6.01	0.13		23.01	36.11	0.27	41.98		
Mar.	3.88	18.73	13.47	32.20	6.06	0.13		22.61	36.08	0.28	41.99		
Apr.	3.92	18.98	13.57	32.55	6.10	0.13		22.90	36.47	0.28	42.42		
May	3.98	19.05	13.70	32.75	6.15	0.13		23.03	36.73	0.28	42.73		
June	4.02	18.85	13.82	32.67	6.19	0.13		22.87	36.69	0.28	42.73		
July	4.01	18.84	13.81	32.65	6.23	0.13		22.85	36.66	0.28	42.74		
Aug.	4.03	18.78	13.90	32.68	6.27	0.13		22.81	36.71	0.29	42.82		
Sept.	4.03	18.92	13.95	32.87	6.31	0.13		22.95	36.90	0.29	43.05		
Oct.	3.99	19.05	14.04	33.09	6.34	0.13		23.04	37.08	0.30	43.25		
Nov.	4.05	19.03	14.13	33.16	6.37	0.13		23.08	37.21	0.30	43.41		
Dec.	4.01	19.16	14.21	33.37	6.40	0.13	2.63	23.17	37.38	0.31	43.60	0.10	46.13
1924													
Jan.	3.92	19.06	14.24	33.30	6.44	0.13		22.98	37.22	0.31	43.48		
Feb.	3.98	18.94	14.44	33.38	6.46	0.13		22.92	37.36	0.32	43.63		
Mar.	4.01	18.97	14.54	33.51	6.51	0.13		22.98	37.52	0.32	43.84		
Apr.	4.00	19.07	14.68	33.75	6.51	0.13		23.07	37.75	0.33	44.06		
May	4.02	19.22	14.73	33.95	6.53	0.13		23.24	37.97	0.33	44.30		
June	3.97	19.50	14.86	34.36	6.59	0.13		23.47	38.33	0.34	44.71		
July	3.94	19.83	15.01	34.84	6.62	0.13		23.77	38.78	0.34	45.19		
Aug.	3.93	20.15	15.13	35.28	6.64	0.13		24.08	39.21	0.34	45.64		
Sept.	3.88	20.47	15.31	35.78	6.68	0.13		24.35	39.66	0.34	46.13		
Oct.	3.93	20.52	15.48	36.00	6.73	0.13		24.45	39.93	0.34	46.45		
Nov.	3.95	20.89	15.58	36.47	6.78	0.13		24.84	40.42	0.34	46.99		
Dec.	3.94	20.70	15.66	36.36	6.84	0.13	3.15	24.64	40.30	0.34	46.93	0.11	49.97
1925													
Jan.	3.96	21.00	15.81	36.81	6.86	0.13		24.96	40.77	0.34	47.42		
Feb.	3.96	21.19	15.94	37.13	6.90	0.13		25.15	41.09	0.34	47.78		
Mar.	3.97	21.07	16.07	37.14	6.92	0.13		25.04	41.11	0.34	47.82		
Apr.	3.95	21.22	16.13	37.35	6.96	0.13		25.17	41.30	0.33	48.06		
May	3.96	21.40	16.29	37.69	6.99	0.13		25.36	41.65	0.33	48.44		
June	3.95	21.65	16.43	38.08	7.04	0.13		25.60	42.03	0.33	48.87		
July	3.97	21.73	16.50	38.23	7.06	0.13		25.70	42.20	0.33	49.06		
Aug.	3.94	22.23	16.61	38.84	7.08	0.13		26.17	42.78	0.33	49.66		
Sept.	3.93	22.54	16.74	39.28	7.06	0.13		26.47	43.21	0.33	50.07		
Oct.	3.96	22.50	16.85	39.35	7.14	0.13		26.46	43.31	0.33	50.35		
Nov.	3.95	22.43	16.96	39.39	7.19	0.13		26.38	43.34	0.33	50.33		
Dec.	3.99	22.33	17.04	39.37	7.24	0.13	3.81	26.32	43.36	0.33	50.40	0.13	54.08
1926													
Jan.	3.99	22.35	17.19	39.54	7.23	0.13		26.34	43.53	0.33	50.56		
Feb.	4.01	22.43	17.24	39.67	7.29	0.13		26.44	43.68	0.33	50.77		
Mar.	3.98	22.36	17.26	39.62	7.32	0.13		26.34	43.60	0.33	50.72		
Apr.	4.04	22.07	17.36	39.43	7.34	0.13		26.11	43.47	0.34	50.60		
May	4.00	22.37	17.47	39.84	7.38	0.13		26.37	43.84	0.34	51.01		
June	4.00	22.31	17.56	39.87	7.43	0.13		26.31	43.87	0.34	51.09		
July	4.05	22.04	17.61	39.65	7.46	0.14		26.09	43.70	0.34	50.96		
Aug.	4.01	22.19	17.69	39.88	7.50	0.14		26.20	43.89	0.34	51.19		
Sept.	4.00	22.13	17.69	39.82	7.55	0.14		26.13	43.82	0.34	51.17		
Oct.	4.00	21.92	17.74	39.66	7.59	0.14		25.92	43.66	0.35	51.04		
Nov.	3.98	21.98	17.73	39.71	7.69	0.14		25.96	43.69	0.35	51.17		
Dec.	4.01	21.68	17.68	39.36	7.70	0.14	4.38	25.69	43.37	0.35	50.86	0.15	55.09

Date	Currency held by the public (1)	Deposits adjusted, commercial banks Demand (2)	Time (3)	Total (4)	Deposits at Mut. sav. banks (5)	Post. sav. syst. (6)	S & L shares (7)	M₁ (Cols. 1 + 2) (8)	M₂ (Cols. 8 + 3) (9)	Duplications betw. col. 9 and cols. 5 + 6 (10)	M₃ (Cols. 9+5 +6 − 10) (11)	Duplications betw. cols. 11 and 7 (12)	M₄ (Cols. 11 + 7 −12) (13)
1927													
Jan.	4.02	21.76	17.92	39.68	7.74	0.14		25.78	43.70	0.35	51.23		
Feb.	4.02	21.89	18.24	40.13	7.78	0.14		25.91	44.15	0.36	51.71		
Mar.	4.04	22.04	18.27	40.31	7.84	0.14		26.08	44.35	0.36	51.97		
Apr.	4.04	21.93	18.39	40.32	7.86	0.15		25.97	44.36	0.36	52.01		
May	4.01	22.40	18.57	40.97	7.91	0.15		26.41	44.98	0.36	52.68		
June	3.98	22.06	18.70	40.76	7.96	0.15		26.04	44.74	0.37	52.48		
July	3.99	22.09	18.81	40.90	8.01	0.15		26.08	44.89	0.36	52.69		
Aug.	3.93	22.29	18.85	41.14	8.05	0.15		26.22	45.07	0.36	52.91		
Sept.	3.97	22.10	18.94	41.04	8.11	0.15		26.07	45.01	0.36	52.91		
Oct.	3.93	22.24	19.02	41.26	8.17	0.15		26.17	45.19	0.36	53.15		
Nov.	3.88	22.76	19.33	42.09	8.24	0.15		26.64	45.97	0.36	54.00		
Dec.	3.89	22.09	19.34	41.43	8.29	0.15	5.03	25.98	45.32	0.36	53.40	0.16	58.27
1928													
Jan.	3.85	22.52	19.63	42.15	8.34	0.15		26.37	46.00	0.36	54.13		
Feb.	3.83	22.62	19.74	42.36	8.38	0.15		26.45	46.19	0.36	54.36		
Mar.	3.90	22.56	20.00	42.56	8.40	0.15		26.46	46.46	0.36	54.65		
Apr.	3.91	22.91	20.09	43.00	8.46	0.15		26.82	46.91	0.35	55.17		
May	3.90	22.72	20.20	42.92	8.49	0.15		26.62	46.82	0.35	55.11		
June	3.95	22.05	20.22	42.27	8.52	0.15		26.00	46.22	0.35	54.54		
July	3.91	22.29	20.12	42.41	8.55	0.15		26.20	46.32	0.35	54.67		
Aug.	3.93	22.11	20.13	42.24	8.60	0.15		26.04	46.17	0.35	54.57		
Sept.	3.90	22.37	20.06	42.43	8.66	0.15		26.27	46.33	0.35	54.79		
Oct.	3.85	22.59	20.25	42.84	8.70	0.15		26.44	46.69	0.35	55.19		
Nov.	3.94	22.69	20.17	42.86	8.74	0.15		26.63	46.80	0.35	55.34		
Dec.	3.86	22.80	20.26	43.06	8.78	0.15	5.76	26.66	46.92	0.35	55.50	0.20	61.06
1929													
Jan.	3.86	22.47	20.20	42.67	8.78	0.15		26.33	46.53	0.35	55.11		
Feb.	3.88	22.60	20.16	42.76	8.81	0.15		26.48	46.64	0.35	55.25		
Mar.	3.93	22.57	20.05	42.62	8.81	0.15		26.50	46.55	0.35	55.16		
Apr.	3.90	22.67	19.89	42.56	8.82	0.15		26.57	46.46	0.34	55.09		
May	3.91	22.37	19.87	42.24	8.83	0.15		26.28	46.15	0.34	54.79		
June	3.94	22.47	19.86	42.33	8.84	0.15		26.41	46.27	0.34	54.92		
July	3.92	22.99	19.85	42.84	8.86	0.16		26.91	46.76	0.35	55.43		
Aug.	3.95	22.75	19.94	42.69	8.87	0.16		26.70	46.64	0.36	55.31		
Sept.	3.85	22.79	20.04	42.83	8.88	0.16		26.64	46.68	0.37	55.35		
Oct.	3.86	24.64	20.02	44.66	8.84	0.16		28.50	48.52	0.37	57.15		
Nov.	3.88	21.86	19.67	41.53	8.82	0.16		25.74	45.41	0.38	54.01		
Dec.	3.83	22.85	19.57	42.42	8.82	0.16	6.24	26.68	46.25	0.39	54.84	0.17	60.91
1930													
Jan.	3.78	22.15	19.76	41.91	8.86	0.16		25.93	45.69	0.40	54.31		
Feb.	3.78	22.42	19.66	42.08	8.91	0.17		26.20	45.86	0.40	54.54		
Mar.	3.75	22.86	19.96	42.82	8.96	0.17		26.61	46.57	0.41	55.29		
Apr.	3.70	22.50	19.85	42.35	8.99	0.17		26.20	46.05	0.42	54.79		
May	3.73	21.88	19.99	41.87	9.02	0.17		25.61	45.60	0.43	54.36		
June	3.71	21.87	20.16	42.03	9.06	0.18		25.58	45.74	0.44	54.54		
July	3.70	21.99	20.10	42.09	9.12	0.18		25.69	45.79	0.46	54.63		
Aug.	3.74	21.63	20.21	41.84	9.16	0.19		25.37	45.58	0.48	54.45		
Sept.	3.67	21.69	20.23	41.92	9.23	0.19		25.36	45.59	0.50	54.51		
Oct.	3.63	21.68	20.27	41.95	9.28	0.19		25.31	45.58	0.52	54.53		
Nov.	3.71	21.64	19.93	41.57	9.33	0.20		25.35	45.28	0.54	54.27		
Dec.	3.84	21.41	19.36	40.77	9.42	0.24	6.30	25.25	44.61	0.56	53.71	0.20	59.81
1931													
Jan.	3.85	21.05	19.33	40.38	9.53	0.28		24.90	44.23	0.59	53.45		
Feb.	3.86	21.21	19.48	40.69	9.60	0.29		25.07	44.55	0.61	53.83		
Mar.	3.90	21.22	19.39	40.61	9.66	0.30		25.12	44.51	0.63	53.84		
Apr.	3.93	20.68	19.49	40.17	9.75	0.31		24.61	44.10	0.65	53.51		
May	3.93	20.33	19.32	39.65	9.82	0.32		24.26	43.58	0.67	53.05		
June	4.03	20.24	19.02	39.26	9.86	0.35		24.27	43.29	0.69	52.81		
July	4.10	20.09	18.85	38.94	9.90	0.37		24.19	43.04	0.73	52.58		
Aug.	4.22	19.60	18.51	38.11	9.94	0.42		23.82	42.33	0.76	51.93		
Sept.	4.33	19.44	17.96	37.40	9.98	0.47		23.77	41.73	0.80	51.38		
Oct.	4.58	18.53	17.08	35.61	10.01	0.54		23.11	40.19	0.83	49.91		
Nov.	4.55	18.21	16.56	34.77	10.02	0.56		22.76	39.32	0.87	49.03		
Dec.	4.65	17.65	15.94	33.59	9.97	0.60	5.92	22.30	38.24	0.91	47.90	0.17	53.65
1932													
Jan.	4.94	16.98	15.58	32.56	9.90	0.66		21.92	37.50	0.94	47.12		
Feb.	4.87	16.86	15.36	32.22	9.90	0.69		21.73	37.09	0.98	46.70		
Mar.	4.79	16.74	15.24	31.98	9.94	0.70		21.53	36.77	1.01	46.40		
Apr.	4.80	16.51	15.16	31.67	9.92	0.72		21.31	36.47	1.05	46.06		
May	4.80	16.16	15.01	31.17	9.89	0.74		20.96	35.97	1.08	45.52		
June	5.01	15.87	14.71	30.58	9.89	0.78		20.88	35.59	1.12	45.14		
July	5.10	15.48	14.69	30.17	9.87	0.83		20.58	35.27	1.14	44.83		
Aug.	5.04	15.58	14.58	30.16	9.85	0.85		20.62	35.20	1.17	44.73		
Sept.	5.00	15.65	14.50	30.15	9.86	0.86		20.65	35.15	1.19	44.68		
Oct.	4.92	15.76	14.62	30.38	9.86	0.87		20.68	35.30	1.21	44.82		
Nov.	4.90	16.08	14.56	30.64	9.88	0.88		20.98	35.54	1.24	45.06		
Dec.	4.89	15.88	14.52	30.40	9.90	0.90	5.33	20.77	35.29	1.26	44.83	0.15	50.01
1933													
Jan.	5.04	16.02	14.38	30.40	9.90	0.94		21.06	35.44	1.28	45.00		
Feb.	5.65	14.76	13.50	28.26	9.84	1.00		20.41	33.91	1.31	43.44		
Mar.	5.57	13.91	11.82	25.73	9.74	1.11		19.48	31.30	1.33	40.82		
Apr.	5.26	14.20	11.64	25.84	9.69	1.16		19.46	31.10	1.35	40.60		
May	5.08	14.79	11.60	26.39	9.62	1.18		19.87	31.47	1.38	40.89		
June	5.01	14.64	11.83	26.47	9.59	1.18		19.65	31.48	1.40	40.85		
July	4.95	14.57	12.03	26.60	9.58	1.18		19.52	31.55	1.38	40.91		
Aug.	4.91	14.64	12.01	26.65	9.53	1.18		19.55	31.56	1.37	40.90		
Sept.	4.89	14.72	12.00	26.72	9.53	1.18		19.61	31.61	1.35	40.97		
Oct.	4.86	14.90	11.96	26.86	9.52	1.19		19.76	31.72	1.34	41.09		
Nov.	4.90	15.11	11.86	26.97	9.52	1.20		20.01	31.87	1.32	41.27		
Dec.	4.90	15.33	11.88	27.21	9.53	1.21	4.75	20.23	32.11	1.30	41.55	0.14	46.16

TABLE A.41 (continued)

Date	Currency held by the public (1)	Deposits adjusted, commercial banks			Deposits at		S & L shares (7)	Consolidated totals					
		Demand (2)	Time (3)	Total (4)	Mut. sav. banks (5)	Post. sav. syst. (6)		M_1 (Cols. 1 + 2) (8)	M_2 (Cols. 8 + 3) (9)	Duplications betw. col. 9 and cols. 5 + 6 (10)	M_3 (Cols. 9+5 +6 – 10) (11)	Duplications betw. cols. 11 and 7 (12)	M_4 (Cols. 11 + 7 –12) (13)
1934													
Jan.	4.55	15.65	12.05	27.70	9.55	1.20		20.20	32.25	1.29	41.71		
Feb.	4.57	16.21	12.10	28.31	9.58	1.20		20.78	32.88	1.27	42.39		
Mar.	4.61	16.63	12.26	28.89	9.61	1.20		21.24	33.50	1.25	43.06		
Apr.	4.61	16.76	12.43	29.19	9.62	1.20		21.37	33.80	1.24	43.38		
May	4.62	16.88	12.52	29.40	9.63	1.19		21.50	34.02	1.22	43.62		
June	4.64	16.94	12.70	29.64	9.65	1.20		21.58	34.28	1.21	43.92		
July	4.66	17.39	12.70	30.09	9.66	1.19		22.05	34.75	1.18	44.42		
Aug.	4.68	17.96	12.75	30.71	9.59	1.19		22.64	35.39	1.16	45.01		
Sept.	4.68	17.86	12.69	30.55	9.68	1.19		22.54	35.23	1.13	44.97		
Oct.	4.64	18.43	12.78	31.21	9.68	1.20		23.07	35.85	1.11	45.62		
Nov.	4.72	18.84	12.73	31.57	9.70	1.20		23.56	36.29	1.08	46.11		
Dec.	4.61	18.67	12.83	31.50	9.70	1.20	4.46	23.28	36.11	1.06	45.95	0.17	50.24
1935													
Jan.	4.67	19.50	12.90	32.40	9.71	1.20		24.17	37.07	1.03	46.95		
Feb.	4.75	20.12	12.90	33.02	9.74	1.20		24.87	37.77	1.01	47.70		
Mar.	4.76	20.01	13.02	33.03	9.76	1.20		24.77	37.79	0.98	47.77		
Apr.	4.76	20.35	13.23	33.58	9.77	1.20		25.11	38.34	0.96	48.35		
May	4.76	20.53	13.22	33.75	9.78	1.20		25.29	38.51	0.93	48.56		
June	4.76	20.96	13.24	34.20	9.79	1.20		25.72	38.96	0.91	49.04		
July	4.74	21.22	13.23	34.45	9.79	1.19		25.96	39.19	0.89	49.28		
Aug.	4.80	22.53	13.21	35.74	9.80	1.19		27.33	40.54	0.88	50.65		
Sept.	4.85	22.06	13.31	35.37	9.81	1.19		26.91	40.22	0.87	50.35		
Oct.	4.89	22.36	13.36	35.72	9.82	1.19		27.25	40.61	0.85	50.77		
Nov.	4.93	22.87	13.39	36.26	9.84	1.20		27.80	41.19	0.84	51.39		
Dec.	4.93	22.63	13.60	36.23	9.84	1.20	4.25	27.56	41.16	0.83	51.37	0.18	55.44
1936													
Jan.	4.98	22.61	13.60	36.21	9.85	1.20		27.59	41.19	0.81	51.43		
Feb.	5.04	23.04	13.63	36.67	9.87	1.21		28.08	41.71	0.80	51.99		
Mar.	5.07	23.04	13.63	36.67	9.89	1.21		28.11	41.74	0.79	52.05		
Apr.	5.06	23.62	13.89	37.51	9.90	1.21		28.68	42.57	0.77	52.91		
May	5.09	24.41	13.87	38.28	9.90	1.21		29.50	43.37	0.76	53.72		
June	5.31	24.87	13.91	38.78	9.93	1.23		30.18	44.09	0.75	54.50		
July	5.28	25.06	14.03	39.09	9.95	1.24		30.34	44.37	0.74	54.82		
Aug.	5.28	24.96	14.11	39.07	9.96	1.25		30.24	44.35	0.73	54.83		
Sept.	5.33	25.40	14.19	39.59	9.98	1.25		30.73	44.92	0.73	55.42		
Oct.	5.37	25.32	14.23	39.55	9.99	1.25		30.69	44.92	0.72	55.44		
Nov.	5.43	25.52	14.20	39.72	10.00	1.25		30.95	45.15	0.71	55.69		
Dec.	5.52	25.86	14.30	40.16	10.02	1.26	4.19	31.38	45.68	0.70	56.26	0.22	60.23
1937													
Jan.	5.52	25.61	14.39	40.00	10.04	1.26		31.13	45.52	0.70	56.12		
Feb.	5.54	25.87	14.59	40.46	10.07	1.27		31.41	46.00	0.69	56.65		
Mar.	5.53	26.07	14.53	40.60	10.10	1.27		31.60	46.13	0.68	56.82		
Apr.	5.57	25.94	14.56	40.50	10.11	1.27		31.51	46.07	0.67	56.78		
May	5.55	25.57	14.70	40.27	10.11	1.26		31.12	45.82	0.67	56.52		
June	5.56	25.55	14.74	40.29	10.10	1.26		31.11	45.85	0.66	56.55		
July	5.60	25.45	14.88	40.33	10.14	1.27		31.05	45.93	0.66	56.68		
Aug.	5.67	25.18	14.97	40.15	10.15	1.27		30.85	45.82	0.66	56.58		
Sept.	5.66	25.02	15.10	40.12	10.15	1.27		30.68	45.78	0.67	56.53		
Oct.	5.64	24.46	15.08	39.54	10.12	1.27		30.10	45.18	0.67	55.90		
Nov.	5.63	24.26	15.01	39.27	10.13	1.27		29.89	44.90	0.67	55.63		
Dec.	5.58	24.05	15.00	39.05	10.13	1.27	4.08	29.63	44.63	0.67	55.36	0.21	59.23
1938													
Jan.	5.54	24.32	15.06	39.38	10.14	1.27		29.86	44.92	0.67	55.66		
Feb.	5.51	24.56	15.12	39.68	10.16	1.27		30.07	45.19	0.68	55.94		
Mar.	5.52	24.64	15.02	39.66	10.18	1.26		30.16	45.18	0.68	55.94		
Apr.	5.49	24.50	15.03	39.53	10.17	1.27		29.99	45.02	0.68	55.78		
May	5.51	24.12	15.00	39.12	10.18	1.25		29.63	44.63	0.68	55.38		
June	5.48	24.25	15.04	39.29	10.16	1.25		29.73	44.77	0.69	55.49		
July	5.51	24.55	14.95	39.50	10.19	1.25		30.06	45.01	0.69	55.76		
Aug.	5.51	25.30	14.99	40.29	10.20	1.25		30.81	45.80	0.70	56.55		
Sept.	5.59	25.58	14.92	40.50	10.20	1.24		31.17	46.09	0.70	56.83		
Oct.	5.61	25.94	14.94	40.88	10.23	1.25		31.55	46.49	0.71	57.26		
Nov.	5.64	26.52	14.86	41.38	10.24	1.25		32.16	47.02	0.72	57.79		
Dec.	5.66	26.70	14.94	41.64	10.24	1.25	4.08	32.36	47.30	0.72	58.07	0.22	61.93
1939													
Jan.	5.74	26.57	15.00	41.57	10.27	1.26		32.31	47.31	0.73	58.11		
Feb.	5.81	26.39	15.02	41.41	10.31	1.26		32.20	47.22	0.74	58.05		
Mar.	5.87	26.81	15.06	41.87	10.35	1.26		32.68	47.74	0.74	58.61		
Apr.	5.96	27.01	15.13	42.14	10.36	1.26		32.97	48.10	0.75	58.97		
May	5.97	27.20	15.11	42.31	10.38	1.26		33.17	48.28	0.75	59.17		
June	6.01	27.27	15.16	42.43	10.39	1.26		33.28	48.44	0.76	59.33		
July	6.05	28.13	15.18	43.31	10.43	1.26		34.18	49.36	0.78	60.27		
Aug.	6.14	28.94	15.19	44.13	10.44	1.27		35.08	50.27	0.80	61.18		
Sept.	6.20	29.64	15.15	44.79	10.44	1.26		35.84	50.99	0.82	61.87		
Oct.	6.24	30.02	15.22	45.24	10.47	1.27		36.26	51.48	0.84	62.38		
Nov.	6.27	30.93	15.18	46.11	10.47	1.27		37.20	52.38	0.87	63.25		
Dec.	6.28	30.56	15.29	45.85	10.48	1.28	4.12	36.84	52.13	0.89	63.00	0.27	66.85
1940													
Jan.	6.36	31.03	15.30	46.33	10.52	1.29		37.39	52.69	0.91	63.59		
Feb.	6.43	31.49	15.39	46.88	10.56	1.29		37.92	53.31	0.93	64.23		
Mar.	6.49	31.98	15.52	47.50	10.60	1.30		38.47	53.99	0.95	64.94		
Apr.	6.52	31.80	15.47	47.27	10.61	1.30		38.32	53.79	0.97	64.73		
May	6.58	32.53	15.54	48.07	10.60	1.30		39.11	54.65	0.99	65.56		
June	6.68	33.04	15.61	48.65	10.58	1.29		39.72	55.33	1.01	66.19		
July	6.74	33.45	15.59	49.04	10.58	1.29		40.19	55.78	1.01	66.64		
Aug.	6.82	33.52	15.63	49.15	10.58	1.29		40.34	55.97	1.01	66.83		
Sept.	6.92	33.93	15.68	49.61	10.59	1.29		40.85	56.53	1.01	67.40		
Oct.	7.04	34.49	15.66	50.15	10.60	1.29		41.53	57.19	1.00	68.08		
Nov.	7.15	34.98	15.68	50.66	10.61	1.30		42.13	57.81	1.00	68.72		
Dec.	7.35	35.52	15.80	51.32	10.62	1.30	4.32	42.87	58.67	1.00	69.59	0.31	73.60

Source: M. Friedman and Anna Jacobson Schwartz, Monetary Statistics, pp. 18 – 32.

Bibliography

General

Federal Reserve System. Annual Reports of the Board of Governors. Washington, D.C.
Federal Reserve System. Board of Governors. Banking and Monetary Statistics. Washington, D.C., 1943.
Moody's Manual of Investments American and Foreign, Banks-Insurance Companies-Investment Trusts-Real Estate-Finance and Credit Companies. New York: Moody's Investors Service, 1929–1935.
Moody's Manual of Investments American and Foreign, Industrial Securities. New York: Moody's Investors Service, 1929–1935.
Moody's Manual of Investments American and Foreign, Public Utility Securities. New York: Moody's Investors Service, 1929–1935.
National Statistical Service. American Underwriting Houses and Their Issues. Vols. 2 and 3. New York, 1930, 1931.
New York Stock Exchange. Annual Reports. New York, 1929–1939.
Secretary of the Treasury. Annual Reports. Washington, D.C.
Securities and Exchange Commission. Investment Trusts and Investment Companies. 5 pts. Washington, D.C.: U.S. Government Printing Office, 1939, 1940, 1942.
U.S. Congress. Stock Exchange Practices Hearings Before the Committee on Banking and Currency. 83rd Cong., 1st and 2nd sess., 1934. 20 pts.
U.S. Department of Commerce. Bureau of the Census. Historical Statistics of the United States, Colonial Times to 1970. Pts. 1 and 2, Washington, D.C., 1975.
U.S. Department of Commerce. Bureau of the Census. Statistical Abstract of the United States, 1939. Washington, D.C., 1940.
U.S. Department of Commerce. The National Income and Products Accounts of the United States, 1929–1965, Statistical Tables: A Supplement to the Survey of Current Business. Washington, D.C., 1966.

Periodicals and Newspapers

The Annalist

Barron's
Business Week
The Commercial and Financial Chronicle
Federal Reserve Monthly Bulletin
Fortune
New York Stock Exchange Bulletin
New York Times
Survey of Current Business
Wall Street Journal

Books

Adams, Jr., Russell B. *King C. Gillette: The Man and His Wonderful Shaving Device*. Boston: Little, Brown and Company, 1978.

Archer, Gleason L. *Big Business and Radio*. New York: American Historical Company, Inc., 1939.

Baldwin, Hanson W., and Stone, Shepard, *We Saw It Happen: The News Behind the News That's Fit to Print*. New York: Simon and Schuster, 1938.

Beaton, Kendall. *Enterprise in Oil; A History of Shell in the United States*. New York: Appleton-Century-Crofts, Inc., 1957.

Bernstein, Irving. *The Lean Years: A History of the American Worker 1920–1933*. 1960; Reprint. New York: DaCapo Press, Inc., 1960.

Bernstein, Michael Alan. *Long Term Economic Growth and The Problem of Recovery in American Manufacturing: A Study of the Great Depression in the United States, 1929–1939*. Ph.D. diss. Yale University, 1982.

Boyle, Andrew. *Montagu Norman*. New York: Weybright and Talley Inc., 1967.

Brooks, John. *Once in Golconda: A True Drama of Wall Street, 1920–1938*. New York: Harper & Row Inc., 1969.

Brown, W. Adams, Jr. *The International Gold Standard Reinterpreted, 1914–1934*. New York: National Bureau of Economic Research, Inc. 1940.

Brunner, Karl, ed. *The Great Depression Revisited*. Boston: Kluwer-Nijhoff Publishing, 1981.

Bryson, A.E. *Halsey, Stuart & Co., Inc., 1901–1937, 1938–1944: A History*. Chicago: 1937–1945.

Buley, R. Carlyle. *The Equitable 1859–1959*. New York: Appleton-Century Crofts Inc., 1959.

Bullock, Hugh. *The Story of Investment Companies*. New York: Columbia University Press, 1959.

Bruner, David. *Herbert Hoover: A Public Life*. New York: Alfred A. Knopf, 1979.

Carosso, Vincent P. *Investment Banking in America*. Cambridge, Mass.: Harvard University Press, 1970.

Carosso, Vincent P. *More Than a Century of Investment Banking: The Kidder Peabody & Co. Story*. New York: McGraw-Hill Book Company, 1979.

Chandler, Alfred D. Jr., *The Visible Hand: The Management Revolution in American Business*. Cambridge, Mass.: Harvard University Press, 1977.

Chandler, Alfred D. Jr., and Salsbury, Stephen. *Pierre S. DuPont and the Making of the Modern Corporation*. New York: Harper & Row Inc., 1971.

Chandler, Lester V. *America's Greatest Depression, 1929–1941*. New York: Harper and Row, 1970.

Childs, C.F. *Concerning U.S. Government Securities*. Chicago: C.F. Childs & Co., 1947.

Clarke, Stephen V.O. *Central Bank Cooperation, 1924–31*. New York: Federal Reserve Bank of New York, 1967.

Cleland, Robert Glass. *A History of Phelps Dodge, 1834–1950*. New York: Alfred A. Knopf, 1952.

Cowles, Alfred & Associates. *Common Stock Indexes, 1871–1937*. Bloomington, Ind.: Principia Press Inc., 1939.

Danielian, N.R., *A.T. & T.: The Story of Industrial Conquest*. New York: Vanguard Press, 1939.

Durand, David. *Basic Yields of Corporate Bonds 1900–1942*, Technical Paper 3, New York: National Bureau of Economic Research, 1942.

Durand, David and Winn, W.J. *Basic Yields of Bonds, 1926–47, Their Measurement and Pattern*, Technical Paper 6, New York: National Bureau of Economic Research, 1947.

Dutton, William S. *DuPont: One Hundred and Forty Years*. New York: Charles Scribner's Sons, 1951.

Farrer, David. *The Warburgs: The Story of a Family*. New York: Stein and Day, 1975.

Feiss, Herbert. *Characters in Crisis, 1933*. Boston: Little, Brown and Company, 1966.

Freidel, Frank. *Franklin D. Roosevelt, Launching the New Deal*. Boston: Little, Brown and Company, 1973.

Friedman, Milton, and Schwartz, Anna Jacobson. *A Monetary History of the United States, 1867–1960*. Princeton: Princeton University Press, 1963.

———. *Monetary Statistics of the United States: Estimates, Sources, Methods*. New York: National Bureau of Economic Research, 1970.

Fuess, Claude M. *Joseph B. Eastman, Servant of the People*. New York: Columbia University Press, 1952.

Galbraith, John K. *The Great Crash, 1929*. Boston: Houghton Mifflin, 1955.

Gibb, G.S. and Knowlton, E.H. *The Resurgent Years, A History of Standard Oil*. New York: Harper & Bros., 1956.

Giddens, P.H. *Standard Oil (Indiana): Oil Pioneer of the Middle West*. New York: Appleton-Century-Crofts Inc., 1955.

Goldenweiser, E.A. *American Monetary Policy*. New York: McGraw-Hill Book Company, 1951.

Gustin, Lawrence R. *Billy Durant: Creator of General Motors*. Grand Rapids, Mich.: Wm. B. Eerdmans Publishing Co., 1973.

Haber, L.F. *The Chemical Industry 1900–1930*. Oxford: Clarendon Press, 1971.

Hamaker, Gene E. *Irrigation Pioneers: A History of the Tri-County Project to 1935*. Minden, Neb.: Warp Publishing Company, 1964.

Hampton, Benjamin B. *History of the American Film Industry from its Beginnings to 1931*. 1970; Reprint. New York: Dover Publications Inc.

Harris, Leon. *Merchant Princes*. New York: Berkley Books, 1980.

Harris, Seymour E. *Twenty Years of Federal Reserve Policy*. Cambridge, Mass.: Harvard University Press, 1933.

Hersh, Benton. *The Mellon Family: A Fortune in History*. New York: William Morrow and Company, Inc., 1978.

Hickman, W. Braddock. *Corporate Bond Quality and Investor Experience*. Princeton: Princeton University Press, 1958.

Homer, Sidney. *A History of Interest Rates*. New Brunswick, N.J.: Rutgers University Press, 1963.

Hoover, Herbert. *The Memoirs of Herbert Hoover*. 3 vols. New York: Macmillan Co., 1952.

Hyman, Sidney. *Marriner S. Eccles: Private Entrepreneur and Public Servant*. Stanford: Graduate School of Business Stanford University, 1976.

James, F. Cyril. *The Growth of Chicago Banks*, Vol. 2, *The Modern Age, 1897–1938*. New York: Harper & Brothers Publishers, 1938.

James, Marquis. *Biography of a Business, 1792–1942: Insurance Company of North America*. New York: Bobbs-Merrill Company, 1942.

———. *The Metropolitan Life: A Study in Business Growth*. New York: Viking Press, 1947.

James, Marquis, and James, B.R. *Biography of a Bank: A History of the Bank of America*. New York: Harper & Row, 1954.

———. *The Texaco Story: The First Fifty Years, 1902–1952*. New York: Texas Company, 1953.

Jones, Jesse H., and Angley, Ed. *$50 Billion: My Years with the R.F.C.* New York: Macmillan Co., 1951.

Josephson, Matthew. *The Money Lords*. New York: Weybright and Talley, Inc., 1972.

Kennedy, Susan Estabrook. *The Banking Crisis of 1933*. Lexington, Ky.: University of Kentucky Press, 1973.

Kindleberger, Charles P. *The World in Depression 1929–1939*. Berkeley, Cal.: University of California Press, 1973.

———. *Manias, Panics, and Crashes: A History of Financial Crises*. New York: Basic Books, Inc., 1978.

Larson, Henrietta M., Knowlton, Evelyn H., and Popple, Charles S. *History of Standard Oil Company (New Jersey) New Horizons 1927–1950*. New York: Harper & Row Inc., 1971.

Lewis, Cleona. *America's Stake in International Investments*. Washington, D.C.: Brookings Institution, 1938.

Loth, David. *Swope of G.E.* New York: Simon and Schuster, Inc., 1958.

Mahoney, Tom, and Sloane, Leonard. *The Great Merchants*. New York: Harper & Row Inc., 1966.

McDonald, Forrest. *Insull*. Chicago: University of Chicago Press, 1962.

McLean, John, and Haigh, Robert. *The Growth of Integrated Oil Companies*. Cambridge, Mass.: Harvard University Press, 1954.

Mintz, Ilse. *Deterioration in the Quality of Foreign Bonds Issued in the United States, 1920–1930*. No. 52. New York: National Bureau of Economic Research, 1951.

Moley, Raymond. *The First New Deal*. New York: Harcourt, Brace & World, Inc., 1966.

Moreau, Emile. *Souvenirs d'un Gouveneur de la Banque de France*. Paris: Librarie de Medicis, 1954.

Myers, Margaret G. *A Financial History of the United States*. New York: Columbia University Press, 1970.

Nevins, Allan, and Hill, Frank Ernest. *Ford: Expansion and Challenge 1915–1933*. New York: Charles Scribner's Sons, 1957.

————. *Ford: Decline and Rebirth 1933–1962*. New York: Charles Scribner's Sons, 1962.

Nurske, Ragnar. *International Currency Experience*. Geneva: Secretariat of the League of Nations, 1944.

Ohlin, Bertil. *Course and Phases of the World Economic Depression*. Geneva: Secretariat of the League of Nations, 1931.

Olson, James Stuart. *Herbert Hoover and the Reconstruction Finance Corporation 1931– 1933*. Ames, Iowa: Iowa State University Press, 1977.

O'Reilly, Maurice. *The Goodyear Story*. Elmsford, N.Y.: The Benjamin Company, Inc., 1983.

Palyi, Melchior. *The Twilight of Gold 1914–1936: Myths and Realities*. Chicago: Henry Regnery Company, 1972.

Pecora, Ferdinand. *Wall Street Under Oath*. New York: Simon & Schuster, 1939.

Perrett, Geoffrey. *America in the Twenties: A History*. New York: Simon and Schuster, 1982.

Pusey, Merlo J. *Eugene Meyer*. New York: Alfred A. Knopf, 1974.

Rees, Goronwy. *The Great Slump: Capitalism in Crisis 1929–1933*. New York: Harper & Row Inc., 1970.

Robert, Joseph C. *The Story of Tobacco in America*. 1967: Reprint. Chapel Hill, N.C.: University of North Carolina Press.

Rothbard, Murray. *America's Great Depression*. 4th ed. New York: Richardson & Snyder, 1983.

Sachs, Walter, Autobiography, Unpublished Manuscript at Goldman, Sachs & Co., New York.

Schlesinger, Arthur. *The Crisis of the Old Order, 1919–1933*. Boston: Houghton Mifflin Company, 1957.

Schwartz, Jordan A. *The Speculator Bernard M. Baruch in Washington, 1917–1965*. Chapel Hill: University of North Carolina Press, 1981.

Sloan, Alfred P. Jr. *My Years with General Motors*. Garden City, N.Y.: Doubleday and Company, Inc. 1963.

Sloat, Warren. *1929*. New York: Macmillan Publishing Co., Inc., 1979.

Smith, Rixey, and Beasly, Norman. *Carter Glass: A Biography*. New York: Longmans, Green and Co., 1939.

Sobel, Robert. *Panic on Wall Street*. New York: Collier Books, 1968.

————. *Amex: A History of the American Stock Exchange, 1921–1971*. New York: Weybright and Talley, Inc., 1972.

Steel, Ronald. *Walter Lippman and the American Century*. New York: Vintage Books, 1981.

Studenski, Paul and Kroos, Herman E. *A Financial History of the United States*. New York: McGraw-Hill Book Company, 1952.

Sullivan, Lawrence. *Prelude to Panic: The Story of the Bank Holiday*. Washington, D.C.: Statesman Press, 1936.

Swanberg, W.A. *Luce and His Empire*. New York: Charles Scribner's Sons, 1972.

Tarbell, Ida M. *Owen D. Young*. New York: MacMillan Co., 1932.

Temin, Peter. *Did Monetary Forces Cause the Great Depression?* New York: W.W. Norton & Company, Inc., 1976.

Thomas, Dana L. *The Plungers and the Peacocks*. New York, G.P. Putnam's Sons, 1967.

Warburg, James P., *The Money Muddle*. New York: Alfred A. Knopf, 1934.

White, Eugene Nelson. *The Regulation and Reform of the American Banking System, 1900–1929*. Princeton, N.J.: Princeton University Press, 1983.

Wicker, Elmus R. *Federal Reserve Monetary Policy, 1919–1933*. New York: Random House, 1966.

Williams, T. Harry. *Huey Long*. New York: Alfred A. Knopf Inc., 1969.

Williamson, Harold F., Andreano, Ralph L., Daum, Arnold R. and Klose, Gilbert C. *The American Petroleum Industry, 1899–1959: The Age of Energy*. Evanston, Illinois: Northwestern University Press, 1963.

Winkler, Max. *Foreign Bonds, An Autopsy*. Philadelphia: Roland Swain Company, 1933.

Worster, Donald. *Dust Bowl: The Southern Plains in the 1930s*. Oxford, England: Oxford University Press, 1979.

Young, H.H., *Forty Years of Public Utility Finance*. Charlottesville, Va.: University Press of Virginia, 1965.

Index

About the Author

BARRIE A. WIGMORE is a corporate finance specialist and partner in Goldman, Sachs & Co., investment bankers.